Democracy

and

Religion

Democracy and Religion

Free Exercise and Diverse Visions

EDITED BY

DAVID ODELL-SCOTT

THE KENT STATE UNIVERSITY PRESS

KENT & LONDON

© 2004 by The Kent State University Press, Kent, Ohio 44242

ALL RIGHTS RESERVED

Library of Congress Catalog Card Number 2004007625

ISBN 0-87338-795-3

Manufactured in the United States of America

08 07 06 05 04   5 4 3 2 1

Library of Congress Cataloging-in-Publication Data

Democracy and religion : free exercise and diverse visions /

edited by David Odell-Scott.

p.   cm.

Includes bibliographical references and index.

ISBN 0-87338-795-3 (pbk. : alk. paper) ∞

1. Freedom of religion—United States—Congresses.

2. Democracy—Religious aspects—Congresses.

3. Violence—Religious aspects—Congresses.

4. Religious fundamentalism—Congresses.

I. Odell-Scott, David W.

BR516.D377 2004

323.44'2'0973—dc22   2004007625

British Library Cataloging-in-Publication data are available.

Contents

Preface and Acknowledgments ix

The Theo-democratic Vision of Religious Fundamentalists
R. SCOTT APPLEBY 1

SECTION I: THE CONSTITUTIONAL DEBATE REGARDING THE
ESTABLISHMENT AND FREE EXERCISE CLAUSE

Exercise Clauses: Introduction and Discussion
CATHARINE COOKSON 19

Explaining the Complexities of Religion and State in the United States:
Separation, Integration, and Accommodation
DEREK H. DAVIS 33

Public Funds and Religious Schools: The Next Prayer Debate?
JOHN E. FERGUSON JR. 48

The Rise of State Law Sanctuary for Minority Religious Liberty in
the Wake of the Fall of Federal Constitutional Protection of
Nonmainstream Faiths
GARY S. GILDIN 89

SECTION II: HOLY AND UNHOLY WAR: RELIGION, VIOLENCE, AND NONVIOLENCE

Religious (Ill)Literacy and (Un)Civil Liberties in the United States: Past and Present
PATRICK G. COY   105

The Search for Meaning in Islam: Between Violence and Nonviolence
SAKAH SAIDU MAHMUD   115

Islam at the Crossroads of Extremism and Moderation: New Science, Global Peace, and Democracy
J. E. RASH (AHMED ABDUR RASHID)   139

The White Man's Wounded Knee, or, Whose Holy War Is This, Anyway? A Cautionary Tale
MARY ZEISS STANGE   156

Yesterday's Love, Today's Ruins: Walker Percy's Apocalyptic Vision
PAUL L. GASTON   175

SECTION III: A DILEMMA FOR DEMOCRACY: THE FREE EXERCISE OF RELIGION AND THE RISE OF FUNDAMENTALISM

Fundamentalism, Democracy, and the Contesting of Meaning
ROGER W. STUMP   185

Dilemmas of Turkish Democracy: The Encounter between Kemalist Laicism and Islamism in 1990s Turkey
ERTAN AYDIN AND YILMAZ ÇOLAK   202

Religious Fundamentalism and Democratic Social Practices: Or, Why a Democracy Needs Fundamentalists, and Why They Need a Democracy
JOHN P. BURGESS   221

On Naming Religious Extremists: The "Fundamentalist" Factor
WILLIAM D. DINGES   243

Section IV: Religion in the Public Square: Challenges to the Free
Exercise of Diverse Religious Practices in a Democratic Society

Exceptionalism and the Immigrant Experience: America, an
Unfinished Project?
AMIRA SONBOL   269

Goddess Amba Unwelcome in Edison, New Jersey: Report of a
Town's Xenophobic Conflation of Race and Religion
VIVODH Z. J. ANAND   282

Liberalism and the Challenge of Multicultural Accommodation
JAN FELDMAN   293

Diverse Religious Practices and the Limits of Liberal Tolerance
POLYCARP IKUENOBE   309

Dealing with the Unfinished Business of America: Fighting Bias,
Bigotry, and Racism in the Twenty-first Century
SANFORD CLOUD JR.   336

Selected Bibliography   348

Contributors   368

Index   372

Preface and Acknowledgments

Beginning with the thirtieth anniversary of the events of May 4, 1970, Carol Cartwright, president of Kent State University, launched the Annual May 4 Symposium on Democracy as a means by which the university might recognize its past and embrace the future by using that time as a platform for examining the present and future challenges of living in a democratic society. The title of that first symposium in 2000 was "The Boundaries of Freedom of Expression and Order in American Democracy." The second symposium, in spring 2001, was "Media, Profit, and Politics: Competing Priorities in an Open Society." At that time, President Cartwright selected the general topic of "democracy and religion" as the theme of the Third Symposium on Democracy, which would be held the following April, and asked that I chair the symposium committee.

The issues of that long-ago spring 2001 that generated conversation related to our theme of democracy and religion were the faith-based initiatives, notably charitable choice, proposed by the recently inaugurated President George W. Bush, and the Supreme Court's decision to consider the case of *Zelman v. Simon-Harris*, commonly known as the Cleveland school-voucher case. These were the most high-profile issues facing the nation at the time that were relevant to our theme, and the school-voucher case had a very local audience. With these issues in mind, the title selected for the Third Annual Symposium became "Democracy and Religion: Free Exercise and Diverse Visions."

It was not our intent to suggest that democracy and religion offer two different visions. Such a characterization would wrongly suggest that there was such a concept or a category as *religion* that offered a monolithic vision of society and human purpose. But then, neither is democracy so singular. By "diverse visions" we had in mind the multiple visions—the diverse religious and democratic perspectives, expectations, projects, narratives, procedures—that influence American society. For example, sharp critique of charitable choice and the school-voucher movement came from both those who sought to protect the government from entanglement with religious institutions and from those who sought to protect the autonomy of religious institutions from government encroachment.

The symposium committee crafted what we concluded would be the final draft of the call for papers on Monday morning, September 10, 2001. And then there was the next morning: September 11. At the same time our focus was on New York City and Washington, D.C., United Flight 98 passed within a few miles of the Kent campus on its journey that ended in a remote wooded area of central Pennsylvania. What we did not know was that somewhere above us in the skies of northeast Ohio or western Pennsylvania, the passengers aboard United Flight 98 quickly convened and voted to overcome their hijackers. In the midst of horrific circumstances, the citizens aboard Flight 98 enacted basic democratic practices and possibly spared the *people's house* from the destruction visited on the World Trade Center and the Pentagon.

Some of the themes that we developed for the call for papers at our Monday meeting faded in relevance and significance in light of the historic events and emergent issues of Tuesday morning, and immediately the themes evolved in sympathy. In the end, three of the four sections comprising the symposium dealt with issues and concerns pertinent after September 11: "A Dilemma for Democracy: The Free Exercise of Religion and the Rise of Fundamentalism," "Holy and Unholy War: Religion, Violence, and Nonviolence," and "Religion in the Public Square: Challenges to the Free Exercise of Diverse Religious Practices in a Democratic Society." The only section to remain unaltered was "The Constitutional Debate regarding the Establishment and Free Exercise Clause."

Our selection of keynote speakers was intended to approach our theme from a plurality of perspectives and disciplines. Thus, we were pleased to welcome Sanford Cloud Jr. and R. Scott Appleby. Two other keynote speakers (Robert Jay Lifton and Azizah Y. Al-Hibri) were forced to cancel in the final weeks leading up to the symposium.

R. Scott Appleby's keynote address, "The Theo-democratic Vision of Religious Fundamentalists," continued his study of the roots of religious violence and the potential of religious peacebuilding. Appleby is the John M. Regan Jr. Director of the Joan B. Kroc Institute for International Peace Studies, professor of history at the University of Notre Dame, the author of *The Ambivalence of the Sacred: Religion, Violence, and Reconciliation* (Rowman and Littlefield, 2000), and editor of *Spokesman for the Despised: Fundamentalist Leaders of the Middle East* (University of Chicago, 1997). Appleby also coedited the five-volume Fundamentalism Project with Martin E. Marty of the University of Chicago, which was sponsored by the American Academy of Arts and Sciences.

Sanford Cloud Jr.'s article, "Dealing with the Unfinished Business of America: Fighting Bias, Bigotry, and Racism in the Twenty-first Century," assumes an activist perspective influenced by religiously and democratically inspired visions of the civil rights movement. Cloud has served as the president and chief executive officer of the National Conference for Community and Justice (formerly known as the National Conference of Christians and Jews) since 1994. As president, Cloud has convened leading thinkers with strongly opposing perspectives to participate in six nationally telecast discussions known as *The National Conversation on Race, Ethnicity, and Gender*. He helped create a collaboration of national organizations to combat prejudice and to build healthy intergroup relations and is an internationally recognized speaker who addressed the United Nations Millennium World Peace Summit.

We invited four discussants, one for each section, to offer comment to the presentations as means to facilitate further conversation. Subsequent to the event, the discussants wrote the introductions to their section for the present volume.

Catharine Cookson, the Joan P. and Macon F. Brock Jr. Director of the Center for the Study of Religious Freedom at Virginia Wesleyan College, introduces the section "The Constitutional Debate regarding the Establishment and Free Exercise Clause."

Patrick G. Coy, associate professor of political science and at the Center for Applied Conflict Management at Kent State University introduces the section "Holy and Unholy War."

The introduction to the section "A Dilemma for Democracy: The Free Exercise of Religion and the Rise of Fundamentalism" is provided by Roger Stump, professor of geography and religious studies at the State University of New York at Albany.

Amira A. Sonbol, associate professor, Center for Muslim-Christian Understanding at Georgetown University, introduces the section "Religion in the Public Square."

In May 1995, prior to instituting the Annual May 4 Symposium on Democracy, Kent State hosted an academic symposium to address the significance of the spring 1970 student protests against the Vietnam War. Called "Legacies of Protest," the symposium examined protest in an international context with insight from renowned scholars, national media, and eyewitnesses to history, including current Kent faculty members who witnessed firsthand the events of May 4, 1970.

I came to understand that a legacy often differs from a bequest of wealth or a specific article delegated to be inherited through a will in that a legacy is often a sense of culture, or heritage, or tradition, or viewpoint, or practice that is passed along from one generation to another. In that vein, a legacy may be intentionally passed forward to succeeding generations from the one who has identified what he or she wishes to delegate to their survivors. Or a legacy may be what those who follow gather from the past as they seek to live in the present and for the future. If the events of that day in May 1970 become only ritualized as a memorial to those who died and were wounded on the field of protest, then the significance, the living influence of those historic events, and the personal, as well as national, tragedy, is diminished.

But May 4 is a legacy of Kent State University from which we may draw as we attend to the present challenges before us. For Kent State University to fail to acknowledge such a legacy in developing its academic pursuits would be to squander its own heritage and purposes and to forget that on May 4, 1970, four Kent State students, Allison Krause, Jeffrey Miller, Sandra Scheuer, and William Schroeder were killed, and nine others were wounded when the Ohio National Guard opened fire on a student protest against the Vietnam War. I prefer to think of the Annual Symposium on Democracy as one of the ways Kent State's learning community honors this legacy with an enduring dedication to scholarship that seeks to prevent violence and to promote the best of democratic values.

A program of the size and complexity of the symposium is a communal undertaking. A number of people deserve to be recognized for their contributions to the symposium itself and this subsequent publication. First and foremost, I acknowledge the members of the symposium committee, who gave of their time and employed their talents to make the event and the book a success: Nawal Ammar, Gail Beveridge, Surinder Bhardwaj, Kenneth Cushner, Kevin Floyd, Joe Harper, Carole Harwood, Thomas Hensley, Leonne Hudson, Ron Kirksey, Janet Meyer, Jackie Parsons, Margaret Ralston Payne, Kim Sebaly, Kathy Wilson, and Thom Yantek. Special recognition is deserved by Elaine Huskins, administrative secretary, not only for her efficient and cheerful service as the secretary for the committee but also for her helpfulness in handling problems as they arose in the midst of the symposium and her continued assistance in the final preparation of the manuscript. And I cannot begin to thank Carole Harwood, public relations and marketing coordinator; and Margaret Payne, senior assistant to the president, for working closely and constructively with me through the difficult situations, especially in those difficult last weeks prior to the event.

I also want to thank those colleagues at Kent State University who served as moderators of the four panels. They were Thomas R. Hensley, professor and chair, Department of Political Science, Kent State University, and the chair of the First Symposium in 2000; Deborah Barnbaum, associate professor of philosophy; Leonne Hudson, associate professor of history; and Surinder Bhardwaj, professor of geography.

I also want to acknowledge the staff of the Kent State University Press for their efforts to bring this volume of the Symposium on Democracy to press. I want to especially thank Kathy Method, managing editor, whose painstaking work with the manuscript and publishing process greatly improved the quality of the final text.

From the beginning of my involvement with the symposium I received the unqualified support of the president of Kent State University, Carol Cartwright. She developed the idea to have the university sponsor an annual May 4 symposium series focusing on the challenges of living in a democratic society and selected the general theme of democracy and religion for the third symposium. I found her leadership and trust empowering. Her perseverance, foresight, and experience served us well in keeping the longterm purpose of the symposium before us in the midst of difficulties in the final weeks leading up to the event.

The Theo-democratic
Vision of Religious Fundamentalists

R. Scott Appleby

Even before the terrorist attacks of September 11, 2001, a debate raged within the academic world, and in certain policy circles as well, regarding the compatibility of Islam and democracy. Participants in this debate who remained skeptical about Islamic openness to democracy often relied on familiar characterizations of religion as being inherently antidemocratic. I will call this position *the skeptical secularist argument about religion.*

The skeptical secularist argument about religion is built around three related assumptions. First, religion is, by definition, *absolutist.* The truths it purports to uphold, advance, and defend are vital for the destiny of humankind. Their origin lies beyond the mundane world, and these truths are revealed to human beings, not created or discovered by them. They come from God, or from a transcendent realm of reality or being. In the monotheistic traditions—Judaism, Christianity, and Islam—these truths are revealed in, by, or through sacred scriptures (the Torah and other parts of the Hebrew Bible, the New Testament, and the Holy Qur'an, respectively). In the traditions of Asia—including Buddhism, Hinduism, and Confucianism—there is a different understanding of both "truth" and "revelation," but these traditions, at least in their modern religious mode, tend also to believe that their worldview is not subject to the same kind of scientific criteria by which mundane "truths" are evaluated, refined, and institutionalized.

Because religions claim that they possess truths or a truth that is absolute, received from on high and beyond criticism, the argument goes, they are unlikely to seek legitimacy from "the people." Revelation occurs quite apart from the needs, desires, or opinions of the people. Truth is not up for a vote, and "the church is not a democracy," as the U.S. Catholic bishops continually remind the American media. (The skeptical secularists tend not to know of, or to know of and disregard, the

1

modern religious movements or groups—including generations of modern Catholic theologians and lay ministers—who hold that "revelation" is an inductive process, ordained by God, but originating in the ongoing experience of the community.)

In consequence, a second assumption about religion is that it is inherently *elitist*. In the course of the historical development of all religions, and, emphatically, of Christianity, Judaism, and Islam, there developed a clerical elite—whether ayatollah or bishop, rabbi or priest—that legitimated their monopoly on power within the community by virtue of their status as a class of men to which the revelation was entrusted, or by virtue of their monopoly on theological or religious-legal expertise.

A corollary of elitism is the patriarchal nature of religious societies. Particularly telling is their leadership in the vanguard of the cultural forces that oppose feminism, or any ideology or philosophy that espouses the social equality of women. Martin Riesebrodt, Helen Hardacre, and other scholars of religious "fundamentalist" movements contend that fundamentalism is best understood as a social protest movement led by men who are defending patriarchy from the encroachment of feminism.[1]

The third assumption, building on the first two, holds that religion, being absolutist and elitist by design, is therefore inimical to democracy. Proponents of this position point to the internal governance of the major religious bodies. The two largest—Roman Catholicism and Islam, whose adherents, taken together, account for nearly one-third of the world's population—are resolutely patriarchal and undemocratic in their internal structures. Catholic laity, who comprise 98 percent of Roman Catholicism, have little or no influence over the governance of the church, its teachings, structures, or policies. And although Islam boasts of "democracy via *shura* (consultation)," one immediately notes that the consultation extends neither to the 1.2 billion Muslims nor to the "laity" in any country or region, but to the *ulema* (religious scholars)—the Islamic equivalent of a male clerical class, which forms a tiny minority of the *umma* (worldwide community of believers).

The skeptical secularist argument is, at base, essentialist. It posits an essence of religion—an unchanging core that defines the religion for all times and places— that is impervious to historical change. In an entertaining twist on this argument, for example, noted controversialist Stanley Fish expressed disdain for those who would expect Islam, or any other religion, to conform its practices to the norms of Western-style democracy or universal human rights, if such conformity would require the religion to abandon, or seriously modify, fundamental tenets of its worldview. A religion is in essence a bid for power, justified by spiritual rather than material ends. Were it to concede the rules of the game to outsiders promoting power sharing and liberal proceduralism, Fish contends, it would cease to be what it is.[2]

History, however, does not bear out the essentialist argument. To the contrary, religions, especially in relation to the temporal order, are preeminently adaptive, fluid, and internally plural. Whatever their form of internal government, which may be deemed "given" (by God) and therefore irreformable, religions have adopted a variety of attitudes toward, and positions on, the external political order. Under the proper circumstances (early twentieth-century U.S. nationalism, for example), religious organizations and communities may be among the most effective promoters of democracy and bearers of the culture underlying and the spirit animating democratic institutions. That is, one must distinguish between the internal governance of the religious community on the one hand, which may remain patriarchal and undemocratic, and the public presence of the religion on the other, which may be an agent of democratization—and, in some cases, of democratic capitalism and free markets.[3]

Religion as Internally Plural and Evolving

"The argument that is tradition" (to paraphrase the philosopher Alisdair MacIntyre) occurs at every level of religious life: in the moral and spiritual life of the individual; in the local community of worship; in seminaries, monasteries, convents, and judicial structures; in diocesan, denominational, religious order and regional bureaucracies; and, among the religions that have them, in hierarchies or centralized governing bodies. Today the argument also takes place among believers in diaspora, unconnected to any religious institution; among people working in nongovernmental organizations (NGOs); and among people who are uncertain about their religious identity.

The argument takes unpredictable turns as believers, drawing on and selectively retrieving the hallowed religious past, interact with one another, with outsiders, and with developments in the structural environment—in the composition and teachings of the host religion itself; in the local, regional, or national political and religious cultures; in the state and its form of government; in the religious and secular educational systems; in social and economic conditions; and in diplomatic and geopolitical relations among nations.

Invariably, believers produce multiple interpretations of the signs of the times. Even were one "religious past" agreed upon by all, the plurality of perceptions of the present would invite a lively argument. Yet the "hallowed religious past" is a vast repository of religio-legal, moral, theological, religio-political, and philosophical precedents developed at different times and under different circumstances, giving different expression to what believers in every religious community assume to be a core set of beliefs and practices (e.g., the Four Noble Truths and Eightfold Path of Buddhism, the Decalogue and the 613 mitzvot of Judaism). To act intentionally in a religious sense the believer, or the religious authority, must discern the meaning of the present circumstances, select the past that speaks most authoritatively to that meaning, and choose an appropriate course of action in response.

Therefore nothing could be further from the truth than the notion that religions are changeless entities, existing above the fray of the temporal, immune to the vicissitudes of history. They tend to present themselves that way, of course, especially when their authority is being challenged. But history shows that religious communities, in their self-understanding and in their orientations to the world, change constantly; indeed, one of the longest-running and liveliest religious arguments concerns the precise relationship between continuity and change within the religious tradition in question—and whether certain changes constitute an "authentic development" or "evolution" of the tradition on the one hand, or its betrayal and regression on the other.

For analysts of religion's relationship to democracy, human rights, and constitutional protections, the idea that religions evolve and reinterpret their mission takes on special significance in an era of globalization. The extension and improvement of cross-cultural communications and transportation; the continual migration of peoples, no longer impeded by vast spaces to traverse, across regions and continents; and the resulting acceleration of the process by which religious actors absorb and integrate exogenous cultural and ideological elements—all this has led to a religious polycentrism unmatched in previous eras.[4]

Particularly within the great traditions unregulated by a centralized government or lacking a hierarchy with comprehensive executive, juridical, or legislative powers—but not only in these religions—one sees a proliferation of para-ecclesial movements, groups, and spokespersons claiming the authority of the great tradition for their special form of advocacy and activism. To some observers the intensity of this disengaging and reengaging process means that religions are fragmenting and squandering the power that comes with purity and uniformity. To others, however, the proliferation of subtraditions, intentional religious communities, and religious NGOs represents an enormous opportunity to mobilize the resources of the religious traditions for democracy, the extension of human rights, and peace building.

As the cold war ended, religious communities were presented with challenging new opportunities to serve the cause of democratization. The context for this development was a renewal of "rights talk" around the world that had its beginnings in the 1960s. The nations of Latin America and Eastern Europe, whose political discourse was impoverished of human rights discourse and characterized by "excessively strong and simple duty talk," embraced democracy and moved to strengthen legal protections of the rights of individuals and minorities. The discussion of democracy and human rights became de rigueur in the Middle East, Africa, and Asia as well—even for governments that preferred to avoid it. In the United States, social critics reassessed an "American rights dialect," impoverished by absolute formulations and excessive concentration on the autonomous and self-sufficient individual at the expense of the community.[5]

In the 1980s and 1990s, religious leaders and scholars initiated internal debates and external dialogues on the religious sources and meanings of universal human rights. Some appropriated elements of the new rights talk or hastened to formulate their own parallel discourses in which rights talk was challenged or complemented by the delineation of responsibilities to religion and society. Protestant, Catholic, and Jewish leaders responded to the excesses of radical individualism in America, for example, by promoting a countervailing discourse of civic responsibility in service to the common good and by reminding their fellow citizens of the long-standing contributions of religious communities to the cultivation of civic virtues and social accountability.[6] Muslims initiated a far-reaching debate over "Islamic democracy" and "Islamic human rights" in the Middle East, Africa, and South Asia.[7]

The Evolution of Roman Catholicism

Roman Catholicism's 1.2 billion members make it Christianity's largest church body. During the course of the twentieth century, the Catholic Church has repositioned itself vis-à-vis the state and civil society, retreating from entangling alliances with the former to assume a constructive and sometimes prophetic democratizing role within the latter. In a striking twentieth-century reversal, the Catholic Church abandoned its previous claims to political privilege, renounced the theocratic model of political order, and became a powerful proponent of religious liberty and universal human rights. This "development of doctrine," ratified in 1965 during the final session of the Second Vatican Council (1962–65), was a dramatic example of internal religious pluralism turned to the advantage of ecumenism, tolerance, human rights, and peace.

It is difficult to overstate the depth and scope of the ecclesial transformation that occurred over the course of the twentieth century. Until 1965 Roman Catholicism had legitimated the denial of civil and other human rights to non-Catholics by teaching, in effect, that "theological error has no rights" in a properly governed (i.e., Roman Catholic) state. The second quarter of the nineteenth century was a defining moment in the initial phase of Catholicism's "internal argument" over the proper role of religion in the modern state. Faced with a popular uprising in Rome and the Papal States, the newly elected Pope Gregory XVI (1831–46 as pope) stood firmly against calls for elected assemblies and lay-dominated councils of state. In the encyclical *Mirari vos* (1832) he denounced the concepts of freedom of conscience, freedom of the press, and separation of church and state, the liberal ideas associated with the French priest Félicité de Lamennais. For our purposes it is instructive to note that Lamennais also held that the common consent of all humanity was a norm of truth. Gregory XVI, by contrast, accepted the basic assumptions of neo-scholastic ecclesiology that the clericalized, monarchical structures of the church were divinely mandated, and he believed that they were to be duplicated in the temporal order. Accordingly, Gregory supported monarchical regimes against the new democratic movements sweeping across Europe, and he declared that the divine origin of the papacy was the basis of the pope's temporal sovereignty over the Papal States.[8]

Subsequent popes followed Gregory's lead. In *Quanta cura* (1864), Pius IX repeated Gregory XVI's attack on "the madness that freedom of conscience and of worship is the proper right of every human being and ought to be proclaimed by law and maintained in every rightly-constituted society."[9] In 1885 Pope Leo XIII reaffirmed the rejection of religious liberty in *Immortale Dei*, an encyclical explicitly focused on "the Christian constitution of States." The Catholic Church had little patience with the human rights reforms and democratic regimes of the later nineteenth and early twentieth centuries. It acquiesced in the authoritative regimes and policies that governed the European, Latin American, and African nations where Catholicism was strong. In liberal democracies, anti-Catholics had little trouble turning the church's own political philosophy against it. As recently as the 1950s, Protestant and secular elites in the United States, for example, were once again joining forces to oppose "an organization that is not only a church but a state within a state, and a state above a state."[10]

On the question of religious liberty in particular, the Catholic Church caught up with the eighteenth century only in the middle of the twentieth. In 1948 John Courtney Murray, a Jesuit professor of theology at Woodstock seminary in Maryland, presented a paper at a gathering of Catholic theologians entitled "Governmental Repression of Heresy," in which he contended that it was *not* the duty of a good Catholic state to repress heresy even when it was practicable to do so. Thus the internal argument was revived, though at first it was not a fair fight. The majority of Catholic authorities, following the papal teachings, opposed Murray; his adversaries included French, German, Italian, and Spanish theologians of his own religious order. In the United States the leading expert on Catholic political philosophy had been Monsignor John A. Ryan, who had concluded in 1941 that protection and promotion of Roman Catholicism "is one of the most obvious and fundamental duties of the State."[11]

Murray's opponents had a certain logic to their position, which can be summarized as follows:

> The Roman Catholic faith is the true religion. It is good for people to believe what is true. The state is obliged to promote Catholic belief, and wherever possible to establish Catholicism as the religion of the state. Advocates of religious

freedom are denying one of the cardinal premises of Roman Catholicism: they are rejecting the absolute truth of Catholic Christianity.[12]

Murray argued that the received Catholic teaching on religious liberty, because it was not complete, was neither permanent nor irreformable. Although consistent with the Catholic teaching since Augustine on the coercion of heretics, the official position ignored both apostolic and subapostolic writings on the priority of conscience, as well as Thomas Aquinas's teachings on the duty to follow conscience. He retrieved the notion of "the indirect power of the Church" first elaborated by the fourteenth-century theologian Jean Quidort, and he insisted that the nineteenth-century encyclicals be read in their proper context, namely, as polemics against the anticlericalism and irreligious rationalism infecting European intellectual life at the time. The American concept of church-state separation, Murray contended, was vastly more congenial to Catholic principles.[13]

In challenging Catholic theologians to learn from the secular world and to reconsider the received doctrine in light of that learning, Murray spoke of "the growing end" of the tradition. By this he meant the contested cutting edge of the ongoing debate about what constitutes authentic Catholic teaching, the place and moment where the internal pluralism of the great tradition crystallizes into a new and profoundly transformative insight into the tradition itself. "The theological task is to trace the stages of growth of the tradition as it makes its way through history . . . to discern the elements of the tradition that are embedded in some historically conditioned synthesis that, as a synthesis, has become archaistic," Murray wrote. "The further task is to discern the 'growing end' of the tradition; it is normally indicated by the new question that is taking shape under the impact of the historical moment."[14]

The "new question" that had confronted the Catholic Church for more than a century was the relationship between "true religion" and the modern liberal state. Murray drew a political distinction between society and the state, defining the former as made up of many diverse communities and forms of association (e.g., families, businesses, labor unions, and churches). State absolutism and totalitarianism occurred, he believed, when the state attempted to control society rather than serve it, as constitutional government requires. Ethically and juridically, Murray distinguished between the common good of society, which all persons and communities are morally bound to pursue, and the narrower juridical notion of public order, which is the proper concern of government.[15]

The French philosopher Jacques Maritain developed themes similar to Murray's. The state may not intervene to coerce a person in the person's search for the truth, he held, for it is the nature of a person to seek the truth freely. Maritain spoke to and for proponents of the idea of a Christian democracy in France, Italy, Germany,

Belgium, and the Netherlands; his writings were also cited by Catholics in Latin America who sought to eliminate military dictatorships.[16]

The debate over religious liberty took a dramatic turn on January 25, 1959, when Pope John XXIII convoked an ecumenical, or worldwide, council of the bishops of the Roman Catholic Church and solicited suggestions as to what the council should consider. In light of the fact that "controversies have arisen about the relation of the Church to the modern State," as one bishop wrote to Rome, there was a need to "supply a new conception of this relation, as the old concepts in force are rooted in political matters no longer in force."[17] In 1960 a papal commission, led by bishops from Switzerland and Belgium, drafted a preliminary document on church-state relations that stressed tolerance as a virtue and discarded the ideal of a Catholic state as the enforcer of orthodoxy.

Pope John's own social encyclicals, especially *Pacem in Terris* (1963), proclaimed "the universal, inviolable, inalienable rights and duties" of the human person and presented a moral framework within which socioeconomic rights were woven together with political and civil rights:

> In endorsing this spectrum of rights, including rights which are immunities and those which are empowerments, the pope took the Catholic church into the heart of the United Nations human rights debates. . . . For *Pacem in Terris,* the foundation and purpose of all rights is the dignity of the human person. The scope of the rights to be endorsed as legitimate moral claims is determined by the specific needs—material and spiritual—each person has to guarantee human dignity.[18]

Murray himself was instrumental in convincing the assembled bishops that religious liberty, as proposed in the draft text under discussion, did not endorse "indifferentism," the notion that it makes no difference what one believes. Nor would the bishops' endorsement of religious freedom exempt the individual from the obligation to seek the truth about God, which could be found in its fullness, Catholics continued to believe, only in the Roman Catholic Church. Rather, the proposed text affirmed the right of the person to the free exercise of religion according to the dictate of the person's conscience and guaranteed the person immunity from all external coercion in such matters.

Murray and his allies carried the day: *Dignitatis Humanae* (Declaration on Religious Freedom), promulgated on December 7, 1965, ratified the postwar development of Roman Catholic doctrine on the inviolable rights of the human person and on the constitutional order of society. Endorsing the approach of Maritain as well as Murray, the council declared that human beings, directed as they are to God, "transcend by their nature the terrestrial and temporal order of things." The civil power "exceeded its limits" when it presumed to direct or impede this relationship to God. Significantly, the council declared that the right to freedom belonged to groups as well as individuals, because both human nature and religion have a social dimension.

Although *Pacem in Terris* maintained a natural law framework, *Dignitatis Humanae* engaged the Enlightenment constitutional tradition of rights and liberties that affirmed the right of religious freedom. By endorsing constitutional limits on the state and by joining religious freedom with other human rights, the church embraced the full range of freedoms needed in the political order for the defense of human dignity. It did not forsake natural law, but situated it within an argument that embraced constitutional ideas previously tolerated but not accepted by the church. This development opened the way for subsequent transformations in Catholic political philosophy and social practice. By identifying innate human dignity, rather than theological orthodoxy and church membership, as the authentic source of civil rights and political self-determination, *Dignitatis Humanae* made connivance with authoritarian (albeit pro-Catholic) regimes untenable. By proclaiming that the great tradition's understanding of the freedom of the church and the limits of the state was compatible with democratic political institutions, it aligned the modern church with democratic polities and against all forms of totalitarianism.[19]

Roman Catholicism, once an accomplice to authoritarian regimes, thus emerged as a powerful advocate of democracy and human rights reform in Brazil, Chile, Central America, the Philippines, South Korea, and elsewhere. Under John Paul II, who became pope in 1978, Rome supported the 1986 People's Power revolution in the Philippines, the revolution against communist rule in Eastern Europe in 1989, and other nonviolent, Catholic-led revolutions against repressive governments.[20]

ISLAM AND "THEO-DEMOCRACY"

Who is correct—the proponents of Islam's compatibility with democracy or Muslims who claim that Islamic core values are antithetical to Western-style democracy and the Universal Declaration of Human Rights (UDHR) and other human rights instruments? There are elements of truth in both descriptions of contemporary Islam.[21]

Islam's (or any other religion's) capacity for bestowing legitimacy on political leaders who advance policies conducive to civic and nonviolent tolerance depends on the situation of its progressive religious leaders and intellectuals—their status within the religious community and the nation, the binding authority of their interpretations of Islamic law, and the popular appeal of those interpretations. It also depends on the range of possibilities contained within the scriptural and traditional sources. The contemporary debate over Islamic polity and the future of Islamic politics demonstrates that shared commitment to the observance of Islamic law does not lead to uniformity or even commensurability of method among Islamists or among Muslims in general. Like any complex legal code, the Shari'a admits many interpretations and diverse applications, each of which is unavoidably selective.[22]

The term "theo-democracy" captures the tension between the populist and absolutist or elitist elements found within some modern Islamist movements. The term comes from the writings of Mawlana Sayyid Abul A'la Mawdudi (1903–79), one of the most important thinkers of twentieth-century Islam. A dynamic orator, seasoned politician, an astute and indefatigable organization builder, and a charismatic leader, he enjoyed a prodigious career as a journalist, editor, and writer that made the Indian-born Pakistani intellectual the chief ideologue of Islamic fundamentalism. Modern Muslim discourse on the social, political, and economic teachings of Islam owes an enormous debt to Mawdudi, who coined and systematically defined terms such as "Islamic politics," "Islamic ideology," "the economic system of Islam," and "the Islamic constitution." More systematically than any other author, Mawdudi recast Islam as an ideological alternative to both Western liberalism and Soviet Marxism.[23]

He described his political vision as "theo-democracy," and refused to see this term as an irreconcilable paradox. Envisioning Islam as a comprehensive political system as well as a way of life, Mawdudi advocated the concept of *iqamat-i-deen* ("the establishment of religion")—the total subordination of the institutions of civil society and the state to the authority of the Shari'a. Islamic law and Islamic governance should extend, Mawdudi taught, "from the mosque to the parliament, from the home to the school and economy; from art, architecture and science to law, state and international relations."[24]

Islam was superior in all respects, he argued, to such contemporary socioeconomic and political ideologies as capitalism, socialism, and nationalism. But he did study their organizational techniques and came to believe that the best way to transform a society was to create a small, informed, dedicated, and disciplined group that would mobilize the masses and work to assume political and social leadership, or Saleh Jamaat: a "holy minority." (Mawdudi was nonetheless cautious about reducing Islam, a universalist ideology, into the ideological underpinnings of a modern nation-state.)

In August 1941 Mawdudi founded the Jamaat-i-Islami (JI), the major Islamist movement of Pakistan, to give institutional shape to his religio-political ideas. The JI pushed for an Islamic constitution of Pakistan; in March 1949 a major victory occurred when the Constituent Assembly of Pakistan passed the Objectives Resolution incorporating the main principles, drawn from Shari'a (Islamic law) upon which the constitution of Pakistan is to be based. The resolution accepted the JI's position that "sovereignty over the entire universe belongs to God Almighty alone, and the authority which He has delegated to the state of Pakistan through its people for being exercised within the limits prescribed by Him is a sacred trust." Thus, "Muslims shall be enabled to order their lives in the individual and collective spheres in accord with the teachings and requirements of Islam." But the resolution also accommodated the modernists' position by stating that "the principles of democracy, freedom, equality, tolerance and social justice, as enunciated by Islam shall be fully observed." The JI interpreted the resolution as a document that laid the foundation for an Islamic state as a "theo-democracy" in order to transform the entire spectrum of collective life in accordance with the teachings of the Qur'an and the Sunna. The acknowledgment of God's sovereignty was seen as an acceptance of the Shari'a as the law of the land.[25]

Mawdudi's influence extended far beyond Pakistan and South Asia. He was, for example, a major influence on Sayyid Qutb, the ideological founder of the school of Sunni extremism to which Osama bin Laden is heir.

FUNDAMENTALISM AND ITS DISCONTENTS

The sweeping judgment that religions tend toward antidemocratic and antisecularist fundamentalism is of course wildly erroneous. Tarring every religiously orthodox, literate, and committed believer with the pejorative label "fundamentalist" erases the enormous distance, for example, between ordinary, pious Muslims and bomb-throwing "Islamic terrorists." It also flies in the face of the fact that many pious Muslims, Hindus, Christians, and Jews strenuously object to the implication that their extremist coreligionists, who are a minority in every religious tradition, are the only believers actually upholding or defending the basic tenets of the faith. And it also conveniently overlooks the fact that radical or extremist religious movements, even those rooted in transnational "world" religions, such as Christianity or Islam, are inherently local in character and incoherent as regional or global entities.

Used properly, the term "fundamentalism" refers to an identifiable pattern of religious militance in which self-styled true believers attempt to arrest the erosion of religious identity by outsiders, fortify the borders of the religious community, and create viable alternatives to secular structures and processes. Their definition of "outsiders" tends to be elastic, frequently extending beyond missionaries of other faiths and foreign troops stationed on the country's sacred ground to Western businessmen, educational and social service volunteers, relief workers, and professional international peacekeepers.

In addition, the extremists count among their enemies their own coreligionists—fellow Muslims or Jews or Christians or Hindus—who advocate pluralism and tolerance, as well as government officials and those with no religious faith at all. In each of these categories, the religious extremists are the sworn enemies of plural- ism, the legally protected coexistence of a variety of religious and secular practices and ways of life.

Fundamentalists perceive their opponents as either intentional or inadvertent agents of secularization, which they see as a process through which traditional reli- gions and religious concerns are gradually relegated to the remote margins of soci- ety. There they can die a harmless death, eliminated by what the Iranian intellec- tual Jalal Al-e Ahmad called the "sweet, lethal poison" of "Westoxication."

To counter these "attacks," fundamentalists instinctively turn to a selective re- trieval of the sacred past—lines or passages from the group's holy book, the tradi- tional teachings of a guru or prophet, or heroic deeds or episodes from a mytholo- gized golden age (or moment of tragedy). These stories and lessons help justify a program of action designed to protect and bolster the besieged "fundamentals" of the religion and to fend off or conquer the outsiders. The agenda expands to in- clude the attainment of greater political power, the transformation of the surround- ing political culture, the moral purification of society and, in some cases, secession from the secular state or the creation of a "pure" religious homeland.

Ideologically, fundamentalists see sacred truths as the foundation of genuine knowledge and religious values as the base and summit of morality—a trait they generally share with traditional believers. But because the fundamentalists them- selves have been formed by secular modernity, or in reaction against it, they are in self-conscious competition with their peers in the secular sciences. Yet they also set the terms of the competition by presenting their sacred texts and traditions—their intellectual resources, so to speak—as inherently free from error and invulnerable to the searching critical methods of secular science, history, cultural studies, and literary theory. Having subordinated secular to sacred epistemology, fundamental- ists feel free to utilize and even develop new forms of computer and communica- tions technology, scientific research, political organizations, and the like.

No matter how expertly or awkwardly they imitate secular moderns, however, fundamentalists remain dualists at heart; they imagine the world divided into un- ambiguous realms of light and darkness, peopled by the elect and reprobate, the pure and impure, the orthodox and the infidel. Many if not all fundamentalists further dramatize this Manichean worldview by setting it within an apocalyptic framework: the world is in spiritual crisis, perhaps near its end, when God will bring terrible judgment upon the children of darkness. When the children of light are depicted in such millenarian imaginings as the agents of this divine wrath, violent intolerance toward outsiders appears justified on theological grounds.

Whatever specific theological resources the host religious tradition may (or may not) have for legitimating a departure from normal operating procedures, funda- mentalists believe themselves to be living in a special dispensation—an unusual, extraordinary time of crisis, danger, apocalyptic doom, the advent of the Messiah, the Second Coming of Christ, the return of the Hidden Imam, and so on. This "special time" is exceptional not only in the sense of being unusual; its urgency requires true believers to make exceptions, to depart from the general rule of the tradition.[26]

This provides an answer to the following puzzling question: How does a religious tradition that normally preaches nothing but peace, compassion, forgiveness, and tolerance adopt the discourse of intolerance and violence? It does so in the belief that "these are not normal times." Thus certain Zionist rabbis in Israel invoked the halakhic norm of *pikuach nefesh* in ruling that the Oslo Accords threatened the very existence of Israel and Judaism itself. This interpretation impelled several "yeshiva boys" to carry out the 1995 assassination of the "traitorous" prime minister, Itzhak Rabin. Similarly, Ayatollah Khomeini made the extraordinary ruling that the survival of the Islamic Republic of Iran demanded that parts of the Islamic law putatively governing it were to be suspended in deference to the Supreme Jurist's (i.e., Khomeini's) own ad hoc rulings.

Organizationally, fundamentalist movements form around male charismatic or authoritarian leaders. The movements begin as local religious enclaves but become increasingly capable of rapid functional and structural differentiation and of international networking with like-minded groups from the same religious tradition. They usually recruit rank-and-file members from the general population, but they are often particularly successful in appealing to young, educated males who are unemployed or underemployed (and, in some cases, from the universities and the military). The movement imposes strict codes of personal discipline, dress, diet, and other markers that serve subtly or otherwise to set group members apart from others in the society.

Fundamentalists draw from radio, television, audiocassettes, faxes, the Internet, Stinger missiles, black markets, think tanks, paleontological "evidence" for the young earth theory, identity politics, and modern marketing techniques to terrorist tactics—all turned to militant or extremist religious ends. Yet fundamentalists' organizational and ideological power remains rooted in the host religious tradition.

If fundamentalists are committed to the consolidation of the host religion's political hegemony within the state, they are weak in the art of "nation building," in bringing together into a viable political coalition the various groups and peoples living within the boundaries of a "nation." As political actors, fundamentalists are exceptionally vulnerable to fissure, fragmentation, and political instability. They are faced with a serious dilemma: abandon the absolutism and exclusivism that inspired and fueled the movement in its formative phase and made it "fundamentalist," or relax religious and moral standards to allow for a broader coalition that enables effective governance.

CONCLUSION

The internal pluralism of Christianity, Islam, and other major religious traditions enables religious actors to select and develop theologies and moral precepts that accommodate democracy and universal human rights. To the extent that religious leaders, educators, and ordinary believers come to be influenced by the progressive thinkers and scholars within their own traditions, the latter have the capacity to transform popular attitudes toward "the Other."

No religious tradition speaks unequivocally about democracy or human rights, however. Their sacred texts and canons devote much more attention to commandments and obligations than to rights and freedoms. Paradoxically, their prelates, supreme guides, theologians, and jurists have cultivated human rights norms while resisting their consistent application. And, as I have argued, powerful forces within the religious communities of the twenty-first century adopt the strategies and discourse of democratization in support of an order that would approach theocracy rather than democracy in its outcome.

Each religion (and its specific schools or subtraditions) has justified and advocated human rights in its own distinctive way and on its own terms, however. Each, as noted, has its own theological and philosophical framework for interpreting human rights, its own constellation of doctrines and precepts modifying the canon of rights, and its own exemplars or champions of human rights. The respective frameworks or doctrines or models of emulation are not readily reconcilable in every respect; even where different religions proclaim essentially the same luminous core truths, this basic unity is not always transparent to the followers of these religions or to others. The challenge of the next phase of the human rights era will be for religious leaders from these different traditions and subtraditions to identify and enlarge the common ground they share.

NOTES

1. Martin Riesebrodt, *Pious Passion: The Emergence of Modern Fundamentalism in the United States and Iran*, trans. Don Reneau (Berkeley: Univ. of California Press, 1993); Helen Hardacre, "The Impact of Fundamentalism on Women, the Family, and Interpersonal Relations," in *Fundamentalisms and Society: Reclaiming the Sciences, the Family, and Education*, ed. Martin E. Marty and R. Scott Appleby (Chicago: Univ. of Chicago Press, 1993), 294–312.

2. Stanley Fish, "Postmodern Warfare," *Harper's* 305, no. 1826 (July 2002): 33–40.

3. David Martin, *Tongues of Fire: The Explosion of Protestantism in Latin America* (Oxford, U.K.: Basil Blackwell, 1990).

4. Anthony Giddens, *The Consequences of Modernity* (Stanford, Calif.: Stanford Univ. Press, 1990), 6.

5. Mary Ann Glendon, *Rights Talk: The Impoverishment of Political Discourse* (New York: Free Press, 1991), 17. Parts of this chapter are adapted from chapter 7 of my recent book, *The Ambivalence of the Sacred: Religion, Violence, and Reconciliation* (Lanham, Md.: Rowman and Littlefield, 2000).

6. For a sampling of the opinions of leading American conservatives on the need for a revitalization of religion in the public sphere, see "The National Prospect," *Commentary* 100, no. 5 (1995): 23–116. For a communitarian perspective that includes but does not privilege religious participation and emphasizes the importance of core religious values that are compatible with secular humanitarian values, see Amitai Etzioni, *The New Golden Rule: Community and Morality in a Democratic Society* (New York: Basic, 1996), 252–57.

7. For a recent overview of the debate, see John L. Esposito and John O. Voll, *Islam and Democracy* (New York: Oxford Univ. Press, 1996).

8. The following discussion of the internal evolution of Roman Catholicism is adapted from my recent book, *Ambivalence of the Sacred*. Richard P. McBrien, *Lives of the Popes: The Pontiffs from St. Peter to John Paul II* (New York: Harper Collins, 1997), 338; Josef L. Althholz, *The Churches in the Nineteenth Century* (New York: Bobbs-Merrill, 1967), 55–90.

9. Pope Gregory XVI, qtd. in John T. Noonan Jr., *The Lustre of Our Country: The American Experience of Religious Freedom* (Berkeley: Univ. of California Press, 1998), 27.

10. Paul Blanshard, *American Freedom and Catholic Power* (Boston: Beacon, 1949), 4.

11. John A. Ryan and Francis J. Boland, *Catholic Principles of Politics* (New York: Macmillan, 1948), 319; Noonan, *Lustre of Our Country*, 26–27.

12. David Hollenbach, "The Growing End of an Argument," *America* 30 (November 1985): 364.

13. Noonan, *Lustre of Our Country*, 28; see also J. Leon Hooper, "The Theological Sources of John Courtney Murray's Ethics," in *John Courtney Murray and the Growth of Tradition*, ed. J. Leon Hooper and Todd David Whitmore (Kansas City: Sheed and Ward, 1997), 106–25.

14. John Courtney Murray, "The Problem of Religious Freedom," *Theological Studies* 25 (1964): 569.

15. Hollenbach, "Growing End of an Argument," 365.

16. Ibid.; see also Jacques Maritain, *Man and the State* (Chicago: Univ. of Chicago Press, 1951); Maritain, *Integral Humanism: Temporal and Spiritual Problems of a New Christendom*, trans. Joseph W. Evans (Notre Dame, Ind.: Univ. of Notre Dame Press, 1973); and James V. Schall, *Jacques Maritain: The Philosopher in Society* (Lanham, Md.: Rowman and Littlefield, 1998), 79–97.

17. Richard J. Cushing, Archbishop of Boston, qtd. in Noonan, *Lustre of Our Country*, 335.

18. J. Bryan Hehir, "Religious Activism for Human Rights: A Christian Case Study," in *Religious Human Rights in Global Perspectives: Religious Perspectives*, ed. John Witte Jr. and Johan D. van der Vyver (The Hague, Netherlands: Martinus Nijhoff, 1996), 103. At the time *Pacem in Terris* was written, debate in the United Nations centered on the question of which rights were to be given primacy, and whether all the claims found in U.N. texts were truly rights. Set in the broader ideological struggle of the cold war, this debate saw the socialist system endorsing socioeconomic rights, with Western democracies giving priority to civil and political rights. *Pacem in Terris* provided an authoritative framework for an understanding of human rights within the church and influenced the public debate as well, Hehir notes.

19. Hollenbach, "Growing End of an Argument," 366. For an analysis of Murray's influence in American public life in the quarter century since his death, see Todd David Whitmore, "Immunity or Empowerment?: John Courtney Murray and the Question of Religious Liberty," in *John Courtney Murray and the Growth of Tradition*, 149–74.

20. The social movements that staged the revolutions were not exclusively Catholic, of course, but they drew heavily on the theological and organizational resources of the church. Spurred by the rise of the Solidarity movement, for example, the Polish revolutionaries drew on explicitly religious symbols, appealed openly to moral warrants and norms in international law, and took a significant part of their moral inspiration from the church and its Polish pope. Summarizing a generation of postconciliar Catholic activism, one outside observer judged the church to have been "a critical force in the new wave of political democratization . . . both through the announcements and interventions of its papal see and curia, and through the efforts of its local clergy." Qtd. in George Weigel, *The Final Revolution: The Resistance Church and the Collapse of Communism* (New York: Oxford Univ. Press, 1992), 26.

21. The debate about Islam raged with particular intensity in the decade following the end of the cold war. For a summary of the various positions, see John L. Esposito, *The Islamic Threat: Myth or Reality?* (New York: Oxford Univ. Press, 1992).

22. See, for example, John Kelsay's discussion of the disagreement involving the statements of representatives of Saudi Arabia and Pakistan at the United Nations with respect to the Universal Declaration of Human Rights: John Kelsay, "Saudi Arabia, Pakistan, and the Universal Declaration of Human Rights," in *Human Rights and the Conflicts of Culture: Western and Islamic Perspectives on Religious Liberty*, ed. David Little, John Kelsay, and Abdulaziz Sachedina (Columbia: Univ. of South Carolina Press, 1988), 33–52.

23. Mumtaz Ahmad, "Islamic Fundamentalism in South Asia: The Jamaat-i-Islami and the Tablighi Jamaat of South Asia," in *Fundamentalisms Observed: A Study Conducted by the American Academy of Arts and Sciences*, ed. Martin E. Marty and R. Scott Appleby (Chicago: Univ. of Chicago Press, 1991), 464.

24. Mumtaz Ahmad, *An Introduction to the Jamaat-i-Islami Pakistan* (Lahore, Pakistan: Jamaat-i-Islami, 1978), 5.

25. Ibid., 469–70.

26. Gabriel A. Almond, R. Scott Appleby, and Emmanuel Sivan, *Strong Religion: The Rise of Fundamentalisms around the World* (Chicago: Univ. of Chicago Press, 2003), 96–97.

.

Section I

The Constitutional Debate
regarding the Establishment and
Free Exercise Clause

Exercise Clauses

Introduction and Discussion

CATHARINE COOKSON

The three papers presented in this section at first blush seem quite divergent: the movement relocating minority groups' efforts to achieve religious freedom to state court venues, school vouchers in Cleveland, and three paradigms of the complex relationship between religion and state. Yet the theories, principles, and controversies discussed in all of these papers can be seen as predicated upon the basic, primary political quest for a just and civil order. Law is the foundation of civil order. The state's primary task is to maintain that order,[1] and clashing conceptions of what is necessary for a just order lie at the heart of the diverse visions of religious freedom.[2]

THE RISE OF STATE LAW SANCTUARY FOR MINORITY RELIGIOUS LIBERTY (GARY S. GILDIN)

Gary Gildin is right: Pure democracy is an inhospitable environment for religious freedom. Constitutional protection for this right has been lost in the fog engendered by the "law and order" hyperbole of the 1990 case of *Employment Division v. Smith*.[3] Instead of viewing free exercise claims as a conflict of principles (the good of the regulatory goal versus the good of religious freedom), the courts now defer to the democratic majority–made law and deem the religious adherent as a criminal seeking to "get away with" deliberate law breaking. Intent to fulfill a religious obligation is equated with intent to commit a crime; religious intent thereby becomes criminal intent.

The courts also emphasize the injustice of unequal treatment: one lawbreaker goes to jail, whereas the religious adherent who breaks the same law goes free. The courts fear anarchy and are wary of those who consider their obligations to God as paramount. As we shall see, such fear of danger to the common good has won out only in the free exercise part of the constitutional equation, with minority religious claimants seen as dangers to the community. Interestingly, the claim for equal treatment is used against free exercise claims, but in support of the erosion of the wall of separation of church and state in establishment clause claims (which tend to favor dominant religious groups).

Fear of free exercise anarchy is misplaced, however: no serious political philosopher or advocate of the right to religious freedom has ever held this freedom to be absolute. There are generally accepted limits; no one can harm the person, property, or common rights of citizenship of another person in the name of their own religious freedom.[4] To show that their free exercise claims will not harm the public good, religious adherents routinely have offered evidence that the harm anticipated by the law either is not present or is not as threatening in their particular case. The state, in turn, is supposed to offer evidence of its compelling interest in overriding the religious obligation. But, lately, the courts haven't felt at all comfortable with this contextual approach. The result has been the demise of the compelling state interest test.

Thus laws and regulations now routinely trump the individual's right to the free exercise of religion. The one narrow exception: if lawmakers *intended* to discriminate against a religious group and uniquely targeted that group. If the law applies generally, then it passes constitutional muster. Here is an example: if there wasn't a sacramental wine exception written into the laws governing alcohol consumption, children under the drinking age of twenty-one could not receive wine as part of communion in the Catholic or Episcopal churches.

Gildin may be letting the government off the hook too easily when he characterizes the crackdown on minority religious groups such as the Amish and the Hmong as unintentional, ignorant, or inadvertent. Not every breach of a regulation results in administrative enforcement and penalties or criminal prosecution, due to the exercise of prosecutorial and administrative discretion. Prosecutors and administrators, agents of the government, are on the scene and do know exactly what they are doing when they use their discretion in a way that harms religious adherents in the name of uniformity.

Gildin examines the only practical resort left to those who are barred by law from adhering to their religious obligations: state courts. The state, he notes, is free to expand protection of individual rights beyond the limits of the federal constitution. Even when the "compelling state interest" test is restored, however, it presents a precarious balancing act that is all too easy to undermine. A state's use of its police powers to protect the health, safety, and welfare of the public can dwarf what seems to be a small and idiosyncratic interest of the religious adherent.

SCHOOL VOUCHERS AND THE ESTABLISHMENT CLAUSE
(JOHN E. FERGUSON JR.)

As discussed in the previous section, in the latest judicial interpretation of the free exercise clause, the bottom line is that civil order requires rigid obedience, and statutes and regulations thus generally trump any claims to religious freedom. Interestingly, notions of the common good, order, equal treatment, and individual religious freedom rights are also key in the movement to dismantle previous establishment clause barriers between church and state.

In looking at the current war over the meaning of the establishment clause, I'll begin again with the question "What is necessary for good order?" One answer favors a narrow, limited establishment clause that does not prevent the government from funding essentially religious institutions when legislatures think it is in the common good and the interests of civil order to do so. Another answer denies the very existence of governmental power either to fund/support or to oppress religion. This debate over government power is as old (if not older) than Patrick Henry and James Madison.

On the one hand, dissenters (Baptists such as Roger Williams, John Leland, and Isaac Backus) and other Christians, such as James Madison, championed a two-kingdom, separation of church and state, approach.[5] The core principle is that government has no power to act on matters of religion—actions and laws that prohibit as well as support religion are null and void, void ab initio. Freedom of religious conscience is retained as an inalienable right—meaning that the state does not and cannot possess the power to support or inhibit religion, even if the majority of the people want the government to have this power.[6] Because the state lacks authority in matters of religion, it has created serious civil disorder by using public tax monies to support religious ministries.

On the other hand, Patrick Henry and others reasoned that because religion was necessary to make citizens virtuous, religion was thus necessary to civil order, and, therefore, government support of religion was vital to civil order. To fill what he perceived to be a dangerous void left when Virginia disestablished the Anglican Church, Henry introduced a bill to provide for teachers (ministers) of the Christian religion. The bill was what we would today describe as "nonpreferentialist" in that it did not prefer one religion to another (albeit the religions in question were all various Christian denominations). In fact, under this bill no one's tax monies went to support the religious institution of another: the bill exacted a tax that went only to the church of one's choice. Henry premised the bill in terms of religion's usefulness to government. He argued the need for religious authority to guide citizens' consciences and raised fear of the anarchy of an immoral, unvirtuous citizenry.[7]

Madison and a groundswell of Christian dissenters wrote petitions opposing this bill, arguing that governments had no authority or jurisdiction over religion and that state support of religion was corrupting and useless.[8] Henry lost this round, and Madison, seizing the moment, quickly introduced a bill Jefferson had written back in 1777. The Virginia Congress considered this bill in October 1785, and it became the Statute of Virginia for Religious Freedom. Part of the statute reads, "No man shall be compelled to . . . support any religious worship, place, or ministry."[9]

But this was hardly the end of the Madison-Henry debate. Three years later, at the Virginia Ratifying Convention, the Henry tradition took the lead in the Virginia debate. Willing to compromise to get Virginia's vote for ratification, the Madisonian side acquiesced to Henry's insistence that Virginia submit a proposed amendment to the United States Constitution. Henry's proposed amendment regarding religious freedom was a rewriting of the 1776 Virginia Declaration of Rights, leaving out "Christian charity and forbearance" in favor of a nonpreferential establishment of religion. This language did not make it into the final Bill of Rights, however.[10]

The lead in this debate continued to be contested as the eighteenth century drew to a close. Dissenters and others of the Madisonian tradition were dying out just as the Second Great Awakening began to reap a harvest of souls for evangelical churches that had benefited from the new free marketplace of religion. As Evangelical Protestantism gained cultural dominance in the nineteenth century,[11] the Henry tradition became the dominant partner in the debate. The United States became caught up in its "Christian Manifest Destiny." In a treatise on the U.S. Constitution written in the nineteenth century, Justice Joseph Story wrote, "It is the especial duty of government to foster and encourage [Christianity] among all the citizens."[12] Public schools, as Attorney Ferguson notes, became sacred places. Although left a weakened debating partner, the Madisonian tradition nonetheless did not leave the debate floor. For example, the House Committee on the Judiciary in 1874 rejected a petition to amend the Constitution to include an "acknowledgment of God and the Christian religion," reasoning that the Founders envisioned the United States as a haven for all, Christian or pagan.[13]

I want to highlight the fact that we've had these two different traditions of establishment clause interpretation with us since the Founding. One would separate church and state, maintaining that government has no authority over religious matters and warning that the power to support religion and the power to suppress religion are one and the same. The other tradition maintains that there is only a minimal separation of church and state and that government has always been free to support religion as a force for the common good.

Moving now to the specifics of the school voucher case, I'm going to eschew the minutiae of case law interpreting the establishment clause because, frankly, the cases are all over the place. Instead, I'm going to look at the political arguments underlying the passage of the school voucher program at issue in the Ohio case of *Zelman v. Simmons-Harris*. First, the following basics (taken from the Sixth Circuit opinion) must be understood. Private schools involved in the voucher program (including all religious schools) "may not discriminate on the basis of . . . religion . . . , [may not] advocate or foster unlawful behavior; or teach hatred of any person or group on the basis of . . . religion" (Ohio Rev. Code section 3313.976[A][6]). Voucher money is unrestricted and can be used for any purpose. The handbooks and mission statements of the sectarian schools participating in the voucher program make it clear that the education offered by these schools is an infused religious ministry.

The sectarian schools vary in their religious affiliation and approaches; however, the handbooks and mission statements of these schools reflect that most believe in interweaving religious beliefs with secular subjects. The sectarian schools also follow religious guidelines, including instruction in religion and mandated participation in religious services; interweaving of Christian doctrines with science and language arts classes; requiring that "all learning take place in an atmosphere of religious ideals" (St. Vincent de Paul School, Parent Handbook [1999–2000], 11); and designing educational scholarship in order "to make . . . faith become living, conscious, and active through the light of instruction . . . religious truths and values permeate the whole atmosphere of the school" (St. Rocco School, Parent-Student Handbook [1999–2000], 1). Other sectarian schools in the voucher program believe that "the one cardinal objective of education to which all others point is to develop devotion to God as our Creator, Redeemer, and Sanctifier" (St. John Nottingham Lutheran School, Parent Handbook [1999–2000], 2) and want to require students to "pledge allegiance to the Christian flag and to the Savior for whose Kingdom it stands, One Savior crucified, risen and coming again with life and liberty for all who believe" (Calvary Center Academy, Parent-Student Handbook [1999–2000], 24).[14]

Those are the religious facts, and I'll summarize what I deem the theoretical and political underpinnings offered for the assertion that public tax monies can be given to these religious ministries without running afoul of the establishment clause.

1. Giving public funds to sectarian school ministries is necessary to solve the problem of failing public schools. This is a utilitarian argument (the ends justify the means): some children are not provided a good education by failing public schools, and their parents cannot afford private schools, and the necessity of a good education (necessary, in turn, for good order and civil peace) demands payment of public funds to parents so they can pay for sectarian school tuition and fees. The noble end (urgently needed decent public education) justifies the means (public tax money funding religious education). Do hard cases make

bad law? Madison called the use of religion as a means to an end, an "unhallowed perversion."

2. Equal treatment requires public funding for sectarian schools. The argument here is that the establishment clause does not mean that there can be *no* government assistance to religion (after all, we provide fire and police protection, don't we?). It means *only* that the government must be neutral and cannot prefer one religion to another. If the ("godless," "liberal," etc.) public schools are funded, then God-fearing Christian schools cannot be singled out and discriminated against. Both are equally entitled to public tax money. Aside from the problems of government support and entanglement in religion, what's lost in this analysis is the truly diverse religious context that we find in our country today. Democratic majorities make laws reflecting the worldview of the majority, tending thus to favor politically dominant religious groups. (Recall that "blue laws" protecting the Sabbath banned Sunday sales, to the detriment of merchants and laborers who kept Sabbath on Saturday.) Interestingly, the equal treatment argument in the establishment context also (as in the free exercise context) works against nondominant religious groups. "Religion" in the establishment clause version of "equal treatment" is assumed to be normatively mainstream Christianity and Judaism. Religions that don't hold the religious obligation to establish sectarian schools, or are too small to afford to do so, now not only do not receive voucher money, but their own members' tax money goes to support religions that are not their own. I wonder how supportive the voucher proponents would be if their tax monies were used to support neo-Pagan, Hindu, or fundamentalist Muslim schools?

3. Individual free exercise choices trump establishment clause limits. This vision sees the establishment clause as less important than, and even an impediment to, individual free exercise. Behind the political voucher arguments, in general, there is a sense of individual entitlement that takes the odd form of a *quasi*–free exercise argument: all children are entitled to a free education from the state, and thus the *state must pay* for the kind of education *my* individual conscience requires. This is a far cry from the early twentieth-century case of *Pierce v. Society of Sisters*,[15] in which the parents sought simply the right to choose to send their children to a private, not public, school. Now, at the beginning of the twenty-first century, parents demand to have the taxpayers pay for their individual choices. What happened to the courts' fear of individual free exercise rights endangering the common good (i.e., in this case, diverting scarce monies away from the common public schools)?

4. Parents mediate between the state and the religious schools. In his paper, Derek Davis defines the separation of church and state as an institutional separation,

and applying this to the voucher debate, the state is indeed supporting religious institutions—the sectarian schools. Voucher supporters argue, however, that the public tax money doesn't go directly to the sectarian religious institutions but is laundered through the parents, because the parents choose the school and must endorse the check. Should this distinction make a difference? Did "choice" matter to Virginians in the debate over Patrick Henry's bill?

5. Parental choice reduces the issue of government entanglement. However, school voucher regulations of necessity involve the entanglement of the government in deciding what "hatred" is. Is a Christian school that teaches that those who do not accept Jesus as their savior are going to hell teaching hatred of a group? Is a school that teaches that Christians are deluded and agents of the devil teaching hatred? And, on the other hand, to the extent that we refuse to fund schools that do not go along with the American virtue of tolerance, are we ultimately back to the business of establishing (i.e., funding) those religious schools whose religion most closely mirrors the liberal, inclusive, American civil religion? This is "equal treatment"?

Since the date of the conference, the U.S. Supreme Court has come down in favor of the constitutionality of the Cleveland voucher program. The strongest emphasis, interestingly, was on the consequentialist argument (ends justify the means). The Cleveland public schools are in dire straights, and poor parents need help.

RELIGION AND STATE: SEPARATION, INTEGRATION, AND ACCOMMODATION (DEREK H. DAVIS)

Derek Davis's section on accommodation focuses on civil religion. Anthropologists, sociologists, and historians all note the importance of a civil religion in creating and maintaining a sense of national identity, especially among an otherwise diverse populace. Trouble occurs, however, when that inclusive and amorphous civil religion becomes sectarian or is coerced by the government. Oaths and civil religious prayers in the form of, for example, the Pledge of Allegiance, are one thing. But in *Engle v. Vitale*,[16] the government wrote an actual prayer for school children to say to God. Where did the state get the authority and theological expertise to author a prayer?

In general, public prayer rituals run the danger of two extremes. The entire, diverse interfaith group may be inappropriately summoned to join in singularly sectarian prayers. On the other hand, the typical rite of civil religion (a generic, one-size-fits-all prayer to an unnamed deity) is also offensive to many because they just don't pray like that.

Interfaith prayer services, especially popular since September 11, have been quite controversial lately in my community. These services, although voluntary and privately sponsored, are very much a vibrant part of the public square. Our local paper describes "a range of clergy most of them conservative Christians" who reject participation in public prayer services because the message that is often conveyed is that we all believe in the same God. The article quotes a local minister: "We can all work shoulder to shoulder to provide food and assistance, absolutely. . . . But when it comes to worshipping, we cannot agree that there is one universal way to meet God's standards."[17] A letter to the editor published in an area weekly paper states, "Christians who worship Jesus as remitting the believers' sin through his death can hardly join in meaningful worship with those who believe otherwise."[18]

Now, keeping in mind these statements about privately sponsored prayer in the public square, let's turn to the issue of state-sponsored prayer. Putting aside the crucial *constitutional* problem of state-sponsored religious worship, how can one *theologically* reject participation in voluntary, nongovernment interfaith prayer services while advocating state-sponsored, group prayer in the public schools (including at graduation and football games), at legislative and judicial proceedings, and at other state-sponsored gatherings? The only way one can maintain theological consistency between the two positions (state prayer yes; interfaith prayer services, no) is to add the contingency—or perhaps the unstated assumption—that only "proper" and "legitimate" ways of prayer (of course, offered only to "proper and legitimate" gods) should be offered by the state. Who makes this theological decision on behalf of the state? (Ironically, government–sponsored ecumenical prayers endorse and establish *liberal* Christianity.)

Something similar can be seen happening in the issue of school vouchers. The same religious groups that oppose public tax funding for *secular, broad-based health and welfare* programs that go against their consciences (e.g., insurance coverage for contraception or medically necessary abortion) also support state-coerced funding for their *sectarian school ministries.* What happened to the inalienable right of conscience that protects persons from coerced tax support of private religious ministries?

Last, I would have us think further about Davis's point regarding the integration of religion and politics, that the free exercise clause gives officeholders the freedom to act and speak out of their personal faith beliefs, sometimes "even when acting in their official capacity." On one end of the spectrum, the president has broad latitude as high priest of the American civil religion. This civil religion works best when it is vague and ambiguous, thus offering a broad umbrella. President George W. Bush, I believe, recently echoed Dwight Eisenhower, who said something to the effect that it is good for people to be religious, and he doesn't care which one they follow. But as we move further down the spectrum away from the ritual obligations of the civil religion and into the activities of government that directly affect people's lives, deferring to government officials' sectarian free exercise rights can put the common good at risk. C. Everett Koop, former surgeon general of the United States, was heavily supported by the Christian Right and came to office in a cloud of controversy over his conservative Christian beliefs. Koop confronted the problem of personal faith versus the public good in formulating the government's response to the AIDS crisis in the 1980s. In an interview for the television program *Nova*, in 1989 after Koop left office, he reflected upon the responsibility of government to act in the best interests of all the people:

> Disappointments come and go in the political arena. I certainly came to Washington as a politically naïve individual. Some people think that I have learned politics very quickly. As I look back on my own accomplishments, I think what I have learned politically is a sense of timing. What I have not learned is to be political about the health of America. It's very difficult to explain to someone the awe, I guess you might say, that goes with the responsibility of this office. You can never divorce yourself from your religious beliefs, from your ethical or moral beliefs, but when you are in the position of being, let's say, what most people consider to be the primary health officer of a country of 240,000,000 people, and they are all your charges—whether you like the way they behave, whether you like their politics, whether you like what they do with their lives or not—you have to have an understanding that when you speak, you not only speak for their benefit, but you are preserving forever, if you can, the integrity of the office you hold.[19]

The government is not a detached, independent entity, but can only act through its agents, government officials. Should the personal free exercise rights of those agents be paramount when they are acting in their official capacity? Consider the matter of every public school teacher having the constitutional right to conduct in her classroom whatever prayers are dictated by his or her conscience. What is required for just order? This is a very difficult question; we want our legislators and elected officials such as the president and our governors to be able to act in accordance with their consciences, but what, if any, are the limits?

This discussion intended to explore how several themes run through both current free exercise and establishment clause debates. The issue of what is required for good order underlies both. The concerns of equal treatment and the extent to which individual rights should be exercised are prominent in both. But these elements intertwine in very different ways in the current court's movement both to narrow the free exercise protections and to narrow the reach of the establishment clause. The bottom line for both parts of our religious freedom protection is that those religious groups with political power win, and those without, lose.

NOTES

1. Major Christian theologians traditionally have acknowledged government as a good ordained by God for the establishment and maintenance of civil order and peace; religion could not flourish in an atmosphere of anarchy. Augustine, in the fifth century, described civil peace as the "well-ordered concord" among those citizens who rule and those who obey. "The peace of all things is the tranquility of order." Augustine, *City of God*, bk. 19, chap. 13, qtd. in Paul E. Sigmund, ed., *St. Thomas Aquinas on Politics and Ethics*, A Norton Critical Edition (New York: W. W. Norton and Co., 1988), 104–5. In the thirteenth century, Thomas Aquinas wrote, "The order of justice requires that inferiors obey their superiors, for otherwise stability could not be maintained in human affairs." Thomas Aquinas, *Summa Theologiae* II-II, qu. 104, art. 6, qtd. in Sigmund, *Thomas Aquinas*, 76.

2. See Catharine Cookson, *Regulating Religion: The Courts and the Free Exercise Clause* (New York: Oxford Univ. Press, 2001), chap. 3.

3. *Employment Div. v. Smith*, 494 U.S. 872 (1990).

4. John Locke wrote, "Nobody . . . neither single persons, nor churches, nay, nor even commonwealths, have any just title to invade the civil rights and worldly goods of each other, upon pretense of religion." John Locke, "A Letter Concerning Toleration," in *John Locke, A Letter Concerning Toleration in Focus*, ed. John Horton and Susan Mendus (New York: Routledge, 1991), 26. Among the civil privileges due all citizens, Locke includes such matters as being "permitted to either buy or sell, or live by their callings; that parents should . . . have the government and education of their own children; they should [not] be excluded from the benefit of the laws, or meet with partial judges." Ibid., 49. Whether a religious adherent can abrogate the common rights of citizenship of another in furtherance of his or her own individual religious freedom has recently become a matter of some contention. The Christian Right, for example, contends that civil rights laws and antidiscrimination laws that prohibit discrimination based on marital status or sexual orientation improperly interfere with an individual's claimed right to employ persons or offer housing in accordance with their religious beliefs. The courts have rejected similar religious claims with respect to racial discrimination. See *Bob Jones University v. United States*, 461 U.S. 574 (1983), in which the university was denied tax-exempt status even though its racial discrimination was based on sincerely held religious beliefs. The Court held that the free exercise clause did not protect these practices because they were contrary to public policy.

5. See William R. Estep, *Revolution within the Revolution: The First Amendment in Historical Context, 1612–1789* (Grand Rapids, Mich.: William B. Eerdmans, 1990); William Lee Miller, *The First Liberty: Religion and the American Republic* (New York: Alfred A. Knopf, 1986); James H. Hutson, ed., *Religion and the New Republic: Faith in the Founding of America* (Lanham, Md.: Rowman and Littlefield, 2000); Cookson, *Regulating Religion*.

6. *Inalienable* is "the characteristic of those things which cannot be bought or sold or transferred from one person to another." *Black's Law Dictionary*, 4th rev. ed. (St. Paul, Minn.: West, 1968), s.v. "Inalienable."

7. The following are excerpts from "A Bill Establishing a Provision for Teachers of the Christian Religion" (Patrick Henry, sponsor, 1784):

> WHEREAS the general diffusion of Christian knowledge hath a natural tendency to correct the morals of men, restrain their vices, and preserve the peace of society, which cannot be effected without a competent provision for learned teachers, who may be thereby enabled to devote their time and attention to their duty of instructing such citizens, as from their circumstances and want of education, cannot otherwise attain such knowledge; and it is judged that such provision may be made by the Legislature, without counteracting the liberal principle heretofore adopted and intended to be preserved by abolishing all distinctions of preeminence amongst the different societies or communities of Christians;

Be it therefore enacted by the General Assembly, That for the support of Christian teachers,   per centum on the amount, or   in the pound on the amount, or   in
the pound on the sum payable for tax on the property within this Commonwealth, is hereby
assessed, and shall be paid by every person chargeable with the said tax at the time the same
shall become due; ...

And be it enacted, That for every sum so paid, the Sheriff or Collector shall give a receipt,
expressing therein to what society of Christians the person from whom he may receive the
same shall direct the money to be paid, keeping a distinct account thereof in his books. ...

And it be further enacted, That the money to be raised by virtue of this act, shall be by the
Vestries, Elders, or Directors of each religious society, appropriated to a provision for a Minister or Teacher of the Gospel of their denomination, or the providing places of divine worship,
and to none other use whatsoever, except in the denominations of Quakers and Menonists,
who may receive what is collected from their members, and place it in their general fund, to be
disposed of in a manner which they shall think best calculated to promote their particular
mode of worship.

See Thomas Buckley, *Church and State in Revolutionary Virginia, 1776–1787* (Charlottesville: Univ. Press
of Virginia, 1977), app., 188–89. For a modern recounting of this argument, see Michael Novak, "The
Influence of Judaism and Christianity on the American Founding," in *Religion and the New Republic:
Faith in the Founding of America*, 159.

8. The following are excerpts from Madison's "Memorial and Remonstrance," written to oppose
Patrick Henry's "Bill to Establish Teachers of the Christian Religion":

To the Honorable the General Assembly of Commonwealth of Virginia:

We, the subscribers, citizens of the said Commonwealth, having taken into serious consideration a Bill printed by order of the last Session of General Assembly, entitled "A Bill establishing a provision for Teachers of the Christian Religion"; and conceiving that the same if
finally armed with the sanctions of a law, will be a dangerous abuse of power, are bound as
faithful members of a free State, to remonstrate against it, and to declare the reasons by which
we are determined. We remonstrate against the said Bill: ...

Because it is proper to take alarm at the first experiment on our liberties. We hold this
prudent jealousy to be the first duty of Citizens and one of the noblest characteristics of the
late Revolution. The free men of America did not wait until usurped power had strengthened
itself by exercise, and entangled the question in precedents. They saw all the consequences in
the principle, and they avoided the consequences by denying the principle. We revere this lesson too much soon to forget it. Who does not see that the same authority which can establish
Christianity in exclusion of all other Religions, may establish with the same ease any particular
sect of Christians, in exclusion of all other Sects? that the same authority which can force a
citizen to contribute three pence only of his property for the support of any one establishment, may force him to conform to any other establishment in all cases whatsoever? ...

Because the Bill implies either that the Civil Magistrate is a competent Judge of Religious
Truth; or that he may employ Religion as an engine of Civil policy. The first is an arrogant
pretension falsified by the contradictory opinion of Rulers in all ages, and throughout the world:
the second an unhallowed perversion of the means of salvation. ...

Because the proposed establishment is a departure from that generous policy, which, offering an Asylum to the persecuted and oppressed of every Nation and Religion, promised a lustre to our country, and an accession to the number of its citizens. What a melancholy mark is
the Bill of sudden degeneracy? Instead of holding forth an Asylum to the persecuted, it is itself
a signal of persecution. It degrades from the equal rank of Citizens all those whose opinions in
Religion do not bend to those of the Legislative authority. Distant as it may be in its present

form from the Inquisition, it differs from it only in degree. The one is the first step, the other the last in the career of intolerance. The magnanimous sufferer under this cruel scourge in foreign Regions, must view the Bill as a Beacon on our Coast, warning him to seek some other haven, where liberty and philanthropy in their due extent, may offer a more certain repose from his Troubles. . . .

Because finally, "the equal right of every citizen to the free exercise of his Religion according to the dictates of conscience" is held by the same tenure with all our other rights. If we recur to its origin, it is equally the gift of nature; if we weigh its importance, it cannot be less dear to us; if we consult the "Declaration of those rights which pertain to the good people of Virginia, as the basis and foundation of Government," it is enumerated with equal solemnity, or rather studied emphasis. Either then, we must say, that the Will of the Legislature is the only measure of their authority; and that in the plenitude of this authority, they may sweep away all our fundamental rights; or, that they are bound to leave this particular right untouched and sacred: Either we must say that they may controul the freedom of the press, may abolish the Trial by Jury, may swallow up the Executive and Judiciary Powers of the State; nay that they may despoil us of our very right of suffrage, and erect themselves into an independent and hereditary Assembly or, we must say, that they have no authority to enact into law the Bill under consideration. We the Subscribers say, that the General Assembly of this Commonwealth have no such authority: And that no effort may be omitted on our part against so dangerous an usurpation, we oppose to it, this remonstrance; earnestly praying, as we are in duty bound, that the Supreme Lawgiver of the Universe, by illuminating those to whom it is addressed, may on the one hand, turn their Councils from every act which would affront his holy prerogative, or violate the trust committed to them: and on the other, guide them into every measure which may be worthy of his blessing, may redound to their own praise, and may establish more firmly the liberties, the prosperity, and the happiness of the Commonwealth.

See James Madison, "A Memorial and Remonstrance" (1785), Miller, *The First Liberty*, app. 2; Edwin S. Gaustad, ed., *A Documentary History of Religion in America to the Civil War* (Grand Rapids, Mich.: William B. Eerdmans, 1982), 262–67; Phillip Kurland, ed., *Founder's Constitution*, vol. 5 (Chicago: University of Chicago Press, 1987), 82.

9. Miller, *The First Liberty*, 1–75; "An Act For Establishing Religious Freedom," written by Thomas Jefferson and enacted as follows by the Virginia General Assembly, on January 16, 1786:

Whereas, Almighty God hath created the mind free; that all attempts to influence it by temporal punishment, or burthens, or by civil incapacitations, tend only to beget habits of hypocrisy and meanness, and are a departure from the plan of the Holy Author of our religion, who, being Lord both of body and mind, yet chose not to propagate it by coercions on either, as was in his Almighty power to do; that the impious presumption of legislators and rulers, civil as well as ecclesiastical, who, being themselves but fallible and uninspired men, have assumed dominion over the faith of others, setting up their own opinions and modes of thinking as the only true and infallible, and as such endeavoring to impose them on others, have established and maintained false religions over the greatest part of the world, and through all time; *that to compel a man to furnish contributions of money for the propagation of opinions which he disbelieves, is sinful and tyrannical, and even the forcing him to support this or that teacher of his own religious persuasion,* is depriving him of the comfortable liberty of giving his contributions to the particular pastor whose morals he would make his pattern, and whose powers he feels most persuasive to righteousness, and is withdrawing from the ministry those temporary rewards which, proceeding from an approbation of their personal conduct, are an additional incitement to earnest and unremitting labors, for the instruction of mankind; that our civil rights have no dependence on our religious opinions any more than our opinions in physics or geometry; that therefore the proscribing any citizen as unworthy the public confidence by laying upon him an incapacity of being called to offices of trust and emolument, unless he profess or renounce this or that religious opinion, is depriving him injuriously of those privileges and advantages to which, in common with his fellow citizens, he has a natural right; that it tends only to corrupt the principles of that religion it is meant to encourage, by bribing, with a monopoly of worldly honors and emoluments, those who will externally profess and conform to it; that though, indeed, those are criminal who do not withstand such temptation, yet, neither are those innocent who lay the bait in their way; that to suffer the civil magistrate to intrude his powers into the field of opinion, and to restrain the profession or propagation of principles on supposition of their ill tendency, is a dangerous fallacy, which at once destroys all religious liberty, because he, being of course judge of that tendency, will make his opinions the rules of judgment, and approve or condemn the sentiments of others only as they shall square with or differ from his own; that it is time enough for the rightful purposes of civil government, for its officers to interfere, when principles break out into overt acts against peace and good order; and finally, that truth is great and will prevail, if left to herself; that she is the proper and sufficient antagonist to error, and has nothing to fear from the conflict, unless by human interposition disarmed of her natural weapons, free argument and debate; errors ceasing to be dangerous when it is permitted freely to contradict them:

Be it enacted by the General Assembly, That no man shall be compelled to frequent or support any religious worship, place or ministry whatsoever, nor shall be enforced, restrained, molested or burthened, in his body or goods, nor shall otherwise suffer on account of his religious opinions or belief; but that all men shall be free to profess, and by argument to maintain, their opinions in matters of religion, and that the same shall in no wise diminish, enlarge or affect their civil capacities.

And though we well know that this Assembly, elected by the people for the ordinary purposes of legislation only, have no power to restrain the acts of succeeding assemblies constituted with powers equal to our own, and that, therefore, to declare this act to be irrevocable would be of no effect in law; yet we are free to declare, and do declare, that the rights hereby asserted are of the natural rights of mankind; and that if any act shall be hereafter passed to repeal the present, or to narrow its operation, such act will be an infringement of natural right.

See William Waller Hening, *The Statutes at Large, Being a Collection of All the Laws of Virginia, from the First Session of the Legislature in the Year 1619*, vol. 12, facsimile reprint published for the Jamestown Foundation of the Commonwealth of Virginia (Charlottesville: Univ. Press of Virginia, 1969), 84–86 (emphasis added). Also found in *Virginia Code Annotated* sec. 57.1; Miller, *The First Liberty*, app. 1.

10. Kurland, *Founder's Constitution*, vol. 5, 88–89.

11. Mark Noll, "Evangelicals in the American Founding," in *Religion and the New Republic*, 137; Jon Butler, "Why Revolutionary America Wasn't a 'Christian Nation,'" in *Religion and the New Republic*, 187.

12. Joseph Story, *A Familiar Exposition of the Constitution of the United States* (1859; reprint, Lake Bluff, Ill.: Regnery Gateway, 1986), 314–15.

13. U.S. House of Representatives, *Acknowledgment of God and the Christian Religion in the Constitution*, 43d Cong., 1st sess., 1874. H. Rept. 143. The report reads as follows:

Mr. Benjamin F. Butler, from the Committee on the Judiciary, submitted the following report:
The Committee on the Judiciary, to whom was referred the petition of E. G. Gould and others, asking Congress for "an acknowledgment of Almighty God and the Christian religion" in the Constitution of the United States, having considered the matter referred to them, respectfully pray leave to report:
That, upon examination even of the meager debates by the fathers of the Republic in the convention which framed the Constitution, they find that the subject of this memorial was most fully and carefully considered, and then, in that convention, decided after grave deliberation, to

which the subject was entitled, that, as this country, the foundation of whose government they were then laying, was to be the home of the oppressed of all nations of the earth, whether Christian or Pagan, and in full realization of the dangers which the union between church and state had imposed upon so many nations of the Old World, with great unanimity that it was inexpedient to put anything into the Constitution or frame of government which might be construed to be a reference to any religious creed or doctrine.

And they further find that this decision was accepted by our Christian fathers with such great unanimity that in the amendments which were afterward proposed, in order to make the Constitution more acceptable to the nation, none has ever been proposed to the States by which this wise determination of the fathers has been attempted to be changed. Wherefore, your committee report that it is inexpedient to legislate upon the subject of the above memorial, and ask that they be discharged from the further consideration thereof, and that this report, together with the petition, be laid upon the table.

14. *Zelman v. Simmons-Harris*, 2000 FED App. 0411P (6th Cir.), 4 of 28, http://laws.findlaw.com/6th/00a0411p.06. Accessed March 27, 2004.

15. *Pierce v. Society of Sisters*, 268 U.S. 5109 (1925).

16. *Engel v. Vitale*, 370 U.S. 421 (1962).

17. Steven Vegh, "Interfaith Services Worry Some: Concerned Christians Fear Prayers of Unity Sanctify All Gods," *Virginian-Pilot*, December 2, 2001.

18. "Forum," *Port Folio Weekly* (Virginia Beach, Va.), January 1, 2002.

19. *Nova*, "The Controversial Dr. Koop," aired on PBS October 10, 1989, show 1612.

Explaining the Complexities of Religion and State in the United States

Separation, Integration, and Accommodation

DEREK H. DAVIS

The interplay between religion and state in the United States is complex, if any-thing. The rules that comprise the American system of church-state relations—rules dictated mostly by judicial interpretations of the First Amendment's religion clauses, but also embracing traditions that the High Court chooses not to interfere with—are frequently criticized as inconsistent and confusing. A common criticism, for ex-ample, is that students in public schools cannot have prayers in their classrooms[1] or at their football games,[2] but the U.S. Congress may have its own chaplains to lead its daily prayers. Another is that the Ten Commandments cannot be posted in public school classrooms, yet the U.S. Supreme Court chamber in Washington, D.C., is decorated with a representation of Moses holding the Ten Commandments.[3] And how is it that ordained preachers such as Pat Robertson and Jesse Jackson can run for president of the United States in the face of the constitutional requirement of separation of church and state? On the face of these circumstances, these seemingly contradictory rules and practices seem rather odd, even bizarre. But understood in the broader, elaborate American framework in which religion and state interact, these apparent consistencies can be understood, even justified.

I suggest here that the American system must be understood as embracing three distinct, yet interrelated sets of rules: *separation* of church and state, *integration* of religion and politics, and *accommodation* of civil religion. All of the various rules, customs, and practices that shape the unique relationship between religion and state in America can be assigned primarily, though not always exclusively, to one of these three categories. Each category is essential to the overall American public phi-losophy, each one part of a nuanced, interconnected system that has as its goal the "good society." And, as I will argue in this chapter, without some appreciation of these three categories, their interrelationship, and the way in which they combine to promote democratic principles, one is certain to become hopelessly confused by the apparent contradictions in the overall system.

SEPARATION OF CHURCH AND STATE

"Separation of church and state" has become the customary way of describing the relationship between religion and state in the American system.[4] Yet the phrase is too broad to accurately describe the whole system, because in many respects there clearly is no "separation." How can a system that proclaims "In God We Trust" as its national motto, invokes the name of God in its Pledge of Allegiance, observes a national day of prayer, and sanctions government-paid legislative chaplains be said to have a commitment to the separation of church and state? Obviously the American tradition of separation of church and state does not mean that a separation of religion from government is required in all cases. So although the phrase is too broad to embrace the whole system, it nevertheless does accurately describe an important part of the system.

A better way to think of separation is as a term that describes an *institutional* separation of church and state. In other words, the Constitution requires that the *institutions* of church and state in American society not be interconnected, dependent upon, or functionally related to each other. The purpose of this requirement is to achieve mutual independence and autonomy for these institutions, based on the belief that they will function best if neither has authority over the other. Affected by this requirement are the institutional bodies of religion, that is, churches, mosques, temples, synagogues, other bodies of organized religion, and the institutional bodies of governmental authority—state and federal governments, but also small local bodies such as school districts, police departments, city councils, utility districts, municipal courts, county commissions, and the like. Consequently, churches and other houses of worship receive no direct governmental funding, nor are they required to pay taxes. Government officials appoint no clergy; conversely, religious bodies appoint no government officials. Governments, even courts, are not allowed to settle church disputes that involve doctrinal issues. And religious bodies, unlike the Catholic Church in the Middle Ages, have no authority to dictate law or public policy.

The institutional separation of church and state is observed most frequently, and most controversially, in judicial decisions that limit religious activity in the public schools. Court decisions limiting schools' ability to entertain vocal prayers and scripture readings, to post the Ten Commandments and other religious texts, or to advance a particular religious worldview are intended to protect the sacred domain of religion from state interference. It is important to remember that in the

SEPARATION OF CHURCH AND STATE

34   DEMOCRACY AND RELIGION

public school context, the precepts and practices of *institutionalized* religion are prohibited from being embraced or proscribed. Courses that teach comparative religion, the historical or literary aspects of religion, or the anthropologized dimensions of religion are permitted, even encouraged. As Justice Tom Clark wrote in *Abington v. Schempp* (1963), "One's education is not complete without a study of comparative religion or the history of religion and its relationship to the advancement of civilization. . . . [S]tudy of the Bible or of religion, when presented objectively as part of a secular program of education [does not violate] the First Amendment."[5]

Likewise, court decisions that place restrictions on the ability of government to fund private religious education are the product of the institutional separation of church and state. Generally the courts have held that these programs, administered by bodies of institutionalized religion, tend to advance religion in a sectarian manner and therefore violate the establishment clause. But funding of "secular" components of private religious schools is permitted. Consequently, the courts have permitted governments to purchase, by way of example, textbooks,[6] computers,[7] equipment for diagnostic testing,[8] and other miscellaneous expenditures on behalf of private religious schools, because these aid programs are not endorsements of religion. Programs that provide benefits that might be used for promoting or advancing religion, however, such as teacher stipends[9] and open-ended subsidies that might be used to purchase religious texts, erect religious statues,[10] or finance field trips in which religious instruction might take place,[11] have been held unconstitutional.

The institutional separation of church and state affects other areas of religion-government interaction as well. Government has passed in recent years a set of measures that attempt to provide government funding of churches and other religious institutions that are willing to administer social service programs—soup kitchens, drug and alcohol rehabilitation programs, clothing pantries, homeless shelters, youth anticrime programs, and the like. Theoretically, these programs advance secular ends, thus passing constitutional scrutiny. But they are a bold challenge to prevailing constitutional doctrine, which holds that churches, temples, mosques, and other houses of worship are "pervasively sectarian," which means that their mission and purpose is so pervaded by religion that it is virtually impossible for them to ferret out "secular" aspects of their activity. This legislation, dubbed "charitable choice" because program beneficiaries may choose either a government-funded religious or secular provider, is a challenge to traditional separationist judicial interpretations of the establishment clause. Proponents of charitable choice advance the ancient fear that without government aid, religion will suffer, potential recipients of assistance will be ignored, and society will experience moral decline. Opponents counter with the argument that religion thrives best when it relies on private rather than government resources and that morality is best fostered in a climate of self-sustaining voluntarism rather than government-sustaining inducements.[12]

The institutional separation of church and state is a novel experiment in human history. Most societies throughout history have operated on the assumption that government should be a moral agent, that it must play a leading role in crafting human beings. It became customary in ancient times for governments to sponsor, even require, religious worship and instruction as the means of inculcating morality into citizens' lives. The American founders were convinced that successful nation building would be impossible in the absence of a moral citizenry, but they believed that moral training, insofar as it was religiously based, must derive primarily from the faith community, not government.[13] The establishment clause was the founders' attempt to end government's coercive role in directing the religious course of citizens' lives; the free exercise clause reflected their goal of putting religion in the hands of the citizens to enable them to shape their own religious commitments. It was a bold experiment, but one that is now central to the American public philosophy. As Supreme Court Justice Wiley Rutledge once declared, "We have staked the very existence of our country on the faith that complete separation between the state and religion is best for the state and best for religion."[14] Justice Rutledge well knew that *complete* separation between church and state is impossible, but his words are a powerful reminder of how central the principle of separation is to the American way of life.

INTEGRATION OF RELIGION AND POLITICS

Separation of church and state is indeed important to the American way of life, but as noted already, it does not describe all aspects of the interplay between religion and state. This is readily seen in the way that the American system encourages the participation of religious voices in the political process. Were the system one of *total* separation, it would not countenance the active involvement of religious persons, faith communities, and religious organizations that vigorously enter public discourse, seeking to persuade government officials of the merits of framing law and public policy to reflect their distinctly religious outlooks.

The right of churches and other religious bodies to engage in political advocacy and to make political pronouncements has never been seriously questioned throughout the United States' history, from the colonial period to the present. In the years leading up to the American Revolution, for example, the churches assumed a leading role in the political debate on the question of whether the colonies should go to war with the mother country. In the nineteenth century, the major causes for political action among the churches and other religious groups were slavery, temperance, and nonsectarian education. In the twentieth century, the engagement of religious bodies in the body politic grew to cover a wide range of issues including economic and social justice, war and peace, abortion, civil rights, and world hunger. Today virtually all of the major religious groups in America and many religious coalitions have public affairs offices in Washington, D.C., to lead their lobbying efforts.[15] These groups, for the most part, do not consider the public affairs offices to exist for the promotion of their self-interests but as an effective means by which they give witness in public affairs based on their understanding of their mission in the world.

Given the time-honored right of religious bodies to be active participants in the American political process, it is not surprising that the U.S. Supreme Court has not seriously challenged this basic right. The strongest affirmation of this right was given by the Court in *Walz v. Tax Commission* (1970): "Adherents of particular faiths and individual churches frequently take strong positions on public issues, including . . . vigorous advocacy of legal and constitutional positions. Of course, churches as much as secular bodies and private citizens have that right."[16] Likewise, in *McDaniel v. Paty* (1978), a case striking down the last of the state statutes prohibiting ministers from seeking state office, the Supreme Court affirmed the importance and protected status of religious ideas in public debate: "Religious ideas, no less than any other, may be the subject of debate which is uninhibited, robust, and wide-open. . . . That public debate of religious ideas, like any other, may arouse emotion, may incite, may foment religious divisiveness and strife, does not rob it of its constitutional protection."[17]

Supreme Court pronouncements such as these, however, should not lead one to assume that organized religion in America enjoys an absolute right to participate in the making of public policy, free from governmental interference of any type. These groups are subject to losing their tax exemptions, for example, for "substantial" political expenditures[18] or for endorsing political candidates (lobbying).[19] Nevertheless they enjoy essentially the same rights as secular groups to participate in the political process. The principles of democracy prevail here, such that the rights of every person or group in American society, religious or secular, that wishes to contribute to democratic governance is free to do so, even encouraged to do so, even though such participation constitutes a technical violation of the principle of church-state separation. *Complete* separation would mean banning the activities of the Christian Coalition and approximately 125 other religious lobbies whose sole reason for existence is to influence lawmaking and public policy according to religiously inspired perspectives. Although many of these lobbies, unfortunately, attempt to issue dictates rather than offer advice, mandates rather than persuasive arguments, the great majority of them have learned to submit their perspectives with some degree of humility, recognizing that America is a democracy shaped by many views, not a theocracy shaped by a few.

Although religious arguments are commonplace in American political discourse, legislation that advances a religious purpose generally is not because of the Supreme

Court's requirement, pursuant to the *Lemon* test, that governmental action reflect a secular purpose, that it not have the primary effect of advancing or inhibiting religion, and that it not create an excessive entanglement between religion and government.[20]

In terms of political theory, the *Lemon* test reflects the Court's understanding that the nation is essentially a *liberal* state rather than a *religious* state. However, according to most scholarly accounts of the liberal state, this designation carries requirements that are in addition to the mandates of the *Lemon* test. Most significantly, participants' dialogue in public discourse within a liberal democracy must be intelligible to other participants. Because religious language is unintelligible to many citizens, it should be translated into secular language accessible to everyone. Religious motivation might lie beneath the veneer of certain legislation, but the legislation itself must be couched in essentially secular language. By most accounts, this requirement is a logical antecedent to the *Lemon* test, which requires that the final product of public discourse—legislation—carry a secular orientation.

The work of John Rawls, of course, is pivotal for the entire tradition of liberal political thought. In *A Theory of Justice* (1971) he makes the basic points just enumerated in support of a secular basis for the liberal state.[21] Rawls's work has been highly influential in the United States and has widespread support among political theorists, albeit in varying degrees.[22] In recent years, however, liberal political theory has been challenged by a host of communitarian thinkers, all complaining essentially that Rawlsian liberal theory unnecessarily undermines the viable contributions to the public good that specifically religious viewpoints can make. Among these critics has been Stephen Carter, who argues in *The Culture of Disbelief* that religious arguments and even religion-based legislation should be countenanced in a liberal democratic framework.[23]

It is this writer's view, contrary to Rawls and affirming Carter, that religious arguments in public discourse generally should be permitted. Common sense may dictate that on many occasions the one advancing a religious argument should translate that argument into secular language in order that it may become more intelligible and convincing to others, but that should be the decision of the one advancing the argument. Nevertheless, it is suggested here, contrary to Carter and affirming Rawls, that when the public debate on a particular issue is completed and legislation is to be enacted—when the relative free-for-all that is American liberal democracy in which every conceivable viewpoint (religious and secular alike) has been entertained—*the legislation that is enacted,* consistent with the *Lemon* test, should reflect essentially secular aims and effects. The great weight of evidence is that the founding fathers intended, as indicated most demonstrably by their purposive omission of God's name in the Constitution, to create what is generally referred to today as a liberal state. The decision to break with traditional political theory that placed human government under divine authority was the result of their belief that the power to frame a new government derived not immediately from heaven, but from the American people. The founders created a government that was to be "of the people, by the people, and for the people." This in no way was a denial of their personal religious (mostly Christian) convictions, but the new federal government was to be one in which the people were the responsible parties, not God. The product of public discourse was to be man's law, not holy law. This always has been, and remains, the essence of a liberal state.

In the modern lawmaking process, politicians, like the Founding Fathers, may personally hold themselves accountable to God. But whether or not they do, they are in fact accountable to the people. Because the people are of diverse faiths, the product of public debate—legislation—should be religiously neutral (secular) so as to reflect the common good, not merely the good of those who prevailed in the debate. The *Lemon* three-prong test and the tradition of American political discourse embody this kind of commitment.

American adherence to the integration of religion and politics also means that potential candidates and officeholders are free to speak about their religious views. They may think it prudent at times to abstain from too much "God speak," but the free exercise clause gives them the freedom to speak freely about matters of faith, even, for the most part, when acting in their official capacities. It is unlikely that a candidate for president could be elected in America without some candid talk about his or her religious views. America is diverse in its religious makeup, but it is unmistakably one of the most religious nations on the globe, and the American people generally demand to know their representatives' religious beliefs. The Constitution forbids the administration of formal religious tests for holding public office (and most states have followed suit), but this is different from the unofficial expectation that an officeholder have at least some religious commitments. This expectation is the product of a religious culture, of a body of citizens who "are a religious people whose institutions presuppose a Supreme Being." This was the perspective of Supreme Court Justice William O. Douglas in 1954,[24] but it remains true roughly a half century later.

ACCOMMODATION OF CIVIL RELIGION

If in the American system the establishment clause is relaxed in sanctioning an integration of religion and politics, it is equally relaxed in accommodating various expressions of civil religion. According to the most celebrated scholar on American civil religion, Robert Bellah, civil religion is about those public rituals that express the nexus of the political order to the divine reality.[25] By most accounts, civil religion is a form of religion that gives sacred meaning to national life. It is a kind of theological glue that binds a nation together by allying the political with the transcendent. Civil religion is a way for Americans to recognize the sovereignty of God over their nation without getting bogged down in theological differences.

Many Americans affirm the separation of church and state, but this does not remove their belief that the nation—as a civil entity—is still somehow obligated to God. For them, nationhood makes little sense unless it is part of a universe ruled by God; consequently, they believe that the body politic should have a religious dimension. Stated in another way, religion is not merely private; it is inescapably public too. Bellah acknowledges this, arguing that separation of church and state does not deny the political realm a religious dimension.[26]

The most common symbols of American civil religion are the national motto "In God We Trust," which also appears on U.S. currency; the invocation of God's name in the Pledge of Allegiance, recited daily by students in many of the nation's public schools; observance of a national day of prayer; the utilization of government-paid chaplains in the military, U.S. Congress, and state legislatures; and the frequent allusion to God and America's religious destiny in political, especially presidential, speeches (every president has acknowledged God in his inaugural address). These civil religious expressions are not promoted exclusively by the state or exclusively by the religious community. Rather, they are promoted by both, serving to embed in the national civil order an unmistakable religious quality.

Civil religion is a sociological reality in every society. It manifests itself in different ways in different contexts, but French sociologist Emile Durkheim (1858–1917) was probably correct in suggesting that every society at its deepest foundations is religious, and the sovereign must act responsibly to respect and acknowledge this, lest the society itself deteriorate and pass into oblivion.[27] For most Americans, of course, a nation that takes steps to acknowledge the sovereignty of God, even if in generic, symbolic ways, is not merely accommodating the wishes of the citizenry in the sense of filling a sociological need, but acting to affirm the divine reality. In any case, the accommodation of civil religion can be said to prevent the nation from steering too far in the direction of a secularized culture.

The U.S. Supreme Court occasionally acknowledges the evidence of civil religion in American life. Legislative prayer,[28] legislative and military chaplaincies,[29] Christmas[30] and Hanukkah displays,[31] and graduation prayers in public schools,[32] as expressions of civil religion, have all been challenged as violations of the separation requirements of the establishment. The Court tends to sanction those civil religious traditions that are generic, long-standing, and not likely to offend persons of tender age. Thus, in the case of legislative prayer, the Supreme Court has held that the practice is constitutional because it has a long and unbroken tradition in American political life.[33] In the public school context, however, given the impressionability of young persons, similar prayers are prohibited as violations of the institutional separation of church and state. The same contrary set of rules, applied in the respective contexts of legislative halls and public school classrooms, can be said to apply to the posting of the Ten Commandments[34] and other sacred texts. Legislative and military chaplaincies are likewise affirmed as long-standing traditions, although it is doubtful that courts would endorse the concept of public school chaplains because of the impressionability and potential for indoctrination of the students they would serve. Holiday displays have been held not to violate the establishment clause if their religious message is muted by surrounding secular symbols.[35] Prayer offered by a clergyman at a public school graduation ceremony, however, has been held to violate the establishment clause as an inappropriate government sponsorship of religion.[36]

The federal courts have struggled in their efforts to assess the constitutional propriety of these kinds of public acknowledgment cases. The difficulty in evaluating such cases is that the religion advanced is typically nonsectarian, symbolic, and without specific theological content—in short, civil religion. The courts, with lawyers sitting as judges, have not been particularly sophisticated in their ability to distinguish civil religion from traditional religion. Occasionally the Supreme Court has applied a vague concept called "ceremonial deism" to justify some practices of civil religion,[37] but for the most part, the Court has seemed to be totally unaware of the large body of scholarly literature that has appeared in recent decades giving analysis to civil religion as a distinctive form of religion.[38] The Court has never defined ceremonial deism; the term seems to be mere shorthand for the Court's judgment that a practice ought to be constitutional because it is not really religious, either because it has culturally lost the significance it once had or because it is used only to solemnize a public occasion.

The increased attention that some courts have given to the civil religion concept has led some legal commentators to suggest that civil religion should be judicially recognized and approved, that indeed civil religion mediates and is the much-needed compromise to settle the debate between those who believe that a strong adherence to separation of church and state is best for America and those who believe that more religion should be accommodated in the public sphere.[39] It is true that the courts have begun to consider the possibility of carving out a special test that might constitutionally sanction certain expressions of civil religion. In a 1987 case, *Stein v. Plainwell Community Schools*,[40] a federal appeals court considered the constitutionality of including prayers in high school commencement ceremonies. The plaintiffs, parents of students at two Michigan high schools, argued that the prayers "invoke[d] the image of a God or Supreme Being" and thus violated the First Amendment values of "liberty of conscience, state neutrality and noninterference with religion."[41] Attendance at the commencement ceremonies was voluntary, and failure to attend did not affect the receipt of a diploma. In one school a student delivered the prayer and, at the other, a member of the local clergy.

The court concluded that the religion clauses, taken together, guarantee "equal liberty of conscience," erecting "a neutral state designed to foster the most extensive liberty of conscience compatible with a similar or equal liberty for others."[42] Treating commencement prayers as analogous to legislative prayers, the court concluded that *Marsh v. Chambers* (authorizing legislative prayers) governed the case, permitting some accommodation to the nation's religious traditions. In analyzing the nature of commencement prayers, the court sought to place them within an overall framework of a civil religion: "So long as the invocation or benediction on these public occasions does not go beyond 'the American civil religion,' so long as it preserves the substance of the principle of equality of liberty of conscience, no violation of the Establishment Clause occurs under the reasoning of *Marsh*."[43] In sustaining commencement prayers generally, the court emphasized that, unlike classroom prayer, they presented little danger of religious coercion or indoctrination. The court, however, found the prayers unacceptable because they were so distinctively Christian that they connoted a governmental endorsement of Christianity. Thus the prayers failed to qualify as permissible invocations and benedictions under a special category of "American civil religion."

In 1992, in *Lee v. Weisman*,[44] the U.S. Supreme Court considered a similar case involving commencement prayer. There, a middle school principal had invited a Jewish rabbi to give the invocation and benediction at the school's commencement ceremony. The rabbi recited nonsectarian prayers, following the school's instructions that prayers reflect "inclusiveness in sensitivity." The plaintiff, the father of a fourteen-year-old student of the school, complained that the prayers were an impermissible governmental advancement of religion contrary to the prohibitions of the establishment clause.

The Court held that the prayers bore the imprint of the Providence school system and were therefore unlawful advancements of religion. The Court stated that even for those students who objected to the religious ceremony, their attendance was in a "fair and real sense" obligatory, even though attendance was not required as a condition for receipt of a diploma. The Court reasoned that this constituted an indirect coercion, which could be as real as any overt compulsion to participate in the state-sponsored religious activity. The atmosphere of the commencement proceeding was distinguished from that of a state legislature, as in *Marsh*. In the latter, the Court said, adults are free to enter and leave with little comment and for any number of reasons, whereas in the former, children are constrained to attend in its entirety the one most important event of their school year.

Of special interest here is the attention that Justice Anthony Kennedy, writing for the majority, gave to the brief discussion of civil religion set forth in the *Stein* case:

We are asked to recognize the existence of a practice of nonsectarian prayer, prayer within the embrace of what is known as the Judeo-Christian tradition, prayer which is more acceptable than one which, for example, makes explicit references to the God of Israel, or to Jesus Christ, or to a patron saint. There may be some support, as an empirical observation, to the statement of the Court of Appeals for the Sixth Circuit, picked up by Judge Campbell's dissent in the Court of Appeals in this case, that there has emerged in this country a civic religion, one which is tolerated when sectarian exercises are not. . . . If common ground can be defined which permits once conflicting faiths to express the shared conviction that there is an ethic and morality which transcend human invention, the sense of community and purpose sought by all decent societies might be advanced. But though the First Amendment does not allow the government to stifle prayers which aspire to these ends, neither does it permit the government to undertake that task for itself.[45]

Kennedy's point here is that "civic religion," whatever its merits and however it might represent consensus, is religion just the same, and if promulgated by government violates the establishment clause. Although Kennedy's was not an extended inquiry into the nature of civil religion, his recognition of it as a distinctive form of religion that is different from creedal religions at least gives Court-watchers some glimpse of how the Court might adjudicate future attempts to seek a special status for civil religion under the establishment clause.

In addition to Kennedy's assertion that civil religion is only another form of religion and therefore suspect under the establishment clause, there are other valid reasons for not enshrining civil religion as a test for measuring the constitutionality of time-honored religious practices. First, an impossible definitional task would ensue. According civil religion a preferred status under the establishment clause would require that its contours be closely defined. As a religion without a formal set of theological tenets, clergy, history, mission, or confessional adherents, civil religion would not possess the content it would have to have as the comparative paradigm for assessing the acceptability of religious symbols and practices in public life.[46]

A second problem with raising the American civil religion to constitutional status is the risk it poses for civil religion's becoming a threat to authentic religious faith. A civil religion tends to enshrine the political order and, as Senator Mark Hatfield once said, for those of traditional faith, borders on idolatry and "fails to speak of repentance, salvation, and God's standard of justice."[47] Finally, constitutionally establishing a civil religion gives the government, through the courts, a tool to justify and reinforce its own policies. As the standard for acceptability, the civil religion would enjoy a preferred status that could be used to exclude traditional religious advocacy from the public arena.[48]

In summary, civil religion has been for much of American history and remains a vital cultural force. It is manifested in our own day in prayers at presidential inaugurations, the invocation used each time the Supreme Court hears argument ("God save this honorable court"), Thanksgiving and National Day of Prayer proclamations, the words "under God" in the Pledge of Allegiance, the phrase "In God We Trust" on coins, various Scripture quotations inscribed on government buildings ("Moses the Lawgiver" is the inscription above the Supreme Court's bench), and even the ritual benediction "God Bless America," used frequently by presidents.

All of these civil religious traditions are violations of a strict notion of the separation of church and state. Yet they form a rich tradition of practices that are culturally and judicially accommodated. Undoubtedly they offend many, but they are for the most part generic practices that are not coercive in the way that, for example, audible school prayers in the public schools are. Indeed, these practices are accepted and celebrated by most Americans, and they contribute to a unique, nuanced, and sometimes contradictory set of concepts, principles, customs, beliefs, and symbols that comprise the American tradition of religion and state.[49]

Conclusion

Although contradictory in many respects, the principles of separation of church and state, integration of religion and politics, and accommodation of civil religion combine to provide unique but important contributions to America's public philosophy. The role of religion in American public life has been controversial since the Founding and will likely remain so far into the future. But perhaps the separation-integration-accommodation triad described in this chapter removes some of the hard edges from the controversy because it embraces elements of both conservative and liberal thought, of competing philosophical and theological beliefs, and indeed of key arguments advanced by both separationists and accommodationists. The final product can be likened to a tossed salad, a blend of items that perhaps are not so tasty if partaken of separately, but quite savory in combination. Such is the way a democracy should work—disparate elements coming together to produce that which hopefully serves everyone, that which we have come to call the common good, indeed that which we might refer to as the Good Society.

NOTES

1. See *Engel v. Vitale*, 370 U.S. 421 (1962), and *Abington School District v. Schempp*, 374 U.S. 203 (1963).

2. *Santa Fe v. Doe*, 530 U.S. 27 (2002).

3. For a discussion of the Ten Commandments in public life, see Derek H. Davis, "The Ten Commandments as Public Ritual," *Journal of Church and State* 44 (Spring 2002): 221.

4. The "separation" principle is explained in a wide range of ways. Those who see separation as requiring only the prohibition against a national church, thus allowing for broader governmental advancement of religion, are often called accommodationists. Those who argue for more extensive prohibitions of governmental support of religion are frequently referred to as separationists. Among the best works presenting accommodationists' interpretations are Chester James Antieu, Arthur L. Downey, and Edward C. Roberts, *Freedom from Federal Establishment: Formation and Early History of the First Amendment Religions Clauses* (Milwaukee, Wis.: Bruce, 1964); Walter Berns, *The First Amendment and the Future of American Democracy* (New York: Basic, 1976); Michael J. Malbin, *Religion and Politics: The Intentions of the Authors of the First Amendment* (Washington, D.C.: American Enterprise Institute for Public Policy Research, 1978); and Robert L. Cord, *Separation of Church and State: Historical Fact and Current Fiction* (New York: Lambeth, 1982). Among the best works with separationist stances are Leo Pfeffer, *Church, State and Freedom*, 2d ed. (Boston, Mass.: Beacon, 1967); Leonard Levy, *The Establishment Clause: Religion and the First Amendment* (New York: Macmillan, 1986); Anson Phelps Stokes, *Church and State in the United States: Historical Development and Contemporary Problems of Religious Freedom under the Constitution*, 3 vols. (New York: Harper and Brothers, 1950); and Isaac Kramnick and R. Laurence Moore, *The Godless Constitution: The Case against Religious Correctness* (New York: Norton, 1996).

5. *Abington v. Schempp*, 225.

6. *Board of Education v. Allen*, 392 U.S. 236 (1968).

7. *Mitchell v. Helms*, 530 U.S. 793 (2000).

8. *Levitt v. Pearl*, 413 U.S. 472 (1973).

9. *Lemon v. Kurtzman*, 403 U.S. 602 (1971).

10. *Pearl v. Nyquist*, 413 U.S. 756 (1973).

11. *Wolman v. Walters*, 433 U.S. 229 (1977).

12. On charitable choice legislation generally, see Derek H. Davis and Barry Hankins, *Welfare Reform and Faith-based Organizations* (Waco, Tex.: J. M. Dawson Institute of Church-State Studies, 1999).

13. See Davis, "Virtue and the Continental Congress," in *Religion and the Continental Congress, 1774–1789: Contributions to Original Intent* (New York: Oxford Univ. Press, 2000), chap. 10.

14. *Everson v. Board of Education*, 330 U.S. 1 (1947), 59.

15. For excellent treatments of religious lobbying, see Ronald J. Hrebenar and Ruth K. Scott, *Interest Group Politics in America* (Englewood Cliffs, N.J.: Prentice Hall, 1982); Jeffrey M. Berry, *The Interest Group Society* (Glenview, Ill.: Scott Foresman, 1989); Allen D. Hertzke, *Representing God in Washington: The Role of Religious Lobbies in the American Polity* (Knoxville: Univ. of Tennessee Press, 1988); Jeffrey M. Berry, *The New Liberalism: The Rising Power of Citizens Groups* (Washington, D.C.: Brookings Institution, 1999); Daniel J. B. Hofrenning, *In Washington, But Not of It: The Prophetic Politics of Religious Lobbyists* (Philadelphia, Pa.: Temple Univ. Press, 1995); and Luke Eugene Ebersole, *Church Lobbying in the Nation's Capital* (New York: Macmillan, 1951).

16. *Walz v. Tax Commission*, 397 U.S. US 664 (1970).

17. *McDaniel v. Paty*, 435 U.S. 618 (1978) at 640.

18. Though there is no clear rule for defining "substantial," one case suggests that there is a "safe harbor" if an organization's lobbying expenses do not exceed 5 percent. *Seasongood v. Commissioner*, 227 F. 2d 907 (6th Cir. 1955). In another case, a court held that a church spending approximately 22 percent of its revenues on members' medical bills under a church medical plan was engaged in a "substantial

nonexempt activity." *Bethel Conservative Mennonite Church v. Commissioner* 80 T.C. 352 (1983), rev'd., 746 F. 2d 388 (7th Cir. 1984). Another court has held that a percentage test is inappropriate. *Haswell v. United States,* 500 F. 2d 1133 (Ct. Cl. 1974), cert. denied, 419 U.S. 1107 (1975). Still, according to one source, no more than 20 percent of expenditures would be deemed "insubstantial." See Lynn R. Buzzard and Sherra Robinson, *I.R.S. Political Activity Restrictions on Churches and Charitable Ministries* (Diamond Bar, Calif.: Christian Ministries Management Association, 1990), 53–59.

19. "Lobbying" is defined in the Internal Revenue Code Section 4911 (d)(1). Various regulations, rulings, and court decisions on the meaning of "lobbying" are explained well in Buzzard and Robinson, I.R.S. Political Activity Restrictions, 42–52.

20. *Lemon v. Kurtzman,* 403 U.S. 602 (1971).

21. John Rawls, *A Theory of Justice* (Cambridge, Mass.: Harvard Univ. Press, 1971).

22. See, for example, Bruce Ackerman, *Social Justice in the Liberal State* (New Haven, Conn.: Yale Univ. Press, 1980); Thomas Nagel, "Moral Conflict and Political Legitimacy," *Philosophy and Public Affairs* 16 (Summer 1987): 232; and Kent Greenawalt, *Religious Convictions and Political Choice* (New York: Oxford Univ. Press, 1988).

23. Stephen L. Carter, *The Culture of Disbelief: How American Law and Politics Trivialize American Devotion* (New York: Basic, 1994).

24. *Zorach v. Clauson,* 343 U.S. 306 (1952), 313.

25. See generally, Robert N. Bellah, *The Broken Covenant: American Civil Religion in Time of Trial,* 2d ed. (Chicago: Univ. of Chicago Press, 1975), esp. 3.

26. Ibid., 169–70.

27. Emile Durkheim, *The Elementary Forms of the Religious Life,* rev. ed. (New York: Free Press, 1965).

28. *Marsh v. Chambers,* 463 U.S. 783 (1983).

29. *Abington v. Schempp,* 374 U.S. 203 (1963), 296–97 (Brennan concurring).

30. *Lynch v. Donnelly,* 465 U.S. 668 (1984).

31. *Allegheny v. Pittsburgh ACLU,* 492 U.S. 573 (1989).

32. *Lee v. Weisman,* 505 U.S. 577 (1992).

33. *Marsh v. Chambers,* 463 U.S. 783 (1983).

34. *Stone v. Graham,* 449 U.S. 39 (1980).

35. *Lynch v. Donnelly,* 465 U.S. 668 (1984; Christmas crèche paid for with public monies constitutional when surrounded by Santa Claus, reindeer, elves, and related secular Christmas decorations); *County of Allegheny v. A.C.L.U.,* 109 S.Ct. 1086 (1989; Jewish menorah displayed on public property constitutional when located next to a Christmas tree and a sign saluting liberty).

36. *Lee v. Weisman,* 505 U.S. 577 (1992).

37. For example, see *Lynch v. Donnelly,* 465 U.S. 668 (1984), 716 (Brennan, J., dissenting), and *County of Allegheny v. A.C.L.U.,* 492 U.S. 573 (1989).

38. Some of the most significant contributions to the literature are Will Herberg, *Protestant, Catholic, Jew: An Essay in American Religious Sociology,* rev. ed. (Garden City, N.Y.: Anchor, 1960); Sidney Mead, *The Nation with the Soul of a Church* (New York: Harper and Row, 1975); and Russell E. Richey and Donald G. Jones, eds., *American Civil Religion* (New York: Harper and Row, 1974).

39. For the leading article expressing the view that civil religion should be applied to establishment clause adjudication, see Yehudah Mirsky, "Civil Religion and the Establishment Clause," *Yale Law Journal* 95 (1986): 1237. For a similar view, see Michael M. Maddigan, "The Establishment Clause, Civil Religion, and the Public Church," *California Law Review* 81 (1993): 293.

40. 822 F. 2d 1406 (6th Cir. 1987).

41. Ibid., 1408.

42. Ibid.

43. Ibid., 1409.

44. *Lee v. Weisman,* 505 U.S. 577 (1992).

45. Ibid., 2652.

46. Arlin M. Adams and Charles J. Emmerich, *A Nation Dedicated to Religious Liberty: The Constitutional Heritage of the Religion Clauses* (Philadelphia.: Univ. of Pennsylvania Press, 1990), 87.

47. Mark Hatfield, *Between a Rock and a Hard Place* (Waco, Tex.: Word, 1976), 92.

48. Adams and Emmerich, *A Nation Dedicated to Religious Liberty,* 87.

49. This position is consistent with the Supreme Court's doctrine of "benevolent neutrality," first expressed in *Walz v. Tax Commission,* 397 U.S. 664 (1970). "Benevolent neutrality" is appropriately sensitive to the institutional difference between religion and government that was intended by the framers while simultaneously allowing for some governmental expressions of religion in public life.

Public Funds and Religious Schools

The Next Prayer Debate?

JOHN E. FERGUSON JR.

"Sic Dues Vult,"[1] cried the Christian Crusaders as they ventured into battle almost a thousand years ago. For centuries, cultures clashed in bloody battles, fighting over differences in religion and worldview. In the end, wars were won not through decisive engagements but through attrition and acquiescence.

How fortunate that in the United States today we no longer have to resolve our religious differences on bloody battlefields. This is not to say that America does not have its own culture wars. And, once again, worldviews and religion form the basis of the conflict over the relationship between religion and government. Without swords, shields, or steeds, today's cultural warriors enter the fray armed with lawyers, lawsuits, and legislation. For decades the schools have been the primary field of battle. Today's fights are not over control of land or cities, but over school-sponsored prayer, devotional Bible readings, holidays, and accommodation of student's religious needs. Although all of these issues have been a cause célèbre at one time or another, recently one issue has risen to the forefront: government funding for private, religious schools in the form of vouchers.

Writing a chapter on the topic of vouchers today is like writing a biography of Thomas Jefferson. What more can be said that has not been said ad infinitum? For one thing, society has reached a crossroads in the debate over the relationship between the government and religion. The case of *Zelman v. Simmons-Harris* will provide the constitutional answers not only about school funding and educational reform but also about such far-reaching issues as charitable choice and President Bush's faith-based initiatives.[2] The Supreme Court's acceptance of this case makes this a unique moment in time, providing an opportunity to formulate an understanding for current and future issues.

Part 1 of this chapter introduces the controversy over vouchers as it exists today in Cleveland, Ohio. Part 2 begins the examination of vouchers by looking at the history of religious liberty and public education in America, with a focus on the genesis of the controversy over public funding of religious schools. This will provide needed context and background for the jurisprudential history that will follow. Part 3 moves beyond the early history and explores various models the Supreme Court has constructed to address establishment clause concerns whenever public funds or benefits are provided to religious organizations. Part 4 returns to the case of *Zelman v. Simmons-Harris* and presents the arguments of the various parties. Part 5 analyzes the arguments of each side, giving special attention to Justice O'Connor and the endorsement test. Finally, part 6 concludes with a prediction of how the Court will decide the *Zelman* case and offers a suggestion of how the voucher debate eventually will be resolved.

1. ZELMAN

The Cleveland school district was and is considered by people on all sides of this debate as being in utter disrepair. Burdened with desegregation busing orders and decades of financial and administrative mismanagement, the Cleveland school district was turned over to state control and oversight by a federal court in the 1990s.[3] In 1995, the General Assembly of Ohio responded to their new duties and, among their modifications, passed the Ohio Pilot Project Scholarship Program.[4] Implemented in the 1996–1997 school year, this program provided vouchers for students to use at participating schools along with a tutoring program for those students who did not take part in the voucher portion of the program.[5]

The scholarship portion of the program provides vouchers for students in kindergarten through eighth grade, with a preference for those students whose families' income is less than 200 percent of the poverty level.[6] Families who do not meet the financial requirements would not qualify to receive a voucher until all requests from low-income families were met.[7] Based on family income, the vouchers pay anywhere from 75 to 90 percent of the tuition with a cap of $2,500 ($2,250 of which is provided by the state).[8] Private schools are prohibited from charging more than the scholarship amount for tuition.[9] A lottery chooses interested students who meet the program criteria, and participating schools are then also required to accept program students by lottery.[10] Private schools meeting the state's educational standards and located within the boundaries of the Cleveland School District may apply but must agree to the financial provisions.[11] They must also abide by the placement provisions of the program and are prohibited from discrimination based on race, religion, or ethnic background; advocating or fostering unlawful conduct; and teaching hatred of a person or group based on these criteria.[12] Public schools from adjoining districts are also permitted to register for the program, allowing them to keep their "average daily membership" funds from the state, while also receiving the $2,500 voucher (for a total of $6,544 per voucher student, according to petitioners).[13] No public school has registered for the program.[14] Of those private schools that do participate, forty-six were church affiliated, and ten were nonsectarian independent schools.[15] Of the students participating in the 1999–2000 school year, 96 percent of the 3,761 students (or 3,611) attended religiously affiliated schools.[16]

In 1996 the voucher program was challenged in state court.[17] After procedural defects were corrected through the state court process, the Ohio Supreme Court found no First Amendment violations in the program.[18] The action was refiled in federal court, where the Northern District of Ohio and the Sixth Circuit Court of Appeals both found that the voucher program did violate the establishment clause of the First Amendment.[19] The case was appealed to the U.S. Supreme Court, and on February 20, 2002, the Supreme Court heard oral arguments in the case of *Zelman v. Simmons-Harris.*[20]

The briefs filed provide an encapsulation of the arguments that have raged in this area for decades. Various entities filed an exceptional thirty-four amicus and party briefs in this case. Not only do the number of briefs filed indicate the importance of this issue for many people, but the range of groups and the alliances created are, to say the least, novel. As one provoucher scholar aptly observed of the new alliances,

> The politics of education reform are a mystery. Millionaire businessmen and conservative activists invoke civil rights ideals to demand equality, freedom, and diversity in education—while liberals join union bosses and anti-religious activists in support of a government monopoly. Strange days indeed, when the NAACP's and ACLU's opponents are black schoolchildren singing "We Shall Overcome" on the courthouse steps.[21]

Yet the variety of groups is not the most interesting element. Although the brief writers couch their arguments for and against vouchers in constitutional terms, it is clear that the more interesting elements are found in the competing worldviews, encompassing issues of parental rights,[22] religious liberty,[23] free markets,[24] education of the next generation,[25] and the very fabric of democracy in this nation.[26] Interestingly, both camps claim religious freedom as their battle cry.[27] Yet to fully understand the alliances and motivations for the various parties, it is important to know the history of educational policy in the United States. It is this history that shapes the Court's decisions and the political actions of those involved.

As with all current controversies, it is important to review history to find the elements that spawned them. America's continuing culture war over public aid to religion has its origins in the late eighteenth century. The contours and motivations one finds in this history propel the current conflicts with emotionally charged rhetoric and characterizations that survived for generations. In addition, knowledge of this history is necessary to understand many of the establishment clause tests, which will be examined later. Historical perspective also will illuminate how the various constitutional principles should be examined in relation to one another.

Sacred Public Schools

From its inception, American education attempted to instill in children skills they would need in order to be good Christians.[28] By the end of the nineteenth century, Andrew S. Draper, superintendent of Massachusetts schools, summed up the situation: "[For] more than sixty years of Massachusetts colonial life, and probably much longer, elementary instruction was held to be only a family duty for the attainment of religious ends."[29] This approach to education continued into private and public institutions that grew up outside the home. As scholar Warren A. Nord describes, "If there was an overriding purpose to American colonial education it was to nurture and sustain a Christian civilization."[30]

In the mid-1800s, America saw unprecedented expansion, and the desire for education grew with it. The common school movement stretched across the emerging states, bringing with it ideals of an educated citizenry that remained heavily imbued with religious overtones.[31] One example of this religious orientation is found in the early common schools' emphasis on reading. The common schools assumed the responsibility for literacy from the Sunday schools that sprung up in several states. In both instances, schools were preparing students to read scriptures in an effort to fortify their souls and prevent eternal damnation.[32]

During the last half of the nineteenth century, public schools began to formalize and to become more inherently a function of communities. Schooling became a focal point for those attempting to create a unique American identity out of differences, working from the assumption that being Christian was a prerequisite to being American.[33] Yet, by "Christian," American polity understood this to mean not an inclusive ideal encompassing all who self-identified as Christian but a Protestant Christianity that vehemently opposed inclusion of non-Protestants, particularly Catholics.[34] Based on these historical underpinnings, *American* became synonymous with *Protestant*.[35] These biases were exacerbated when an influx of Catholic immigrants began to flood the Northeast at the turn of the century.[36] Nativist movements, such as the Know-Nothings, railed against these new immigrants and targeted much of their activity on keeping the newly created public schools American (Protestant).[37]

The inevitable conflicts that followed stained both the nation and Christianity. One of the most virulent battles was fought over which version of the Bible should be read to begin the school day.[38] For the Protestant majority, there was no question but that the 1611 authorized King James Version of the Christian scriptures should be used by the public schools.[39] Although newly immigrated Catholic families eagerly enrolled their children in public schools in order to educate and assimilate them into American citizenship, the King James Version of the Bible soon became a massive stumbling block.[40] In particular, the preface castigated the pope as an oppressor who attempted to keep Christians in "darkness and ignorance."[41] For devout Catholics, imparting American ideals and identity to their children was vitally important, but could not come at the expense of their faith.[42] After a brief attempt at requiring equal time for the Douay version of the Bible, anti-Catholic sentiment reached a crescendo, with violent attacks against Catholics. In Philadelphia, Catholic-Protestant tensions over the Bible and control of the schools led to Protestants dragging a cannon through the city streets and blowing holes into the sides of a Catholic church downtown.[43] In Boston, Lyman Beecher whipped a mob into such a frenzy that it burned down the Ursuline Convent.[44] New York and Cincinnati also saw protests and occasional violence. In Massachusetts, the state legislature went so far as to begin hearings by the Nunnery Investigation Committee into the evil activities of convents.[45]

In light of this backdrop of bigotry, Catholic parents who were able began to pull their children out of public schools and sought alternate educational opportunities.[46] In response to this plight, Catholic parishes and communities came together and formed parochial schools for local children.[47] In an effort to level the educational playing field, these parents began lobbying legislators for economic relief to help with the tuition they were now forced to undertake.[48]

Less-than-Christian responses to the Catholic community's activities were swift.[49] At the federal level, the Blaine Amendment to the U.S. Constitution was introduced, forbidding any public money from ever going to a religious institution. After its failure, Blaine Amendment look-alikes began to sprout up in the states, many of which passed and are still on the books.[50] State legislatures even passed laws forcing Catholic parents to keep their children in public schools as an attempt at "Protestantizing" them into good Americans.[51] During this period, terms such as *pervasively sectarian* became code words for Catholic schools and were used as justification for marginalization of parochial schools and the avoidance of state funding for these schools.[52] This era of public education has been characterized as the "sacred schools," due to its pervasively Protestant flavor and disposition.[53]

Although public schools began with a heavy religious emphasis in both texts and curriculum, by the beginning of the twentieth century the official common school movement began to shift away from the religious focus it began with and instituted training in more secular aspects of citizenship, including a new focus on broader disciplines such as mathematics, the sciences, and technological skills.[54] This move mirrored the changes occurring in society at large, as America moved from an agrarian-based economy to an urban, technological orientation.[55] Science and objectivity became the new watchwords for public schools.[56]

Useful knowledge was the knowledge one needed to be prosperous, and this quickly became paramount in the schools.[57] Religion was still nominally present, but only in a ceremonial function, found in morning prayers and daily Bible readings.[58] Society increasingly privatized study and reflection on religion, relegating these functions to the family.[59] By the 1960s the space race and cold war realities resulted in a national policy explicitly preferring science education to the traditional liberal arts curriculum.[60]

Diversity within the population also became increasingly important to schools. Homogenization that had first begun with the Protestant compromises over how the Bible should be read in schools led to the ideal of America as a melting pot.[61] When immigration led to a more diverse population, such homogenization was no longer realistic. The schools began to reflect the diverse population, and people were no longer willing to be molded into a quasi-Protestant ideal of what it meant to be an American.[62]

These changes caused religion to become largely irrelevant in the curriculum.[63] The final nail in the long-closed coffin of religious indoctrination in schools came with the often-misunderstood Supreme Court decisions in *Engle v. Vitale* and *Abington v. Shempp,* where even the ceremonial elements of religion were eliminated.[64] This caused many in the education profession to believe that schools were required to avoid religion, even to the point of hostility in some situations.[65] Where public schools once reflected the shared values and practices of a homogenized nation, these schools soon became bastions of secularization. Through no evil intent or grand conspiracies, public schools gradually became overwhelmingly secular.[66]

By the 1970s many parents and educators became concerned over the public schools' perceived hostility to religion and began to demand changes. This uproar came to a head in the 1980s with the textbook trials in the South and a number of research efforts from a broad spectrum of groups about religion's role in American public education.[67] The results of both the trials and the studies astounded many people and led to an increased awareness of this issue. The textbook studies in particular were especially troubling, as social studies texts actively ignored religion and its influence on the world.[68] From the treatment given in many textbooks, it appears as though religion vanished in America after the Civil War.[69] Other textbooks defined Pilgrims as "people who take long journeys."[70] One textbook even edited Nobel laureate Isaac Bashevis Singer's stories, changing references such as "thank God" to "thank goodness."[71] For many civil libertarians, this indicated an illiberal education, whereas religious groups found something far more insidious.[72] This modern era of public education is sometimes referred to as the "sanitized schools."[73]

Although the pioneering work of people such as Charles Haynes and Warren Nord attempts to provide a new model for public education in which religion is treated with fairness and respect, many religious parents still feel disaffected by the public education system.[74] For many religious parents, public schools continue to bear a striking resemblance to the discriminatory institutions that sent so many Catholics fleeing almost a century earlier. Once again, based on a desire for an educational environment that would not be hostile to their faith, religious parents pull their children out of public schools and place them in newly created private religious schools. And again, just as Catholic parents did before, parents argue that they should not be economically disadvantaged based on their religious needs, so they also seek economic assistance in educating their children. With few exceptions, these requests meet the same resistance and rejection that parochial school parents have received.

Today an extensive community of private religious schools exists in tandem with public schools.[75] Begun first by Catholics fleeing the Protestant-dominated public schools, these days many private religious schools are just as likely to be Protestant. In many cases, private religious schools flourished and gained the respect of the broader community, even among those who do not share their faith commitments.[76]

The history of parochial schools must be set in the context of the public school system. For the most part, America's public schools are remarkable institutions, staffed by professionals who care deeply about their charges. Despite this level of interest and care, external factors of financing, judicial intervention, and political influence combined with internal realities of management, politics, and lack of professional growth potential create an abysmal educational environment in some places.[77] These conflagrations occurred before, but modern society is far more mobile and better informed. If schools were failing in the past, people just assumed there was no choice but to fix the community's schools. After years of desegregation rulings, parents are now aware that students can be bused just about anywhere. Coupled with better information about how students are performing across town, across the country, or even across the world, parents are increasingly frustrated when their community school fails to meet their increasingly high standards.[78] Many parents in underperforming schools cast longing eyes at institutions that seem to be performing at a higher level.[79] In many lower-income areas, these are the private religious schools. Whether these perceptions of higher performance coincide with any objective standards is irrelevant. The fact is that many parents perceive these private, oftentimes religious schools as better options, and they are eager to find ways to get their children into these institutions.[80]

What was once the fight of Catholic parents and became the cause of a broader community of religious parents has broadened once again to include lower-income and middle-class families, each group for decidedly different reasons. But despite their motivation, their goal remains the same: to get the government to provide them with the means to send their children to the school of their choice. Several funding mechanisms have been proposed, but many education reform proponents return to vouchers as the solution. It is from this desire for aid that we begin to examine the legal constructs that have arguably had the greatest impact on the debate for the past seventy years.

3. ESTABLISHMENT CLAUSE MODELS

Almost absent from the fray until the 1930s, the Supreme Court suddenly emerged as the primary arbiter in the culture war battles.[81] The court cases that inevitably follow in the wake of each conflict provide a number of paradigms for understanding the establishment clause and its applicability to state funding issues. The dominant establishment clause criteria that emerged included no-aid, direct versus indirect, the *Lemon* test, neutrality, and, finally, endorsement.[82] These tests often run concurrently through many of the same cases: in concurring opinions, dissents, and sometimes even within the same opinion. For illustrative purposes these tests will be examined conceptually and individually instead of chronologically, even though they are often intertwined within the decisions.[83]

One of the earliest and arguably most influential aid to religion cases came in the 1947 decision in *Everson v. Board of Education of Township of Ewing*.[84] The Court has since used Justice Hugo Black's prose as the foundation for the establishment clause models that would follow.

No Aid

In 1946, for the first time, the Supreme Court heard arguments that a state violated the First Amendment by providing aid to a private religious school.[85] The case arose when Arch Everson, a taxpayer in Ewing Township, New Jersey, objected to a state statute authorizing reimbursement to parents for bus transportation to and from public or nonprofit private schools.[86] His concern stemmed from the fact that most of the nonprofit private schools were Catholic parochial schools.[87] Everson filed suit, arguing that because money went to transporting parochial school students, this program constituted an establishment of religion in violation of the establishment clause of the First Amendment to the U.S. Constitution.[88] The Supreme Court decision in *Everson v. Board of Education of Township of Ewing* provided one of the first principles in modern establishment clause jurisprudence: no public aid shall go to a religious organization.[89]

As this was the first time the Court examined such issues, Justice Black based much of his analysis on history, examining the foundations of religious liberty in this country.[90] Looking first to the Puritans, Justice Black pointed out that the earliest European settlers fled Europe and the state-sponsored religions found there.[91] He then turned to James Madison's *Memorial and Remonstrance.*[92] Reference to the *Memorial* seemed apropos, considering that Madison's pamphlet responded to the Virginia legislature's 1785 attempt to establish a tax in support of "Teachers of the Christian Religion."[93] From the *Memorial,* Justice Black quotes, "No person, either believer or non-believer, should be taxed to support a religious institution of any kind."[94] Justice Black concludes his historical review by referring to Thomas Jefferson and his "Virginia Bill for Religious Liberty."[95] Claiming that the First Amendment should protect the same rights that Virginia's bill sought to protect,[96] Justice Black quotes Jefferson, "No man shall be compelled to frequent or support any religious worship, place, or ministry whatsoever."[97]

Based on this history, Justice Black penned some of the most oft-quoted language concerning the establishment clause:

> The "establishment of religion" clause of the First Amendment means at least this: Neither a state nor the Federal Government can set up a church. Neither can pass laws which aid one religion, aid all religions, or prefer one religion over another. . . . No tax in any amount, large or small, can be levied to support any religious activities or institutions, whatever they may be called, or whatever form they may adopt to teach or practice religion. Neither a state nor the Federal Government can, openly or secretly, participate in the affairs of any religious organizations or groups and vice versa. In the words of Jefferson, the clause against the establishment of religion by law was intended to erect "a wall of separation between church and State."[98]

This last line, pulled from a letter sent by Jefferson to a congregation of Baptists in Danbury, Virginia, provides the imagery for Justice Black's concept of "no aid."[99] For the last sixty years, many have used this image of a "wall of separation" to illustrate the relationship between church and state.[100]

After providing the previously discussed history and an analysis section that has been worn smooth through use by modern courts, Justice Black addressed the obvious point that when referring to governmental aid to religious institutions, surely any wall of separation cannot be an absolute prohibition on all government aid.[101] Fire and police protection, water, power, and sewer infrastructure are just some of the general government services that any community institution would need to survive.[102] Justice Black confirmed that it would not be a violation of the establishment clause to provide these basic services.[103] Yet this begs the question of where to draw the line between what aid is allowed and what is not. In order to answer this, the Court looked to the purpose behind the establishment clause and its historical context.[104] The Court concluded that the real purpose and concern for the establishment clause was to make sure that the religious mission and teaching of a place was not being aided.[105] Fewer establishment clause concerns arise over funding elements of the church associated with the "secular" or "social" accoutrements of religion, such as homeless shelters and soup kitchens.[106] This assumes a dichotomy between the cultic elements of a religion, which cannot be aided, and the ethical or social elements of a religious entity, which can be assisted.[107] Yet even this raises issues, for simple economics dictates that if funds are not needed in one place, then they can be used in another.[108]

In the end, the Court concluded that it was the aid itself with which they were concerned.[109] The prohibition should consist only of that which could be converted to religious use.[110] Therefore, although police and fire protection, sewer service, and electricity were all considered aid, they were deemed sufficiently secular that there was little or no likelihood that they would be converted to religious use.[111] On the other hand, the Court considered money easily divertible, as it could be used to buy Bibles, hymnals, and crucifixes.[112]

Some justices continue to either follow the "no aid" rhetoric of *Everson* or allow it to influence their reasoning, though they are currently in the minority on the Court.[113] The dissent in *Mitchell v. Helms* expressed a triumvirate of reasons for adhering to this paradigm.[114] First, compelling support for religion violates a person's freedom of conscience.[115] Historical references to Madison and Jefferson provide the rather clear explanation of this concern.[116] Second, public aid to religion harms religion.[117] History has demonstrated time and again that when the government supports religion, the religious endeavor becomes corrupted in both word and deed.[118] Finally, whenever the government entangles itself with religion, conflict follows.[119] In any democratic form of government, when the government is supposed to represent the people, supporting one religious group leaves the others feeling like outsiders. This leads to disaffected sections of the populace, which eventually results in conflict that often becomes violent.[120]

Despite the obvious importance of these concerns, adherents to the no-aid test seem to ignore the change and evolution that occurred in society, while pulling Madison and Jefferson from their historical context and adhering literally to their words. The situation today finds religious institutions facing a massive, all-encompassing government, as opposed to the limited, skeleton governments Madison and Jefferson confronted. Two-hundred fifty years ago a tax to specifically support religious teachers would disproportionately represent religion in a government that did little more than deliver the mail and protect the borders. Contrast this to modern times, where a multitrillion-dollar federal government creates a benefit and allows any institution to participate except those that are religious. As the situation has changed, so should understanding of the constitutional parameters. The modern Court should look to the balance that Justice Black sought in *Everson*, being careful "in protecting the citizens of New Jersey against state established churches, to be sure that we do not inadvertently prohibit New Jersey from extending its general state law benefits to all its citizens without regard to their religious belief."[121] It remains true that government providing special benefits for religion—such as a special tax just for religious teachers, favoring a specific state religion, funding religion, or any other entanglement in religion—should not be tolerated in a liberal democracy.

Although cases continue the trend of disallowing aid to religious schools, they seldom return to the no-aid paradigm, at least overtly. Instead, the Court has other avenues of questioning in these matters. One avenue involves the question of whether the route the aid takes in getting to the religious school matters.

Direct versus Indirect

The Court realized, even within the *Everson* decision, that the absolute prohibition of aid to religious organizations was impossible. The Court also understood that even though the type of aid is important, the route the aid takes to religious institutions is ultimately more determinative of whether the government has established a religion, or even a preference for one. The Court seemed impressed with the argument that the aid in *Everson* went not to the religious school, but directly to the parent, thus benefiting the individual instead of the religious entity.[122]

Justice O'Connor best articulated the reasoning behind this in her concurring opinion in *Mitchell v. Helms*. There she explained that although previous Supreme Court decisions "provide[d] no precedent for the use of public funds to finance religious activities," surely "a State may issue a paycheck to one of its employees, who may then donate all or part of that paycheck to a religious institution, all without constitutional barrier; and the State may do so even knowing that the employee so intends to dispose of his salary."[123]

In *Everson v. Board of Education*, the fact that the aid was part of a general benefit program with the benefit flowing to the parents, and only remotely benefited religious schools, greatly influenced the Court.[124] Justice Black emphasized this point:

"The State contributes no money to the schools. It does not support them. It does no more than [get children,] regardless of their religion, safely and expeditiously to and from accredited schools."[125]

Twenty-five years later, the Court took the next case examining the direction of the aid in *Committee for Public Education and Religious Liberty v. Nyquist*.[126] Breaking with the *Everson* decision earlier, the Court took a more economic approach to aid situations. At issue were three aid programs, all provided only to private schools, of which a majority were religious.[127] In fact, it was clear that the purpose of these programs was to bail out private parochial schools.[128] These programs included a direct money grant for maintenance, a tuition reimbursement for low-income parents, and tax relief for those who did not qualify for the reimbursement.[129] By a six to three majority, the Court found that all three programs were unconstitutional.[130] Unimpressed by arguments that the aid in question went to parents or for secular purposes such as maintenance, the Court instead found that

> if the grants are offered as an incentive to parents to send their children to sectarian schools by making unrestricted cash payments to them, the Establishment Clause is violated whether or not the actual dollars given eventually find their way into the sectarian institutions. Whether the grant is labeled a reimbursement, a reward, or a subsidy, the substantive impact is still the same.[131]

Yet *Nyquist* seems a bit of an aberration from *Everson* before it and the cases that follow. In many later cases, the Court differentiates *Nyquist* and seeks alternate rationales.[132] For example, in the 1983 case of *Mueller v. Allen*, a sharply divided Court upheld a Minnesota tax break to parents for educational expenses, despite arguments that *Nyquist* should control.[133] Returning to earlier ideas from *Everson* on direction of aid, one of the primary factors the Court examined was whether the aid went directly to the school or to the parent. Justice Rehnquist wrote:

> It is true, of course, that financial assistance provided to parents ultimately has an economic effect comparable to that of aid given directly to the schools attended by their children. It is also true, however, that under Minnesota's arrangement public funds become available only as a result of numerous private choices of individual parents of school-age children.[134]

This return of focus on direction of aid was strengthened by many of the cases that followed, particularly the 1986 decision in *Witters v. Washington*.[135] This case required the Court to analyze whether a blind man could use his state rehabilitation assistance grant to attend a religious school to study for a religious vocation.[136]

The Court rejected the state's claims that allowing such uses of a state grant would constitute a violation of the establishment clause.[137] In Justice Marshall's majority opinion, the question came down to "whether, on the facts as they appear in the record before us, extension of aid to petitioner [*Witters*] and the use of that aid by petitioner to support his religious education is a permissible transfer similar to the [salary donation from a person's government paycheck], or is an impermissible direct subsidy"[138] (internal quotations omitted). Once again, the Court found the private choice determinative in the outcome.[139]

Clearly the Court is concerned with the distinction between direct and indirect aid. The break in the chain where state control ends and private or individual choice begins is crucial. As will be discussed later, the distinction becomes paramount for some members of the Court, such as Justice O'Connor. But these cases also demonstrate that the direct and indirect question is only one aspect of the equation.

Lemon *Test*

Almost twenty-five years after the *Everson* decision, establishment clause jurisprudence went through a major reformulation in the 1971 Supreme Court decision of *Lemon v. Kurtzman*.[140] Another case involving government aid to parochial schools, the *Lemon* case arose when taxpayers in Rhode Island sued over government supplements to teachers of secular subjects in private religious schools.[141] The Justices analyzed three areas of establishment clause concern in finding that such an arrangement was a constitutional violation. These three reasons would become the three prongs for analyzing establishment clause concerns for decades to come.

A patchwork of earlier decisions and the concerns expressed in them, the three elements of what would eventually become known as the *Lemon* test provide an intellectual history of establishment clause theory. Beginning with the idea that the government should only concern itself with secular activities, the first prong requires that government action be based on a secular purpose.[142] This prong is no longer much of an obstacle for most government action, as even the most novice state actor intuitively knows they must articulate a secular rationale for their actions.[143]

The second prong of the *Lemon* test requires that even if the challenged action is found to have a secular purpose, it must not inadvertently have the primary effect of advancing or inhibiting religion.[144] This primary effect prong has by far been the most determinative element of the *Lemon* test. The basis for this prong is that the government should not help or hinder any particular religion.[145] In post-1971 cases, the Court consistently evaluates the direct and indirect funding issue previously discussed under the rubric of this prong.[146]

Finally, the Court focuses on issues of excessive entanglement. The concerns addressed by this prong include giving the appearance of government involvement with religion and the desire to keep religion free from government interference.[147] The test for this prong is whether there is a discernible line of demarcation between government and religion. In cases where government regulation or oversight is so extensive that the religious enterprise is subsumed into it, excessive entanglement has occurred.[148]

By encapsulating the rationales of earlier cases, the *Lemon* test left a far more lasting impression in that it provided a comprehensive approach to examining establishment clause situations. From 1973 through the beginning of the twenty-first century, these three prongs have in one way or another been used to shape almost every establishment clause case before the Supreme Court. Yet, despite its omnipresence throughout this area of the law, jurists and scholars alike routinely criticize the *Lemon* test.[149] Justice O'Connor is especially concerned as she is unable to tie the elements of the *Lemon* test to any historical or philosophical hierarchy that would explain why these elements are important or which elements should be weighted the most.[150] Justice Scalia has questioned how, after repeated attempts to bury *Lemon*, it is able, time and again, to raise its head from the grave, as if it were some sort of ghoul from a late-night horror movie.[151]

Although seemingly eager to overrule this test, the justices have yet to explicitly do so. Instead, their response to the plethora of criticisms is to transform elements of each prong. Most recently, in *Agostini v. Felton,* the three-prong test underwent a major reorganization into a two-question test.[152] The second prong of the new test merges the effects and entanglement prongs and then uses three separate criteria to analyze the applicability of the new effects or entanglement prong on a specific issue.[153] In 1985 the Court ruled in the case of *Aguilar v. Felton* that the state of New York could not place teachers of secular subjects in private religious schools, even to meet the requirements of Title I remedial assistance for disadvantaged children.[154] In 1997 the Court revisited this issue and overturned their previous ruling to better coincide with recent precedent.[155] As part of their analysis, the Court still looks to see if a secular purpose is the motivation for the government action.[156] The change occurred in the second part of the analysis, when the Court looked at the second prong, which now determines if the primary effect is to advance or inhibit religion by examining three factors: does the program involve government indoctrination;[157] does the program in question define its recipients by reference to religion;[158] and does the program excessively entangle government and religion?[159]

Yet even with these modifications, the Court continues to search for a better establishment clause test. The two most prevalent contenders—neutrality and endorsement—follow.

Although the *Lemon* test remains good law, four members of the Supreme Court have given primacy to another concern when determining establishment clause questions in the context of government programs and benefits: neutrality. For Justices Rehnquist, Scalia, Thomas, and Kennedy, the line of establishment clause cases beginning with *Everson* and ending with *Helms* all point to one rule: the government must remain neutral in matters of religion.[160]

The word *neutrality* frequently shows up in precedent. In *Everson*, Justice Black wrote that the First Amendment "requires the state to be neutral in its relations with groups of religious believers and non-believers; it does not require the state to be their adversary. State power is no more to be used so as to handicap religions than it is to favor them."[161] Since that time, case after case has returned to the concept of neutrality. In *Everson v. Board of Education*, the Court found that the government could not advance or hinder religion, thus remaining neutral.[162] In the case of *Board of Education v. Allen*, the Court found that loaning secular textbooks to students in religious schools was constitutional because the aid provided was neutral.[163] In *Bowen v. Kendrick*, a case over public funding of religious organizations' pregnancy counseling, the Court found that the "neutrality of the grant requirements" obviated the establishment clause claims.[164]

As the dissent in *Helms* points out, although the term "neutral" is frequently used, the previous lineage of cases illustrates an evolution in the way it has been defined by the Court as a test for constitutionality. Justice Souter explains:

> In sum, "neutrality" originally entered this field of jurisprudence as a conclusory term, a label for the required relationship between the government and religion as a state of equipoise between government as ally and government as adversary. Reexamining *Everson*'s paradigm cases to derive a prescriptive guideline, we first determined that "neutral" aid was secular, nonideological, or unrelated to religious education. Our subsequent reexamination of *Everson* and *Allen*, beginning in *Nyquist* and culminating in *Mueller* and most recently in *Agostini*, recasts neutrality as a concept of "evenhandedness."[165]

The dissenters agree that "neutrality" should play some part in the analysis of constitutionality (at least in some of its manifestations), but they are adamantly opposed to placing it in a position of singular primacy.[166] Their concern stems from the results of such a test, especially when using the most recent "evenhandedness" definition of neutrality. Specifically, they are concerned that it will lead to public money eventually getting to religious institutions, thus violating the no-aid approach to the establishment clause to which they still cling.[167]

There are other concerns about using this approach. For one, not every case that is facially neutral is really intended to be neutrally beneficial to all in its applicable class. As some have argued with vouchers, although the programs seem neutral on their face, the way they are designed creates benefits for some and disadvantages for others.[168] Although this test holds sway over four members of the Court, it has failed to gain the support of Justice O'Connor, who prefers a broader examination of issues in establishment clause cases.

Endorsement

Finally, the endorsement test currently receives a great deal of attention due to its proponent, Justice O'Connor. Because she has become the swing vote on so many cases in this area, her test often receives disproportionate attention, from both her fellow justices as well as the attorneys coming before the Court.

First elucidated in Justice O'Connor's concurring opinion in the 1984 case of *Lynch v. Donnelly*, the endorsement test and the ideals it purports to protect have quickly become the touchstone of establishment clause arguments before the Court.[169] Based on a controversy over the annual practice in Pawtucket, Rhode Island, of erecting a holiday display that includes a crèche, Justice O'Connor reviewed *Lemon* and other previous establishment clause tests.[170] Justice O'Connor began her inquiry by looking first to "the central issue in this case . . . whether Pawtucket has endorsed Christianity by its display of the crèche."[171] To answer this question, Justice O'Connor looked at two factors: what the state intended to communicate and what was actually conveyed.[172] These factors are based on the purpose prong and a combination of the effects and entanglement prongs of *Lemon*.[173] The real change provided comes not in the novelty of the test's elements, but in the effects of its reformulation. Justice O'Connor clarifies that the primary effect of a government action can advance religion, as long as the message sent and received is not one of government endorsement.[174]

Although the intended endorsement element is a rather conservative construct, the question of perceived endorsement remains another question. For one, how does the government control what people perceive to be, in either intent or action? Actual intentional endorsement raises few questions, as most would agree that government endorsing a particular religion or religious activity is unconstitutional, but once the issue becomes a question of impression and perception, how far must the government go? Justice O'Connor explains in *Lynch* that the focus of the inquiry should not be on the divisiveness created by the action, but on the character of the government activity itself.[175] This indicates that Justice O'Connor's focus may be on requiring some level of reasonableness, as a kind of commonsense safeguard against actions that appear constitutionally questionable due to the incompetence of a government actor.

It is also of some import that Justice O'Connor, when first proposing this approach to the establishment clause in *Lynch*, stated that the purpose should be ascertained by looking at the broader context and not examining the element in question in isolation.[176] Justice O'Connor provides this as a prophylactic measure against requiring a lowest common denominator approach to perception analysis. This requires an assumed level of knowledge by the body politic of at least the circumstances surrounding the government action.

A more in-depth review of the endorsement test will be provided later, as it is best understood as applied to an actual situation. The previous summary is provided to allow the following comparisons.

Relationship to Other Establishment Clause Tests

This new approach has in many ways so dominated this area of constitutional inquiry that special attention will be given to it based on its relationship with the other tests preferred by other members of the Court. Although neither separationists nor accommodationists are completely happy with this approach, the questions recently raised during oral arguments in the *Zelman* case demonstrate the tacit acceptance by the other justices that Justice O'Connor's endorsement test must be addressed.

First, the endorsement test will be examined in light of the three most frequently cited concerns of the separationists who still prefer a no-aid approach. As stated earlier, separationists on the Court look at freedom of conscience, corrupting effects on religion, and creation of conflict.

The issue of freedom of conscience is one that must be viewed not only through historical context but also in light of current cultural realities. When Jefferson and Madison wrote against the use of public funds for particular religious groups, they lived within a context of a very limited government.[177] They could not have begun to conceive of the pervasiveness of government in modern life. Their context of a simple government with few roles would have highlighted support of religion, thus making such action a far more magnified event serving to single religion out for benefits no other group received. In today's modern state, government taxes and funds impact every level of life.[178] Although a specific tax for religion would still be noxious, it is a far cry from pulling funds from the general tax fund to finance programs that religious groups may in some way take part.

The second issue of concern for separationists is that of harm to religion.[179] The Court addresses this issue either to point out why accommodationists should be concerned with such approaches to the establishment clause or as a way of addressing the free-exercise issues that arise with excessive entanglement between government and religion. In any event, it is questionable as to whether the Court should concern itself with such matters. Such paternalistic approaches are beyond the scope of constitutional purview of the Court in a liberal society. Particularly when one of the Court's stated goals is to retain a level of neutrality that neither advances nor inhibits religion, it comes across as rather superficial to then say that the Court's desire is to protect religion.[180]

Finally, the question of conflict is indeed an important one and should probably be given primacy in the separationists' dissents. It is one of the most fundamental goals of any government to minimize conflict, especially when it leads to infringements on other interests and goals of government. Yet this is the area where the endorsement test proves most effective. Political conflict is the issue that troubles Justice O'Connor most and arguably is why she formulated this test in the first instance.[181] In *Lynch,* she explained, "Endorsement sends a message to nonadherents that they are outsiders, not full members of the political community, and an accompanying message to adherents that they are insiders, favored members of the political community. Disapproval sends the opposite message."[182] By focusing not on the effects of the government action on religion but on the message that such action sends, political alienation can be avoided. Under the endorsement test, the government no longer has to guess as to whether their actions will positively or negatively impact religion; instead they can concern themselves with creating criteria for their actions that will neither discriminate against nor unfairly advantage religion's interests. This avoids the conflict that concerns separationists in these situations.

On the other end of the religious liberty spectrum, accommodationists also express anxiety over the endorsement test. Accommodationists believe that religion and religious people should have a robust presence in public life and are leery of any establishment clause test that does not allow such involvement. For many years, accommodationists have been concerned over separationist ideas that they feel treat religious people as second-class citizens, especially in the area of government funding. Any test that does not, in their view, level the field for all people is suspect.[183] Although some members of the Court feel that the endorsement test unnecessarily excludes religion from areas where it should be allowed, others seem to consider the test a valid compromise.

The endorsement test alleviates these concerns by allowing religion to participate in the public arena of government aid while avoiding the preferences or special treatment that were of concern to Jefferson and Madison and that would alienate many in society today. In this sense, the accommodationists' favorite establishment clause test, neutrality, is similar to endorsement. In reality, they are probably two points on a continuum. Although neutrality seems concerned only with facial and actual neutrality, endorsement seeks to also hold the government accountable, to a degree, for how people perceive their actions. Endorsement is not as accommodationist as neutrality, yet both efforts allow government to engage religious communities and avoid discrimination based on religious identity.

Although Justice Powell may not have been convinced in *Nyquist* that establishment clause jurisprudence has become "as winding as the famous serpentine wall [that Jefferson designed for the University of Virginia]," the diversity in the previously mentioned tests demonstrates that there may be some truth in Justice Jackson's prediction.[184] For those looking for clarity, the difficult arena of church-state jurisprudence is a nightmare. Yet these are the tools the Court has decided to use, and they are the tools applied by all sides to the issue of vouchers. This is most notable in the case of *Zelman v. Simmons-Harris* that is currently before the Supreme Court.

4. ARGUMENTS IN *ZELMAN V. SIMMONS-HARRIS*

Attention must now turn to the question presented before the Court today. Part 1 of this chapter already laid out the facts of the case before the Court. Next I will introduce how the parties to this controversy chose to cast their arguments in light of the history and jurisprudence that led to this point.

To better understand the issues, each side's positions will be presented. Although both groups tend to couch many of their arguments in terms of education policy, for purposes of this chapter, only the constitutional issues raised will be examined.

Respondents

The respondents raise three constitutional questions as to whether the Cleveland voucher program violates the establishment clause of the First Amendment. Each of these claims will be viewed in turn.[185]

"Unrestricted funds . . . attributable to the state."

First, petitioners contend that the system in Cleveland provides unrestricted funds to a religious organization that are attributable to the state.[186] They claim that this is a violation of Supreme Court precedent, referring to the *Nyquist, Sloan,* and *Witters* trilogy of cases.[187] The pieces of this analytical puzzle are painstakingly laid out in the respondent's brief, with each layer providing the foundation for the next. The result is a pyramid of reasoning, from which the respondent stands atop to analyze the linchpin pieces of the final analysis, as well as to claim the requisite height to appropriately analyze precedent.

The analysis begins with the axiomatic principle that the state cannot finance religious indoctrination.[188] They explain that in practical terms, this means that if a government program provides unrestricted funds that are attributable to the state directly to a religious organization, the program is unconstitutional.[189] From this first layer, the respondent begins building the second layer, arguing that if the previous is true, then per-capita aid, even if distributed neutrally among private religious, private nonreligious, and public schools, is unconstitutional.[190] This draws on the idea that unrestricted aid to a religious school by the state, irrelevant of context, is a violation of the establishment clause because the aid will eventually help in indoctrination.[191] Finally, the pinnacle of the pyramid is drawn from the idea that in a model program where voucher aid goes only to sectarian schools, the reality of such a program would in effect be a per-capita aid program for sectarian schools, and that would be unconstitutional, as the limitation of only religious choices creates attribution to the state.[192] In the *Zelman* case, the money is clearly unrestricted, leaving respondents with what seems to be the primary question in this case: Is the aid attributable to the state, or do the actions of a third party break the lines of control and influence?[193]

This question hinges on whether there is a genuine, independent choice available to parents, or if the choices are structured in such a way as to push people toward religious options.[194] Within the choice analysis, respondents focus on three issues. First, respondents argue that the high number of religious schools participating in the program (82 percent) and the percentage of vouchers used at religious schools (96 percent) make the program almost the same as a situation where 100 percent of religious schools participate, the model of which was argued as unconstitutional previously.[195] In effect, they argue that there is no real choice because voucher recipients may only choose from the participating, and therefore religious, schools.[196] They contend that the decision in *Witters* found the scholarship to a religious school constitutional simply because there were a number of choices, only a few of which were religious.[197] Therefore they posit that *Witters* requires a range of nonreligious options—a criterion that the Cleveland program fails to meet.[198] Elliot Mincberg, legal director for People for the American Way, described the situation as being the difference between the government giving you a check and allowing you to spend it wherever you wanted, and the government giving you a check and requiring you to spend it at one of ten stores, eight of which are religious.[199] In any event, respondents argue that it gives the impression that the government supports religion.[200]

Second, respondents attempt to avoid arguments surrounding the numbers game that will eventually have to be addressed.[201] Avoidance of this issue in oral arguments seemed to irritate the justices the most, as both Justice Kennedy and Chief Justice Rehnquist chided respondents' attorney Chanin when he refused to answer questions about where a bright line could be drawn.[202] Eager to avoid having to provide arbitrary bright lines, respondents argue that these are matters on a continuum, and the numbers of schools in the program that are religious place the Cleveland plan in the same point on the continuum as *Nyquist* and *Sloan* and far away from the plethora of choices available in *Witters*.[203] They continued by arguing that even if bright lines had to be drawn, this would be an easy case in which to do so, because the ratios are so skewed toward religious schools.[204]

Finally, Justice O'Connor seemed to take the greatest interest in whether the voucher portion of the program should be viewed in isolation or in the context of all educational opportunities available to students.[205] As Justice O'Connor indicated in her concurrence in Helms, true independent choice by an individual obviates the connection with the state.[206] As respondents argue based on the *Witters* case, in order to have a truly independent choice, the voucher recipient must have a range of choices that are not limited to religious schools.[207]

In order to examine the question of choice, the parameters of the choice options must be demarcated. Respondents address this issue by arguing that the voucher program must be examined in isolation for two reasons. First, they claim that to look at all of the educational choices available would prove too much, as it would logically lead to per-capita funding, which respondents contend that they have already proven to be unconstitutional.[208] Second, they also argue that it would violate precedent, as *Nyquist* had already ruled that voucher programs must be viewed in isolation and not in the context of all available educational options.[209]

"Violates the Establishment Clause in two additional separate and independent ways."

The second and third issues are raised in a more cursory fashion in the respondents' brief. The second issue questions whether the Cleveland program creates a financial incentive for participants to choose private religious schools.[210] Conceptually similar to the arguments mentioned earlier, here the argument focuses on the *Agostini* prohibition against identifying beneficiaries based on religion.[211] The argument is that if a program is structured in such a way that the only schools that can participate are religious schools, then the effect is the same as if the government only allowed religious schools.[212] Respondents argue that the program criteria for participating schools that limit tuition and the geographic area from which schools can apply are designed to limit participation to those schools that are religiously affiliated.[213] This leaves those who wish to participate with an incentive to choose a religious school.[214] Respondents claim that these criteria themselves have the effect of encouraging parents to send their children to a religious school, thus violating one of *Agostini*'s new elements in the revised *Lemon* test.[215]

Finally, respondents argue that a program creates the public perception that the state is endorsing religion.[216] Because so many of the participating schools are religious, "public perception could hardly be otherwise."[217] The approach seems to rest on the somewhat facile assertion that any government program made up of primarily religious entities will obviously appear to endorse religion. The assumption is based on looking at the program in rather extreme isolation.[218] Respondents do not address this point in much detail as a separate issue, relying instead on their analysis under the funds attributable to the state portion.[219]

Although much is made of the continuation of principles throughout the cases, the brief predominantly returns to the *Nyquist* case. In fact, without *Nyquist*, there is little left of the respondent's primary argument. To this end, the respondents focus the conclusion of their brief not only on the parallels between the Cleveland program and the voucher program in *Nyquist*, but also on the doctrine of *stare decisis*, arguing that deviation from previous rulings requires special justification before departing from precedent.[220] Respondents claim that no such special justification is found here.[221]

Petitioners

On the other side of this issue are those who claim that the Cleveland voucher program does not violate the establishment clause, but instead provides opportunities for students who are stuck in failing schools.[222]

"Satisfies . . . test applied to individual benefit cases."

Petitioners begin their analysis with the claim that the Cleveland program satisfies the two criteria found in every individual benefit case from *Everson* to *Zobrest;* namely, that true private choice exists and that "the program 'neutrally provides state assistance to a broad spectrum of citizens.'"[223]

Petitioner's arguments start where the respondents left off, over the issue of true choice. The analysis consists of looking to the reimbursements for bus fare in *Everson* and *Mueller's* tax deductions for education expenses, *Witters's* provision of aid to a blind student for a religious education, and *Zobrest's* allowance of a state-funded sign language interpreter for a student in a parochial school.[224] In each case, petitioners contend that the Court held in high regard whether genuine private choice existed.[225] As evidence that this kind of private choice has been accomplished in the Cleveland plan, petitioners point to the terms of the program, which explicitly place the choice of where the voucher is to go with the parent.[226] They also point out the number of affidavits of participants who, without exception, claimed to have unconstrained choices and their rationales for making said choices.[227] Petitioners further bolster their argument by emphasizing that parents are making these decisions, not the easily influenced minors who will be attending the schools.[228] Finally, petitioners point out that the only financial incentives in this program tend to favor nonreligious schools.[229] If students remain in public school, their education is completely free of charge, whereas students in the scholarship program are required to provide at least 10 percent of their tuition.[230]

Petitioners argue that the other criterion required in individual benefit cases is neutrality.[231] Petitioners look at neutrality in three different contexts. First, they claim that the program is neutral regarding the religious affiliation of the recipient.[232] They argue that neutrality means not only that the state cannot favor religion, but that the state also cannot discriminate against religion.[233] Quoting *Everson*, petitioners point out that the establishment clause does not require the state to be an adversary to religion.[234] The criterion is merely that the aid program "neutrally provides state assistance to a broad spectrum of citizens."[235] Petitioners claim that this has been met because of the second context, neutrality of eligibility criteria.[236] Petitioners argue that if the eligibility criteria are truly neutral, then they cannot prefer any one religion, or even religion to nonreligion.[237] Petitioners point out that the factors determining eligibility in the program are neutral regarding religion.[238] They contend that the only initial criterion is whether the family resides in a failing school district and that the only other criterion is for preference in the program, which is based on family income.[239] Finally, petitioners point out that the type of aid in question is religiously neutral, as money is more like a bus or school lunch than a religious tract or other kind of indoctrinational implement.[240] For these reasons, petitioners contend that the Cleveland voucher program passes constitutional muster as an individual benefit provided to citizens by the state.[241]

Direct-aid cases.

Petitioners continue by arguing that not only is this program constitutional under the individual benefit paradigm, but even if the Court were to find that the schools are the beneficiaries instead of the students, the Cleveland program also meets the *Agostini* requirements for direct-aid cases.[242] Neither petitioner nor respondent argue that the secular purpose or excessive entanglement prongs of *Lemon* or *Agostini* are in question in this case.[243] Instead, the focus is on governmental indoctrination and whether the program defines its recipients by reference to religion.[244]

Petitioners cast the first question as "whether any religious indoctrination that occurs in those schools could reasonably be attributed to governmental action."[245] In determining the answer to this question, petitioners return to neutrality and private choice.[246] Referring back to their reasoning in the individual aid cases, petitioners contend that both of these requirements have been met, thus removing the taint of perceived endorsement.[247]

The question as to whether recipients are defined by their religion is looked at in two ways. Overtly, petitioners point out that no one is chosen based on religious affiliation.[248] The terms of the program specifically prohibit such biases.[249] Petitioners follow the *Agostini* reasoning and ask the additional question of "whether the criteria for allocating the aid in question 'creates [sic] a financial incentive to undertake religious indoctrination.'"[250] In both the explicit and incentive approaches to this second prong, petitioners contend that the Cleveland voucher program is acceptable.[251]

This case is not Nyquist *redux.*[252]

Finally, all three petitioners' briefs take great pains to address the question of *Nyquist.* The plan of attack is threefold: differentiate *Nyquist* on the facts;[253] analyze the Cleveland plan under the *Nyquist* requirements;[254] and, finally, due to the confusing nature of *Nyquist,* ask the Court to either clarify in light of recent precedent or overrule it.[255]

First, petitioners argue that the facts of *Nyquist* are substantially different from the facts surrounding the Cleveland plan.[256] In *Nyquist,* the stated purpose of the program was to "rescue religious schools" that were foundering.[257] The *Nyquist* program also allowed schools receiving state aid to discriminate on the basis of religion in both admissions and in requiring obedience to a particular faith.[258] The petitioners heavily emphasize the distinction between the *Nyquist* program's application only to private schools and the Cleveland program's application to both private and public schools.[259]

Second, petitioners claim that even within *Nyquist,* the Cleveland situation is presaged, and *Nyquist* itself forestalls judgment on the issue, thus removing the *Nyquist* restrictions from the current controversy and placing the Cleveland program under the purview of more recent establishment clause constructs.[260] As proof, they point to footnote 38 in *Nyquist,* which states that *Nyquist* could be differentiated from "a case involving some form of public assistance (e.g., scholarships) made available generally without regard to the sectarian-nonsectarian, or public-nonpublic nature of the institution benefited."[261] They follow with examples from more recent decisions that indicate Cleveland-like programs would be acceptable (for many of the previously mentioned reasons).[262]

Finally, petitioners contend that *Nyquist* "continues to spawn nationwide confusion" and as such should not be used to invalidate the Cleveland program.[263] The petitioners are asking the Court to either clarify *Nyquist* or overrule it outright.[264] In either instance, petitioners contend that it should not be controlling.[265]

5. ANALYSIS

For veteran Court watchers, the analysis of the Court on this case is generally straightforward. Chief Justice Rehnquist, along with Justices Scalia, Thomas, and Kennedy, understand the First Amendment in a way that clearly allows vouchers.[266] On the other end of the spectrum, Justices Souter, Breyer, Ginsburg, and Stevens adhere to a First Amendment construct that is not likely to allow vouchers for religious institutions.[267] Most agree that the constitutional question of vouchers rests with Justice O'Connor.[268] The key to convincing Justice O'Connor lies in the endorsement test. But before addressing the principle issue, other arguments were made by both parties, and these should be addressed.

Respondents' Arguments

For the respondents, there are really only three claims that need to be addressed at any length: the use of unrestricted funds that are attributable to the state, the similarities with *Nyquist*, and the question of endorsement. Arguments based on *Agostini*'s prohibition against using religion in determining beneficiaries are conceptually identical to claims about unrestricted funds attributable to the state, and the issues of endorsement will be addressed at the conclusion of this part. This leaves two issues.

First, it is important to examine unrestricted funds attributable to the state. "Unrestricted funds" is a red flag for respondents, not because of recent jurisprudence, but because of a desire to adhere to ideals of no aid to religion by the state.[269] Although there are still some members of the Court who hold this concept dear, it is anachronistic for purposes of modern jurisprudence for two reasons. First, looked at from a free-exercise perspective, providing aid in religious schools in these situations could be viewed as not hindering religion.[270] Giving aid to any qualified entity, except religious ones, requires the religious entity to bear the burden of costs that their secular counterparts are not required to undertake, thus inhibiting religion. Second, distinctions between secular or nondivertable aid are specious at best. Any first-year economics student understands the concept of opportunity costs. Whether using time or money as the medium, any time aid is provided to a group for one purpose, it frees up resources for other uses. This has always been the case, and the Court should drop the facade and admit the reality of the situation.[271] The biggest problem with the question of unrestricted funds analysis is that it fails to take into account the interconnected and interdependent nature of modern social structure, thus prompting the difficult questions that arise over the reality that no part of a community can realistically be completely separated from governmental aid, whether through general services or financial assistance.

In any event, the unrestricted funds argument is of secondary importance to the current situation as the other half of this construct is where the case will turn. This case will ultimately be decided based on whether the flow of money is attributable to the government or whether it is attributable to the independent choice of a nongovernmental entity. Respondents contend that no choice exists because the program looks skewed toward religion due to the large numbers of primarily religious schools that chose to participate.[272] Accompanying this argument is the claim that the program funding levels were designed to encourage religious schools and not nonreligious schools.[273]

There are two major problems with this argument. First, the program seems to function adequately for both religious and nonreligious schools, as some nonreligious private schools have been able to provide places in their programs at the specified amount.[274] The respondents' line of reasoning assumes that religious groups are the only ones with enough eleemosynary proclivities to support education in the private sector. Yet this does not necessarily coincide with current trends in corporations and other secular groups that have found a new interest in funding education.[275]

The second problem is that the program is not skewed toward private religious schools, but toward private nonreligious schools. The Cleveland program provides additional economic incentives for nonreligious schools, both public and private. If a private nonreligious school participates in the program, it has the option of either accepting the voucher as is or applying with the state to become a "community school," whereby it receives additional funding, up to twice the amount it would have received had it remained a strictly private school.[276] The realities of this situation are born out by the several nonreligious schools that have opted to take the plunge and become community schools.[277] Public schools from neighboring communities would also receive the scholarship amount along with their per-capita funding they already receive, thus also creating greater incentive for their participation than for a private religious school.

Respondents attempt to bolster their choice argument by pointing out that the ratio of parents choosing religious schools is greater than the percentage of religious schools participating.[278] This proves a rather odd argument, as it demonstrates the desire of the people for religiously oriented education, not any incentives offered by the state to attend a religious institution. If people were ambivalent, or were seeking nonreligious education, then the numbers attending the various institutions would coincide more closely with the number of schools participating. This indicates a level of choice. For this part of the analysis, it is important to point out that no one who has sought a nonreligious option has been denied an opportunity to participate.[279]

The other portion of the "attributable to the state" argument depends on whether the choices that are available should include only those in the voucher portion of the program, all elements of the program, or all educational choices available. If a situation exists due primarily to state action and influence where only religious options are available, it does indicate at least an arguable preference for religion. Respondents wish to demonstrate that the participants are overwhelmingly religious, thus creating such a presumption of preference.[280] In order to make this claim, respondents contend that the voucher portion of the Cleveland program should be viewed in isolation.[281] Yet even if viewed in isolation, there is a question as to whether numbers alone are enough to make a program a violation of the establishment clause.[282] It raises the specter of requiring the state to affirmatively discriminate against religion in the event a program's participants consist of religious entities, even if the state has done nothing to encourage the makeup of participants. This creates a number of questions about whether the establishment clause requires the state to violate the free-exercise and equal-protection clauses.

The other portion of the respondents' arguments rests heavily on the Court's decision in *Nyquist*.[283] Though they claim these situations are identical, there are significant factual differences, as petitioners point out. More importantly, the Court has failed to follow *Nyquist* in any other case. Instead, the Court differentiates *Nyquist* and finds other cases on which to base their ruling.[284] This behavior does not indicate a strong preference by the Court for *Nyquist*, and it therefore may not be the strongest peg on which to hang one's case. In any event, footnote 38 provides the ambiguity needed for members of the Court to make their cases for or against. This is not likely to move anyone on the Court from a position they are already in. Instead, it provides bolstering material for their eventual decisions.

Petitioners' Arguments

Petitioners' arguments will be given short shrift, as their central argument will be addressed under the following endorsement analysis. The bulk of the petitioner's argument ultimately revolves around the question of choice by the parent, as choice is the prerequisite for their argument that this is actually an individual benefit case.[285] If true choice is found, then the Cleveland program surely qualifies under the requirements of individual benefit cases. Although all of the elements of a true choice are present and seemingly well established, there is still a question of whether there is a perception that there is no true choice.[286] As perception of state endorsement is the important second prong of Justice O'Connor's endorsement analysis, the question of perception will be examined later.

The second issue raised focuses on the question of direct aid and the petitioners' contention that the *Agostini* standard for direct-aid cases is met.[287] In this regard, the petitioner seemingly fails to fully understand the elements of *Agostini*, as the

Court indicates that, if nothing else, the threat of government indoctrination is met if unrestricted money is directly given by the state to an organization that intends to use the money to further its religious mission.[288] The petitioner may try to argue that such an arrangement should be constitutional, but a majority of the Court has yet to agree. The Court has always required some intermediary between the state and the eventual religious recipient[289] or has required that there be some restrictions on the aid, such as it being of a neutral character or it only going toward secular endeavors.[290] This point seems to be a nonstarter and, given the following analysis, is superfluous.

Finally, the question of clarifying *Nyquist* goes without saying. The Court should clarify the parameters of the *Nyquist* decision, though whether that is done by overturning it or by distinguishing it further is more a matter of form than of function. The final fate of *Nyquist* will rest with Justice O'Connor's application of the endorsement test.

Endorsement Test

In Justice O'Connor's formulation of the endorsement test, she explains, "To answer [the establishment clause] question, we must examine both what [the state] intended to communicate . . . and what message [the state] actually conveyed. The purpose and effect prongs of the *Lemon* test represent these two aspects of the meaning [of the state action]."[291] She also clarifies that questions of endorsement are not merely questions of historical fact. Instead, for questions of governmental endorsement of religion, "[though] evidentiary submissions may help answer it, the question is, like the question whether racial or sex-based classifications communicate an invidious message, in large part a legal question to be answered on the basis of judicial interpretation of social facts."[292]

The Court analyzes the first element of this dual-pronged test, intentional endorsement, in nearly identical ways as the purpose prong of the *Lemon* test.[293] Although antivoucher pundits and some of respondents' briefs allude to issues of sub-rosa attempts at propping up parochial schools, neither side has placed much emphasis on the purpose prong.[294] Respondent Harris-Simmons's brief practically concedes this point when it points out that in the *Nyquist* and *Sloan* decisions a secular purpose was found, yet the programs were still found to be unconstitutional.[295] In any event, the state of education in Cleveland provides ample credence to claims of a secular purpose in the lower courts, irrespective of whether these claims are mere masks for alternate purposes by some legislators.

Justice O'Connor also indicates in *Lynch* and other establishment clause cases that there should be no inference that the state has intended to endorse religion merely because a larger program contained a religious element.[296] Although Justice O'Connor does not expand this into a presumption of constitutionality, at the very least this indicates a starting point of neutrality when evaluating possible establishment clause violations.

The second prong, perceived endorsement, creates greater conceptual difficulties. Analogous to the effects prong, the question of perceived endorsement requires the Court to stand in the place of the "general public" and view a particular government action or program to see if the general public would perceive an endorsement of religion by the government.[297] This presumably places the Court in the place of the "reasonable observer," representing neither the most informed and intelligent in the community nor the most ignorant and slow.

In the case of funding religious schools, the problem quickly becomes where one draws the line. Looked at from a historical perspective, public schools in America have a long history of bias against religion, particularly Catholicism. Should the reasonable observer have to take into account historical bias against religion when determining endorsement? If so, the stronger case would be that vouchers are required to avoid discrimination against religion. When viewed from a modern perspective of all publicly funded educational opportunities in the system, the funding allocations between private religious, private nonreligious, nonreligious community, and public schools hardly indicates an endorsement of religion at any level.

The only method by which endorsement could possibly be conceived would be to look at the Cleveland program in the limited context of voucher recipients. This would be quite a stretch for the average person, for as a legal construct many attorneys who work in this area have difficulty segmenting government funding into such distinct segments. It seems absolutely counterintuitive and is but a breath away from requiring each individual voucher to be viewed independently. Yet even in this constrained view, a person should be imputed with an awareness of the particulars of the program, which allow any school that meets the religiously neutral requirements to become part of the program and receive vouchers from students. To do otherwise would require the state to actively discriminate against religion by requiring artificial limits on the number of religious groups that could participate in a government program or would require religious groups to be prohibited from participating. In either instance, the state would be required to identify the participants in a government program by their religious character, which is specifically prohibited in *Agostini*.[298]

Concern over perceived endorsement is certainly understandable, but in the end, such concern must be tempered by the reality that government can only do so much to avoid misperceptions. Justice Scalia's complete dismissal of this form of endorsement can be excessive, but allowing this approach to endorsement to provide a veto by the ignorant is equally misguided.

6. Conclusion

If the Court follows their recent precedent, they will eventually find vouchers to be constitutional. It is highly likely the Court will find the Cleveland voucher program constitutional in this case, with many Court watchers predicting either a five to four or even six to three majority in favor of petitioners. The tone of recent opinions, the creation of new establishment clause paradigms, and the direction of the questions presented at oral arguments all indicate this result. If the Court fails to find vouchers constitutional this time, provoucher groups have already indicated that a loss would merely provide a roadmap on how to construct a constitutional model the next time.[299]

Fortunately, modern America is not the crusades. America's culture wars do not require a resort to violence. Instead, interested parties look to the Supreme Court to provide the constitutional principles that govern the issues in question. These principles do not end the debate, but provide the parameters inside which the parties must formulate their policies and practices. Eventually, once the constitutional questions are settled, the debate will return again to the political arena, where the ultimate fate of vouchers will be worked out through the newly constrained political process. Thus the principles the Court provides about vouchers today will illuminate and direct the next culture war battle, whether it be over charitable choice or public school curriculum.

In the end, it is a great nation, with a well-founded system of government that requires its culture wars to be fought with words instead of swords. The warriors of today emerge from the battlefield shaking hands and trading good-natured jibes, instead of holding aloft the head of the defeated. Yet even today, culture warriors still make a petition to a higher power as they enter the field, though it is usually not in Latin. Instead, the culture war today follows the petition "God save the United States and this honorable Court."

Addendum

On June 27, 2002, the U.S. Supreme Court handed down its decision in *Zelman v. Simmons-Harris*. By a five-to-four majority, the Court found the Cleveland voucher arrangement to be constitutional. Although this case is one of the most important establishment clause cases in the last fifty years, it comes in such proximity to the far more visceral, yet less important ruling in the Ninth Circuit over the Pledge of Allegiance that it will receive little attention in the media. Yet for those alert to the ramifications, the *Zelman* decision caps a line of semiambiguous precedents that some will cheer, some will mourn, but all will have to come to terms with.

Chief Justice Rehnquist wrote the majority decision, which was joined by Justices Thomas, Scalia, Kennedy, and O'Connor. The majority found that because the Cleveland program provided a genuine choice between a neutral range of educational options, and the benefit went to the parent instead of to the school, the program was constitutional.

Justice O'Connor provided a concurring opinion, noting that no preferences were given to religious schools when all of the educational options were examined. The most surprising element of Justice O'Connor's concurrence was not in what it said, but in what it did not say. Known for concurrences that have limited the scope of majority decisions, her concurrence merely shored up Justice Rehnquist's arguments. Justice Thomas also provided a separate concurring opinion. In it he questioned the validity of the incorporation doctrine, using the Fourteenth Amendment to incorporate the establishment clause onto the states. He then pointed out the irony of using the Fourteenth Amendment, which was designed to counter the effects of slavery, in a way that denies black children a better education.

Justices Stevens, Souter, Breyer, and Ginsburg dissented. Justice Stevens's dissent consisted of three brief rebuttals of the majority's main points. Justice Souter's dissent, on which Justices Stevens, Breyer, and Ginsburg joined, provided a lengthy response to the majority. Turning first to the history of the various aid to parochial school decisions, he contended that the *Everson* no-aid approach to these cases most accurately represents the best constitutional position. He also argued that even if formal neutrality is to be the criteria, the Cleveland program fails because the set of choices to be analyzed must be limited to the schools accepting vouchers, and not all educational options. Justice Souter also argued that the idea of vouchers goes against the spirit and principles of the First Amendment and will lead to sectarian strife and harm to religion.

Finally, Justice Breyer provided a dissent onto which Justices Stevens and Souter joined. Justice Breyer extrapolated the concerns of Justice Souter and argued at length that aid to religious schools will create sectarian strife that will harm society. He argued that concern over the nation's social fabric is of such overriding concern that it cannot be countered by arguments of parental choice.

With this important decision, the battle has shifted from questions of whether vouchers are constitutional to whether they are beneficial. Instead of lawyers and judges, parents, school boards, and educators must debate and decide what best serves the interest of children and communities.

NOTES

1. "God wills it so."

2. *Simmons-Harris v. Zelman*, 234 F. 3d 945 (6th Cir. 2000).

3. Ibid., 948.

4. Ibid. The specifics of this program can also be found in Ohio Rev. Code Anno. §§ 3313.974–3313.979.

5. *Simmons-Harris v. Zelman*, 948.

6. Ibid., 949.

7. Ibid.

8. Ibid.

9. Ibid.

10. Ibid.

11. Ibid.

12. Ibid., 949–50.

13. Brief on the Merits for Petitioner, 2–3, 2000 U.S. Briefs 1779 (November 9, 2001), citing Ohio Rev. Code §§ 3317.03(I)(1), 3327.06, 3317.08(A)(1).

14. *Simmons-Harris v. Zelman*, 949.

15. Ibid.

16. Ibid.

17. Ibid.

18. Ibid. The program originally failed the one-subject rule required by the Ohio Constitution. The legislature reauthorized the program with the procedural defect corrected, although the program particulars remained unchanged.

19. Ibid. The sensitivity of this issue is seen at the appeals level, where the 2–1 panel drafted an exceedingly acerbic opinion and dissent, leveling rather acrimonious remarks at one another.

20. *Zelman v. Simmons-Harris*, 122 S. Ct. 23 (2001).

21. Nicole Stelle Garnett and Richard W. Garnett, "School Choice, the First Amendment, and Social Justice," *Texas Review of Law and Politics* 4 (2000): 301, 305–6.

22. Brief of Amicus Curiae, The Claremont Institute Center for Constitutional Jurisprudence in support of Petitioners, 4, 2000 U.S. Briefs 1751 (November 9, 2001).

23. All of the parties' briefs, as well as most of the amicus briefs, touch on this topic.

24. Amicus Brief of Ohio Association for Public Education and Religious Liberty in Support of Affirmance for Respondents, 4, 2000 U.S. Briefs 1751 (December 10, 2001).

25. Brief for California Alliance for Public Schools as Amicus Curiae Supporting Respondents, 3, 2000 U.S. Briefs 1751 (December 13, 2001).

26. Brief of Anti-Defamation League, Amicus Curiae, in Support of Respondents, 20, 2000 U.S. Briefs 1751 (December 13, 2001).

27. Again, both sides are replete with examples of this theme. See, generally, Brief on the Merits for Petitioner, 2000 U.S. Briefs 1779 (November 9, 2001), and Brief of Respondents Sue Gatton, et al., 2000 U.S. Briefs 1751 (December 14, 2001).

28. Warren A. Nord, *Religion and American Education: Rethinking a National Dilemma* (Chapel Hill: Univ. of North Carolina Press, 1995), 63.

29. Lloyd P. Jorgenson, *The State and the Non-Public School: 1825–1925* (Columbia: Univ. of Missouri Press, 1987), 2.

30. Nord, *Religion and American Education*, 63.

31. Ibid., 64.

32. Jorgenson, *State and the Non-Public School*, 13. This is an extension of the much earlier "Old Deluder Satan" laws that were passed by the Puritans in an effort to require literacy for colonial children. See Nord, *Religion and American Education*, 64.

33. John C. Jefferies Jr. and James E. Ryan, "A Political History of the Establishment Clause," *Michigan Law Review* 100 (2001): 279, 297. Also see, generally, Jorgenson, *State and the Non-Public School,* chaps. 5–6.

34. Jorgenson, *Religion and American Education,* 129–32.

35. Catholics in particular were considered un-American because of their ties to the Vatican, which frequently pronounced democracy as evil during this period. This conflicted with the French ideals of liberty that were sweeping the country. Jeffries and Ryan, *Political History of the Establishment Clause,* 302–3; A. James Reichley, *Religion in American Public Life* (Washington, D.C.: Brookings Institution, 1985), 137–38.

36. Jeffries and Ryan, *Political History of the Establishment Clause,* 299–300; see, generally, Jorgenson, *Religion and American Education,* 69–110.

37. Jorgenson, *Religion and American Education,* 69–110.

38. Reichley, *Religion in American Public Life,* 137–38.

39. Jorgenson, *State and the Non-Public School,* 73.

40. Catholic students faced persecution at school, such as expulsion for failing to read from the King James Bible, *Donahoe v. Richards,* 38 Me. 379 (1854); expulsion for failing to bow their heads during the Protestant Bible reading, *Spiller v. Woburn,* 94 Mass., 127, 129 (1866); and corporal punishment for failing to read the King James Version of the Bible, Jorgenson, *State and the Non-Public School,* 90–93. At the Eliot School in Boston, a student was beaten across the hands for half an hour with a rattan cane until they were cut and bleeding for refusing to recite the Protestant version of the Ten Commandments. Jorgenson, *State and the Non-Public School,* 91–92, citing Robert H. Lord, et al., *History of the Archdiocese of Boston in the Various Stages of Development, 1604–1943,* vol. 2 (New York: Sheed and Ward), 587–91.

41. "So that if, on the one side, we shall be traduced by Popish Persons [Catholics] at home or abroad, who therefore will malign us, because we are poor instruments to make God's holy Truth to be yet more and more known unto the people, whom they desire still to keep in ignorance and darkness; or if, on the other side, we shall be maligned by self-conceited Brethren, who run their own ways, and give liking unto nothing, but what is framed by themselves, and hammered on their anvil; we may rest secure, supported within by truth and innocency of a good conscience, having walked the ways of simplicity and integrity, as before the Lord; and sustained without by the powerful protection of Your Majesty's grace and favour, which will ever give countenance to honest and Christian endeavours against bitter censures and uncharitable imputations." Epistle Dedicatory to the Authorized King James Version [1611].

42. Patrick W. Carey, *The Roman Catholics in America* (Westport, Conn.: Praeger, 1996), 37–38.

43. Jorgenson, *State and the Non-Public School,* 82.

44. Ibid., 29. Although Bible controversies were certainly part of the tension, other issues also influenced these conflicts. In particular, Maria Monk's nativist propaganda book, *Awful Disclosures of the Hotel Dieu Nunnery of Montreal,* led to investigations and attacks on convents.

45. Garnett and Garnett, *School Choice,* 337.

46. Jeffries and Ryan, *Political History of the Establishment,* 300–301.

47. Ibid., 304; Jorgenson, *State and the Non-Public School,* 74–76.

48. Jorgenson, *State and the Non-Public School,* 74–76.

49. Know-Nothings and other xenophobic groups attempted to destroy the parochial school system through political means by passing discriminatory laws, in particular, laws that required students to attend public schools. Jorgenson, *State and the Non-Public School,* 70.

50. Reichley, *Religion in American Public Life,* 139. Many voucher programs may prove to violate not the federal Constitution, but state constitutions. Between 1877 and 1913, thirty-seven states drafted and passed prohibitions against public funding of "sectarian instruction." This was largely due to congressional requirements that all states entering the Union after 1876 include in their constitutions provisions for the maintenance of nonsectarian public school systems. See Michael Ariens and Robert Destro, *Religious Liberty in a Pluralistic Society* (Durham, N.C.: Carolina Academic Press, 1996), 168.

51. One of the earliest Supreme Court cases in religious liberty arose around this controversy. In *Pierce v. Society of Sisters*, 268 U.S. 510 (1925), the Supreme Court found that parents have a fundamental right in the upbringing of their children.

52. Jorgenson, *State and the Non-Public School*, 70.

53. Charles Haynes, "Religion in the Public Schools," *The School Administrator* (January 1999): 7.

54. Nord, *Religion and American Education*, 91.

55. Ibid. See, generally, 63–97.

56. Ibid.

57. Ibid.

58. Ibid., 96. Even this perfunctory recognition of religion became scarce as religious groups formed uneasy alliances to avoid allowing any particular religious entity to gain control of the schools. Thus secularization by the faithful became politically expedient and necessary due to the fear of Catholic power in particular. Jeffries and Ryan, *Political History of the Establishment*, 312–14.

59. Jeffries and Ryan, *Political History of the Establishment*, 309.

60. Nord, *Religion and American Education*, 91–92.

61. Many still hold to the idea that the core mission of public education is to meld various backgrounds into an idealized "American." See Molly O'Brien, "Free at Last, Charter Schools and Deregulated Curriculum," *Akron Law Review* 34 (2000): 137, 169–70; Nomi Maya Stolzenberg, "'He Drew a Circle That Shut Me Out': Assimilation, Indoctrination, and the Paradox of a Liberal Education," *Harvard Law Review* 106 (1993): 581.

62. Nord, *Religion and American Education*, 96.

63. Ibid.

64. *Engle v. Vitale*, 370 U.S. 421 (1962); *Abington v. Shempp*, 374 U.S. 203 (1963). Many commentators referred to the era of these decisions as when "God was kicked out of schools." These decisions specifically prohibited state-sponsored prayer and state-sponsored devotional Bible readings. Nothing in these decisions removed religion from school. Students and teachers still retain their free-exercise rights, and the curriculum may still (and arguably should) teach about religion. See, generally, Warren Nord and Charles Haynes, *Taking Religion Seriously across the Curriculum* (Alexandria, Va.: Association for Supervision and Curriculum Development, 1998). It should also be noted that to a large extent most schools in the country had already done away with such ceremonial activities as a devotional at the beginning of the day.

65. For a more sinister approach to this situation, see Paul C. Vitz, *Censorship: Evidence of Bias in Our Children's Textbooks* (Ann Arbor, Mich.: Servant, 1986).

66. See, generally, Nord, *Religion and American Education*, 63–97.

67. See *Mozert v. Hawkings County Board of Education*, 827 F. 2d 1058 (1987); Charles C. Haynes, *Teaching about Religious Freedom in American Secondary Schools* (Silver Spring, Md.: Americans United Research Foundation, 1985); Vitz, *Censorship;* O. L. Davis, et al., *Looking at History: A Review of Major U.S. History Textbooks* (Washington, D.C.: People for the American Way, 1986).

68. Vitz, *Censorship;* Davis, *Looking at History.*

69. Vitz, *Censorship*, 18.

70. Ibid., 3–4.

71. Ibid.

72. Compare Nord, *Religion and American Education*, 63–97, and Davis, *Looking at History*, 9, to Vitz, *Censorship*, 89–90.

73. Other terms include "naked public schools" and "secular public schools." See John Ferguson, "Religion in Public Schools: Who Decides?" *Liberty* 96, no. 3 (2001): 17.

74. Jefferies and Ryan, *Political History of the Establishment*, 337. Some evangelical Christian groups have gone so far as to support initiatives such as Exodus 2000 and the Exodus Mandate, projects dedicated to removing all Christian children from the public schools. See Robert Haly McCain, "Christians

Urged to Abandon Public Schools as Irreparable," *Washington Times,* August 26, 1999; National Desk, "Take Your Kids Out of Public Schools," *U.S. Newswire,* April 19, 2002.

75. National Center for Educational Statistics, Findings from the Condition of Education 1997: Public and Private Schools: How Do They Differ? Report NCES 97–983 (July 1997).

76. Examples of this can be seen in the *Zelman* case, where often more than 90 percent of the students enrolled were not of the same religious faith as the enrolling institution.

77. See, generally, Carol A. Langdon, "The Fifth Phi Delta Kappan Poll of Teachers' Attitudes toward Public Schools," April 15, 1999, www.pdkintl.org/kappan/klan9904.htm (accessed March 26, 2002); David Young, Petitioner's Brief 00–1777, 3–5.

78. See, generally, Paul E. Peterson, "School Choice: A Report Card," *Virginia Journal of Social Policy and the Law* 6 (1998): 47.

79. Ibid., 56–57.

80. Ibid.

81. Before 1940 the Court had been unable to evaluate state attempts at establishment, as the First Amendment religion clauses were not interpreted by the Court to be applicable to the state through the doctrine of incorporation of the Fourteenth Amendment. In the 1940 decision of *Cantwell v. Connecticut,* 310 U.S. 296 (1940), the Court initially applied the First Amendment religion clauses to the states.

82. It should be noted that another test that has gained some popularity in the area of establishment clause jurisprudence is the coercion test espoused by Justice Kennedy in *Lee v. Weisman,* 505 U.S. 577 (1992). Despite its use, it typically focuses on government expression that indicates a preference for a religion and as such is only tangentially connected to the question of funding. Many of the concerns found in this test are given heightened scrutiny in O'Connor's endorsement test.

83. For example, the case of *Mitchell v. Helms,* 530 U.S. 793 (2000), examines all of the previously mentioned standards in an attempt to articulate their various rationales.

84. *Everson v. Board of Education,* 330 U.S. 1 (1947).

85. Ibid., 3–5.

86. Ibid., 3.

87. Ibid., 5.

88. Ibid.

89. Ibid., 16.

90. Ibid., 8–15.

91. Ibid., 8–9. It should be noted that Justice Black's foray into history is questionable. Puritans did not seek religious freedom as modern audiences understand it. Toleration and protection of minority viewpoints and beliefs were not a primary concern. Puritans were concerned with freedom for their faith, not that of others, and they quickly institutionalized many of their religious practices and enforced them through the power of the state. For an analysis of how modern jurisprudence is philosophically situated, see Jeffries and Ryan, Political History of the Establishment Clause.

92. *Everson v. Board of Education,* 10–13.

93. Ibid., 11–12.

94. Ibid., 12.

95. Ibid.

96. Ibid., 13.

97. Ibid.

98. Ibid., 15–16.

99. Ibid., 16.

100. It should be noted that the terminology "church and state," although seemingly exclusive, is being used as a term of art as it is universally recognized in the field. This term includes any interaction between religious adherents, their institutions, and the state (in its broadest terms).

101. *Everson v. Board of Education*, 17–18.

102. Ibid.

103. Ibid.

104. Ibid., 18.

105. Ibid., 16.

106. Although *Everson* implies this differentiation, the full nature of the issue comes to light in later decisions such as *Tilton v. Richardson*, 403 U.S. 672 (1971) (regarding the use of government bonds to finance a gymnasium at a religious school) and *Bowen v. Kendrick*, 487 U.S. 589 (1988) (allowing government funds for religiously oriented counseling services).

107. This is at best a very Western ideal of religion and at worse a misleading dichotomy. Many religious traditions find no distinction within the tradition between cultic or sacramental elements of one's faith and the socio-ethical requirements.

108. Justice Black alluded to this in *Everson v. Board of Education*, 17–18, and later cases explained this issue more fully. See *Committee for Public Education and Religious Liberty v. Nyquist*, 413 U.S. 756 (1973) and *Mitchell v. Helms*.

109. Differentiating between aid given to help religious institutions versus aid provided to parents to get their children safely to school. *Everson v. Board of Education*, 17–18. This issue will be more fully explored in the next section.

110. Again, *Everson v. Board of Education* (19) provides the groundwork for this idea, and later cases extrapolate the concept into a more robust concept. See *Board of Education v. Allen*, 392 U.S. 236 (1968).

111. *Everson v. Board of Education*, 19. Another oft-cited reason for providing such services is that they serve a prophylactic function for adjacent property and other community businesses, thus ensuring the safety of not only the religious entities interests, but the broader interests of the community as well.

112. The Court most recently addressed this issue at some depth in *Mitchell v. Helms*, 822–23.

113. In the *Helms* decision, Justices Ginsburg, Stevens, and Souter all joined in a dissent that indicates their continued adherence to the no-aid paradigm. In the simplest terms, these justices believe that the First Amendment "bars the use of public funds for religious aid." Ibid., 793, 868. Later they reiterate, "Today, the substantive principle of no aid to religious mission remains the governing understanding of the Establishment Clause as applied to public benefits inuring to religious schools." Ibid., 878. This seems a rather marked contradiction to the views of the other six justices. See, generally, the majority and concurring opinions in *Mitchell v. Helms* and *Lynch v. Donnelly*, 465 U.S. 668 (Justice O'Connor's concurrence, 1984).

114. *Mitchell v. Helms*, 870 (concurring opinion).

115. Ibid., 870–71.

116. Ibid. In particular, Madison's *Memorial and Remonstrance* and Jefferson's "Virginia Bill for Establishing Religious Freedom" are consistently referred to by the Court as rationale for many of these views.

117. Ibid., 871–72.

118. Ibid. Again, frequent reference is made to the works of Madison and Jefferson.

119. Ibid., 872–73.

120. Ibid. Justice O'Connor used this concern as the foundation of her later endorsement test.

121. *Everson v. Board of Education*, 16.

122. Ibid., 18.

123. *Witters v. Washington Dept. of Serv. for the Blind*, 474 U.S. 481, 485–86 (1986).

124. *Everson v. Board of Education*, 16–17.

125. *Everson v. Board of Education*, 18.

126. *Committee for Public Education and Religious Liberty v. Nyquist*.

127. Ibid., 761–68.

128. Brief on the Merits for Petitioner, 18–19, citing N.Y. Educ. Law, art. 12-A, § § 549(2), 559(3) and *Committee for Public Education and Religious Liberty v. Nyquist*, 764–65.

129. *Committee for Public Education and Religious Liberty v. Nyquist,* 762–64.

130. Ibid., 768.

131. Ibid., 786.

132. Interestingly, the Court most frequently refers to *Nyquist* for a quote from footnote 38 about Constitutionality requiring "even-handedness" when providing aid. See *Mitchell v. Helms,* 881–82; *Witters v. Washington Dept. of Serv. for the Blind,* 491; *Zobrest v. Catalina Foothills School District,* 509 U.S. 1 (1993), 12–13.

133. *Mueller v. Allen,* 463 U.S. 388 (1983).

134. Ibid., 399.

135. *Witters v. Washington Dept. of Serv. for the Blind.*

136. Ibid., 482.

137. Ibid., 482–85.

138. Ibid., 487.

139. Ibid., 488.

140. *Lemon v. Kurtzman,* 403 U.S. 602 (1971).

141. Ibid., 606–7.

142. Ibid., 611–12.

143. This is not to say that this prong has not proven the undoing of some legislative action, as the Court is more than willing to review an action to make sure that it is not merely a cover for unconstitutional purposes. See *Wallace v. Jaffree,* 472 U.S. 38 (1985).

144. *Lemon v. Kurtzman,* 613.

145. Ibid.

146. *Witters v. Washington Dept. of Serv. for the Blind,* 486–488; *Agostini v. Felton,* 521 U.S. 220–21 (1997); *Mitchell v. Helms,* 816.

147. *Lemon v. Kurtzman,* 201.

148. Ibid., 201–3.

149. Carole F. Kagan, "Squeezing the Juice from Lemon: Toward a Consistent Test for the Establishment Clause," *North Kentucky Law Review* 22 (1995): 621, 632–33; Douglas Laycock, "A Survey of Religious Liberty in the United States," *Ohio State Law Journal* 47 (1986): 409, 449–50.

150. "It has never been entirely clear, however, how the three parts of the test relate to the principles enshrined in the Establishment Clause." *Lynch v. Donnelly,* 688–89; *Kiryas Joel Sc. Dist. v. Grumet,* 114 S. Ct. 2481, 2498–2500 (1994).

151. *Lamb's Chapel v. Centers Moriches Union Free Sch. Dist.,* 113 S. Ct. 2141, 2149 (1993; Justice Scalia concurring).

152. *Agostini v. Felton,* 203, 233.

153. Ibid., 234.

154. *Aguilar v. Felton,* 473 U.S. 402 (1985).

155. *Agostini v. Felton,* 209.

156. Ibid., 218–19.

157. Ibid., 234.

158. Ibid.

159. Ibid.

160. *Mitchell v. Helms,* 809–14.

161. *Everson v. Board of Education,* 18.

162. Ibid., 18.

163. *Board of Ed. v. Allen,* 392 U.S. 236 (1968).

164. *Bowen v. Kendrick,* 487 U.S. 589 (1988).

165. *Mitchell v. Helms,* 882–83.

166. Ibid., 869.

167. Ibid., 913.

168. Opponents of vouchers in the *Zelman* controversy claim that the funding system requires a cap on tuition that is set at such a level that only religious schools with additional funding can compete. *Brief of Amicus Curiae, The American Jewish Committee in Support of Respondents,* 21–22. This argument will be addressed more fully in part 4.

169. *Lynch v. Donnelly,* 465 U.S. 668 (1984).

170. Ibid., 671.

171. Ibid., 690.

172. Ibid.

173. Ibid.

174. Ibid., 691–92.

175. Ibid., 689.

176. Ibid., 691.

177. Barely able to service war debts, the federal government focused almost all of its attention on matters of defense and revenue collection.

178. In March 2002, Congress prepared to pass a proposed $2.1 trillion budget. Available online at http://w3.access.gpo.gov/usbudget/fy2003/budget.html.

179. *Mitchell v. Helms,* 871.

180. *Everson v. Board of Education,* 18. The author does not dispute the fact that government involvement with religion does and will lead to the detriment of religion. The author's contention is that harm to religion should be a policy question asked by those involved, not an element of constitutional calculus.

181. *Lynch v. Donnelly,* 690.

182. Ibid., 688.

183. Chief Justice Rehnquist's dissent in *Santa Fe v. Doe,* 530 U.S. 290, 318 (2000), found that the separationist opinion of the majority not only infringed on the rights of students, but it "bristled with hostility to all things religious in public life."

184. *Committee for Public Education and Religious Liberty v. Nyquist,* 761. Justice Jackson had warned in McCollum that if the Court was not careful, it would end up with too many establishment clause cases, and establishment clause jurisprudence would end up based on the peculiarities of the Court instead of logic and principle. *McCollum v. Board of Education,* 333 U.S. 203, 238 (1948).

185. It should be noted that the case before the Court is a consolidated case, and therefore there are several briefs for differing groups of both respondents and petitioners. For purposes of clarity, only one brief will be discussed, and in cases of difference or additional analytical constructs, such distinctions will be noted.

186. Brief for Respondent Doris Simmons-Harris, 6. *Zelman v. Simmons-Harris,* 536 U.S. 639 (2002).

187. Ibid., 11–12.

188. Ibid., 12.

189. Ibid., 13.

190. Ibid., 14.

191. Ibid.

192. Ibid., 18.

193. Ibid., 19–20.

194. Not only do the briefs focus on this issue, but also the questions asked, particularly by Justices O'Connor, Rehnquist, Kennedy, and Stevens. Tony Mauro, "All Eyes on O'Connor during Voucher Arguments," *Freedom Forum News Service,* February 21, 2002, www.Freedomforum.org.

195. Brief for Respondent Doris Simmons-Harris, 19.

196. Ibid., 24–25.

197. Ibid., 24.

198. Ibid., 25.

199. Fredreka Shouten, "Supreme Court Tackles Landmark Vouchers Case," *Gannett News Service*, February 15, 2002.

200. Brief for Respondent Doris Simmons-Harris, 24–26. The endorsement question in the brief will be brought up separately later.

201. Ibid., 25.

202. During oral arguments, Chanin eventually conceded that if less than 1 percent of the schools that participated were religious, he would have less of a problem with the program. See Mauro, "All Eyes on O'Connor."

203. Brief for Respondent Doris Simmons-Harris, 25.

204. Ibid.

205. Ibid., 26–33.

206. *Mitchell v. Helms*, 841–42.

207. Brief for Respondent Doris Simmons-Harris, 31–32.

208. Ibid., 27–29.

209. Ibid., 29–31.

210. Ibid., 35.

211. Ibid.

212. Ibid., 35–36.

213. Ibid.

214. Ibid.

215. Ibid.

216. Ibid., 37.

217. Ibid., 37–38.

218. Ibid., 38.

219. Ibid., see note 15.

220. Ibid., 42.

221. Ibid.

222. As with respondents, multiple briefs were filed on behalf of petitioners. And again, for purposes of clarity, most of the focus in this section will be on the state's brief, as the brief for the Perkins school parallels most of the arguments in the state's brief, and the brief on the merits tends to wander into issues of educational policy more than issues of constitutional validity.

223. Brief of State Petitioners, 22, *Zelman v. Simmons-Harris*, 536 U.S. 639 (2002).

224. Ibid., 22–24.

225. Ibid., 24.

226. Ibid., 24.

227. Ibid.

228. Ibid., 25.

229. Ibid., 27–28.

230. Ibid., 27.

231. Ibid., 28.

232. Ibid., 28–29.

233. Ibid.

234. Ibid., 29.

235. Ibid., 28–29.

236. Ibid., 29.

237. Ibid., 29–30.

238. Ibid.

239. Ibid., 30–31.

240. Ibid.

241. Ibid., 32.

242. Ibid., 33.

243. Ibid., 33, citing lower court *Simmons-Harris v. Zelman*, 234 F. 3d 1945 (2000), 845.

244. Ibid., 34.

245. Ibid., citing *Mitchell v. Helms*, 809.

246. Ibid., 34–35, citing the majority, concurrence, and dissent in the *Mitchell* decision.

247. Ibid., 35.

248. Ibid., 36.

249. Ibid.

250. Ibid., citing *Agostini v. Felton*, 231.

251. Ibid., 37.

252. Ibid., 19.

253. Ibid., 42–44.

254. Ibid., 44–47.

255. Ibid., 47–48.

256. Ibid., 42.

257. Ibid., 42–43.

258. Ibid., 42.

259. Ibid., 42–43.

260. Ibid., 44.

261. Ibid., citing *Committee for Public Education and Religious Liberty v. Nyquist*, 782n 38.

262. Ibid., 45.

263. Ibid., 48.

264. Ibid.

265. Ibid.

266. See, generally, Mauro, "All Eyes on O'Connor"; Jeffrey Rosen, "The Liberal Roots of Vouchers: Class Action," *New Republic*, March, 18, 2002.

267. Judge Breyer may be another wild card in this situation. His pragmatic leanings led him to join in Justice O'Connor's concurrence in Mitchell, and he may once again if he perceives the situation in Cleveland as bad enough. See Rosen, "Liberal Roots of Vouchers."

268. Mauro, "All Eyes on O'Connor"; Rosen, "Liberal Roots of Vouchers."

269. *Mitchell v. Helms*, 868 (Justice Souter's dissent).

270. Due to the Supreme Court's decision in *Employment Division v. Smith* that eviscerated the free exercise clause, free exercise clause jurisprudence has had to take the form of either an equal protection claim or a reverse establishment clause claim (meaning that the government cannot create special barriers for a particular religion or group of religious entities, as this would have the effect of establishing all other religions over the group facing the hindrances).

271. Justice Rutledge's dissent in *Everson* points out this very reality from the beginning. *Everson v. Board of Education*, 48.

272. Brief for Respondent Doris Simmons-Harris, 37.

273. Brief of Anti-Defamation League, Amicus Curiae, for Respondents, 6.

274. All parties recognize that ten out of the fifty-six schools were nonsectarian. See Brief for Respondent Doris Simmons-Harris, 1; Brief on the Merits for Petitioner, 3.

275. "Oracle Help Us Help Foundation Donates to Twenty New Orleans Schools," *PR Newswire*, January 22, 2002; Joy Dryfoos, "Partnering: Full-Service Community Schools: Creating New Institutions," *Phi Delta Kappan* 83, no. 5 (2002): 393.

276. Brief of State Petitioners, 9–10.

277. Ibid., 10.

278. Brief of Respondent Sue Gatton, 37; Brief for Respondents Doris Simmons-Harris, 2.

279. This type of factual distinction is not relevant in later endorsement analysis, as perceptions of endorsement are considered matters of law, not fact, and the Court will examine the situation based on judicially recognized facts, not the facts of the specific situation. *Lynch v. Donnelly,* 694.

280. See Brief for Respondent Doris Simmons-Harris, 38.

281. Ibid., 26–27.

282. Respondents address this by arguing that the situation is more like areas on a continuum, with *Nyquist, Sloan,* and the Cleveland program on one end and the circumstances in *Witters* on the other. Ibid., 24–25.

283. Respondents' briefs are rife with references to *Nyquist.* See generally Brief for Respondent Doris Simmons-Harris.

284. *Mitchell v. Helms,* 820 (differentiating based on aid only provided for private nonprofit schools); most often, it is cited only for the quote requiring neutrality in government programs; *Agostini v. Felton,* 225; *Zobrest v. Catalina Foothills School District,* 10.

285. Brief of State Petitioner, 22–28.

286. Respondents frequently point out that the numbers of religious entities involved in the program make it look like government sponsorship of religion. See Brief for Respondents Doris Simmons-Harris, 38.

287. Brief of State Petitioner, 38.

288. *Agostini v. Felton,* 228.

289. See, generally, *Zobrest* (allowing state funding for a sign-language interpreter for student in religious school) and *Witters* (allowing the use of a disability aid grant for a student to be used in a religious school, for a specifically religious education).

290. See, generally, *Agostini v. Felton* (Title I assistance for teachers in parochial schools); *Wolman v. Walters* (allowing loans of secular textbooks); *Mitchell v. Helms* (allowing the loans of computers and other educational material to religious schools).

291. *Lynch v. Donnelly,* 691.

292. Ibid., 695.

293. Ibid., 690.

294. See, generally, Brief of Respondents Sue Gatton, et al., 45–46.

295. Brief for Respondent Doris Simmons-Harris, 11.

296. *Lynch v. Donnelly,* 692.

297. Justice Scalia has frequently rejected the notion of perceived endorsement, arguing that it is not the Court's job to protect people from their own willful ignorance and stupidity. See *Good News Club v. Milford,* 533 U.S. 98, 121 (2001; dissent by Justice Scalia); *Capital Square Review and Advisory Board v. Pinette,* 515 U.S. 753 (1995); and *Lamb's Chapel v. Centers Moriches Union Free School,* 508 U.S. 384 (1993).

298. *Agostini v. Felton,* 234.

299. Elizabeth Auster, "Constitutional Impact May Be Far Reaching in Voucher Case," *Cleveland Plain Dealer,* February 17, 2002.

The Rise of State Law Sanctuary for Minority Religious Liberty in the Wake of the Fall of Federal Constitutional Protection of Nonmainstream Faiths

GARY S. GILDIN

INTRODUCTION

The overarching title of this year's symposium, Democracy and Religion: Free Exercise and Diverse Visions, appears to presume that democracy is a hospitable environment for religious liberty. Certainly the popular understanding is that democracies—in stark contrast to regimes that lean toward totalitarianism, such as the Taliban, which imposed its own brand of fundamentalist Islam on the populace of Afghanistan, or the former Soviet Union, which essentially banned religion—extend equal rights to followers of a multiplicity of denominations. The more particularized title of section I, "The Constitutional Debate regarding the Establishment and Free Exercise Clauses," intimates that the First Amendment of the U.S. Constitution stands as the primary legal stronghold of religious freedom for worshipers of diverse faiths in the American democracy.

This chapter submits that, in reality, neither of the suppositions is accurate. Adherents of nonmainstream sects remain vulnerable to hindrances, unintentionally imposed by democratic majorities, to pursuit of their beliefs. Moreover, since 1990 the free exercise clause of the First Amendment to the U.S. Constitution has offered negligible security to constituents of minority creeds whose religion is burdened by neutral laws of general applicability. In the twenty-first century it is state law rather than the federal constitution that affords the greatest capacity to ensure that disciples of diverse persuasions may follow their religious conscience in the American democracy.

It is true that the history and maturation of our American democracy renders *intentional* discrimination against a particular religion improbable. As Justice O'Connor observed, "The principle that government may not enact laws that suppress religious belief or practice is so well understood that few violations are recorded in our opinions."[1] The nation was founded in part on rebellion against the bonds of state-sanctioned orthodoxy. Our polity is sufficiently stable that the coexistence of diverse systems of religious belief is considered a strength, not a threat. Even in the earliest days of the horror and grieving following the September 11 attacks, our leaders cautioned against letting the thirst for revenge manifest itself in animosity toward followers of Islamic faith traditions.

Although purposeful incursions on religious liberty may be unlikely, the diversification of American society has vastly increased the probability that a secular law, meant to apply to the entire citizenry in a nondiscriminatory fashion, will turn out to conflict with the rituals of nonmainstream denominations. As Timothy Hall observed, "Especially when a religious belief is held by a small minority of individuals, legislators may simply be unaware of the crisis of religious conscience a neutral law may occasion."[2] The Wisconsin legislature undoubtedly was not cognizant that its compulsory education law requiring pupils to attend school until age sixteen endangered the salvation of the children of the Old Order Amish.[3] It is doubtful that legislators in South Carolina knew that by denying benefits to persons who refused Saturday work, its Unemployment Compensation Act served to disqualify a member of the Seventh Day Adventist Church whose teachings precluded her from laboring on Saturday, her sabbath.[4] Congress did not anticipate that its mandate that participants in welfare programs provide the Social Security numbers of their offspring as a condition of receiving benefits would conflict with the credo of a descendant of the Abenaki tribe that providing a number for his daughter, Little Bird of the Snow, would rob her of spiritual power.[5] The U.S. Supreme Court has acknowledged that democracy alone will not ensure that smaller orders remain free to practice their religion; to the contrary, the Court understood that "leaving accommodation to the political process will place at a relative disadvantage those religious practices that are not widely engaged in."[6]

The U.S. Constitution traditionally has been viewed as the guardian of minority religious liberty against burdens imposed knowingly or unknowingly by democratic majorities. Those lacking political power to inform or affect the majoritarian legislative process turned to the courts to enforce the guarantees of the federal Bill of Rights, asking to be exempted from the strictures of laws that had the effect of encumbering the individual's religious exercise.

As of 1990, the U.S. Supreme Court had interpreted the free exercise clause of the First Amendment to generously secure religious liberty, applying strict scrutiny to laws that had either the purpose or the effect of impeding an individual's religion. The person claiming an invasion of free exercise was required first to prove the governmental regulation in issue infringed a sincerely held theological belief. In applying this prong of the analysis, the Court was solicitous of minority religious precepts. The Court abnegated inquiry into either the centrality of the tenet or the validity of the individual's interpretation of the doctrine.[7] Nor were the courts to assess whether the asserted belief was consistent, logical, or officially sanctioned;[8] to the contrary, religious views merited safekeeping even when they were considered "rank heresy to followers of the orthodox faiths."[9]

Although deferential to the professed belief, the Court rigorously evaluated the government's insistence that the demands of civil society necessitated subordinating the individual's religious obligation. To justify the burden on religious exercise, the government had to prove both that it had a compelling, not merely a rational, interest at stake and that the government's compelling interest could not be accomplished by alternate means less restrictive of the individual's religious beliefs.[10] The Court not only applied the test to laws that intentionally discriminated, but equally scrutinized legislation, enacted in good faith, that unknowingly impinged upon the practice of an individual's religion. Under the compelling interest/no less restrictive alternatives test, the Court provided the shelter to minority denominations that the legislative body, through ignorance rather than animus, had neglected to extend. The Court exempted the Old Order Amish from the Wisconsin compulsory attendance laws,[11] excused the Seventh-Day Adventist from the general requirement to accept Saturday work as a condition of eligibility for unemployment compensation,[12] and freed the Native American father from supplying a Social Security number for his daughter in order to procure food stamps for his family.[13]

In 1990, however, a divided U.S. Supreme Court stripped the federal Constitution of its role as the guardian of nonmainstream faiths against barriers unwittingly erected by secular laws. In *Employment Division v. Smith*,[14] the Court upheld the denial of unemployment compensation to two members of the Native American Church who had been fired from their jobs because they had ingested peyote for sacramental purposes at a ceremony of the church. Although the State argued that laws criminalizing the use of peyote served a compelling governmental interest, the Court chose instead to refashion the free exercise test. It held that laws of general applicability that had the effect, but not the intent, of interfering with an individual's religious obligations no longer would be gauged under the compelling interest/no less restrictive alternatives test, but now would pass constitutional muster so long as there was a rational basis for the rule.[15]

Abandonment of strict scrutiny in favor of the rational basis test has had the predictable consequence of upholding a series of governmental regulations that have the effect of impeding nonmainstream persuasions, even where the regulation serves no compelling governmental interest. For example, in *Yang v. Sturner*,[16] the Court held that Rhode Island's medical examiner did not violate the First Amendment rights of the Yang family by performing an autopsy on their son, who had died after a seizure suffered while sleeping. The Yang family followed the teachings of the Hmong, holding as an article of faith that the autopsy constituted a mutilation that would impair the freedom of their son's spirit, which would cause the spirit to return to take away another member of the family. Even though the government did not demonstrate a compelling interest in performing the autopsy, the court sustained the constitutionality of the Rhode Island statute ordering autopsies, because it was a generally applicable law enacted without animus toward the Hmong faith.[17] The *Smith* majority was cognizant of the fact that minority denominations, lacking the visibility to inform or the political force to defeat legislation that inadvertently offends their canons, would be the sects most likely victimized by the deference to government inherent in the rational basis test; this inequity, ruled the Court, is "an unavoidable consequence of democratic government [that] must be preferred to a system in which each conscience is a law unto itself or in which judges weigh the social importance of all laws against the centrality of all religious beliefs."[18]

Interestingly, the very democratic government that *Smith* preferred over individual conscience responded to the Court's opinion by attempting to dismantle the majority's capacity to inflict hardships on nonmainstream religions by across-the-board legislation. Relying on its power under Section 5 of the Fourteenth Amendment, the U.S. Congress overwhelmingly passed the Religious Freedom Restoration Act of 1993 (RFRA).[19] Finding the *Smith* decision unacceptably "eliminated the requirement that the government justify burdens on religious exercise imposed by laws neutral towards religion,"[20] the statute set forth as its purpose "to restore the compelling interest test as set forth in *Sherbert v. Verner*, 374 U.S. 398 (1963) and *Wisconsin v. Yoder*, 406 U.S. 205 (1972) and to guarantee its application in all cases where free exercise of religion is substantially burdened."[21] As suggested by its title, RFRA restored by legislation strict scrutiny that the Supreme Court had abrogated for governmental actions whose effect is to arrest the exercise of an individual's religion.[22]

In passing RFRA, Congress recognized that democracy alone affords insufficient sanctuary to nonmainstream sects. The Senate Report acknowledged, "state and local legislative bodies cannot be relied upon to craft exceptions from laws of general applicability to protect the ability of religious minorities to practice their faiths."[23] Congress further recognized that intentional discrimination is not the lone evil threatening worshipers of minority faiths, expressly finding that "laws 'neutral' towards religion may burden religious exercise as surely as laws intended to interfere with religious exercise."[24]

The same Court that subordinated individual religious liberty to the interest of democracy, however, annulled democracy's effort to safeguard adherents of nonmainstream faiths through federal legislative restoration of the compelling interest/no less restrictive alternatives test. In *City of Boerne v. Flores*,[25] the Supreme Court held RFRA unconstitutional on two interrelated structural grounds. First, the Court found that Congress' Section 5 power to enforce rights guaranteed by Section 1 of the Fourteenth Amendment does not entitle the legislature to expand the definition of the rights. Through legislating strict scrutiny of unintended burdens on religion, the Court found, Congress substantively broadened the contours of the free exercise clause. Consequently, RFRA manifested "a considerable congressional intrusion into the States' traditional prerogatives and general authority to regulate for the health and welfare of their citizens."[26]

The *Boerne* Court found that not only did Congress intrude on the province of the state, but by designing to trump the Court's *Smith* decision, encroached upon the judicial power as well. Through RFRA, Congress arrogated the Court's exclusive authority "to say what the law is."[27] Under our constitutional scheme, the Court admonished, "it is the Court's precedent, not RFRA, which must control."[28]

In sum, contrary to the suppositions of this symposium, neither democracy nor the U.S. Constitution secures diverse religious visions from unintended burdens inflicted by secular laws. Rather than shielding religion, the interest in democracy has served as the justification for withholding guarantees of individual conscience under the free exercise clause. The fall of federal constitutional guardianship of minority religions, however, has spawned the resurrection of the original font of religious liberty—state law.

The Rebirth of State Law Preservation of Minority Religious Liberty

Although neither the free exercise clause of the U.S. Constitution nor federal legislation ensures that democratic majorities do not invade the religious liberty of smaller sects, progress in securing freedom of religion for minority believers has been achieved by resort to state law. Through statute or by constitution, the laws of twenty-one states now supply the bulwark of minority faiths previously erected by the federal Constitution, mandating strict scrutiny of laws that have the effect of burdening an individual's religious beliefs.

The first of the state law protectorships of minority persuasions to emerge in the wake of *Smith* and *Boerne* has been legislative grace. Religious freedom acts in nine states debar the power of majorities to unintentionally hinder the religious practices of less widespread faiths. These acts restore under state law the vigilance abandoned by the *Smith* and *Boerne* Courts, requiring the exemption of religious objectors from across-the-board regulations unless the state can prove a compelling interest that cannot be satisfied by alternatives less restrictive of the exercise of religion.[29] Interestingly, these statutes are not infected by the constitutional maladies that led to the demise of the federal RFRA. To the contrary, the very grounds that impelled the Supreme Court to strike down the federal RFRA sanction comparable guarantees of nonmainstream religious exercise under state statutes.

As discussed earlier, the first basis on which the *Boerne* Court declared RFRA unconstitutional was that by redefining the outlines of religious liberty under the free exercise clause, Congress had impinged upon "the States' traditional prerogatives and general authority to regulate for the health and welfare of their citizens."[30] It is the same police power that Congress was held to have invaded in enacting RFRA that supplies state legislatures with the means to insulate minority faiths against hardships imposed by laws of general applicability. As the Arizona legislature proclaimed in enacting its Religious Freedom Restoration Act, "Under its police power, the legislature, may establish protections that . . . supplement rights guaranteed by the Constitution."[31] State legislation that widens religious liberty against unintended infringement falls squarely within the ambit of the state's "traditional prerogative" to preserve the welfare of its citizens that the U.S. Congress arrogated when it enacted RFRA.

State religious freedom acts likewise do not usurp the Supreme Court's power to interpret the federal Constitution, the second ground on which the Court struck down RFRA. In a decision issued the day after *Boerne,* the Court endorsed the rightful authority of state legislatures to prescribe rights that surpass the liberties afforded by the U.S. Constitution. Holding that the due process clause of the Fourteenth Amendment does not furnish the right to physician-assisted suicide, the Court in *Washington v. Glucksberg* reasoned that its decision "permits this debate to continue, as it should in a democratic society."[32] Likewise, the *Smith* decision left the people of each state the option to preserve religious freedom not only against intentional discrimination but also from inadvertent burdens. In repudiating strict scrutiny under the free exercise clause of the U.S. Constitution, the *Smith* Court recognized that its decision would "leav[e] accommodation to the political process."[33] The fact that the public debate in nine states concluded that civil society can and should accommodate diverse individual religious beliefs in the absence of a compelling governmental interest professes no lack of obedience to U.S. Supreme Court strictures on the scope of the First Amendment to the U.S. Constitution. Rather, the constitutional scheme empowers each state to resolve the controversy over affording rights, above the threshold fixed by the Bill of Rights, as the majority finds appropriate.

Followers of less prominent sects have not depended entirely upon the good graces of state representatives of majority faiths to secure religious liberty. In twelve states where democratic majorities have not opted to instate the compelling interest test by legislation, insurance of religious freedom against unintentional usurpation by the majority has been founded in state constitutions.[34]

Although the federal Constitution sets a floor of rights that under the supremacy clause the states are not free to reject,[35] a state is not barred from offering greater liberties to its citizenry under its own constitution.[36] Independent interpretation of state constitutions to afford wider protection of religious liberty maybe justified by textual, historic, or structural differences between state and federal constitutions.

The first rationale for differential construction of liberty of conscience under a state constitution is the text of the charter. Even where the language of a state constitution is similar or identical to the words of the federal Constitution, courts are not obliged to assign identical meaning to the provisions.[37] The presence of significant differences in language, however, weighs more emphatically in favor of independent interpretation of the two charters.[38] Accordingly, the Ohio Supreme Court held that because the religious freedom clause of the state's constitution says, "nor shall any interference with the rights of conscience be permitted,"[39] it affords broader asylum than the First Amendment proscription of any law "prohibiting the free exercise [of religion]."[40] Applying strict scrutiny, the Court exempted a Native American from the general prison grooming policy limiting hair length of guards because the policy could be served by the less restrictive means of permitting the correctional officer to pin his hair under his uniform cap.[41]

History too may support distinct interpretation of religious liberty provisions of state constitutions. Many state constitutions predated ratification of the federal Bill of Rights or were derived from state constitutions that preceded ratification. Obviously these constitutions were not modeled after the free exercise clause and deserve autonomous construction. Courts also have relied on the states' history of religious tolerance to extend a wider swath of liberty. For example, the Wisconsin Supreme Court pointed to the heterogeneity of its populace in adopting the compelling interest test, concluding that the framers of the state constitution crafted a document codifying the ideal that the religiously diverse citizenry should be free to honor the dictates of their faith.[42]

Beyond textual and historic differences, the structure of American government sanctions—indeed encourages—more inclusive treatment of religious liberty under state constitutions. The U.S. Supreme Court has admitted that its construction of individual rights provisions of the federal constitution always is constrained by considerations of federalism as well as by the concern that the Court cannot reliably ascertain the effect of mandating a right that must be respected by each of the fifty states and their subdivisions. As the Court wrote in *San Antonio Independent School District v. Rodriguez:*

> It must be remembered that every claim arising under the Equal Protection Clause has implications for the relationship between national and state power under our federal system. Questions of federalism are always inherent in the process of determining whether a State's laws are to be accorded the traditional presumption of constitutionality, or are to be subjected instead to rigorous constitutional scrutiny.[43]

State courts, whose decisions have no extraterritorial force, are not similarly saddled with anxiety over the unknown feasibility of implementation of rights across the nation. As Justice Brandeis wrote, "It is one of the happy incidents of the federal system that a single courageous State may, if its citizens choose, serve as a laboratory; and try novel and economic experiments without risk to the rest of the country."[44] Hence the institutional and structural factors that caused the U.S. Supreme Court to reject strict scrutiny in *Smith* liberate state courts to afford more liberal sanctuary for minority faiths under state constitutions.

CONCLUSION

One possible conclusion that may be gleaned from the phoenix-like rise of state law guardianship of minority religious from the ashes of the collapse of federal law shelter is that state statutory and constitutional adoption of strict scrutiny vindicates the Supreme Court's vision of American democracy ultimately without cost to minority religious liberty. Neither the Supreme Court's abrogation of the compelling interest test under the free exercise clause in *Smith* nor its nullification of the Religious Freedom Restoration Act in *Boerne* was founded overtly upon hostility to freedom of religion in general or to minority faiths in particular. Instead, both opinions were premised upon the means by which separation of powers in American democracy serves to promote freedom, preventing federal legislative majorities and unelected Supreme Court members from usurping the prerogative of citizens of the states to strike the appropriate balance between the demands of the civil order and the liberty of each individual in a pluralistic society to pursue his or her faith tradition.

There certainly is some historical precedent for leaving the states to prescribe the boundaries of religious freedom. For the first 150 years of our nation, it was state law exclusively that guaranteed religious freedom against encroachment by state and local governments. Although the Bill of Rights secured the blessings of liberty against federal invasion, the first eight amendments to the U.S. Constitution did not shield against state or local overreaching.[45] It was not until 1940 that the Supreme Court held rights under the free exercise clause to be fundamental and thus made applicable to the states through the due process clause of the Fourteenth Amendment.[46] As Justice O'Connor observed after canvassing the historic record in *Boerne*, "Long before the First Amendment was ratified, legislative accommodations were a common response to conflicts between religious practice and civic obligation."[47] State laws have provided exemptions from civil duties, criminal prosecution, education, employment, licensing requirements, and medical testing and health regulations otherwise mandated by neutral laws of general applicability.[48] Similarly, absent a federal constitutional shelter, believers invoked state constitutions to ensure the liberty to practice their religion.[49] Hence returning the mantle of free exercise to the states arguably poses no irredeemable threat to free exercise.

The wistful proposition that the reawakening of state law guardianship of religious liberty is a benign correction in the market of constitutional structure, restoring power to the states at no expense to minority religious freedom, ignores the realities confronting smaller persuasions in the twenty-first century. The emotional courtroom outburst of the Yang family, and the silent tears shed by the numbers of Hmong faithful who had gathered to witness how the grief caused by the sudden death of the Yangs' son was compounded by the chief medical examiner's insistence on performing an autopsy notwithstanding that it served to enslave the spirit of their son, went without redress because the Rhode Island legislature had not seen fit to prescribe an exemption for religious objectors.[50] Minority believers in California were left to endure obstacles to their practice resulting from general laws when the governor vetoed the state statute that instated the compelling interest test.[51] The religious liberty of followers of nonmainstream faiths in Tennessee and Oregon remain in jeopardy as the courts have refused to construe the provisions of the state constitution more broadly than the diluted free exercise clause of the U.S. Constitution.[52] The restoration of the power of state democratic majorities to shape religious liberty is scant consolation to Jonas Swartzentruber and the eleven families of the Swartzentruber Amish who reside in the area of Ebensburg, Pennsylvania. These members of the senior order Amish in the United States, clinging to the traditions of the old world, refuse to display the fluorescent yellow-orange reflective triangle on their horse-drawn buggies, because to do so would violate the central religious tenet that they remain "plain." Because the Pennsylvania legislature neither promulgated an exemption to the yellow-orange triangle requirement nor enacted a religious freedom act adopting the compelling interest/less restrictive alternative test, Jonas was jailed for contempt of court after refusing, based on religious scruples, to pay the fine assessed for neglecting to display the triangle.[53]

These instances of discrimination should come as no surprise. From the Founding, states did not uniformly endorse the principle that all persons are entitled to full and free exercise of religious conscience. To the contrary, all but two of the original colonies mandated or preferred followers of an established church.[54] As the struggle for racial justice has amply demonstrated, state majorities are not inherently reliable safe havens for the rights of minorities.

Although twenty-one states have responded to the diminution of federal constitutional refuge for religious liberty in *Smith* by endorsing strict scrutiny of neutral laws, adherents of nonmainstream sects in the balance of the states presently lack any positive law preservation of their ability to pursue their faith, save as against intentional incursion. Small congregations in these jurisdictions are vulnerable to the majority's ignorance of the obligations of their faith and lack the political capital to effect legislative exceptions to shield the free exercise of their religion. So although seeking conservation of minority faith in state law has been a pragmatic response to the abrogation of federal protection, it has not universally succeeded in restoring the liberty that, before *Smith*, was afforded under the free exercise clause of the Fourteenth Amendment. In those states who neither by statute nor constitution demand a compelling interest before government may refuse to exempt a believer from the law, democracy has supplanted rather than safeguarded the full and free exercise of religion of adherents of nonmainstream faiths, without hope of rescue by the free exercise clause of the U.S. Constitution.

NOTES

1. *Church of Lukumi Babalu Aye, Inc. v. Hialeah*, 508 U.S. 520, 523 (1993).

2. Timothy L. Hall, "Omnibus Protections of Religious Liberty and the Establishment Clause," *Cardozo Law Review* 21 (1999): 539. See also Michael W. McConnell, "The Origins and Historical Understanding of Free Exercise," Harvard Law Review 103 (1990): 1409, 1420, "Judicially enforceable exemptions . . . are needed to ensure that unpopular or unfamiliar faiths will receive the same consideration afforded mainstream or generally respected religions by the representative branches."

3. See *Wisconsin v. Yoder*, 406 U.S. 205, 209 (1972).

4. See *Sherbert v. Verner*, 374 U.S. 398, 399 (1963).

5. See *Bowen v. Roy*, 476 U.S. 693, 695–96 (1986).

6. *Employment Div. v. Smith*, 494 U.S. 872, 890 (1990).

7. See *Hernandez v. Commissioner*, 490 U.S. 680 (1989).

8. See *Frazee v. Illinois Dept. of Employment Sec.*, 489 U.S. 829, 834 (1989).

9. *United States v. Ballard*, 322 U.S. 78, 86 (1944); see also *Thomas v. Review Bd. of the Ind. Employment Sec. Div.*, 450 U.S. 707, 715–16 (1981).

10. See, for example, *Hernandez v. Commissioner*, 689; *Frazee v. Illinois Dept. of Employment Sec.*, 835; *Hobbie v. Unemployment Appeals Comm'n*, 480 U.S. 136, 141 (1987); *Bowen v. Roy*, 693, 732 (Justice O'Connor concurring in part and dissenting in part); *Bob Jones Univ. v. United States*, 461 U.S. 574, 604 (1983); *United States v. Lee*, 455 U.S. 252, 257–58 (1982); *Thomas v. Review Bd. of the Ind. Employment Sec. Div.*, 718; *Wisconsin v. Yoder*, 213; *Sherbert v. Verner*, 406–7.

11. *Wisconsin v. Yoder*, 234.

12. *Sherbert v. Verner*, 410.

13. *Bowen v. Roy*, 693. A majority of the justices agreed that requiring Mr. Roy to provide a Social Security number for Little Bird of the Snow violated the free exercise clause. 476 U.S., 716 (Justice Blackmun concurring); 476 U.S., 726–32 (Justice O'Connor, Justice Brennan, and Justice Marshall concurring in part and dissenting in part); 476 U.S., 733 (Justice White dissenting). However, the Court held that the plaintiff could not enjoin the government from using the number for which the mother of Little Bird of the Snow had unknowingly applied.

14. 494 U.S. 872 (1990).

15. Strict scrutiny would continue to apply only in three narrow circumstances: (1) the law had the purpose of interfering with the free exercise of religion; (2) the regulation in issue not only trammeled freedom of religion, but also invaded a second and independent fundamental constitutional right; or (3) there was an extant protocol for conferring secular exemptions from the generally applicable rule that did not afford religious exemptions. *Employment Div. v. Smith*, 883–84; see *Fraternal Order of Police Newark Lodge No. 12 v. City of Newark*, 170 F. 3d 359 (3d Cir. 1999; applying strict scrutiny to police department's refusal to exempt Sunni Muslim officers from policy prohibiting wearing of beards where exemptions were permitted for medical reasons). See generally Carol M. Kaplan, "The Devil Is in the Details: Neutral, Generally Applicable Laws and Exceptions from Smith," *NYU Law Review* 75 (2000): 1045.

16. 750 F. Supp. 558 (D. R.I. 1990).

17. *Yang v. Sturner*, 750 F. Supp., 560. See also *Miller v. Reed*, 176 F. 3d 1202 (9th Cir. 1999; California statute requiring applicants for renewal of a driver's license to provide a Social Security number constitutional notwithstanding that Social Security number is tantamount to sin under Miller's theological beliefs).

18. *Employment Div. v. Smith*, 890. Justice O'Connor rejected the notion that hampering smaller religions was an inevitable cost of democracy:

> In my view . . . the First Amendment was enacted precisely to protect the rights of those whose religious practices are not shared by the majority and may be viewed with hostility. The history of our free exercise doctrine amply demonstrates the harsh impact majoritarian rule has had on unpopular or emerging religious groups such as the Jehovah's Witnesses and the Amish.

Employment Div. v. Smith, 902 (Justice O'Connor concurring).

19. 42 United States Code § 2000bb-1 to -4. RFRA passed the House of Representatives without opposition, and only three senators voted against the act. 139 Cong. Rec. 2356–03, 2363; 139 Cong. Rec. 8713–04, 8715; 139 Cong. Rec. S14461–01, S14471.

20. 42 U.S.C. § 2000bb(a)(4).

21. 42 U.S.C. § 2000bb(b)(1).

22. See 42 U.S.C. § 2000bb-1. The person whose religious exercise is invaded may raise a violation of RFRA "as a claim or defense in a judicial proceeding and obtain appropriate relief against a government." 42 U.S.C. § 2000bb-1(c). The government may legitimately maintain the burden on religion only by demonstrating both a compelling interest as well as the absence of any less restrictive means of furthering that compelling interest. 42 U.S.C. § 2000bb-1(b).

23. S. Rept. 103–11, 1 (1993), reprinted in U.S.C.C.A.N. 1892, 1897.

24. 42 U.S.C. § 2000bb(a)(2).

25. 521 U.S. 507 (1997).

26. Ibid., 520–21.

27. Ibid., 536 (qtg. *Marbury v. Madison*, 5 U.S. [1 Cranch] 137 [1803]).

28. Ibid. After the Court declared RFRA unconstitutional, Congress passed the Religious Land Use and Institutionalized Persons Act of 2000, 42 U.S.C. § 2000cc (2000). Rather than purporting to enforce the Fourteenth Amendment, Congress relied upon its spending and commerce powers to instate

the compelling interest/no less restrictive alternatives test for hurdles to religion imposed by land use regulations in programs that receive federal financial assistance or that affect commerce, 42 U.S.C. § 2000cc-1(b), and burdens on religion inflicted on persons confined in institutions governed by the Civil Rights of Institutionalized Persons Act, 42 U.S.C. § 1997 (1994), 42 U.S.C. § 2000cc-1(a).

29. See R.I. Gen. Laws § 42–80.1–3 (1998); Conn. Gen. Stat. § 52–571(b) (1997); 775 Ill. Comp. Stat. 35 (1998); Fla. Stat. Anno. § 761.01 (West 1998); S.C. Code Anno. § 1–32–30 (Law. Co-op. 1999); Ariz. Rev. Stat. § 41–1493 (1999); Tex. Civ. Prac. and Rem. Code Anno. § 110 (West 1999); Idaho Code § 73–402 (Michie 2000); N.M. Stat. Anno. § 28–22–5 (2000). In California, the legislature passed a religious freedom act, but the governor vetoed the legislation. See Veto Message of Governor Pete Wilson, California Dept. of Consumer Affairs Legislative Digest—Religious Freedom Protection Act, A.B. No. 1617 (September 28, 1998), www.dca.ca.gov/legis/ab1617.htm.

30. *City of Boerne v. Flores*, 521 U.S. 507, 534 (1997).

31. S. 1391, 44th Leg., 1st Reg. Sess. § 2 (Ariz. 1999).

32. *Washington v. Glucksberg*, 521 U.S. 702, 735 (1997).

33. *Employment Div. v. Smith*, 872, 890.

34. Courts in eleven states—Massachusetts, New York, Minnesota, Alaska, Montana, Wisconsin, Washington, Ohio, Maine, North Carolina, and Kansas—have determined that their state constitutions furnish more protection than the federal constitution and demand that the state government prove a compelling interest/no less restrictive alternative to justify burdens on religion imposed by across-the-board laws. See *Soc'y of Jesus of New England v. Boston Landmarks Comm'n*, 564 N.E. 2d 571 (Mass. 1990); *Rourke v. N.Y. State Dept. of Corr. Servs.*, 603 N.Y.S. 2d 647 (N.Y. Sup. Ct. 1993), affirmed by 615 N.Y.S. 2d 470 (N.Y. App. Div. 1994); *State v. Hershberger*, 462 N.W. 2d 393 (Minn. 1990); *Swanner v. Anchorage Equal Rights Comm'n*, 874 P. 2d 274 (Alaska 1994); *Davis v. Church of Jesus Christ of Latter Day Saints*, 852 P. 2d 640 (Mont. 1993); *State v. Miller*, 549 N.W. 2d 235 (Wis. 1996); *First Covenant Church of Seattle v. City of Seattle*, 840 P. 2d 174 (Wash. 1992); *Humphrey v. Lane*, 728 N.E. 2d 1039 (Ohio 2000); *Rupert v. City of Portland*, 605 A. 2d 63 (Me. 1992); *In the Matter of Tommy Browning and Robert Browing*, 476 S.E. 2d 465 (N.C. Ct. App. 1996); *State v. Evans*, 796 P. 2d 178 (Kan. Ct. App. 1990). A twelfth state—Alabama—amended its constitution to instate strict scrutiny of neutral laws of general applicability. See Alabama Constitution, amend. 622 (ratified January 6, 1999).

35. U.S. Constitution, art. 6, cl. 2.

36. See *Pruneyard Shopping Ctr. v. Robbins*, 447 U.S. 74 (1980).

37. See *Commonwealth v. Edmunds*, 586 A. 2d 887 (Pa. 1991; holding that the state cannot assert a good faith exception to the exclusionary rule under Article 1, Section 8 of the Pennsylvania Constitution to admit evidence that was obtained pursuant to a search warrant issued without probable cause).

38. See *State v. Hunt*, 450 A. 2d 952, 965 (N.J. 1982; Justice Handler concurring. Language "may be so significantly different from the language used to address the same subject in the federal Constitution that we can feel free to interpret our provision on an independent basis"); *Kroger Co. v. O'Hara Township*, 392 A. 2d 266, 274 (Pa. 1978; "While there may be a correspondence in the meaning and purpose between the two, the language of the Pennsylvania Constitution is substantially different from the federal constitution. We are not free to treat that language as though it was not there. Because the Framers of the Pennsylvania Constitution employed these words, the specific language in our Constitution cannot be readily dismissed as superfluous").

39. Ohio Constitution, art. 1, § 7.

40. *Humphrey v. Lane*, 1039, 1044. The Minnesota and Wisconsin Supreme Courts likewise relied upon differential language in their state constitutions to adopt the compelling interest/no less restrictive alternatives test. See *State v. Hershberger*, 393, 395 (reasoning that although the First Amendment constrains only governmental *prohibition* of the exercise of religion, Article 1, section 16 of the Minnesota Constitution forbids "even an *infringement* on or an *interference* with religious freedom"); *State v.*

Miller, 235, 239 (language of the Wisconsin Constitution "operate[s] as a perpetual bar to the state . . . from the *infringement, control or interference* with the individual rights of every person").

41. *Humphrey v. Lane*, 1047.

42. *State v. Miller*, 239.

43. 411 U.S. 1, 44 (1973).

44. *New State Ice Co. v. Liebmann*, 285 U.S. 262, 311 (1932).

45. See *Barron v. The Mayor and City Council of Baltimore*, 32 U.S. (7 Pet.) 243 (1833).

46. See *Cantwell v. Connecticut*, 310 U.S. 296, 303 (1940).

47. See *City of Boerne v. Flores*, 559 (Justice O'Connor dissenting).

48. See Haw. Rev. Stat. § 612–16 (1993; a person may claim exemption from service as a juror if she is a minister or priest); Idaho Code § 37–2732A (1994; persons of Native American descent are exempt from criminal penalties for sacramental use of peyote); S.D. Codified Laws § 13–27–1.1 (Michie 1991; crafting exception from compulsory attendance laws for members of recognized churches that object to mandated public high school attendance and provide alternative supervised program of instruction); Or. Rev. Stat. § 653.010 (1997; exempting seasonal employees at organized religious camp from minimum wage standard); Ariz. Rev. Stat. Anno. § 32–1421A (West 1992 and Supp. 1998; medical licensing requirements do not apply to any person engaged in treatment by prayer or laying on of hands as a religious rite or ordinance); and Ala. Code § 16–30–3 (1995; schoolchildren exempt from immunization conflicting with religious tenets).

49. See *Updegraph v. Commonwealth*, 11; Serg. and Rawle 155 (Pa. 1824).

50. *Yang v. Sturner.*

51. See veto message of Governor Pete Wilson, *City of Boerne v. Flores.*

52. See *Wolf v. Sundquist*, 955 S.W. 2d 626 (Tenn. Ct. App. 1997); *Meltebeke v. Bureau of Labor and Indus.*, 903 P. 2d 351 (Or. 1995); *State v. Loudon*, 857 S.W. 2d 878 (Tenn. Crim. App. 1993).

53. Following the consolidated trial of several members of the Swartzentruber Amish on charges of failing to display the fluorescent triangle, the Court of Common Pleas of Cambria County, Pennsylvania, found the defendants guilty of violating the Pennsylvania Motor Vehicle Code. *Commonwealth v. Jonas Miller et al.*, no. 0624–2002 (June 6, 2002). The case is currently on appeal before the Pennsylvania Superior Court. *Commonwealth v. Miller, et al.*, no. 1124 WDA 2002.

54. See McConnell, "Origins and Historical Understanding of Free Exercise of Religion," 1409, 1421–25.

Section II
Holy and Unholy War: Religion, Violence, and Nonviolence

Religious (Ill)Literacy and (Un)Civil Liberties in the United States

Past and Present

PATRICK G. COY

The symposium for which these chapters were originally written and presented is educational in its primary orientation. More specifically, this version of Kent State University's annual symposium was focused on increasing our interrelated understandings of how freedom, religion, and democracy intersect. Thus, in introducing this section of the book, it is useful to tarry over how freedom, religion, and democracy intersect with the educational enterprise through the four chapters that make up this section.

In Sakah Saidu Mahmud's wide-ranging and ambitious paper "The Search for Meaning in Islam: Between Violence and Nonviolence," one of the many issues with which he wrestles is the role of the teacher in the religious formation of the faithful. Mahmud pursues this as part of his inquiry into what there is in "the nature of Islam that may make a Muslim commit violence" in the name of religion. One variable Mahmud identifies that is particularly relevant for this symposium and volume is the role of the teacher.

He argues, "The absence of intermediaries in Islam means that Muslims can seek knowledge and communicate with their God directly and independently." But in matters of faith and religion few things are as simple or as clear-cut as they may initially appear, particularly to outsiders or nonbelievers. Mahmud goes on to emphasize the influential and even primary role that the independent Islamic scholars and teachers often hold among their students. He includes the teacher in his category of "intervening variables" in a Muslim's "search for meaning," which Mahmud says influences how that individual believer responds to the social and political world as a Muslim. In fact, Mahmud argues, the role of the teacher is the most significant of his intervening variables, which also include poverty or whether or not the believer has lived in democratic societies. Mahmud claims that in "most cases" the teacher serves as a "lifetime mentor," has the "final say as far as the student is concerned," is the source of "almost all" of the student's knowledge, and the teacher's interpretations are considered "almost divine." It is not clear if Mahmud's formulation is an entirely accurate description of the epistemological enterprise for most of today's Muslims, but to the extent that it manages to approximate a common reality, we are presented with a rather disquieting circumstance, one amply acknowledged by Mahmud in his chapter.

Such an approach to the role of the teacher and the gathering of spiritual knowledge may too easily lead away from developing a personally mature system of beliefs. It may also make the creation of an inquisitive epistemology, and the development of critical thinking and scholarship on the part of the faithful, the student, and even the teacher, that much less likely. Mahmud cautions that this approach has left many Muslims open to manipulation through faulty—and what can become literally dangerous—interpretations of Islam by their teachers.

Similarly, in his chapter, "Islam at the Crossroads of Extremism and Moderation: New Science, Global Peace, and Democracy," J. E. Rash suggests that those Muslims who seek "open-minded experts" and who eschew exclusivist interpretations and rigid rules are also less likely to fall prey to faulty interpretations of Islam's nuanced treatment of the ethical and conditioned use of force. Both Mahmud and Rash point to the crude and broad brushstrokes with which Islam is being painted in much of the U.S. media following the September 11 terror attacks. The views and actions of a small Islamic minority, a minority that both Mahmud and Rash criticize as having perverted the true teachings of the faith and that they label "extremist," have too often been seen as representative of Islam and granted spokesperson status by mainstream U.S. media. This is, of course, an old and recurring phenomenon in U.S. religious and political history, even if it is a millstone most often attached only to the necks of minority religious traditions. One need only recall, for example, the disproportionate influence that accrued to Rev. Charles Coughlin, the Detroit-area Catholic priest who in the 1930s became a leading media darling and radio spokesman for American Catholicism. It actually mattered little that Coughlin's demagogic views were far outside the Catholic mainstream and represented only a tiny minority sequestered in the far right pews of the U.S. Catholic Church. Much like today's Islamic militants and supposed spokesmen, who Rash and Mahmud show have distorted Islamic teachings by pedaling fearmongering, Reverend Coughlin's influence also stemmed from his "amazing capacity to manipulate the rhetoric of hate and fear."[1]

As Benjamin Barber and others have argued, democracy and education are usefully viewed as being in an interdependent relationship: at its best, democracy is fundamentally about public education and involvement, just as education in a democracy must also be about democracy itself.[2] We might pursue this more generally by simply asking, "What makes a good teacher?" Is it simply being able to attract a bevy of faithful followers deeply devoted to a shared cause, as Mary Zeiss Stange shows in her chapter that Joseph Smith of Mormon fame and David Koresh of Branch Davidian notoriety were each eminently capable of doing? On this point, bell hooks advises that true education is actually best thought of as the practice of freedom,[3] whereas Paulo Freire argues elegantly and eloquently for a specific understanding of what it means to teach. We do well to note the multiple ways Freire's formulation of the teaching mission impinges implicitly and explicitly on the themes of this volume: "The teaching task is above all a professional task that requires constant intellectual rigor and the stimulation of epistemological curiosity, of the capacity to love, of creativity, of scientific competence and the rejection of scientific reductionism. The teaching task also requires the capacity to fight for freedom, without which the teaching task becomes meaningless."[4]

Rash argues in his chapter that Jeffersonian democracy and Sufism each recognize, in their own ways, not only that human beings are basically good in their orientation but also that the individual retains ultimate responsibility for her or his growth and realization. Rash also usefully extends this analysis into the political economy of the present day. He does this through a relevant critique of the homogenizing aspects of globalization and the many negative ways it impacts both cultural diversity and what in this context I think we might profitably call the sovereignty of the individual spirit. Rash's careful and sound argument that a dynamic and meaningful peace[5]—one that endures even as it changes and adapts to the conflicting demands of various groups—depends on what he calls flexible, democratic spiritualities, of which he ably argues Islam is one, when in informed hands. This is put forward in contradistinction to other approaches to teaching and to influencing the behavior of the faithful in Islam, approaches that Rash labels as "extremist," "exclusivist," and "dictatorial."[6] This is one of the many crossroads for Islam that Rash suggests today's Muslims cannot avoid. But Rash goes further by arguing that neither religious nor political legislation, neither rituals nor enforcement of any kind can ultimately compel people to believe certain things, to say nothing of living up to what he refers to as "their highest spiritual calling." We might note that these measures, and others like them, are also ultimately bereft of any definitive power to force individuals (Muslim or otherwise) to behave in particular ways. In this way, Rash's argument complements that put forward by Paul Gaston in his chapter "Yesterday's Love, Today's Ruins: Walker Percy's Apocalyptic Vision," a literary exegesis of Percy's 1972 novel *Love in Ruins*.

Gaston's chapter demonstrates that yet another approach to the intersection of education, freedom, religion, and democracy asks what it means to be an effective novelist. More specifically for our purposes in this section of the volume, what does it mean to be a novelist concerned with the moral and political dimensions of life, a designation for which Gaston shows us Percy is most assuredly qualified? Percy's novel *Love in Ruins* is actually a satire, and an existential one at that. Consequently, the peculiar dynamics of the satirical enterprise are worth a brief consideration.

Nearly all satire relies on varying degrees of irony, parody, or even ridicule to engender a variety of critical judgments, including "amused contempt."[7] For our purposes here—in a volume devoted to the messy intersections of education, democracy, religion, and freedom—what is most attractive politically and socially about satire is that it does not desire to simply discredit. The far more powerful purpose of most satirists is to nurture an independent critical awareness within his or her audience. Critical awareness, however, is not the end goal for satire worth its social salt. This critical awareness theoretically leads the individual to informed participation in initiatives for political reform, social and religious change, or personal transformation. In this way, although satire can be initially seductive, it is eventually politically powerful, socially significant, and personally transformative in its consequences. The frequently unsuspecting audience (in our case, the reader, student, citizen, or believer) is drawn deeply into the satirical web and finds themselves immersed in a critical conspiracy that calls into question literary locutions, social patterns, political practices, and even religious beliefs or rituals that previously escaped questioning. In the end, however, the enduring legacy of successful political, social, or religious satire is precisely this nurturance and practiced refinement of the skills of critical thinking, what the great Brazilian educator Paulo Freire referred to simply as "critical consciousness."[8]

Gaston shows us that Percy accomplishes something very similar to this by highlighting the alienated and morally rudderless world toward which Percy believed we were heading when he was writing. The novelist's critique of the triumph of technology and the spiritual malaise that he thought it engendered makes ample use of satire, while including suggestions of morally preferable alternatives. But the emphasis and the power lie more in the presentation of the critical satire and less in the exposition of alternatives. For satire is always open and conditioned, dependent as it is not just on the sagacity and truths contained in the critique, but just as much on the insights of the reader, the student, the believer, or the democratic citizen. That is also partly why satire is sometimes leaden and falls so flat, like the lame joke to which it is closely related.

What does all this mean for democracy, freedom, religion, and education, including religious education? The satirist—much like the teacher, religious or otherwise—can only lead the listener to the edge of the overlook, pointing to a horizon of possible conclusions. But what the student, the citizen, or the believer comprehends and ultimately does in response is quite beyond the teacher's or the politician's or the satirist's control, much less to dictate, as too many religious teachers are too often too wont to do.

In this regard, Gaston's chapter shows us that one of the enduring lessons of Percy's novel is that the book's central character, Dr. Thomas More, finally achieves meaning and some sense of success in life through his personal struggle to live independently and with integrity in the face of increasing determination in his society. This deterministic understanding of human experience—where the horizon of individual human choices is severely constrained—is rejected in Percy's novel by Dr. Thomas More. What is additionally significant for our purposes is that this rejected worldview is similar in some broad outlines to the black-white, either-or dualisms that lurk in Samuel Huntington's thinking about today's world, popularly known as his theory of the "clash of civilizations."[9] In Huntington's truncated analysis, water, territory, economics, oil, military weaponry, and other natural and human "resources" fade away as significant conflict generators and escalators. In their place, Huntington posits "civilization," or more properly, diametrically and essentially differing cultures and worldviews, as the primary source of conflict today and in the near future. As both Rash and Stange indicate, this approach to understanding world affairs has enjoyed a second wind of late, partly blown in by the terrorist attacks of September 11. Despite its popular currency and simplicity (or perhaps because of it), Huntington's thesis on contemporary conflict has many shortcomings.[10] Some of these shortcomings give rise, in turn, to rather significant dangers, which are graphically enumerated in different ways in the chapters by Stange and Rash, each of whom also calls into question Huntington's analysis.

Gaston explains how it comes to pass that the Thomas More character in Percy's novel resolutely refuses to be told what to do, what to say, or even what to think. It is instructive to realize that in today's world a similar character would likely refuse to be told what to say, think, or do by a David Koresh, by an independent Islamic scholar, or by a teacher or a university professor. Nor would such an individual agree to be told what *not* to think, what *not* to do, or what *not* to say by John Ashcroft's FBI, by George W. Bush's Homeland Security Office, or by the U.S. Congress' terribly ill-considered U.S. Patriot Act, which we do better to consider more an antidote to U.S. democracy than any remedy to international terrorism.

Today the United States' experiment in democracy—and Stange's account in this volume of the treatment accorded to various religious groups demonstrates that it has only ever been an experiment, never an accomplished fact—faces threats as grave as those presented in Percy's novel. Many of those threats are external, originating beyond our shores. But we do well to recognize as well that some of the more enduring threats are internal They emanate not just from within our own citizenry but from the highest elected and appointed offices in this country. As a result, these sorts of threats are particularly pernicious and carry with them the longest-lived consequences for the republic.

Stange's chapter, "The White Man's Wounded Knee, or, Whose Holy War Is This, Anyway? A Cautionary Tale," is an erudite and compelling comparative analysis of the shortsighted and tragic treatments accorded to various religious groups and practices at different points in U.S. history. Stange's focus is on the following three groups: Joseph Smith and the Mormons in the mid-1800s, the Plains Indians and their Ghost Dance religion in the late 1880s, and David Koresh and the Branch Davidians in the 1990s. The multilayered research that Stange conducts into what at first seems to be disparate events in U.S. religious and political history eventually reveals them to be connected in ways that are both culturally fascinating and politically significant, not least for our current situation, in which the United States is engaged in a far-flung "war on terrorism" and has invaded and occupied both Afghanistan and Iraq. In fact, the interpretive lessons she draws from these various cases for our current situation is an example of historical scholarship put to its best and most useful service. Her insightful analysis of this tragic past leads her to ask about today: "At what point does divergence from the religious norm become a justification for the imposition of violence" by the state? In much of her chapter, Stange asks about religious norms, but she also broadens the questions and suggests that we should too. Let us do so now.

Expanded versions of this remarkably relevant question might include: At what point does divergence from *political norms* justify widespread violations of civil liberties of U.S. citizens by the FBI, or widespread violations of international human rights agreements and the rules of war with regard to detainees in this country's war on terrorism? The Muslim and Arab-American communities have, of course, experienced the worst of these excesses and violations of deeply held democratic freedoms, as is usefully pointed out in three of these chapters.

At what point does divergence from *economic norms* about the benefits of globalized and unregulated capital justify preemptive arrests and destructive police strikes on the headquarters of social movement organizations planning legitimate, nonviolent demonstrations in Washington, D.C., and Philadelphia, as occurred recently? At what point does a divergence from *social norms* about campus quietude compel university administrators at places such as New Mexico State University, the University of Wisconsin-Whitewater, the University of South Florida, West Virginia University, and elsewhere to designate certain spaces on their campuses as "free speech zones," effectively hamstringing constitutional liberties and disallowing the free exercise of expression anywhere else on their campuses?

Stange draws sobering conclusions from the striking similarities between the massacre by government troops of American Indian men, women, and children at Wounded Knee, South Dakota, in 1890 and the FBI assault on the Branch Davidians near Waco, a little more than a hundred years later, in 1993. She demonstrates a tendency in the United States to do more than simply misunderstand minority religious traditions, but to demonize divergent religious groups, even as political leaders routinely invoke the symbols, dualisms, terminologies, and teachings of mainstream religions.[11] Both Rash and Stange wisely highlight, but in different ways, the manifold manifestations of this tendency in the current "war on terrorism," chiefly by President George W. Bush and by Attorney General John Ashcroft. These officeholders have been overly fond of manipulating traditional dualisms of good and evil, right and wrong, light and darkness, just and unjust, and civilized and barbaric, often enveloping them in the cloak of mainstream religion at the same time. What is particularly salient for our purposes is that these actions are preformed—historically, and also in the present instance—in a bald attempt to legitimize government actions and effectively place them beyond the critique of most of the citizenry. The use of these religious symbols and traditions by government officials in conflict situations is actually intended as an antidote to any development of the critical consciousness called for by Freire and other proponents of democratic education. One can cynically, but accurately, think of these actions as a bid to muzzle contrary citizen voices, especially the voices of those free-thinking and independent citizens that are the lifeblood of any democracy trying to move beyond its experimental stage.

Whereas Stange's analysis of historical and contemporary events leaves us with rather little hope for the future, Rash is cautiously optimistic. He argues that contemporary Islam is at a critical crossroads: he maintains that one path leads to what he calls "extremism," whereas the other leads to "moderation." But Rash pushes deeper and also insists that Islam is not alone in having come to a crossroads; in his considered view, the United States faces a similar juncture, "with the potential to impact the route ultimately pursued by Muslims." Clearly, this is not an inconsiderable responsibility. Rash argues that if the seeds of moderate as opposed to extreme versions of Islam are to take further root and proliferate, they ought to find the most congenial climate and fertile soil on the shores of the United States, given its founding ideals of democracy, pluralism, and respect for the individual. But he too is rightly worried about the future, given the erosion of civil liberties and the widespread finger pointing and scapegoating of Muslim Americans in the wake of September 11.

Both Mahmud and Rash convincingly demonstrate that Islam is much more complex in general and more nuanced in particular with regard to the ethical uses of violence and war than some self-appointed and mainstream-media-appointed "spokesmen" for Islam would have us believe. Rejecting reductionist approaches to understanding Islam, their chapters are part of a wider movement within Islam to retrieve and accurately articulate the nonviolent components of the faith. But when the widespread misunderstandings and distortions of Islam pointed to by Mahmud and Rash are combined with Stange's analysis of the mainstream culture's utterly tragic failure to understand the Branch Davidians and the Plains Indians, we are left with a clear pedagogic and political mandate: the need for what I call religious literacy among both policymakers and the mass media. This is nowhere more important at this moment than in reference to Islam, as the recent ignorant remarks of certain U. S. politicians and Christian leaders have embarrassingly indicated.[12]

Because Gaston's chapter on Percy's novel closes this section, let us return to it in this conclusion. The protagonist in Percy's novel, Dr. Thomas More, finally saves himself and even contributes to his society through a two-pronged approach: first, through his personal struggle with contrary social and political forces, and, second, by relying on the legacy of those who have gone before him, particularly those who have faced similar struggles with all-too-rare degrees of integrity. This reliance on those who have struggled before us is what I want to briefly highlight. We are not facing the fictionalized apocalyptic circumstances of Dr. Thomas More, but as the restrictive boundaries of the Patriot Act are revealed in the next few years, our democracy will be tested in profound ways. Although a sober assessment of what's ahead indicates that these are dark times for free expression, the fact is that this American experiment in democracy has faced similarly dark times in the past.

There was the original "Red scare" occasioned by the Russian revolution, World War I, and the massive migration of Eastern Europeans to these shores at the beginning of this century. A different attorney general, A. Mitchell Palmer, ran roughshod over civil liberties via what became known as the "Palmer raids" of 1918–1921, arresting thousands suspected of falling into the catch-all categories of "communist" or "Bolshevik." Hundreds were summarily deported, with no recourse to law whatsoever. Later generations dealt with the excesses of J. Edgar Hoover, Joseph McCarthy, Richard Nixon, and many others who employed the considerable powers of a bureaucratic government in the service of fear. The blacklisting of artists, writers, musicians, teachers, and civil servants in the United States, as well as the smearing of candidates for elected offices was as widespread as it was odious shortly after World War II and at least through the first half of the cold war.

But in each of these periods, there were also individual Americans, and associations of Americans, who valiantly came to the defense of the free expression of ideas, the free practice of religion, and the right to free association. We ought to study those struggles for what they have to teach us today, in much the same way that Stange's scholarship into religious history illuminates our contemporary situation. If the restrictions so far undertaken on behalf of the war on terrorism and under the repressive powers of the Patriot Act are any indication whatsoever, we will need to take inspiration and even courage from the stories of others who in earlier times stood for civil liberty and freedom at significant personal costs.

Gaston's chapter analyzes the fictional Dr. Thomas More, who in Percy's novel is a descendant of the real-life St. Thomas More. In the novel, it was the fictional Dr. Thomas More's reliance on the legacy of his real-life ancestor, St. Thomas More, that eventually turns the tide for him. Therefore let us turn to Robert Bolt and his play about St. Thomas More, *A Man for All Seasons.* In the play St. Thomas More responds to the accusation leveled at him by his daughter and her suitor (Mr. Roper) that his fixation on the law means that he is letting an evil man slip away. More responds, "And go he should, if he was the Devil himself, until he broke the law!" Thomas More's argument is swiftly rejected by Mr. Roper, who proclaims that he is prepared to "cut down every law in England" to get at the Devil. But Thomas More has the final word when he plays the part of the democrat, the good saint, and the good educator: "Oh? And when the last law was down, and the Devil turned round on you—where would you hide, Roper, the laws all being flat? This country's planted thick with laws from coast to coast—man's laws, not God's—and if you cut them down—and you're just the man to do it—d'you really think you could stand up-right in the winds that would blow then? Yes, I'd give the Devil benefit of law, for my own safety's sake."[13]

NOTES

1. Sydney E. Ahlstrom, *A Religious History of the American People*, vol. 2 (Garden City, N.Y.: Image, 1975), 420. According to James Hennesey, Coughlin's brand of demagogy defined America's villains as "godless capitalists, the Jews, Communists, international bankers and plutocrats." See James Hennesey, *American Catholics: A History of the Roman Catholic Community in the United States* (Oxford: Oxford Univ. Press, 1981), 274.

2. Theodore K. Becker and Richard A. Couto, introduction to *Teaching Democracy by Being Democratic*, ed. Theodore K. Becker and Richard A. Couto (Westport, Conn.: Praeger, 1996), 18. Also see Benjamin R. Barber, *An Aristocracy of Everyone: The Politics of Education and the Future of America* (New York: Ballantine, 1992).

3. bell hooks, *Teaching to Transgress: Education as the Practice of Freedom* (New York: Routledge, 1994), 13 and throughout.

4. Paulo Freire, *Teachers as Cultural Workers: Letters to Those Who Dare to Teach* (Boulder, Colo.: Westview, 1998), 4.

5. Rash relies on the work of Hans-Peter Dürr for his reconceptualization of peace. The most prolific and preeminent thinker on the multiple manifestations of both violence and peace is the Norwegian scholar Johan Galtung. His classic and influential treatment of peace can be found in Johan Galtung, "Three Approaches to Peace: Peacekeeping, Peacemaking and Peacebuilding," in *Essays in Peace Research: War, Peace, Defense*, ed. Johan Galtung (Copenhagen: Christian Ejlers, 1976), 282–304. See also Johan Galtung, *Peace by Peaceful Means: Peace and Conflict, Development and Civilization* (Thousand Oaks, Calif.: Sage, 1997).

6. But Rash also says, "The way of the Sufi seems to demonstrate Islam at its most progressive, its most personal, its most genuinely reflective of fundamental principles, its most democratic, and its

most conducive to change." These are expansive and curious claims from someone who also offers quite helpful arguments against the dangers that certain varieties of fundamentalism present to today's world, marked as they often are by certitude regarding their supposed monopolies on truth and best or proper practices. The reader is also well advised to note that Rash's claims and characterizations about Sufism's position within Islam are much contested.

7. This understanding is found in *The Oxford Companion to the English Language*, ed. Tom McArthur (1992), www.xrefer.com/entry/443731 (retrieved April 23, 2002), s.v. "Satire."

8. Freire, *Education for Critical Consciousness* (New York: Continuum, 1990), 17–20.

9. Samuel Huntington, *The Clash of Civilizations and the Remaking of World Order* (New York: Simon and Schuster, 1993).

10. For contrary and more nuanced and fully developed views on the complicated dynamics of human conflict than those put forward by Huntington, see two of the most influential approaches in the field of conflict resolution: Louis Kriesberg, *Constructive Conflicts: From Escalation to Resolution*, 2d ed. (Lanham, Md.: Rowman and Littlefield, 2002); and John Burton, *Conflict: Resolution and Prevention* (New York: St. Martin's, 1990). On the role of collective identity in conflict, see Patrick G. Coy and Lynne M. Woehrle, eds., *Social Conflicts and Collective Identities* (Lanham, Md.: Rowman and Littlefield, 2000).

11. This demonizing of the "Other" and the "enemy" is not peculiarly American; on the contrary, it is widely practiced across cultures and political generations. For an especially useful, if disturbing, cross-cultural and cross-generational analysis of this phenomenon, based largely on graphic visual characterizations of the "Other" and the "enemy," see Sam Keen, *Faces of the Enemy: Reflections of the Hostile Imagination* (San Francisco: Harper and Row, 1991).

12. To cite but two examples, in November 2001, U.S. Attorney General John Ashcroft was quoted in an interview with conservative columnist Cal Thomas as saying, "Islam is a religion in which God requires you to send your son to die for him. Christianity is a faith in which God sends his son to die for you." These remarks were deeply offensive to Muslims. Ashcroft later "clarified" his remarks by saying that Thomas's rendition of the interview "does not accurately reflect what I believe I said." Thomas stood by the interview as published. See Dan Eggen, "Alleged Remarks on Islam Prompt an Ashcroft Reply," *Washington Post*, February, 14, 2002.

Then in October 2002 Southern Baptist Convention leader and Moral Majority president Rev. Jerry Falwell was quoted on the CBS television show *60 Minutes*, saying, "I think Muhammad was a terrorist. I read enough of the history of his life written by both Muslims and—non-Muslims, (to know) that he was a—a violent man, a man of war." More important, Falwell went on to say that "Jesus set the example for love, as did Moses. I think Muhammad set an opposite example." CBS News Online, "Falwell Sorry for Bashing Muhammad," www.cbsnews.com/stories/2002/10/11/60minutes/main525316.shtml, October 14, 2002 (retrieved October 16, 2002).

13. Robert Bolt, *A Man for All Seasons: A Play in Two Acts* (New York: Vintage, 1962), 37–38.

The Search for Meaning in Islam

Between Violence and Nonviolence

SAKAH SAIDU MAHMUD

Islam was and is one of the most powerful means of explaining human life and giving meaning to our activity.—Anthony Black

The September 11, 2001, terrorist attacks on the United States by Muslim extremists have put the Islamic religion on the defensive. Whichever way one looks at the terrorist attacks—whether Islam was responsible for the terrorism or whether Islam is a religion of peace—the fact is that Islam is called upon to explain and re-evaluate itself[1] regarding the practice and role of Islam in contemporary world affairs. The attacks raised major questions for Muslims and their religion: What is the role of Islam in the attacks? Is Islam responsible for such acts of violence? Answers to these questions are not easy. And this may be the reason why satisfactory answers have escaped the public.

So far there have been three interrelated perspectives on the relationship between the attacks and Islam. The first perspective sees Islam as the root cause of the terrorism. In this perspective, the success of the Iranian Revolution in 1979 has revived Islam as a major rival civilization to the West and a potential source of conflict between the two.[2] The terrorist attacks on New York and Washington, D.C., on September 11, and the earlier attack on the World Trade Center in 1993 only added weight to this perspective.[3] It is in fact this perspective that initially informed the understanding of the tragedy to most Americans. The hijackers' claim to a "holy war" against the West provided an easy proof. For example, in "This *Is* a Religious War," Andrew Sullivan only had to quote bin Laden:

Osama bin Laden himself couldn't be clearer about the religious underpinnings of his campaign of terror. In 1998, he told his followers, "The call to wage war against America was made because America has spearheaded the crusade against the Islamic nation, sending tens of thousands of its troops to the land of the two holy mosques over and above its meddling in its affairs and in its politics and its support of the oppressive, corrupt and tyrannical regime that is in control."[4]

In his response to this perspective, Edward Said was right to observe, "Labels like Islam and the West mislead and confuse the mind, which is trying to make sense of a disorderly reality."[5] It may be true that Osama bin Laden is a Muslim, but does his position and actions represent Islam? Does Islam determine all actions of all Muslims? In fact, should any religion be held responsible for all actions of its believers? These are questions that such a perspective cannot answer. It fails to see the overwhelming majority of Muslims in the world for whom the religion means only peace through observing the five basic principles in their search for meaning in life.[6] Explaining how and why a few would take the violent path, whereas others take a peaceful approach to life is one of the goals of this chapter.

The second perspective (and perhaps a direct response to the first) comes from Islamic leaders within the United States and from across the Islamic world who claim that Islam is a religion of peace[7] and that violent acts against civilians is un-Islamic, that suicide is especially not condoned by Islam. This view implies that the perpetrators of such terrorism are not Muslims, nor do they represent Islam. Although I accept that the terrorists do not represent Islam, I do accept that they could be Muslims. I find the perspective, therefore, intellectually simplistic under these circumstances. In the face of Islamic resurgence and militancy, it obscures the fact that something in the nature of Islam may make a Muslim commit such violence thinking (mistakenly in my view), that he or she is acting for the religion. A more intellectual approach would be to acknowledge the complexity of Islam and to ask what is in the religion that would make such criminals feel that they are acting in the name of Islam.

A third perspective that falls in between the two previous perspectives explains the terrorist acts as directly caused by the social conditions in most countries of the Middle East. These conditions include the existence of poverty in Muslim countries, as well as the undemocratic nature of the governments that led the extremists to resort to violence and to seek justification in Islam for their actions.[8] In this perspective, the independent variables are the social conditions. However, the problem with this perspective is that in many Muslim societies around the world where material poverty is widespread there is a relative absence of violence. The religion actually provides the basis for peaceful existence among members of the communities. Such societies actually enjoy more stability and peace than their neighbors. Thus we cannot say that Islam determines violent response to these situations, although justifications may be found in the religion for actions taken. None of the three perspectives, therefore, provide a credible explanation for the association made between the violence witnessed and Islam as a religion even though they all have implications for Islam.

As someone who grew up Muslim and who still practices the religion,[9] I do not identify myself in any of the perspectives relating Islam to violence. However, my academic training informs me that an intellectual understanding of Islam could lead one to see the correlation (not causation) between Islam and violence. Such explanation avoids the simplistic association or dissociation of violence with Islam. So how does one explain the correlation between Islam and violence? I propose in this chapter that the process of the search for meaning in life for a Muslim provides the clue to the explanation. This process does not begin with a personal knowledge in Islam. Rather, it starts with a worldview that is constructed beginning with the process of socialization that includes Islamic teachings but that may also include other values that are influenced by history, customs, and other agents of socialization. As a Muslim however, one's belief is that such socialization is based on Islam. This worldview is the antecedent variable.[10] Following this stage, one moves on to acquire knowledge in Islam through the Qur'an and the Sunnah (the independent variables). At this stage, a reversal of the worldviews constructed earlier is still possible but unlikely, as one tends to look for the sources that would legitimize the acquired worldview. This is perhaps the point where Islam can be said to play an independent role in the search for meaning in life.

Finally, there are the intervening variables such as one's teacher and the sociopolitical conditions of one's environment. In the final analysis, the actions taken in search of meaning are thus influenced at these various stages by many factors that vary from person to person or from region to region depending on particular historical and political experiences. In this quest for meaning in life, therefore, the action taken by a Muslim is influenced by those variables that are not deterministic, but are negotiated and renegotiated throughout life. The variables explaining the process function like the following negotiation model of policy making:

ANTECEDENT		INDEPENDENT		INTERVENING		ACTION
Worldviews		Nature/Sources Quran, Sunnah		Teachers/Social Conditions		Violence/ Nonviolence

The different variables may constitute different stages in the process, but they are inextricably interrelated. It is not a process that has a clear beginning and a clear end. At each stage one negotiates within oneself and with external factors from the wider environment.

From the previous analysis, it is therefore hypothesized that if, on the one hand, a Muslim starts the search for meaning in life with a radical worldview, he or she is more likely to adopt a political strategy that could lead to a violent action. Within that political strategy, any means necessary could be taken. On the other hand, and as will be explained later, most Muslims may not even have a worldview as such, and their approach to life is more focused on spiritual salvation. In that case, the search for meaning would not extend beyond the literal interpretation of the five basic principles of Islam within which only peaceful actions and prayers are the only approaches. As the decision model analogy shows, the process is not deterministic, and changes at any stage are still possible. What this says about the relationship between Islam and violence or nonviolence is that Islam is not the determining factor, but because a particular Muslim may be acting with the conviction that he or she is acting according to the principles of the religion, Islam becomes implicated in a Muslim's action. The analysis that follows explains why this could be the case. This may often be confusing to the casual observer.

ISLAM AND THE SEARCH FOR MEANING IN LIFE

In Islam, what is expected of a Muslim is complex. There are rights, duties, and obligations that stipulate not only how to live a good and purposeful life but also how to comport oneself in the hereafter. Life is not worth much if what one does here does not guarantee the hereafter. How to achieve both goals is also very complex. There are no straightforward paths. And it is here that internal struggles become part of everyday life. Life itself becomes a struggle to understand the complexity of life. As Thomas Lippman stated,

> Islam tells its adherents not only what to believe about God, angels, and the afterlife, but also how to live on earth in such a way as to find favor with God, within the principles of social justice, communal peace, and individual dignity.[11]

To a Muslim, achieving these qualities is what gives meaning to life. As John Esposito further observes, "Islam, like other world religions, is a faith of peace and social justice, moving its adherents to worship God, obey His laws, and be socially responsible."[12] This sounds simple, and most Muslims take it as is. But there are those for whom the road to fulfilling these obligations can be complex and who seek a deeper search that could lead to more serious consequences. Because there are broad but not specific guidelines, a Muslim refers to prayers for divine guidance, while acting socially responsible with others in the community. One's community is also there for support, but in the final analysis, results are based on the individual's beliefs and actions. Finally, there are the authoritative sources—the Qur'an and the Sunnah—to guide one through the complex path. Actually, in most cases, the Sunnah is taught as part of a Muslim's socialization.

In the process of finding meaning, one is actually involved in the greater jihad—the struggle within oneself. This involves seeking answers to many questions. What should one do to satisfy the command of Allah? What behavior is socially responsible? Or, when Islam is defined as "total submission to the Will of Allah," how does one attain such total submission? How much is total submission? Answers to these questions are sought throughout a Muslim's entire adult life: as a wife, a husband, a mother, a father, a leader, a follower, and so on. Achieving the right answers poses major challenges for a Muslim. Such struggles are not static and conservative, as most non-Muslims often believe. They involve many debates. One way out for most Muslims is to pray for guidance against doing the wrong things or going astray. The significance of prayers for guidance is found in the first surah,[13] and as Fazlur Rahman wrote, prayer "prevents from evil and helps man to conquer difficulties, especially when combined with patience."[14]

Besides prayers one also pays Zakaat (obligatory tax on Muslims), where officially in place, and in its absence gives Sadaqua (alms, or giving to the poor). A Muslim shows respect and helps out the less fortunate. These are all peaceful ways of seeking the meaning in life. These deeds also prepare one for the "Day of Judgment" and, God willing, a place in heaven. Achieving both a desired life in this world and assurance of the hereafter are equally and mutually significant. The Qur'an is specific about a Muslim's worldly and heavenly duties:

> And seek, in whatever God has bestowed upon you, the next world, but do not forget your participation and share in this world, and be nice as God has been kind to you, and never seek doing corruption in the earth. Verily God does not love the corruption.[15]

For most Muslims this search for meaning in life takes a spiritual path dominated by prayers, doing what is considered good and accepting as forbidden what is unlawful in the religion. However, there are those for whom that may not be enough, and those individuals may look for more meaning beyond this. Theoretically, my position is that there are many variables that might make one look for more or less within the religion in their search for meaning. The answers one gets from searching further and deeper determine whether one follows the nonviolent means as described earlier or a violent path as a small minority do. This is the point at which the religion is implicated in the actions of its adherents. What determines how far a Muslim might go in search for meaning? Worldviews held are a major determinant, and they provide one explanation for violent or peaceful actions by Muslims.

What determines how far one goes in search for meaning in life? Generally, there is no one answer for all Muslims. Answers to these questions are determined by factors outside the religion even though believers may feel that the answers are in response to religious demands. The first place to start, I believe, is the construction of worldviews that different Muslims may hold. The term "worldview" is used here not in a deeply philosophical sense but simply as "a set of presuppositions (or assumptions) which we hold (consciously or subconsciously) about the basic makeup of our world,"[16] or, as Brian Walsh and Richard Middleton observe, "A worldview provides a model of the world which guides its adherents in the world."[17] An important characteristic of worldviews is that they are not just a way of looking at the world, but they also form our views *for the world.*"[18]

These presuppositions or assumptions shape our ideas and beliefs not only of the world but also of our everyday life. The process of acquiring these worldviews includes our socialization beginning with the family, the historical time, and the social environment (including politics of the modern nation-state and the international system within which these states function). Thus a worldview could be as narrow or as wide as one's exposure to the rest of humanity. For some, a worldview may not extend beyond their immediate community if that is the extent of one's consciousness of the universe. For others this could be a view of the entire universe and how one fits in it. A religious worldview, although informed by one's belief, is equally affected by the same factors. This is why it is possible to find a wide spectrum of worldviews between Muslims.

For our purposes, the acquisition and construction of a worldview (even for most Muslims) precede any thorough knowledge of Islam. And in those cases where knowledge of the religion comes first, a worldview becomes a powerful tool for interpretation and action. Knowledge and ideas acquired during the early socialization process could create a certain mindset in a Muslim. Such a mindset is not simply forgotten and may linger on and determine various actions later in life. How do we characterize the subsequent actions that are determined by such worldviews? Should we attribute those actions as determined by the religion? It is at this point of constructing a worldview that the decision is made concerning how one responds to the world, as well as how one would pursue the calling of one's religion in response to the wider world. The choices become more social and political than spiritual.

To demonstrate this process, I will present brief background material on the leading Islamic fundamentalist (the Ayatollah Khomeini) and three Islamic extremists (Qutb, bin Laden, and Sheikh Omar) to demonstrate how their worldviews determined their actions in response to their situations. First, beginning in the 1960s, the Ayatollah Khomeini progressed from his strictly spiritual devotion to political protest. The reasons for such change were the Shah of Iran's tyrannical rule. Karen Armstrong pointed out that

> at a time when nobody else dared to speak out against the regime, Khomeini protested against the cruelty and injustice of the Shah's rule, his unconstitutional dismissal of the Majlis, the torture, the wicked suppression of all opposition, the Shah's craven subservience to the United States, and his support of Israel, which has deprived Palestinians of their homes."[19]

Except for the dismissal of the Majlis (Muslim council or assembly), the rest of the accusations are political and social. However, he later translated these charges in religious terms, saying that "Islam is the religion of militant individuals who are committed to faith and justice. It is the religion of those who desire freedom and independence. It is the school of those who struggle against imperialism."[20]

There are millions of Muslims around the world who would not understand these statements as Islamic. It takes a political consciousness to make sense of these statements. The Ayatollah himself admitted that he had to take a political approach, observing that at the time "Islam lives among the people as if it were a stranger. If somebody were to present Islam *as it truly is* [my emphasis], he would find it difficult to make people believe him."[21] And it is evident from the earlier discussion that Khomeini's fundamentalism, which a decade later led the first successful Islamic revolution in modern times, had its roots in a worldview that could have been constructed mostly by social factors. The specifics of such a worldview could not have been found in the Qur'an. Even Bernard Lewis, who considers such actions as Islamic, admits that the ideas that lead to labeling opponents as "enemies of God" are from the "dualist religions of ancient Iran—which had also influenced a number of Christian and Jewish sects, through Manichaeism and other routes."[22]

Of the extremists who advocated violence and called their mission Islamic using the "holy war" slogan, Sayyid Qutb (1906–66) of Egypt was the most prominent. Born in a village from humble beginnings, Qutb was in elementary school during the Egyptian revolution of 1919 when his school was closed and

> the Principal addressed the students on the duty to revolt. Meanwhile his father started selling parts of his land in order to meet the necessities of life since his salary was insufficient. In a dialogue with his mother, she made him promise her to get the land back.[23]

It is not surprising then to learn that fifty years later, Qutb referred to Egypt as "a *jahiliya* society (period of ignorance, often in reference to pre-Islamic Arabia) . . . not to be transformed (but) destroyed and rebuilt from the ground up. Against it

Jihad was not merely lawful but imperative. A true Muslim had no choice but to struggle to overthrow it by whatever means necessary."[24] In his extremist version of fundamentalism, Qutb went on to draw a large following and to write numerous political and ideological papers. Unlike the Ayatollah Khomeini, however, many who studied Qutb's activities admit that he was not intellectually trained in Islam. It was after he started his campaigns that he turned to the academic training in Islam. Walter Laqueur said of him:

> Qutb, a secular Egyptian writer, returned to the religion of his forefathers following a two-year stay in the United States in the late 1940s. . . . Qutb also advocated violence—not only against Christians and Jews but also against fellow Muslims who did not accept his version of Islam.[25]

The Egypt of Qutb's time created for him a following, amongst whom were "students who could not find jobs; the religiously observant lower class, distrustful of modernity; and, generally speaking, all those disaffected by the state of affairs in the Muslim world who had become intellectually homeless after the failure of Arab nationalist ideology and Marxism."[26] Qutb's worldview was created by his political and social experiences and not by his understanding of the religion. Living in a society that was predominantly Muslim, and to achieve the kind of world he wanted to see established, he had to appeal to Islam. Islam simply became a tool for realizing his worldview.

As for the most recent extremists (bin Laden and Ahmed Sheikh Omar), both had extensive exposure to the Western world and had Western educations. Neither seems to have had an early scholarly training in Islam beyond the basic education as Muslims. Bin Laden, the alleged mastermind of the September 11 terrorist attacks, is the son of a Saudi millionaire and an engineering student. His first activism was to oppose the Soviets in Afghanistan in the early 1980s. It is not clear how much he thought of Islam at the time, but those who knew him observed that his knowledge of Islam was at best rudimentary. A Saudi prince recently recalled how, ten years ago, bin Laden was "floundering when guests questioned him about interpretations of Islamic texts."[27] His attention was drawn to the United States in 1991 during the Gulf War when U.S. troops were stationed in Saudi Arabia. The common knowledge is that he saw this as an intrusion on the holy land. But there have been other Westerners in the country working for oil companies and other industries, and the U.S. troops were not in the holy cities of Mecca and Medina. So how does their presence threaten Islam? Bin Laden's claim that his hatred of the United States is based on Islam does not appear credible.

Bin Laden's hatred of the United States seems more political than Islamic. In 1998, an Arab newspaper introduced to the world the "*International Islamic Front for Combating Crusaders and Jews."* Its founding document was signed by "Sheikh" bin Laden, Zawahiri "Amir" of the Jihad Group in Egypt, and others. In its inaugural statement, the Front

> condemned the "sins" of American foreign policy for declaring "war" on God, his messenger, and Muslims. And it called "on every Muslim—to comply with God's order to kill the Americans and plunder their money wherever and whenever they find it."[28]

The overtly political tone of this statement is clearly a construction of the proponents' worldview, not that of the Qur'an or the Sunnah. And as for "God's order," that could come only through the Prophet. Is the statement claiming that there is now a new prophet of Islam? The contradiction of this call on religious grounds is self-evident.

As for the latest extremist in the news, Ahmed Sheikh Omar, the Pakistani militant indicted for the murder of *Wall Street Journal* reporter Daniel Pearl, it is evident that his political beliefs emerged from the territorial dispute between Pakistan and India over Kashmir. From the information available on his background, there is nothing to show that his commitment to Islam led to his activities. "Mr. Sheikh was born in London, the son of Pakistani clothes merchants. He studied at the London School of Economics for a year beginning in 1992, then left to join the fight for the independence of Kashmir, the only Muslim-majority state in predominantly Hindu India."[29] With such evidence, the previous story still referred to Mr. Sheikh as a "prominent Muslim Militant," which may not be adequate, even though better than the label "Islamic militant." The population in Kashmir is Muslim, but does that necessarily mean that the war is *for* Islam?

It is evident from these profiles, especially of the extremists who advocated violence, that their actions were determined by their political worldviews after which justifications were found in Islam. The fact that they found a following also has little to do with Islam but stems from the social and political issues of their time. Given similar situations, it is probable that any advocate would get the same response from the population.

This pattern of constructing worldviews is illustrated in the observation of the education of ten- and eleven-year-old students of an Islamic school (madrassa) in Pakistan as narrated by Lisa Anderson for the *Chicago Tribune.* The U.S. war in Afghanistan has already begun to shape a worldview that is likely to live with them. Their views about the war did not come from what they read in the Qur'an, but they had to make sense of the situation from a religious perspective. One of the two students introduced to the reporter was quoted as saying that "he regrets that he was not old enough to fight in Afghanistan against the Americans." He was further quoted as saying that "they (Americans) are cruel. They are doing bad things to Muslims. It is our duty to fight. *It is part of Islam*" [my emphasis].[30]

How could an eleven-year-old student of Islam who is only just learning to recite and memorize the Koran (and not in his first language) know what the religion says about America, war, and violence? Answers to these questions clearly indicate that these children's responses are shaped more by what they know and are told about the current war rather than by what is written in the religious texts. As they grow up, it will be difficult to differentiate between their worldviews and Islamic views. At a similar age, going through the same memorization of the Qur'an, it would have been impossible for me to make such a statement even though everything I thought about life was slanted through an Islamic perspective. The difference has nothing to do with Islam as a religion, but with the time and the geographical situations. At that stage for me, the extent of my learning was what the teacher of the previously mentioned school later said to the reporter.

> The most important goal of *Jamiat-ul-Arabia* (name of the school) is to assure [*sic*] that each student has memorized the entire Koran and can recite its poetic verses with perfect rhythm and pronunciation. . . . This is the quality of the Koran. That it can be learned by heart. . . . If the followers of the Holy Prophet learn it by heart, then, on the day of judgment they will not be punished."[31]

As a child going through a similar training in the Qur'an, identifying "enemies" of Islam and fighting them had never occurred to me. Unbelievers were supposed to be left on their own. Allah knows what he would do with them.

The analysis so far has been to demonstrate that, especially for Muslims who choose the violent approach to finding meaning in life, such actions are more political than spiritual. How to deal with the "enemy" so identified by that worldview depends on one's calculations in terms of powers of the adversary. As Michael Ignatieff eloquently puts it,

> When one side—the state—has all the power, and the other side has only the shock value of violence to compensate for its military weakness, terror soon begins to pay better than restraint. Radical asymmetries of power, more than moral barbarity alone, are what make [it] seem like a logical strategy for the weak. The barbarians who attacked the World Trade Center knew, unfortunately, that violence is the force multiplier of the weak.[32]

What made any Muslim commit such violence as the attacks on the United States could only have come from a worldview that sees the enemy as strategically overpowering. Even then, a spiritual approach in this century would leave such an "enemy" to Allah the Most Powerful. However, as the next section will explain, the nature of Islam makes it susceptible to interpretations in such a way that perpetrators of such violent actions could look to the religion for justifications. What then does the Qur'an and the Sunnah say about violence and nonviolence? The Qur'an is full of both conditional and unconditional requirements, but whichever interpretations particular Muslims choose are in turn conditioned by their worldviews.

THE NATURE AND SOURCE OF KNOWLEDGE IN ISLAM: THE QUR'AN AND THE SUNNAH

There are two aspects of Islam that are often agreed upon by both Muslim and non-Muslim scholars of the religion. One is the totality of the religion, and the other is its political aspect. To understand Islam as a total religion, one turns to its definition, as "total submission to the Will of Allah." By this is meant that the religion has stipulations for all aspects of a Muslim's life. Islam is the guide to every aspect of life. It is the perfection of life. In the Qur'an, Allah says, "This day have I perfected for you your religion, and I have given to you Islam as your religion." It states emphatically, "Truly, the only way of life acceptable to Allah is Islam."[33] There are regulations on how to deal with one's neighbors, how to be happy in life, how to manage one's family, how to conduct private and public life, how to conduct economic transactions, and how to deal with issues of justice, kindness, and forgiveness. Anything in life is contained within the guidelines of the religion.

The Qur'an deals with issues of morality, establishing a society that is just and free of oppression. "Be just; it is closest to being pious."[34] There is great emphasis on value of human life. "Whoever kills a person, unless it be for manslaughter or for mischief in the land, it is as though he had killed entire humanity. And whoever saves a life, it is as though he has saved lives of all men."[35] Islam calls on believers to look into the Qur'an for all answers to their actions and problems. Yet how Muslims do so differs from society to society. In fact, some go as far as doing things contrary to what the religion prescribes and still believe that they are acting according to the religion. As Lippman observes,

In Islam, as in Christianity, there are differences between what the believers are taught by their faith and what they actually think and do. For instance, while there is no Muslim priesthood, the Mullahs of Iran, who are often referred to as clergy, hold a special place in the form of Islam practiced there. Folk practice has ascribed to various men a role analogous to that of saints in Christianity.

Muslims have created shrines and devotions to these "saints" in the belief that they can do what the Koran says they cannot do—intercede with God.[36]

In places where such shrines are built, people go on "pilgrimages" to them, seeking all kinds of divine help, ranging from success in business, fertility, promotion in jobs, and other kinds of worldly desires even though such acts are forbidden in the religion.

A Muslim lives in constant awareness of what to do and what not to do. Doing what is required and expected then gives life its meaning. Under such circumstances, it is easy to understand why Muslims would believe that whatever happens to them and however they behave is ordained by God (Allah). This characteristic of Islam makes it difficult to convince some believers that their actions are not Islamic. This is where a correlation can be established between the actions of Muslims and their religion. But the fact remains that all Muslims do not approach their problems in the same way. Other factors play intermediary roles in every Muslim's approach to their worldly concerns.

The other aspect of Islam—the political aspect—relates more to violence or non-violence by Muslims in their search for meaning in life. Ruthven states that "in theory, Islam is an inherently political religion. Classically, the state's legitimacy depended on its role as protector of the Islamic community or Ummah and the preservation of the Sharia, or divine law, by 'enjoining the good and forbidding the evil.'"[37] But even in its political aspect, there are variations from one society to another. In those Muslim societies where there is a substantial separation between secular and religious authority, the political manifestation of Islam is not pronounced. These Muslims would seek justice and some other aspects of life from other realms. Where such separation has not been implemented, the religion becomes a source for seeking legitimacy by those in power as well as the source of protest against the established order.

In this power struggle, the actions taken are strategic but regarded by each party as sanctioned by Islam. Therefore if it takes violence to achieve the means (which in this case is political), so be it; after all, those in power use political (and sometimes violent) means to maintain their rule. It then becomes a matter of who is better able to find the necessary supporting evidence for their claims and their actions. Both sides in the political struggle then use Islam as their rationale. Although the religion emphasizes justice for all, it also demands obedience from subjects and believers. The Qur'an itself leaves a lot of areas unresolved in terms of power relations. It says in one chapter, for example,

O, ye who believe, obey God and obey the Prophet and those who are in power amongst you. Thereupon, if you have any matter of dispute, refer it to God and to the Prophet if you certainly believe in God and in the last Day, that is the best deed and it is better to interpret.[38]

At the time of the revelation, the Prophet was in power, and there could not have been any confusion between the Prophet and "those in power." But after the Prophet and when political power is contested, who does a believer respond to for problems or disputes?

This leads to a lesser problem emerging from the nature of Islam, that is, its lasting significance for all times. This is true for all religions. But this very nature poses a problem of interpretation. To what extent should all the specifics revealed during the revelation be applied to contemporary life? Those who seek deeper understanding might claim that every bit of the revelation still applies completely, whereas there are those who would argue that some aspects of the religion were specific to the time of revelation and that it should be applied relatively. The latter would say that the five basic principles cannot be sacrificed and should remain unchanged; other provisions should be treated based on their merit for contemporary times. Those who would interpret all aspects of the religion into actions for contemporary times face a more complex case. If Islam is a religion for all times, they would argue, then one could find analogous cases for the lesser jihad (fighting wars for Islam) in contemporary times. And as the Prophet fought a Jihad, Muslims are enjoined to do so today. To this one can counter that even the Prophet did not fight on every occasion that he was provoked. He used his discretion and reasoning and took every case on its own merit. But this response, of course, is just an opinion.

What has been demonstrated is that the nature of Islam creates a problem of interpretation that is determined by different worldviews. And to observers of Muslims and their religion this poses tremendous problems of understanding the extent to which Islam provides meaning and dictates what Muslims do and the extent to which they believe their religion makes them do what they do. To some observers, this makes Islam an agency that transforms adherents into vessels for the religion, Muslims having no will of their own. Such perceptions are, however, incorrect, for Islam only serves as a guide to life. A Muslim can find as much or as little as he or she seeks in the religion. One can do as little as observing the five basic principles, or one can embed oneself in search of deeper knowledge and meaning. A Muslim with a radical worldview would look for deeper meaning and use Islam to realize his or her goal with the belief that such actions are sanctioned by the religion. Seeking more or less knowledge, however, does not make one a better or a worse Muslim, but merely a more or less learned Muslim. Humans at least cannot make such a judgment; that judgment is the domain of Allah the All Knowing. However, it does not stop some from seeking more and more knowledge.

How far one pursues life based on Islam and what actions he or she takes as a result is determined by a worldview constructed out of the existing conditions and experiences of the particular believer. This is why devout Muslims from different parts of the Muslim world would respond differently to similar world affairs. It is wrong, therefore, to assume, as the popular media does, that there is a uniform Muslim response to all events.

Sources of Knowledge: The Qur'an and the Sunnah

Where do Muslims get their knowledge concerning what the religion regards as meaningful in life? The two universally accepted authoritative sources of knowledge are the Qur'an and the Sunnah (the practices and sayings of the Prophet). To a lesser extent some would add the *Ulema* (the group of Islamic scholars who actually consult the former two sources for their knowledge as well). What do these sources say about violence and nonviolence in Islam? It is important to ask this because the perspectives we have been discussing all refer to these two sources for evidence.

Evidence from the sources of knowledge in Islam is often of the general type. In most cases, specifics are not given. And beyond that, the general instructions are not always clear, and the Qur'an testifies that some of its verses "are precise in meaning—they are the foundation of the Book—and others ambiguous. Those whose hearts are infected with disbelief follow the ambiguous part, so as to create dissension by seeking to analyze it. But no one knows its meaning except Allah."[39]

The specifics are to be filled in depending on one's situation and circumstances. There are a few agreed-upon specifics as in the five basic principles of Islam. Further than that, major issues are left open to different interpretations. One such issue centers on the meaning of the term "jihad," a concept that is directly related to the issues of violence and nonviolence in Islam.

Jihad and Holy War in the Qur'an and the Sunnah

The issue that is most contested concerning Islam and violence or nonviolence centers on the notion of jihad, or "holy war" as popularly interpreted. For those who hold the view that Islam is responsible for violence, the foundation for this belief is that Islam sanctions jihad against the unbelievers. What does Islam say about jihad as found in the sources?

Although some Muslims may deny the "holy war" meaning of the term "jihad," I accept that there is a notion of holy war in Islam. It is not as complicated as most people make it appear. The fight *for* Islam can be referred to as a Holy War. And there have been fights for Islam, just as there have been wars in Judaism and Christianity. It could not have been otherwise. Under the circumstances in which the religion found itself at its beginning, the believers were called upon to be courageous and fight the enemies. And the language is brutal, just as wars are inherently political, violent, and cruel. This is the other version of jihad. Some may say it is the lesser jihad, but it is still jihad when fought for the sake of the religion as during the Prophet's time. The greater jihad, as I have already mentioned, is the personal struggle to do the right thing according to Islam and not to go astray from the prescribed way of life. As for the lesser jihad, one verse of the Qur'an often quoted runs as follows:

> Therefore, when ye meet the unbelievers (in fight), smite at their necks; At length, when ye have thoroughly subdued them, bind a bond firmly (on them); thereafter (is the time for) either generosity or ransom:—But those who are slain in the Way of Allah, He will never let their deeds be lost.[40]

One finds similar and even more graphic examples calling on the faithful to fight to the last. During the early years, the Prophet and his followers were a very small minority facing a majority with a superior means of fighting. What the Muslims had on their side was their belief and resilience. Such wars were *Holy Wars,* and like any war they were violent. The chapters and verses dealing with war in the Qur'an were revealed during those wars; Muslims should not deny these facts. What are debatable, however, are the conditions under which Muslims are enjoined to fight in the cause of Islam. It is here that the nature of the religion and a Muslim's worldview combine to explain the choices made by a Muslim.

Under what conditions should a Muslim fight such a Holy War as stipulated in the sources? There are numerous chapters in the Qur'an that stipulate such situations: "Permission to fight is given to those upon whom war is made because they are oppressed, and Allah is well able to assist them; those who have been expelled from their homes without a just cause except that they say, Our Lord is Allah."[41] In another instance the Qur'an says, "And fight against them until there is no more persecution, and religion is only for Allah."[42] And furthermore it says, "And had there been Allah's repelling some people by others, there would have been pulled down cloisters and churches and synagogues and mosques in which God's name is much remembered."[43]

Conditions were also laid down for fighting: "And if they incline to peace, do thou incline to it and trust in Allah; He is the Hearing, the Knowing. And if they intend to deceive thee, then surely Allah is sufficient for thee."[44] Also it says, "And fight in the way of Allah against those who fight against you, *and do not exceed the limits* [my emphasis], for Allah loves not those who exceed the limits."[45]

In reference to offensive wars, the Qur'an says, "Allah forbids you not respecting those who have not made war against you *on account of your religion* [my emphasis], and have not drawn you forth from your homes, that you show them kindness and deal with them justly; for Allah loves the doers of justice."[46] It also states that "there is no compulsion in religion."[47] Thus just as there are cases calling on the faithful to fight, there are also other numerous occasions for restraint. The problem Muslims face is when to accept which conditions. Those on the one hand who take these conditions strictly in their spiritual sense take the nonviolent path in their search for meaning in life. Any acts of war or violence that do not heed these conditions would be unholy—that would be terrorism. Those on the other hand who reject these conditions and believe that jihad is for all times take the violent approach. These are most likely to be those whose worldviews are more political than spiritual. There have been and continue to be renowned Islamic scholars who take the nonviolent interpretations to the extreme. Listening to some of them is like listening to Gandhi on nonviolence. The scholar Maulana Wahiduddin Khan, for example, made the following remarks:

> Islam is a religion, which teaches non-violence. According to the Qur'an, God does not love *fasad*, violence. What is meant here is that *fasad* is clearly expressed in verse 205 of the second surah (chapter). Basically, fasad is that action which results in disruption of the social system, causing huge losses in terms of lives and property.[48]

He gave evidence from the Qur'an to support nonviolence, saying that "only defensive war is permitted in Islam. Such a war is one in which aggression is committed by some other party so that the believers have to fight in self-defense. Initiating hostility is not permitted for Muslims. The Qur'an says: 'they were the first to attack you.'"[49] He gave further examples of nonviolence in the Prophet's approach even to his enemies, saying that "of the first 23 years of Prophethood, the initial 13 years were years of pacifism and non-violence."[50] And in another presentation on the "Principles for Success," Khan used the Prophet's example to show how the power of peace is stronger than the power of violence:

> When Mecca was conquered, all the Prophet's direst opponents were brought before him. They were war criminals in every sense of the word. But the Prophet did not order to kill them. He simply said: "Go, you are free." The result of this kind behavior was miraculous. They immediately accepted Islam.[51]

A scholar of the Islamic state and its constitution under the Prophet also observed that "the Islamic Holy Constitution has restricted the exertion of Muslims themselves to the cause or path of God in three areas: to defend the Islamic Nation (Umma from outside attack; to liberate people from any aggressive power; and to call people to Islam and convey its message to all people in terms of courtesy and consideration."[52]

Any actions by Muslims that stem from the previously mentioned positions (which are held by the overwhelming majority of Muslims in the world) are bound to be nonviolent. In fact, as early as the beginning of the twentieth century, the Qadianis (an offspring of Ahmadiya of Pakistan, then part of British India) adopted doctrines that "'Jihad' or 'holy war' has lapsed."[53] The Ahmadiya has influenced much of Islam in Southeast Asia and sub-Saharan Africa. This could have contributed to the silence over the use of the term "jihad" in those parts of the Muslim world.

Who then would take the violent alternative despite the evidence? The answer is those with political agendas or those for whom the political aspect of Islam is more important, such as the cases of the extremists examined earlier. Sayyid Qutb, for example, was one of the proponents of jihad as an Islamic injunction in contemporary life. In his response to those Muslims who denounce jihad in the modern world, he said,

> We ought not be deceived or embarrassed by the attacks of the orientalists on the origins of Jihad, nor lose self-confidence under the pressure of present conditions and the weight of the great powers of the world to such an extent that we try to find reasons for the Islamic Jihad outside the nature of this religion, and try to show that it was a defensive measure under temporary conditions. The need for Jihad remains and will continue to remain whether these conditions exist or not.[54]

One should note the propagandist nature of this statement. One weakness in Qutb's statements is their lack of reference to the sources of knowledge in Islam. Most of his arguments are placed in general terms and without specific reference to the Qur'an. There seems to be a deliberate intention to avoid dealing with religious facts.

The contemporary references to America and unbelievers were not instances in the Qur'an or the Sunnah. The unbelievers referred to in the Qur'an were not outsiders, but Arabs of Mecca who were persecuting the Prophet and the new religion. Any conception of the enemy and of America today has to be constructed in light of current circumstances determined by a worldview that is shaped by politics. A scholar of Islamic fundamentalism is right in his observation of Qutb in saying, "There is thus in Qutb something of the Western individualist and existentialist;— His approach makes the interpretation of Islam highly subjective. Truth and therefore, authority derive from personal aesthetic vision."[55]

Why then do I still regard the nature of Islam and the teachings as found in the sources as the independent variable? It is difficult to answer that question directly.

It has to do with belief systems, in which, even though Muslims might be acting differently, all believe they are acting in compliance with the religion. The nature of the religion makes it vulnerable to such belief. But this difficulty is lessened in the evidence of the antecedent variable, the worldviews held by individual Muslims for which they see justification in the religion. Thus if Muslims approach the religion with a peaceful outlook, their actions would be nonviolent. If, however, one maintains a worldview that has designated an "enemy" who is to be confronted violently, then his or her approach would be violent. Islam is implicated here in the sense that such diverse actions are taken with the feeling (right or wrong) that the actions are sanctioned by their faith. Although the sources of knowledge are clearly on the side of nonviolence, the nature of the religion as described coupled with radical worldviews held by some Muslims explain why they would take a violent approach to life. But as another Muslim scholar warns,

> The question of violence has to be dealt with great caution as far as the Islamic tradition is concerned. At the level of the value Qur'an upholds non-violence and exhorts Muslims to use wisdom and benevolence (*hikmah* and *ihsan*) while dealing with others. Whenever violence has taken place in the Islamic history it is Muslims and . . . their norms that could be held responsible than the teachings of the Qur'an.[56]

The Social Environment and the Scholars

There are also lesser influences that can affect a Muslim's actions and response to their search for meaning in life. These I refer to as the intervening variables that may account for violent or nonviolent actions by Muslims. Among the intervening variables the most important are the nature and character of one's teacher in their search for knowledge and the social conditions of one's environment.

On the role of Islamic scholars, it is ironic that the aspect of Islam that gives it its democratic nature has turned out to be a source of disruption. This is the independent scholar. The absence of intermediaries in Islam means that Muslims can seek knowledge and communicate with their God directly and independently. But the same provision has contributed to the emergence of learned individuals who, because of their knowledge, claim special positions in Muslim societies. Islam enjoins Muslims to seek knowledge wherever it can be found, and those with the resources and the time do so. Some actually devote their entire life to learning. This is where the scholars get their social and religious prestige. Unfortunately, what these scholars say is often interpreted as the final truth as far as their students are concerned.[57]

The special knowledge allows such teachers to use their position for an expression of their worldview rather than the propagation of a strictly spiritual worldview. How does this translate into ideas of violence or nonviolence in the student? Most students of Islamic scholarship depend on their teachers for nearly all of the sources of knowledge. Interpretations by the teacher are considered almost divine because he or she is expected to say only what is true. Thus the teacher serves as both an intellectual and a spiritual mentor. Such is the nature of the teacher-student relationship coupled with a preconceived worldview that a Muslim in search of deeper knowledge would choose a teacher whose views he already knows are congruent with his worldview. This is usually more likely to be the case when the student is an adult. For younger students, the parents choose the teacher. For example, bin Laden's teacher in the 1980s was Abdullah Azzam, a Palestinian who lived in Pakistan and who was murdered in a car bomb in 1989.

> Azzam was the man who developed the idea of Jihad in a complete way. He enshrined the need for armed struggle as part of daily life, to deal with problems deemed by Islamic scholars to be unjust. He first started with an anti-Israeli agenda. But then he takes it further.[58]

An expert on the Taliban noted that, without this teacher, bin Laden "would have been nothing."[59]

If one sticks with the teacher, one is likely to emerge with the teacher's entrenched worldview, because one could not say that the teacher's views are not religious. The teacher in most cases serves as a lifetime mentor. But what may be unknown is that the teacher's interpretation may not be neutral and may be selective, mirroring his or her personal worldview. As an intervening variable, the teacher can influence the outcome of a Muslim's lifelong thinking and actions.

As for social conditions and their role as intervening variables affecting how a Muslim might respond to the search for meaning, these are not as strong as the role played by one's teacher. Some of the social conditions often mentioned are poverty and lack of democratic institutions in some Muslim societies. As for poverty, evidence from the lives of those who have led most of the violent movements show that they came from privileged backgrounds. In fact, bin Laden dismisses poverty as the cause of violence. In an interview with John Miller, the question was posed directly: "You came from a background of wealth and comfort to end up fighting on the front lines. Many Americans find that unusual." His response was

> They claim that this blessed awakening and the people reverting to Islam are due to economic factors. This is not so. It is rather a grace from Allah, a desire to

embrace the religion of Allah. And this is not surprising. When the holy war called, thousands of young men came from the Arab peninsula and other countries answered the call and they came from wealthy backgrounds.[60]

If poverty occurs in an urban setting, it usually leads to violent reactions, whereas poverty in rural settings among Muslims hardly ever leads to violent reactions. Instead people seek solace in their spiritual calling and hope that prayers will change their fates. Along with the prayers, Muslims work hard while waiting for God to reward their efforts. Violent reactions are however prevalent in the urban environments where more political worldviews are easily acquired. This tends to support the significance of the worldview hypothesis. The terrorist Atta, for example, had his initial experiences in Cairo, and even though he was not from a poor background, his experiences in Europe triggered his resort to violence. As narrated by Ajami, "Religion came to Atta unexpectedly, in Hamburg, where he had gone for a graduate degree in urban planning. In *bilad al kufr* (the countries of unbelief), he needed the faith as consolation, and it was there that he shaped it as a weapon of war."[61]

The other factor of the social environment that may lead to violence is the political aspect of the religion. In Muslim societies where the leaders use the religion for legitimation, failure to produce desired results also reduces their legitimacy, and citizens find reasons for protest against the system. To find justification for protests, they have to refer to the religion in the same way the leaders do for legitimation of their rule. Even then, one cannot categorically say that the social condition is the independent variable. The conditions could at best be intervening factors. There must have been some preconceived views that culminated into a package that says violence is the final answer. The religious undertones of such violence were a way of believing that the actions would be rewarded with heaven. In reference to Islam however, it is still difficult to claim that any violent responses are struggles *for* Islam.

CONCLUSION: VIOLENCE OR NONVIOLENCE IN THE SEARCH
FOR MEANING IN LIFE

For Muslims the search for meaning in life takes a long journey that is truly defined by the greater jihad (the struggle within oneself). It is not a linear process, with a clear beginning and a clear end. It goes through various stages and turns, the outcome of which is not predictable because only God knows how it would end. During that long journey Muslims constantly seek whichever deed would satisfy God as well as their fellow humans. This is what provides meaning in life. What is complicated about the search is that there are only broad instructions and conditions that are subject to different interpretations. So where does this lead us?

This chapter has demonstrated the complexity of the Islamic religion, which has been responsible for the misrepresentations of actions of Muslims often regarded as sanctioned by Islam. However, this chapter proposes that the religion acts like a theory, which a Muslim can use in many different ways to derive at an explanation of life. And just as there are often some presumptions about how a particular theory may work out, so most Muslims often start from some presumptions about the meaning of life and how to seek and achieve that desired life. In so doing, nonspiritual factors may play significant roles; these I referred to as worldviews that serve as antecedent variables. The factors responsible for the worldviews are more political and social than spiritual, even though the recipient may assume that they are religious.[62]

Following from this and because of the nature of Islam that demands complete submission from adherents and that makes believers look to it for all answers, it becomes an easy target for explanations of actions taken by its adherents. Still, the fact that different Muslims from different regions of the world respond to social and political problems differently means that the religion could not be held responsible for the actions of all Muslims. What accounts for these differences include the worldviews held by Muslims, which in turn leads to different interpretations of the religion. Other variables that may affect a Muslim's action in search of meaning in life include the nature and character of the teacher and the nature of politics in the modern state system. A state deemed to be unjust could easily fall prey to violent actions against that regime by Muslims. Even then, others would find evidence in the Qur'an that denounce violence in such cases. In the final analysis, the responses taken by Muslims to the same situations vary between regions, countries, and individuals. This enables us to understand that because of the nature of Islam (total and political) the religion becomes implicated by all these actions. In short, one may even say that Islam is the victim of its adherents' behavior.

What are the implications of these findings? There are those who demand that Islam be transformed.[63] But is it Islam that should be transformed or the behavior of Muslims? I believe that it is the latter. In this debate following the September 11 terrorist attacks, therefore, Muslims have a duty to explain and demonstrate what the true religion is all about. The charge from some Muslims that Islam is misunderstood is correct. One could even say that Islam has been wrongly singled out to explain the diverse actions of its adherents, something that other religions are exonerated from.[64]

Finally, regarding the theme of this symposium, one might even go to the extent of saying that there is potential for democracy within Islam. The decentralized nature of its organization and interpretation offers a democratic potential. Unfortunately, many of those who could promote these aspects are the very ones who abuse it for political reasons. It should be noted, however, that there are various groups and individual scholars around the world who are making efforts to realize the humane and democratic potential of Islam. The voices of this latter individuals and groups deserve to be heard.

1. See John F. Burns, "Bin Laden Stirs Struggle on Meaning of Jihad," *New York Times on the Web*, www.nytimes.com/2002, January 27, 2002 (accessed January 27, 2002). The article covers debates and opinions of Islamic scholars around the Middle East on the relationship between Islam and violence. Although most scholars condemned the terrorist attacks, younger generations tended to admire bin Laden. The overwhelming opinion of the scholars point to the fact that the terrorist acts are political, not religious.

2. See Bernard Lewis, "The Roots of Muslim Rage," *Atlantic* (Sept. 1990); Samuel P. Huntington, "The Clash of Civilizations?" *Foreign Affairs* (Summer 1993). John L. Esposito, "Political Islam: Beyond the Green Menace," *Current History* (Jan. 1994), explained the differences between the terms, showing that in most cases the fundamentalists pursue peaceful approaches to Islamic revival. Militant Islam (extremists) is "characterized by its readiness to use violence." Mary-Jane Deeb, "Militant Islam and the Politics of Redemption," *Annals of American Academy of Political and Social Sciences* 524 (Nov. 1992): 52.

3. Also, reviews of the works of these two scholars by both Paul Kennedy (on Lewis) and Robert Kaplan (on Huntington) praised both scholars as visionaries in foreseeing the "Islamic Threat." See Kennedy, Review of *What Went Wrong? Western Impact and Middle East Response* by Bernard Lewis, *New York Times Book Review*, January 27, 2002; and Kaplan, "Looking the World in the Eye," *Atlantic Monthly* (Dec. 2001).

4. See Andrew Sullivan, "This *Is* a Religious War," *New York Times Magazine* (Oct. 7, 2001). Six months after the attacks and despite the U.S. government's clear statements to the contrary, some senior clergy in the United States continue to make categorical statements that Islam is the root cause of the violence. Franklin Graham Jr. actually said that he believed Islam to be "a very evil and wicked religion." In Gustav Niebuhr, "Muslim Group Seeks to Meet Billy Graham's Son," *New York Times*, November 20, 2001.

5. Edward Said, "The Clash of Ignorance," *Nation* (Oct. 22, 2001): 12.

6. For the uninitiated, the five basic principles (pillars) of Islam are (1) the Shahada (declaration that there is no God but Allah and that Muhammad is His Prophet), (2) to pray five times a day, (3) to pay Zakaat (and where this is officially not in place, give Sadaqua), (4) to fast during the entire month of Ramadan, and (5) to perform the pilgrimage to Mecca and Medina (if one can afford it) at least once in one's lifetime.

7. See Roy Mottahedeh, "Islam and the Opposition to Terrorism," *New York Times*, September 30, 2001. See also Burns, "Bin Laden Stirs Struggle," ibid.

8. See Fouad Ajami, "Nowhere Man," *New York Times Magazine*, October 7, 2001. The subtitle reads "Islam Alone Didn't Produce Mohamed Atta. He was born of his country's struggle to reconcile modernity with tradition."

9. I grew up in a predominantly Muslim community in Nigeria, where there was tolerance and peace with the minority groups of Christians and practitioners of traditional African religions. It was common to find members of extended families practicing the three different religions. That was some forty years ago and is still the case.

10. Antecedent variables are independent variables that precede the independent variable in time or "a variable that causes variation in the variable that, for purposes of a given hypothesis, is regarded as the independent variable." Jarol B. Manheim, Richard C. Rich, and Lars Willnat, eds., *Empirical Political Analysis: Research Methods in Political Science*, 5th ed. (New York: Longman, 2002), 420.

11. See Thomas W. Lippman, *Understanding Islam: An Introduction to the Muslim World*. 2d rev. ed. (New York: Meridian, 1995), 70.

12. See Esposito, "Political Islam," 19.

13. See Abdullah Yusaf Ali, trans., "Al-Fatiha" ("The Opening"), *The Glorious Qur'an*, chap. 1 (New Delhi, India: Islamic Book Service, 2002).

14. See Fazlur Rahman, *Islam* (New York: Anchor, 1968), 33.

15. Qur'an, 28:77.

16. See James W. Sire, *The Universe Next Door,* 2d ed. (Downers Grove, Ill.: InterVarsity, 1988), 17.

17. Brian J. Walsh and Richard J. Middleton, *The Transforming Vision: Shaping a Christian World View* (Downer's Grove, Ill.: InterVarsity, 1984), 32.

18. W. Gary Phillips and William E. Brown, *Making Sense of Your World* (Chicago: Moody, 1991), 29.

19. Karen Armstrong, *The Battle for God* (New York: Random House, 2000), 248.

20. Ibid., 256.

21. Sayed Ruhollah Khomeini, *Islam and Revolution: Writings and Declarations of Imam Khomeini,* trans. Hamid Algar (London: KAI, 1985), 28.

22. See Lewis, "Roots of Muslim Rage," 222.

23. Ahmad S. Moussalli, *Radical Islamic Fundamentalism: The Ideological and Political Discourse of Sayyid Qutb* (Beirut, Lebanon: American University of Beirut, 1992), 21.

24. See R. Stephen Humphreys, *Between Memory and Desire: The Middle East in a Troubled Age* (Berkeley: Univ. of California Press, 1999), 194.

25. Walter Laqueur, "A Failure of Intelligence," review of *Jihad* by Guilles Kepel, *Atlantic Monthly* (March 2002): 127.

26. Ibid.

27. Reported in Robert Marquand, "A Special Report on the Ideology of Jihad and the Rise of Islamic Militancy," *Christian Science Monitor* (Oct. 18, 2001): 4.

28. Ibid., 8.

29. Douglas Jehl, "Prominent Muslim Militant Is Named a Suspect in Pearl Case," *New York Times,* February 7, 2002.

30. See Lisa Anderson, "Classes, the Koran and Jihad: Religious Schools in Pakistan Teach Extremist Islam," *Chicago Tribune,* December 21, 2001.

31. Ibid.

32. Michael Ignatieff, "Barbarians at the Gates," review of *The Lessons of Terror: A History of Warfare against Civilians: Why It Has Always Failed and Why It Will Fail Again* by Caleb Carr, *New York Times Book Review* (Feb. 17, 2002): 8.

33. Qur'an, 3:19.

34. Qur'an, 5:8.

35. Qur'an, 5:2.

36. Lippman, *Understanding Islam,* 3.

37. Malise Ruthven, "Islamic Politics in the Middle East and North Africa," in *The Middle East and North Africa,* Europa Year Book, vol. 30 (London: Europa, 1989): 93.

38. Qur'an, 4:59.

39. Qur'an, 3:7.

40. Qur'an, 47:4.

41. Qur'an, 22:39 and 40.

42. Qur'an, 2:193, and repeated in 8:39.

43. Qur'an, 22:40.

44. Qur'an, 8:61 and 62.

45. Qur'an, 2:190.

46. Qur'an, 60:8.

47. Qur'an, 2:256.

48. Maulana Wahiduddin Khan, "Non-Violence in Islam," paper presented at the Symposium on Islam and Peace, sponsored by Non-Violence International and the Mohammed Said Farsi Chair of Islamic Peace at the American University, Washington, D.C., February 6–7, 1998. Available online at www.alrisala.org (accessed January 24, 2002).

49. Ibid.

50. Ibid.

51. Khan, "Principles of Success in the Light of Seerah," Al Risala Forum International, www.alrisala.org/Articles/mailing_list/principles_of_success.htm, January 24, 2002 (accessed January 24, 2002).

52. Abdulrahman Abdulkadir Kurdi, *The Islamic State: A Study Based on the Islamic Holy Constitution* (London: Mansell, 1984), 100.

53. Alfred Guillaume, *Islam* (Harmondsworth, U.K.: Penguin, 1956), 126.

54. Sayyid Qutb, "Paving the Way," *Nida'ul Islam* (April–May 1998). Available online at www.islam.org.au, February 9, 2002 (accessed February 9, 2002).

55. Anthony Black, *The History of Islamic Political Thought: From the Prophet to the Present* (New York: Routledge, 2001), 323.

56. Asghar Ali Engineer, "Islamic Ethic," Center for the Study of Society and Secularism, www.ecumene.org//IIS/csss24.htm, 2000, January 3, 2000 (accessed January 24, 2002).

57. See Anderson, "Classes, the Koran and Jihad."

58. See Marquand, "Special Report," 4, qtg. Mukahil Zia of the Islamic Center at Peshawar University.

59. Ibid.

60. See John Miller, interview, program *Frontline: Hunting Bin Laden*, www.pbs.org/wgbh/frontline/shows, April 1999 (accessed January 16, 2002).

61. Ajami, "Nowhere Man," 20.

62. It is the case in general that Muslims in urban settings and those exposed to a wider world often construct elaborate worldviews that makes them search for more meaning, whereas those in rural settings may be satisfied by the basic five principles. These differences explain in most part the choice of actions (violence or nonviolence).

63. For example, the panel "Transforming Islam" in the symposium "September 11 as a Transformative Moment," University of Southern California Center on Law, History, and Culture, University of Southern California Law School, May 24, 2002.

64. Asma Barlas, "Will the 'Real' Islam Please Stand Up?" delivered at the Master's Tea, Sillman College, Yale University, February 21, 2002. This provides a good summation of the arguments in this essay by stating the need to "distinguish between the Qur'an and its exegesis on the one hand, and between the religious texts, cultures, and histories on the other, both of which we must learn to do in order to challenge oppressive readings of Islam."

Islam at the Crossroads of Extremism and Moderation

New Science, Global Peace, and Democracy

J. E. RASH (AHMED ABDUR RASHID)

The ingredients of the discussion of Islamic extremism versus moderation are familiar. On the one hand, we have the picture of Islam as gentle, peaceful, and tolerant that has been periodically presented by the media (as, for example, on the fall 2001 Oprah Winfrey broadcast, "Islam 101"), as well as by Muslims themselves. On the other hand, we find the stereotype of Islam reinforced by September 11 and touted by neoconservatives as the new great global evil. On the one hand, the Grand Mufti of Syria, Shaykh Ahmad Kaftaro, says, "To be a good Muslim, one must first be a good Jew and a good Christian"; on the other, Osama bin Laden declares all Muslims duty-bound to bring Palestine under their control. There is more to these contrasts than the obvious chasm that divides them. At stake in their interplay lies the potential for a significant segment (about one-sixth) of our global population either to reassert Islam as a worldview with a capacity for uplifting individuals and benefiting humanity or to allow extremists to marginalize moderates, using partial truths and the normal challenges each generation faces to distort the potential for dynamic civilizational development and to impose doctrinaire and dangerous interpretations of Islam.

We hear much talk about a "clash of civilizations" that pits the West against the Muslim world. Even skeptics of all-embracing black and white paradigms have trouble denying that such a clash underlay the attacks of September 11. But seeing the world in terms of civilizational clashes is little help to those looking for practical ways to ease tensions. More useful are questions such as, "How can diverse peoples peaceably coexist? Is cultural homogenization really our best hope for reducing conflict? Can consensus be achieved without at least some groups having to compromise core beliefs?" In short, can we humans, in all our multiplicity, get along?

We can, according to Hans-Peter Dürr, a quantum physicist and former director of the Max Planck Institute who brings his scientific knowledge to peace studies. To do so, we must recognize that the real clash at hand is not a clash of civilizations but rather a clash of centuries, of old and new perspectives on an ever-changing universe.

A key ingredient in today's conflicts is the attempt to hold on to nineteenth-century thinking. Professor Dürr describes this thinking as centering on a mechanistic or materially oriented view of reality, according to which the future unfolds from the present in a deterministic progression governed by immutable laws of nature. Struggle dominates interactions in a world where only the fittest survive. Differentiation breeds conflict.[1]

Twentieth-century thinkers began to realize that this deterministic, competition-oriented worldview failed to acknowledge deeper, more profound elements underlying outer phenomena. Discoveries in quantum physics suggested that nature was surprisingly unpredictable, disorderly, and nonlinear. Scientists in particular started to awaken to the role of human consciousness, which defied explanation in conventional scientific terms; to see science as a metaphor, revealing not just one truth, but many dimensions of truth; and to regard the future as open-ended.

According to this newer worldview, differentiation among peoples allows for a pooling of wide-ranging capabilities, a cross-fertilization of insights, and an array of options for organizing and reorganizing society as circumstances warrant. Peace is possible: not, Dürr explains, peace as a "tension-free state of static equilibrium," but peace that "has color, variety, and tensions, and has challenges, even disagreements and conflicts struggling for balance." Peace is regarded as "a poised, statically unstable state that seeks a dynamic equilibrium through an interaction of forces and counterforces. Like life, . . . it is a homeostasis, in which the counterforce is not the enemy of the force it opposes, but only the combination of the two makes vitality, openness, and freedom possible."

This definition rejects the nineteenth-century view that peace happens when one competitor neutralizes others. It equally rejects the idea that the road to harmony lies in the type of economic globalization we are witnessing today. As Benjamin Barber points out, so far, international market forces have done little to "improve the chances for civic responsibility, accountability, or democracy." Instead, they have imposed the "sterile cultural monism" that he dubs "McWorld." Side effects include "the resentments and spiritual unease of those for whom the trivialization and homogenization of values is an affront to cultural diversity and spiritual and moral seriousness."[2]

Rather than tapping each person's and each civilization's unique riches, globalization buries them. Dürr writes, "We should not forget that the modern doctrine of salvation, namely the Western scientific, technical, and economic ideology, is today in danger of becoming the worst fundamentalism, and is putting other major cultures, that are very important for the survivability of humanity, in great difficulties."

The writings of Dürr, Barber, and others point to the importance of rethinking conflict and peace. They suggest that solutions lie not in nineteenth-century paradigms of "good versus evil" but in philosophical constructs and practical structures that respect, value, and benefit from human diversity.

Long before the fundamentalism that would put a McDonald's on every corner and a PDA in every hand, the valuing of diversity characterized the United States. Before the fundamentalism that strives to put a chador on every woman and a man at the wheel of every car, valuing of diversity also characterized Islam. Indeed, when it comes to matters of individual difference and collective well-being, the teachings of the Qur'an and the Prophet Muhammad (pbuh)[3] are strikingly similar to those of Thomas Jefferson, Benjamin Franklin, James Madison, and some of our nation's other founders. The rubric under which these teachings may be loosely grouped is "democracy." (Although the Prophet Muhammad [pbuh] and early Muslims did not use this label, they advanced public participation and representative governance through such principles and practices as *ijtihad* [the exercise of independent judgment], *shura* [consultation], and *ijma* [consensus].)

According to a basic definition, "both the theory and the practice of democracy rest on the notion that all people possess equal worth and have the right to share in their own governance—to rule themselves either directly or through leaders of their own choosing. The ruled, in short, must consent to their rulers, who are in turn accountable to the governed."[4] Each element of this definition is paralleled in Islamic and American sources.

All people possess equal worth: There is little need to repeat the eloquent assertion of human equality set forth in the Declaration of Independence: "We hold these truths to be self-evident, that all men are created equal." Less familiar in the West, but central to the teachings of Islam, is the understanding that God "created the human being of the best stature" (Qur'an 95:4).[5] Reinforcing this statement, the Prophet Muhammad (pbuh) said, "Every person is born in fitra," that is, in a state of essential goodness.

All people . . . have the right to share in their own governance—to rule themselves either directly or through leaders of their own choosing. The ruled, in short, must consent to their rulers: From Islam's affirmation of human beings' innate goodness grows the view that individuals have the potential for sound decision making. Hence we find the Prophet (pbuh) frequently consulting his companions and expressing respect for their insights. He also was known to defer to the consensus of the majority. In at least one instance (the Battle of Uhud), the majority decision of his associates led to disastrous results. Soon thereafter a newly revealed passage of the Qur'an told the Prophet (pbuh) to continue seeking others' opinions: "Consult with them on the conduct of affairs" (3:159), God enjoined, with "them" referring to the very people who had recently given poor advice.

Thomas Jefferson similarly expressed confidence in the decision-making abilities of the people, writing, "Civil government being the sole object of forming societies, its administration must be conducted by common consent." He too continued to hold this view despite experiences of consensual government's occasional flaws. In an 1820 letter he wrote, "I know no safe depository of the ultimate powers of the society but the people themselves; and if we think them not enlightened enough to exercise their control with a wholesome discretion, the remedy is not to take it from them, but to inform their discretion by education."[6]

The rulers . . . are in turn accountable to the governed: The Prophet Muhammad (pbuh) is reported to have said, "The best fighting through the path of Allah is to speak a word of justice to an oppressive ruler." Abu Bakr, chosen (based on the consensus of a group of Muslim leaders) to lead the Muslim community following Muhammad's death, said during his first inaugural address, "If I act rightly, help me, but if I act wrongly, correct me and set me right." 'Umar, the second caliph, observed the same principle. When one of his associates tried to prevent someone from criticizing him, 'Umar insisted on allowing the person to speak, saying, "There is no good in them if they do not speak out, and there is no good in us if we do not listen to what they say." Once after 'Umar had publicly given a judicial opinion (*fatwa*), a woman in the assembly corrected him on the basis of Shari'a. He said, "This woman is right, and I am wrong" and amended his ruling.

Paralleling these Islamic examples is George Washington's second inaugural address, which focused solely on accountability. "This Oath I am now about to take—and in your presence—that if it shall be found during my administration of the Government, I have in any instance violated willingly, or knowingly, the injunctions thereof, I may (besides incurring Constitutional punishment) be subject to the upbraidings of all who are now witnesses of the present solemn Ceremony." Jefferson stressed the need to preserve individuals' freedom to censure government even when they were in the wrong; in 1799, he wrote, "I am . . . against all violations of the Constitution to silence by force and not by reason the complaints or criticisms, just or unjust, of our citizens against the conduct of their agents."[7]

On the basis of these tenets, the United States and Muslim communities (most notably the community of the Prophet Muhammad [pbuh] and the first four caliphs, but also some others, historically) have set up democratic institutions. These institutions in turn have facilitated the peaceful coexistence of diverse peoples. One way of defining crossroads in the lives of these communities is in terms of junctures where their democratic institutions have either been affirmed or undermined (such as the change that took place among Muslim leaders of the Abbasid dynasty

[750–1258 CE] who generally dropped any pretense of accountability to their subjects). Crossroads in the evolution of institutions, however, reflect only one level of the types of changes that may affect how well a given society accommodates diversity. Analyzing developments on this level alone flattens the landscape of reality.

Consider, for example, developments in Chechnya during the 1990s. Traditionally, the Chechens' understanding and practice of Islam reflected Sufi, or mystical, teachings, but after Russia's incursions, Wahhabi-type attitudes displaced Sufism. This shift is certainly significant on the level of political and religious institutions. Yet it could have even deeper repercussions in shaping thousands of people's understanding of faith, of the purpose of life, and of their relationship with the Divine. In the long run, its impacts on individuals' inner sense of balance, security, and peace could influence events in the region as much as changes in government and religious structures will influence them.

In my work and travels, I have spent many years dealing with the grassroots implications of various political and social approaches. Most significant to me has been the extent to which issues are influenced not just by outer conditions but also by people's spiritual condition. I have found the lens of Sufism to be helpful in understanding this interior dimension. At the risk of being esoteric, I would like to share some observations that a Sufi might make regarding the inner workings of democratic principles shared by the United States and Islam.

As already noted, these sets of principles posit that human beings are essentially good. From this capacity for goodness grow qualities that are conducive to collective well-being, such as tolerance, compassion, generosity, justice, and a willingness to sacrifice and serve. Jefferson detected in these qualities the working of something more than human reason:

> It has been said that we feed the hungry, clothe the naked, bind up the wounds of the man beaten by thieves, pour oil and wine into them, set him on our own beast and bring him to the inn, because we receive ourselves pleasure from these acts. . . . These good acts give us pleasure, but how happens it that they give us pleasure? Because nature hath implanted in our breasts a love of others, a sense of duty to them, a moral instinct, in short, which prompts us irresistibly to feel and to succor their distresses. . . . The Creator would indeed have been a bungling artist had He intended man for a social animal without planting in him social dispositions.[8]

A Sufi would agree with Jefferson's assessment and would perhaps add that these dispositions, seeded in us by our Creator, are potentials that each of us is responsible for bringing forth in himself or herself, step by step, through intention, knowledge, and experience. The fulfillment of these potentials cannot be legislated or enforced by one group upon another. Nor are religious rituals any guarantee of their realization. The Qur'an cautions, "Woe to those who pray—and are unmindful of their prayers—who want to be seen—and [yet] refuse small kindesses" (107:4–7).

If legislation, enforcement, and ritual cannot compel people to live up to their highest potential, what can? Sufis address this question through the concept of *ihsan*, which may be interpreted as seeing God in everything, and if one is not able to accomplish this, then knowing that God is, is seeing one.[9] In this act of consciousness, the Sufi strives for attunement to a power higher than oneself—to a timeless, unchangeable Truth. In the tranquility of the mosque, in the call to prayer, in the five daily pauses for reflection, in the guidelines of Shari'a, Muslims may find a constant metaphor that appeals to the core of one who looks behind the apparent phenomenon called life. The beauty of the recitation of Qur'an, the contemplative calm of meditation, the natural satisfaction found in serving others, the heart's yearning to experience a nearness to the Divine—all foster inner peace. All help to create a means of communication between the outer realities of day-to-day life and the inner reality of one's self.

It is said that God revealed to the Prophet Muhammad (pbuh), "Who knows himself knows his Lord," emphasizing that a person's identity ultimately lies in his or her relationship with God. (A similar understanding may be reflected in Jesus' statement "the kingdom of Heaven is among [or within] you" [Luke 17:20, New Revised Standard Version].) This realization fosters harmony within and without, under the principle of "being in the world and not of the world." In this, Sufism differs from religious sects that regard the material world as a barrier and threat to piety. Life to the Sufi is a series of experiences that lead one toward Truth. It provides the opportunity to refine the self and to serve God by serving God's creatures. Much is to be learned by working toward the "good life" *(hayat-i-tayybah)* for oneself and others in the material world while respecting values that precede and extend beyond this physical existence.

In these and other perspectives, the way of the Sufi seems to demonstrate Islam at its most progressive, its most personal, its most genuinely reflective of fundamental principles, its most democratic, and its most conducive to peace. Sufi scholar Fadhlalla Haeri writes, "Islam is not an historical phenomenon that began 1400 years ago. It is the timeless art of awakening by means of submission. Sufism is the heart of Islam. It is as ancient as the rise of human consciousness."[10]

Extremists readily perceive danger in such a comprehensive and nonlinear perspective. Not surprisingly, they have for centuries worked to discredit Sufi teachings. If fascism is the political extreme that negates the democratic frameworks necessary for peace, then movements such as the Wahhabis, the Taliban, Hizbu-l Tahrir, Takfir wa Hijrah, and their Christian, Jewish, and other counterparts in various faiths represent a corresponding religious extreme that negates the democratic spirituality on which peace depends.

Islam as interpreted by extremists has been used to cultivate qualities that are anathema to peace, including coerciveness, envy, revenge, hatred, selfishness, materialism, tribalism, and disregard for human rights and choices. Under the guise of education, extremists have spent decades teaching hate and misrepresenting Islam's essential teachings. They have distorted Shari'a in ways that abrogate its democratic principles. Three aspects of their doctrines are especially disruptive: their insistence that they are sole proprietors of pure Islam, their attempts to legislate human beings' relationship with God through rigid and oppressive rules of conduct, and their failure to honor any rules of engagement in their relations with perceived enemies (of which they have many).

Benjamin Franklin, in a speech at the conclusion of the deliberations of the Constitutional Convention in 1787, observed that "most men, indeed, as well as most sects in religion, think themselves in possession of all truth, and wherever others differ from them, it is so far error. Steele, a Protestant, in a dedication, tells the Pope, that the only difference between our two churches in their opinions of the certainty of their doctrine, is, the Romish Church is infallible, and the Church of England is never in the wrong."[11] Going a step beyond the good-natured antagonists in Franklin's anecdote, Muslim extremists assert their monopoly on the "whole truth" in uncompromising and frequently politicized terms.

Members of the first such movement in Islam were known as Kharajites: literally, "those who depart." The Kharajites did indeed depart from the mainstream, declaring both sides wrong in the seventh-century civil war over succession and launching attacks on both parties' leaders. On the intellectual front, narrow, exclusionary understandings of Islam found voice in the works of eleventh-century scholar Ibn Hazm, who denounced "all forms of deduction, analogy, opinion . . . [and] theological discourse." In the thirteenth century, Ibn Taymiyah confined the legitimate sources of truth to "the Qur'an and the hadith as interpreted by the Companions of the Prophet or their immediate successors."[12] Subsequent movements, such as the Wahhabis (founded in the eighteenth century), have continued to strictly circumscribe the sources of spiritual knowledge. Some have reinforced their monopoly on truth by going so far as to modify hadith or to attribute to weak hadith the status of affirmed or strong.[13] Their claims to proprietorship over the only pure Islam have been matched by their denunciation of variant interpretations, particularly Sufism.

Muslim extremists' exclusivity runs counter to the Qur'an and the teachings of the Prophet Muhammad (pbuh). The central, nonnegotiable teaching of Islam is belief in one God—the same God worshiped by other monotheistic faiths. The Qur'an states, "He has ordained for you the same religious way of life (diin) that was enjoined upon Noah, and that We have revealed to you, and which We had already enjoined upon Abraham and Moses and Jesus, [saying], 'Establish the religion, (diin) and do not be divided in it'" (42:13). Muslim nonviolent activist Karim Crow notes that these and other Islamic teachings allow no room for "religious exclusivity or ethnic election." Rather, they call for "a harmonious religious pluralism."[14]

The Qur'an does indicate that by the time of its revelation in the early seventh century CE, misinterpretations had crept into the doctrines and practices of both Jews and Christians. Yet only some of these religions' followers were said to have gone astray: "Of the People of the Book there is an upright community that recite the Signs of Allah in the night—and they prostrate. They believe in Allah and in the Final Day and enjoin the doing of the right and forbid the doing of what is wrong and vie with one another in good works. And it is they who are from the righteous" (Qur'an 3:113–15).

If Muslims are to respect other monotheistic faiths, how much more so should they respect varying points of view among themselves? As for Muslim sects that assert their interpretation of Islam as superior to other Muslims', the Qur'an cautions, "And do not be from those . . . who have split up their religion (diin) and become partisans [of one school of thought or another]—each faction rejoicing in what they have" (30:31–32). Another passage warns, "Do not dispute, lest you lose heart and your strength depart you" (8:46).

Nevertheless, extremists are convinced that they alone are right—and that this justifies making rigid rules for behavior. "Religious correctness" is not just desirable but mandatory and subject to imposition through legal penalties and appointed enforcers. The strictures imposed by the government of Saudi Arabia on individuals' attire, women's freedom to travel, non-Muslims' right to worship, public dancing, movie viewing, and other aspects of day-to-day life demonstrate a highly narrow, selective understanding of permissible behavior. The Taliban went further, banning television, music CDs, kite flying, chess, and the building of snowmen. Beyond crippling huge venues of human activity, the extremists' policies often undermine the dignity and capacity of those whom they govern or control.

This distrustful and dictatorial approach belies the trust that the Prophet Muhammad (pbuh) exemplified in his dealings with even the common people. He is reported to have said, "Beware of excessiveness in religion, before you have perished as a result of such excessiveness." In keeping with this guidance, he strove always for the middle way, for balance and harmony. When approached by particularly devout individuals who wished to fast continually or to opt for celibacy instead of marriage, he recommended a more moderate spiritual course, reminding them that Muslims have a duty to respect the body's physical needs. In political terms, he strove to harmonize the Jewish and Muslim populations of Medina by establishing a written constitution, according to which both parties were equal before the law, both were to guarantee the rights of the other, and both were to aid the other if either was attacked.

The Prophet Muhammad's moderate approach reflected a deep understanding of Islam in its most universal sense. It is valuable to recall that the Arabic language has no capital letters, and that therefore, when Muhammad (pbuh) spoke of Islam, he was not invoking a capitalized label. For him, and for those who first heard the revelations of Qur'an as he recited them, "islam" meant surrender or submission. Extracted from the same root as *salaam*, it connoted an active process of coming to peace, safety, security, wholeness, and well-being through consciousness in the Presence of the Divine. Nothing in the term implied institutional structure, hierarchy, or dogma. Nor did the term prescribe a political agenda. For these early Muslims, Islam was first and foremost a framework for deepening the relationship between individuals and their Creator in moment-to-moment life.

In general, this framework was neither arduous nor inflexible. The Prophet Muhammad (pbuh) said, "Make things easy, not difficult." He was sensitive to his followers' tendency to take every aspect of his example as incumbent to imitate. During Ramadan, he often performed a supererogatory prayer known as Taraweeh. One night, he arrived at the mosque for Taraweeh, saw people gathered, and left, realizing that if he did the prayer every evening, it would be interpreted as a mandatory practice.

Once, as a party of Muslims was leaving for a military campaign, the Prophet (pbuh) instructed them, "Do not perform the mid-afternoon prayer until you get to the place of Banu Qurayzah." The time of the prayer came before they had reached their destination. Some companions said, "We will not pray until we get to the place of Banu Qurayzah." Others said, "We should pray here, on time. The saying of the Prophet will not prevent us from praying now." When the matter was brought before the Prophet (pbuh), he did not disapprove of either group.

These and other teachings make evident the degree to which Islam recommends flexible approaches rather than dictatorial rules of behavior.

In a 2002 *U.S. News and World Report* interview, Muslim scholar Khaled Abou El Fadl reflected on his transformation from a rigidly doctrinaire youth to an open-minded adult. Contrary to what one might expect, the change came about as a result of learning more about the teachings of his faith. Having driven his family to exasperation by "railing against television, trousers, and mixed gatherings" (not to mention ruining his sister's Rod Stewart cassettes), he finally took up their challenge to study at the local Shari'a school. There, he "was shocked when the sheik handily dismantled his pious pronouncements on everything from the proper manner of dress to the sinfulness of all music and art. 'If I cited a single hadith,' Abou El Fadl recalls, 'I would be challenged with ten others plus the precedent of [the Prophet's] Companions and a meticulous accounting of the evidence at hand.' The experience reduced him to tears, he says, but it changed the course of his life by spurring him to master the traditional learning that had defeated him."[15]

Openminded teachers helped Abou El Fadl learn to apply Shari'a flexibly to today's world. In contrast, those who adopt exclusivist interpretations of truth and insist on rigid rules place themselves at odds with their surroundings. The Taliban roused antagonism long before September 11 through their "refusal to cooperate with UN humanitarian agencies or foreign donor countries, or to compromise their principles in exchange for international recognition, and [in] their rejection of all Muslim ruling elites as corrupt."[16]

Outside influences of any kind are perceived by extremists as a threat; feeling threatened, they believe that they have grounds to take any steps necessary to neutralize the threats' sources. Hizballah ideologue Sheikh Fadlallah has argued, "when Islam fights a war, it fights like any other power in the world, defending itself in order to preserve its existence and its liberty, forced to undertake preventative operations when it is in danger."[17] Dr. Magnus Ranstorp observes that "the totality of the struggle . . . purely defined in dialectic and cosmic terms as believers against unbelievers, order against chaos, and justice against injustice . . . is mirrored in the total and uncompromising nature of the cause." The perception of being engaged in an all-out war "is often used to justify the level and intensity of the violence."[18] No parameters for engagement and disengagement need apply.

The extremists' frequent failure to observe limits on armed engagement contradicts Islamic guidelines for using force. To be a Muslim is by definition to be a person who actively works for the peace, security, and well-being of all people. In this context, there are circumstances under which Islam permits or even mandates the use of force—but always, the use of force must support long-term peace. As Shaykh Ahmad Kaftaro, the Grand Mufti of Syria, has noted, "The Prophet (pbuh) never said, 'I have been raised for militancy or for fighting.' Rather, he said, 'I have been raised as a teacher, to complete the structure of moral values.'"[19]

Muslims were first authorized to fight in the following words: "[Fighting is] permitted to those who are fought against, because they are wronged; and surely Allah has the power to help them—those who have been driven unjustly from their homes only for the reason that they have said, 'Our Lord is Allah.' For had it not been for Allah repelling some people by the means of others, monasteries, churches, synagogues and places of prostration (*masajid*) in which the Name of Allah is much remembered, would have been demolished" (Qur'an 22:39–40). What are Muslims obligated to defend? The freedom to say, "Our Lord is God" and the spaces where people meditate, pray, and turn their attention to the Divine—be those spaces sacred to Jews, Christians, Muslims, or other believers.

Elsewhere the Qur'an poses the question: "And what is with you, that you do not fight in the Way of Allah and [for] the oppressed among men, women and children who say, 'Our Lord! Take us out of this city of unjust oppressors [of themselves and others] and appoint from Yourself [a] protector and appoint from Yourself [a] helper'" (4:75). The limited use of force in Islam to defend "basic human rights—security, [life] and property, freedom of thought—corresponds to what [we might call] 'humanitarian intervention.'"[20] Mark Juergensmeyer notes that even within the Gandhian philosophy of nonviolence, "conditions could be so extreme that those who stood for truth were faced with the necessity of choosing between violent resistance and none at all. Gandhi said that in these cases 'vengeance is any day superior to passive and helpless submission.'"[21]

In keeping with its humanitarian ends, the use of force within Islam is bounded by strict limitations.

- Force may be employed only in defense of religion. During the civil strife that followed the death of the caliph Ali, supporters of one party tried to enlist the support of the eldest remaining companion of the Prophet (pbuh). They quoted Qur'an in an effort to prove that he was obligated to take part. He retorted that the Qur'an calls for battling religious coercion, not for political infighting.[22]
- Muslims' responses to violence must be proportionate and measured. According to the Qur'an, "If you retaliate [in an exchange], then retaliate only at the level at which you were attacked; but if you are steadfastly patient—then it is better for the patient" (16:126).
- Muslims should not harm innocent people or destroy an enemy's livelihood. The caliph Abu Bakr instructed his soldiers, "Do not kill the [enemy's] children, old people, and women. Do not . . . burn their harvest, nor cut the fruit-bearing trees."[23]
- Muslims must terminate hostilities as soon as possible. The Qur'an states, "If they lean towards peace, then you should lean as well, and trust in Allah" (8:61).

In sum, extremists have tended to preach and act in ways that diverge from teachings given in the Qur'an, by the Prophet Muhammad (pbuh), and through the historical example of some Muslim leaders and societies. Open-mindedness, flexibility, and restraint are firmly established concepts in Islam. Why, then, do the statements and actions by subgroups of Muslims today reflect the opposite? Although a comprehensive answer is outside the scope of this chapter, contributing factors include:

Cultural Overlays—As Islam spread, its teachings and practices often became mixed with already existing customs. Some customs gave rise to distorted interpretations. For example, the complete covering of women in public reflects Persian customs that predate Islam. In the Qur'an, both men and women are enjoined to dress modestly. The Qur'an does not specify that women must cover themselves completely from head to foot.

Politicization of Faith—Competing claims to leadership splintered the Muslim community soon after the death of the Prophet Muhammad (pbuh). More recently,

Muslims' experiences under European colonial powers gave rise to new forms of political Islam. In some countries, Western-style modernization efforts prompted extremist reactions. Ongoing superpower intrusions (real or perceived) into the affairs of Muslim countries further bolstered extremists' popularity. In the quest for autonomy and prosperity, the word *Islam* became an umbrella excuse for actions motivated less by piety than by political expediency.[24]

Demographic Pressures—Population trends have also contributed to extremism. Many Muslim societies are experiencing a "youth bulge." For example, on average, sixty-five percent of the Arab world's population is under the age of eighteen.[25] Countries lack sufficient schools and jobs for this mass of young adults. Parents are sending their sons to extremist-sponsored schools for lack of educational alternatives. Meanwhile, the numbers of unemployed youths are swelling. Scores of young men from rural areas have flocked to the cities in search of work. There they confront the chasm between traditional and Western ways of life. Caught between old and new, East and West, Islamic and secular, frustrated by the inequities of a materialist world, and goaded by personal experiences of discrimination or humiliation, some have found a voice and promise of future power and security in the simplistic worldview offered by extremism. Often they do so at the expense of permitting themselves to be misguided by leaders with multiple agendas.

There is a danger, however, in dwelling too long on the causes of extremism, as it may give the impression that extremism is the dominant strain of Islam. Even in Pakistan prior to President Musharraf's 2002 crackdown, extremist parties had never won more than ten percent of the vote. In Egypt, they are a significant but by no means dominant force.[26]

Despite their minority status, extremist Muslims have frequently benefited from the Western media's tendency to portray them as spokespersons for Islam. Some (such as Osama bin Laden) have been able to manipulate public opinion and portray Islam as the enemy of the West and its values. Policy makers in the United States have been known to buy into this portrayal, for reasons that may serve shortsighted political agendas more than the nation's long-term well-being.

The question of who may legitimately speak for Islam is complex, which makes manipulation of Islam's public image easier. According to Shia Muslims, the Ayatollahs represent Islam. But Shias make up only about ten percent of the Muslim population worldwide. The Sunni majority views the question "Who speaks for Islam?" in a different way, one that is simultaneously liberating and disabling. Sunnis hold that unless there is a living Amir al-Mu'mineen—that is, a "commander of the faithful"—then anyone may speak for Islam in the sense of advancing her or his interpretation, yet no one is authorized to speak for Islam with binding authority. Muslims have not been unified behind a single Amir al-Mu'mineen since Mu'awiya came to power in 660 CE (and some would say the invalidation of the Amir's position began even earlier), nor is any framework in place for authorizing a new Amir al-Mu'mineen. (Although the Taliban call Mullah Omar the Amir al-Mu'mineen, in fact no sect has the power to bestow this title.) As a result, although any Muslim is free to speak about Islam, and many movements would like the world at large to believe that they speak for Islam, it is critical to weigh which individuals or movements speak with greatest legitimacy.

Perhaps the most obvious sign of the crossroads between extremism and moderation in Islam lies in the gap between the voices who speak most loudly and the majority opinion. Those who were once on the margin have become spokespersons for the mainstream, neither by virtue of their merit nor by consensus of those they claim to represent, but through the force of their actions.

Islam is not alone in confronting a crossroads. The United States also stands at a critical juncture, with the potential to impact the route ultimately pursued by Muslims.

Prior to September 11, 2001, many American Muslims had come to the conclusion that the best hope for a revivification of moderate Islam lay in this country. The democratic institutions, multiculturalism, and a wide spectrum of educational and professional opportunities in the United States hold promise for enabling Muslims to live Islam as a dynamic and progressive faith. The religious and personal freedoms guaranteed by the Bill of Rights create an environment where Muslims can integrate their values and beliefs with the world of the twenty-first century, not by imposing monolithic interpretations, but rather by tapping Islam's capacity to be flexible without losing its firm foundation.

American Muslims approach Islam differently than do their counterparts in the Muslim world. What they see in Islam is democracy, diversity, a commitment to justice, equity, equality, reluctance to stereotype, and a commitment to community well-being, among other strengths. They recognize and appreciate the parallels between Islamic concepts such as *ijma, ijtihad,* the affirmation of individuals' rights, and the structures established by the Constitution.

Young Muslim Americans are aware of—and generally are unsympathetic toward—narrow-minded, dogmatic, exclusionary, accusatory forms of belief. They recognize that whatever the faults of U.S. policies, the domestic mindset overall affirms freedom of choice and mutual respect. Whereas some Muslims might crave acceptance, and others might see themselves as warners who are going to change the American landscape through force or doctrinal argumentation, most see themselves as either American Muslims or Muslim Americans with a role to play in contributing to the future through their knowledge, faith, and creativity.

It is critical that moderates within the American Muslim community be acknowledged and supported rather than undermined in their efforts to play a constructive role in society. Certain extremist Muslims have worked diligently over the last century, and the last fifty years especially, to introduce or to strengthen narrow and often ethnocentric attitudes in the minds, politics, and social structures of Muslim peoples and countries from India to Indonesia, from Central Asia to Europe. Islamic institutions in the United States are not immune to these efforts. Khaled Abou El Fadl, speaking at the Islamic Center of Greater Austin (Texas), was jeered by a group of audience members who then followed him out to his car, threatening violence. Other congregations have displayed similar hostility. The president of the Graduate School of Islamic and Social Sciences in Leesburg, Virginia, Taha Alalwani, "worries that many of [the] imams [in America's mosques and Islamic centers] 'are just Islamists,' often supported by Saudi organizations and more concerned with ideology than with complexities of faith. 'I would love to see the Muslim community try to enrich their traditions and revive their values, and I try to encourage this in my school,' he says. 'Unfortunately, many imams think in a different way.'"27

The potentials for doctrinaire and exclusivist interpretations of Islam to gain footholds in U.S. mosques make the decisions that face policy makers all the more challenging. Since September 11, recognition of the parallels between Islamic teachings and the United States' founding ideals of democracy, pluralism, and diversity has become more difficult. Extremists' acts have overshadowed the voices of moderate Muslims. Some Americans' attention has shifted to guarding against the perceived threat of Islam rather than proactively affirming moderate Islam. The result is a negative feedback loop in which the potential for progressive Islam, on the one hand, and the potential for the United States to provide a genuinely inclusive and moderating environment for religious expression, on the other, are moving out of synch. (As of late April 2002, the deepening polarization among Israel, Palestine, and other parties involved in the Middle East crisis seems to be accentuating this trend.)

In a February 2002 television interview, Azizah al-Hibri, a law professor at the University of Richmond and a Lebanese Muslim immigrant, commented:

> The American experience does something to people. When you come to the U.S. [as an immigrant], you might come with a different perception, you might even come from those societies which feel that the U.S. has not treated them well in its foreign policy, but when you come to the U.S., you are under the protection of the Constitution, you are under the umbrella of democracy, you are sharing in all the economic opportunities. . . . Suddenly, you find out that your perception of the U.S. is changing, and that you are becoming an American. . . . We [Americans] need to be thinking about what this society does to people. . . . Even if [extremist groups] sent someone as a sleeper ten, twenty years ago, are they going to stay the same? If they . . . saw this society the way it is, are they going to stay the same? I think we should have confidence in who we are.28

If Muslims are to revivify Islamic teachings of tolerance, justice, open-mindedness, and respect for diversity, then the best—if not the only—environment conducive to that effort is in the United States. Future developments within the Muslim American community cannot be separated from choices facing U.S. policy makers as they decide how to interpret principles of democracy, civil liberty, and civil rights in the post–September 11 era. Worries prevail among Muslims in the United States regarding the course of our policies and the extent and motivators for what appears to be an erosion of civil liberties. The rise of neoconservative influence has created resonances of previous places and times in the hearts and minds of many in the Muslim community who came to the United States precisely for its guarantee of freedom and human rights. American Muslims are increasingly feeling isolated due to their minority status and to what they perceive as a pattern of targeting by individuals and government agencies.

As for Muslims worldwide, September 11 could be a nexus that inspires some who had looked for security in the false promises of extremism to trade in that allegiance for the security of moderation. The Kharajites—"those who depart[ed]"— were as marginalized as their name implied. During the latest phase of politicization of Islam, the extremist minority has been allowed to permeate the Muslim world, moving in from the fringes to dominate a significant portion of Islamic thought and education. September 11 has forced previously passive Muslims to identify and to understand more deeply the moderate message of Islam by having to defend it. This may be a first step toward taking the groups that have traditionally been marginalized and marginalizing them again.

Thomas Jefferson wrote, "When principles are well understood, their application is less embarrassing."[29] Human beings have proven their skill in applying principles that they presume to understand through decisions that end up being embarrassing or—more ominously—dangerous. Today, Islam and the United States stand at intersecting crossroads. In-depth understanding, not nineteenth-century rhetoric, is needed to chart the course ahead. Muslims the world over have an opportunity to revivify the essential democratic and pluralistic principles of their heritage. Citizens and leaders of the United States also have an opportunity: to revisit and reaffirm the original writings and the institutional precedents that have made their nation, for much of its history, a testimony to the potential for diversity to thrive under democracy.

There are causes for suspicion on all sides, for questions of intent and motivation, for careful examination of long-term visions. From an Islamic point of view and, I believe, equally from a point of view that is expressed in the writings of this nation's founders, much could be accomplished toward establishing peace if a strong and honorable leader were to stand before the citizens of this country and other nations and repent of the wrongs that have been committed against many peoples, declaring a sincere intention to reconcile differences, act with fairness and equity, and reaffirm the principles of freedom and democracy that have drawn diverse individuals from across the world to this land. This declaration must be matched equally by statements from the Islamic world, where leadership of high character has been sorely lacking.[30] Idealistic as this suggestion may sound, it is a practical part of the solution to the tragic and globally threatening circumstances in which we find ourselves.

NOTES

1. All quotations from and references to comments made by Hans-Peter Dürr are taken from his speech, "Peace as the Crisis" (delivered at the meeting of the Institute of Peace Research and Security Policy at the University of Hamburg and the Association of German Scientists, Berlin, October 12, 2001), and from private conversations with the author, April 2002.

2. Benjamin R. Barber, *Jihad vs. McWorld* (New York: Ballantine, 2001), xii, xiii, 14.

3. "(Pbuh)" following the name of the Prophet Muhammad stands for "peace be upon him," the traditional invocation offered by Muslims in respect and gratitude whenever Muhammad is mentioned.

4. Herbert McClosky and John Zaller, *The American Ethos: Public Attitudes toward Capitalism and Democracy* (Cambridge, Mass.: Harvard Univ. Press, 1984), 2.

5. Translations of Qur'anic passages are drawn from The Tajwidi Qur'an: Transliterated by A. Nooruddeen Durkee with Meanings Rendered in Contemporary American English (Charlottesville, Va.: an-Noor Educational Foundation, 2003), with the exception that English names have been substituted for names translated to Arabic equivalents.

6. Thomas Jefferson: Notes on Virginia Q.VIII, 1782, *The Writings of Thomas Jefferson*, Memorial Edition, ed. Andrew A. Lipscomb and Albert E. Bergh (Washington, D.C.: Thomas Jefferson Memorial Association, 1903–04), 2:120; Jefferson to William C. Jarvis, 1820, *Writings*, 15:278. The author gratefully acknowledges the Electronic Text Center of the University of Virginia Library for making Jefferson's writings available online at http://etext.lib.virginia.edu/Jefferson, May 6, 2002.

7. George Washington, Second Inaugural Address (Philadelphia), in secretary's hand (probably Tobias Lear), March 4, 1793, Washington, D.C., Library of Congress Manuscript Division, mssmisc pin0201.

8. Jefferson to Thomas Law, 1814, *Writings*, 14:141.

9. *Ihsan*, which ranks with Islam (submission) and *iman* (faith) as one of the cornerstones of Muslim life, was defined by the Prophet Muhammad (pbuh) as "to worship God as though you are seeing Him, and while you see Him not yet truly He sees you." This concept inspires the Sufis' quest to become conscious of God in all circumstances and at all times.

10. Fadhlalla Haeri, *The Elements of Sufism* (Rockport, Mass.: Element, 1990), vii.

11. Benjamin Franklin, "Speech in the Convention at the Conclusion of Its Deliberations," delivered before the Constitutional Convention, Philadelphia, Pennsylvania, September 17, 1787, in *Benjamin Franklin: Representative Selections with Introduction, Bibliography, and Notes*, rev. ed., ed. Chester E. Jorgenson and Frank L. Mott (New York: Hill and Wang, 1962), 491.

12. Majid Fakhry, "Philosophy and Theology from the Eighth Century CE to the Present," in *The Oxford History of Islam*, ed. John L. Esposito (Oxford: Oxford Univ. Press, 1999), 289–90.

13. Hadith (reports of the sayings and actions of the Prophet Muhammad [pbuh]) are classified from most to least reliable; knowing the status of a given hadith helps Muslims weigh its validity relative to other Islamic sources.

14. Karim Crow, *Islamic Peaceful-Action (*al-Jihad al-Silmi*): Nonviolent Approach to Justice and Peace in Islamic Societies* (Washington, D.C.: Nonviolence International, 1999), 6.

15. Jay Tolson, "Defender of the Faith (Portrait: Khaled Abou El Fadl)," *U.S. News and World Report* (Apr. 15, 2002): 37.

16. Ahmed Rashid, *Taliban: Militant Islam, Oil and Fundamentalism in Central Asia* (New Haven, Conn.: Yale Univ. Press, 2000), 93.

17. Muhammad Hussein Fadlallah, qtd. in Magnus Ranstorp, "Terrorism in the Name of Religion," *Journal of International Affairs* 50, no. 1 (Summer 1996): 41–62.

18. Ibid.

19. Shaykh Ahmed Kaftaro, telephone conversation with author, November 26, 2000.

20. Marcel Boisard, *Humanism in Islam* (Indianapolis, Ind.: American Trust Publications, 1988), 181.

21. Mark Juergensmeyer, *Fighting with Gandhi* (San Francisco: Harper and Row, 1984), 106. Islamic history also offers precedents for nonviolent resistance. For an account of nonviolent leader Khan Ghaffar Khan's efforts in the North-West Frontier during the 1930s and 1940s, see Eknath Easwaran, *Nonviolent Soldier of Islam: Badshah Khan, A Man to Match His Mountains* (Petaluma, Calif.: Nilgiri Press, 1999). For additional remarks on the use of force in Islam, see Ahmed Abdur Rashid, "Islam's Commitment to Peace and Nonviolence," lecture delivered at Johns Hopkins University, Baltimore, Maryland, March 9, 2001.

22. Maulana Wahiduddin Khan, "Non-Violence and Islam," www.alrisala.org/Articles/papers/nonviolence.htm (accessed March 1, 2001).

23. 'Abdur Rahman I. Doi, *Shari'ah: The Islamic Law* (London: Ta Ha, 1984), 446.

24. One telling anecdote concerns Dzhokhar Dudaev, who was elected president of Chechnya in 1991 and who (according to some) tried to enlist the aid of Islamic sentiments and Muslim governments only after failing to woo the West with a secular approach. He is said to have stated in a press conference that Muslims were required to pray four (rather than five) times daily. When the mistake was pointed out, he said that praying five times was even better. Edward W. Walker, "Islam in Chechnya," lecture delivered at the Berkeley-Stanford Conference, "Religion and Spirituality in Eastern Europe and the Former Soviet Union," Stanford, California, March 13, 1998), in *Contemporary Caucasus Newsletter*, no. 6 (Fall 1998): 10–15.

25. Fareed Zakaria, "The Allies Who Made Our Foes," *Newsweek*, October 1, 2001, 34.

26. Fareed Zakaria, "Why Do They Hate Us?" *Newsweek*, October 15, 2001, 40.

27. Tolson, "Defender of the Faith," 38.

28. Azizah Y. al-Hibri, television interview with Bill Moyers, *Now* (Public Broadcasting Service), February 15, 2002.

29. Jefferson to Gouverneur Morris, 1793, *Writings*, 9:36.

30. Leadership of high character in the Muslim world has been not only lacking but also neither encouraged nor supported, for reasons outside the scope of this chapter, but which need to be discussed and understood.

The White Man's Wounded Knee, or, Whose Holy War Is This, Anyway?

A Cautionary Tale

MARY ZEISS STANGE

ARMIES OF THE LORD

Consider the religious careers of two American "prophets" who lived and died approximately 150 years apart. They had much in common. Both had scant formal education but possessed remarkable facility with scripture, charismatic personalities, and impressive preaching skill. Both claimed to have received revelations from God that sharply diverged from the conventional Christian beliefs and practices of their times. Both attracted fiercely devoted followers, most of whom felt disillusioned by the secular culture of their day and were searching for a message deeper than the customarily superficial interpretations of the Bible that they encountered in more "mainstream" Christian churches. These followers, in both cases, willingly signed over all their worldly assets to their religious leaders. They also tended to overlook their leaders' obvious moral and ethical lapses. Both prophets practiced plural, "spiritual" marriage, taking to themselves the daughters and wives of their male associates in the community. And both amassed sizeable arsenals of weapons, so that when the time came, the Children of Light would be equipped to battle the Sons of Darkness—the latter being represented primarily by the armed forces of the secular state.

In each case, the news media played a crucial role. Rumors swirled around both separatist communities, generated for the most part by disgruntled former followers. Allegations of rape, child abuse, and worse were fanned into frenzy by reporters who published stories laced with innuendo, though short on hard fact. Gradually, in each case, there emerged in the media a portrait of the religious leader as a power-crazed madman, a con artist who practiced some sort of "mind control" over his hapless followers. Inevitably, in both cases, it was judged to be in the public interest to eliminate the prophet, with the goal of eliminating, by attrition, his errant flock. One prophet, Joseph Smith, was assassinated in what amounted to a lynching by members of the Illinois Militia, in the Carthage jail in 1844. The other, David Koresh, was killed along with roughly eighty of his followers by agents of the FBI, in circumstances that may never be fully understood, outside of Waco, Texas, in 1993.

The historical parallels between Joseph Smith and David Koresh are instructive in a variety of ways. In their broadest outlines, of course, the stories of these men and the religious communities they led are deeply American and not all that unfamiliar. Radical communitarian groups founded on principles that sharply diverge from the religious and social norm in one way or another, frequently having to do with sexual practices or "antisocial" behaviors, have dotted the landscape of Christian history for two millennia. But, nurtured perhaps by the crosscurrents of a frontier spirit and the constitutional separation of church and state, such movements took root with particular vigor in the United States. Most of them became little more than historical footnotes, but some proved to have genuine staying power. They evolved into churches, none more spectacularly than Smith's Church of Jesus Christ of Latter-Day Saints—popularly known as the Mormon Church. Surely, few if any of Smith's contemporaries would have predicted that his renegade sect would be, a century and a half down the road, among the most prosperous and fastest growing Christian churches in North America. It is a moot point whether Koresh's Branch Davidian movement—itself an offshoot of another American sectarian success story, Seventh-Day Adventism—could have similarly established itself as a freestanding church. That is the sort of question that only time can answer, although the Davidian remnant is far less substantial, in numbers or in leadership, than the Mormons Brigham Young led to Utah after Smith's murder.

The point of making the comparison between Smith's Latter-Day Saints and Koresh's Branch Davidians in this context is that the sins of which these groups and their leaders were judged guilty, both by the civil authorities and in the court of public opinion, were essentially the same: sexual misconduct involving plural marriage and alleged (though unsubstantiated) patterns of child abuse and the possession of large caches of firearms (the nature and number of which were in both cases inflated in press accounts). The matter of these arsenals, in particular, led to a public perception that these groups were violence-crazed and quite obviously dangerous to the common good.

Of course, every village on the nineteenth-century American frontier had its local militia. Smith's settlement in Nauvoo, Illinois, was therefore exceptional not for the existence of its Nauvoo Legion, but for its size and organization. Comprised of every able-bodied male between eighteen and forty-five, this was no ordinary militia. It was an "Army of the Lord," and it numbered four thousand by 1844, at which time the Saints were also building an armory and gun-powder factory.[1] Smith, who had a heavily armed twelve-man bodyguard, "took an expansive view of his powers,"[2] proudly wore his rank of general (he had been commissioned a lieutenant-general in the Illinois state militia by the governor), and fashioned an appropriately smart uniform for himself. Visitors to Nauvoo were often "troubled by the unmistakable military atmosphere that pervaded the city."[3]

Among these visitors were journalists, drawn by tales of Mormon debauchery, many of which were circulated by former members of the Saints community who had left or been expelled. The most prominent of these ex-Mormons was John Cook Bennett, whom Smith excommunicated for having used the evolving doctrine of celestial marriage as a cloak for serial fornication. In 1842, Bennett wrote a series of letters to a Springfield newspaper, detailing the crimes of "Holy Joe and his Danite band of murderers," which were subsequently collected and published in book form as *The History of the Saints: or, An Exposé of Joe Smith and Mormonism*. Among other things, Bennett—who had helped organize the Nauvoo Legion in the first place—vastly exaggerated the number of cannons and rifles in Mormon hands.[4] Bennett's book was the first in a long series of anti-Mormon propaganda, most of it fixating on the horrors of polygamy coupled with a purportedly endemic tendency to violence, which newspapers nationwide gleefully, and uncritically, reiterated.[5] These press reports, in their turn, fueled two generations of anti-Mormon public sentiment and popular support for government suppression of the Latter-Day Saints.

Smith had, in many ways, welcomed the controversy his prophetic career generated. Some anti-Mormon literature, reflecting an early strain of American "orientalism," likened him to Mohammed, who in the conventional wisdom of the mid-nineteenth century represented the classic case of the religious imposter who proclaimed a false message to a deluded band of followers so blindly loyal to him that they would kill at his behest.[6] Smith himself picked up the analogy in 1838, in a speech declaring Mormonism to be the "Islam of America:"[7]

> If the people will let us alone, we will preach the gospel in peace. But if they come on us to molest us, we will establish our religion by the sword. We will trample down our enemies and make it one gore of blood from the Rocky Mountains to the Atlantic Ocean. I will be to this generation a second Mohammed, whose motto in treating for peace was "the Alcoran or the Sword." So shall it eventually be with us—"Joseph Smith or the Sword!"[8]

When it reported the news of Smith's killing in 1844, the *New York Herald* remarked, "The death of the modern Mahomet will seal the fate of Mormonism. They cannot get another Joe Smith."[9]

What they got instead, of course, was the "American Moses," Brigham Young. Antipathy against the Mormons did not die with Smith. Under Young's leadership, polygamy became a much more prominent element of Mormon practice (spurring further Islam/Mormon comparisons), and violence perpetrated by and against Mormons accelerated to the extent that the U.S. government was essentially (often literally) at war with the Latter-Day Saints from 1852 until 1890, when the church discontinued the practice of plural marriage in Utah Territory, in order to pave the way for statehood.

In the preface of her classic biography of Smith, *No Man Knows My History,* Fawn Brodie wrote, "If one were unscrupulously selective in choosing details, one could make him out to be not only a prophet, but also a political menace—a dictator complete with army, propaganda ministry, and secret police who created an authoritarian dominion on the American frontier." Of course, she concluded, to present Smith in such fashion would be to "reject history for yellow journalism."[10] However, the pull to characterize the divergent religious leader as a danger to society is as strong today as it was in the nineteenth century, and the temptation to resort to yellow journalism in the name of the public good is, if anything, stronger. Many of the same allegations used to indict the character of Smith and his followers resurfaced in the press coverage of, and subsequent federal action against, David Koresh and the Mount Carmel community.

Few Americans had ever heard of the Branch Davidians before 1993, when the phrase entered the American public lexicon to describe a sinister "doomsday cult" founded by a charlatan named David Koresh. In fact, however, although press accounts routinely characterized Koresh and his followers as renegades or upstarts, the Davidian sect had been in existence since the 1920s, as an offshoot of the Seventh-Day Adventist Church. Indeed, the apocalyptic worldview that united the community at Mount Carmel, Koresh's role in that community, and the content of his preaching is incomprehensible without some understanding of Adventist theology. The failure of federal law enforcement authorities to gain such understanding was, arguably, the primary cause of the trail of events that left a total of ninety people dead outside of Waco, Texas, by April 19, 1993.

It was assumed then, as indeed it continues to be by most Americans today, that federal agents were justified in laying siege to Mount Carmel because of the threat a fiendish Koresh, the "wacko from Waco," posed to the community at large. As had been the case with Joseph Smith, the perception of Koresh as dangerously deranged was a direct result of propaganda generated by a former associate and sometime rival for power within the group, Marc Breault. Having "escaped" the Davidians in 1990, Breault, a self-styled "cultbuster," collaborated with Australian documentary filmmaker Martin King on *Inside the Cult,* the purpose of which was, as King later put it, "to expose [Koresh] as a cruel, maniacal, child-molesting, pistol-packing religious zealot who brainwashed his devotees into believing he was the Messiah, the reincarnation of Jesus Christ, and who would eventually lead them into an all-out war with the United States government and, finally, to their deaths."[11] Breault and King compared Mount Carmel to Jonestown, the American press followed their lead, and the two "cult" communities, although in historical reality quite distinct, became virtually interchangeable in the popular imagination.

In February 1993, shortly before the Bureau of Alcohol, Tobacco, and Firearms (BATF) raid on Mount Carmel, the *Waco Tribune-Herald* began a series of feature articles inspired by Breault. Immediately following the BATF action that killed four federal agents and six Davidians, this series entitled "The Sinful Messiah," was picked up by the national press and set the tone for subsequent media coverage. During the fifty-one-day siege, the national media fell into lockstep reportage regarding the sins of Koresh and his followers: They were child-abusers (the Texas Department of Child Welfare had investigated the community a year earlier and found no irregularities or reasons for concern); they were brainwashed zombies (videotaped interviews, withheld at the time from the media, demonstrated otherwise); they were engaged in the production of illegal drugs (a totally unsubstantiated charge, apparently created for the purpose of invoking the Posse Comitatus Act to allow the use of military force against civilians); and, most damning of all, they had amassed a huge arsenal, which included illegal weapons, and they were engaged in converting semiautomatic firearms to fully automatic machine guns, a violation of federal law.

As to this last charge, it is clearly true that the Branch Davidians were heavily armed—a fact, in itself, by no means unusual in Texas, historically a "gun culture" with some of the most liberal firearms statutes in the nation. The Davidians' motives for firearms possession were undoubtedly complex, and, alas, died with them. As religious historian Philip Jenkins puts it:

> The justification for this arsenal is uncertain. Some believe that the Davidians were training to fight the forces of evil in the coming Apocalypse, while law enforcement authorities have charged that the weapons might have been intended for terrorist violence. As the sect supported itself by legally trading weapons, the supposed arsenal might more properly be called a commercial inventory.[12]

What is clear is that there was no solid evidence that the Branch Davidians were engaged in illegally converting firearms, either for their own use or for sale on the black market. It is also clear that Koresh himself had strong feelings about the right to armed self-defense. In an interview taped during the siege against Mount Carmel, Koresh said, "I don't care who they are. Nobody is going to come to my home, with my babies around, shaking guns around, without a gun back in their face. That's just the American way." As James Tabor and Eugene Gallagher point out, "under

Texas law, he was correct . . . a citizen had the right to use armed force in self-defense, even against law-enforcement agents, if in his best judgment those authorities were exercising improper force in carrying out their duty."[13]

Of course, Koresh's judgment was assessed, by the Justice Department and its agents, to be that of a lunatic; they could only justify the assault against Mount Carmel on the grounds that they were not dealing with a reasonable person.[14] Agents of the FBI persisted in referring to Koresh's claim that he would only leave when he had completed his interpretation of the Seven Seals of *Revelation* as "Bible babble." Purportedly, some agents were so ignorant regarding Koresh's language that they thought the seals in question were aquatic mammals. This, in spite of the fact that religious scholars James Tabor and Phillip Arnold had endeavored to convince the FBI that Koresh's theological language was consistent with the Adventist style of biblical exegesis—a style at least as old as the allegorical hermeneutic developed by the church father Origen in the third century. Inspired by the inflammatory accounts of Breault and other defectors from the group, however, the FBI preferred to rely on expert advice from anticult psychologist Murray Miron and psychiatrist Park Dietz.[15] These men neither interviewed Koresh, nor were they versed in the language and dynamics of religious apocalypticism; they did, however, derive both prestige and income from the "deprogramming" industry.

Even as the FBI's aggressive actions depended on demonizing Koresh and stripping his message of any religious legitimacy, those same actions established for the Branch Davidians the fact that they were living "in the message" of the Fifth Seal. Armageddon was indeed at hand. Whether or not they had intentionally been arming themselves in conscious preparation for cosmic battle, they were now de facto an Army of the Lord. Not only did the federal authorities willingly, if unwittingly, walk right into the demonic role Davidian apocalypticism assigned them, throughout the siege they consistently performed according to type. This did not mean, however, that the tragic events of April 19 were preordained. As one Davidian survivor put it:

> Whilst it is true that we were aware of the fact they were coming even before they knew they were coming, it was not inevitable that events had to end the way they did. The final outcome was contingent on our adversaries' response to our efforts to communicate our position of faith. It will be clearly seen that all our efforts were ignored. Evidently the government wanted its deception, both for itself and its people.[16]

According to their reading of the Fifth Seal, the Davidians were willing to die as martyrs, if this was what God truly willed. The FBI obliged, as if fulfilling the wishes of this "doomsday cult." Philip Jenkins neatly sums up the dynamic that was at work:

Doomsday cult language came close to making millenarian expectation *ipso facto* a token of cultlike behavior and even a warning symptom of likely mass suicide. The "doomsday" label was applied indiscriminately to those who prophesied catastrophe no less than those who tried to provoke it, even to those like the Davidians who had Armageddon visited upon them. The terminology made possible a kind of grim comedy of errors in which official expectations would lead a sect to become more paranoid and defensive, which would in turn cause even more official nervousness and intervention. There are few limits to the force that can be levied against any group once it has been designated a doomsday cult, a self-fulfilling title if ever there was one. Invoking the specter of mass suicide almost ensures that mass deaths will ensue.[17]

What was it about the Branch Davidians, and before them the Mormons, that set this dynamic in tragic motion? At what point does divergence from the religious norm become a justification for the imposition of violence? It may be argued that in arming themselves the Mormons and Davidians provoked aggression by government authorities. It may just as readily be argued that, in light of the violence ultimately brought to bear against these communities, they had good reasons to arm themselves for the purpose of self-protection. When the siege at Waco ended on April 19 with the deaths of eighty Branch Davidians, sixteen of them under the age of five, Lakota activist Russell Means called it "the White's Man's Wounded Knee."[18] The comparison is instructive.

"Barbarism Personified"

I should let the dance continue. The coming of the troops has frightened the Indians. If the Seventh-Day Adventists prepare their ascension robes for the second coming of the Savior, the United States Army is not put in motion to prevent them. Why should not the Indians have the same privilege? If the troops remain, trouble is sure to come.—Indian Agent Valentine McGillycuddy, Pine Ridge, South Dakota, 1890

The Ghost Dance was a product of despair commingled with desperation. Sometime in 1870, a band of Paiute Indians, trapped by the U.S. Cavalry, were inspired by a young visionary named Wovoka. They began dancing. They fell into trance states, in which they saw visions of the dead. They came to believe they were living at the end of the world, with the dawning of a new age imminent: the native dead would return to life, the whites would retreat from Indian lands, peace and prosperity would prevail.[19] Wovoka came to be recognized as the Messiah, and his Ghost

Dance religion was a syncretistic blend of native and Christian elements, founded on three basic principles: "You must not fight. Do no harm to anyone. Do right always."[20] During the next twenty years of the Indian Wars, the Ghost Dance slowly spread throughout the Plains Indian territories. Its popularity increased in direct proportion to the deterioration of the native peoples' material situation. In one of the bitterer ironies in history, this pacifistic spiritual movement led indirectly to the deaths of three hundred Lakota, most of them women, children, and the elderly, in the bloody snow of Wounded Knee in December 1890.

From the government's point of view, a necessary component of the westward expansion of the American frontier, the Indian Wars were conducted largely by the forces of a post–Civil War Union Army in need of a military campaign to keep itself occupied. Although the motivation was economic—to overtake the Indian lands with their resources—the rationale was that this war was being fought for the sake of civilization. The spirit of the "War Policy" was summed up by Gen. Philip Sheridan: "Kill the buffalo, kill the Indians."[21] He recognized not only that the bison was the "Indians commissary" but also that the most effective way to crush the Plains tribes was to deprive them of their most potent religious symbol.

Opposing Sheridan and his colleagues in the military, supporters of the "Peace Policy," represented largely by Christian missionaries, urged restraint. This did not mean, however, that they were any less hostile to native religion. Both camps saw the Sun Dance as nothing short of barbaric. The goal of the Peace Policy was to Christianize the Indians in order to civilize them—in effect, to save the Indians from themselves, by stripping them of their Indianness. Government agents and missionaries alike therefore regarded holy men such as Sitting Bull, Black Elk, Wovoka, and other spiritual leaders as the most dangerous elements in Indian society. The following report by Agent McGillycuddy of Pine Ridge reservation captures the official spirit:

With the American Indian, as with other savage nations, the native medicine-man combines the calling of physician, priest, and prophet. He is, above all others, barbarism personified, and is through his influence over a superstitious following, one of the principle obstacles in the way of civilization. Therefore no effort or means should be neglected to destroy his influence and himself in his peculiar capacity.[22]

He penned these words in 1884, a year after the U.S. government—in direct violation of the First Amendment—had outlawed the Sun Dance.

Missionaries, of course, welcomed the ban on the Plains Indians' central religious and social ceremony because they believed it would make it easier to convert them. For partisans of the War Policy the ban was equally desirable because they perceived, with some accuracy, the connection between the Sun Dance and a warrior culture. Although the Sun Dance cannot be reduced to the stereotypical "war dance," there was a distinct correlation.[23] A huge Sun Dance, involving perhaps as many as thirty thousand people and apparently organized by Sitting Bull, was held shortly before the defeat of Custer's Seventh Cavalry at the Battle of the Little Big Horn in June 1876.

The rise in popularity of the Ghost Dance religion among the Lakota can be directly linked to the ban on the Sun Dance. The two rituals were in no way commensurate—indeed they were quite different in spirit and intent—yet in the awful circumstances in which the people found themselves by the late 1880s, the Ghost Dance apparently provided some hope for the future and for a return to essentially Indian values, to those who refused to become "hang-around-the-fort-people." Sitting Bull himself, under house arrest at Pine Ridge, began to perform the Ghost Dance, with eventually devastating outcome. According to Congregationalist missionary Mary Collins, who witnessed it:

> [Sitting Bull's Ghost Dance] became almost like the Sun dance and was continued from evening until morning and from dawn till night. . . . As the excitement grew, the dance became wilder and more excited. People gathered by the thousands and the dance became more and more like the sun dance which was forbidden by the government.[24]

Military men cared little for the ritual distinctions between the two forms of dancing; when they saw something that began to look like a war dance, they assumed that trouble was brewing. That assumption was reinforced by erroneous press reports that Wovoka was really a Mormon in Indian disguise and "had been preaching a bloody campaign against the whites."[25] It was against this background that McGillycuddy, who appears to have been something of a pragmatist, issued the recommendation of tolerance quoted at the beginning of this section. His wise advice was not heeded. By the close of 1890, Lakota were Ghost Dancing at Pine Ridge and Rosebud, at Standing Rock and on the banks of Wounded Knee Creek. And on December 15, Sitting Bull was assassinated, in much the same fashion as Crazy Horse had been, under the pretense of "resisting arrest."

The attention of the Seventh Cavalry then turned to the holy man Big Foot and his encampment at Wounded Knee. Big Foot himself was gravely ill with pneumonia. His camp of 350 persons, mostly women, the elderly, and children, included about a hundred warriors, most of whom had already given up their weapons. Colonel James Forsyth surrounded the camp, on the pretense of preparing to help Big Foot's people relocate to Pine Ridge, although the actual plan (which may or may not have leaked to the Lakota) was to transport them by train to a federal prison camp in Oklahoma. When the morning of December 29 dawned cold and sunny, it is possible neither cavalrymen nor Indians knew what carnage lay ahead.

Accounts of exactly what happened conflict sharply, depending upon who is doing the telling, but the essential outline is clear: the Seventh Cavalry, nursing a fourteen-year-old grudge after the Little Big Horn, were prepared for battle; they outnumbered the Lakota warriors five-to-one, they were armed not only with rifles and sidearms but also with Hotchkiss guns (wagon-borne cannons). Forsyth ordered the warriors to forfeit whatever remaining arms they had. When the number of guns surrendered seemed too low to him, he ordered his men to search the camp: they ransacked tipis and manhandled the women and children. Additional weapons were discovered, and tempers flared on both sides. All the while, a medicine-man named Yellow Bird had been Ghost Dancing and singing. The soldiers assumed he was inciting violence. He blew on an eagle-bone whistle, threw a handful of dust into the air, and at about the same time a shot was fired by a young warrior named Black Fox.

At this point, the army and Lakota versions of the story diverge—the former asserting that Black Fox freely fired this first hostile shot, the latter claiming either that his gun went off accidentally in the struggle that ensued when a soldier tried to wrest it from him or that he was framed after the fact, and no Lakota shots were fired. In any event, what happened next is clear: Forsyth's men returned fire with a volley that killed as many as half the warriors immediately. Hand-to-hand combat ensued, the Indians fighting primarily with knives, as the Hotchkiss guns delivered two-pound explosive shells at the rate of fifty per minute. According to an eyewitness account:

> In a few minutes 200 hundred [sic] Indian men, women, and children, with 60 soldiers, were lying dead and wounded on the ground, the tipis had been torn down by the shells and some of them were burning above the helpless wounded, and the surviving handful of Indians were flying in wild panic to the shelter of the ravine, pursued by hundreds of maddened soldiers and followed up by a raking fire from the Hotchkiss guns, which had been moved into position to sweep the ravine.[26]

The bodies of some of the women and children were found as far as two miles from the camp. Many of the roughly three hundred killed were wearing the Ghost Dance shirts that they believed would make their bodies impervious to bullets.

Wounded Knee, of course, would become the predominant symbol among American Indians for the fact that the policy of the U.S. government in their regard amounted to genocide. By the mid-twentieth century, when under the Eisenhower administration the official program with regard to Indian culture was chillingly dubbed "Termination," the legacy of Wounded Knee was all too clear: a trail not only of broken treaties, but of thwarted lives, and a native culture in many ways at war with itself.[27] That tide began to turn with the rise of the American Indian Movement (AIM), under the leadership of such activists as Russell Means, Dennis Banks, and the medicine man Leonard Crow Dog. Although AIM was primarily a political movement, it coincided with a renewed interest among young activists in the "old ways." There was a spiritual subtext to the stand that the Lakota and other Indian people took in 1973: Wounded Knee II, their seventy-one-day occupation of the site of the massacre, which evoked a government response that amounted to the largest armed action in the United States since the Civil War. It was as if the Ghost Dance religion had returned—and in a sense it had, to the extent that the U.S. government deemed violent counterforce the only appropriate response to an assertion of Indian autonomy. When Means and Banks were tried in 1974 on federal charges arising from the occupation, they invoked the broken Fort Laramie Treaty of 1868 and declared, "It's really the United States that's on trial, not us." The judge ultimately agreed, dismissing all charges against them "because of federal and prosecutorial misconduct, including evidence of illegal wiretapping, withholding of evidence, and the U.S. military's clandestine involvement in the occupation of Wounded Knee."[28] Meanwhile, as Peter Matthiessen and others have documented, the FBI had declared war on AIM in ways strikingly similar to the actions it subsequently took against the Branch Davidians.[29]

It was against this background that Means placed Waco and Wounded Knee on the same political and symbolic plane:

INTERVIEWER: Were you being literal, or symbolic, or both?

MEANS: Both. The massacre of my people at Wounded Knee was symbolic to us in that that was our last chance to be free. Koresh represented the same thing: The last chance to be free in America . . . for people to be different. The fact that the government killed men, women and children with impunity . . . the scariest part is that Waco's even more dangerous, a bigger warning light . . . it's like the miner's canary. You see, Felix Cohen, a legal scholar back in the 1920s put together all of the spare Indian laws into one collection and called it Indian Law in the United States. . . . He said "the American Indian is the miner's canary for liberty in this country."

INTERVIEWER: What happened to you will happen to the rest of us . . .

MEANS: Exactly. He was very prophetic. This was the last light that went out, when the government will attack white people, white women and children and babies, and massacre them and then lie about it, that is the worst sign.[30]

Despite the constitutional guarantee of religious freedom, there has long been a tendency in America to be highly selective when it comes to which forms of divergence from the religious norm our government is willing to tolerate. There has also been a tendency to use the perceived "craziness" or "extremeness" or "dangerousness" of certain perspectives as an excuse for violent government interference in the beliefs and practices of religious communities—too often, as at Wounded Knee and Waco, with disastrous consequences.

The same dynamic that has become so familiar in American religio-political history is arguably now at work in the "War against Terror." It is far easier to pathologize or to demonize religiously rooted political perspectives that we don't really want to understand than to make any move toward comprehending them that might lend them even a fragment of credibility—or that might bring us to the point of acknowledging the degree to which American domestic and foreign policy are shaped by a militaristically inspired mainline Christianity. In this climate, the question "Why do so many Muslims hate us?" rings both hollow and naïve.

The ultimate question, to which we must now turn, has to do with the extent to which the U.S. government is capable of waging "holy war" against divergent religious and political forces—indeed, has been, with increasingly intense ferocity, and with a correspondingly blatant unself-consciousness.

"Black and White, Heaven and Hell"

As the cases of the Mormons, the Branch Davidians, and the Plains Indians make clear, the characteristic American response is to demonize armed and potentially dangerous divergent religious groups. This demonization rests on the firm (Protestant-inspired) foundation of truth, justice, and the "American Way." One fights emergent holy wars by becoming a holy warrior oneself. As Mark Juergensmeyer has pointed out regarding religiously motivated violence, the fact that some groups are "marginal . . . does not mean that they are intrinsically different from mainstream religion. . . . These movements are not simply aberrations but religious responses to social situations and expressions of deeply held convictions." He goes on to remark that in interviewing "supporters of these cultures of violence," he was "struck with the intensity of their quests for a deeper level of spirituality than that offered by the superficial values of the modern world."[31] Tabor and Gallagher make a kindred point, that for many people one of the most troubling things about groups such as the Branch Davidians is the depth of their commitment to an alternative ideal. "The anticultists' vigorous defense of traditional religion, the nuclear family, personal autonomy, and other core values against the challenge of the 'cults' allows them to locate the vexing problems of Americans and American society outside themselves in a dangerous and alien 'other.'"[32]

If this dynamic has been observable in American domestic relations, it is even more obvious in the Bush administration's stance since September 11, 2001. From his first comments characterizing Osama bin Laden as the "Evil One" and his followers as "the evildoers," President Bush has employed explicitly Christian theological language to characterize, and to justify, American foreign policy. In his Easter weekend radio address, he commented, "For those who observe Easter and Passover, faith brings confidence that failure is never final, and suffering is temporary, and the pains of the earth will be overcome. We can be confident, too, that evil may be present and it may be strong, but it will not prevail." The war against terrorism, he reaffirmed, is a conflict between cosmic forces of light and darkness: "In this season, we are assured that history is of moral design. Justice and cruelty have always been at war, and God is not neutral between them. His purposes are often defied, but never defeated."[33] Speaking in China a few weeks earlier, President Bush had remarked that "faith points to a moral law beyond man's law and calls us to duties higher than material gain." In this context, he called the United States "a nation with the soul of a church."[34]

Attorney General John Ashcroft is of like mind. "We are," he told a group of Christian broadcasters, "a nation called to defend freedom—a tradition that is not a grant of any government or document, but is an endowment from God.[35] Given such a lofty commission, it is not surprising that Ashcroft has assumed that anyone calling into question the American conduct of the war against terror is, ipso facto, giving aid and comfort to the enemy. His world, as journalist Jeffrey Toobin remarked recently, is a world of binary oppositions, "black and white, heaven and hell." Toobin tied this oppositional view directly to Ashcroft's being "a very religious man."[36] The same fact was, of course, frequently and accurately remarked during his presidency about Jimmy Carter, who shares Ashcroft's fundamentalist Christian perspective. Yet, tellingly, neither did this lead Carter into a polar opposition of heavens and hells (rather the opposite, in fact), nor—more importantly— did it provide the basis for a public affirmation of the conflation of public officials' private religiosity and the public policy they craft.

What makes it more possible for the public to accept this conflation today than it did twenty-five years ago has largely to do with the nature of the enemy: during the cold war, the Communist Bloc may have been "godless," but they looked in other obvious respects pretty much like us. The enemy America faces today is not only more shadowy but also more divergent from the American religious and social norms, and hence far easier to "satanize"[37] in the terms already familiar from the federal government's handling of religious divergence at home. As several commentators have pointed out, this essentializing of the "evildoers" has profound implications for the ability of the American people to think through the meaning of American foreign policy. Benjamin Barber, editor of *Jihad vs. McWorld*, observes:

"Bad seed" notions of original sin ("the evil ones") actually render perpetrators invulnerable—subject only to a manichean struggle in which the alternative to total victory is total defeat. Calling bin Laden and his associates "the evil ones" is not necessarily inaccurate, but it commits us to a dark world of *jihad* and counter*jihad* (what the President first called his crusade), in which issues of democracy, civil comity, and social justice—let alone nuance, complexity and interdependence—simply vanish. It is possible to hate *jihad* without loving America. It is possible to condemn terror as absolutely wrong without thinking that those who are terror's targets possess absolute right.[38]

In a similar vein, jurist Patricia Williams remarks the oddity of invoking the language of "Evil Ones" or "Bad Guys"

as though our leaders were speaking to very young children. By this, Al Qaeda is placed in an almost biblical narrative, ready to be smote and cast out. In this forum, giving The Evil Ones so mundane a forum as a trial is literally "courting" the devil. While this sort of embedded language has certainly galvanized the people in a time of great crisis, I don't believe it's a useful long-term model for a democratic secular government trying to fight real political foes, particularly stateless enemies who are religious zealots in their own right. . . . They are humans, not demons.[39]

The black hats–white hats approach to international justice nonetheless appeals to those who want to keep the distinction between a righteous Us and a demonic Them in place, who counter criticisms of American foreign policy with a complacent, "We're right, they're wrong, get over it."[40]

If it has been easy for the American majority, prompted by government rhetoric and a cooperative press, to demonize such homegrown groups as we considered earlier, it almost comes naturally to extend the stigma of "dangerous other" to Muslims. We are, as Edward Said has demonstrated, well versed in our Orientalism. We assume that Arabs and Muslims (and the terms are in the popular mind virtually interchangeable) are rigorously conformist and shame-obsessed, that they "can function only in conflict situations," that in their culture prestige is strictly a matter of dominance over others, that they are fundamentally less objective or rational than we are, that in short everything about their behavior, "which from *our* point of view is 'aberrant' . . . for Arabs is 'normal.'"[41] They are further, as Bernard Lewis has argued in a number of works,[42] trapped in their historical past, collectively conscious that in world-historical terms their culture and influence "peaked" a millennium ago. Thus for the past several months we have heard in the media a near-constant refrain about the "clash of civilizations" symbolized by the September 11 attacks. The appeal here is to the thesis first advanced in 1993 by Samuel Huntington,

> that the fundamental source of conflict in this new world will not be primarily ideological or primarily economic. The great divisions among humankind and the dominating source of conflict will be cultural. Nation states will remain the most powerful actors in world affairs, but the principal conflicts of global politics will occur between nations and groups of different civilizations. The clash of civilizations will dominate global politics. The fault lines between civilizations will be the battle lines of the future.[43]

This essentializing opposition of irreducibly different civilizations meshes perfectly with the binary worldview driving the Bush administration's policy making. But as Said remarks, what we have here is actually a clash of ignorance: "'The Clash of Civilizations' thesis is a gimmick like 'The War of the Worlds,' better for reinforcing defensive self-pride than for critical understanding of the bewildering interdependence of our time."

It must be observed, in this light, as Avishai Margalit and Ian Buruma did in an important essay in *The New York Review of Books*, that a concomitant "Occidentalism" has long been at work in Asiatic cultures, and to similarly self-limiting effect. In that regard, "West" and "East" mirror each other:

> When politics and religion merge, collective aims, often promoted in the name of love and justice, tend to compass the whole world, or at least large chunks of it. The state is a secular construct. The Brotherhood of Islam, the Church of Rome, All the World Under One Japanese Roof, world communism, all in their different ways have had religious or millenarian goals. Such goals are not unknown in the supposedly secular states of the West either. Especially in the US, right-wing Christian organizations and other religious pressure groups have sought to inject their religious values and agendas into national politics in ways that would have shocked the Founding Fathers. That Reverend Jerry Falwell described the terrorist attacks on New York and Washington as a kind of punishment for our worldly sins showed that his thinking is not so far removed from that of the Islamists.[44]

Thinking along lines not too far removed from Falwell, if admittedly different in spirit, Andrew Sullivan argued in the *New York Times Magazine* that the real war America is fighting is against religious fundamentalism—with the clear, if unintentional, implication that it is up to the United States to defend mainstream religion against divergence.[45]

At what point does religious divergence become sufficiently dangerous that the state needs to move in to protect the public from it? As the historical cases cited earlier demonstrate, government-sponsored violence against ostensibly dangerous religious groups has not served our democracy well. Nor has the assumption that the truly dangerous "Other" is external to our culture—recall the first two days after the Oklahoma City bombing, when government and the media jumped to the conclusion that the perpetrators of what was then the largest terrorist crime on American soil must have been Islamic militants. Muslims were detained for interrogation here and abroad. It turned out, of course, that the mastermind was not only American born and bred, but also a Gulf War veteran who chose the second anniversary of the assault at Mount Carmel to make his antigovernment statement. Timothy McVeigh was trained in the methods of attack by the U.S. military. He appears to have had sympathetic ties to the far-right-wing "Christian Identity" movement; indeed, his worldview was no doubt closer to Jerry Falwell's than to Osama bin Laden's.[46]

A government that exerts violent force against its own citizens, and perhaps especially one that does so believing God is on its side, will continue to create the likes of McVeigh, as well as Osama bin Laden—a point McVeigh himself ironically put his finger on, when at his sentencing hearing he chose to quote Supreme Court Justice Louis Brandeis: "Our government is the potent, the omnipresent teacher," Brandeis had written, "for good or ill, it teaches the whole people by its example."[47] Now, as perhaps never before in our history, it is crucial that the government learn the lessons of its own history.

In the wake of World War II, Reinhold Niebuhr warned that in the world-political battles between the Children of Light and the Children of Darkness, it is the former who are, ultimately, more to be feared—not because their intentions are bad, but rather because they are so good as to warrant universal application. If religion has any place in political rhetoric undergirding the war against terrorism, it is the one Niebuhr discerned for it:

There is a religious solution to the problem of religious diversity. This solution makes religious and cultural diversity possible within the presuppositions of a free society, without destroying the religious depth of culture. The solution requires a very high form of religious commitment. It demands that each religion, or each version of a single faith, seek to proclaim its highest insights while yet preserving an humble and contrite recognition of the fact that all actual expressions of religious faith are subject to historical contingency and relativity. Such a recognition creates a spirit of tolerance and makes any religious or cultural movement hesitant to claim official validity for its form of religion or to demand an official monopoly for its cult.[48]

Niebuhr's sentiment is as apt—and, sadly, as fresh—today as it was a half-century ago. The task facing our policy makers is to keep religion in its proper place and to keep America out of the business of waging holy war.

NOTES

1. Stanley P. Hirshson, *The Lion of the Lord: A Biography of Brigham Young* (New York: Alfred A. Knopf, 1969), 50; Fawn M. Brodie, *No Man Knows My History* (New York: Alfred A. Knopf, 1945), 357.

2. Leonard J. Arrington, *Brigham Young: American Moses* (New York: Alfred A. Knopf, 1985), 103. Arrington, writing from within the Mormon perspective, asserts reasonably enough that Joseph Smith's somewhat inflated view of himself as a military leader and his militia as a standing army was owed at least in part to fear of repetitions of the violence that had been visited on the Mormons by their neighbors and by civil authorities in Ohio and Missouri.

3. Brodie, *No Man Knows My History*, 270–71.

4. Ibid., 314. The Danites were originally Smith's "Armies of Israel"; however, with the formal development of the Nauvoo Legion, the name reverted to an undercover paramilitary brotherhood, at best loosely related to the Nauvoo Legion itself, which often engaged in criminal activity. As to the number of armaments, when the Nauvoo Legion was chartered by the state of Illinois, they were provided with three cannons and about two hundred and fifty small arms; Bennett inflated the number of cannons to thirty, and contributed to rumors that the Army of the Lord was in possession of five to six thousand long guns.

5. See, for example, the anti-Mormon tract about "how women and girls are snared" by Mormonism, *Uncle Sam's Abscess: Hell upon Earth! Startling Revelations, for Saints and Sinners*, by William Jarmon, "ex-Mormon priest," reproduced in Hirshson, *Lion of the Lord*.

6. On the history of this idea, see Edward Said, *Orientalism* (New York: Vintage, 1979), 60–65.

7. Philip Jenkins, *Mystics and Messiahs: Cults and New Religions in American History* (New York: Oxford Univ. Press, 2000), 31.

8. Brodie, *No Man Knows My History*, 230–31. Smith was, it should be remarked, speaking in the heat of passion and at the height of anti-Mormon violence in Missouri.

9. *New York Herald*, July 8, 1844, qtd. by Hirshson, *Lion of the Lord*, 48. It bears noting that, in general, the *Herald* was less critical of Smith than most of the mainstream press.

10. Brodie, *No Man Knows My History*, viii.

11. Qtd. in James D. Tabor and Eugene V. Gallagher, *Why Waco? Cults and the Battle for Religious Freedom in America* (Berkeley: Univ. of California Press, 1995), 84–85. On the role the press played in constructing Koresh as "the wacko from Waco," see chapter 6, 117–45.

12. Jenkins, *Mystics and Messiahs*, 217.

13. Tabor and Gallagher, *Why Waco?* 64–65.

14. It bears noting, in this regard, that one need not see Koresh as either sane or a religious leader to come to the conclusion that what the federal authorities did at Waco was terribly wrong. Lawyers David B. Kopel and Paul H. Blackman, although taking a dim view of Koresh's character, nevertheless mount a powerful indictment of the Waco siege and subsequent government justifications of it in *No More Wacos: What's Wrong with Federal Law Enforcement and How to Fix It* (Amherst, N.Y.: Prometheus, 1997).

15. See Tabor and Gallagher, *Why Waco?* on these men and their credentials. Dietz, more recently, distinguished himself as the only psychiatrist testifying for either side in the trial of Andrea Yates, who was not willing to say that she was psychotic on the day she killed her five children. He was testifying for the prosecution.

16. Livingstone Fagan, qtd. by Tabor and Gallagher, *Why Waco?* 78. Fagan, imprisoned for aiding and abetting the commission of voluntary manslaughter as a result of the February 28 BATF raid, emerged as the major spokesperson for the Branch Davidians after Koresh's death.

17. Jenkins, *Mystics and Messiahs*, 222.

18. Robert L. Jones, "A Conversation with Russell Means," interview conducted March 15, 2000, www.home.flash.net/~park29/means_1.htm (accessed June 2000).

19. The classic study of the Ghost Dance as a product of desperation is Weston LaBarre, *The Ghost Dance: Origins of Religion* (London: Allen and Unwin, 1972). For a good description of the visionary experience of the Ghost Dancer, see John G. Neihardt, *Black Elk Speaks: Being the Life Story of a Holy Man of the Oglala Sioux* (Lincoln: Univ. of Nebraska Press, 1979), 230–47.

20. James Mooney, *The Ghost-Dance Religion and Wounded Knee* (New York: Dover, 1973), 777. Mooney was one of the early ethnologists to study the Plains Indian cultures firsthand. This is a facsimile edition of his "The Ghost-Dance Religion and the Sioux Outbreak of 1890," originally published in the *Fourteenth Annual Report (Part 2) of the Bureau of Ethnology to the Smithsonian Institution, 1892–93, by J. W. Powell, Director*, U.S. Government Printing Office, in 1896.

21. Cited in Linda Hasselstrom, *Bison: Monarch of the Plains* (Portland, Ore.: Graphic Arts Center, 1998), 62. In an endnote, Hasselstrom points out that, like so many other familiar slogans, these words entered the public lexicon as a shorthand form of what Sheridan had actually said. Speaking before the Texas state legislature and referring to the bison as the "Indian's commissary," Sheridan went on to remark: "Instead of stopping the hunters, they ought to give them a hearty, unanimous vote of thanks, and appropriate a sufficient sum of money to strike and present to each one a medal of bronze, with a dead buffalo on one side and a discouraged Indian on the other" (122). Sheridan also bequeathed to history the idea that the only good Indian was a dead one: "The only good Indians I ever saw were dead," a remark he made in 1869, is his sole entry in the 16th edition of *Bartlett's Familiar Quotations*.

22. Qtd. in Clyde Holler, *Black Elk's Religion: The Sun Dance and Lakota Catholicism* (Syracuse, N.Y.: Syracuse Univ. Press, 1995), 123.

23. See Holler, *Black Elk's Religion*, for example, on the warrior elements in Black Elk's variation on the theme—elements that John Neihardt for the most part eliminated in *Black Elk Speaks*.

24. Holler, *Black Elk's Religion*, 135.

25. Mooney, *Ghost-Dance Religion*, 766.

26. Mooney, *Ghost-Dance Religion*, 869. I have relied largely on his account, drawn from several eyewitnesses. For the most comprehensive compilation of documents relating to the massacre at Wounded Knee, see William S. E. Coleman, *Voices of Wounded Knee* (Lincoln: Univ. of Nebraska Press, 2000).

27. On these themes, see Vine Deloria Jr., *Custer Died for Your Sins: An Indian Manifesto* (New York: Macmillan, 1969), and the documentary film *The Spirit of Crazy Horse* (Pacific Arts Video Productions/PBS Home Video, 1991).

28. Brian Wagaman, review of John William Sayer, *Ghost Dancing and the Law: The Wounded Knee Trials*, H-PCAACA, H-Net Reviews, December 1998. www.h-net.msu.edu/reviews/showrev.cgi?path=21313913131882.

29. See Peter Matthiessen, *In the Spirit of Crazy Horse* (New York: Penguin, 1992), and Michael Apted's documentary film *Incident at Oglala* (Carolco International N.V. and Spanish Fork Motion Picture Company, 1991).

30. Jones, "A Conversation with Russell Means."

31. Mark Juergensmeyer, *Terror in the Mind of God: The Global Rise of Religious Violence* (Berkeley: Univ. of California Press, 2000), 221–22.

32. Tabor and Gallagher, *Why Waco?* 181.

33. "Bush Strikes Religious Note in an Address for Holidays," *New York Times*, March 31, 2002.

34. "Bush Urges Freedom of Worship in China," *New York Times*, February 22, 2002.

35. Qtd. by Rob Morse, "The Gospel According to John (Ashcroft)," *San Francisco Chronicle*, February 22, 2002.

36. Jeffrey Toobin interview on CNN, *American Morning*, April 8, 2002.

37. The term is Juergensmeyer's. For his helpful discussion of the process of satanization, see *Terror in the Mind of God*, 182–86.

38. Benjamin R. Barber, "Beyond *Jihad* vs. McWorld: On Terrorism and the New Democratic Realism," *The Nation* (Jan. 21, 2002): 17.

39. Patricia J. Williams, "The Beloved Community," *The Nation* (Feb. 11, 2002): 9.

40. Paul Mulshine, "We're Right, They're Wrong, Get Over It," *Boston Herald*, March 10, 2002. Mulshine concluded this column celebrating American freedom as opposed to Muslim repression thusly: "Either we have to change or they have to change. I vote for them."

41. Said, *Orientalism*, 48. He is here summarizing a psychological profile of "the inner workings of Arab behavior" by Harold W. Glidden, published in the February 1972 issue of the *American Journal of Psychiatry*.

42. See, for example, Lewis, *Cultures in Conflict: Christians, Muslims and Jews in the Age of Discovery* (New York: Oxford Univ. Press, 1995), and *What Went Wrong? Western Impact and Middle Eastern Response* (New York: Oxford Univ. Press, 2002).

43. Qtd. by Edward Said, "The Clash of Ignorance," *The Nation* 273, no. 12 (Oct. 22, 2001): 11–13.

44. Avishai Margalit and Ian Buruma, "Occidentalism," *New York Review of Books* 49, no. 1 (Jan. 17, 2002): 4–7.

45. Andrew Sullivan, "This *Is* a Religious War," *New York Times Magazine*, October 7, 2001.

46. On this theme, see Juergensmeyer, *Terror in the Mind of God*, 30–36.

47. Qtd. ibid., 164.

48. Reinhold Niebuhr, *The Children of Light and the Children of Darkness* (New York: Scribner's, 1953), 134–35.

Yesterday's Love, Today's Ruins

Walker Percy's Apocalyptic Vision

Paul L. Gaston

In 1972, within months of the publication of Walker Percy's third novel, *Love in the Ruins*, I published an article detailing the principal elements of what the book jacket concedes is a "not wholly serious apocalypse." Given the depth of the novel's grounding in the novelist's immediate circumstances and environment, I described it, with a glance at the New Testament, as Percy's *Revelation*.[1] Shortly afterward, Percy wrote me a thoughtful note to express his thanks and concluded with a postscript: "St. John of Patmos: pretty classy company!"

Since then, there have been several far more extensive and discerning studies of the apocalyptic elements in Percy's novel, most notably that of Gary Ciuba in his 1991 book, *Walker Percy: Books of Revelations*.[2] As a result, it is now widely appreciated that Percy's novel follows through on the design he intimated in a 1967 letter to his friend Shelby Foote. His "futurist novel" would deal with both democracy, that is, "the decline and fall of the U.S.," and with religion, that is, "the goodness of God."[3] Subtitled *The Adventures of a Bad Catholic at a Time Near the End of the World*, the novel would describe "bad times" in both spiritual and political terms: "Principalities and powers are everywhere victorious. Wickedness flourishes in high places" (5).[4]

The fabric of this "futurist novel" is reasonably straightforward. The protagonist, Dr. Thomas More, is a semiretired, apathetic physician and a descendant of the English saint and politician Sir Thomas More. From his southeastern Louisiana perspective on the late 1970s, Dr. More believes that society is on the point of collapse and that the world may end soon. He has attempted to prepare for this eventuality by creating a haven for himself and three girlfriends in an abandoned motel. His great invention, a device capable of diagnosing and treating ills of the spirit, has fallen into the hands of a sleazy salesman, and his delight in gin fizzes, to which he is allergic, may well kill him. The novel reaches its climax in a brief confrontation between Dr.

More and the salesman, then concludes with a subdued portrait of a society five years later that has made room for Dr. More as a contented physician, husband, and father.

What prompts a return to a novel now largely neglected is the theme of the third annual Kent State University Symposium on Democracy, "Democracy and Religion: Free Exercise and Diverse Visions," which both justifies a fresh look at Percy's handling of democracy and religion and poses direct questions about the kinds of tension he creates between the two. By examining these tensions, we may be better able to appreciate more fully why Percy's novel should continue to interest us and to gain a clearer awareness of what it accomplishes.

To be sure, in one respect, the thirty years that have passed since the novel's publication in 1971 have been unkind to it. Its pointed observations regarding the 1970s now seem dated, and its topical prescience, although in many respects more striking now than when the novel was published (see, for instance, Percy's diagnosis of "a secret and paradoxical conviction that America is immovable and indestructible"),[5] seem at best peripheral to the novel's principal values and, at worst, distracting.

But it is the increasing obscurity of the novel's contemporary context, its targets and determinations, that has thrown into clearer relief its ultimate concerns: faith, government (broadly understood), and the unstable but essential relation between the two. No longer troubled by references to "Dutch theologians," research on sexual dysfunction, or the John Birch Society, we may be better able to gain a clearer impression of just how high the stakes were for Percy in this novel—and just how high they remain for us today.

One clue to the close connection between issues of religious faith and those of polity lies in the novel's persistent reference to Dr. More's illustrious ancestor, namesake, and alter ego. For Sir Thomas More, as for many of his sixteenth-century contemporaries, there was a firm correspondence between a proper order within the beliefs and observances of individuals, on the one hand, and order in the state, on the other. Indeed, the word *government* was understood to refer both to the administration of a state and to the management of one's life, one's "conduct" and "behavior." (It is in this sense that Spenser's Red Cross Knight relies on "wary government" to avoid the moral "darts" thrown at him.) As suggested by the affinity between the two senses of the word, the "government" of a state expresses the extent to which those who belong to it observe "wary government" in their lives, just as individual behavior finds its authority in that of the monarch and the court.

For Percy's failed physician, Dr. Thomas More, this connection becomes all too vivid. From his perspective as a "bad Catholic at a time near the end of the world," the "coming apart" of the United States follows inevitably, indeed expresses, the "secret ills of the spirit" that have undermined the integrity of individuals before God. In Dr. More's words, it is "the very soul of Western man that is in the very act of flying apart HERE and NOW" (115). Speaking in 1971, just months before the publication of the novel, Percy made the link explicit. The split shown in the novel "between left and right, white and black, young and old; between Los Angeles and San Francisco, between Chicago and Cicero" mirrors "a split within the person, a split between the person's self, a ghostly self which abstracts from the world and has identity crises, and the person's body."[6]

It is only in the light of this apocalyptic awareness that Dr. More's halting, only partly intended, but at least temporarily successful, effort to spare humankind from catastrophe can be fully appreciated. Through the days leading up to the confrontation that represents the climax of the novel, Dr. More comes to understand that the social and political directions he has ineffectually resisted and in part adopted are the expression of a force that is offensive to him personally, dangerous to the country, and menacing for all creation. He concludes that he must resist this force with all available effort if the restoration of government, in both senses of the word, is to be made possible.

Both the novel itself and Percy's comments on it suggest just how seriously he took the fable he created. The concerns for American society and for the human soul embodied in the novel are not mere mimetic devices framed to float a fiction, but animating perceptions that propel and sustain what would otherwise be a dated experiment in futuristic satire. These perceptions of correspondences between the decay of democratic values and the festering of spiritual lesions prompt the organization of the novel, sustain its development, and interpret its denouement.

Although a full exposition of the alignments between social and spiritual decay in *Love in the Ruins* is beyond the scope of a brief essay, a review of three broad concerns—imbalance, irreverence, and insecurity—can suggest the more important of the novel's two thematic emphases. (A reminder that apocalyptic writing is characteristically dynamic, that is, moving toward catastrophe, suggests the other.) By observing the alignments among these concerns as they appear within the impetus of the plot, we can understand more clearly just how critical to the novel's purpose is its juxtaposition and correlation of political and spiritual issues, its relating of democracy to religion.

Of course, there must be a caveat. "Democracy" in this context represents not an objectively defined political system, but the welter of cultural, political, and even physiological perspectives on American society assembled within the novel. Similarly, "religion" refers to the idiosyncratic impressions (on skepticism, denominational schism, Catholicism) and the singular experiences (including active commerce with the diabolical) of the protagonist/narrator.

With this caveat in mind, the three broad concerns pursued within the novel (imbalance, irreverence, and insecurity) can be seen to describe both a democratic society that has lost its grip and the deterioration of a physician whose health, "especially my mental health," is "very poor" (11). And it is no coincidence that each of these terms points to the degradation of a value—balance, reverence, and security—typically associated both with sound government, in the usual political sense, and with the psychological and spiritual stability of the individual.

Imbalance may be the most conspicuous and important of the symptoms afflicting both the body politic and the spirit of the protagonist. A collapse of equilibrium in both political and personal terms has resulted in the clash of competing dualisms. Traditional political dichotomies, for example, liberal and conservative, Democrat and Republican, northern and southern, wealthy and poor, no longer invite compromise and an effort to achieve consensus but move inexorably to confrontation and schism. One consequence of such divisions and a cause of their having grown deeper is the nation's abiding materialism, which in turn leads to a tolerance for the very disparities that help to fuel the threatened revolution. But as Percy indicated, these dichotomies, as serious as they may be for American society, attest in Dr. More's eyes to an even more important crisis, the sundered souls of American citizens who are as divided within themselves as the nation itself.

The concern is not so much that polarities exist, but that instead of moving closer to synthesis, they are flying further apart. On the political level, the prevailing centrifugal force creates ever smaller and more intransigent factions. On the spiritual level, the creative tension in humanity between earthly sovereignty and heavenly aspiration has become an excruciating contest for dominance. "Angelism" and "bestialism" threaten to pull the creature apart, effectively thwarting the realization of either human capacity. It is an indication of Dr. More's hubris that he proposes to address this threat, to bridge "the dead chasm between body and mind that has sundered the soul of Western man for five hundred years" (90).

Moreover, as Percy suggests, comparison of these two arenas, political and spiritual, points not only to the presence of such correspondences but also to the possibility of causal links between them. That is, just as the corrosive dichotomy on a personal level creates a myopic intensity appropriate to narrow interest groups, so too does the fragmented political landscape exacerbate the individual's leaning toward insularity and fanaticism.

Irreverence, in the broad sense of a lack of respect for established values, beliefs, and authorities, is hardly less important, for, even more than social and spiritual *imbalance*, irreverence propels the progress of the novel toward its climax and helps to account for the plangent tone of its afterword. Just as the imbalance shown in the novel rests on an unhealthy tension between persuasions that may possess some value in themselves, so too does irreverence represent a distortion of rational standards: democracy's separation of church and state on the one hand, and the individual's respect for the implicit distinction between the church as social institution and as mediator between heaven and earth on the other.

Both principles survive as vestiges in the world of *Love in the Ruins*, yet each has become diluted and ineffectual. The separation of church and state hardly matters anymore, given the inconsequentiality of multiple faiths distributed among ever more fragmentary remnants of the faithful. And respect for the multiple roles of the authoritative institutional church has largely given way to an expectation that the church will indulge and reflect the predilections of its few communicants. In its efforts to survive, Dr. More's small Catholic splinter group offers its parishioners neither the support of a vigorous social community nor the mediation of confident sacramental worship.

Finally, *insecurity*, in both a political and a spiritual sense, emerges as a crippling encumbrance both to governmental and to personal renewal. Even worse than the legitimate threats confronted by the American democracy is a pervasive personal sense of dread and dislocation, all the more debilitating for its ambiguity and uncertainty. And the wide variety of inappropriate responses to this insecurity, from dogged effort to sustain an illusion of normalcy to the paranoid belief in the imminent collapse of civilization, further illustrates the polarities of divided individuals in a divided society. Here as well, the link between the political and personal senses of "government" is unequivocal, for Dr. More's own sense of vulnerability, which prompts him to create a survival bunker in an abandoned motel, closely mirrors his society's preference for isolated, defended neighborhoods.

Observation of these elements within the world of *Love in the Ruins* sustains much of the novel's force as commentary. Yet their greater importance lies in the propulsive force they offer the novel as it moves to and beyond its cosmic climax. For in the course of the events described by the novel, the relation between political and personal government shifts as Dr. Thomas More moves progressively through three distinct postures of the individual relative to the society in which he lives. It is by doing so that he comes in time to accept the prominent eschatological role he has endeavored so diligently to avoid.

During his first marriage and in the early stages of the developing political and social upheaval the novel describes, Dr. More appears as an oblique *microcosm* of his society, a skeptical but in some ways typical embodiment of its culture. He is rootless, self-absorbed, and dissolute, suffering the characteristic physical ailments of both conservative and liberal. The death of his daughter has turned him from metaphysical concerns to purely physical ones, and if he suspects that the things of the world will not offer enduring pleasure, he is determined at least to exploit them so far as possible.

Later, as a sense of impending catastrophe tests him and his assumptions, he becomes the individual distinct from his society, a skeptic, an exile, even a counterterrorist of sorts. This is the Thomas More we meet at the beginning of the novel, before the extended flashback begins. He is at this point awaiting but not yet actively confronting the threat of apocalypse.

In the novel's dramatic climax, Dr. More becomes the *redeemer* of society, the individual whose actions can effect change in society as a whole. The determinant of these changes is, of course, Dr. More's half-hearted but nonetheless grave struggle to achieve some measure of self-government in contrast with the increasing determination of his society to destroy itself both materially and spiritually. And the measure of that struggle is his capacity, finally, to call upon his illustrious forebear for the grace to repulse the diabolical in the figure of one Art Immelman:

> I cry, but I can't seem to move. I close my eyes. *Sir Thomas More, kinsman, saint, best dearest merriest of Englishmen, pray for us and drive this son of a bitch hence.*
>
> I open my eyes. Art is turning slowly away, wheeling in slow motion, a dazed hurt look through the eyes as if he had been struck across the face. . . . Art disappears into the smoke swirling beyond the bunker. (376)

Dr. More's course through the events of the novel toward this experience of grace can be appreciated in terms of the novel's three broad dichotomies, in that he finally achieves—or, more properly, receives—a sense of balance, a renewed capacity for reverence, and an assurance of security. And, in turn, we may imagine, his society gains its own opportunity to achieve greater balance, to make room for reverence, and to offer its citizens at least a measure of security.

That is the world described in the novel's final scene, as Dr. More, now happily married to his solid Georgia Presbyterian, stands on his small patio, barbecuing a turkey late on Christmas Eve, wearing a patch of sackcloth given him for penance. He dances to keep warm, his hands in his pockets, in an explicit pantomime of balance and reverence taken together: "It is Christmas Day and the Lord is here, a holy night and surely that is all one needs" (492). And his sense of security could not be made clearer by the novel's final line: "To bed we go for a long winter's nap, twined about each other as the ivy twineth, not under a bush or in a car or on the floor or any such humbug as marked the past peculiar years of Christendom, but at home in bed where all good folk belong" (493).

To be sure, Dr. More's own "government" stands in contrast with the continuing political fragmentation of the nation. His victory over Satan may have prevented (or at least has postponed) the end of the world, but five years later it is clear that the schisms that had contributed to the risk of catastrophe remain. The state of affairs sketched in the epilogue is by Percy's admission calculated to "infuriate Catholics, Protestants, Jews, Southerners, Northerners, liberals and conservatives, hawks and doves."[7] The problems left unresolved are both that of the divided nation and that of the divided individual.

Dr. More is at last the individual *sui generis,* a remnant, an architect by grace of a separate peace denied to many others. But in that remnant is hope, and that hope, in the manner of the *Revelation,* can speak not only about society but to individuals, and not only to its own time, its highest priority, but to future generations as well.

For the remainder of his life, Walker Percy was to continue his pursuit of these concerns. Through *Lancelot, The Second Coming,* and *The Thanatos Syndrome,* he would establish as a legacy the insistence that the health of the American democracy and that of the individual soul are indissolubly linked and that the prognosis for both, given the signs of his times, is none too good.

Are those signs better now?

Walker Percy's *Love in the Ruins* speaks to us still. It does so in part because its futuristic satire camouflages substantive perceptions and compelling concerns. The social polarizations he exaggerates have in fact become more pronounced in the years since the novel's publication. A pervasive indifference to widening schisms has become near blindness. "Sentimentality," having encouraged an indifference to "terror,"[8] allows an illusion of safety, even as ignored forces swell into "acts of desperation." Distressingly prescient, Percy writes in 1971, "Blowing up a building is, after all, a nutty thing to do. The fact is that America is not immovable and indestructible."[9]

Similarly, it would be difficult to argue that the spiritual ills taken seriously in this novel have become either less conspicuous or less consequential. Percy's observation in 1971 regarding a pervasive "alienation and boredom in the face of an affluent life"[10] has if anything become more trenchant. How else to explain the passion driving magnates to sacrifice morality and risk imprisonment so as to multiply incomes already immeasurably generous?

Like his protagonist, Walker Percy, a physician both in fact and metaphorically, leaves us with a diagnosis, an informed perception more sure of the disease than of the cure. Having run all the tests, he sits before his patient and offers a quiet warning. Not a diatribe nor an evangelical exhortation, but a prognosis grounded in an acute observation of present symptoms. In short, in the "pretty classy company" of St. John, Walker Percy offers us—there is still no better word—a "revelation."

NOTES

1. "The Revelation of Walker Percy," *Colorado Quarterly* 20 (Spring 1972): 459–70.

2. Gary Ciuba, *Walker Percy: Books of Revelations* (Athens: Univ. of Georgia Press, 1992).

3. Jay Tolson, ed., *The Correspondence of Shelby Foote and Walker Percy* (New York: DoubleTake, 1997), 129.

4. Walker Percy, *Love in the Ruins* (New York: Farrar, Straus and Giroux, 1971). All subsequent page references to the novel will appear parenthetically within the text.

5. Percy, "Concerning *Love in the Ruins,*" in *Signposts in a Strange Land,* ed. Patrick Samway (New York: Farrar, Straus and Giroux, 1991), 249.

6. Ibid., 248–49.

7. Tolson, *Correspondence*, 148.

8. Percy, "Novel Writing in an Apocalyptic Time," in *Signposts in a Strange Land*, 156.

9. Percy, "Concerning *Love in the Ruins*," 246.

10. Charles C. Bunting, "An Afternoon with Walker Percy," in *Conversations with Walker Percy*, ed. Lewis Lawson and Victor A. Kramer (Jackson: Univ. Press of Mississippi, 1985), 54.

Section III

A Dilemma for Democracy:
The Free Exercise of Religion and
the Rise of Fundamentalism

Fundamentalism, Democracy, and the Contesting of Meaning

ROGER W. STUMP

The rise of various forms of religious fundamentalism over the past century has created a significant dilemma for contemporary democracies. Commitment to the free exercise of religion represents one of the most basic democratic ideals, as recognized, for example, in Article 18 of the United Nation's Universal Declaration of Human Rights. The protection of religious rights has consequently become a hallmark of the constitutional systems of democratic polities. At the same time, the guarantee of religious freedom can make possible the articulation of religious ideologies whose exclusivity and absolutism challenge the very principles of equality and accommodation on which a democratic polity is founded. In particular, religious fundamentalism has posed such a challenge in many different contexts, first by asserting the certainty of a rigidly defined worldview based on a specific interpretation of religious tradition and then by insisting on the right of adherents to enact their religious certainty in diverse realms of public life. Given their certainty in the truth of their own religious system, fundamentalists strive to ensure that their beliefs are not contravened. As a result, for fundamentalists, the free expression of religion involves an ongoing struggle against aspects of society that are inconsistent with their absolutist ideology, a struggle that potentially may impinge on the freedoms of others.

The problematic relationship between fundamentalism and democracy thus represents a critical concern within the more general consideration of the interactions between democratic principles and religious practice. As the following chapters in this section illustrate, moreover, the relationship between the concepts of fundamentalism and democracy is neither simple nor straightforward. Each of these concepts possesses varied and unresolved meanings, and fundamentalist and democratic ideologies both represent social constructs that can take diverse forms and that in themselves often contain internal incongruities. In addition, the mutability of these concepts complicates the actual ramifications of one for the other as they are articulated by social actors in specific contexts. The consideration of religious fundamentalism as a dilemma for democracy must therefore take into account the complex and occasionally paradoxical nature of these phenomena as social constructs, individually and in interaction with one another.

The purpose of this introductory chapter is to examine a number of broader issues related to the multifarious character of these phenomena and their interactions, to provide a foundation for the more detailed discussions presented in the subsequent chapters of this section. The following discussion focuses specifically on the contested meanings of fundamentalism and democracy as considered from two perspectives. The discussion first addresses the contested nature of the concepts of fundamentalism and democracy themselves, identifying some of the difficulties that arise in generalizing about these complex ideological expressions and briefly analyzing some of the ambiguities and paradoxes associated with them. The discussion then turns to an examination of the role of contested meanings in conflicts between fundamentalism and democracy. Here the meanings in question refer not to fundamentalism and democracy as abstract concepts, but rather to the conflicting assumptions and principles that are posited by fundamentalist and democratic ideologies, which lie at the heart of the dilemma posed by the former for the latter.

The Meanings of Fundamentalism

In its application to a variety of different religious movements and ideologies, fundamentalism has in recent decades become a contested term in both academic and popular usage. The term itself was first used in the 1920s to describe a conservative branch of American evangelical Protestantism committed to the preservation of certain fundamental Christian doctrines. The original fundamentalists placed particular emphasis on unqualified belief in the divine authorship and literal accuracy of the Bible, a doctrine that in their view was being undermined by the influence of modernism and secularism in American culture. It can be argued that the term "fundamentalism" only makes sense when narrowly applied to this particular movement, and possibly to similar movements that strongly emphasize the literal interpretation of sacred texts. Over time, however, the term has been used to describe a more diverse array of religious movements and groups that define themselves in opposition to perceived threats to tradition, such as the secularizing effects of modernism or the cultural relativism of postmodernism. This broader use of the term has achieved widespread academic currency, particularly in the wake of the influential Fundamentalism Project sponsored by the American Academy of Arts and

Sciences.[1] Acceptance of a more inclusive understanding of fundamentalism has been particularly useful in comparative and cross-cultural studies of contemporary religious trends.[2]

Nonetheless, fundamentalism continues to be a contested term, subject to diverse interpretations and meanings. One major difficulty associated with use of the term has been the negative connotation that it has acquired in many contexts. The description of a group or belief system as being fundamentalist often carries with it implications of fanaticism, irrationality, intolerance, or cultural atavism. These pejorative undertones are not universally recognized, as many Christian fundamentalists continue to identify themselves with that label in a positive sense. In other contexts, however, popular use of the fundamentalist label has become highly politicized, serving to stigmatize groups or individuals who are perceived by others as threats to social stability. In South Asia, for example, accusations of fundamentalist tendencies are regularly directed at certain Hindu and Muslim groups by one another, as well as by Hindu and Muslim moderates.[3] Given this process of stigmatization, many groups and individuals identified as fundamentalists object strongly to the label, even when (as in much academic writing) the term is used for the purpose of classification and comparison rather than to deprecate those to whom it has been applied. Militant or political Islamists have often taken exception to being identified as fundamentalists, to cite one example, arguing that this designation marginalizes them or imposes on them ideological boundaries rooted in Western culture.[4] Calling someone a fundamentalist, in sum, represents in many contexts a political act fraught with underlying meanings. Characterizing terrorist actions such as those of September 11, 2001, as expressions of fundamentalism likewise stigmatizes and politicizes the term, as discussed at length in the chapter by William Dinges later in this section.

The acceptance of a more inclusive interpretation of fundamentalism also does not solve the problem of defining the exact nature of the phenomenon. Again, some have argued that the term should be applied only to groups that emphasize the inerrancy of sacred texts, whereas others have found such a definition to be too limiting. Still others have found such a definition to be too broad, as in the case of Islam. Because the worldview of Islam is predicated on belief in the perfection of the Qur'an as the Word of God, this interpretation of the term would make all Muslims fundamentalists.[5] Indeed, the difficulty of drawing precise boundaries around the concept of fundamentalism remains as long as we consider it from an essentialist perspective, as a discrete phenomenon with a fixed set of intrinsic traits. A more useful approach, and one that is consistent with the methods and findings of the Fundamentalism Project, employs the concept of fundamentalism as a heuristic device to identify significant correspondences among diverse religious movements and groups. From this perspective, fundamentalism has come to signify an overlapping cluster of related traits that find expression in varied forms and combinations as they are articulated within particular contexts.

The most basic of these fundamentalist traits is belief in a set of unassailable certainties derived from a religious tradition. These certainties often focus on sacred texts, but they can relate to other issues as well, such as belief in a sacred national identity in some forms of Jewish and Hindu fundamentalism. At the same time, expressions of fundamentalism differ from other forms of religious traditionalism in their vital concern with contemporary threats to the religious certainties on which they focus. The threats identified by fundamentalists take different forms in different contexts, but in most cases involve the perceived impacts of modernism, secularism, imperialism, or postmodern pluralism on the authority of the fundamentalists' religious certainties as organizing principles within society. Fundamentalists tend to see these challenges to their religious certainties in dualistic terms, as a contest between absolute good and absolute evil, and therefore typically draw an impermeable ideological barrier between themselves and their perceived antagonists. The resulting sense of identity shared by members of a particular group or movement represents a key element of fundamentalism and typically fosters and is reinforced by a strong commitment to public activism in defense of traditional certainties. The activist dimension of fundamentalism can again take many forms: some groups have emphasized withdrawal from the rest of society, others have attempted to promote their agenda on a broader scale through legitimate political action, and still others have resorted to violent confrontations with their antagonists. But no matter how it is expressed, fundamentalist activism manifests a powerful desire for coherence between the certainties of religious belief and other realms of personal and social life.

In more theoretical terms, then, fundamentalism represents an interaction between particular social expressions of structure and agency. It draws in a positive sense from cultural structures based on traditional concepts of religious authority, including specific patterns of belief and identity that are accepted as irrefutable. At the same time, fundamentalism also develops in response to negatively perceived structures, such as cultural trends and social institutions, which are perceived as threats to once uncontested religious certainties. Fundamentalists then are primarily concerned with the conflicts between two sets of structures, one set related to an idealized religious tradition and the other related to antagonistic forces or trends perceived as undermining that tradition. The role of human agency comes into play as fundamentalists attempt first to define the terms of the conflict between these two sets of structures and then to influence the outcome of that conflict, with the goal of ensuring that the structures with which they identify prevail. Human agency may also enter into the conflict through the activities of individuals opposed to the fundamentalists' agenda. Fundamentalists themselves tend to be primarily concerned, however, with combating structural threats, such as the moral decay of society or the organization of a political state in accordance with secularist principles. In this sense, fundamentalist groups or movements typically emerge as their adherents take deliberate action to shape broader social structures to conform to their own religious certainties. In the process, the interaction between fundamentalist agency and the relevant social structures may take many different forms, based on the characteristics of the particular context in which that interaction takes place. Quite often, though, fundamentalist goals and actions come into conflict with democratic principles, because the former are rooted in religious certainties that, from the perspective of their adherents, are not subject to democratic debate.

Although the general interpretation of fundamentalism outlined earlier has achieved fairly widespread scholarly acceptance over the past decade, some significant questions regarding the nature of fundamentalism persist, as discussed in the chapters that follow. In his chapter, William Dinges raises one crucial issue in the aftermath of the terrorist attacks of September 11, 2001: that is, can and should terrorist actions of this magnitude be labeled as expressions of fundamentalism? He makes a convincing case against using the term in this context, arguing that to associate these horrific acts with fundamentalism would inevitably weaken the descriptive value of the term and instead charge it with political meanings that could serve various ideological agendas, either in support of or against Islam, or against religion generally. Moreover, the September 11 attacks deviate in significant ways from the phenomena that by scholarly consensus have been grouped under the rubric of fundamentalism. Simply the scale and gratuitous nature of the destruction involved appears to make these actions categorically distinct, of course, but the destruction also does not appear to have been tied to an internally consistent set of religious objectives. Although the intended goals of fundamentalists are often seen by others as undesirable outcomes, fundamentalists themselves invariably understand their goals in constructive terms: to improve society, to restore the harmonious order of an idealized past, to somehow make the world "right" in terms of their religious worldview. Moreover, these goals are typically pursued by fundamentalists in a highly pragmatic fashion, not just to make symbolic statements but also to achieve concrete, positive ends. The destruction of September 11 lacks any evidence of such a constructive strategy. As gratuitous acts of violence, the September 11 attacks were inherently self-defeating, only leading to more violence and to the destabilization of existing structures (such as al Qaeda and the Taliban regime). Indeed, the primary objective of the attacks appears merely to have been the self-aggrandizement of their organizers within the culture of violence that has emerged in the Islamic militant fringe over the past several decades. As Dinges suggests toward the end of his chapter, the use of religious meanings and structures to legitimatize violence represents a phenomenon of great contemporary significance, but one that cannot be effectively explained within the conceptual context of fundamentalism.

In addition to questioning its boundaries as an analytical concept, the following chapters raise a number of other important issues concerning the problematic nature of fundamentalism. Most importantly, these chapters reveal some of the paradoxes inherent within fundamentalism as a form of ideological expression. Perhaps most significantly, fundamentalism in most of its guises represents an ideological rejection of modernity (and postmodernity), but in some ways it also reproduces certain features of modernity. An often-cited example of the latter trend is the widespread adoption of technological advances by fundamentalists in spreading their message, such as the early development of cable television networks by Christian fundamentalists in the 1970s or the more recent use of the Internet by many different fundamentalist groups. But the incorporation of elements of modernity into expressions of fundamentalism also takes more substantive forms, a point clearly made in the chapter by John Burgess. He specifically notes, for instance, that expressions of fundamentalism often reveal a distinctly modern emphasis on the authority of law rather than of custom or personal influence. Moreover, this emphasis on the law often displays a modern concern with practical objectives, such as the personal well-being of the adherent. The focus on law does not appear in all fundamentalist movements, of course. Hindu fundamentalists, to cite one example, are much more concerned with issues of identity than with the observance of law.[6] Nonetheless, their emphasis on identity again reflects contemporary concerns, such as the postmodern preoccupation with difference and distinctiveness. Despite their assimilation of such contemporary elements, however, fundamentalist movements maintain worldviews that at their core are essentially incompatible with either modernism or postmodernism. The incorporation of modern or postmodern elements thus should not be overemphasized in defining the nature of fundamentalism as an ideological expression. Although fundamentalism as it is generally defined exists only in contemporary settings, it is invariably grounded in the premodern belief in a single view of truth validated by faith. The assimilation of certain modern and postmodern elements in this sense remains secondary in fundamentalist ideologies to an underlying worldview based on premodern understandings of authority.

A similar paradox appears in the practical use of the instruments of democracy by fundamentalist groups and movements. In their insistence on the existence of a single understanding of truth based on a particular reading of religious tradition, fundamentalist ideologies are inherently at odds with democratic concepts concerning freedom of thought, the nature of popular rule, the accommodation of diversity, and the like. At the same time, in various contexts fundamentalists have made use of the workings of democracy to promote their own agendas. The chapter by Yilmaz Çolak and Ertan Aydin provides a useful illustration of this paradox in examining the strategies of Islamists in Turkey in recent years. Because they represent a political minority within Turkey, Islamist groups have sought to achieve greater influence in the public sphere by pushing for the broader implementation of democratic measures designed to protect minority interests. These efforts have focused in part on the issue of electoral representation but in recent years have also addressed more basic questions of human rights, particularly as they relate to public displays of the practice of Islam. Similar efforts to employ democratic structures and institutions have been adopted by fundamentalists in other contexts as well. Christian fundamentalists in the United States, for example, have repeatedly tried to reshape the content of public school curricula to conform to their own beliefs concerning creation, first in the 1920s and 1930s through state legislation and toward the end of the twentieth century through the control of locally elected school boards. Along somewhat different lines, Hindu fundamentalists in India have used the electoral process to assert political hegemony as representatives of the Hindu majority within a core group of states as well as at the federal level. Both as majorities and minorities, then, fundamentalists have developed strategies that make use of democratic practices even though they advocate ideologies that challenge certain democratic principles.

A third ambiguity inherent within fundamentalism, as that term is currently used, involves the complex role of tradition in fundamentalist ideologies. As stated earlier, the most basic fundamentalist characteristic is belief in religious certainties associated with a particular understanding of religious tradition. In articulating their understanding of tradition, however, fundamentalists tend to be selective, emphasizing some elements of tradition over others. As Burgess suggests in his chapter, this selectivity in the idealization of tradition often centers on matters of law, but it may comprise other concerns as well, such as issues of identity or the control of sacred space. Whatever their emphasis, though, fundamentalist ideologies do not generally propose a wholesale recreation of some idealized past. Instead, fundamentalists tend to accentuate those elements of tradition that stand in sharpest contrast to the perceived threats that they oppose. As a result, the conflicts between fundamentalists and their antagonists typically develop around very specific issues rather than around a broader debate of the role of religious tradition in society. These specific issues in turn take on considerable symbolic significance for fundamentalists and their antagonists. The conflict in Turkey over the wearing of headscarves and other public displays of Islam, discussed by Çolak and Aydin, provides a telling example of this tendency for fundamentalists to become embroiled in narrowly defined but symbolically potent controversies. In such instances, again, fundamentalists may use tradition in very modern or postmodern ways as the basis for contesting political meanings or promoting a particular social agenda.

The concept of fundamentalism thus encompasses a complex set of meanings. The term itself has been contested in many ways, both in a scholarly context and by those to whom it has been applied. Fundamentalism as a form of ideological expression also contains various inherent ambiguities, particularly in relation to the appropriation of modern and postmodern strategies in the defense of tradition. As the following chapters reveal, these complexities are very much involved in the dilemma that fundamentalism poses for democracy in various settings.

The Meanings of Democracy

Democracy is perhaps a less ambiguous concept than fundamentalism and does not carry the same potential for negative connotation. Nonetheless, democracy too represents a contested term with its own problems and paradoxes, and the latter play an important role in the complex interactions between fundamentalism and democracy discussed in subsequent chapters.[7] In contemporary Western usage, the term "democracy" generally denotes a polity having a representative form of government whose leaders are chosen through free and fair elections. Diverse interests are typically represented by a multiparty political system, and a formal constitution provides certain protections for minority and individual rights. Democracies so described can take different specific forms, however. Some are structured around an adversarial system among different parties, for example, whereas others emphasize rule through consensus. Some democracies make regular use of plebiscites or public referenda, thereby allowing voters to have a direct voice in policy decisions, whereas others do not. Democracies constructed according to the Western model have also varied over time in the scope of electoral enfranchisement and in the past often restricted voting rights to a minority of the adult population. The understanding of what makes an election "free and fair" has thus been contextualized, depending on prevailing social structures within the polity in question.

Moreover, a democracy need not be structured according to this contemporary Western model. Marxism, for example, presents a radically different conception of democracy that, at least in theory, eliminates the distinction between the ruling class and the populace at large.[8] Of greater relevance to the chapters presented here is the nature of Kemalism as a form of democracy, as described by Çolak and Aydin. Unlike contemporary Western democracy, which generally places a strong emphasis on pluralism and the coexistence of diverse groups within society, Kemalism represents a democratic ideology that explicitly discourages pluralism. It instead stresses the need for a secular, homogeneous society organized around a shared sense of national identity, such a society being deemed necessary for the creation of a stable nation-state. The implications of the Kemalist model for the public practice of religion are thus very different from those of the contemporary Western model of democracy. Both models assert the essential secularity of the government, but in the former the free practice of religion may become suspect as a potential source of social divisiveness or political fragmentation, whereas in the latter it remains an important individual right protected by secular political structures. A third interpretation of democracy relevant to the discussion of fundamentalism appears in the concept of theodemocracy posited by Mawlana Sayyid Abul A'la Mawdudi, a leading twentieth-century Islamic scholar.[9] This view of democracy defines the state as a divine instrument, deriving its authority from God and created for the purpose of enacting divine law. In the ordinary business of government, however, the state functions according to democratic principles, particularly through the popular election of leaders or representatives. The government thus rules at least in part through democratic institutions, but under the ultimate sovereignty of God. Iran after the Islamic Revolution is often cited as an example of such a theodemocracy, although in that case the system of government articulated by Ayatollah Khomeini emphasized the divine selection of the ruling Jurist or Faqih along with the democratic election of popular representatives.[10]

As the previous examples illustrate, then, democracy can take different forms in different places and at different times. The resulting contextuality of democracy as an ideological system has important implications for its interactions with expressions of fundamentalism. It is in the contemporary Western model that fundamentalism most clearly poses a dilemma for democracy, as the protection of individual rights and the emphasis on pluralism within this model allow fundamentalist groups to exist freely within society, even though such groups may advocate ideologies that contain undemocratic elements. Within the Kemalist form of democracy described by Çolak and Aydin, fundamentalism poses less of a dilemma in the sense that under such a system the state has no ideological responsibility to protect socially divisive religious expressions. Fundamentalism nonetheless remains a problem in its opposition to the secular homogeneity promoted by Kemalism. Within a theodemocracy, finally, the state is likely to draw its legitimacy from a prevailing fundamentalist ideology. In such a context, the primary dilemma involving democracy and fundamentalism thus focuses on the former rather than the latter, specifically with regard to the protection of the rights of those who do not adhere to the dominant religious tradition. The persecution of Bahais in Iran since the Islamic Revolution represents an extreme example of the violation of democratic rights within a fundamentalist state ostensibly organized as a republican democracy.[11]

In addition to taking different forms in different contexts, the realization of democratic ideologies has also frequently resulted in certain problems and paradoxes relevant to the interaction with fundamentalism. One such problem derives from the interconnected relationships between the rise of democratic movements over the past century and the concurrent rise of political movements centering on local, ethnic, communal, or even transnational identities.[12] These two types of movements have often developed hand in hand with the establishment of democratic institutions serving in part to promote the political representation and participation of distinct groups within an explicitly heterogeneous society. Within this context, the essentially modernist political concept of "the people" has increasingly given way to a more complex, postmodern notion of diverse "peoples" or identity groups as key political actors. Democratization has thus been associated with the social fragmentation that has accompanied the rise of the politics of difference in some contexts. By creating political and institutional structures through which different groups can promote their separate agendas, the establishment of democracy can in turn lead to significant tensions and even conflict within (and between) states. This trend is significant within this discussion because religion—and more to the point, fundamentalist religion—can play a significant role in defining the boundaries of identity for distinct groups within a polity or broader region. Again, Turkey provides a telling example of this problem. The Kemalist ideology assumes that Turkey's inhabitants represent a homogeneous people committed to a unified nation-state; the Islamists, on the other hand, claim a distinct identity based on religious adherence and assert their democratic right to seek social and political change in accordance with their beliefs. Comparable problems have developed in other contexts as well. The constitution of India as a secular democracy has provided a context for the complexities of communal politics, which have become increasingly radicalized through the growing influence of both Hindu and Muslim fundamentalism. To cite another significant example, democracy in Israel has provided a context in which the very meaning of the state has been contested by the secularist majority and various fundamentalist groups, including some who in fact challenge the legitimacy of the state.[13]

A further problem that has appeared in many attempts to put an avowedly democratic ideology into practice has been the adoption of undemocratic means to achieve long-term democratic goals. Again, the analysis of the case of Turkey by Çolak and Aydin effectively illustrates this paradox. The "certainties of Kemalism" to which they refer in their chapter have provided military leaders with a rationale for intervening in democratic processes as a means of protecting the secular character of Turkish society and minimizing fundamentalist influences. In this instance, those in power see the concession of democratic rights to certain groups as a threat to democracy, but in trying to avert that threat they have in some sense violated democratic principles. The Kemalist ideology grounded in the ideal of a homogeneous, secular nation-state, in other words, exists in continuing tension with an ideological commitment to the ideals of democracy, and that tension has resulted in the contesting of meaning concerning the role of religion in the public sphere.

The converse of this paradox arises when the establishment of diverse freedoms—freedom of religion, of movement, of assembly—makes a democracy vulnerable to undemocratic forces or influences. From this perspective, the guarantee of democratic freedoms can carry with it the risk of allowing the germination and growth of unambiguous challenges to democracy. In most instances, perhaps, such challenges are in the end unsuccessful, merely giving a political voice to those at odds with prevailing democratic values. Such has often been the case, for example, when religious fundamentalists have used the workings of democracy to promote their sectarian agendas through legitimate political action. More rarely and more tragically, however, the freedoms taken for granted within a democracy can be exploited by extremists in the commission of violence. Recent examples abound, from the attacks of September 11, 2001, to the recurring suicide bombings in Israel, from communal violence in India to political kidnappings and executions in the Philippines.

Thus, democracy, like fundamentalism, represents a complex and sometimes contested concept, comprising different forms in different contexts and containing intrinsic stresses arising from the tensions between individual freedoms and the good of society at large. The resulting ambiguities complicate any consideration of the interactions between fundamentalism and democracy and indeed are partially responsible for the difficulties that have emerged from such interactions. The dilemma of fundamentalism for democracy, however, does not stem solely from the contested nature of these concepts and the diverse ways in which each has been articulated in specific settings. This dilemma also arises from the ideological character of both fundamentalism and democracy as they are actually put into practice. Proponents of both of these forms of ideological expression are essentially concerned with defining and controlling the application of basic meanings within society, based on their own particular set of assumptions and principles. These meanings therefore become the focus of conflict between the two ideological cohorts as each seeks to ensure that its worldview prevails. This discussion concludes, then, with a brief examination of some of these contested meanings and the role that they play in fundamentalism's dilemma for democracy.

THE DILEMMA OF CONTESTED MEANINGS

The varied conflicts that have developed between fundamentalism and democracy have ultimately focused on the meanings of concepts relevant to both of these forms of ideological expression. Indeed, fundamentalist reactions against modernity and postmodernity are organized around the defense of meanings believed to have been corrupted within and by contemporary society; and from the fundamentalist point of view, the secularism and cultural relativism fostered by democratic ideologies represent principal sources of this corruption of tradition. The contesting of meanings has thus become a central feature of the interaction between fundamentalism and democracy. In turn, the difficulty of resolving conflicts between fundamentalist and democratic ideologies typically reflects the problem of reconciling distinct interpretations of meanings based on divergent worldviews. It is this unresolved incongruity between different understandings of crucial meanings that in the end poses the dilemma of fundamentalism for democracy.

Of the various meanings contested by fundamentalist and democratic ideologies, perhaps the most important involves the concept of authority. The divergence between fundamentalist and democratic understandings of authority is particularly evident in how such ideologies define the character of law. As Burgess notes in his chapter, there are some important similarities between fundamentalist and secular democratic notions of law: both share an emphasis on rationality, for example, and both see law as a means of regulating society. Nonetheless, these notions of law derive from two very different understandings of authority, which have significant implications for the role of law in society.

From the secular democratic perspective, law derives its authority from the general consent of the people. Its primary purpose is to provide a workable set of rules by which a society comprising diverse interests can function. Democratic law may be based on underlying certainties—such as belief in certain inalienable rights in the American case—but because it derives its force from the people, the law is constantly subject to change. Democratic law is thus not absolute. As a result, it can be resisted by those who oppose it. Indeed, opposition to unjust laws—for example, through civil disobedience—has appeared as an important feature of many democratic traditions. Within this context, acts of conscience (often based on religious belief) can take on a certain legitimacy, even though they violate the law.

The fundamentalist view of law is, of course, quite different. Alongside secular law, fundamentalists recognize the existence of sacred law that derives its authority from an eternal, divine source. From the fundamentalist perspective, this law is based on absolute certainties, is explicit in its meaning, and therefore is not subject to change through democratic processes. The primary purpose of this sacred law is to articulate and preserve the ordained order of things as revealed in divinely inspired texts or teachings. Because fundamentalists consider sacred law to be absolute and unequivocally just, they do not recognize the legitimacy of efforts to resist or oppose it. In the Manichean worldview typical of fundamentalism, violators of sacred law are therefore seen not just as wrongdoers but as evildoers. Moreover, from the fundamentalist perspective the incontrovertible authority of sacred law requires that secular law conform to it.

Clearly, then, the fundamentalist and secular democratic perspectives conceptualize law very differently, reflecting different understandings of law as an expression of authority. A legal system based on the ideals of secular democracy is basically incapable of accommodating the absolute sense of certainty and authority that fundamentalists ascribe to their understanding of sacred law. Nonetheless, fundamentalists in various democratic contexts have frequently sought to achieve congruity between secular and sacred law as a means of perfecting society according to their religious vision. The difficulty of reconciling these two interpretations of law thus represents a major challenge for democratic polities in which fundamentalism represents an influential force.

In a more practical sense, the conflict between fundamentalism and democracy has also often involved contention over the meaning of the right of religious expression. Again, democratic principles place significant emphasis on religious rights, but in most democratic contexts such rights have been defined in reference to individual, private thought and behavior. The right to free religious expression generally becomes more limited within the public sphere. A public schoolteacher in the United States thus cannot organize his curriculum to promote his personal religious beliefs, for example, nor can the owner of a public place of accommodation limit service to other adherents of her own faith. Of course, the boundary between the public and private spheres can be defined in different ways in different settings. Women have been banned from wearing headscarves at Turkish universities, as discussed by Çolak and Aydin, because in that context those in power assert that wearing a headscarf represents a divisive, political act, not a matter of private religious practice. A similar restriction on Muslim women at an American public university would probably not be countenanced, because in this context the practice would most likely be interpreted as falling within the domain of private religious choice.

Fundamentalists, on the other hand, have typically opposed the establishment of a boundary between public and private spheres in the practice of their religion, asserting that such boundaries inhibit their right to free religious expression. This assertion reflects the fundamentalist conviction that religion must be fully integrated into all aspects of life. From the fundamentalist perspective, then, the right of religious expression cannot be limited to a narrowly defined private sphere. Islamists in Turkey have thus emphasized the issue of human rights in their efforts to expand their ability to practice Islam publicly. Christian fundamentalists in the United States have similarly contested the concept of religious rights—for example, in opposing the teaching of biological evolution in public schools—arguing that their right to religious freedom includes the right to have their children attend schools in which the curriculum does not contradict their basic religious beliefs. Ultra-Orthodox Jewish fundamentalists in Israel have in a like manner sought to promote their religious rights in the public sphere, for example, by demanding that traffic be barred from public streets near their neighborhoods on the Sabbath and that public buses running through their neighborhoods provide separate seating for men and women.[14] The meaning of religious rights thus becomes contested between fundamentalism and democracy when fundamentalists insist on restructuring both the private and public domains in accordance with their religious beliefs. Although fundamentalists may consider reform of the public domain to be a necessary part of the free expression of their religion, for others, such religiously inspired reform may be seen as an infringement of their own democratic rights. Again, the incompatibility of these different views of the public role of religion in society poses a significant dilemma for democracy.

A third important focus of the meanings contested by democratic and fundamentalist ideologies is the nature of national identity. Democratic ideologies generally define national identity in terms of some shared sense of citizenship, through which individuals acquire rights and accept responsibilities within the context of a larger polity. That sense of citizenship may contain within it strong cultural connotations, such as the association with a particular linguistic or ethnic identity, but according to basic democratic principles the rights and responsibilities of citizenship apply universally, regardless of other factors. Fundamentalist ideologies have contested this understanding of national identity in two ways: in some cases by denying the concept of a unified citizenry and in others by proposing a radically different basis for national identity. Again, the actions of Islamists in Turkey serve as a useful illustration of the first of these two patterns: by drawing an ideological boundary between Muslims and non-Muslims, Islamists in Turkey have undermined the conception of national homogeneity and unity promoted by Kemalism. To cite a somewhat different example of this first pattern, many of the strictest ultra-Orthodox Jews in Israel deny the legitimacy of the state of Israel itself, reject their own citizenship, and attempt to remain as isolated from the surrounding society as possible. The second pattern, of asserting a different basis for national identity, has been more common in settings where fundamentalists see themselves as representatives of the national majority. To some extent this pattern has also emerged in Turkey as Islamists have attempted to redefine the boundaries of the national community around a Muslim identity. The focus of Hindu fundamentalists on Hindutva, or Hinduness, as the essential feature of India's national identity represents another explicit example of this pattern, as does the attempt by Christian fundamentalists to define the United States as an essentially Christian nation. Fundamentalists in various contexts have thus rejected the secular democratic construction of national identity, based on an inclusive conception of citizenship, and in its place have promoted more exclusive and problematic interpretations of national identity based on religious adherence.

In sum, different understandings of authority, rights, national identity, and related concepts lie at the heart of the conflicts between democratic and fundamentalist ideologies. These conflicts ultimately focus on the clash between the totalizing worldviews associated with fundamentalism and the democratic emphasis on secular or pluralistic values in the organization of society. Such conflicts have taken distinctive forms in different settings, however, reflecting the nature of local expressions of fundamentalism as well as the local articulation of democratic ideals. The encounter between democratic and fundamentalist ideologies in the United States thus differs in important ways from the corresponding encounter in Turkey. As a result, the resolution of such conflicts will also likely proceed in diverse ways, reflecting opportunities and constraints defined in part by local circumstances.

At least two factors may have a widespread impact on this process of resolution, however, as democracies address the dilemma of fundamentalism. First, as seen in the case of Turkey analyzed by Çolak and Aydin, fundamentalists may appropriate the use of certain democratic concepts, such as civil rights, in pursuing their objectives. This pattern is perhaps most likely to develop in settings where a fundamentalist movement or group must contend with another totalizing ideology whose adherents hold greater political power, as in the encounter between Islamic fundamentalism and Kemalism in Turkey. The situation of Islamists in contemporary India, where Hindu fundamentalists have acquired considerable power at the federal level and in various state governments, provides another case in point. The encounter between ultra-Orthodox anti-Zionists and the dominant, secular Zionist society in Israel perhaps reflects this pattern as well. In such cases, fundamentalists have a strong interest in supporting democratic practices, which provide a means of protecting their status within the larger society. Even in more pluralistic settings, moreover, fundamentalists may acknowledge the importance of democratic principles in protecting their right to assert their own views. In this sense, as Burgess argues in his chapter, fundamentalists need democracy. And fundamentalists' recognition of the ways that democratic structures can support their own interests may in turn serve as the foundation for further reconciliation between fundamentalist and democratic ideologies.

A second, related factor that may ultimately contribute to the resolution of conflicts between fundamentalism and democracy is the inherent mutability of fundamentalism as a form of cultural expression. All elements of human culture are in a perpetual state of transformation, constantly changing over time and space as they are reproduced by those who practice them. In the context of religion, adherents typically understand their faith as a representation of universal, unchanging truths and meanings, transcending the contingencies of particular moments in time and space; but as cultural systems, religions continually evolve in relation to the specific times and places in which they are acted out by communities of believers.[15] The same pattern holds true for fundamentalist ideologies, even though they are even more likely than other forms of religious expression to emphasize the absolute, unchanging certainty of their core beliefs and values. In particular, contemporary expressions of fundamentalism are likely to be transformed by their encounters with democracy. The recent emphasis by Turkish Islamists on their basic human right to practice Islam openly provides a useful example of this process. The encounter with democracy may thus serve to temper the absolutism of fundamentalist ideologies over time, as adherents of the latter adopt democratic strategies in pursuing their own objectives. Of course, the influence may not be unidirectional: democracy may itself be transformed in various ways by its contacts with fundamentalism. The lessons of the past two centuries of human history suggest, however, that in the encounter between any form of absolutism and more pluralist, populist, or democratic ideologies, the latter are ultimately more likely to prevail.

In this context, then, the mutability of human meanings represents perhaps the most significant factor in the potential resolution of fundamentalism's dilemma for democracy.

NOTES

1. The results of the Fundamentalism Project appear in the series of volumes edited by Martin E. Marty and R. Scott Appleby, *Fundamentalisms Observed* (Chicago: Univ. of Chicago Press, 1991), *Fundamentalisms and Society* (Chicago: Univ. of Chicago Press, 1993), *Fundamentalisms and the State* (Chicago: Univ. of Chicago Press, 1993), *Accounting for Fundamentalisms* (Chicago: Univ. of Chicago Press, 1994), and *Fundamentalisms Comprehended* (Chicago: Univ. of Chicago Press, 1995).

2. See, for example, Roger W. Stump, *Boundaries of Faith: Geographical Perspectives on Religious Fundamentalism* (Lanham, Md.: Rowman and Littlefield, 2000); Judy Brink and Joan Mencher, eds., *Mixed Blessings: Gender and Religious Fundamentalism Cross Culturally* (New York: Routledge, 1997); and Lawrence Kaplan, ed., *Fundamentalism in Comparative Perspective* (Amherst: Univ. of Massachusetts Press, 1992).

3. Alex Ninian, "Hindu and Muslim Strife in India," *Contemporary Review* 280 (June 2002): 340–43.

4. This issue is discussed, for example, in a number of the essays included in David Westerlund and Eva Evers Rosander, eds., *African Islam and Islam in Africa: Encounters Between Sufis and Islamists* (Athens: Ohio Univ. Press, 1997).

5. Jeff Haynes, *Religion in Third World Politics* (Boulder, Colo.: Lynne Reiner Publishers, 1994), 3.

6. Stump, *Boundaries of Faith*, 194–97; C. Ram-Prasad, "Hindutva Ideology: Extracting the Fundamentals," *Contemporary South Asia* 2, no. 3 (1993): 285–309.

7. A useful discussion of democracy as a contested term appears in John L. Esposito and John O. Voll, *Islam and Democracy* (New York: Oxford Univ. Press, 1996), 11–32.

8. Esposito and Voll, *Islam and Democracy*, 17.

9. John L. Esposito, *Islam: The Straight Path* (New York: Oxford Univ. Press, 1996), 152. The term "theodemocracy" was also used by various Mormon leaders in the nineteenth century to describe the idealized state they hoped to create. Compare with Eugene E. Campbell, "Governmental Beginnings," in *Utah's History*, ed. Richard D. Poll (Provo, Utah: Brigham Young Univ. Press, 1989), 153–73.

10. Parviz Daneshvar, *Revolution in Iran* (London: Macmillan, 1996), 143–45.

11. U.S. Congress, House, Committee on International Relations, and Senate, Committee on Foreign Relations, *Annual Report, International Religious Freedom, 1999*, 106th Cong., 2d sess., 2000, 350–56.

12. Esposito and Voll, *Islam and Democracy*, 14–15; David B. Knight, "People Together, Yet Apart: Rethinking Territory, Sovereignty, and Identities," in *Reordering the World: Geopolitical Perspectives on*

the Twenty-First Century, ed. George J. Demko and William B. Wood, 2d ed. (Boulder, Colo.: Westview Press, 1999), 209–26.

13. Among Jewish fundamentalists, those characterized as religious Zionists support the state of Israel as the first step in the redemption of the Jewish people, whereas many of those characterized as ultra-Orthodox reject the legitimacy of Israel, based on the belief that restoration of the Jews to the promised land can be achieved only by divine action, not by human agency. See Stump, *Boundaries of Faith,* 41–48.

14. Stump, *Boundaries of Faith,* 184–85.

15. Max Charlesworth, "Universal and Local Elements in Religion," in *Religious Inventions: Four Essays* (Cambridge: Cambridge Univ. Press, 1997), 81–104.

Dilemmas of Turkish Democracy

The Encounter between Kemalist Laicism
and Islamism in 1990s Turkey

ERTAN AYDIN AND YILMAZ ÇOLAK

The experience of Turkish secularism and the participation of Islamically oriented political parties in the Turkish democratic process demonstrated peculiar paradoxes that challenge predominant notions of the relationship between democracy and religion.[1] In the 1990s, the secular Kemalist establishment in Turkey favored military involvement in democratic processes in spite of their pro-Western and democratic ideas, whereas Islamist groups began to advocate Turkey's entrance into the European Union and adoption of an American model of secularism. What does the clash of identities in Turkey, as evident in the conflict between Kemalist and Islamist political groups, teach us about the dilemma for democracy in the most modern and secular nation of the Muslim world?

This chapter examines the political implications of the rising Islamic demands for being represented in the democratic public sphere and the reactions of the Kemalists in Turkey in the 1990s. Historically, Kemalism, the official ideology of the Turkish state, posed laicism in pseudoreligious terms and symbols and, in doing so, aimed at diminishing the public appearances of Islam for the sake of the creation of a homogenous, laic culture that presupposes the eradication of all particularities in the society. Secularization in Turkey thus took the form of a kind of a Weltanschauung that had claimed to redraw the boundaries between religious culture and the political community. Further, this study will depict the nature of the dilemmas of the Kemalist vision of democracy that takes secularism (*laiklik*) as the essential constituent of democracy.

The central difficulty in the democratic consolidation in Turkey is that the Kemalist elite considers a kind of radical secularism as the prerequisite and even sine qua non of democracy. Therefore, the Turkish revolutionary rulers feel themselves obliged to hinder the public visibility of religion for the sake of democracy. This is, historically, justified by the understanding that every country has its own peculiar way to democracy; the way to attain it should rely on forming a national unity and a secular social structure.

This chapter will argue that since the early period of the Kemalist project of cultural modernization, the revolutionary elite considered the religious symbols and images as the primary impediment to democratization of society. In that sense, cultural symbols of the new Turkish republican regime were overpoliticized since the early cultural modernization of Kemalism. This overpoliticization of cultural symbols narrows the boundaries of the public sphere and restricts the individual freedoms and further debilitates democracy. Therefore, the paradox of democracy in Turkey will be broadly unraveled through analyzing the tension between democracy and secularism that the early republican practices elicited. This tension still appears to have a greater impact on the Turkish politics, especially during the last decade. Social and cultural polarization among society inherited from the impact of secularist reforms led activists groups within the Kemalist elite to maintain symbolic violence on groups opposing the Kemalist definition of secularism. Moreover, it also led highly Westernized and educated segments of Turkish society to support military interventions in the name of protecting the dominant laicist vision of secularism, which distanced itself from liberal democratic norms in its response to the rising visibility of political Islam in the public sphere.

However, when the other pillar of the medal is concerned, as a reaction to the radical secularist policies, Islamic political opposition wanted to de-Kemalize culture and turned religious practices into a means of politics and thus further triggered the Kemalist prejudice and predisposition about the dangers of religious manifestation in the public sphere, and in this sense, the Islamist politics became part of the augmentation of the tension between democracy and secularism. This tension, in fact, serves as a resource base to rise up against Kemalist discourse. As a result, aggravation of this tension engenders an antagonistic aura in Turkey that limits the scope of the political participation and even restricts the freedom of individuals even when the majority of the Turkish population favors democratization up to the standards of Western Europe or the United States. Our main argument is that the political consequences and legacy of the early republican cultural revolution and radical secularist practices shaped the historical development of state-Islam interaction and created the paradoxical support of the secular democrats in Turkey for the military intervention during the February 28 process and the Islamists advocating an Anglo-Saxon model of liberal secularism.

In the 1990s, Turkish democracy, as Özbudun aptly argues, has faced a "number of constitutional problems" stemming from "the increasing importance of religious and ethnic issues, . . . such as Islam versus secularism, nation-state versus minority rights, and centralization versus decentralization. A full consolidation of Turkish democracy depends on the peaceful resolution of these ideas."[2] These difficulties might be related to the weakness of a "liberal 'thick' democracy, [which] stresses limited government, basic freedoms, the rule of law and a political culture of moderation, non-violence, compromise and tolerance," whereas "'thin' or 'procedural' democracy" includes a multiparty system, free elections, and parliamentary consolidation of opponents.[3]

Turkish democratization has not resulted in a serious attempt to expand the scope of the political, embracing successfully various interests and identities on the grounds of mutual respect and compromise. One might argue that this stems mainly from the certainties of Kemalism[4] and demands of new social movements, which become very clear in the Islamic quest for recognition and Kemalist resistance. In the struggle between political Islamism and Kemalist laicism, the early republican modernization came to the fore as the object of debate, revisited by both critics and revitalization. In fact it was the period in which state-Islam interaction was to a greater extent determined on the basis of Kemalist laicism called *laiklik*. Here *laiklik* constituted the basis of Kemalist modernization equated with Westernization, which meant transforming state and social structure.

The Kemalist project of modernization had a close tie with Ottoman legacy in general and Ottoman modernization. That is, the Turkish Revolution, launched during the 1920s and 1930s, was not a rupture in the Turkish history, but rather was the most radical outcome of the preceding modernization attempts initiated with the Tanzimat script toward the end of the Ottoman Empire.[5] In the process, Western models including scientific thinking, technological developments, administrative and social organizations gradually appeared to be grounds for legitimization for the Ottoman elite. The validity of "local" values for the Young Turks, especially in the last decades of the empire, began to be verified with regard to the "universal" Western ideas seen as a privileged category. For the Turkish nationalists, this "modern" outlook became the name of the attempt to transform the empire into a nation-state model.

The republican regime, during the formative years of the republic, initiated a modernist project to civilize the society on the basis of a sort of state-led nationalism. The Turkish polity was based principally on "state-dominant monoparty authoritarianism," eliminating any potential and alternative power centers.[6] Here the state came as an active agent and sole authorized power in launching a cultural revolution. The revolutionary elite established new cultural institutions such as the Turkish Historical Society (*Türk Tarih Cemiyeti*), the Turkish Language Society (*Türk Dil Cemiyeti*), and the People's Houses (*Halkevleri*) to promote and forge "the modern way of life" to reshape the society, to create future generations, and to tame the masses.[7] This state-led modernization is based on a specific concept of modernity that the Kemalists conceived only through its "institutional, ritual, symbolic, and aesthetic manifestations to set the official standards of exterior form and behavior against which people, ideas, and events have been measured and judged."[8] In this regard, the prescriptions for how to talk and listen, how to dress, how to eat, and so on all were necessary for being publicly visible. New standards, those of the "civilized" world, became obviously uncontested subject matters of Turkish identity coming to terms as a process of culturalization through which each Turkish citizen carries out such aim on the basis of dress, bearing, and physical and verbal manners.

Laicism, constituting the basis of the Kemalist project of modernity, was the crucial component of the official attitude to democracy and Islam. For the Kemalists, laicism meant the separation of state from religious life where religion would remain as a matter of conscience; on the other hand, in practice, it resulted in state control over religion. They attempted to control and domesticate Islam by institutionalizing it under state control; as in French conception, laic refers to nonreligious authorities' control over religion.[9] As a project, laicism also, perhaps most importantly, aimed to end the hegemony of Islamic concepts and popular Islamic practices, which were seen as the sources of a social and cultural archaism, over the mind of the Turks. At the beginning, as part of a controlling mechanism, the idea of reform in Islam was commonly accepted among the ruling circles; so the modernizing rulers strove to reform Islam and even create new rituals for it. Here the aim was to make a creation something like Protestantism; and the enlightened form of Islam would serve to justify the new reforms at some initial stages of reform. But, due to some popular reactions against reforms in Islam in the early 1930s, the policy ended. After that time, because Islam, and even religion in a general sense, was regarded as "archaic" and would lose its significance in the course of modernization, it was completely negated in the official discourse.[10] By means of efforts to describe new principles for the state and society, Kemalist laicism became a constituent part of new Turkish cultural identity and imposed it on the rest of the society. In short, laicism was not only the name of secularization of institutional, legal, and educational structures of the state, but also, perhaps more importantly, the name of the quest for creating a laic cultural identity.

Together with laicism, republicanism that was mainly inspired from "the centralist Jacobin model of republicanism"[11] constituted another basis of the Kemalist view of democracy. The notion of republic in the discourse of Kemalism is not simply the name of the political system nor the change of the regime from a sultan-ate to a republic but also the elimination of superstitious mentalities and manners that had "poisoned" the consciousness of the Turks throughout history; it is rather the name of a civilizational shift. For the Turkish revolutionary elite, democracy can only flourish in a laic and republican system coupled with the enlightenment of society. In fact, the elite were torn between the competing goals of emancipating and enlightening the people: the first implied trust; the second seemed to require strict control. The Turkish revolutionary elite of the 1930s discovered that the exis-tent "corruption" of the majority ensures a transition to democracy only by exter-nal involvement. In order to emancipate people from the bondage of tradition and religion, they felt themselves responsible to enlighten people via certain authori-tarian means. In that sense, for instance, as one of the policy makers of the period held, the revolutionary formulas should be injected into the minds of people even by force to emancipate and order the society.[12] In his famous İnkilap Dersleri (Revo-lutionary Courses), Recep Peker, under the subtitle "Using Force in Revolution," argued that the Turkish Revolution had to use force and violence against irtica (reactionism) so as to pave the way for the progress and prosperity of the coun-try.[13] For the revolutionaries of the 1930s, there was the "tyranny" of tradition and customs among people; that tyranny had to be swept away through "people's edu-cation," which was necessary for the emancipation and hence democratization of society, because "the rule of freedom means the predominance of an educated rea-son."[14] In order to smother the domination of tradition, the Kemalists portrayed themselves as the apostles and missionaries in the new crusade to enlighten the Turkish populations.

What is most paradoxical is that the Revolutionary elite applied religious termi-nology to embark on a revolutionary mission to "democratize" society. It used reli-gious terms and notions interchangeably with the revolutionary symbols. The People's Houses, the adult education centers of the 1930s, were labeled as "the Temples of Ideal" (Ülkü Mabetleri)[15]; the "apostles" (havari)[16] of revolution were recruited for the "village mission" (köy misyonerliği)[17]; the "divine revolution" (manevi inkilap)[18] was said to be disseminated by the zealous efforts of the "resplendent" (nurlu)[19] devotees of Kemalism. It might be argued that the revolutionary radical-ism of the Kemalist elite generally borrowed from religious forms and built on tra-ditional rituals. It is worthwhile to stress that the adult education institutions of the Republic such as the People's Houses and the Village Institutes became the sites of converting Turkish populations from Islamic codes of morality into the values of the Turkish revolution so as to redress them with a laic identity for attaining an ideal democracy. Hence, revolutionary acculturation of society entailed a barrage of laic rituals, some practiced through the revolutionary institutions of education.

That quest for establishing new symbolic codes for future democracy finds its true expression in the words of Mustafa Kemal:

> Turkey is going to build up a perfect democracy. How can there be a *perfect* democracy with half the country in bondage? In two years from now, every woman must be freed from this useless tyranny. Every man will wear a hat instead of a fez and every woman have her face uncovered; woman's help is absolutely necessary and she must have full freedom in order to take her share of her country's burden.[20]

The previous statement shows how significant modern standards and symbols are in crystallizing the role of symbols in the Kemalist democratic vision. In this crystallization, the new cultural institutions of the republic worked to remove all outer signs of conflict and the suppression of alternative value systems to preserve the harmony and uniformity of the society.

What is most important for our purposes is that these centers of culture functioned as crucial venues to the establishment of Turkey's particular notion of democracy. However, the revolutionary elite's perceptions of democracy are totally different from contemporary visions. The European Enlightenment tradition implanted in the Turkish revolutionary elite a profound commitment to the concept of democracy—the ideas of freedom, equality, representation, and, above all, the rule of the people. Most of the revolutionary elite had retained those commitments, but their philosophic and practical expression of the concepts had taken considerably different forms. They, consciously or unconsciously, often misconstrued the ideas concerning democracy and representation. Whatever and whenever such misapprehension occurred, the democratic idea was likely to have a certain appeal among the Turkish revolutionary elite. Nonetheless, they had the tendency to retain their commitment to the more broad and theoretical values of democracy—as a utopian and irresistible ideal—while freeing themselves from the traditional democratic forms and practices. The "ideal democracy" was based on the tutelage of the masses by the revolutionary elite who felt themselves obliged to mature the people believed to be "ignorant." Theoretically, the people continue to be the objects of worship, the source of supreme authority, and the fountainhead of truth. In practice, however, they become the subjects of intensive indoctrination and total commitment to the purposes of state as defined by their "vanguards." It can be maintained that the Kemalists were not interested in the representation of the existing structure of society, but in the representation of an imaginary people, which they intended to construct in the future. This kind of understanding of democracy led the republican elite to consider politics in a messianic fashion. This "political Messianism" based on secular, social morality postulated an enlightened, civilized, and prosperous tomorrow "to which men are irresistibly driven, and at which they are bound to arrive."[21] This postponed representation of society, or to put it another way, this sense of understanding of "belated democracy" constituted a great problem for the later generations. As a consequence, based on a kind of Jacobin utopianism, the Turkish revolutionary elite generally felt themselves responsible for "maturing" and "taming" the people, which would raise them up to a position at which they could be represented.

In a sense, the newly established cultural institutions became the centers of political Messianism to prepare the people for the belated democracy. As a matter of fact, they are sites of apostolic craft to disseminate the Truth, which can be captured only through the realization of revolutionary ideals. In other words, their goals of consolidation of power and social restructuring are intertwined with a peculiar conception of democracy; the education of the people went to other ends, which created a tension among the people because that priority was given to a revolutionary ideal, and this ideal came to grips with traditional values and vernacular culture. This is justified by the understanding that every country has its own peculiar way to democracy; the way to attain it should rely on forming "collective habits," and "amalgamated" social structure. Of course, this understanding refracted the elites' march to democracy in such a way that it turned out to be a serious obstacle to democracy; it was redressed with their view that in a society without laic revolutionary culture, democracy is not possible.

THE PROCESS OF TURKISH DEMOCRATIZATION

Turkish democratization began with the transition from authoritarian to competitive politics in 1946. The main reason that led Turkish leaders to make the decision was the previously mentioned Kemalist notion of democracy; "the success of Kemalist reforms," wrote Özbudun, "undermined the long-term legitimacy of the single-party system."[22] However, the early Kemalist reforms failed to successfully socialize and transform most of the population on the path of its laic and revolutionary culture, due to the lack of technological development hindering communication and transportation. The result would be a widening gap between the values of the center and that of the masses, leading to some loss of the legitimacy of the national culture produced by the state's agencies. In the multiparty context of the 1950s, political and economic liberalization and urbanization provided the suitable ground for the rise of "alternative" cultural forms as new political projects. In other words, internal political and social conflicts inevitably made the struggle among various definitions of national culture the hottest issue on the political agenda. This process was accelerated by the policies of the Democrat Party governments (1950–60) that tried to justify Islamic practices as well as traditional and local values.

In 1960 the Turkish military intervened in the democratic process, because in the eyes of the officers the politicians deviated for the most part from the Kemalist vision of democracy and laicism. Thus their goal was to restructure the life of the Turkish population culturally as well as politically, which also constituted the basic motives for those of the later 1971 and 1980 military interventions. The leaders and supporters of the coup sought ways to regulate and reorganize politics on the basis of the "preferences of modernity, positivism and secularism in their earlier official definitions of the early Republican cultural revolutions."[23] The 1961 constitution was indeed the product of the will to maintain the project of social transformation. The efforts on the part of the state elite, particularly those of the military, came to naught in procuring the wanted "order" for both politics and the society in the 1960s and 1970s. The result was the repetition of two other military coups in 1971 and 1980.

During the process of Kemalist military interventions into the dynamics of state-society relations during the multiparty political system, the cultural restructuring of the 1980 military intervention and the 1982 constitution did introduce compromises between the certainties of Kemalist ideology and the pressures of popular Islamic culture. The new constitution emphasized the importance of the traditional and historical values of the Turks, namely Islamic culture, signifying to some extent a rupture of the orthodox Kemalist discourse. Although Islam still had to remain outside of politics, the interventionists recognized Islam as a necessary ethical base for personal identity and as a crucial antidote to communism and other fractional and divisive movements. However, such limited recognition did not stop their insistent struggle against the rising visibility of symbols and images of Islam in the public realm, regarded them as synonymous with *irtica*. As a matter of fact, democratization and globalization made the Islamically oriented groups more visible in both the political and public spheres. The Motherland Party governments under Prime Minister Turgut Özal provided a successful synthesis between Kemalism and the religiosity of the masses. At that optimistic point, the democratic aspects of Turkish secularism were on the rise as well. But, thanks to democratization, Islamic groups began to gain roots in the civil society and political sphere. These groups, together with ethnic (Kurdish) and sectarian (Alevi) movements, were able to question the Kemalist certainties and made claims to new rights and entitlements.

A War of Cultures in the 1990s and the Rise of the Welfare Party

In the 1980s and 1990s the previously mentioned cultural war had a negative effect on Turkish politics, partly due to the impact of globalization. It was an era in Turkey, as well as in other countries, when universalization and particularization simultaneously crystallized, with the certainties of the nation-states beginning to erode in the face of effective claims to identity by various societal elements. In the process, particular values began to be recognized as elements of the rising politics of culture and identity.

Together with the Kurdish movement, the Islamic one (which has questioned the very principles of Kemalism, especially laicism and republicanism), was the most prominent of the new social movements encouraged by globalization.[24] Its demands, especially in the 1990s, created one of the biggest political crises Turkey has faced throughout the history of the republic. It was this February 28 process that was a turning point in state-Islam and state-culture relationship in Turkey, and it was mainly against the Islamic groups in the country. The Welfare Party (WP, *Refah Partisi*), founded in 1983 as heir to the National Salvation Party (NSP; one of the major political movements in the 1970s), came to the fore as the political reflection of Islamic critiques of the Kemalist legacy. Having favored a new community based on a shared religious identity, the WP no doubt became the rival of the state-sponsored ideology. Since the 1970s, the NSP-WP line has used Islamism as a counterideology against their secular "Other" to legitimize their political actions. The new Islamists were under the effect of "traditionalizing" and "authenticating" the discourse of Islamism of the late Ottoman era, in which this discourse was critiqued with the unrestricted imitations of Western manners and symbols. Islamist thought began to be systematized under an ideology from the work of a group of intellectuals of the *İkinci Mesrutiyet* (the Second Mesrutiyet, 1908–18). Islam was not an obstacle to progress; it could even provide both technological and political awakening and so had to command the spheres of state and society. It was obvious from the views of the Islamists that the culture of each society was a historically unique entity incommensurable with Western culture.[25]

However, in the 1970s, the Islamists of modern Turkey developed a counterideology against their secular "Other" and within the confines of the modern nation-state. This orientation began to gain wide popular support, especially in rapidly urbanizing areas in the 1960s and 1970s, where the secular, positivistic ideology of the Kemalists had failed to provide an ethical base to replace traditional values. The leaders of the NSP accused the state elite as being materialistic and alienated from their own authentic values. The rejection of Kemalist symbolism was at the center of their discourse preaching the pride of being Muslim as members of an idealized religious community. Thus it can be argued that this was a period of elevation of countersymbols against those of the Kemalists. This sort of open challenge to the legitimate use of cultural codes by the state elite could hardly be welcomed. It was one of the reasons that paved the way to the 1980 military intervention.

Islamism in Turkey appeared to be a political cultural movement essentially antithetic to the Kemalist model of modernization. The 1990s, coupled with the globalization process, signified the remarkably augmenting weight of the Islamic demands in Turkey.[26] The expanding market and liberal openings made these demands more and more publicly visible. Since the early 1990s, partly because of the vacuum in the center of Turkish politics and the rising tide of globalization, the religious segments of Turkish society began to side more with the WP. In the 1994 local elections, it won the majority of the votes in most of the big cities including Istanbul and Ankara, and in the 1995 elections received almost 22 percent of the votes.

Following the NSP tradition, the WP put strong emphasis on Islam as the primary focus of loyalty. The two components forming the core ideological basis of the WP were the themes of "justice" and "identity."[27] The party used the term "justice," especially in its manifesto *Adil Düzen* (the Just Order), as a panacea for economic decline, moral corruption, social inequalities, and, perhaps most importantly, for the alienation resulting from the Kemalist way of modernization. Dealing with the problems of identity and justice, the party leaders intended to constitute a new moral base aside from socioeconomic issues. This new moral base was regarded as necessary to project a holistic vision of community, a "secure shelter" for all, an antidote to the evils of modern individualism and alienation. In this sense, in the election campaigns the discourse of the WP had a populist tone embracing all segments and differences of the country.

When the WP was in the opposition, it maintained a very conflictual and aggressive discourse that compartmentalized the society as "infidels" and "Muslims," or enemies of Islam and supporters of Islam. This was an antagonizing discourse for the functioning of democracy, which led to increasing polarization in Turkish politics. In some ways, the WP in general publicized the restrictive categories of Kemalism. In other words, paradoxically, the WP had internalized Kemalism's authoritarian conceptions of democracy and society as well as its symbolic use of politics.[28] It might be argued that Kemalism, by influencing its rivals, rendered possible a resemblance between itself and its adversaries. WP's program aimed at determining the boundaries of a new community by offering a prescription to define the symbols of sociopolitical and socioeconomic life. Like the Kemalists, its leaders conceived the democratic mechanism to establish their "alternative" symbolic universe, setting some prescriptions for a new public identity.

After the 1995 general elections, the WP came to power as a coalition partner of the True Path Party (TPP, *Doğru Yol Partisi*) on June 28, 1996. Shortly after coming to power, the WP's pragmatic leaders began to confirm their commitment to the regime and Kemalism, highlighting their own interpretation.[29] This was very obvious, especially in the fifth general congress of the party held on October 13, 1996. For example, compared with the previous congress at which the party had declared "a reform program which included recognizing Kurdish identity and cultural rights," at the fifth congress it declared that "it was not possible to find even one word about Kurds except the statement that terrorism should be fought to the end."[30]

But the WP's ruling cadre gave their adherents several clues confirming that the primary ideals of the party continued. The WP leaders in power frequently depicted their different views of secularism by causing intense discussions over the decisions of the Military Council (*Askeri Şura*) on the dismissal of military officers and the headscarf (*türban*) issue. For instance, State Minister Abdullah Gül of the WP stated that their view of secularism differed from that of the army and voiced the party's disagreement with the council's pressure on certain military officers to resign. He went on, saying, "We will change Article 125 of the Constitution so that these former [purged army] officers can apply to the court."[31] In a parallel decision, on the prohibition of headscarves, especially at the universities and in public offices, Minister of Justice Şevket Kazan prepared a circular that would enable female law school graduates with headscarves to be lawyers, public prosecutors, and judges. Moreover, Prime Minister Necmettin Erbakan told the university rectors and the Higher Education Authority (YÖK) officials that they should not get involved in the headscarf issue. During the rule of the WP-led coalition, women with headscarves became more and more visible in the public realm, and even some public offices.

The situation disturbed the secular sensibilities of many social segments and provided the Kemalist wing with an opportunity to push the army, the judiciary, and academia into confrontation with the WP. Kemalist and secular-inclined dailies became the voice of the campaign against such moves. This emerging front of Kemalist opposition to the WP was especially utilizing the following events that unexpectedly gave rise to a crisis for the regime: the official proposal of building a mosque in a Westernized section of Istanbul (Taksim) that to the WP's leaders symbolized a "reconquest" of the city; Erbakan's invitation to the religious order leaders, who dressed up in religious form, to an Ramadan dinner reception (*iftar*) at the Prime Ministry building; the minor speeches of some mayors and deputies of the WP who criticized and denounced the Kemalist ideology. These were all prominent symbolic acts that were considered by the state elite as disturbing the basis of "Kemalist democratic regime."

There were two main reactions: the first and most important one was the military's reaction, and the second was that of mainly state-led, civil groups, including the mass media, judiciary, civil associations, and academia with secularist inclinations. In fact, the second reaction led to a homogenized Kemalist front cheering the attitudes of the military by organizing several meetings, conferences, and rallies. Actually, these responses of different Kemalist sectors had been loudly voiced after the WP's success in the 1994 municipality and 1995 general elections. These "social" reactions developed as a response to the WP's leaders' claim that they were the true representatives of society. When they came to power, especially in influential municipalities, they began to revive the symbols and values of the society. To prove that their culture not only belonged to the state but also to society, the Kemalists mobilized a secular front (including the state agents, media, private sector, labor unions, and civil organizations) to celebrate, for example, the Republic Days, a commemoration of the direct participation of the people since 1994.[32] In fact, the Kemalist emphasis on the celebration of the Republic Days aimed at meeting the efforts of WP leaders who began to unofficially celebrate May 29, the "Conquest of Istanbul," as an "alternative national day" in order to "construct an alternative national identity, evoked as an Ottoman-Islamic civilization as opposed to the secular, modern Turkish Republic."[33] Several national festivals and celebrations were employed as rallies against the Islamic groups in such an unusual way that their foremost agenda was to preserve and perpetuate the values and norms of the republic.

In general, the counter-acts by the Kemalist front mainly came to the fore as symbolic forms; large numbers of secularists began to wear badges of Atatürk, and they made public visits to the mausoleum of Atatürk.[34] This in fact was a simple reflection of their struggle over the "essential" symbols of the nation. The Kemalist strand since 1994 had revived and expanded countrywide the tradition of organizing "republican balls and dance parties," like the ones held in the 1930s, particularly in the commemorations of the republic on October 29. Participation in such activities in itself was deemed proof of being Kemalist and modern. Similar acts reached their peak points during the celebrations of the seventy-fifth anniversary of the republic on October 29, 1998. It is important to note that after the fall of the WP the interest in these sorts of activities drastically declined. It appears that civil reactions to the WP are directly related to the military's sensitivity.

However, the reaction of the military was the most effective and most determining. As the chief guardian and protector of the Kemalist regime, the military labeled the rise of the WP and its emphasis on countersymbols as a serious and, of course, symptomatic reaction to Kemalist "modern" principles. Their belief was in line with the classical Kemalist belief that Islam, seen as a reactionary attitude to modernization, should be swept away from the political domain. The regime crisis came to the fore during the meetings of the National Security Council (NSC), in which both WP ministers and army leaders were members, especially after the last quarter of 1996. Turkey once more profoundly experienced the involvement of the military in politics in such a way that "it [had] placed itself above the restrictions, scrutiny, and public criticism that apply to all other sectors of society."[35] Actually, through utilizing the NSC, the military became the primary actor of politics. The military has taken a firm stand against Islamic politics via several NSC decisions recommending to the government certain measures to be taken against the rising antisecular activities.

The February 28 Intervention and Crises of Turkish Democracy

The NSC meeting of February 28, 1997, was critical; it has been considered as a "postmodern" military intervention against Islamic groups. It was evaluated as postmodern even by one of its initiators because the military changed the political structure without direct intervention, by only using and mobilizing the media, universities, some interest groups, and bureaucracy.[36] The object behind the intervention was that the Islamists would harm democracy by way of misusing it. Nevertheless, the military violated the democratic principles for the sake of democracy. By intervening once again in politics, the military had undermined the very consolidation of democracy in Turkey with the aim to protect democracy from Islamic fundamentalism. For this purpose, the Turkish Armed Forces founded the so-called *Bati Çalişma Grubu* (West Working Group) to inspect the administrators and officers aiding the Islamists by deciphering their activities and urging the government to dismiss them from their jobs.[37]

For the Kemalist bloc, the military used its legitimate power in its struggle against *irtica*. The military justified its activities as necessary for the preservation and perpetuation of the secular regime. For example, Ahmet Taner Kişlali, a journalist in the pro-Kemalist newspaper *Cumhuriyet*, approved the involvement of the military in politics in order to prevent Islamist activities:

> [The Turkish army] is fighting against the *shariatists* in every part of the country. The name of this is a "total war"! A "Death or survival (*ölüm kalim*)" combat. It is a war between who want[s] to save the *laic* democratic republic and who has been destroying the fundamental character of the Republic. . . . There is no more a possibility to keep the game hidden. Both sides should play the game overtly.[38]

The February 28 NSC decisions comprised certain measures aimed at diminishing the public visibility of Islam and its symbols.[39] The recommendations intended to resume the state control over religion, education, culture, and economy. The recommendations consisted of the articles that highlighted the very threat that the cultural symbols and public visibilities of political Islam have posed against the Kemalist laicism: dress of people (such as headscarves for women and religious garb and beards for men), Qur'an recitation schools, the large number of clergy (*imam-hatip*) schools, and "Islamic" capitals and foundations were singled out as threats to the regime.

Another significant act of February 28 that was aimed to shape the public opinion was the military briefings presented by the army to the judiciary, businesspeople, trade union representatives, academics, and the mass media about the antisecular activities of Islamists. These briefings signified a total cultural war eliminating all "anti-laic" life forms. The last briefing, called *İrtica Brifingi* (Briefing on Reactionism), was held on June 11, 1997, to again warn the government about the rise of Islamism as a political movement.[40] As a complementary declaration of the February 28 NSC decisions, an attempt was made to describe the movement as *Siyasal İslam* (Political Islam)—a political movement that uses the Islamic symbols and discourses to come to power by using democratic mechanisms and to reorganize the Turkish Republic according to the Shari'a. In this view, all organized groups with a religious orientation, such as political parties, foundations, interest groups, economic cooperations, and civil initiatives, were identified in one way or another as the instruments of political Islam. The WP, therefore, was regarded as the chief organization responsible for that organized reactionary movement, though it did not represent all religious groups in Turkey. Various Islamic groups were no longer able to define themselves outside of the WP, whereas all the secularists, even the very democratic ones, had to advocate the Kemalist front, which symbolized the secular front against the WP. This briefing also mentioned the resumption of the state authority over religious affairs, which were said to have gradually come under the control of religious foundations and orders. In sum, the briefing portrayed political Islam as the primary threat to the republic, giving first priority to the elimination of *irtica* for the survival of the "laic-democratic" regime.[41]

An end product of this process was the economic embargo that the military institutions placed over the so-called Islamic companies following a general staff command. What made a company "Islamic" was any financial support it gave to *irtica*. The general staff's black list covered nearly one hundred companies.[42] After the publication of this list, some of these companies declared that they had not given any support to Islamism and that they were devoted to Atatürkism and the principles of the republic. Another striking case that manifests the military's sensitivity on the symbolic appearance of political Islam was the issue of dress. In both the NSC meeting of February 28 and the *irtica* briefing, those men in religious garb (*sarik ve cübbe*) and those women with a special religious clothing (*çarşaf*) had been presented as the public images of *irtica*, especially those of the so-called conservative Fatih district of Istanbul. It was stated that the clothing that violated the dress code should be banned. Therefore women with headscarves could not attend universities, and in some cases men in *sarik* and *cübbe* (traditional head covers and long garb) were arrested, as they were incompatible with the civilized vision of Turkey. In addition, other measures of the February 28 process that have directly affected the everyday lives of the ordinary people were sending teams of state inspectors who monitor Friday prayers around the country whether or not there were any acts against laicism, and dictating the charities of animal skins that Muslims can present after the traditional annual sacrifice to semiofficial Türk Hava Kurumu (the Turkish Aeronautical Association).[43]

The NSC decisions and these briefings, by enhancing the public pressure against the WP-led government, gave rise to a process that ended with the resignation of that government. Shortly after the resignation and displacement of the WP-TTP coalition government, the Motherland Party (MP, *Anavatan Partisi*), the Democratic Left Party (DLP, *Demokratik Sol Parti*), and the Democratic Turkey Party (DTP) formed a minority coalition government under the prime ministry of Mesut Yilmaz by the initiative of the military. The anti-*irtica* measures were accelerated under this government. Parallel to the developments during the preceding government, the NSC promulgated a Report of National Security Politics. In this report, prepared by the military, *irtica* is stated as the first and foremost threat for the security of the country. Islamic groups severely reacted to this report, because, in this report, *irtica* was equated with separatism (the most serious crime in the Turkish civil law), justifying several anti-Islamic implementations.[44]

A case was filed against the WP to close it down on the grounds that the party had brought the country near "civil war." The public prosecutor of the Supreme Court, Vural Savaş, argued that "[the] Welfare Party has become the locus of the all anti-laic activities."[45] The indictment resembled a Kemalist manifesto more than a formal charge. The party was closed down in accordance with the judgment of the Constitution Court—Turkey's highest court and a bulwark of Kemalist sentiment—for violating the principles of the state in January 1998. Its principal leaders, including Necmettin Erbakan and Şevket Kazan, were banned from politics for five years.

This time, its followers came with a new party, the Virtue Party (VP, *Fazilet Partisi*), as heir to the WP. They tried to readjust themselves to the legal and political frameworks in an attempt to not be discounted. In their new discourse, there is very little reference to Islam and much more emphasis on the rule of law, democracy, civil rights, and liberties.[46] In other words, when their claims to new rights and entitlements were rejected, the leaders of the WP-VP party strived to look for the alliances in the West previously condemned as sources of decadence and corruption. This search for a global alliance transcending the nation-state may be seen as part of the globalization process.[47] At the beginning, the leaders of the WP, during both opposition and power, were in search of alliances in the Islamic world, which was the expression of their wish for transcending the boundaries of the existing nation-state to attain an Islamic community, but after the February 28 decisions we witnessed the opposite tendency among the leaders of the VP as they considered some basic issues such as the headscarf ban and religious education in terms of civil liberties. This is very clearly seen in the case of Merve Kavakci who was elected an MP from the list of the VP in the 1999 general election. She was the first woman to seek to wear a headscarf in parliament, but was not allowed to do so during her oath in the parliament. She was then stripped of her parliamentary status and her citizenship due to accusations of previously acquiring U.S. citizenship. Merve Kavakci and the VP's leaders emphasized wearing a headscarf as her democratic right, and so for them it should be considered as a matter of human rights.[48]

In the days following, Turkey's chief prosecutor, Vural Savaş, launched a new attempt to close the VP, citing the headscarf issue and the VP's being a continuation of the Welfare Party as the two main reasons. He charged its leaders with "inciting enmity and hatred through religious and doctrinal differences."[49] This criminal investigation had been on the agenda for two years, serving to make the VP a more loyal party to the principles of the regime. At the end, it was banned in June 2001 for undermining Kemalist secular order, in which the headscarf issue was mentioned as the main reason.

CONCLUSION

In this study our main conclusion is that radical interpretation of secularism has set limits to the scope of Turkish politics. Thus "alternative" political and social movements with different identity claims have been regarded as divisive and reactionary and so are excluded and marginalized for the consolidation and optimization of democratic ideals. In the 1990s, the Islamic quest for recognition came to the fore mainly as a reaction to Kemalist laicism, and so Islamic political opposition developed alternative cultural forms and symbols, which became a means of politics for them. The radical Kemalist elite felt themselves obliged to hinder the public visibility of Islam for the sake of democracy. That movement caused the Kemalist elite to redefine their idea of modernism on the basis of early republican notions shaped during the single-party period of Jacobin laicism. The result is a cultural war between laic and Islamic groups.

The culmination of this war manifested itself in the February 28 military intervention, which paved the way for the revitalization and further normalization of the tension between secularism and democracy in Turkey. The forces of February 28 that were working to "democratize" the country sought to produce new forms of discipline and new ways of organizing the masses. It was this process whereby secularism was reduced to a version of Kemalism, its radical version, and Islam was reduced to a political party, the WP. Thus, as a result of the politicization of symbols, democracy has been relinquished and subordinated at the expense of a certain interpretation of Kemalist laicism and political Islam.

In this process, the state elite not only suppressed the WP but also tried to control and ban the symbolic aspects of popular Muslim culture, such as Qur'an recitation schools, headscarves, and the like, which had hitherto been associated with the Islamic groups in participating in the modern public sphere. Henceforth, it began to be problematic for a religious person to practice politics by asserting the religious sensibilities and traditional symbols. The only way to practice politics left for the Islamist is to highlight the liberal democratic concepts and values against the Kemalist notion of democracy. This new political style of the Islamists was accused of practicing a form of trickery. Although Islamic groups failed to promote a political attitude toward cultural pluralism, they now are utilizing a liberal democratic discourse as an emancipation tactic to avoid Kemalist symbolic violence.

Nowadays in Turkey an atmosphere is beginning to manifest in which most identities make efforts to recognize the Other, but do not make a point of learning from the Other. In order to establish a functioning democracy in a global context, recognition should go hand in hand with learning on the basis of a constant dialogue. Nevertheless, the orthodox interpreters of Kemalism who are politically hegemonic continue to be unfamiliar with and hostile to the idea of dialogue between the political establishment and social segments who feel strongly about their religious and ethnic identities and practices. This might be the main reason behind the failure of transforming the state into a more democratic form.

NOTES

1. The introductory section of this article is adapted from Ertan Aydin's article "The Peculiarities of Turkish Revolutionary Ideology in the 1930s: The Ulku Version of Kemalism, 1933–1936," *Middle Eastern Studies* 42, no. 3 (July 2005).

2. Ergun Özbudun, "Turkey: Crises, Interruptions, and Reequilibrations," in *Politics in Developing Countries*, ed. Larry Diamond, Juan Linz, and Seymour Lipset (Boulder, Colo.: Lynne Rienner, 1995), 259.

3. For "thin" and "thick" democracy, see Benjamin Neuberger, "Democracy and Democratization in Africa," in *Identity, Culture and Globalization*, ed. E. Be-Rafael and Yitzhak Sternberg (Boston, Mass.: Brill, 2001), 193.

4. Kemalism, first and foremost, has been the official ideology of the Turkish state since the early years of the republic. As the unique ethos of legitimacy for political authority, Kemalism plays a significant part not only in determining the boundaries of the political, but also in comprising the standards of judgment in every sphere of social life. For this definition of Kemalism, see Taha Parla, *Türkiye'de Siyasal Kültürün Resmi Kaynaklari, Cilt I, Atatürk'ün Nutuk'u (The Sources of Political Culture in Turkey, vol. 1, Atatürk's Speech)* (İstanbul, Turkey: İletişim, 1991), 13–15.

5. See Şerif Mardin, "Religion and Secularism in Turkey," in *Atatürk: Founder of a Modern State*, ed. Ali Kazancıgil and Ergun Özbudun (London: Hurst and Company, 1997), 209.

6. See Andrew Davison, *Secularism and Revivalism in Turkey: A Hermeneutic Reconsideration* (New Haven, Conn.: Yale Univ. Press, 1998), 141.

7. It was about the creation of a "new national entity" and opening a "new historical phase for the Turkish nation." Ahmet Asim, "Türk İnkilabinin Mana ve Mahiyeti" ("Meaning and True Nature of the Turkish Revolution"), *Ayin Tarihi* (March 1934): 74–75.

8. Sibel Bozdoğan and Reşat Kasaba, "Introduction," in *Rethinking Modernity and National Identity in Turkey*, ed. S. Bozdoan and R. Kasaba (Seattle: Univ. of Washington Press, 1997), 5.

9. Davison, *Secularism and Revivalism in Turkey*.

10. For example, for Necmeddin Sadik, one of the legislators of Kemalism, religious feelings and ideas belong to "the Middle Ages," where there was no "freedom of mind, and no freedom of conscience. Everyone was required to think according to the judgments of religion." Necmeddin Sadık, "Laik Ne Demektir?" ("What Is Laicism?"), *Ülkü* 2, no. 12 (1933): 371.

11. Nilüfer Göle, "The Freedom of Seduction for Muslim Women," *New Perspectives Quarterly* 15, no. 3 (1998): 49.

12. Necip Ali, "İnkilap ve Türk Kanunu Medenisi" ("Revolution and Turkish Civil Law"), *Ülkü* 2, no. 9 (1933): 178.

13. Recep Peker, *İnkilap Tarihi Ders Notlari (Lecture Notes of History of Revolution)*, (İstanbul, Turkey: İletişim Yayinlari, 1984).

14. Mehmet Saffet, "İnklap Terbiyesi" ("Revolutionary Education"), *Ülkü* 2, no. 8 (1933): 107.

15. Necip Ali, "Halkevleri Yildönümünde Necip Ali Bey'in Nutku" ("Necip Ali Bey's Speech at the Anniversary of the People's Houses"), *Ülkü* 1, no. 2 (1933): 104.

16. Hamit Zübeyr, "Halk Terbiyesi Vasitalari" ("The Means of People Education"), *Ülkü* 1, no. 2 (1933): 152.

17. Nusret Köymen, "Köy Misyonerliği" ("Village Missionarism"), *Ülkü* 2, no. 7 (1933): 150.

18. Mehmet Saffet, "Kültür İnklabimiz" ("Our Cultural Revolution"), *Ülkü* 1, no. 5 (1933): 351.

19. Nusret Kemal, "Halkçilik" ("Populism"), *Ülkü* 1, no. 3 (1933): 190.

20. Cited in Grace Ellison, *Turkey To-Day* (London: Hutchinson and Co., 1929), 8.

21. Jacob L. Talmon, *The Origins of Totalitarian Democracy* (Suffolk, U.K.: Penguin Books, 1952), 4.

22. Ergun Özbudun, *Contemporary Turkish Politics* (Boulder, Colo.: Lynne Reinner, 2000), 22. Besides this, two other motives were the changing international system and socioeconomic transformations in Turkish society (19).

23. Hasan Bülent Kahraman, "A Journey of Rupture and Conflict: The Culture in Purgatory," *Privateview* (Autumn 1997): 109.

24. The Orthodox Kemalist establishment has regarded Kurdish and Islamic movements as the main "enemies within." For further details, see Eric Rouleau, "Turkey's Dream of Democracy," *Foreign Affairs* 76, no. 6 (Nov.–Dec. 2000): 100–115.

25. For the views of Islamists of this period, see Niyazi Berkes, *The Development of Secularism in Turkey* (Montreal: McGill Univ. Press, 1966), 362–63.

26. On this see Haldun Gülalp, "Globalization and Political Islam: The Social Bases of Turkey's Welfare Party," *Int. J. Middle East Studies* 33 (2001): 433–48.

27. M. Hakan Yavuz, "Political Islam and the Welfare (*Refah*) Party in Turkey," *Comparative Politics* (Oct. 1997): 73–76.

28. Menderes Çinar, "Postmodern Zamanların Kemalist Projesi," *Birikim* (1996): 35.

29. See Jenny B. White, "Pragmatists or Ideologues? Turkey's Welfare Party in Power," *Current History* (Jan. 1997): 27.

30. Burhaneddin Duran, "Approaching the Kurdish Question via Adil Düzen: An Islamist Formula of the Welfare Party for Ethnic Coexistence," *Journal of Muslim Minority Affairs* 18, no. 1 (1998): 118.

31. *Zaman* (İstanbul daily newspaper), September 26, 1996.

32. Yael Navaro-Yashin, "Travesty and Truth: Politics of Culture and Fantasies of the State in Turkey" (unpublished Ph.D. diss., Princeton University, January 1998), 289–302.

33. Alev Çinar, "National History as a Contested Site: The Conquest of Istanbul and Islamist Negotiations of the Nation," *Comparative Studies in Society and History* 43, no. 2 (2001): 364–91.

34. In fact Atatürk's "'personality cult' in the shape of numerous huge banners of his likeness reached new heights on Republic Day of 1994." Hugh Poulton, *Top Hat, Grey Wolf and Crescent: Turkish Nationalism and the Turkish Republic* (London: Hurst and Company, 1997), 191.

35. Jeremy Salt, "Turkey's Military 'Democracy,'" *Current History* (Feb. 1999): 72.

36. See "Mor Üniformalinin' Gerçek Öyküsü" ("Real Story of One with Purple Official Dress"), *Milliyet* (İstanbul daily newspaper), January 15, 2001.

37. Murat Belge, "Ordu Yaparsa Meşru . . ." ("All the Army Does Is Legitimate . . ."), *Radikal* (Istanbul daily newspaper), July 13, 1997.

38. Ahmet Taner Kişlali, *Cumhuriyet* (Istanbul daily newspaper), January 11, 1997.

39. For the decisions, see *Turkish Daily News* (Ankara daily newspaper), March 3, 1997.

40. See Muzaffer Şahin, ed., *MGK 28 Şubat Öncesi ve Sonrasi (MGK Before and After February 28)* (Ankara, Turkey: Ufuk Kitabevi, 1997), 111–24.

41. *İrtica* was portrayed as the main internal threat, regarded more dangerous than the other internal one, the armed secessionist Kurdish movement organized under the Kurdistan Labor Party (PKK, *Partia Karkeran Kurdistan*). See Duran, "Approaching the Kurdish Questions," 123.

42. *Milliyet*, June 6, 1997.

43. See "Fundamental Separation," *The Economist*, June 10, 2000, 11.

44. *Gazete Pazar* (İstanbul weekly newspaper), November 9, 1997.

45. *Sabah* (İstanbul daily newspaper), May 22, 1997.

46. See Whit Mason, "The Future of Political Islam in Turkey," *World Policy Journal* 17, no. 2 (2000): 56–70.

47. See Elisabeth Gerle, "Contemporary Globalization and Its Ethical Challenges," *The Ecumenical Review* 52, no. 2 (April 2000): 158–71.

48. See Stephen Kinzer, "An Official's Head Scarf Upsets a Turkish Taboo," *New York Times*, May 2, 1999.

49. "Fundamental Separation," 11.

Religious Fundamentalisms and Democratic Social Practices

Or, Why a Democracy Needs Fundamentalists, and Why They Need a Democracy

John P. Burgess

Fundamentalist religious movements in North American Protestant Christianity interact in complex ways with the secular, pluralistic, democratic social order within which they find themselves. On the one hand, these movements arise as a reaction against the larger social, political order. The secular and pluralistic values of Western democracy threaten the ultimate, religious meanings that fundamentalists find embedded in their religious traditions. On the other hand, fundamentalist religious movements are deeply influenced by secular, pluralistic, democratic society. These movements align themselves with a great religious past, but they are a thoroughly modern phenomenon.[1]

The role of holy texts in fundamentalist religious movements helps to illustrate these complex interactions.[2] Central to secular, pluralistic, democratic social orders is the assumption that matters of truth are subject to critical examination and debate. In contrast, fundamentalist religious movements argue that their holy texts establish absolute truths. What is needed is not critical inquiry but submissive acceptance. Yet fundamentalists use these texts in ways that betray the sensibilities of the wider culture. Like democratic societies, fundamentalist religious movements root standards of belief and practice in authoritative texts, not in social custom or personal authority. Texts become the source of abstract, universal laws—that is, principles for regulating social behavior. The fundamentalist appeal to the "text" is simultaneously an act of protest against a democratic culture and an accommodation to it.

The fact that fundamentalist religious movements are as much a product of modernity as a turn away from it ought to give members of a democratic society pause. The very characteristics of fundamentalism that are most disturbing—its adherents' sense of self-certainty and absolutism and their tendencies toward moral self-righteousness and legalism—mirror, even if in exaggerated form, aspects of a modern democratic society that most of us would rather not acknowledge. Fundamentalism may distort the values of a secular, pluralistic, democratic society, but these distortions also point to dangers inherent in modern democratic society itself.

A democratic society needs its fundamentalists because they help it to look at itself more honestly. At the same time, fundamentalists need a democratic society, both because it checks their worst tendencies toward absolutism and because it offers them the social space in which they can make their critique.

I.

In a provocative essay published as part of the American Academy of Arts and Sciences' Fundamentalism Project, Jewish scholar Haym Soloveitchik explores the role of texts in fundamentalist, or haredi, Judaism in North America, Europe, and Israel. Soloveitchik notes that traditional Jewish practice has never been dictated by the halakah alone, that is, Jewish law as borne by the Talmud and its commentaries. As Soloveitchik observes, "A way of life is not learned but rather absorbed. Its transmission is mimetic, imbibed from parents and friends, and patterned on conduct regularly observed in home and street, synagogue and school."[3] In the Jewish past, this way of life often but not always accorded with halakhic requirements. The weight of custom sometimes led interpreters to try to bring the text in accord with popular practice, rather than the other way around. Soloveitchik says, "The written word was reread in light of traditional behavior."[4]

As Soloveitchik notes, traditional Jewish practice in Eastern Europe began to break down in the late nineteenth and early twentieth centuries. The precipitating factors were many, including the influence of new political ideologies (such as socialism and Zionism), the impact of Enlightenment secularism (especially in the urban setting), and the mass migration of Jews to the United States and Israel. The Holocaust was the final, crowning blow. In its aftermath, "tradition" was no longer a way of life that a Jew could simply assume; rather, one now had to make a choice— either to acculturate partially or fully to a society defined by secular, pluralistic, democratic values or to embrace Jewish tradition and to reject that brave, new world.

The haredim chose tradition. Unable to rely any longer on the socializing power of custom, they made a conscious effort to practice a Jewish identity and appealed to sacred texts to assist them. One would now turn to the Talmud and its commentaries alone, not to social custom, in order to know what one as a Jew was supposed to do. The texts would provide a standard for behavior (201–2).

Soloveitchik notes that this concern for texts has translated into a greater concern for formal Jewish education. The school has come to play a new role in Jewish life; it now bears "most of the burden of imprinting Jewish identity" (216). In addition, haredi Judaism has given birth to a flood of publications on how Jews can practically observe the requirements of the halakah. "A way of life has become a *regula*, and behavior, once governed by habit, is now governed by rule" (201). For the haredim, "religious life must be constructed anew and according to the groundplan embedded in the canonized literature and in that literature alone" (205).

Soloveitchik notes, however, that Jewish religious texts do not easily lend themselves to this kind of use. The haredim go to the texts in order to know what in a practical sense they are supposed to do—what under the new and complex conditions of the modern world they are to eat, how they are to keep the Sabbath, and when and where they are to interact with Gentiles—but the texts do not always provide a clear answer. What the practitioner typically finds is not one point of view but several, and the text rarely offers a precise way of reconciling the differences. One gets a slice of the ancient community's debate about what a Jew is supposed to do rather than a precise law code that is clearly applicable to the present.

Moreover, texts require interpretation, and interpretation inevitably results in a degree of uncertainty. As Soloveitchik observes, "One learns best by being shown, that is to say, mimetically. When conduct *is* learned from texts, conflicting views about its performance literally proliferate and the simplest gesture becomes acutely complicated" (202). In this thicket of possible behaviors, practitioners increasingly turn to legal experts to provide authoritative answers. The scholar plays an increasingly prominent role in shaping Jewish identity (217–18).

Among Soloveitchik's conclusions, two stand out. First, Soloveitchik suggests that the haredi concern for personal and communal regulation has emerged at the very moment Jews' sense of living in the presence of the divine has radically diminished. Jewish ritual is no longer the occasion for a dramatic encounter with the Holy One of Israel; rather, it is the occasion for constantly questioning whether one is doing things right—that is, by the book. What distinguishes the observant Jew is not "the perception of God as a *daily, natural* force" but the rules by which one has chosen to live:

> Zealous to continue traditional Judaism unimpaired, [the haredim] seek to ground their new emerging spirituality less on a now unattainable intimacy with [God] than on an intimacy with His will, avidly eliciting Its intricate demands and saturating their daily lives with Its exactions. Having lost the touch of His presence, they now seek solace in the pressure of His yoke. (215)

Second, the concern with regulation has changed the way Jews read their holy texts. "In traditional Jewish society, the purpose of study (*lernen*) was not information or even knowledge but a lifelong exposure to the sacred texts and an ongoing dialogue with them" (210). Reading the text was an end in itself, an act of devotion. When, as for the haredim, the principal concern is for determining how one is supposed to behave in a specific situation, the student of the text wants an immediate answer. He or she looks for handbooks and scholarly guidance that will unlock the secrets of the holy book as quickly, efficiently, and accurately as possible.

Soloveitchik suggests that this way of reading sacred texts, like the loss of a sense of personal intimacy with God, reflects the impact of the larger democratic social order on religious communities:

> The world now experienced by the haredim, by us all, is rule-oriented and, in the broadest sense of the term, rational. Modern society is governed by regulations, mostly written and interpreted by experts accounting for their decisions in an ostensibly reasoned fashion. . . . As men, moreover, now submit to rule rather than to custom, they have a like perception of what makes a just and compelling claim to men's allegiance, a corresponding belief in the kind of yoke people ought and do, in fact, willingly bear. (216)

Soloveitchik's argument is suggestive of key characteristics of not only Jewish but also Christian fundamentalism in the West today. Scholars have noted that fundamentalism is a reaction against modernism—and therefore against key aspects of a secular, pluralistic, democratic social order, which refuses to privilege one religious voice over another. Yet as these scholars have also noted, fundamentalism reflects important aspects of the very world that it rejects.[4] In appealing to absolute, divinely revealed truth (embedded for Jews and Christians in the sacred texts of their traditions), fundamentalists react against the pluralizing, relativizing forces of modernity. In deriving practical rules and guidelines from these texts, fundamentalists reproduce modernity's reliance on law, rather than on custom or personal authority, as the foundation of social life.

Fundamentalism is shaped by the deepest assumptions of modernity, even as it rejects it. For fundamentalists, as for members of a democratic society, laws embedded in texts should provide reliable, accurate information. For both, laws are the glue that holds a community together.

II.

German Protestant theologian Michael Weinrich observes tendencies in Protestant Christian fundamentalism similar to those that Soloveitchik finds in haredi Judaism. Weinrich argues that the growing complexity of modern societies and their rapid rate of change prove disorienting to many people. Traditional belief and practice no longer hold sway. People have many lifestyle options but little clarity about what commends one option over another. In such a world, fundamentalism offers people a new sense of certainty. One can know what is absolutely right, based as it is on divine decision, not simply on personal preference. Sacred texts are key because they establish what God requires. Belief and practice are to be regulated by direct appeal to the text.[5]

Weinrich identifies three key assumptions that characterize Protestant fundamentalist approaches to the Bible: (1) it is divinely inspired; (2) it is factually true; and (3) it provides practical, moral guidance. Fundamentalists argue that each assumption is grounded in the claims of the text itself and has been guarded over the centuries by tradition.[6] Weinrich notes, however, that each of these assumptions is distinctively modern. Whatever roots they have in the Christian tradition, these assumptions have been profoundly shaped by modernity and have attained prominence because they somehow correspond to it. Each assumption reflects the complex interactions between fundamentalism and a secular, pluralistic, democratic social order, similar to those that Soloveitchik observes in his analysis of haredi Judaism.

Inspiration

Key to Protestant fundamentalism since its emergence in early twentieth-century America has been the belief that every part of the Bible is true because God ultimately guided its writing. This position does not deny that the Christian scriptures include diverse materials, some of which must be read more symbolically, others more literally. It does claim that all these materials are God's direct word to humans (the theological principle called plenary inspiration). If there are errors in the text, they can only be the result of mistakes that ancient scribes introduced into the text as they copied it. God determined, at least in the original manuscripts, every jot and tittle (the theological principle called verbal inspiration).[7]

Weinrich argues that theories of inspiration function in Protestant fundamentalism to give the reader a sense of absolute certainty. Fundamentalists reason that if these texts are divinely inspired, they must be authoritative and binding.

A popular bumper sticker that appeared in the United States several years ago sums it up: "God said it. I believe it. That settles it." For fundamentalists, the Bible is a collection of divine certainties. As sociologist James Davison Hunter has observed, "Such objective and transcendent authority defines, at least in the abstract, a consistent, unchangeable measure of value, purpose, goodness, and identity, both personal and collective. It tells us what is good, what is true, how we should live, and who we are. It is an authority that is sufficient for all time."[8]

Some like Hunter label this way of approaching scripture "traditional" or "orthodox." Yet fundamentalist readings of scripture are out of step with much of the Christian tradition. Fundamentalists appeal to the principle of divine inspiration in order to read the scriptures with absolute certainty. The inspired character of the Bible taught many ancient, medieval, and Reformation Christians to approach it with a degree of reservation and self-criticism.[9] Major theologians of the Christian tradition have used the language of inspiration to characterize the unique authority of scripture, but they have also insisted that the reader needs as much divine assistance in understanding the texts as the biblical authors needed in writing them. There is nothing automatic or sure about opening the book and correctly reading it.

For fundamentalists, inspiration functions to guarantee that the texts are clear and accessible to any reader who is willing to accept their authority. The meaning of the text is plain. Those who refuse to accept the texts and to orient their lives by the text's teachings merely demonstrate their hardness of heart. For the greater part of the Christian tradition, however, inspiration has functioned to remind the reader that the scriptures are not under human control. One has to engage in a process of interpretation, whereby one opens oneself to a living word that may not accord with what one first takes the words on the page to mean.

In developing an understanding of the role of sacred texts in the world's great religions, historian of religions Wilfred Cantwell Smith captures this traditional (rather than fundamentalist) stance well: "What is proffered in scripture is transcendent truth. The words that we read are 'deep in mystery,' and present us with a mystery that we must struggle to explore—that it is our privilege to explore."[10]

The believer goes to the text in the confidence that it speaks a living word and directs one into right relationship with the divine. Yet this confidence is accompanied by a profound sense of humility about one's ability to rightly hear and obey the text. One must constantly test one's apprehensions about the meaning of a particular text by testing them against other texts and the accumulated wisdom of the tradition. Smith concedes that readers have always brought their own presuppositions to the text, often finding there what they wanted to find. They nevertheless had a profound sense of being shaped by the text itself.[11]

> Those involved [in reading the sacred texts of their tradition] . . . have consistently reported that their scriptures—and this is indeed those scriptures' *raison d'etre*— open up a window, or constitute that window, to a world of ultimate reality and truth and goodness. Over against the mundane world of sorrow, of self-interest and its loneliness, of injustice and failure, scriptures have played a role of enabling human beings to be aware of and indeed to live in relation to the other [i.e., transcendent] dimension of reality that characterizes our humanity.[12]

Karl Barth, the great Swiss Protestant theologian of the twentieth century, offered a similar understanding of Christian scripture. Although often labeled "neo-orthodox," Barth rejected fundamentalist understandings of inspiration, even as he sought to recover the Bible's religious authority. Barth argued that one could not claim to have comprehended the divine will simply by reading the Bible. The Bible is a thoroughly human book. It reflects the historical and personal limitations of its authors. It has error, even theological error. scripture is not a divine object dropped from heaven to earth. It is not a direct revelation of God. God speaks through these texts, but only as they become the occasion for God to speak a living word that transcends them.[13]

Barth feared that theories of verbal and plenary inspiration inevitably represent human efforts to control God. Inspirationists want scripture to yield a fixed meaning by which they can make themselves the judge of truth and falsehood, right and wrong. Barth argued that scripture becomes the word of God only as it takes hold of believers and displaces them from the judgment seat.

Barth noted that theories of verbal and plenary inspiration first emerged in the late seventeenth century, at the very birth of the Enlightenment. Orthodox Protestants began to approach the text with the same assumptions as their Enlightenment opponents. The text no longer mediated an encounter with the divine; a sense of living fellowship with the divine no longer shaped one's interpretation of the text. Rather, one now approached the text directly, confident that one could immediately grasp its meaning through one's own interpretive powers. One sought to read the Bible historically, equating its divine meaning with the meaning that the original author intended, insofar as the interpreter was able to reconstruct it. The result was to secularize the Bible—that is, to read it as one would any other text.[14]

These analyses of theories of inspiration demonstrate again the complex ways in which fundamentalist movements interact with secular, pluralistic, democratic values. In appealing to an inspired, unchanging text, the fundamentalist protests against the pluralizing, relativizing tendencies of the modern West. In a world in which matters of belief and practice are reduced to matters of personal preference, the fundamentalist asserts a basis for absolute certainty. Yet the antimodernism of the fundamentalist is thoroughly modern.[15] Fundamentalists want to hear and read scripture "with the same obviousness and directness with which we can hear and read other human words."[16]

A postmodern age may eventually change the social landscape. In recent years, some literary scholars have argued that texts are indeterminate in meaning, that no text has a fixed meaning.[17] Yet such approaches to sacred texts remain the pastime of a small, intellectual elite. The basic assumptions of a technological information society remain unaltered. Most people approach texts as carriers of information and knowledge, and they expect scripture to function in the same way. The fundamentalist's self-certainty in dealing with scripture merely exposes a larger cultural confidence in the capacity of texts to record and transmit what is true. Soloveitchik makes a similar observation:

The new generation [that was attracted to the haredim] . . . obtained its knowledge in business and in daily affairs from books, and these books imparted their
information in a self-contained, straightforward, and accessible format. They
saw no reason why knowledge of the Torah should not be equally available to
them in so ready and serviceable a format.[18]

Weinrich has further noted that the fundamentalist use of scripture reflects modernity's emphasis on the individual.[19] If the text has fixed meanings that are in principle available to any reader, then the reader can make sense of scripture on his or
her own. The fact that scripture does not always yield meaning quickly and clearly
merely encourages members of a technological information society to do what they
already know to do with other texts—that is, to consult those experts who are able
to reduce the complexities of the text and clarify its meaning. Like haredi Judaism,
fundamentalist Christianity has given birth to a vast array of publications that assist the lay reader in making sense of the Bible on his or her own. Meaning emerges
not slowly and tentatively out of extended debate within a community of interpretation, but directly and clearly out of expert analysis of the text.

Factual Truth

Fundamentalists acknowledge that scripture uses the language and reflects the historical context of its human authors, but they are confident that the Bible ultimately
reveals divine, eternal facts. scripture has reliable information about every area of
life, including science and history. It accurately describes matters that human reason can investigate and confirm. In recent years, adherents of creation science have
vividly exemplified this position, both in their insistence that Genesis 1 be taught in
public school science classes and in their confidence that Genesis 1 can be confirmed
by the geologic record. What scripture gives us is not only certain ("inspired") but
also rational. It is true for everyone, not only for people of faith. It applies not simply to a special spiritual dimension of our lives but to our lives as a whole.

Even where fundamentalists do focus on specifically religious truths, rather than
on scientific or historical matters, they tend to frame these truths in what one scholar
has called "cognitive-propositional" terms.[20] Scripture does not simply provide symbols that interpret the human condition; it offers true statements about God and
God's will that one can master intellectually. Even where the Bible works with narrative or poetry, these materials are best understood as illustrations or embellish-
ments of factual truths, not as symbolic, metaphorical ways of expressing ultimate
truths that go beyond rational articulation.

Historically, North American Protestant fundamentalism arose as an effort to
define and explicate core statements of truth about the Christian faith. As one

scholar has noted, the contributors to the twelve volumes that came to give the fundamentalists their name (*The Fundamentals*, 1910–15) "were scholarly, well-reasoned, carefully nuanced and polite. In time, however, fundamentalists learned to narrow their list of concerns and become more militant in their approach."[21] Different groups began to formulate short lists of nonnegotiable beliefs. By the 1920s, fundamentalists in the Presbyterian Church (USA) had reduced the essentials of the faith to five: the inerrancy of the Bible, the virgin birth, the substitutionary atonement, Jesus' physical resurrection, and Jesus' miracle-working power.[22]

Fundamentalists drew each of these points from their reading of scripture itself; conversely, they interpreted the Bible in terms of its capacity to illustrate these truths. The miracle stories demonstrated Jesus' miracle-working power. The resurrection accounts offered proof that Jesus' body had returned to life. Confident in the rational truth of the biblical witness, fundamentalists believed that they could rationally explain and harmonize apparent discrepancies in the biblical accounts. Convinced that they could rationally persuade nonbelievers to accept these biblical truths, they developed extensive apologetic theologies that sought to demonstrate the rational truth of the Christian faith to a secular world.[23]

Fundamentalists of the early twentieth century—and sometimes their opponents as well—believed that fundamentalism was defending the great truths of scripture that had been self-evident to earlier generations of Christians but had now come under fire from developments in biblical criticism and liberal theology. But, again, a careful analysis of fundamentalist language demonstrates that the fundamentalist focus on rational factuality has always been more modern than "traditional."

Jewish and Christian holy texts have traditionally functioned in metaphorical, iconic ways. Ancient and medieval interpreters did not expect to find one right meaning in a biblical passage. Rather, the text had several levels of meaning, and it could speak in different ways at different times to different readers. scripture was best understood not simply as words on a page but as a dynamic process in which a community of interpreters struggled with a text in the confidence that the community would eventually hear a living word of God. The text promised to draw its readers into the presence of the divine, not simply to give them unchanging information. The text set forth an encounter with God, not simply an authoritative report about God and God's will.[24] James Kugel has described ancient Jewish and Christian exegesis in this way:

> Everything was held to apply to present-day readers and to contain within it an imperative for adoption and application to the readers' own lives. . . . The Bible is not *essentially* a record of things that happened or were spoken in the past. That they happened is of course true; but if they were written down in the Bible, it was not so much to record what has occurred in some distant past, but "for

our instruction," so that, by reading the sacred text whose material comes down to us from the past, we might learn some vital lesson for our own lives.[25]

Kugel also notes that the ancient interpreters regarded scripture as a "fundamentally cryptic document. . . . The Bible could be demonstrated time and again to contain some meaning other than the apparent one."[26] The text rarely had a single, fixed meaning. Rather, the text became the occasion for the interpreter to reflect on the most profound questions of life and death. It was through the interpreter's encounter with the text that the interpreter sought to receive a living word that would speak definitely and concretely into the interpreter's situation. The Bible had eternal truths, but they could never be reduced to a list of intellectual propositions. They were truths that individuals absorbed as they were shaped by a communal process of engaging and debating the texts.

The doctrines that were distilled into five fundamentals have a long, complex history of interpretation in the Christian tradition and have rarely been reduced to statements of indisputable fact. As Jaroslav Pelikan, eminent historian of Christian thought, has noted, the Christian tradition has consistently maintained the authority of the Bible, yet "on the details of biblical interpretation itself, orthodoxy had, repeatedly if not quite consistently, manifested and tolerated a hermeneutical pluralism that could not easily be accommodated to the fundamentalist mold."[27] Pelikan points out that Augustine, writing in the fifth century, understood the six days of creation to be symbolic. Creation established time; it did not occur within time. In the thirteenth century, Thomas Aquinas refuted Augustine's position, arguing that Genesis 1 was literally true. But, notes Pelikan, "there is not even a hint in Saint Thomas that Saint Augustine should be declared a heretic. . . . Historic Christian orthodoxy was able to speak about biblical 'inerrancy' only because its hermeneutic was sensitive to the multiple senses of a biblical text."[28]

Significantly, North American Protestant fundamentalists of the early twentieth century did not agree among themselves about how to interpret Genesis 1.[29] The interpretive pluralism that they were able to acknowledge in regard to the creation story might have suggested to them that none of the five fundamentals could simply be read off the sacred page. To the majority of the Christian tradition, matters such as the virgin birth and the physical resurrection have functioned not so much as rational propositions but rather as poemlike language. The language of scripture has been understood to point to acts of a transcendent God that cannot be wholly contained in human language. Biblical language has been first of all the language of prayer and contemplation, of worship and meditation, rather than of science and history. The fact that the Christian tradition has supported a variety of communities of interpretation, each appropriating biblical images in its own ways, has ensured a continuing debate about the meaning and application of the sacred text.

American Protestant fundamentalism has frequently found its heroes among Calvinists, especially those of the nineteenth-century Princeton School (such as Archibald Alexander, Charles Hodge, and Benjamin Warfield). Yet Calvin himself is closer to the orthodox tradition that Pelikan describes than to modern fundamentalism. Although Calvin gives rational proofs for the authority of scripture, he concedes that they are of limited value. It is the divine Spirit alone who can persuade a person of the truth of scripture.[30]

Moreover, what one finds in scripture is not so much a set of propositions for the intellect but a way of seeing that evokes a deep existential trust. In a famous section of his *Institutes of the Christian Religion*, Calvin writes:

> Just as old or bleary-eyed men and those with weak vision, if you thrust before them a most beautiful volume, even if they recognize it to be some sort of writing, yet can scarcely construe two words, but with the aid of spectacles will begin to read distinctly; so scripture, gathering up the otherwise confused knowledge of God in our minds, having dispersed our dullness, clearly shows us the true God.[31]

Calvin is convinced that the Bible not only tells a person about God but also draws a person into the very presence of God. scripture offers more than factual information about God; it invites one into relationship with the God who for Christians has entered human history in the life, death, and resurrection of Jesus. The scriptures point their readers to Christ, and Christ is not simply a name of the past but a living, spiritual presence today: "If through the Spirit [the word] is really branded upon hearts . . . it shows forth Christ."[32] The Bible for Calvin has a sacramental quality. It becomes a means by which humans are fed spiritual truths.[33]

As in the case of fundamentalist understandings of inspiration, the fundamentalist assumption that the Bible reveals unchanging facts illustrates fundamentalism's reliance on modern culture, even as it reacts against it. Historian George Marsden has noted the influence of Scottish Common Sense Realism on nineteenth-century American intellectual life. The intellectual skepticism of European philosophers never found a firm foothold in the broader American scene. The pragmatic bent of Americans corresponded well to Scottish Realism's assurance that truth consisted of basic facts about the structure of the world and that these facts were accessible to the average person as he or she looked at the world. Scottish Realism also fit well with emerging fundamentalist understandings of truth. One could trust the scriptures to mean what they said.[34]

Even in the pluralistic world of the twenty-first century, the language of rational fact continues to play a significant role. People perhaps sense that different kinds of language and different kinds of truth characterize different areas of life. Yet most of us continue to live our everyday lives with a confidence in factual knowledge. We look to scientific experts to provide us the facts that we need to make informed decisions about personal or social matters. We look for patterns of predictability in human behavior, whether the question is how to market new consumer products or how to prevent school shootings. A pluralistic situation may complicate our ability to sort through the facts, but we do not doubt that they exist or that we can ultimately understand them.[35]

Theologian Langdon Gilkey has observed the paradoxical character of the creation science movement in the United States. How can it be, Gilkey asks, that many of the leading exponents of creation science are not antiscientific bigots, but have received a secular scientific training from some of the nation's top universities? He notes in reply that creation scientists typically come from technical rather than theoretical fields. They are fact-oriented people. They have been trained to distill knowledge into essential principles that can be efficiently communicated and applied.[36]

The rise to power of an information technology class in American economic and political life is mirrored, in however distorted a form, in the rise of an American fundamentalism that assumes the wider culture's confidence in information, reason, and factual knowledge. Like the technologist, the fundamentalist assumes that knowledge can be transmitted in texts that people study and master. Fundamentalists react against some of the purposes to which a secular, pluralistic, democratic society employs reason and science. But they do not dispute that reality can be understood rationally and factually.

Practical, Moral Guidance

Fundamentalists expend considerable time and energy in demonstrating the rational truth of holy scripture, but their principal interest is not in doctrine but in practice.[37] Because they understand the sacred text to be rationally true, they also hold it to be authoritative for regulating moral behavior. Moreover, scripture's law code is applicable not only to the community of faith but to society as a whole. Not surprisingly, public displays of the Ten Commandments have in recent years become a rallying point for some Protestant fundamentalists in the United States. To their thinking, the commandments are rational, self-evident truths that American society once widely accepted and that once held American society together. They believe that renewed attention to the commandments would save the nation today from the ills of a secular, pluralistic society.[38]

Modern societies, as numerous scholars have observed, tend to undermine traditional sources of religious authority such as the Ten Commandments. Public institutions, such as state-supported schools, which once helped to transmit religious ideas and values, become increasingly secularized; religion becomes privatized and understood as a matter of individual choice.[39]

Modern societies are also characterized by pluralistic values. People become ever more aware of the fact that they can choose a practical life orientation from a variety of religious and nonreligious sources. Sociologist Wade Clark Roof has recently written of the "spiritual marketplace."[40] People in modern societies learn to cobble together a spirituality for themselves, rather than to accept traditional sources of authority. As wise consumers, people are ever ready to make adjustments in what they believe, in order to find what works best for them. The flexibility and innovation that modern societies value so highly in matters of economic production and consumption also come to define religious life.

Although such a society appears to enhance individuals' ability to control their lives, it also gives them a profound sense of their limitations. Within the carefully circumscribed and protected boundaries of the private sphere, a person enjoys considerable freedom of choice. At the same time, a person may easily feel overwhelmed by the complexity of public life, with its competing interest groups and its concentration of power in large, anonymous social organizations. Social consensus appears elusive; moral values seem arbitrary and subject to constant renegotiation and reinterpretation. One is never quite sure where one fits in such a world and whether one's moral values are anything more than a matter of personal taste.[41]

Fundamentalist movements arise as a reaction against the apparent moral chaos of modern societies. By idealizing and seeking to revive certain religious traditions, they offer their members a renewed sense of moral orientation. Central to this moral program is a stance of resistance. Fundamentalism calls people to fight the corrosive effects of a secular, pluralistic world. It argues that traditional religious values alone can save society from impending moral collapse. As cultural geographer Roger Stump has noted, fundamentalism lives from a sense of moral opposition and conflict.[42] The world is divided in two: "Either you are for us or you are against us." What sustains fundamentalists' confidence that they are fighting for a righteous cause is their sacred text. The text offers an Archimedean point from which they attempt to lift the world and bring it back into order.

Just as the Bible provides absolute, nonnegotiable truths about God, it also defines an absolute moral code for human behavior. To quote James Davison Hunter again:

> God, [fundamentalists] would say, is real and makes Himself tangibly, directly, and even propositionally known in the everyday experience of individuals and communities. . . . In matters of moral judgment, the unequivocal appeal . . . is to these uncompromisable standards. [The Bible] is, then, an authority that is universally valid—adequate for every circumstance and context.[43]

Christians throughout the ages, not only fundamentalists, have turned to their sacred texts for practical, moral guidance. Yet obedience to scriptural imperatives threatens in fundamentalism to become an end in itself. (One is reminded of Soloveitchik's remark that the haredi assume the yoke of the law in order to compensate for the seeming absence of God.) A look at the broader Christian tradition suggests a significant contrast. For the greater part of the tradition, scriptural imperatives have served to describe a way of life that aims at deepening communion with the divine life and with other human beings. These imperatives have served explicitly religious ends, rather than the purpose of assuring us that we can have a clean conscience because we now know what is morally right.

In classic treatments of the Ten Commandments, both Catholic and Protestant, the commandments have helped to discipline and make concrete the contours of Christian love.[44] They have represented disciplines at which one must work over a lifetime in order to advance, however tentatively and incompletely, in the spiritual life. For some Protestant fundamentalists, "thou shalt not kill" is a straightforward moral imperative that prohibits certain discrete moral acts, such as abortion or euthanasia (but not necessarily war!).[45] Classic Christian interpretations of the commandment, however, have never reduced it to an abstract legal standard. "Thou shalt not kill" has been nothing less than a summons to a way of life that promises to bring one more fully into correspondence with the life ordained by God.

Three features of these classic treatments of the commandments are noteworthy. First, each commandment is understood to do more than simply forbid certain discrete acts, as though it could be developed into a checklist that one could use to ensure one's own righteousness or to accuse others of unrighteousness. Rather, each commandment describes a broad category of behaviors that ultimately implicates every human being in wrongdoing. In the case of "thou shalt not kill," any action that hurts our neighbor or hinders our neighbor's capacity to live in health and safety—not only physical murder—is enjoined. Few people commit murder, but every person is guilty of seeking his or her own good at the expense of others' well-being.

Second, classic treatments of the commandments have applied each commandment not only to outer behaviors but also to inner dispositions. "Thou shalt not kill" is not only about restraining ourselves from physically harming others but also about our very thoughts toward others. Do we harbor anger? Do we dismiss the neighbor as a fool? Do we wish the neighbor harm or deprivation of some necessary good? The commandments have as much to do with attitudes as with actions. Again, this interpretive strategy has the effect of radicalizing and broadening the reach of each commandment, so that no one can claim ultimate righteousness—but also so that anyone seeking to grow in the spiritual life has a clearer sense of the direction in which he or she must proceed.

Third, classic treatments of the commandments have insisted that each commandment is as much a positive injunction as a negative prohibition. "Thou shalt not kill" also means that one should seek the good of one's neighbor and enhance the neighbor's ability to live well. One should do everything possible to deepen bonds of care and community. Once again, the commandment is radicalized and broadened. The effect is to remind one that one needs divine forgiveness and guidance as one seeks to obey and that one is summoned to a process of continuing self-transformation, by which one might grow more fully into the divine life.

Given the complexity of each commandment, obedience is never a cut-and-dried affair. Rather, one is called into an extended process of moral deliberation that necessarily draws from the best wisdom of the larger religious tradition. The commandments are not a checklist; rather, they initiate a way of life that develops over a lifetime. The commandments are never simply a linchpin for guaranteeing personal righteousness; rather, they call one to continual self-examination and repentance.

Classic Christian treatments of the Ten Commandments have further suggested that this way of life becomes possible only in disciplined communities of faith. The commandments are not abstract moral imperatives that one can choose to obey on one's own. They require structures of mutual accountability and encouragement. They must be embedded in larger patterns of communal worship and service.[46]

Protestant fundamentalists typically look to scripture to resolve moral questions, not to raise them. They want to know that they can do the right thing here and now, not that they are perpetually doomed to fall short. What the Bible should provide is personal reassurance that a person is on the right track, not that he or she is just beginning a slow process of self-transformation.

Such a stance again owes more to the assumptions of a secular, pluralistic society than to the religious traditions to which fundamentalists appeal. In recent decades, sociologists of religion have noted that therapeutic language and concerns have grown increasingly prominent in North American Christianity. Religion should assist the individual in living a more satisfied life. It should help heal personal hurts, help relieve personal stresses.[47] The religious life is viewed not as a difficult, extended process of submission to the divine, but as a means for achieving a sense of personal, emotional well-being. What people seek is practical counsel for how to keep their marriages together, how to raise their children, how to succeed at their vocation, and how to deal positively with the inevitable stresses of modern life. The pragmatic bent that some historians have recognized as characteristic of American religion from its beginnings also shapes the fundamentalist concern to say clearly and concisely, "Here's what you need to do to be a good, happy person."[48]

Protestant fundamentalism blames secularity and pluralism for many of the moral problems that afflict contemporary American society. It appeals to sacred texts for moral values that stand in sharp opposition to what it takes to be the excessive hedonism of Western culture. But Protestant fundamentalism also reflects the wider culture's interest in personal well-being. In a world of self-help manuals and self-help groups, it is not surprising that religious institutions, including those of Protestant fundamentalism, devote a great deal of energy to addressing individuals' everyday life problems. Protestant fundamentalists use the freedom of expression that a democratic society guarantees and the technological means that modernity provides in order to persuade individuals that biblical values offer them a better, more satisfying way of life. Moreover, Protestant fundamentalists argue that adherence to these values will protect the high economic standard of living that Americans have achieved but will likely lose if moral decline continues.[49]

The complex interplay in North American fundamentalism between a posture of protest and a posture of accommodation is again evident. The fundamentalist emphasis on the Bible as a source of practical, moral guidance reflects aspects of the very world that fundamentalism claims to reject.

III.

Fundamentalist religious movements are a modern phenomenon, deeply influenced by scientific, technological, rationalistic ways of thinking, even as these movements react against the secular, pluralistic framework in which these ways of thinking flourish in Western democracies. The growing complexity of modern societies—characterized by competing truth claims, as embodied in competing communities of discourse—destabilizes human efforts to find ultimate, religious meaning to existence. One response is fundamentalism and its appeal to divinely revealed, absolute wisdom. Fundamentalists insist that democratic social practice is dangerous when it undermines confidence in divine truth and therefore in human efforts to achieve right belief and practice.

Traditional, sacred texts play a key role in giving fundamentalists a new sense of certainty. The text is inspired; therefore, its meaning is clear, its truth is absolute, and its standards are nonnegotiable. The text is factually true; therefore it tells a person the way things really are, it offers reliable information about the world and our place in it, and it can be applied logically and rationally to every area of life. The text offers practical, moral guidance; therefore it tells us clearly what we must do to live a righteous and a personally satisfying and rewarding life.

In a world in which the divine seems increasingly remote from everyday human experience, human beings long more than ever to know that their way of life has some greater, even ultimate significance. They want their way of life to correspond to the grain of the universe, not simply to the particular quirks of their own personalities or cultures. For fundamentalists, the holy text, because it clearly communicates what God wants of us, provides this reassurance.

But this way of approaching scripture reflects the assumptions of modernity and is therefore in contrast to much of the Jewish and Christian tradition. In fundamentalism, the text no longer functions in metaphorical, iconic ways, but as a collection of regulatory principles. It no longer points beyond itself to a living divine presence but is understood to be a collection of divinely revealed, holy laws that require not interpretation but implementation. The text is no longer inextricably embedded in communal practices of worship and meditative study but is transformed into a handbook of individualized moral instruction, whose abstract knowledge and absolute facts offer the reader practical guidance for negotiating everyday life in the modern world.

The particular moral values that fundamentalists find in their texts may or may not correspond to the moral values of the wider society, but the fundamentalist interest in texts does reflect the wider society's emphasis on written rules and laws as guarantors of personal and social well-being. Fundamentalist religious movements develop elaborate theologies of law, and their emphasis on textually based rules and principles for moral behavior reflects their dependence on modern ways of thinking, in which behaviors are regulated more by law than by social custom.[50]

In a modern democratic society, where multiple lifestyle niches exist side by side, written laws and procedures are supposed to guarantee that public life will be governed by one set of rules—that is, that the playing field will be level. Where secularization and pluralism have eroded the binding power of social custom, written moral codes seem to offer the next best thing. Corporations develop employee handbooks that set forth codes of ethical conduct. Employees attend special ethical training sessions and certify in writing that they have read these codes, understand them, and will adhere to them. The corporation puts these written statements on file, in the event that it is ever sued for sexual or racial harassment. Governments develop large bureaucracies that develop intricate, written procedures for dispersing monies or implementing legally mandated programs. In academic life, catalogs, even class syllabi, come to function as semilegal documents. "Back to the texts" is the motto of our day. The fundamentalist reliance on texts and the tendency to interpret these texts as authoritative moral, legal handbooks merely mirror the larger culture.

Although their way of using sacred texts has been shaped by the wider democratic culture, fundamentalists sometimes appeal to these texts in order to advance an antidemocratic vision.[51] In a secular, pluralistic democracy, law is instrumental to human ends; for fundamentalists, law must ultimately reflect the divine will. In a secular, pluralistic democracy, law offers a framework in which competing interest groups negotiate their differences; fundamentalists appeal to the divine law as an absolute to which all members of society should conform.[52] Secular civil law has its authority from the people; it can be revised and altered. Fundamentalism, by contrast, argues for laws that have their authority from God; one must simply submit—there are no grounds for resistance. As we have seen, fundamentalism uses modernist assumptions in the service of an antimodernist program. When fundamentalism becomes religious extremism, divine law becomes the foundation for authoritarian theocracy, rather than a guarantor of democratic social practice.

Is fundamentalism inevitably a danger to a secular, pluralistic, democratic society? Few fundamentalists become political extremists, and few Protestant fundamentalists in the West seek actively to overthrow the democratic governments in which they live. Yet fundamentalists' sense of self-righteous opposition to the morality of the wider culture makes them an easy target for popular disdain. Their opposition to secularism and pluralism seems profoundly antidemocratic.

Ironically, the aspects of fundamentalism that trouble many of us reflect the most basic assumptions of a secular, pluralistic democracy. One might think of the funny mirrors that one finds at a circus or carnival. They distort our features, stretching out one part of our body and pressing together another. We are nevertheless looking at ourselves, and the exaggerations that we see and at which we laugh may also remind us how ambivalent we are about our bodies and their appearance (too fat, too skinny, too tall, too short). So too fundamentalism holds up a curvy, wavy mirror to a secular, pluralistic, democratic society and asks its members to look at themselves again. Even if what we see is exaggerated and hard for us to take seriously, it nevertheless reminds us of potential dangers in a secular, pluralistic, democratic society that we might rather refuse to acknowledge.

Those of us who are committed to secular, pluralistic values look in the mirror of fundamentalism and see absolute self-certainties that repel us. But where do we operate with similar self-certainties? Are not too many Americans all too sure that the American way of life is the end of history and that the rest of the world will inevitably trod the path that we have laid down? We look in the mirror of fundamentalism and see notions of science and reason (such as creationism) that strike us as arbitrary and nonsensical. Yet how often do we appeal to the "plain facts" to hide our own ideologies? How often do we forget that the "facts" of social life are rarely neutral, self-evident realities but are interpretations of highly complex phenomena? Where do we appeal to science and reason to silence debate rather than to become humbled at how little we really know about how to solve the basic social problems that ail our society and world?

We look in the mirror of fundamentalism and belittle its moralistic, legalistic tone. But are we equally adept at recognizing how often we reduce the mystery of existence to simplistic self-help moralities? Do we detect how skillfully we appeal to the language of law and justice and moral rectitude to justify our lifestyles of excessive individualism and prosperity, even when that individualism and prosperity come at the expense of others, including the poor of the greater part of the world? Are we willing to assess where appeals to right and procedure enhance the capacity of humans to live with each other, and where they merely divert us from the task of forging deeper bonds of community and friendship that are necessary if we are to break through the anonymity that so dominates life in modern societies?

Fundamentalist religious movements need the checks and balances of a democratic society. No one committed to a secular, pluralistic democratic society can wish its fundamentalists to achieve political power, for their power would come only at the cost of freedoms that we prize. But no one committed to a democratic society can afford simply to dismiss its fundamentalists. The self-righteousness and absolutism that most frightens us in fundamentalism merely reflects what we should find most frightening in a secular, pluralistic democracy, which continually faces its own temptations to abuse power.

The young Karl Marx asserted that religion was not simply a false consciousness but also a protest against social, economic inequality.[53] Similarly, fundamentalist religious movements, despite their reactionary dangers, ultimately expose some of the deficits of democratic societies. In their absolutizing of law, fundamentalists represent a necessary protest against the tendency of a secular, pluralistic, democratic order to rely excessively on law and procedure for social cohesion. The phenomenon of fundamentalism ultimately challenges a democracy to acknowledge that values of secularity and pluralism, even values of democratic freedom, do not answer the longings of the human spirit for ultimate meaning. Beneath the language of toleration and diversity, a secular, pluralistic democracy hides its own potential for distortion unless it makes room for religious values—not religious values of absolutism and extremism, but those that humble the human spirit before the ultimate mysteries of life and death and promise to lead us into deeper, more just community with one another.

NOTES

1. The term "fundamentalism" is notoriously difficult to define and is often used in a pejorative, dismissive sense. I focus on religious movements that react, sometimes militantly, against social processes of secularization and pluralism; that claim absolute, uncompromisable truth, based on divine revelation; and that revive selected aspects of the moral code of their religious traditions, in order to resist selected aspects of the moral code of the wider culture in which they find themselves. For general discussions of fundamentalism that have informed my own, see the editors' summations in the five volumes of the Fundamentalist Project edited by Martin E. Marty and Scott Appleby (Chicago: Univ. of Chicago Press, 1991–95); Martin Riesebrodt, *Pious Passion: The Emergence of Modern Fundamentalism in the United States and Iran*, trans. Don Reneau (Berkeley: Univ. of California Press, 1993); and Roger W. Stump, *Boundaries of Faith: Geographical Perspectives on Religious Fundamentalism* (Lanham, Md.: Rowman and Littlefield, 2000).

2. For the critical role of sacred texts in fundamentalism, see Bruce B. Lawrence, *Defenders of God: The Fundamentalist Revolt against the Modern Age* (San Francisco: Harper and Row, 1989), 15. Says

Lawrence, "Remove scripture, and you no longer have fundamentalism. . . . Religious ideology arises out of scripture. It entails a specific plan of action that translates the 'clear' teaching of scripture. . . . Religious ideology is textually based before it is contextually elaborated and enacted."

3. Haym Soloveitchik, "Migration, Acculturation, and the New Role of Texts in the Haredi World," in *Accounting for Fundamentalisms*, ed. Martin E. Marty and Scott Appleby (Chicago: Univ. of Chicago Press, 1994), 197. Subsequent references to this work are cited parenthetically in text.

4. Besides the general literature cited in n. 1, consult Robert Wuthnow and Matthew P. Lawson, "Imagining the Last Days: The Politics of Apocalyptic Language," in *Accounting for Fundamentalisms*, ed. Martin E. Marty and Scott Appleby (Chicago: Univ. of Chicago Press, 1994), 44–45.

5. Michael Weinrich, *Kirche Glauben: Annäherungen an eine ökumenische Ekklesiologie* (Wuppertal, Germany: Foedus-Verlag, 1998), 262–302.

6. For general studies of conservative Protestant interpretation of scripture (which also underlies fundamentalist approaches), see James Barr, *Fundamentalism* (Philadelphia, Pa.: Westminster, 1977); and Kathleen C. Boone, *The Bible Tells Them So: The Discourse of Protestant Fundamentalism* (Albany: State Univ. of New York Press, 1989).

7. Benjamin B. Warfield (1851–1921), professor of theology at Princeton Theological Seminary, was a principal exponent of this position. See his essays in Mark Noll, ed., *The Princeton Theology: 1812–1921* (Grand Rapids, Mich.: Baker Book House, 1983).

8. James Davison Hunter, *Culture Wars: The Battle to Define America* (New York: Basic, 1991), 44.

9. Weinrich, *Kirche Glauben*, 278.

10. Wilfred Cantwell Smith, *What Is scripture? A Comparative Approach* (Minneapolis, Minn.: Augsburg Fortress, 1993), 32.

11. Ibid., 32, 36.

12. Ibid., 232.

13. For Barth's explication of his position, see his *Church Dogmatics*, vol. 1, part 2, *The Doctrine of the Word of God*, trans. G. T. Thomson and Harold Knight (Edinburgh, Scotland: T. and T. Clark, 1956), 457–740.

14. Ibid., 514–26.

15. Weinrich, *Kirche Glauben*, 297–98. Weinrich uses the phrase "modern antimodernism," which he borrows from G. Küenzeln, "Fundamentalismus und säkulare Kultur," in *Fundamentalismus in der verweltlichten Welt*, ed. H. Hemminger (Stuttgart, Germany: Quell, 1991), 196–221.

16. Barth, *Church Dogmatics*, 525.

17. For one example of this postmodern approach, see Stanley Fish, *Is There a Text in This Class? The Authority of Interpretive Communities* (Cambridge, Mass.: Harvard Univ. Press, 1980).

18. Soloveitchik, "Migration, Acculturation, and the New Role of Texts," 210.

19. Weinrich, *Kirche Glauben*, 273.

20. George A. Lindbeck, *The Nature of Doctrine: Religion and Theology in a Postliberal Age* (Philadelphia, Pa.: Westminster, 1984), 16.

21. T. P. Weber, "Fundamentalism," in *Dictionary of Christianity in America*, ed. Daniel G. Reid (Downers Grove, Ill.: InterVarsity Press, 1990), 463.

22. Good reviews of this history are available in Lefferts A. Loetscher, *The Broadening Church: A Study of Theological Issues in the Presbyterian Church since 1869* (Philadelphia: Univ. of Pennsylvania Press, 1954); and Bradley J. Longfield, *The Presbyterian Controversy: Fundamentalists, Modernists, and Moderates* (New York: Oxford Univ. Press, 1991).

23. For one example, see Clarence Edward Macartney, *Christianity and Common Sense: A Dialogue of Faith* (Philadelphia, Pa.: John C. Winston, 1927). For a recent analysis of fundamentalist efforts to harmonize the scriptures rationally, see Paul J. Achtemeier, *Inspiration and Authority: Nature and Function of Christian scripture* (Peabody, Mass.: Hendrickson, 1999), 36–63.

24. Smith, *What Is scripture?* 212–42.

25. James L. Kugel, *The Bible As It Was* (Cambridge, Mass.: Belknap, 1997), 20.

26. Ibid., 18.

27. Jaroslav Pelikan, "Fundamentalism and/or Orthodoxy? Toward an Understanding of the Fundamentalist Phenomenon," in *The Fundamentalist Phenomenon,* ed. Norman J. Cohen (Grand Rapids, Mich.: Eerdmans, 1990), 6–7.

28. Ibid., 8.

29. See Longfield, *Presbyterian Controversy,* 13.

30. John Calvin, *Institutes of the Christian Religion,* ed. John T. McNeill (Philadelphia, Pa.: Westminster, 1960), 79 (bk. 1, chap. 7, sec. 4).

31. Ibid., 70 (bk. 1, chap. 7, sec. 1).

32. Ibid., 95 (bk. 1, chap. 9, sec. 3).

33. I have explored this sacramental approach to holy texts in *Why scripture Matters: Reading the Bible in a Time of Church Conflict* (Louisville, Ky.: Westminster John Knox, 1998).

34. See George M. Marsden, *Fundamentalism and American Culture: The Shaping of Twentieth-Century Evangelicalism, 1870–1925* (New York: Oxford Univ. Press, 1980).

35. For a trenchant analysis of this phenomenon, see Neil Postman, *Technopoly: The Surrender of Culture to Technology* (New York: Knopf, 1992).

36. Langdon Gilkey, *Creationism on Trial: Evolution and God at Little Rock* (Minneapolis, Minn.: Winston, 1985).

37. Weinrich, *Kirche Glauben,* 281–82.

38. For a critique of fundamentalist efforts to lift up the Ten Commandments as moral foundations for public life, see Stanley Hauerwas and William H. Willimon, *The Truth about God: The Ten Commandments in Christian Life* (Nashville, Tenn.: Abingdon, 1999).

39. Of continuing significance is the analysis in Peter L. Berger, *The Sacred Canopy: Elements of a Sociological Theory of Religion* (Garden City, N.Y.: Doubleday and Co., 1967).

40. Wade Clark Roof, *Spiritual Marketplace: Baby Boomers and the Remaking of American Religion* (Princeton, N.J.: Princeton Univ. Press, 1999).

41. See Peter L. Berger, *The Heretical Imperative: Contemporary Possibilities of Religious Affirmation* (Garden City, N.Y.: Anchor/Doubleday, 1979); and Robert Bellah et al., *Habits of the Heart: Individualism and Commitment in American Life* (Berkeley: Univ. of California Press, 1985).

42. Stump, *Boundaries of Faith,* 8. Also see Riesebrodt, *Pious Passion.*

43. Hunter, *Culture Wars,* 121.

44. The following observations are based on my own extensive analysis of Reformation and post-Reformation explications of the commandments. Key documents include Martin Luther's treatment of the Ten Commandments in his Large Catechism, John Calvin's sermons on Deuteronomy, *Sermons on the Ten Commandments,* ed. and trans. Benjamin W. Farley (Grand Rapids, Mich.: Baker Books, 1980), and the Catechism of the Council of Trent (also known as the Roman Catechism).

45. One could argue that the biblical prohibitions against Christian participation in war are at least as strong as its strictures on abortion and euthanasia. See Richard B. Hays, *The Moral Vision of the New Testament* (San Francisco: HarperSanFrancisco, 1996), 317–46, 444–61.

46. Reading the Ten Commandments aloud has been a standard part of the liturgy for the Lord's Day in many Reformed churches. See the examples of Martin Bucer and John Calvin in Bard Thompson, *Liturgies of the Western Church* (Philadelphia, Pa.: Fortress, 1961). Catechetical use of the commandments has been important in both Catholic and Reformation traditions.

47. See Robert Wuthnow, *The Restructuring of American Religion: Society and Faith since World War II* (Princeton, N.J.: Princeton Univ. Press, 1988); and Donald E. Miller, *Reinventing American Protestantism: Christianity in the New Millennium* (Berkeley: Univ. of California Press, 1997).

48. Aspects of this pragmatic approach to religion are treated in Nathan O. Hatch, *The Democratization of American Christianity* (New Haven, Conn.: Yale Univ. Press, 1989).

49. See Weinrich, *Kirche Glauben,* 276–77, 281–82.

50. Riesebrodt writes of fundamentalism's "rigorous adherence to statutory thinking, with its literalist rationalism and its statutory ethical regulation of life conduct." Riesebrodt, *Pious Passion,* 185.

51. I leave unanswered why certain of these groups become militant, even violent, whereas others work more quietly within the possibilities of the very societies that they distrust. For an excellent study of the dynamics of religious extremism, see Mark Juergensmeyer, *Terror in the Mind of God: The Global Rise of Religious Violence* (Berkeley: Univ. of California Press, 2001).

52. For a helpful analysis of the role of rules and laws in democracies, see Giuseppe Di Palma, *To Craft Democracies: An Essay on Democratic Transitions* (Berkeley: Univ. of California Press, 1990).

53. Karl Marx, "Zur Kritik der Hegelschen Rechtsphilosophie," in *Deutsch-Französische Jahrbücher (1844),* ed. Arnold Ruge and Karl Marx (Leipzig, Germany: Verlag Philipp Reclam, 1981), 150–51.

On Naming Religious Extremists

The "Fundamentalist" Factor

WILLIAM D. DINGES

My response to the events of September 11 went something like this: speculation, shock, disbelief, and then a deep and profound sense of bewilderment. I spent nearly a week in an emotional mindset akin to the "psychic numbing" that Robert Lifton described among Hiroshima survivors—a state devoid of affectivity or the ability to focus on anything.[1] I could not listen to music, which, for me, is a sure and definitive sign that something is profoundly wrong.

As it became increasingly clear that the events of September 11 included a lethal fusing of religion and violence, the question arose, not only why would someone or some group do something like this, but *why would they do this in the name of God?* How does a suicidal attack on unarmed civilians translate into a salvific act? How is faith a weapon of war? Why is killing planned and executed in the name of religion or perceived as a spiritual imperative? What *level* of religious certitude is necessary or sufficient to legitimate an act of terror?

I am not unaware that religion has a shadow-side relationship with violence, or that religious ideologies can rouse, legitimate, and exacerbate deadly conflict. The tragic mix of religion and violence is hardly new. The Crusades, the Inquisition, and the bloody European religious wars of the sixteenth and seventeenth century easily come to mind. In the American experience, colonial expansion and the destruction of indigenous cultures had religious underpinnings. The Puritan "errand unto the wilderness" cost Quaker missionary lives; mystical religious visions inspired violent slave revolts; millennial religious eschatology animated the American struggle for independence; and nineteenth-century Catholic and Protestant animosity reached occasional bloody dimensions.[2] In more recent times, radicalized elements of the "pro-life" movement and paranoid groups on the margins of America's contemporary cult milieu have also engaged in homicidal and self-destructive behavior.[3]

In the wake of the attacks of September 11, I became increasingly intrigued by how Americans talk about and name these events, particularly where the complexities of religious motives and agency—which are invariably intertwined with non-religious ones—are at work. How do we call the horrendous events of that day: "terrorist attacks," "surprise attacks," "mass murder," "the catastrophe"?[4] And how do we name the underlying motives of the attacks insofar as they derive from religious values and agency?

The events of September 11 present a challenge in terminology. As a religious studies scholar, I was particularly intrigued by the use of the word *fundamentalism* in public discourse on the religious dimensions of the attacks. In reference to Islam—both before and after September 11—the word is often used interchangeably with emotionally laden terms such as "extremists," "militants," "fanatics," "radicals," "zealots," and "terrorists." Note that the operative label here is not Islamic "traditionalists" or "conservatives"; it is Islamic "fundamentalists."

Naming Osama bin Laden's al Qaeda network and its role in the September 11 attacks an expression of "fundamentalism" lacks the politically charged implications of the controversy over the use of the term "terrorism." Terrorism signifies an act that can be interpreted in a more benign or even positive way as one of liberation—where one person's "terrorist" is another's "freedom fighter." This is not the case, however, with use of the word *fundamentalism* with its overwhelmingly negative connotation.

This is not a purely academic or semantic issue. Sociologist Erving Goffman has observed that humans create frames for interpreting actors and situations. These frames include specific metaphors, symbolic representations, and cognitive clues. Religious ideologies are master frame sets. They provide individuals with labels, problem definitions, explanations, and goals. As situations change, frame alignments, or ideological alterations, become necessary.[5] Frames as vocabularies of meaning are obviously important because the way people discuss issues necessarily constitutes the issues.[6]

How we name the religious dimensions of the events of September 11 has important implications as a framing process. Names and labels count in public discourse. They have social and political consequences. They carry residual imaginative meaning and shape how we perceive and remember something. The power to name is the power to define. The power to define is the power to socially locate and designate and (in some cases) to condemn what is labeled deviant or nonnormative. And although labels have the power to facilitate comparison and analysis, they also run the risk of stereotyping. They can become shorthand abstractions that miss what is essential or different about the topic at hand.[7]

As Charles Long has noted, categorizing a religio-political phenomenon as "fundamentalist" is an act of signification, a discursive act of power grounded in the fact that the relationship between the signifier and the signified is an arbitrary and value-laden one. Whether certain groups (Muslims) wish to be denominated in this way is not for them, but for scholars, politicians, journalists, and others outside their community to decide.[8] The naming process also begs the question about whether labeling a particular type of movement "fundamentalist" improves or impedes our understanding of the phenomenon within its own theological and cultural frameworks. How do critics who do not share the ethical, theological, and philosophical assumptions of fundamentalists regarding human dignity and autonomy, science and technology, or progress and prosperity do fundamentalism justice?[9] Nor should it be forgotten that language is always vulnerable to manipulation and misuse in times of conflict and warfare. It is one of the first casualties of both. Having your own vocabulary to define a conflict is already a victory.

The reflection that follows examines the association between the acts of September 11 and their framing as an expression of "fundamentalism." I address three issues: (1) Why is this label employed, and what is its meaning? (2) Is the term an appropriate signifier vis-à-vis the profile of fundamentalism that grew out of the American Academy of Arts and Sciences Fundamentalist Project (FP)? (3) What agendas are served by how the events of September 11 are named qua fundamentalism and in reference to critiques of "holy" violence by religious communities themselves?

WHY "FUNDAMENTALISM"?

The obvious starting point for use of the fundamentalist label surrounding the attacks is the religious rhetoric of the perpetrators themselves. Although it is one thing to assert that the September 11 events represent a "twisted version of Islam,"[10] it is something else to attempt to divorce them completely from Islam—however culturally and theologically diverse the tradition, and however much moderate or progressive voices within the Islamic community may wish to distance themselves from the bloodshed of that ill-fated date.

At face value, what happened on September 11 is very much about religion, notably religion inspired by a radical and militant vision of Islam. The planes that slammed into the World Trade Center, the Pentagon, and a rolling Pennsylvania field were not piloted by hijackers opposing a tyrannical government or defending a secular ideology. Al Qaeda acts in the name of one religion, not one state or political or ethnic identity. Osama bin Laden's rhetoric with its frequent invocation of Allah is unambiguous in this regard. His cause is jihad in defense of Islam. His videos before and after September 11 repeatedly cite Islamic scripture. In a *fatwa* (religious ruling) delivered in February 1998, months before the bombing of the American embassies in Kenya and Tanzania, bin Laden made clear that the world was at war, that this war had been started by American actions in the Middle East, and that these actions constituted "a clear declaration of war on God, His messenger and Muslims." According to bin Laden, it was the "duty of every Muslim" to kill Americans and their allies—civilian and military. In taped remarks on Qatar's al-Jazeera television in the wake of September 11, bin Laden asserted that through the attacks America had been "hit by God" and that God had "blessed on the groups of Islam [that] destroyed America." Two years earlier he told his followers that his terrorism was of the "commendable kind, for it is directed at the tyrants and the aggressors and the enemies of Allah." According to bin Laden, the course on which he and his al Qaeda organization have embarked is historic and grandiose. It is "part of our religion," a matter of "religion and creed,"[11] a war of civilizations, a religious war against "unbelief and unbelievers"—jihad against the infidel West and "the Great Satan."[12]

My point is that religious values, symbols, and ideals are central to the meaning of the acts of September 11. They certainly are to the actors themselves and cannot be ignored or denied on these grounds, however irrational or irreligious they may appear to outsiders.[13] Nor is it insignificant that bin Laden's claim to religious legitimation carries greater plausibility in the context of the absence of centralized interpretative authority in Islam over the whole *umma* (community).[14]

If we accept that religiously inspired motives animated the September 11 attacks, the question naturally arises, what kind of religion? The answer, of course, is the bad kind. And the generic name for bad religion in American cultural parlance is "fundamentalism."[15]

FUNDAMENTALISM

The word *fundamentalism* came into widespread usage in American Protestant circles in conjunction with the publication of a series of theological tracts between 1910 and 1915 called *The Fundamentals: A Testimony to the Truth.* The term was originally no more than a (self-)descriptive referent for conservative evangelicals devoted to defending Christianity against the inroads of modernity and for asserting the fundamental beliefs in the Virgin Birth, the deity of Jesus Christ, biblical miracles, Christ's bodily Resurrection, and the belief that the Bible is without error and that its truths are valid for all eternity. Within a short period of time, however, the word metamorphosed into a label of cultural derision.[16] This shift in the meaning of the term occurred in the wake of fundamentalists' loss of power and control of their parent denominations. However, the process was dramatically accelerated by the public ignominy heaped on fundamentalism during a courtroom spectacle in Dayton, Tennessee, during the hot summer of 1925.

The Scopes "Monkey trial" was one of America's first judicial mass media extravaganzas. Local businessmen intent on stimulating a sagging economy and working in collusion with the American Civil Liberties Union orchestrated the affair. The much-hyped trial pitted a clique of Northern lawyers led by the caustic and agnostic Clarence Darrow against the "great commoner" and World's Christian Fundamentals Association's chosen potentate and would-be biblical exegete, William Jennings Bryan.

Although Scopes was convicted of violating Tennessee's anti-evolution law, the trial stamped the entire fundamentalist movement with an indelible negative image.[17] Darrow's scathing ridicule and humiliation of Bryan during cross-examination, the secular mocking of H. L. Mencken's base and derisive dispatches to the *Baltimore Sun*, and attacks on the fundamentalist creed in liberal Protestant theological quarters created much of the disparaging symbolism surrounding the phenomenon[18]—all of which was gleefully promoted in the national press. By the 1930s, fundamentalism had come to mean for many Americans not only unswerving biblical literalism and bad science, but the specter of bigotry, fanaticism, intolerance, dogmatism, antimodernism, exclusivism, and moral and pietistic rigorism. Things got worse.

Within the next two decades, fanatical anticommunism, hyper-masculinity, sexual repression, the subordination of women, and the abhorrence of homosexuality joined the list of pathologies associated with fundamentalism. All of these traits were cardinal sins in the modern conception of civil society earmarked by growing pluralism, relativism, open-mindedness, sexual liberation, and scientific and secular cultural hegemony. As a pugnacious and high-tension expression of religious identity, fundamentalism also violated the ascending liberal vision of a de-fanged and accommodationist form of denominational Christianity that was ecumenical, inclusive, and tolerant.

In the wake of the Age of Aquarius and the subsequent resurgence of the Moral Majority and New Religious Right in the 1970s and 1980s, the term "fundamentalism" again raced to the cultural fore with its negative signifying power—even as the leadership of this resurgence Moral Majority defiantly proclaimed themselves "fundamentalists."[19] The word became a popular mantra of many who opposed the muscular Christianity of the time. Liberals readily deployed the term—not unlike the way the political right used the word *communist* during the 1950s—as a label of derision and intimidation. By the mid-1980s, one observer noted that

labeling various people fundamentalists has become stock-in-trade in political and journalistic discourse in recent years. . . . [T]he major American newspapers contained advertisements deploring the rising tide of religious fundamentalism on the political shores at home and abroad. The avowedly secularist signatories of these advertisements, citing specific examples of what they meant by religious fundamentalism, named such diverse figures as the Rev. Jerry Falwell, the Ayatollah Ruhollah Khomeini and Pope John Paul II.[20]

The cultural construction of the negative animus surrounding fundamentalism also reflected academic prejudice, notably social scientific disdain for religion in general, and against strong or more sectarian affirmations of faith in particular. Throughout the first half of the twentieth century, American social scientists routinely dismissed religion as primitive, childish, authoritarian, irrational, and dogmatic. As Stark and Finke recently pointed out, even "authentic" social scientists of religion (meaning those with personal religious beliefs) freely expressed hostility toward any group showing the slightest sign of "fundamentalist" proclivities—as indicated over the last several decades by the overwhelming preponderance of articles warning against the Christian Right and exploring the social psychology of its adherents, relative to the paucity of similar articles focusing on the Christian Left.[21]

My point here is that throughout most of the twentieth century, religion perceived in the public square as aggressive, high-tension, literalist, insistent upon adherence to orthodoxy, and rhetorically militant came to be identified and derogated as fundamentalism. Little wonder that the term found widespread cultural deployment in the wake of the events of September 11. It was a ubiquitous, convenient, and culturally charged label for framing the religious dimensions of the attacks.

THE FUNDAMENTALISM PROJECT

The Fundamentalism Project (FP) was a Herculean academic initiative undertaken in the 1990s to examine the global dimensions of fundamentalism. Under the auspices of the American Academy of Arts and Sciences and the leadership of Martin Marty and R. Scott Appleby, an international group of scholars constructed a model of fundamentalism addressing the variety of data, the multitude of forms, and the distinct circumstances in which a particular variant of fundamentalism might emerge. The project culminated in academic and public conferences, films, and, most notably, a five-volume magnum opus edited by Marty and Appleby.[22]

The work of the FP was driven, in large part, by less derogatory assumptions about fundamentalism than were operative in public discourse at the time. Scholars working on the project tried to understand fundamentalism on its own terms while laboring to sharpen the word's descriptive and comparative utility. The work also conveyed a growing conviction that fundamentalism is a generic and global phenomenon related to conflicts over modernization. There is nothing inherently nationalistic or denominational about fundamentalism. Rather, fundamentalism pertains to a wide array of tensions attending the accommodation of religion to modernity/postmodernity, particularly in more traditional societies, and especially in those with unyielding autocratic governments.

The FP brought together an immense body of scholarly data and reflection. Although the work is difficult to summarize because of its scope and nuanced treatment, certain characteristics (in a Wittgenstein "family resemblances" sense) emerged as patterns and conceptual boundaries of the term. Accordingly, fundamentalism is a reaction to marginalization; an assertion of a minority or disenfranchised viewpoint against those internal and external forces perceived as tainted or corrupt; and an attempt to stop the erosion of a religious identity. Fundamentalism is always selective in engaging its host tradition and cultural surroundings. It is dualistic ("moral Manichaeism") and marked by a penchant for absolutism derived from a sacred text, book, or law. Fundamentalism is also millennial or messianic in flavor.

In addition, the organizational properties of fundamentalism include elect or divinely inspired leadership, often in the form of a charismatic figure; sharper and more distinct boundaries with which fundamentalists differentiate themselves and their communal identity from others ("us" vs. "them"); authoritarian and autocratic patterns of organization structures; and strict behavioral requirements (commitment mechanisms) to which members must adhere.

The FP editors summarized much of the work of the project by linking fundamentalism with those who "fight back" against perceived threats to their traditions and identity; "fight for" principles, policies, and programs that promise to achieve their goals; "fight with" resources that will best reinforce their identity and achieve their goals; "fight against" whoever or whatever threatens "all that is held dear"; and "fight under" God, or under the signs of "some transcendent reference." All this makes clear that fundamentalist movements have an inherently antagonistic relationship with the world beyond their own enclave.[23]

The FP editors were also adamant in asserting that fundamentalism is a genuinely religious phenomenon, an "attempt to preserve religious orthodoxy, integrity and 'purity' against compromise and corruption by malevolent religious and secular actors."[24] This is an important point, and one that distinguishes fundamentalist movements from other types of social and political ones. However, the FP editors also observed that fundamentalists are "inevitably political," although the actual weight or salience of the political—as opposed to the religious character of the phenomenon—varies by circumstance.[25] What is important is how the particular dynamics of fundamentalism interact (structure, chance, choice) in the world in which fundamentalists find themselves and in various relation-to-the-world patterns. Despite the world-conquering rhetoric, the high-tension dimensions of fundamentalism are inevitably blunted by the economic, political, and social realities of the "outside world." To be in the world is necessarily to be of it in some unwanted fashion or the other—even for fundamentalists.

If the FP accurately described essential characteristics of fundamentalism, the applicability of these characteristics to Osama bin Laden and his al Qaeda network, to the actions of September 11, or to any other radicalized expression of Islam remains an empirical question. In what sense are marginalization, selectivity, dualism, absolutism, millennialism, charismatic leadership, strict boundaries, and behavioral patterns part of the worldview and organizational dynamics of this and other religiously inspired terrorist groups? Many of these fundamentalist characteristics appear to apply to al Qaeda and bin Laden. In addition, linking the actions of the September 11 perpetrators with fundamentalism implicitly articulates the religious nature of the attacks—given the FP's emphasis on the intrinsic religious nature of any truly fundamentalist phenomenon.

Aside from the apparent symmetry between bin Laden's motives and the FP's definition of the term, other factors also facilitate linking the September 11 attacks with fundamentalism. For example, it has been argued that Islam produces the greatest number of fundamentalist movements today. Appleby summarizes why: first, spread of the mass media has increased the awareness of the social, economic, and political inequalities and unrelieved injustices that abound in many Muslim societies. Collaterally, the media has also highlighted the corruption, mismanagement, false promises, and incompetence that bedevil many Muslim governments and state-run institutions in what are sham democracies, military dictatorships, and one-party tyrannies reflecting a colonialist legacy. The ensuing relative deprivation coincides with exhaustion and disgust at the string of failed secular or liberal "solutions"— from socialism to Arab nationalism. These and other failures are easily blamed on the lingering hegemony of Western colonial powers, on the humiliating military defeat at the hands of the Israelis, and on the abandonment of Islam itself as the basis for the ordering of society. Appleby also notes that the Islamist "solution" to this malaise is fundamentalist rather than nationalist because the glorious Islamic empires and civilization serve as precedents antedated to, or resisted the rise of, the modern secular nation-state as it arose in the West. Islam's own internal vocabulary and conceptual repertoire conceives of a transnational, transregional spiritual community of believing Muslims as the basic political entity.[26] (In a similar vein, Bernard Lewis recently observed that Muslims tend to see not a nation subdivided into religious groups, "but a religion subdivided into nations.")[27] It is also commonly acknowledged that the response to this perceived deprivation is religious in nature because of the absence in virtually every Muslim country of democratically inspired venues for airing social protest and political grievance.

Second, the pervasiveness of fundamentalist responses in Islamic countries to deprivation and social malaise also stems from the fact that Islam has been remarkably resistant to the differentiation and privatization processes accompanying secularization in the West. Islam has yet to undergo a reformation such as the one that led Christianity to a more pronounced differentiation of sacred and secular, religious and political. Fundamentalist movements in Muslim countries are viewed, therefore, as nervous and inevitable reactions to the possibility that Islamization of the political sphere is slipping.

Finally, Appleby notes that the alleged pervasiveness of fundamentalist movements in Muslim countries stems from practical considerations: their preachers, leaders, and organizations have competed effectively with other Islamic leaders for resources and respect. They demonstrate integrity and efficiency in service to the poor and needy, as well as militant dedication to their cause. They are more sincere and committed to self-sacrifice, purity, and discipline. Their organizations provide a better social network than do corrupt governments.[28]

An Appropriate Term?

In light of the previous discussion, fundamentalism seems a legitimate way of framing the religious dimensions of the events of September 11. Some concerns remain, however.

To begin with, doubts persist about the appropriateness of the term outside the Western context. Some scholars of Islam have objected to the use of "fundamentalism" in reference to Islam or Muslims because of differences in ideology, organization, and behavior—especially where Muslim movements have a genealogy that predates the fundamentalist roots of conflict with modernity,[29] or where politics and history rather than Qur'anic literalism are seen as the progenitors of Islamic militancy.[30] From this perspective, fundamentalism is a term best left to Protestant Christians in North America and not applied to contemporary Islamic militancy. Although this is a cautionary position, it is a weak argument in light of the cross-cultural patterns and family resemblances of global fundamentalism amply and convincingly illustrated by the FP.

A second objection is that fundamentalism arose within the Christian tradition because of conflicts over doctrine. It has been observed, however, that in Islam, as in Judaism, the primary fissures (aside from questions of succession) have not centered around correct belief as much as around correct practice. In these traditions, how one eats, dresses, and acts are hardly trivial matters. They are core components of religious identity, of authentic actualization of revealed law.[31] This is a different locus of internal conflict from disputes over doctrinal subtleties. Such an argument, however, misses the point.

Although external factors are important in the etiology of fundamentalism, the movement stemmed first and foremost from the perception that Christian beliefs were being perverted from within by theological and scholarly elites bent on accommodating the tradition to modernity. This sense of internal subversion is one of the central *leitmotifs* in the rise of fundamentalism. It is especially notable in J. Gresham Machen's classic fundamentalist attack on liberalism and its theological apologists.[32]

Although conflicts over practice rather than creed may be more prevalent within Islam, the relevant factor is not the focus of conflict, but fundamentalism's essence as a form of pollution behavior concerned with defilement and subversion. In much of the Islamic world today, as in much of the Christian context from which fundamentalism arose in the late nineteenth and early twentieth centuries, subversion from within is a defining concern. The perceived dangers to the Islamic *umma* come not only from the external sources of Western hegemony ("McWorld") but more insidiously from an array of "Western enemies at home, who have imported and imposed infidel ways on Muslim people."[33] This concern with subversion from within, and not its specific locus or content (belief or practice) per se, is the defining factor in the fundamentalist dimensions of contemporary Islamic militancy.

Third, it has been argued that if we use the term "fundamentalism" in regard to Islam, all of Islam has to be labeled fundamentalist—despite the tradition's obvious diversity. This is because the Qur'an is not simply the Muslims' bible. As Aldridge notes, Muslims are held to believe that the Qur'an is uncreated and coexistent with God. The text is the word of God delivered to the Prophet Muhammad by the Angel Gabriel. Strictly, it is untranslatable from Arabic. In Christian terms, the Qur'an functions more as Christ than the Bible. Like Christ, it is a hierophany of the divine. It is an object of reverence in ways that the Bible usually is not, even to Christian fundamentalists. In reference to the Qur'an, therefore, it is "not possible to distinguish between liberal and conservative interpretations in the Christian sense."[34] All interpretive processes in Islam are necessarily "fundamentalist"—making bin Laden's motives and rhetoric indistinguishable in this regard.

This argument, too, is inadequate because it too narrowly confines the meaning of fundamentalism to the issue of verbal inerrancy. The fundamentalist dimensions of social protest in many Muslim countries today go far beyond the literal reading of a sacred book. Textual literalism cannot be separated from other social and political motives. Although a hermeneutic of verbal inerrancy surrounding a sacred text may be a necessary factor in fundamentalist identity, it is not a sufficient one.

Although I find the earlier arguments weak indictments of the use of the fundamentalist label in reference to the events of September 11, a more serious challenge to use of the term arises from the nature of the events themselves. The horror and confounding character of the attacks rest in the scope and intensity of their violence and destruction. In the context of mass murder, the fundamentalist appellation falls seriously short. I will return to this issue in the conclusion.

It is axiomatic that how something gets named or framed tells you as much about those doing so as about the phenomenon itself. Predictably, certain patterns or frames emerged in the wake of September 11 in how various religious and nonreligious groups and individuals named the attacks. These frames carry ideological agendas—of which the term "fundamentalism" is a key component. I call these patterns the nothing-to-do-with, something-to-do-with, and everything-to-do-with Islam frames.

Nothing-to-Do-With

In the wake of the attacks, most American politicians proclaimed that Islam is a religion of peace. Its core values have been "perverted" by violent extremists. In a nationally televised speech in September 2001, President Bush tried to assure American Muslims by reiterating this motif: "We respect your faith. Its teachings are good and peaceful, and those who commit evil in the name of Allah blaspheme the name of Allah."

Although there have been complaints of Muslim feebleness in this regard, especially the unwillingness or inability to take on their own extremists, the dissociation of "authentic" Islam from September 11 has come from within the tradition itself. Muslim voices have sought to discredit bin Laden and al Qaeda on religious grounds. Accordingly, the attacks of September 11 violate "true Islam" and have "nothing to do" with the tradition.[35] They "distort" a great religion[36] and are the desperate and horrific acts of a "cult of fanatics."[37] According to Prince Bandar bin Sultan, Saudi Arabian ambassador to Washington, bin Laden was "deluding himself" in trying to wrap his actions within the tenets of Islam.[38]

Other Muslim commentary has emphasized that the attacks of September 11 cannot be sanctioned by Islam or Shari'a because innocent victims were killed and property destroyed. They violate Qur'anic prescriptions and the ethics of battle spelled out by Muhammad. They pervert the true meaning of jihad, a term more correctly understood as a metaphor for spiritual struggle, moral self-improvement, and activism on behalf of justice—not the killing of innocent human beings.[39]

Muslims have also charged that bin Laden's actions represent a warping of Islam to suit political goals to achieve power. They emphasize the al Qaeda leader's criminal bent and predilection to use piety in the service of terror. They also charge that bin Laden has had no formal religious education and, therefore, no right to speak for Muslims, to issue fatwas, or to legitimate the attacks by Qur'anic injunctions.[40]

In more bizarre and denial-like allegations that sustain the motif of Islamic victimization and circumvent self-analysis and self-criticism, the attacks have also been described by some Muslims as the product of a "Jewish" or "Zionist" conspiracy.[41]

While defending "true Islam" against the attacks, many Muslim leaders and groups have also distinguished the message from the method. Radical Muslims are said to act out of a deep sense of injustice. The perpetrators who fuel violence with religion are allegedly blinded by these feelings of oppression and hatred.[42]

Muslims also remind Americans of U.S. culpability: Al Qaeda is a form of highly politicized Islam previously nurtured by the United States as a cold war anticommunist tool.[43] Nor can any country expect immunity from problems emanating from regional conflicts, especially when its own foreign policy is deeply implicated in such the conflict.

The nothing-to-do-with-Islam frame is also an understandable reaction of the American religious mainstream, notably individuals and denominations attuned to perceived religious intolerance and the persecution of minority faiths. It is likewise a predictable response of those who, in the current climate of multiculturalism, want to avoid any direct criticism of other groups or who are concerned about the possible ill effects of September 11 on public interfaith dialogue and harmony.[44] Fear of hate-violence, lashing out, and harassment and attacks on American Muslims and citizens of Middle Eastern descent also animate much of this type of response.

Much of this mainstream religious discourse surrounding September 11 makes generalized references to "evil" in the world, preaches patience and understanding, and admonishes citizens not to blame loyal, law-abiding American Muslims for terrorist acts committed by the coreligionists.[45] In addition, where the term "fundamentalism" is used, much of the commentary focuses (ironically) on "hijacking" imagery[46]—suggesting that Islam qua religion had been taken over by something external to it. The events of September 11 are framed as a struggle for the "soul" of Islam, a struggle between fundamentalist (notably Saudi Arabian Wahabism) and progressive forces within the tradition. They are a "test" of Islam's standing as a great world religion.[47] Exculpating emphasis has also been placed on Islam's history of tolerance before the enlightenment of the West and on the dangers of cosmologizing the events of September 11 such that the language of "good" and "evil" gives rise to a disproportionate military response or feeds an unwarranted social imagination that sees Muslims as fanatics and enemies of Christianity.[48]

Ironically, this attempt to dissociate Islam completely from the events of September 11 implicitly denies that religion—especially traditions of "the Book,"—involves hermeneutical acts that produce selective and, in some cases, different and contradictory interpretations. To deny this possibility implicitly recapitulates the fundamentalist penchant for literalism that refuses the social and historical imbeddedness of the interpretive act. In addition, such denial also expresses a weak understanding of the ambivalent potential for violence, militancy, and destructiveness within religious traditions themselves.

Another variant of the nothing-to-do-with-Islam response, more pronounced on the Religious Right, has been to frame the events of September 11 not as a critique of Islam, per se, but in terms of the Religious Right's premillennialist eschatology and contemporary political agenda. This approach generally avoids the fundamentalist term and reflects the standard right-wing pattern of combining themes of retribution with dramatic news events and complaints about secularism in American society. The public relations faux pas of Revs. Falwell and Robertson in proclaiming that the September 11 attacks were a divine punishment for the nation's sinful ways, notably the actions of a deviant assortment of liberal culprits—gays, abortionists, lesbians, liberal advocacy groups, and those who removed prayer from public schools—exemplifies this approach.[49] According to Falwell and Robertson, these forces have been trying to "secularize America."[50] The corruption, immorality, and secularism of America that they have reaped, along with the separation of God from governance and our failure as a Christian nation, have provoked divine wrath. As other conservative pundits have echoed, Islam is simply an instrument of retribution for America's sins.[51]

A collateral but more tempered view, popular across the religious spectrum, but more so on the Religious Right, is that the events of September 11 are a catalyst for a religious revival. The catastrophe presents the nation with an opportunity to arouse spiritual energies and a renewed interest in God—all of which runs contrary to persistent left/liberal attempts to secularize American public life. James Dobson, head of Focus on the Family, observed that in light of September 11, American leaders are once again "reweaving" rituals of God and country. Revivalism notwithstanding, the events of September 11 have proven a prime marketing opportunity for Dobson's organization and others to promote and sell books, tapes, and other items to help Christians "cope" with the tragedy.[52]

Not all voices in the nothing-to-do-with-Islam frame are concerned with religious causality or exonerating Islam per se. Some have focused attention on secular or sociological factors that define the conflict between bin Laden and the West as one of cultural identity, pitting tribalism, intolerance, and narrow-mindedness against cosmopolitanism and modernity—as symbolized by the choice of the targets, especially the World Trade Center in New York City.[53] Rather than Islam, per se, the pervasiveness of protracted poverty and helplessness across generations is seen as the nucleus of the problem. Related causes include profound cultural confusion among the masses of young, disaffected, middle-class Muslim students who have been placed close to modernity, but who have been unable to partake of it.[54] Or the problem is defined as a product of global forms of political disintegration challenging the existing multicultural nations.[55]

Occidentalism, a cluster of "images and ideas in the West in the minds of its haters," is another culprit. These images and ideas include the city, the bourgeoisie, reason, feminism, and their alleged cultural attributes—arrogance, feebleness, greed, depravity, decadence—all of which are evoked as typically Western and inherently threatening to traditional societies.[56]

Psychological explanations of the motives behind the attacks also carry nothing-to-do-with-Islam overtones. These explanations focus on gender issues or problematic definitions of manhood. Fear of women and traditional cultural needs for dominating and violent patriarchal definitions of manliness (and, by implication, submissive womanhood) are primary factors.[57]

Overromanticized death wishes[58] coupled with bin Laden's own grandiose psychological need for power and attention via the destruction of others have also been identified as motives for the September 11 attacks.[59]

Aside from the desire to protect the integrity of religion in general, and religious orthodoxy from defamation in particular, the attempt to exculpate Islam completely from September 11 has also been linked to crasser political maneuvering, notably attempts by conservative Republican operatives to curry favor with American Muslims and bring them into the Republican party. Grover Norquist, a Republican activist with White House connections, has purportedly worked aggressively toward disassociating Islam from bin Laden-inspired fanaticism to achieve this political end.[60]

Something-to-Do-With

A second perspective on the attacks gradually emerged after September 11. Within this frame, the onus for September 11 rests within Islam itself. The term "fundamentalism" is a key component of the discourse of this perspective.

In the something-to-do-with frame, the fundamentalist nature of the strand of Islam that has opted for political violence, along with its militant offshoots, is not a distortion of the tradition or, for that matter, a "hijacking" of it. Bin Laden is not just another "violent cult leader"; he is someone who has tapped into Islamic theological foundations and sources with a "wide following and a deep history"[61]—in much the same way one can talk about the deep theological roots of anti-Semitism in the Christian tradition.[62] Certain theological shortcomings, along with alleged fascist and totalitarian characteristics at the heart of Islam, are deeply implicated in his actions. These shortcomings are partially reflected in the "religious space opened up by the revelation Islam presupposes."[63] They must be acknowledged and taken seriously—as must the general absence of theological defenses in Islam against the spread of militant extremism in many Muslim countries. The most salient of these theological sources are values and orientations associated with absolutism and exclusivism.[64]

One of the more widely read something-to-do-with-Islam arguments is Andrew Sullivan's October *New York Times Magazine* essay, "This *Is* a Religious War."[65]

Sullivan insists that the religious dimensions of the events of September 11 (and conflict with Islam in general) are central to their meaning. The terrorists represent a "radical, fundamentalist" part of Islam. Their actions are a religious problem, not simply a political or social one. This religious dimension needs to be acknowledged in order to figure out how and why it is the case.

Sullivan ties the "fundamentalist mentality" animating the September 11 attacks with blind recourse to texts, the subjugation of reason, judgment, and conscience to dogma, and the impetus to coerce others with the "word [Islamic, in this case] of absolute truth." In particular, he focuses on the deep undercurrent of "fundamentalist" intolerance in Islam toward unbelievers, especially those perceived as a threat to the faith. Sullivan draws on the eminent scholar Bernard Lewis in support of this charge:

> What is truly evil and unacceptable is the domination of infidels over true believers. For true believers to rule misbelievers is proper and natural, since this provides for the maintenance of the holy law and gives the misbelievers both the opportunity and the incentive to embrace the true faith. But for misbelievers to rule over true believers is blasphemous and unnatural, since it leads to the corruption of religion and morality in society and to the flouting or even the abrogation of God's law.[66]

The basic flaw is Islam's theocratic impulse to dominate all social and political life, along with its fusing of the claim to absolute truth with politics. Drawing on secular horrors of the twentieth century, Sullivan argues that Nazi Germany and Soviet Russia represented the same lethal fusing of politics and ultimate meaning—even in the service of radically different ends (racial purity and revolutionary class consciousness). Islam has yet to learn the lessons of history in regard to its own totalizing ideology. Where the tradition has been tolerant, it is a tolerance premised on its own power.

Sullivan concludes that the present conflict is an even greater threat than the "discarded lies" of Nazism and Communism. This is because the power of Islam's logic is greater than that of Hitler's or Stalin's. In its general failure to embrace the pluralism of modernity, and in its fusion with the political sphere that turns conflict about right and wrong into cosmic (and lethal) debates over "good" and "evil," Islam promotes a dangerous and dichotomous capitulation to an "unbelief or radical strike" mentality.[67]

A similar perspective on "Islamic fundamentalists" occurs in the journalistic commentary of Thomas L. Friedman. Friedman, too, argues for the theological roots of September 11. The current conflict with Islam is a battle against its "religious totalitarianism," an exclusivist orientation at variance with modern pluralism. The problem is rooted in the tradition's inability to reinterpret the past and to develop a dominant religious philosophy that allows equal recognition of alternative faith communities. Friedman insinuates too that Islam has failed to follow the development of Christianity and Judaism in their respective engagements with modernity and remains instead captive to a retrograde and intolerant theological ethos.[68]

A counterargument to this, and one closer to the nothing-to-do-with-Islam point of view, can be found in the commentaries of David F. Forte, a Catholic legal scholar from Cleveland-Marshall College who has written on international religious persecution. When President Bush told Congress that bin Laden and his supporters "follow in the path of fascism, Nazism, and totalitarianism," he was following Forte's line of thought.[69]

According to Forte, al Qaeda operatives give expression to certain Islamic theological impulses. These impulses, however, are heretical ones. Bin Laden and other radicals practice an esoteric strain of Islam going back to a seventh-century sect. Their theological lineage derives from the tradition of the Kharajites, an early faction that violently opposed all other adherents of Islam as impure. Though long-ago defeated, Kharajite beliefs have been revitalized by bin Laden and other radicals.

Like Sullivan, Forte links the contemporary zealots with a new form of "fascist tyranny." However, unlike Sullivan, Forte divorces this tyranny not only from Islam in particular, but from religion in general—alleging that "nothing this evil could be religious." His point is that bin Laden's real enemy is "traditional Islam" and, by implication, traditional religion of any kind. Islamic militants are not "true Muslims" at all.[70]

Forte's assertions deflect attention away from contemporary theological currents in Islam, notably the Wahabism in Saudi Arabia that has been linked with Islamic radicalism. More importantly, they derive from the general need (more pronounced on the religious right) to distance orthodox religion of any kind from the events of September 11. Because the attacks implicitly cast aspersions on all variants of militant or high-tension religion, conservative expressions of Christianity—more or less aggressive and exclusive in their own right—cannot be linked with the excesses of militant Islam lest all forms of religious orthodoxy be tainted with the stain of fanaticism.

Everything-to-Do-With

The most explicit charges of direct Islamic culpability for the events of September 11 have come from more radically sectarian groups on the Christian Right. These voices assert that the attacks are another manifestation of Islam as a false, degenerate, aggressive, and blood-thirsty religion. In mirror imitation of bin Laden's own Manichean worldview, they cosmologized the attacks as the work of Satan.[71] Because Islam is not an authentic religion to begin with, September 11 is not an "extremist," "heretical," or "fundamentalist" expression of the tradition or of its purported failure to develop in ways compatible with modernity. Arguments that Islamic rage is a distortion of traditional Islam are dismissed as no more than political correctness.[72] Where religion spawns violence, it is by "unbiblical gods" and the work of Satan. Militant Islam is such an agency. The violence of September 11 is not the consequence of a true religion or a fundamentalist one; it is the product of an entirely false religion engaged in a centuries-long conflict with the West.

Similar sentiments can be found among radical right-wing Catholic sources. Rev. Jacque Emily of the traditionalist Society of St. Pius X described the attacks of September 11 as another "escalation" in a long-running war by the Islamic world to conquer Western countries. Islam is a false religion, a "blatant revolt against God and his Christ." Like many radical right Protestant counterparts, Emily views Islamic aggressiveness and expansionist propensities as the consequence of Western impotence. Those who assert that there is nothing that could justify terrorist actions "are lying." The ultimate aim of Islam is "Islamization" of the world. In a distinctly Catholic version of Protestant retribution themes, Emily alleges that nations that betrayed their Catholic heritage in 1789, will pay under the "Islamic yoke."[73]

Other traditionalist Catholics have also promoted retribution motifs in conjunction with September 11. These motifs are typically situated in the context of denunciations of the alleged "about-face" of Vatican II on non-Christian religions. Traditionalist Catholics also reject the idea that the current conflict is an aberration of fundamentalist Islam. They emphasize instead—like their far-right Protestant counterparts—that Islam itself is a "false religion."[74]

CONCLUSION

The word *fundamentalism* has a long-standing history in American cultural discourse as a term of derision and a label of symbolic degradation. The symbiotic relationship between fundamentalism and modernism in the West has been one of fundamentalists as the "Other"—an alien, retrograde, and threatening presence. The fundamentalist epithet is appealing because it telescopes into a single term an entire range of negative attributes associated with retrograde, deviant, and dangerous religion.

The Fundamentalism Project made significant strides in describing and clarifying the characteristics associated with fundamentalism and their interplay in various geopolitical settings. The project moved usage of the word beyond its American Protestant moorings and illuminated fundamentalism's various cultural and national variants. The work also promoted a more descriptive rather than normative meaning of the term. Nevertheless, the concept has limited utility in discussing the tragedy of September 11.

Although we can infer certain affinities between the motives and mentalities of the perpetrators of September 11 and the characteristics of fundamentalism, use of the term continues to serve various ideological agendas. These agendas include either exonerating Islam as having been taken over by alleged fundamentalists or contributing to a negatively charged atmosphere by indicting Islam as fundamentalist in essence and therefore deficient and culpable. Two additional problems surround use of the word beyond the question of its applicability to contemporary expressions of radicalized Islam.

First, as I intimated earlier, although it is easy to associate extremism with a fundamentalist mentality, not every fundamentalist movement advocates or propagates violence—even while individual fundamentalists may be angry, rhetorically militant, and intolerant of outsiders. Mark Juergensmeyer, Appleby, and others have made this point. Juergensmeyer notes, for example, that individuals he interviewed in his studies of religious-inspired violence (predating September 11 and particularly antiabortion opponents) did not come from fundamentalist backgrounds, but from mainline (Lutheran, Presbyterian) Protestant ones. They were not "fundamentalists" in any traditional understanding of the term. Some could quote Bonhoeffer at length.[75]

Furthermore, fundamentalism in America has no historical legacy of organizational violence, per se, even while often being associated in the public mind with violence-prone organizations such as the Ku Klux Klan. The history of the movement is largely one of internal doctrinal controversy and ecclesial conflict. Nor are contemporary radical movements such as the American Christian Patriot movement and Christian Identity fundamentalist initiatives. As Appleby notes, these movements draw their primary ideological and organizational resources and recruits from radical political or racist ideologies rather than, as the classical fundamentalist movement has, from historical, multigenerational religious communities or denominations.[76] In addition, until recently, American fundamentalists have generally followed the logic of their own dispensational premillennialism and steered clear of political power. They have vacillated instead among periods of political assertiveness, rhetorical militancy, and withdrawal into their own cultural enclaves as a remnant faithful besieged by a hostile and reprobate world. Roger Stump, too, has noted that many global fundamentalist movements dissociate themselves from extremist destructive tactics and adopt strategies of participation, in large part because they believe that their own tradition embodies the larger values of the society to which they belong.[77]

Much of the violent imagery linked with fundamentalism is a by-product of the movement's penchant for verbal pugnaciousness, coupled with its association with the warfare metaphor and imagery and military paradigm animating cultural "battles" ("wars") between science and religion and evolution and creation in modern American history.

My point here is that fundamentalism is not an inherently violent expression of religious self-understanding—in Islam or otherwise. Although a fundamentalist disposition may be a precondition for religious-inspired violence, this does not make fundamentalism a cause of such violence. Militancy and incivility toward "secular humanists" is hardly mass murder.

Second, as a concept, fundamentalism carries a diagnostic frame of attribution. Juergensmeyer has observed (and I agree) that use of the word *fundamentalism* in reference to religious violence in general, and to the attacks of September 11 in particular, implies that there is something *inherently* wrong with religion.[78] Because the term is linked so intrinsically with religion in public discourse—a view reinforced by the Fundamentalism Project—any movement or action associated with fundamentalism necessarily implies religious causality and culpability.[79] The deeds of a few (fundamentalists) necessarily indict the phenomenon (religion) as a whole.

A more helpful frame for discussing the relationship between religion and violence growing out of the events of September 11 would shift the focus of this relationship. It would not ask first and foremost why or how religion causes or rationalizes violence; it would ask instead how and why violent behavior necessitates or makes more probable religious agency and legitimation. What conditions of conflict or oppression compel engagement of the religious imagination? What structural characteristics of a society facilitate such a link? What forces of geopolitics provoke religious violence? What psychological conditions of alienation or victimization do likewise? What level of spiritual and political collapse leads to religious-inspired terrorism? How does violence empower religion? Or what organizational conditions of a religious establishment facilitate the emergence of violence from within a tradition?

The issue here, in other words, is not how religion radicalizes politics or motivates terrorism; it is how the exigencies of political and social conflict or individual alienation radicalize religion, thereby transforming religion's ambivalent potential for violence into real violence. This reframing of the question—implicit in Juergensmeyer's and Appleby's studies of religious-inspired violence—does not mean that religion is merely a dependent variable; the question must also be addressed about how moderation and affirmation within a tradition break down or give way to violence and extremism. Reframing the issue addresses a collateral problem.

I see no satisfactory resolution to the question of whether religion is a cause of or restraint on the use of violence. The fundamentalist appellation assumes it is a cause. Religion can obviously be both, however. As various scholars have noted,[80] religion is inherently ambivalent in this regard—and likely to remain so. Religious traditions (texts, precepts, rituals, ethical practices) have the capacity to motivate humans toward goodness, love, peace, hope, and reconciliation. They can also breed violence, destruction, and death. The adulation of sacrifice and martyrdom, the penchant for absolutism and satanization, and the tendency to cosmologize conflict are but a few of the characteristics of religion that facilitate the sacralization of violence.[81] Nor is it clear why it is so often assumed that it is an alleged distortion of a tradition to amplify the more aggressive passages in its sacred texts, especially when the tradition is perceived as being under attack.

Prevailing paradigms among scholars and political and editorial pundits can lead to the wrong questions and a focus on the wrong sorts of information. This is what has happened with the deployment of the term "fundamentalism" in relation to the events September 11.

Reframing the question into one of how religious symbols, sensibilities, and organizations are activated or mobilized on behalf of violent conflict shifts the focus away from the stigma of religious fundamentalism and all of its negative connotations. We are on firmer ground labeling religiously linked or rationalized violence an act of *extremism*, rather than an expression of fundamentalism. Extremism is a potential endemic to all channels and modes of human culture. Whether religion has a natural propensity toward extremism given the totalistic principles of eternity and inerrancy as some have claimed remains to be seen.[82] What is clear is that the fundamentalist label assumes that it does.

NOTES

1. Robert J. Lifton, *Death in Life: Survivors of Hiroshima* (Chapel Hill: Univ. of North Carolina Press, 1968).

2. Richard Hofstadter and Michael Wallace, eds., *American Violence: A Documentary History* (New York: Alfred A. Knopf, 1970), especially part 4, 295–336.

3. Catherine Wessinger, *Millennialism, Persecution, and Violence: A Documentary History* (Syracuse, N.Y.: Syracuse Univ. Press, 2001); Tom Robbins and Susan J. Palmer, eds., *Millennium, Messiahs, and Mayhem: Contemporary Apocalyptic Movements* (New York: Routledge, 1997).

4. We seem to have settled on the terse "9-1-1" tag—a play on the number used for emergency calls. See William Safire, "On Language," *New York Times Magazine*, October 7, 2001, 24.

5. Erving Goffman, *Frame Analysis* (Cambridge, Mass.: Harvard Univ. Press, 1974).

6. In relationship to the mobilization of fundamentalist movements in this regard, see Rhys H. Williams, "Movement Dynamics and Social Change: Transforming Fundamentalist Ideology and Organizations," in *Accounting for Fundamentalisms*, ed. Martin E. Marty and R. Scott Appleby (Chicago: Univ. of Chicago Press, 1994), 785.

7. Consider, for example, President Bush's initial employment and subsequent retraction of the term "crusade" (with all of its historically laden anti-Muslim connotations), and the Defense Department's faux pas in naming the military campaign against terrorism "Operation Infinite Justice," a label eventually replaced with the less transcendent-sounding title, "Operation Enduring Freedom." Another example of this labeling issue is the use of the term "martyr" (*shaheed*) rather than "suicide bomber"—given the Islamic belief that suicide is contrary to the Qur'anic injunction and teaching of the Prophet.

8. Charles H. Long, *Significations: Signs, Symbols, and Images in the Interpretation of Religion* (Philadelphia, Pa.: Fortress, 1986).

9. On these issues see Frederick Mathewson Denny, "The Fundamentalism Project: An Islamic Scholar's Perspective," *Religious Studies Review* 24 (Jan. 1998): 8–9.

10. *Christian Century* 118, no. 26 (Sept.–Oct. 2001): 3.

11. "November 3 Videotape Broadcast," *New York Times*, Sunday, November 4, 2001.

12. For a summary compilation of bin Laden's remarks, see Lynn Ludlow, "Osama Speaks: Inside the Mind of a Terrorist," *San Francisco Chronicle*, October 7, 2001, www.sfgate.com/cgi-bin/article. cgi?file=/chronicle/archive/2001/10/07/IN176521.DTL. See also "Declaration of War against Americans Who Occupy the Land of the Two Holy Mosques" and "Jihad Is an Individual Duty," *Los Angeles Times*, August 13, 1998; "Bin Laden Hails Attacks on U.S." and "Text of bin Laden's Remarks" *Washington Post*, October 8, 2001. Mohammed Atta's five-page letter to his fellow hijackers is also replete with religious exhortation.

13. An axiom of symbolic interactionism is that in order to understand behavior, we must know how the actor defines the situation. See George Herbert Mead, *Mind, Self, and Society: From the Standpoint of a Social Behaviorist* (Chicago: Univ. of Chicago Press, 1934); also, Herbert Blumer, *Symbolic Interactionism: Perspective and Method* (Englewood Cliffs, N.J.: Prentice-Hall, 1969). The rationality of a choice must be seen from the "insider" perspective. As James S. Coleman has observed, "Much of what is ordinarily described as nonrational or irrational is merely so because observers have not discovered the point of view of the actor, for which the action *is* rational." *Foundations of Social Theory* (Cambridge, Mass.: Belknap, Harvard Univ. Press, 1990), 18.

14. I recognize the role of respected leaders in Islam, notably scholars and legal experts who study the Qur'an and the hadith and are responsible for determining the application of law.

15. I do not address the question of what Muslims understand by the term "fundamentalist." Frederick Denny notes in his assessment of the Islamic component of the Fundamentalism Project ("Fundamentalism Project," 8–12) that, where Muslims have accepted the term "fundamentalist" or "fundamentalism," it is in reference to a person who upholds the "fundamentals" of Islam and expects all other sincere Muslims to do so. This is the same understanding associated with the initial coinage of the term by conservative American evangelicals.

16. Standard works on fundamentalism include George M. Marsden, *Fundamentalism and American Culture: The Shaping of Twentieth-Century Evangelicalism, 1870–1925* (New York: Oxford Univ. Press, 1980), and *Reforming Fundamentalism: Fuller Seminary and the New Evangelicalism* (Grand Rapids, Mich.: Eerdmans, 1987); Ernest R. Sandeen, *The Roots of Fundamentalism: British and American Millenarianism, 1800–1930* (Chicago: Univ. of Chicago Press, 1970); Lawrence Kaplan, ed., *Fundamentalism in Comparative Perspective* (Amherst: Univ. of Massachusetts Press, 1992); Bruce Lawrence, *Defenders of God: The Fundamentalist Revolt in the Modern Age* (San Francisco: Harper and Row, 1989).

17. Marsden, *Fundamentalism and American Culture*, 184–95.

18. One of the best-known was Harry Emerson Fosdick's classic sermon, "Shall the Fundamentalist Win?" Sinclair Lewis's 1927 novel *Elmer Gantry* also contributed significantly to the negative public caricature of fundamentalism.

19. George Marsden, *Understanding Fundamentalism and Evangelicalism* (Grand Rapids, Mich.: William B. Eerdmans, 1991), 106.

20. Patrick J. Ryan, "Islamic Fundamentalism: A Questionable Category," *America* 29 (Dec. 1984): 437.

21. Rodney Stark and Roger Finke, *Acts of Faith: Explaining the Human Side of Religion* (Berkeley: Univ. of California Press, 2000), 21.

22. Martin E. Marty and R. Scott Appleby, eds., *Fundamentalisms Comprehended* (Chicago: Univ. of Chicago Press, 1995); *Accounting for Fundamentalisms* (Chicago: Univ. of Chicago Press, 1994); *Fundamentalisms and Society* (Chicago: Univ. of Chicago Press, 1993); *Fundamentalisms and the State* (Chicago: Univ. of Chicago Press, 1993); *Fundamentalisms Observed* (Chicago: Univ. of Chicago Press, 1991).

23. Marty and Appleby, *Fundamentalisms Observed*, ix–x.

24. Marty and Appleby, "Conclusion: An Interim Report on a Hypothetical Family," *Fundamentalisms*

Observed, 814–42. That fundamentalism is a type of religious movement is a position also emphasized in Lawrence's *Defenders of God*, 83, 100.

25. Marty and Appleby, *Accounting for Fundamentalisms*, 503. See also John R. Fitzmier's, "The Fundamentalist Project: An American Perspective," *Religious Studies Review* 24 (Jan. 1998): 3–8.

26. R. Scott Appleby, *The Ambivalence of the Sacred: Religion, Violence and Reconciliation* (Lanham, Md.: Rowman and Littlefield, 2000), 106.

27. Bernard Lewis, "The Revolt of Islam," *The New Yorker*, November 19, 2001, 51.

28. Appleby, *Ambivalence of the Sacred*, 106–7.

29. See, for example, Martin Van Bruinessen, "Muslim Fundamentalism: Something to Be Understood or to Be Explained Away?" *Islam and Christian-Muslim Relations* 6 (1995): 157. For an excellent treatment of problematic aspects of use of the term "fundamentalism" in reference to Islam in general, see Riffat Hassan, "The Burgeoning of Islamic Fundamentalism: Toward an Understanding of the Phenomenon," in *The Fundamentalist Phenomenon*, ed. Norman J. Cohen (Grand Rapids, Mich.: Eerdmans, 1990), 151–71.

30. Patrick J. Ryan, "Islamic Fundamentalism: A Questionable Category," *America* 29 (Dec. 1984): 437–40.

31. Alan Aldridge, *Religion in the Contemporary World: A Sociological Introduction* (Malden, Mass.: Blackwell, 2000), 124.

32. J. Gresham Machen, *Christianity and Liberalism* (Grand Rapids, Mich.: Eerdmans, 1923).

33. Lewis, "Revolt of Islam," 60. Curiously, Lewis seems to miss this point and instead associates the term "fundamentalism" with Protestant churches that "differed in some respects" from more mainstream Christian churches. Although it is correct that these differences "bear no resemblance to those that divide Muslim fundamentalists from the Islamic mainstream," they are not essential to fundamentalism. The perception of subversion from within is.

34. Aldridge, *Religion in the Contemporary World*, 125.

35. See the remarks by Sheik Zafzaf of Al Azhar, the revered mosque and distinguished university, the leading voice of the Sunni Muslim establishment, in Douglas Jehl, "Moderate Muslims Fear Their Message Is Being Ignored," *New York Times*, October 21, 2001; see also Mona Eltahawy, "My Islam," *Washington Post*, January 3, 2002.

36. Abdallah Awad Abbud bin Laden, head of the bin Laden family, qtd. in *Christian Century* 118, no. 26 (Sept.–Oct. 2001): 15.

37. The words of Iranian President Mohammad Khatami in *Washington Post*, November 11, 2001. Also, "Muslim Leaders Speak Out," *Washington Post*, October 13, 2001.

38. *Washington Post*, December 28, 2001; See also Douglas Jehe, "Speaking in the Name of Islam," *New York Times*, December 2, 2002.

39. Colin Nickerson, "Not Easy to Define 'Jihad,'" *Milwaukee Journal Sentinel* Online, October 13, 2001, www.jsonline.com/news/editorials/Oct01/Nickerson/4101301.asp, accessed April 2002. See also the comments of Shaykh "Abdul-"Azeez Aalash-Shaykh, the *muftee* (one qualified to pass fatwa) of Saudi Arabia, September 17, 2001, www.fatwa-online.com/news/0010917_1.htm, accessed April 2002, and M. A. Muqtedar Khan, "Muslim to Muslim," *Christian Century* 118, no. 30 (Nov. 7, 2001): 5.

40. See comments in Nora Boustany, "Bin Laden Now a Target in Arab Media," *Washington Post*, November 23, 2001; Eltahawy, "My Islam."

41. On this and more generalized problems of an alleged Jewish conspiracy against Muslims, see Thomas L. Friedman, "Blunt Question, Blunt Answer," *New York Times*, February 10, 2002. See also the remarks of Muhammad Gemeaha of Al Azhar University in Richard Cohen, "Where Bigotry Gets a Hearing," *Washington Post*, October 30, 2001.

42. Bill Broadway, "Looking for Answers In Islam's Holy Book," *Washington Post*, September 29, 2001.

43. Saad Mehio, "How Islam and Politics Mixed," *New York Times*, December 2, 2001.

44. See, for example, Adrain Dominican Sisters, "In Response to Events of September 11, 2001," *New York Times*, October 7, 2001.

45. See, for example, *Origins* 31, no. 16 (Sept. 2001) for a series of articles and statements by Roman Catholic bishops on the events of September 11.

46. Karen Armstrong, "The True, Peaceful Face of Islam," *Time*, October 1, 2001, 48.

47. Gilbert Meilaender, "After September 11," *Christian Century* 118, no. 26 (Sept.–Oct. 2001): 8. See also the remarks of Muslim leaders in Mark Silk, "Islam Is Everywhere," *Religion in the News* (Fall 2001): 6–8, 28; William Pfaff, "Seeds of War: What Drives Islamic Fundamentalists," *Commonweal* 128, no. 18 (Oct. 2001): 9–10; Armstrong, "True, Peaceful Face of Islam," 48.

48. John Gunneman, "Naming the Terror," *Christian Century* 118, no. 26 (Sept.–Oct.2001): 4–6.

49. The specific remarks were made by Reverend Falwell. Pat Robertson subsequently protested that he did not make the statements attributed to Falwell. His response has included evoking Lincoln's use of retribution language during the Civil War. See "Pat Robertson's Letter to U.S. Newspaper Editors," September 17, 2001, www.patrobertson.com/pressreleases/newspapeditors.asp, accessed April 2002.

50. Robertson never actually apologized, noting simply that Falwell's remarks were "totally inappropriate." See Michael E. Naparstek, "Falwell and Robertson Stumble," *Religion in the News* (Fall 2001): 5, 28.

51. Dave Clark, "Understanding Islamic Fanaticism," *Family News in Focus*, September 21, 2002, www.family.org/cforum/fnif/news/a00177764, accessed April 2002.

52. See, for example, James Dobson, "How God Continues to Bless America," *Dr. Dobson's Monthly Newsletter*, December 2001, http://family.org/docstudy/newsletters, accessed April 2002.

53. Aryeh Neier, "Warring against Modernity," *Washington Post*, October 9, 2001.

54. See Fouad Ajami's reflections on Mohamed Atta, the Egyptian who may have been at the controls of the jet that crashed into the North Tower of the World Trade Center. "Nowhere Man," *New York Times Magazine*, October 7, 2001, 19–20. For a similar perspective regarding a world getting more out of reach of "simple people" who have "only religion," see the interview with V. S. Naipaul, interview in *New York Times Magazine*, October 28, 2001, 19.

55. Naill Ferguson, "2001," *New York Times Magazine*, October 28, 2001, 19.

56. Avishai Margalit and Ian Buruma, "Occidentalism," *New York Review of Books*, January 17, 2002, 4–7.

57. Judy Mann, "Terrorism and the Cult of Manly Men," *Washington Post*, December 19, 2001; Maureen Dowd, "Cleopatra and Osama," *New York Times*, November 18, 2001.

58. Robin Morgan, *The Demon Lover: On the Sexuality of Terrorism* (New York: Norton, 1989).

59. Jim Hoagland, "We're Still Chasing a Criminal," *Washington Post*, November 2, 2001.

60. See Franklin Foer, "Fevered Pitch," *New Republic*, November 12, 2001, 22–24.

61. Robert Worth, "The Deep Intellectual Roots of Islamic Terror," *New York Times*, October 3, 2001.

62. An important background element in the something-to-do-with-Islam frame is Samuel Huntington's widely read 1993 essay on the impending "clash of civilizations," in which the author argues that future wars will not be fought between nations, but between competing cultures, notably between Islam and the West. See "The Clash of Civilizations?" *Foreign Affairs* 72, no. 2 (Summer 1993): 22–28.

63. Mark Lilla, "America at War: Voices in a Nation on Edge; Roles of Religion," *New York Times*, October 9, 2001.

64. The "promise of paradise" attending de facto acts of suicide done as righteous deeds in defense of Islam can be considered another theological motif. See Joseph Lelyveld, "All Suicide Bombers Are Not Alike," *New York Times Magazine*. October 28, 2001, 49–53, 62, 79.

65. Similar perspectives can be found in the *Washington Post*, Outlook sec., October 21, 2001; Salman Rushdie, "Yes, This Is about Islam," *New York Times*, November 2, 2001; and Amir Taheri, "Islam Can't Escape Blame for September 11," *Wall Street Journal*, October 24, 2001.

66. Andrew Sullivan, "This *Is* a Religious War," *New York Times Magazine*, October 7, 2001, 44–52.

67. In Sullivan, "This *Is* a Religious War," 49. For similar views regarding the fusion of the religious and political in Islam, see Robert Malley, "Faith and Terror," *Washington Post,* October 11, 2001; and William Pfaff, "An Old Story: Muslim-Western Conflict," *Commonweal* 128, no. 19 (Nov. 9, 2001): 8–9.

68. Thomas L. Friedman, "The Real War," *New York Times,* November 27, 2001.

69. Dana Milbank, "Professor Shapes Bush Rhetoric," *Washington Post,* September 26, 2001.

70. Forte's views are treated in Franklin Foer, "Blind Faith," *New Republic,* October 22, 2001.

71. See Jeffrey De Yoe's "Homegrown Extremism," *Christian Century* 118, no. 21 (Oct. 10, 2001): 7, for reports on sermons in conservative Protestant churches in the wake of the September 11 events.

72. Andy and Berit Kjos, "The Four Faces of Islam," American Family Association Online, November 6, 2001, www.afa.net/culture/bk120401.asp, accessed April 2002.

73. Jacque Emily, "On the Topic of Islam," *Angelus* (Dec. 2001): 20–29.

74. Michael Boniface, "Real Islam vs. Imaginary Islam," *Angelus* (Oct. 2001): 3–4; also, Michael Matt, "The Power of Fear," *Remnant* (Oct. 31, 2001): 7, 10–11.

75. Mark Juergensmeyer, *Terror in the Mind of God: The Global Rise of Religious Violence* (Berkeley: Univ. of California Press, 2000), esp. 19–36.

76. Appleby, *Ambivalence of the Sacred,* 103.

77. Roger W. Stump, *Boundaries of Faith: Geographical Perspectives on Religious Fundamentalism* (Lanham, Md.: Rowman and Littlefield, 2000), 137.

78. See also Juergensmeyer's remarks at the October 20 annual meeting of the SSSR and RRA in Columbus, Ohio, quoted in *Christian Century* 118, no. 23 (Nov. 7, 2001): 4.

79. For the same reason it is better to avoid adjectival use of Muslim or Islamic in reference to terrorists, extremists, or fundamentalists and instead use "violent extremists" with the prepositional phrase *within the Islamic tradition.* To do so would help to counter the spread of further negative, stereotypical images of Islam. See Charles A. Kimball, "Examining Islamic Militancy: Roots of Rancor," *Christian Century* 118, no. 22 (Oct. 24–31, 2001): 18–23.

80. Notably Rene Girard, *Violence and the Sacred,* trans. by Patrick Gregory (Baltimore: Johns Hopkins Univ. Press, 1972). On monotheism's penchant for violence—particularly when under threat—see Rodney Stark, *One True God: Historical Consequences of Monotheism* (Princeton, N.J.: Princeton Univ. Press, 2002).

81. Juergensmeyer, *Terror in the Mind of God,* esp. chaps. 10 and 11.

82. Charles S. Liebman, "Extremism as a Religious Norm," *Journal for the Scientific Study of Religion* 22 (1983): 75–86.

Section IV

*Religion in the Public Square:
Challenges to the Free Exercise
of Diverse Religious Practices
in a Democratic Society*

Exceptionalism and the Immigrant Experience

America, an Unfinished Product?

AMIRA SONBOL

The chapters by Vivodh Z. J. Anand, Jan Feldman, and Polycarp Ikuenobe[1] are about immigration, cultural and religious differences, and American liberal and democratic traditions. They raise many important questions about three immigrant communities, namely, the Jewish Chassidim, who migrated mainly from Eastern Europe following World War I; the Gujarati Indian community, whose members began to arrive in America following the 1965 relaxation of immigration laws; and Muslim communities, which are the most recent arrivals and perhaps the most contentious given the long history between Christianity and Islam.

The most important issue dealt with by the three chapters is the tension that exists between American liberalism and democracy. Are the two essentially compatible or do they actually clash when confronted with culturally different communities whose members' loyalties may be more oriented to their group than to the state? How liberal can the system be with groups that resist assimilation into the dominant Anglo-white culture (to use Anand's definition of American elite culture) and whose belief in individualism is guided by their group affiliation? Unlike the dominant culture that considers secularism and separation of church and state to be essential requirements for liberalism and democracy, minority groups often define liberalism and democracy in ways different from those espoused by the dominant culture even though they, at the same time, accept both liberalism and democracy and use them to achieve freedoms that reinforce their resistance to assimilation against the wishes of the dominant culture. In other words, the dominant culture expects and demands that minorities assimilate, and the law is one instrument in achieving that end. Minority communities are differentiating between liberalism and democracy on one side, and the dominant culture on the other. Clearly clashes, physical and otherwise, have resulted and continue to be experienced by non-European immigrant communities such as Indian or Muslim that appear to be so culturally different. Here, tolerance of difference, an essential claim of American exceptionalism, becomes highly strained, putting into question the very basis of liberalism and individualism that allows the individual to worship and live as he or she will, as long as that does not harm the larger community. Ikuenobe's conclusion regarding liberalism and intolerance is significant: "A liberal society must be *intolerant* of and *nonneutral* toward the forms of life that are inconsistent with or threatening to its liberal values of human society and the values necessary for its preservation." That was the experience of workers of the Gujarati Indian community in their battle to preserve their religious festivals against the bigotry of members of the wider community who challenged their right to freedom of religious practices by complaining about the noise produced in these festivals without presenting evidence of their allegations. As Anand concludes, what the Indians experienced were "prejudices of difference that erupt from time to time as ugly demons of stereotypic otherness." Otherness and difference are largely based on clothing, diet, language, and social and family traditions. Race and class are important, but are not as widely acknowledged.

The contrast between tolerance of the Chassidic community and lack of tolerance toward the Indian or Muslim communities illustrates the importance of race. Although the latter communities have faced violence and various forms of intolerance, the Chassidic community has not. Yet like Gujarati Indians, the Chassidim are very group oriented, much more so in fact than the Muslim community. They are also visible in contrast to the invisible Amish, as Feldman has pointed out. The Chassidic community has faced serious clashes with the state because of loyalty to the group and the need for special treatment in public spaces. But one can probably hypothesize that no matter how different the Chassidim may appear to be, different and aloof and unwilling to assimilate, holding on to specific forms of dress, dietary rules, and family values, including a strong patriarchal order, still they fall within the terrain of Caucasianism in America and the privileges that go with it. The emphasis here is a discussion of white as a race metaphor.

This brings us to a discussion of "othering" and difference. Why are certain groups "othered," whereas other groups are not? Exceptionalism is a term popularized by Seymour Martin Lipset[2] to define a discourse that considers the American experience to be unique and different from that of other peoples. According to this discourse, American culture is exceptional because it was founded by immigrants imbued with a heritage of individualism and a work ethic that they brought with them from their native European countries. Escaping from European political and religious oppression, they built a society and political system on positive aspects of Western traditions, on liberalism and natural rights guaranteeing an individual's right to bear arms, freedom of speech and worship, freedom from oppression, and the right to sanctity of life and property. Such principles imbue Americans with a feeling of correctness, righteousness, and superiority to other cultures that may or may not hold to these same beliefs. Obfuscation of similarities is helped through representation, dismissal, and "othering." Whole communities are essentialized into simplistic symbols and clichés that are then compared to "superior" American cultural symbols. Clothing, food, skin color, or forms of worship all become instruments of difference and hence discrimination as Anand, Feldman, and Ikuenobe show in their contributions to this volume.

America's perception of immigrants today is framed against a background of the experiences of earlier masses of European immigrants from northern and southern Europe who came to America between the 1840s and 1920s, and the Africans forced to migrate between the seventeenth and nineteenth centuries. Although the former were able to assimilate into the dominantly English culture, easily if not immediately, helped by similarities in culture and language, Africans were forced to serve in a system that treated them as private property, and after emancipation, they were oppressed as second-class citizens under Jim Crow laws. Even today, notwithstanding a civil war and a civil rights movement, African Americans have yet to fully enjoy the fruits of liberalism, freedom, and democracy promised by American exceptionalism. Race and discrimination continue to be realities in defining relations between groups in the United States, and the idea of America as a "melting pot," another of its claims to exceptionalism, seems to be a receding dream even as, or perhaps because, there is a growing racial intermixing between younger generations of Americans and the multiracial nature of America's contemporary popular culture continues to emerge.

The African American experience presents a valuable comparison to the communities discussed by Anand and Feldman, namely, the Indian and Sephardic. It is also a valid comparison to Arab and Muslim communities that have become so prominent in the news these days, the latter being the focus of Ikuenobe's stimulating discussion of liberalism. In all, differences of culture, religion, symbols, and skin color play important roles in the problems faced by these communities in their efforts to live as equal citizens in the United States. It is true that the system of slavery has been repudiated, and even theories of white racial superiority are no longer accepted except by a few on the fringe. But the remnants of belief in differences accentuated by cultural and religious divisions have meant the continuation of racial and religious prejudice and of "othering," which became an umbrella covering new immigrants from other than Europe. With the increased volume of immigration caused by the easing of immigration laws, the growth of illegal immigration, and the flight of refugees from political and religious repression globally, prejudice against immigrant communities has become more active and vocal. Immigration has been a driving force during the last decades, turning America toward greater ethnic and cultural diversity. These new immigrants come from Asia, Central and South America, and Africa. A good example is that of the Gujarati Indian immigrants who came to the United States following the 1965 Immigration Act of America, the subject of Anand's article. Focusing on the town of Edison in Middlesex County, New Jersey, Anand illustrates the latent prejudices of white people involving race, religion, and language, "Prejudices of difference that erupt from time to time as ugly demons of stereotypic otherness," as Anand puts it.

The nature of these new immigrants is different from that of the earlier European, African, and even earlier Chinese or Japanese labor immigrants. These new immigrants came in substantial numbers and tended to set up communities in particular spots, such as Gujarati Indians in northern New Jersey or Arabs in Dearborn, Michigan. These groups are not interested in mimicking their Anglo predecessors, but rather hold on to ethnic peculiarities such as dress, food, language, and religion. Sephardic Jews, unlike other Jews who assimilated easily into the white Anglo culture, kept their distance through choice of dress, language, marital and gender traditions, and even in their business dealings, preferably within their own communities, are very much like the European Amish communities. Here we can point to one of the most important issues pertaining to immigration, namely assimilation.

THE QUESTION OF ASSIMILATION

Pointing to the Chassidic experience, Feldman explains the dilemma regarding assimilation in very articulate terms:

> The danger . . . is that if we legitimize the "politics of difference" or confer explicit rights upon groups, we may also create a politics of grievance and a fragmented citizenry. The danger of the latter is that if we minimize differences, we risk making assimilation to a single, universal standard of citizenship the price that minority cultures or religions must pay in order to enjoy the benefits that other American citizens take for granted. Exclusion from these benefits will not be easier to swallow simply because it is justified in terms of the facial neutrality of the law or policy.

All three chapters consider the difficulties in addressing this question, particularly for liberals, who see America as a multicultural society, yet at the same time see cultural uniformity as a necessary ingredient for the pursuit of equality and the "American way." This is particularly problematic for religious groups that identify their culture and religion synonymously and that see both in terms of First Amendment rights. Feldman asks if "the associations of civil society buttress the democratic state, or do they compete with the state for moral authority over their members?" She finds an answer in liberal theory, which she considers to be recognizing subnational loyalties, "but would prefer to see them in a cooperative light, as building blocks of democracy rather than as competitors creating a centrifugal pull against the state." Ikuenobe throws in a twist pertaining to the America experience:

> The Constitution and laws are inconsistent with diversity of religions and cultures, in that they primarily do not recognize cultural and religious groups as entities with valid-right claims. Liberal individualism seeks a Constitutional or normative framework for social unity, which provides the basis for assimilating and integrating individuals as citizens of a state. This principle ensures equal liberty and justice for all, avoids discrimination, and limits state's power against individuals. This view assumes that there are no significant cultural differences that could trump the normative basis for assimilation.

The presupposition that assimilation into the dominant culture is the ultimate goal of American citizenry, which Ikuenobe considers as integral to the American Constitution and laws, is based on America's historical experience during its formative period and the system's focus on individual rights. Agreeing with Will Kymlicka,[3] Ikuenobe opines that this "has resulted in, or has been, a cover for injustices to minority cultures . . . because it does not adequately appreciate that the deeper issues raised by freedom of religious practices are about freedom of cultural expression and identity." The American experience is based on resolving a conflict between two religious traditions that stemmed originally from common cultural roots. "This is illuminating because it is *easier* for people to be tolerant of each other's religious differences, such as, Catholics and Protestants, in a nation-state with a homogenous culture, because the religions emerged from one culture. Tolerance is more difficult if religious differences derive from substantially different cultures, ethnicity, or nationalities." It is therefore hard for Christians to accept the Muslim idea of polygamy and insist that Muslims follow Christian dictates of monogamy, even though both are sanctified by religious beliefs and the Constitution provides for freedom of religion.

The contradictions between individual rights, particularly freedom of religion and the demand for the cultural assimilation of immigrant communities called for by the same Constitution, established by a nation-state with the normal demands for political allegiance, as Feldman shows, may work theoretically but is hard to achieve practically when faced with exclusionary sects that prefer their own schools, language, and religious practices. Here it is relevant to cite the issue of state power and the connection between the power of a dominant culture and the power of a state structure that the dominant culture brought into being. The more dominant a particular culture and the more entrenched it is in the power structure of the state, the greater the need of the immigrant community to assimilate. Thus, in the American experience, early immigrants found that they had to assimilate because they were weaker and smaller in number, often one at a time, as in the case of Lebanese immigrants who came earlier in the century. These immigrants tried to mimic the "thinking and behavior of the Anglo," as Anand puts it. Recent immigration, in contrast, has brought new waves of culturally different people who have tended to live in particular communities. The more closely they lived together, the more they kept their traditions, language, food, and dress. In Dearborn you can hear both Arabic and English spoken in the street. The food, shop signs, and food reflect their Middle Eastern origin. The same is true in the communities of the Gujarati Indians. It is important to recognize that these groups are latecomers; American society has become more hardened, more entrenched, more complete. It becomes harder for the new groups to assimilate, particularly because they migrated as families and groups and settled in particular places where their cultural community established itself and became a magnet for others of the same culture. Furthermore, these newcomers are different from earlier immigrants from the same countries who left their homes when their countries were under colonial rule. These later groups of immigrants had experienced independence, national pride, and a stronger affiliation with the homeland. Having migrated after their homelands had achieved independence from European imperialist powers, these new immigrants do not stand in awe of Western culture and power. Therefore, they do not espouse a discourse of exceptionalism when viewing America, notwithstanding their thrill of being in America and their strong loyalties to America. But they also bring with them pride in their own cultures, a pride reinforced by the cohesiveness of the group. The revolution in communication and media also meant that they were more in contact with their homeland and families than earlier generations of immigrants. Therefore there was greater cultural affinity with the countries they left behind even as their own cultures were being transformed by world events, cultural diffusion, modernization, and globalization.

The Chassidim are a good example illustrating the complexities of assimilation and historical context. The first Chassidic migration took place following the first world war and was largely caused by the Holocaust of Eastern European Jews. They arrived on American shores, bringing with them a strong affiliation to their religious and cultural heritage in Eastern Europe. To them the Christian-dominant culture of post–World War II America was quite alien. This was in clear contrast to the majority of American Jews who had arrived on American shores in several waves from the end of the nineteenth and beginning of the twentieth centuries in search of political freedom and fleeing racial discrimination that denied them full rights of citizenship. The infamous Dreyfus Affair was but one example illustrating the anti-Semitism of Western Europe that Jewish immigrants hoped to escape. Even though they were religiously different from the dominant Christian culture of the time, Jewish immigrants who came from Western Europe were quite familiar with Western culture and traditions, and assimilation was therefore easier for them, particularly because America represented the political system in which they hoped to find full citizenship while being able to practice freedom of religion. They therefore worked for "full access to American political, social, and economic life." Unlike the Chassidim later on, they found American public and private schools to be an important vehicle toward Americanization. As Feldman points out, "The obstacles to success were perceived by many of these Jews to be discriminatory laws and disabilities placed upon them. Not surprisingly, their political activity was aimed at getting the courts to strictly uphold the establishment clause on the belief that they had more to fear from the establishment of Christianity than from a secular public sphere." In other words, Jewish Americans worked for a secular America in which there would be no discrimination based on religion, and they were quite successful in their legal battle that ensured freedom of religion and establishment of a religion-free public space. Religious minorities of all types owe gratitude to the Jewish community for having fought this battle, the achievements of which are today being fought by the Christian Right and other conservative elements who find that this clashes with their wish for cultural exclusivism and the association of civil rights with secular culture.

Although the legal struggles of early Jewish immigrants changed the cultural discourse from what was once seen as a dominant Christian culture to a Judeo-Christian appellation—itself an indication of the power of the Jewish community's influence on the American political, economic, and legal spectrum—the Chassidim rejected the very Judeo-Christian formula that they were required to assimilate into. The differences between the two immigrant groups are based not only on when and why they immigrated but also on the historical conditions they left behind and the ones they immigrated to. Feldman's conclusions explain this:

The Chassidim, on the other hand, cut their political teeth in Russia, fighting for survival under the Tsars, Hitler, and Stalin. When they arrived in the United States, it was with the intention of regrouping and recreating their semiautonomous, traditional enclaves. Not surprisingly, their political focus has been on the First Amendment rights of association and free exercise of religion. In fact, they believe that a society devoid of religion is devoid of morality and therefore truly threatening to its citizens. They are not bothered by the Christian undertone of American culture. They do not participate in it, avoiding television, the malls, and public schools . . . [and] hold a different underlying conception of political identity. In their view, territory is replaced by Diaspora, or the sense that their primary geographic orientation is somewhere other than where they currently reside. Chassidim understand their territorial residence to be temporary. They feel themselves to be in exile (golus), both physically and spiritually. Home, to them, means the rebuilt Jerusalem in the era following the arrival of the Messiah (Moshiach).

In other words, the Chassidim do not see themselves as part of the fabric of America; they are in America because the utopia that their traditions prophesied has yet to come about. This is why the Chassidim do not support the state of Israel as it stands, not because they do not want to build a home for the Jews around Jerusalem, but because this rebuilt Jerusalem can only happen after the arrival of the Messiah. Assimilation into any culture other than the Chassidic is vocally refused even if the dominant culture is partly Judeo; after all it is a different "Judeo" than the Chassidim believe in.

The Indian and Muslim communities present similar problems, as they are more oriented toward family, clan, or group than they are toward individualism, at least in the sense of individual rights as holding precedence over group goals. Among the three communities, the Muslim community presents perhaps the least cohesive fundamentally because Muslims in America come from different ethnic and national backgrounds, differing in race, color, language, and cultural traditions. Today, even with increased immigration and a community numbering anywhere from six to ten million—exact estimates are not known—Muslims in America have yet to form a cohesive community, but are rather a basket of diversity.

CLASS AND GENDER

Class plays an important role in defining various immigrant communities into different groups. Many are professionals, others are nonprofessional, many are white- or blue-color workers, and still others come from the poorest sectors of their societies. This is best exemplified by the American Latin community, which ranges from Cabinet members to CEOs of major corporations to industrialists to members of the various professions, and yet this community maintains a significant percentage of illegal agricultural workers and labor that emigrate clandestinely from Mexico and other Latin American countries.

What we have seen in immigrant communities is interesting: the more educated and professional the immigrants, the more there is a tendency toward integration, particularly in the second generation. Furthermore, the more antagonistic the dominant culture is to the particular immigrant group, the more this group tends to remain unwilling to integrate or the more the dominant culture is suspicious of the efforts to integrate. In this respect, the Muslim and Arab communities contrast sharply with the Indian community. Politically and culturally, the Arab community, Christian and Muslims alike, have kept more to their culture, food, names, and so on than other communities, even though early Arab Christian immigrants (e.g., the Syrian and Lebanese) were able to integrate and enter the political scene and gain seats in the legislatures and political offices. However, when it is a case of Arab Muslim or Pakistani or Indian Muslim, it is that much harder; Arab because of the political dominance played by the Israeli lobby in American politics and public life, and Pakistani because of their purist form of Islam that keeps the community pretty tight. Pakistani traditions, like Indian traditions, continue to emphasize allegiance to family and clan, discouraging marriage with outsiders and emphasizing economic interdependence between the members of the community. Still, Indians are much more acceptable to the wider community and the dominant white culture because they are anti-Islam and have managed to capitalize on this animosity in being part of the "us" versus "them" struggle; hence their expertise is more acceptable and, at least the men among them, are able to become better accepted as experts in various professions from computers in which they excel to media and financial expertise.

In other words, assimilation is a question that goes beyond religion; it is also a question of class, and as African immigrants found out centuries before, class is not a question of money alone but is also concerned with ethnicity and skin color. Two mass demonstrations that took place in Washington, D.C., during April 2002 illustrate this clearly. The first rally involved supporters of Israel who were greeted by a White House representative with a message from the president of the United States; members of Congress showed up in support of Israel, and the media put in hours of media coverage. The other, much larger demonstration in support of various causes such as the Palestinians, Columbians, anti–World Bank, and globalization was shunned by all of political Washington and by the media. Except C-Span, there was hardly a minute of coverage, even on local Washington, D.C., television channels. There is obviously something wrong with this picture, when the people's representatives and a media that claims fair coverage of the news confine the democratic discourse to their own self-interest. Where are the freedoms, the liberal ideals, and democracy in this picture? What we are seeing is the actual struggle that has characterized the rest of the globe finally coming home to the United States. The two demonstrations illustrate a hegemonic elite in control of world power on the one side, and people of color who have migrated voluntarily in search of the American dream on the other. With them stand intellectuals who are still hoping to see the realization of the American democratic, liberal, and "free-hand" capitalist dream, as well as labor activists fighting the impact of globalization on local labor. To these groups America does not appear to be a finished product; rather they see it as a melting pot still ready for new ingredients. To use Ikuenobe's wonderful example of the heat stirring the pot, these groups do not see Anglo-white or Judeo-Christian culture as providing that heat, but rather look at the ideals of democracy and liberalism as providing the heat. In doing so they make a clear distinction between the dominant culture and the ideals underlining American exceptionalism, an exceptionalism that they buy into and want to make into a reality. It is no wonder that the intellectuals of the American Right see themselves on the cusp of a crisis of civilization, and they fear for the passing of the Anglo-American culture. Samuel Huntington's *The Clash of Civilizations and the Remaking of World Order* [4] and Pat Buchanan's *The Death of the West* [5] are but examples of these unwarranted fears among politicians of the Right who can see no good coming of American cultural diversity, even though they believe strongly in American democracy and liberalism.

As for gender, exceptionalism dismisses the role of women, the power of women, and the agency of women in other than Western societies. Liberals often point out that women are the symbols of their societies, that oppressed women come from oppressed societies, and that liberated women are indicators of the freedoms enjoyed by their peoples. The symbols of oppression and freedoms provide the structures around which definitions of oppression and freedoms are embroidered. The best examples here are the constant references by the Western media, feminists, and liberals to the veiled Muslim women, the female genital mutilation among Africans, or the wife-burnings among Indians. In contrast, the life of women in the West and Westernized societies are symbolized by sexual freedom, the working woman, jeans and other "liberating" forms of clothing, and so on. Because the symbols differ between the Western and non-Western, expectations differ from one community to the other. A veiled Muslim woman is hence not expected to be as good a worker or student as her unveiled counterpart, a fact that is dismissed quickly in workplaces and classrooms if and when the veiled woman is given the chance to compete with her unveiled sister. The feminist liberal discourse is so contradictory here as to warrant censure. Even though feminists have considered models of clothing and beauty as hegemonic instruments meant to confine women's freedoms from sexist paradigms, it is these very models that they use to deny equality to women who do not accept the models of beauty and clothing that Western feminists consider to be essential to their struggle against sexist discourses. So feminists who fought against the confinement of the bra and the right to choose whatever fashion they fancy rather than follow the dictates of conservative society deny that same right of choice to women who choose to wear a veil or to wear the Indian sari as their right to free choice. Nudity or seminudity becomes acceptable and a norm, whereas women who find being covered more liberating are looked at as being antiAmerican. Here culture conflicts directly with ideology even though the two are confused in the minds of feminists and liberals. Even more serious is that symbols became a gauge for legal rights, job opportunity, and chances at political participation. The actions of the various enforcement powers of the state under the leadership of Ashcroft following the September 11, 2001, terrorist acts in New York and Washington, although justified in their duty to provide protection to the United States from further terrorism, exemplify the intolerance of conservative America and the acceptance of this intolerance by liberals already antagonized by symbols of difference. It is no secret that a veil or a beard were symbols used by the FBI and other agencies to single out Muslims for search of self, computers, homes, personal and business records, just as they were seen as "just cause" for imprisonment without legal process. One wonders if this could have been possible if it had been other than the Muslim community that was suspected of the terrorist activity; after all, other communities have been responsible for terrorist acts in the United States, and the Oklahoma bombing by Timothy McVeigh brought very little similar retaliation among white militants like himself.

Sexual freedom seems to have predominated Western feminist claims to equality. This does not mean that most Americans approve of sexual freedoms, but it is the discourse espoused by liberals and is, perhaps consequently, central to the political discourse of the Christian Right. The Gujarati, Chassidim, and Muslim communities all refuse to accept sexual freedom as part of the cultural makeup of the America they want to be part of. The Latin American community is no different in this, and given the sexual freedoms that young Latinos have been exposed to in American public schools, the community continues to hold closely to its Catholicism even if it means marrying their children very young, even while still in school due to juvenile pregnancy. Attitudes toward gender freedoms put immigrant communities at odds with the political system in America; their political inclinations as minorities push them toward the Democratic Party, but their social conservatism makes them natural allies to the Republicans. So far, political needs have meant the success of the Democratic Party in garnering the minority vote. This assumption may be questioned in the future, particularly in regard to the immigrant Muslim community, which voted overwhelmingly Republican in the last elections thereby helping George W. Bush win the elections (a purported 59,000 Muslim voters, normally Democratic, went Republican at the urging of their mosques and leaders in Florida).

Anand's discussion of the goddess Amba and the people's reaction to the Navratri's adoration of her explains the problematic of American liberalism and gender. Even though liberals call for equal participation of women in the political process, there is no concept of matriarchy in the minds of these liberals or in the political system itself. Rather, both are essentially patriarchal. The idea that a community worships a woman God or that a community may be matriarchal or offering a combination of the patriarchal and matriarchal in a complex form does not seem to have significance to liberals or feminists who look at gender relations through dominant symbols familiar to Western feminism. As Anand points out, "the idea that women could actually be agents and political activists within their communities, is simply disregarded" if the community concerned does not practice the sexual freedom supported by American liberals. Indians may not practice sexual freedom, but the "Navratri's affirmation of community and the power of women is central to the adoration of Amba." In the epic of Amba, the goddess saves the world after male gods lost it in battle. The epic shows Navratri as a "fierce, independent, and not vanquished" woman who "reminds its celebrants of the duality of woman—gentle, bending, and compassionate on one hand, and fierce, unrelenting, and driven on the other."

Although the goddess Amba is probably a better representative of the kind of women that feminists hope for, her symbolism is dismissed because of cultural differences. In a melting pot, new cultures are supposed to melt into the original mix and not create new symbols even if these new symbols are more powerful or more representative of the very ideologies underlining the original mix. That is the function of exceptionalism, which in its patriarchal Western setting dismisses the role of women, the power of women, and the agency of women in other than Western societies. The example of Amba should give us "pause to question paradigms that have been at the very heart of our understanding of gender through prisms of patriarchy. We forget that patriarchy is really based on Christian and particularly Greek Orthodox images of relations between male patriarch and his flock, in the form of a priest, of a father, or of a husband. That image is certainly questionable for other areas of the world, if it is even acceptable for Greek society whose women are very strong matriarchs and who have been celebrated in powerful myths of women goddesses." Anand concludes, "I think that the image of Amba throws a curve to the prisms through which we have seen gender and its connection to culture and calls for different ways of approaching social relations."

Feldman makes similar comments about American liberal feminists and their dismissal of gender equality among Jews. Critiquing in particular Susan Okin's finding that "most traditional cultures oppress women,"[6] which leads Okin to conclude that, given the treatment of women, she—meaning Okin—"would not regret the extinction of these groups," Feldman points to the ignorance of feminists like Okin who cannot see beyond their own paradigms and their dismissal of "deeply imbedded, gender-based roles" such as that among the Chassidim. "Although liberal feminists may be unmoved by the Chassidic woman's power to influence as well as transmit the norms of her community, radical feminists would find much to sympathize with in the ability of Chassidic women to create a distinctive women's world of meaning from which they derive palpable and irrefutable joy."

One wonders at American liberal feminism's refusal to see beyond the paradigm of sexual liberation to the lessons to be learned about gender-equality among immigrant communities. These communities, such as the Chassidim or Muslims, may have strong religious prohibitions against gender mixing, but why this should mean a lesser role for women or their inferiority is not clear. Certainly the matriarch is the uncontested head in Muslim families: sons, daughters, and grandchildren all bow to her wisdom and honor her. She is the symbol of unity, and many Muslims will tell you that the family breaks up when the mother dies, but remains together if the father or grandfather dies as long as the matriarch still lives. The role of mother, worker, or professional is very much part of the life of women in immigrant communities; there is a lot that American feminism and immigrant communities can learn from each other in a mutually respecting relationship. The dominant culture, however, does not allow for cultural diffusion except from the dominant to the immigrant and, to ensure this, establishes and calls for laws that discriminate against specific groups because of the "fear of cultural contamination [and] the need to keep the communities religiously and racially pure."

NOTES

1. Vivodh Z. J. Anand, "Edison's Navratri: A Report on Communal Religious Conflict"; Jan Feldman, "Liberalism, Chassidim, and the Challenge of Multicultural Accommodation"; Polycarp Ikuenobe, "Diverse Religious Practices and the Limits of Liberal Tolerance."

2. Seymour Martin Lipset, *American Exceptionalism: A Double-Edged Sword* (New York: Norton, 1997), and "American Exceptionalism Reaffirmed," in *Is America Different? A New Look at American Exceptionalism* (London: Oxford Univ. Press, 1991).

3. Will Kymlicka, *Multicultural Citizenship: A Liberal Theory of Minority Rights* (Oxford, U.K.: Clarendon, 1995), 195.

4. Samuel Huntington, *The Clash of Civilizations and the Remaking of World Order* (New York: Touchstone, 1998).

5. Pat Buchanan, *The Death of the West: How Dying Populations and Immigrant Invasions Imperil Our Country and Civilization* (New York: Thomas Dunne, 2001).

6. Susan Moller Okin, "Is Multiculturalism Bad for Women?" *Boston Review* 22, no. 5 (Oct.–Nov. 1997).

Goddess Amba Unwelcome in Edison, New Jersey

Report of a Town's Xenophobic Conflation of Race and Religion

Vivodh Z. J. Anand

Friday and Saturday nights during four consecutive weekends in October the Gujarati Indian community, ten thousand strong, converges on the floodplain at the mouth of the Raritan River. In massive communal festivity, devotees in colorful holiday attire dance barefoot throughout the night into the early hours of the morning as they celebrate the epic victory of good over evil. With graceful swirls and twirls, thousands circumambulate the image of the great female deity Amba who, holding in her eight arms the sacred weapons of successful combat against the evil demon Mahishasuara, rides triumphant astride a tiger.

This is the famous Navratri festival of Edison, New Jersey, and the raison d'être for its organizers, the Indo-American Cultural Society. Between 1994 and 1998 the metaphor of epic battle against the demonic became concrete reality for those who regularly celebrate Navratri. The extended Indian immigrant community, and its worldwide diasporas, closely watched the combat as it played out in a modern-day court action known in the federal docket as *Indo-American Cultural Society, Inc. v. Township of Edison, New Jersey, et al.*, Civil Action No. 95–4690 (JCL).

Edison's Navratri and its court battle is now a major mile marker in the history of South Asian immigration. The landmark federal case fought by the Gujarati community to protect First Amendment rights is a major immigration victory story.

The 1965 Immigration Act of America has brought large numbers of Indian expatriates who have sunk their roots in metropolises all over the United States. In Edison and its environs of Middlesex County, New Jersey, many Gujaratis have established themselves in often deteriorating longtime working-class neighborhoods. The immigrant influx has stimulated the white psyche's latent prejudices of race, religion, and language—prejudices of difference that erupt from time to time as ugly demons of stereotypic otherness. Storms of conflict in immigrant communities regularly surface in Middlesex County as they do elsewhere in New Jersey, the nation, and, it must also be said, in Europe.

Navratri, translated as "the festival of nine nights" is celebrated throughout India in the fall or the harvest season. India's diversity, pluralism, and differences interpret the story of Navratri as differently as its myriad cultures, and these differing interpretations often confuse those who expect monolithic single-expression traditions. Calendar dates and the names of principal protagonists, including the name of the festival itself, varies from locale to locale as is common for most Hindu festivals. The prevailing story is as follows:

Brahma of the triune Brahma, Vishnu, and Shiva granted Mahishasura the "buffalo demon," or simply Mahisa (buffalo), a boon that protected him from any man in the world. Empowered by this gift, Mahishasura set out to conquer heaven and the world, to bring about the defeat of Indra king of deities. At the pleading of Indra, the trinity created Durga the female through an amalgamation of its own triune shakti or divine power. Endowed with the trinity's shakti, Durga was a formidable opponent and defeated Mahisa after nine vicious night battles, finally beheading him on the tenth. Simply translated, Navratri symbolizes the nine nights of battle, while the tenth day, "vijayadashami"—literally means the victorious tenth day of conquest.

This great epic is recounted and celebrated slightly differently in various regions, often taking on different forms and names. In West Bengal, Navratri and vijayadashami are respectively celebrated as Durga Puja and Dasara. In South India, the festival includes other female deities and dedicates three days of the festival to Lakshmi, the female archetype of wealth and fortune, and another three to Saraswathi, archetype of learning, music, and knowledge. In northern India, it takes the form of the great epic Ramyana where Rama, an incarnation of Vishnu, is victorious over the evil king Ravana.

Regional variations of the epic saga also bring with them changes in the names and physical forms of the triumphant female deity. In Gujarat, the western-most province of India just north of Bombay and home to the folk who celebrate Edison's Navratri, she is Amba. Amba, also known as Mata, is adored for her victory over Mahisa the evil, and the celebration centers around her. The festival starts with an oil lamp arti followed by devotional songs and colorful dances of the Garba and Raas Dandia. Garba, traditionally a women's dance, revolves around earthen lamps, devotional songs, and a syncopated clapping of hands. Dandia, the dance that follows the Garba, is a group dance for both men and women who rhythmically click each other's short handheld sticks as they whirl clockwise in large groups around the deity. Traditionally, devotees fast during the nine days of the festival, taking only sweets and nonalcoholic drinks for nourishment.

Navratri's affirmation of community and the power of women is central to the adoration of Amba. In contrast to cultural norms of patriarchy, Navratri portrays women as fierce, independent, and not vanquished. In this epic, the female shakti save a world lost in battle by mighty male deities. Navratri reminds its celebrants of the duality of woman—gentle, bending, and compassionate on one hand, and fierce, unrelenting, and driven on the other.

Community, collective effort, extended family, village, and neighborhood are celebrated in nightlong music and traditional dance. The triune deity's power integrated in a single shakti defeats evil and marks the unity and strength of family and community through power in the female. Navratri is an ethnic celebration not seen before 1965. Pre-1965 immigrants never "bought" into the assimilative "melting pot" of white dominance. Instead Asian immigrants suffered and struggled for five hundred years, seething in silence from enthrallment sanctioned by the church and colonial commission.

In post–1965 Immigration Act America, South Asian immigrants of northern New Jersey brought with them typical immigrant patterns of neighborhood and community. Ethnic accoutrements of language, religion, food, and dress have emerged. Long gone is the silent pre-1965 individual immigrant struggle to gain acceptance through mimic of white Anglo behavior and culture.

The droves of post-1965 immigrants, whose movement to the United States is stimulated by racist and economically motivated immigration policies, are professionals, nonprofessional workers, and businesspeople who come to fill the need for the "dangerous, difficult, and dirty," the three Ds of international migration patterns: work that the majority white population finds unpalatable. These present-day immigrant fixtures of the bottom-line oriented economy have radically changed monochromatic single culture and religion dominated landscapes. They celebrate their unique ethnicity unabashedly and openly.

Immigrants and their lawyers are a new face of pluralism and an expression of personal cultures and styles. When the power of the law is coupled with a media eager to report the complaints and tensions of individuals and groups who demand equality and rights, it makes for a constant and vexing background noise. This strategy is well known and has been refined for demonstration in the "public square" by twentieth-century change agents such as Mr. Gandhi, a Gujarati himself.

The massive influx of immigrants has brought neighborhoods, ethnic shopping districts, public celebrations, and a visibility dictated by critical mass. The downside of critical mass and visibility is the emergence of naked hatred of visible "Otherness." Unfettered conflict surfaces as "Otherness" drives wedges between new communities and the older neighborhoods. In this atmosphere, it is not surprising that South Asian immigrant communities experience prejudices etched into the European psyche since its "Renaissance," that is, the period of colonial expansion. In New Jersey the story of the vicious Jersey City gang that called itself the Dot Busters is a well-remembered response to Indian immigrant "critical mass." The Dot Busters conflated race and religion as they attacked a Parsi Indian man, Navroze Mody. In bitter hate they shouted "Hindu, Hindu, Hindu" as they bludgeoned him to death.[1] A similar gang that called itself "The Lost Boys" terrorized the Indian community of Edison. My good friend Pradip (Peter) Kothari, president of the Indo-American Cultural Society, the group that organizes Edison's Navratri celebration, has experienced numerous drive-by shootings that smashed the windows of his travel agency as recently as 1997. During the summer of 1998, in unabashed and naked racist venom, a group of Euro-Americans drove through the Oak Tree Road shopping district spitting, hurling racist epithets, and shooting BB pellets at Indo-American shoppers in front of the well-known Chowpatty Restaurant owned by Chandrakant Patel, cofounder of the Indo-American Cultural Society.

It is in this hostile atmosphere that Edison's populous ethnic Gujarati community celebrates Navratri each fall. This the largest Navratri held outside of India, originating in 1990 with humble beginnings on a local school property by a small group of individuals headed by Pradip (Peter) Kothari and Chandrakant Patel in the spirit of the Divikaruni poem. The Indo-American Cultural Society (IACS), as this small group called itself, found that their early efforts were immensely popular. When 12,000 people attended the 1991 festival revue, it was moved to Expo Hall, a large indoor facility in Raritan Center, Edison. The festival gained enormous popularity, so when thousands more met each Navratri night, the IACS was forced to seek a larger facility.

To accommodate the large numbers of celebrants, the 1992 festival was moved to a giant tent on an undeveloped portion of Raritan Center's industrial park. The popularity of the 1992 celebration was used by local politicos, for reasons of personal gain, to fan latent anti-immigrant sentiment and xenophobia. To cater to the xenophobia, the township council passed a public entertainment ordinance that sought to curb the festival. The ordinance was crafted with criteria specifically aimed against the festival and included a string of new rules, some of which could be "waived by Council resolution for bona fide nonprofit service organizations."[2]

In 1993 and 1994 the IACS was told that it had to comply with the ordinance in order to hold the festival. The IACS dutifully made these applications in accordance with the unfair rules. The applications themselves were approved only after bureaucratic nitpicking and stonewalling. In 1995 when the IACS again applied for its permit, a number of additional restrictions were placed on how the festival was to be conducted.

Members of the township council claimed that this was because of noise complaints reported to the police by neighbors. The IACS immediately requested police reports of the complaints and asked to meet informally with any and all concerned individuals including the complainants—the reports never materialized.

A meeting was held on June 19, 1995, where about fifteen Euro-American residents of Edison showed up to voice their complaints about the festival. This meeting became an open attack on the IACS by non-Indian residents. Because it recounts the happening and sentiments of that evening, the letter that the IACS sent two days later to the three councilmen who arranged this meeting follows in its entirety.

June 21, 1995
Hon. Robert Julius Engel
Hon. James F. Kennedy
Hon. David Papi
Township Council of Edison
100 Municipal Boulevard
Edison, N.J. 08817
Gentlemen:
Thank you for arranging a meeting with residents of Bonhamtown and Clara Barton who are concerned about sound levels during our annual Navratri festival. We were happy to dispel some misconceptions that existed about the requirements for the festival, and glad to formally hear of concern about the sound level.

We had assumed sound not to be problematic in view of natural barriers created by the extensive highway infrastructure between the festival and its nearest residential neighbors. The first of these highways is Woodbridge Avenue that looms at least 100 feet above the festival grounds. Surprising was the vehement outpouring by residents of Clara Barton who live as far as two miles away to the north of Woodbridge Avenue, the Turnpike and Route 287—some of these individuals wore hearing aids.

As you know, we will be happy to submit to sound monitoring with accurate devices widely used to measure ambient noise created by surface and air traffic and other noise pollutants. Several residents did bring up the fact that truck traffic noise from the Turnpike and the adjacent New York Times complex contiguous to Bonhamtown is an unresolved issue along with aircraft noise associated with surrounding airports. We certainly hope that our music does not reach the decibel levels generated by these. We suspect that you must regularly measure these for compliance with town ordinance.

Very perturbing were the anti-festival sentiments that Mr. Engel holds, and that he injected into the conversation. Dispute resolution is dependent on mediator impartiality—a function we understood that you were to provide at the meeting. Mr. Engel several times brought up the fact that he had voted against the festival each time it came to the Council floor. We did not take issue publicly at the time, but would like to know why Mr. Engel is against the festival. Shocking was Mr. Engel's insinuation that we negatively effect the neighborhood and the "homes that people have worked so hard for."

Lastly we were subjected to fifteen people including the Council President each taking turns to say when the festival should close for the night. We wonder if there is any awareness in Edison of freedoms of assembly and religion. We are immigrants to a democracy that provided the model for the constitution India adopted less than fifty years ago. We wonder how the folk who inspired our struggle against colonialism can arbitrarily dismiss our rights. Ridiculous is the assertion by some that the festival be held at a different time of year. Navratri's timing is dictated by our religious calendar in much the same way as the Jewish and other religious calendars make for changeable holidays during the Christian calendar year. It would be insulting to Christians to have people suggest that Christmas be celebrated more conveniently in July.

As we pointed out time and again, we will be happy to comply with appropriate and measurable sound level requirements. We are glad to be finally appraised of something that has existed for the three years for the few weekend nights we celebrate every fall. We consider it strange that such venom about our celebration is only expressed now when we are applying for a permit and never during any of the festivities for the past three years. This year, as you know, we have curtailed celebrating our festival on Sunday nights.

We look forward to your early reply so that we can appraise our two thousand festival goers and voters in Edison of the true sentiments of their neighbors and elected leaders.
Sincerely,
Vivodh Z. J. Anand, Ph.D.
Director of Communications
cc. Pradip (Peter) Kothari
Jerald Baranoff, Esq.
Township Fax: 908 248–3738 on 6/21/95
Original mailed

Following this disastrous meeting, the township council met on July 8 and passed a new ordinance specifically aimed at the IACS. About 250 Gujarati residents of Edison attended this meeting. TV Asia broadcast the meeting via satellite around the world, and other ethnic media, both radio and print, covered the story as well. Below is the letter the IACS wrote the president of the township council a week later.

July 14, 1995
Hon. Raymond Koperwhats, President
Township Council of Edison
100 Municipal Boulevard
Edison, N.J. 08817
Mr. Koperwhats:
The Indo-American Cultural Society anticipating possible difficulties in obtaining the permit for the 1995 celebration of Navratri was forced to mobilize some two hundred and fifty Edison residents of Indian origin to attend last Wednesday's Council meeting.

Fortunately the council seeing resident support of this very important festival did grant the permit. The reason this letter is coming to you is to register our protest of the way the permit was handled by the Council. First, the permit was finally granted over 90 days after date of application instead of the 30 days required by town ordinance. The delay caused by bureaucratic snafu, perhaps willful, and council indifference to our need for an early start to a large and complex project is typical of the pattern in this and our former applications.

We believe that in this election year matters were made even worse through political stirring of some residents' inability to deal with our cultural, and ethnic difference. We regret that those supporting the Navratri festival were stifled by you during the Council meeting. Mr. Baranoff, our attorney was interrupted and as was Mr. Kothari our president, neither were these two individuals permitted the courtesy of rebuttal.

Some of those opposed spoke long and more than once in their often vituperative opposition to the permit. We heard our most important religious and cultural festival compared among other things to a carnival and to bars that close at 2.00 a.m. Even Edison's permit process under an entertainment rubric is all ready [sic] unpalatable making our religion invisible.

What hurt most was the "Three strikes and you're out" threat that dominated the entire proceedings and remains as an item on the resolution for us to ever wear as a "Scarlet letter" of disgrace for practicing our religion and culture. Our constant reiteration that we always have, and always do insist on meeting all legal, sanitary and safety requirements have been drowned out in a political atmosphere that marginalizes and trivializes us through questioning our integrity and veracity.

Lastly Edison's bureaucratic ineptitude kept us uninformed of any complaints by neighbors. In addition to being burdened with legal expenses and volunteer time and effort to protect our simple rights, we have the added expense of sound monitoring. Because of the shortened interval, we are managing the festival project in a crisis mode.

Sincerely,

Vivodh Z. J. Anand, Ph.D.

Director of Communications

cc. Pradip (Peter) Kothari

Jerald Baranoff, Esq.

Township Clerk for distribution to Council and Administration

The IACS realized that it was unlikely that the festival would be held unless drastic action was taken. The Hackensack, New Jersey, law firm of Loughlin and Latimer was retained as counsel. Unsuccessful in negotiating terms for the celebration with the township of Edison, Steve Latimer and Michaelene Loughlin were forced to file a complaint on September 13, 1995, just weeks before the festival, seeking an injunction against the township's unfair ordinance. Although the injunction to hold the festival was granted, it did have a proviso that, much to the chagrin of the devotees, required the festival to close at 2:00 A.M. each morning.

The festival was held and diligently closed at 2:00 A.M. each day. Each night rigorous sound monitoring was conducted by me and by several other members of the IACS trained by Dr. M. G. Prashad, head of sound and vibration engineering at Stevens Institute of Technology. Independently the Edison township engineer and the Edison police force also conducted sound monitoring that revealed no infractions of any local, state, or federal codes of noise standards.

In this Navratri season, some spurious complaints of noise were filed by a few residents—some before the festival and its music had even begun. At election time the entire township council was voted out, some like to think by the Indian community that showed up in greater numbers than usual at the polls. As an aside, I would like to add that it may be useful to explore voter turnout as it is reflected in a desire to express individual and communal personal concerns over and above strategic political manipulation of public opinion.

In a July 10, 1996, landmark ruling, a precedent-setting historical first for Hinduism in America, John C. Lifland, United States district judge, upheld the constitutional rights of Navratri. In 1997 the township tried to impose further restrictions on the festival only to be rebuffed by Judge Lifland in mid-September.

On October 3, 1997, the first day of the festival that year, the township of Edison sought injunctive relief against Judge Lifland's ruling by filing an appeal in the Third Circuit Court of Philadelphia. The motion was denied, and festive music and dance continued until about 4:00 A.M.

In carrying forward the Navratri metaphor of the tenth day or vijayadashami, the day of victory, a final settlement between the IACS and the township of Edison, New Jersey, was signed on June 19, 1998. Although all the requirements sought by the IACS were met in the settlement, the following letter to the *Edison Home News Tribune* remains a grim reminder of the reality that communal conflict continues to simmer:

Keep Public Money away from Festival

July 7, 1998

It is reprehensible and a slap in the face of every resident of Edison that taxpayers must fork over $95,000 to a group of Asian Indians who have shown disdain for the people of the United States by making horrible caricatures of Americans at its festival at Middlesex County College.

This group has thumbed its nose at the curfew laws in Edison, and despite petitions to quiet its members at a decent hour, the Edison Township Council and Mayor George Spadoro are paying them to break the law so they could bang their heathen drums in obeisance to their heathen gods until 4 a.m. on the Sabbath.

By paying $95,000 to this undeserving group, the Edison leadership is breaking the so-called "Separation of church and state" by funding a religious festival. If there is but one copy of the Vedic Scriptures present or one statue of Brahma, Vishnu or Shiva, then it is a religious festival and no government money is allowed to be given to it. Edison opens itself to a lawsuit. If the mayor and council want to give the money away so badly, let them give it out of their own pockets, not stealing from taxpayers.

I can guarantee that if I played "Amazing Grace" or "Rock of Ages" out of my window at 4 a.m., I would be arrested for disturbing the peace and the mayor wouldn't be running to my aid with a checkbook.
The Rev. Kenneth Matto
Edison

On October 19, 1999, to follow up on the previous letter, I telephoned the Rev. Kenneth Matto, who refused to talk or comment on his letter, only asserting that his views remained unchanged.

As a New Jersey State civil rights commissioner and as an immigrant who arrived on these shores in February 1963, I am familiar with the American civil rights movement and the struggle for equity. I can report that the courts seem to be the only venue available to resolve vexing communal conflicts. Although advocacy groups for a wide spectrum of social issues exist, the onus of resolving issues of religious freedom and rights, and in this case the more complex conflation of religious and racial "Otherness," seems to rest only on those who are wronged and whose rights have been compromised. Jenny Bourne in her essay "The Life and Times of Institutional Racism" writes that the Institute of Race Relations (IRR) in Britain where she works

> underwent a revolutionary transformation, shifting the focus of race research from black people to white institutions from the done-to to the do-er, from the victim to the perpetrator.

And I would hasten to add that the present worldwide religious conflagration indicates that those who work in the religious arena have not learned to articulate religious dissonances in the unequivocal way the IRR is able to discuss race. Religious leadership itself, with the exception of very few voices, seems profoundly silent and invisible.

Other than the late Eric Neisser, then professor of constitutional law at Rutgers University, and some of his students from the school's constitutional law clinic, there was no outside support for the IACS. In Edison, no religious group or ethnic or community leader stepped up to the plate in support of the IACS during this well-publicized case.

Our democracy has a paucity of institutions to study, educate, arbitrate, and promote the credence of the religious "Other." Yet for a democracy to flourish, it is imperative that both individuals and groups learn about and provide advocacy for the stories and lives of fellow citizens who appear dissimilar from themselves.

To maintain and preserve our democratic institutions, those of us involved in the study of religion and culture could perhaps be even more vocal, responsive, concerned, and actively involved in institutional and community innovation that promotes a national agenda of interreligious arbitration and conciliation. In our commitment to the rights of all citizens, we must continue to support religious pluralism for both individual believers and for groups. This is the bedrock of our religious and democratic freedom. We must be vigilant and protect the rights and beliefs guaranteed by the Constitution of the United States.

Notes

1. Diana Eck, "Neighboring Faiths," *Harvard Magazine* 99, no. 1 (Sept.–Oct. 1996): 43.
2. Conversation between author and Councilman David Papi, Edison, New Jersey, June 1993.

Liberalism and the Challenge of Multicultural Accommodation

JAN FELDMAN

The case for multicultural accommodation has become tougher to make in the wake of September 11. It seems reasonable to scrutinize religious and cultural minorities in order to determine if they pose a threat to our democratic institutions. If the pendulum had begun to swing from liberal universalism, with its demand for assimilation, toward cultural particularism, with its demand for accommodation, any number of impassioned voices would now warn us of the dangers of the latter position.

Although it is certainly in vogue in many circles to respect, even celebrate diversity, there is a pervasive ambivalence toward cultural minorities that is not merely a response to recent events; rather, it is a deeply imbedded characteristic in our public philosophy, liberalism. One specific type of diversity, that constituted by nonliberal religious groups, seems more than other types to test the extent to which we as a nation are willing to honor our commitments to pluralism and toleration.

The religious group that I intend to discuss is a subset of Judaism known as Chassidim. There are only several hundred thousand of members of the group in the United States, most concentrated in New York and several other urban centers. There are about thirty groups of Chassidim, known as courts. They are named for the eastern European and Russian towns of their origin. Chassidim are recognizable by their distinctive dress, which, for men, with some variations among groups, include black coats and hats, white fringes called tsitsit, a yarmulke, or skull-cap, beards, and side locks, called payot. Women are less visible. The requirements of their dress are not specified beyond wearing longish skirts, high collars, long sleeves, stockings, and a head covering that may be a hat, scarf, or wig, called a sheitel.

As a relatively recent (about three hundred years old) offshoot of traditional Judaism with roots in what is now Eastern Europe, Russia, Ukraine, and Belarus, Chassidic Judaism came to this country with political traditions shaped by corporate, centralized, and certainly undemocratic governments. The Enlightenment and the emancipation movements of middle and Western Europe had passed Chassidim by, leaving them to be buffeted by hostile governments, legal disabilities, pogroms, and war. The good side of their situation, as compared to that of other European Jews, was that they did not face that peculiar threat to their existence that the Enlightenment and later that political emancipation represented. The offer of full rights of citizenship came with a high price tag for minorities, especially Jews, in that central aspects of religious life had to be hidden from public view. This requirement, although formally applicable to all religions, did not impose the same burdens upon Christian observance because Christianity was congruent with the dominant culture. The resulting fusion created the illusion, for them, of state neutrality.

Judaism did not fare well in such a bifurcated situation. Becoming an abstract, universal French or German citizen in reality meant ceasing to be a Jew or, if not, being relegated to the margins of society. Meanwhile, Chassidim and other Orthodox Jews of Eastern Europe and Russia, although ghettoized and persecuted, were permitted a certain amount of communal religious and political autonomy. The Jewish political and social response was the kehillah or Kahal, a fairly democratic form of self-government that exercised power and jurisdiction within the corporate-style state. This entrenched tradition of communal life, political autonomy, and self-sufficiency was transported with the Chassidim who immigrated to the West. This has been a defining feature of Chassidim in the United States, one that has created a distinctive approach to life and politics in North America.

Chassidim were relative latecomers to this country compared to other European Jews, arriving after World War II as a handful of survivors of the original communities that were destroyed by the Holocaust. The majority of American Jews had arrived in several waves at the end of the nineteenth and beginning of the twentieth centuries. These earlier immigrants had cut their political teeth on struggles to end legal discrimination and to secure full rights of citizenship, meaning full access to American political, social, and economic life. Americanization schools set them on the path to assimilation with the full approval of the immigrants themselves. The obstacles to success were perceived by many of these Jews to be discriminatory laws and disabilities placed upon them. Not surprisingly, their political activity was aimed at getting the courts to strictly uphold the establishment clause on the belief that they had more to fear from the establishment of Christianity than from a secular public sphere.

The Chassidim had as their inauguration into political life in Russia the fight for survival under the czars, Hitler, and Stalin. When they arrived in the United States, it was with the intention of regrouping and recreating their semiautonomous, traditional enclaves. Not surprisingly, their political focus has been on the First Amendment rights of association and free exercise of religion. In fact, Chassidim believe that a society devoid of religion is devoid of morality and therefore truly threatening to its citizens. They are not bothered by the Christian undertone of American culture. They do not participate in it, avoiding television, the malls, and public schools. They feel confident that they can transmit their religion to the next generation, not simply by walling themselves off from the mainstream but, more importantly, by strengthening their own internal community life. Unlike their counterparts in mainstream Jewish life, Chassidim have no desire to reap the social or economic fruits of assimilation to American culture. Yet they are appreciative of the nonmaterial benefits of life in America, not the least of which, in their judgment, is the right to be left alone.

Chassidim pose conceptual problems for political theorists. They clearly do not conform to the model of voluntary association that is the only model of group life that is congruent with liberal principles. By and large, they do not hold liberal values, yet they not only hold but also practice democratic ones. They have not removed themselves from politics like the Amish, who tend to evoke a sense of nostalgia. Instead, Chassidim tend to draw fire from precisely those quarters where they might expect to garner respect: among political theorists who advocate participatory democracy. Chassidim are politically active in ways that irritate many of these theorists. They deploy their considerable political acumen in order to reinforce and secure the boundaries of their group. For this reason, more than for reasons of their distinctive dress, habits, and language, they find little acceptance within the conventional liberal framework. Yet they are not so anomalous as to be politically irrelevant. In fact, they serve democratic purposes quite well by highlighting a critical question for our political system: whether it is better and more effective to attain equality for all citizens by recognizing or by minimizing differences.

The danger of the former is that if we legitimize the "politics of difference" or confer explicit rights upon groups, we may also create a politics of grievance and a fragmented citizenry. The danger of the latter is that if we minimize differences, we risk making assimilation to a single, universal standard of citizenship the price that minority cultures or religions must pay in order to enjoy the benefits that other American citizens take for granted. Exclusion from these benefits will not be easier to swallow simply because it is justified in terms of the facial neutrality of the law or policy. Historically, neutrality has rarely lived up to its name. The "neutral citizen" has made women appear to be deviant men, Jews appear to be deviant Christians, and African Americans appear to be deviant whites.

Chassidim dramatize three areas of discomfort that liberal theorists experience when confronted by multiculturalism. The first aspect of the discomfort is generated specifically by religious groups like the Chassidim, centering on the interpretation of First Amendment religion clauses. The second and third aspects of the discomfort are generated by all groups, the one centering on the conceptual role of groups in liberal democratic theory and the other on the tension between the state and subnational competitors for jurisdiction over members. All three areas of discomfort are intensified in the face of nonliberal groups because of a tendency among political theorists to conflate liberal values and attitudes with the requirements of democratic citizenship.

The first area of discomfort among liberal theorists involves religious groups, specifically, and is traceable to the eighteenth century European experience of internecine warfare among religions vying for political supremacy. The framers of our Constitution recognized that the state must be above the fray, neither allowing itself to become the captive of one religion nor throwing its weight behind any particular religion. Accordingly, it has become axiomatic that the state must maintain strict official neutrality with respect to its citizens' conception of the good.

In principle, religion was banished from the public sphere by the establishment clause of the First Amendment. The exception is the adoption of the most general and amorphous symbols that might comprise a sort of civic religion. Some have claimed that this is the price we all equally pay for the social contract that put an end to religious strife. Arguably, all citizens, perhaps those professing minority religions most of all, benefit from the "wall of separation" in that no religion, even that of the majority, can monopolize the public square.

Some theorists have called into question the putative neutrality of the state, charging that liberalism itself constitutes an ideology or even a religion of secularism.[1] They maintain that the religious have been reduced to second-class citizens, sidelined in the public square because they cannot voice their real concerns without violating the rules of civil, that is, neutral, public speech. If one is required to frame one's political discussion in terms determined to be accessible and intelligible to all, and religious reasoning is categorized as the product of special revelation rather than universal rationality, then religious citizens must either couch their concerns in secular terms or remain silent.

But this issue goes deeper than the language or terminology that we employ in public deliberations, be it religious or secular. The conflict is really one that pits two competing styles of knowing and reasoning about the world against each other in a rigged fight in which the supremacy of Enlightenment rationality is already assumed. The fight is rigged because Enlightenment principles and liberal principles are congruent. In addition, these principles, inclinations, or habits of thinking are also considered democratic virtues. What emerges is a set of false dichotomies between reason and tradition, freedom and authority, open and closed societies, universal and particular attachments, the free and the unfree, authentic and encumbered selves, self-actualized and repressed individuals, and flourishing and stunted lives.

A more useful and less judgmental distinction is drawn by Robert Lipkin between two types of cultures: deliberative and dedicated.[2] The deliberative culture is certainly derivative of the Enlightenment. It understands human reasoning as mobilizing and deploying formal methods of problem solving, linear logic, and analytical skills. Only by critically evaluating, constantly revising, and laying bare the fallibility of all received truths is human progress possible. Of course, this mentality might call into question the very existence of truth. At any rate it ought to generate intellectual humility and therefore tolerance toward contrary views. But in fact deliberative cultures tend as much as any to possess their own prejudices and conceits; notably among them is the claim of universality and neutrality. In our society, the ascendance of the deliberative culture is nearly unchallenged. It has dominion, significantly, in the huge bureaucracy of public education, thereby giving it an edge over dedicated cultures in perpetuating itself.

Within the pervasive, quasi-official deliberative culture are islands of minority cultures, many of them conforming to Lipkin's model of dedicated cultures. These communities are often based on traditional religions that set the boundaries, norms, and behaviors of their members' lives according to ancient rhythms, truths, and narratives. The Chassidim are one such dedicated culture surrounded by a deliberative culture. Chassidim live their lives down to the tiniest detail in accordance with the 613 commands of G-d[3] set out in the written and oral Torah. That the contract with God goes back to Sinai does not suggest to them that it is in need of reevaluation, revision, or updating. If the authentic, eternal truth is known and clear, there does not seem to Chassidim any defensible reason for tinkering with it.

These are a rigorously scholarly people, but their quest is not for a novel interpretation or a paradigm shift that upends accepted truths. Progress and change are not valuable in their own right. The relevant question for democratic theorists is not whether Chassidim are self-actualized, authentic, unencumbered, critically rational individualists prepared to revise or even jettison their deepest convictions and dearest projects. The question is whether or not individuals with the mental habits acquired in a dedicated culture are capable of adopting the habits of a deliberative culture if that is what is required in order to assess political candidates' capabilities and fitness.

The evidence is that Chassidim are quite capable of shifting into a deliberative mode with respect to politics. They call this ability to evaluate candidates and political issues "common sense." This is a pretty good argument for accepting Rawls's distinction between "comprehensive liberalism" and "political liberalism,"[4] with the latter setting the threshold for a common political culture based on a set of fair procedures. Chassidim have no problem meeting the standards of "political liberalism" and are therefore solid candidates for the title "rational democratic actors."

Yet a simple admission that the deliberative attitude, or critical rationality, is a skill that is accessible to any citizen in some aspects of his or her life—say politics—does not carry the day. Those who see critical rationality as a habit of thinking about the world will not be happy to admit that it can be exercised in one area of life without spilling over into other areas of life. They argue that a bifurcated existence would produce cognitive dissonance and ultimately be untenable. To question is to question everything. Skepticism about even one's deepest convictions is claimed to produce a more authentic life. But more significantly, it is also claimed that deliberative cultures produce individuals with commitments to liberty, equality, privacy, and the rule of law in ways that dedicated cultures cannot.

In short, liberal habits are harnessed to democracy in such a way that it can be claimed that only liberal cultures can support democracy. Liberal habits are part and parcel of the good, rather than instruments for attaining it. This closes the circle that shuts out nonliberal or dedicated cultures. When liberalism embraces liberal attitudes as part of the good itself, it can justify intolerance toward nonliberal cultures. Liberalism thus exposes its nonneutrality.

Defenders of the secular public square are unbothered by the accusation that liberalism has betrayed its neutrality. They never shared the pretense that liberalism is neutral or creates a level playing field for religious, dedicated communities and secular, deliberative ones. They share Kathleen Sullivan's view instead, that the framers of the Constitution intended that the establishment and free exercise clauses, taken together, create a positive, secular public sphere.[5] To the extent that some religions find it difficult to survive in a secular milieu, we need not regret their demise.

These theorists often voice concern about what they view as the tendency of some nonliberal and traditional religious groups to deprive members of autonomy and the possibilities for an "open life." In this case, they would advocate that the state eschews its official neutrality in favor of intervention on behalf of these individuals. They argue that cultural particularism often collides with individual freedom and that they do not want the state to become an unwitting party to oppression. In these cases, the state's hands-off policy may actually reinforce a group's internal, often patriarchal power structure. With varying degrees of militancy, these theorists would have the state use all legal measures at its disposal to rescue vulnerable individuals and promote internal changes in conformity with liberal principles. They assert that the expectation of assimilation is implicit in our Constitution, justifying, if anything, the reuniversalization of citizenship rather than cultural particularism or differentiated citizenship.

Among the vocal critics of traditional religions are liberal feminist theorists who understand that accommodating multiculturalism may come at the expense of upholding the civil rights of female members of these groups. Susan Okin, for one, finds that most traditional cultures oppress women.[6] If there is a trade-off between the survival of the culture and the freedom of women (even those that seem willingly to accede to their oppression and contribute to the shaping and transmission of these traditional norms), she would not regret the extinction of these groups. Okin is particularly harsh in her evaluation of Orthodox Judaism because of its deeply imbedded, gender-based roles.

Any Orthodox Jew can defend this division of roles. Of course, liberal critics would likely dismiss claims based on the authority of G-d. They are just as likely to dismiss as "false consciousness" claims made by women themselves as to their satisfaction with their lives. Would it help to point out that if Chassidic women don't seem to embrace careers or conventional notions of success, neither do Chassidic men? If anything, Chassidic girls receive a much stronger secular education than do the boys (many of whom are barely competent in English) and are therefore better equipped than the boys to exercise the option of "exit" from the community. Chassidic men are, in almost every way, more "burdened" by the stringency of dress and daily, time-bound obligations than are the women. Finally, although liberal feminists may be unmoved by the Chassidic woman's power to influence as well as to transmit the norms of her community, radical feminists would find much to sympathize with in the ability of Chassidic women to create a distinctive women's world of meaning from which they derive palpable and irrefutable joy.

Rather than accept the gauntlet thrown out by Okin to Orthodox Judaism—"liberalize or die"—Chassidic women would clearly maintain their loyalty to their current way of life. In addition, if given a forum to voice their views, they would have quite a bit to say about the deficiencies and betrayals of the liberal promise made to American women since the 1960s. It is not that Chassidic women are ignorant of the ways of the liberal world, it is that they are simply not attracted by them.

In fact, the state rarely intervenes in order to "rescue" women from traditional religious groups unless actual crimes have been committed against them or unless the women bring a dispute before the courts. Some theorists contend that if the state could ensure that individuals had the skills necessary to function in the wider world, as well as the option of free exit, then groups that fail to liberalize would most likely be unable to compete with the dominant culture. They would lose their "market share," as the product of a benign market adjustment. A more proactive approach would deploy the strongest weapon at the state's disposal, which is public education,[7] but this can only be triggered if girls of minority cultures enter the public schools, which Chassidic girls do not.

The state's approach to religious groups' internal norms must be delicate. Religious practice falls under the protection of the First Amendment and therefore benefits from a certain permissiveness or leniency that secular groups do not. The putative asymmetrical treatment of religious groups by the courts irks critics because they claim it allows some religions to engage in discriminatory practices that would not be tolerated if practiced by secular associations.[8]

In fact, I think this fear is overstated. Both Fourteenth Amendment claims and establishment clause claims often trump free-exercise claims when legal disputes arise. Framed this way, almost any attempt by the state to accommodate a religious practice or tenet on free-exercise grounds can potentially run afoul of establishment prohibitions. The application of the Lemon test makes it likely that accommodation will be read as entanglement or endorsement, triggering intense scrutiny. The court will likely enunciate the state's "compelling interest" in preventing establishment, thereby burdening, if unintentionally, some groups' free-exercise rights.

An example of this tendency is the successful sex discrimination suit by female bus drivers involving the Satmar Chassidic private boys' school, United Talmudic Academy.[9] The dispute centered on the refusal of the boys and their teachers to be served by a female bus driver on a public school bus provided under state law. There is a very strong religious prohibition against men and women coming into casual contact in this community. There was no intention on the part of the Chassidim to imply inferiority of women or to insult the driver. The school district tried to work out an accommodation by replacing the female with a male driver, but this violated the acceptable assignment procedures based on seniority. The bus driver union filed suit against the district alleging violation of the collective bargaining agreement. The court expressed the view that a plan requiring the district to provide male drivers for the Chassidic school would create an impermissible symbolic union between church and state and that Chassidic children would perceive the government's provision of male drivers as an endorsement by the court and district of their religious beliefs. "In effect, riding the school bus would no longer be a neutral activity, but rather, would be akin to a government sponsored religious experience."

The court concluded that the provision of male drivers would have "the fatal primary effect of advancing religion and would, therefore, violate the dictates of the Establishment Clause of the First Amendment." The court expressed the additional view that although the decision infringes upon the Chassidim's right to the free exercise of religion, the burden on the Chassidim's religious freedom is "based upon a compelling state interest."

That the courts have been uneven in their treatment of religious groups, arguably unduly broad in their reading of the establishment clause and unduly narrow in their reading of the free exercise clause, does not seem to level the playing field in the evaluation of theorists who want the state to act as a stronger lever against the internal practices of nonliberal religions. They would keep the focus squarely on the threats that religious groups purportedly pose to democracy rather than ways in which our democracy poses a threat to the free exercise and even survival of religious minorities.

DISCOMFORT OVER THE ROLE OF GROUPS

The second area of discomfort generated by groups is general, multicultural, religious, or otherwise. It reflects our emphasis on the individual as the basic unit of analysis, an emphasis that has in part confounded our ability to make sense of group life. Ever since Hobbes portrayed our social life as a series of freedom-curtailing collisions between atoms in pursuit of self-interest, liberal theory has had a problem fully conceptualizing the role of groups both with respect to their individual members and with respect to the political life of democracies. Do the associations of civil society buttress the democratic state, or do they compete with the state for moral authority over their members?

Liberal theory recognizes two parties to political relationships, two political actors, two units of analysis: state and individual citizen. Theorists of multiculturalism presuppose three parties in any relationship: the individual citizen, the group, and the state. Our Constitution recognizes only abstract and undifferentiated individuals with respect to bearing rights, with respect to political representation, and with respect to citizenship. Yet, in reality, there is a myriad of groups that take on the characteristics of political actors vying either for state benefits and protections or simply for the right to be left alone. If all of the potential repositories of citizen loyalty were arrayed along a continuum from the most local, immediate, and particular to the most universal and remote, we would discover that most individuals possess multiple subnational loyalties that they may or may not rank above the state. Liberal theory recognizes these subnational loyalties, but would prefer to see them in a cooperative light, as building blocks of democracy rather than as competitors creating a centrifugal pull against the state.

Yet recognizing that individuals have affinities for associational life is nothing new. From de Tocqueville to Putnam, theorists have noted that group affiliations are a major component of social life, constituting what we call civil society. A thick, vibrant layer of private associations is held to be healthy for, and perhaps essential to, a vigorous, stable democracy. Yet the role played by groups in the lives of their individual members, and the mechanism whereby associations (many not themselves internally democratic) promote the democratic collective political life of the state, remains somewhat undertheorized in liberal thought.[10]

Of course, it will be pointed out that groups have long been accepted as informal political actors. Interest groups have been part of the political landscape and accounted for in the political science literature. But interest-group politics have always shared the liberal presupposition that the group is simply a vehicle for securing the interests and goals of their members. In other words, membership is both voluntary and self-serving. The integument of the group is the interest that they accidentally share. Each member retains his autonomy and the group exists only as long as the shared interest does.

Communitarians represent a refinement of classical liberalism, compensating to an extent for its traditional lack of attention to groups. They claim that liberalism's excessive emphasis on the individual not only clashes with democracy's need for collective civic behavior but misses the fact that humans are constituted by nature to live in groups. They credit associations with acting as incubators of democratic habits, thereby serving the state. They credit competition among groups with checking the pretensions of other individuals, groups, and, importantly, the state to monopolize power. They also regard associational life as the setting in which individuals discover their values and identity. Groups, to communitarian liberals, are essential to human flourishing.

But communitarians share a certain blind spot about group life with the liberals that they criticize. They are therefore unlikely to hold up Chassidim as the ideal model. Their perspective is still an instrumental one, in that groups serve either the needs of the state or the needs of their individual members, but beyond that, have no valid ends in their own right. Even for the advocates of formal group rights within the democratic polity, the justification for the group is that it is a superior vehicle for securing individual rights, autonomy, and interests than the individual facing off against the state would be.[11]

They are reluctant to grant that groups, particularly ascriptive and religious groups, might have an existence and purpose that is not reducible to the aggregate of goals and interests of its individual members. It is difficult even for communitarian theorists to understand individuals as totally identified with their groups. We can accept that an individual might vote straight self-interest, and we can accept, even applaud the noble individual who puts aside self-interest to vote for a common good. But an individual who intends his political action to further his group is regarded with suspicion as if he has sacrificed his autonomy and marched lockstep with other members of his group to the polls to do his master's bidding.

This brings to light one of the most significant differences between religious groups and voluntary associations. Chassidim, for instance, do not regard their membership as voluntary or contractual. It is not a matter of conscious choice, but of prior commitment. They see themselves as claimed by the group. They do not imagine life apart from the group because they would be unable to fulfill the obligations of an individual Jew if they were isolated from the community. Therefore, they do not regard the group as a vehicle for securing their self-interest. Moreover, they do not regard their bond to other members as one created by an accident in which they share an interest or concern. They do not regard the group as the backdrop against which they achieve self-actualization or fulfillment of a personal sort. They have accordingly had a difficult time making themselves understood by wider society.

Judicial opinions and legal commentary regarding Chassidim share an underlying assumption about the relationship between the individual and the polity, according to Jonathan Boyarin.[12] The premise of liberal theory is that the polity consists of individual citizens of a neutrally bounded territory, be it a municipality or a state. The citizen is assumed to be an individual person. Chassidim, on the other hand, hold a different underlying conception of political identity. In their view, territory is replaced by Diaspora, or the sense that their primary geographic orientation is somewhere other than where they currently reside. Chassidim understand their territorial residence to be temporary. They feel themselves to be in exile (golus), both physically and spiritually. Home, to them, means the rebuilt Jerusalem in the era following the arrival of the Messiah (Moshiach).

In addition, they do not regard the individual as the basic unit of consideration. Instead, they understand the individual in the context of family, history, descent, and group, which Boyarin refers to as "genealogy." Chassidim and liberals are operating in different cultural contexts, confounding the search for "neutral principles" of adjudication. The liberal context is consonant with Protestant Christian traditions of individual liberty and conscience, as well as American traditions of political representation centered on territory and residence. Yet individualism and territoriality are no less contingent than genealogy and Diaspora as ways of understanding political life, though they implicitly guide the court's response to Chassidim.

In short, religious groups such as Chassidim pose a vexing problem because they do not conform to the liberal model of voluntary associations and therefore tend to disturb liberal sensibilities and confound liberal assumptions. Their existence prompts questions such as "what are the limits of the state's obligation to tolerate groups that monopolize their members' loyalty?" "Do liberal principles require that we exercise toleration even toward groups that are not themselves tolerant?" "Does the state have an obligation to intervene in these groups when it judges that members are not exercising our notion of autonomy?" These questions become all the more acute when the groups under scrutiny appear not to share liberal values and attitudes. As Martha Minow notes, nonliberal groups are much more likely to have their practices scrutinized than are groups that subscribe to the values of the dominant culture.[13]

THE THIRD AREA OF DISCOMFORT: SHARING AUTHORITY WITH SUBNATIONAL GROUPS

Perhaps the best theoretical context for understanding the relationship of groups such as Chassidim and the state is offered by Robert Cover in his remarkable "Nomos and Narrative."[14] Chassidim, in his framework, would be characterized as a nomos, or subnational group, producing an authoritative world of meaning for its members. Cover held that there are no universally and eternally valid principles of law and that the state should recognize the existence of any number of self-governing, substate jurisgenerative authorities. Although Cover would welcome the proliferation of legal meaning, states, not surprisingly, resist yielding the monopoly they claim over the right to make and interpret law to other contenders. Cover envisioned the nomos in a perpetually adversarial relationship to the state. The state demands a monopoly over the making of laws, but in doing so, it confronts groups with ironclad loyalties to ancient faith, tradition, narratives, and laws of their own.

For Chassidim, the ultimate authority is Torah, or G-d's law. Ordinarily, this is not problematic. Chassidim, in fact, are remarkably law-abiding citizens. They would not relish being cast in the role of Cover's nomic heroes. Occasionally, caught between nomos and state, they have been forced to play that role, and not to a unanimous standing ovation by political theorists.

This was nowhere more in evidence than in a legal dispute involving Chassidim that came before the Supreme Court twice before ultimately being resolved in favor of the plaintiffs against them.[15] The plaintiffs challenged the constitutionality of the enactment under Chapter 748 of New York State law, of a public school district coinciding with the already legally incorporated village of Kiryas Joel, the residents of which were predominantly Satmar Chassidim.

The motive behind the creation of the school district was to allow Chassidic children with profound learning disabilities to receive special education services, ordinarily provided by the state, in their own communities. It had already been attempted to provide these services in a consolidated public school setting outside of the village, but the hostile reception by the other children to the Satmar children, with their distinctive garb and language, had made the continued provision of special education in this setting untenable. The parents of the Chassidic children cited the "panic, fear, and trauma" experienced by their children as the reason for withdrawing them from the public school.

Despite the fact that both the language of the statute and the physical space that the Satmar allocated for special education were both meticulously neutral, meaning free of religious symbols and language, the Court ruled that the creation of the school district serving Chassidim violated the second prong (the "effects test") of the Lemon test.[16] The plaintiff's central argument, that the primary effect of the statute involved "the state in sponsorship of Satmar separatist precepts," was adopted by the Court in its ruling that the legislation was a violation of the establishment clause of the First Amendment.

The case turned not simply on concerns about establishment, but on the fear that the state, by granting this sort of authority to the Satmar community, would be giving its imprimatur in principle to separatism. Underlying the Court's ruling in the Kiryas Joel case was the desire not to grant or acknowledge a right of semiautonomy to groups that demonstrate a strong, religiously based desire to separate themselves geographically.

The Chassidim realize that they cannot exist as autonomous nomic islands within the state. They must constantly engage in a bee-dance of shared jurisdictions and multiple, overlapping authorities. The sort of concessions and indulgences that Chassidim occasionally request from the state are, in my view, congruent with the

Constitution and provide us with the opportunity to carve out law-protected space for enclaves, giving real meaning to our claims of toleration and respect for multiculturalism. Some political theorists share this view, notably Thomas C. Berg, Martha Minow, Maya Nomi Stolzenberg, Robert Lipkin, and Abner Greene.

Other political theorists do not share this view, among them Christopher Eisgruber, Ira Lupu, Judith Failer, and Jeff Spinner. Eisgruber, for instance, holds that the Constitution clearly promotes assimilation to a common culture. It permits dissent but creates the expectation that dissenting groups will be willing to express their dissent publicly, thereby providing the service to democracy of showcasing alternative conceptions of the good, which in turn expands the menu of lifestyle choices available to other citizens.[17] Chassidim, however, have no desire to proselytize. Moreover, their lives require such rigorous discipline that they are not likely to serve as a countercultural model for alienated liberals.

The concern expressed by Ira Lupu is that Chassidic communities are not internally democratic and may engage in "Constitution flouting."[18] Another commonly expressed concern is that granting semiautonomy to Chassidim creates a demonstration effect and a bad precedent. Finally, it is noted that Chassidim violate the principle of political unity by seeking, in effect, "exit" from the larger community, accomplished by making use of the accoutrements of state power to reinforce social isolation.[19]

This allegedly makes Chassidim "bad" citizens who want to snub their neighbors. No distinction is recognized here between autonomy in order to practice their religion and autonomy based on racial or social prejudice, such as earlier "white flight" from the cities. The boundary-maintaining measures of Chassidim are intended to be inclusive and protective, designed to ensure the survival of their way of life, yet they are likely to be perceived as exclusive, clannish, snobbish, and hostile. That the Chassidim are visible, unlike the Amish, exacerbates the problem. It is one thing to reject the majority culture in favor of a remote and isolated apolitical existence, but quite another to reject that culture while seemingly employing its procedures and institutions in what appears to be a bid to reinforce the boundaries of a group. It is this trait, the combination of political acuity and influence, with the stark, nonliberal "Otherness" of the Chassidim that rankles their critics.

Yet it seems almost mean-spirited to begrudge the Chassidim, or other minorities, the limited means at their disposal to perpetuate their cultures against the odds. The dominant culture is attractive, not necessarily because of its intrinsic superiority, but because it is pervasive and easy. It is corrosive of more demanding ways of life. The dominant culture effortlessly has the edge, whereas minority cultures, without concerted effort to transmit their values to the next generation, will be entirely absorbed. For their efforts, they may be branded as intolerant. Yet demanding reciprocal toleration misses the point. This is not a quid pro quo because of the asymmetry of power. Minorities, in effect, have no option but to exercise tolerance toward the majority, yet tolerance is only recognized as a virtue when it is exercised by the majority.

CONCLUSION

It seems logical enough to claim that democratic institutions require the support of a shared democratic culture. Although interfering in group life would seem to violate the liberal principles of neutrality and toleration, it can be justified according to the view that the state has a stake in creating a citizenry equal to the task of upholding democratic institutions. Every regime, it is argued, has a right to ensure its own survival, which, for a democratic regime, implies a right to produce competent democratic citizens.

In this sense, the problem is not with the Chassidim or the dictates of their religion, but with our tendency to enunciate a higher standard of citizenship than is required for the operation of democratic institutions—higher, in fact, then the majority of Americans could meet. This high hurdle is created by unnecessarily linking liberal values and democratic virtues, making us more suspicious and skeptical of minority cultures' prospects for producing good citizens. Chassidim, in terms of their political activities and goals, are reasonably good citizens, if not modern-day Pericleses.

This is not to say that it is never justified to scrutinize the private workings of nonliberal groups. Not all of them are benign. The groups that violate the law, amass weapons, or otherwise threaten civil peace and security should certainly not be tolerated. That being said, I would argue that as a democracy, we can afford to give rather wide latitude to minority cultural and religious groups. There is no reason to believe that the skills required in order to exercise effective and responsible democratic deliberation and participation are the sole province of those citizens who hold liberal values.

My goal is to demonstrate that there are valid reasons to reverse the lens and to try to see the world from the perspective of the religious group rather than from the perspective of the state. After all, requiring that groups serve state purposes, even when those purposes are democratic purposes, puts the group at a disadvantage. The group must legitimize its existence to outsiders, namely the dominant cultural majority, instead of fulfilling its own mission, namely allowing its members to live their daily lives as the embodiment of their norms. In short, Chassidim are interested in fulfilling their contract with God rather than with the state. They have no desire to live their lives publicly. They have no desire to win adherents or to impose their values on the majority.

I do not want to overstate my case by claiming that the Chassidim are in danger of being actively oppressed and driven out of existence by the state. Their survival is not in jeopardy. But they do experience the state as anything but neutral. Their encounter with the state, with liberalism and secularism, does put them at a disadvantage relative to individuals and groups that are more at home in the mainstream culture. We do not want to make assimilation the price of full citizenship. We do not want to force religious groups to choose exit in order to avoid gradual extinction through assimilation. If we do, groups such as the Chassidim will forego state benefits by exiting rather than compromising religious law.

My guess is that without going to the extreme of a formal group rights model, we can accommodate a fair amount of multicultural constitutionalism. Like Ayelet Shachar, I believe that we must engage in novel rethinking of traditional, hard and fast jurisdictions between state and nomoi.[20] I do not believe, however, that we should be in the business of offering multicultural accommodation with the ulterior motive of radically or even gradually transforming these cultures. The mere necessity of interacting with the wider world probably already has had more influence on these groups than is immediately apparent, because it is subtle, long-term, and indirect.

I would stand by the claim that mainstream America will benefit from multicultural accommodation as much as Chassidim will, if for no other reason than groups such as Chassidim prod us to examine and live up to one of our highest liberal ideals, that is, toleration. By toleration I mean respect for differences—not merely superficial or cosmetic differences in food or costume, but real and profound differences in core values. In my view, respect for diversity demands no less.

NOTES

1. In this group would be included Stephen L. Carter, Ronald Thiemann, Kent Greenawalt, David Smolin, Richard Neuhaus, among others.

2. Robert Justin Lipkin, "Liberalism and the Possibility of Multicultural Constitutionalism: The Distinction between Deliberative and Dedicated Cultures," *University of Richmond Law Review* 29, no. 5 (Dec. 1995): 1263–326.

3. Chassidic Jews are prohibited from representing and thereby limiting the infinite nature of G-d through any depiction of G-d, including the writing of the name.

4. John Rawls, "The Priority of Right and Ideas of the Good," *Philosophy and Public Affairs* 17, no. 4 (1988): 251–76.

5. Kathleen Sullivan, "Religion and Liberal Democracy," *University of Chicago Law Review* 59 (1992): 195.

6. Susan Moller Okin, "Is Multiculturalism Bad for Women?" in *Is Multiculturalism Bad for Women: Susan Moller Okin with Respondents,* ed. Joshua Cohen, Matthew Howard, and Martha C. Nussbaum (Princeton, N.J.: Princeton Univ. Press, 1999), 7–26.

7. There is an extensive literature on the use of public education as a lever for loosening the grip of values received in the family. It raises many controversies, of course, related to the jurisdictional authority over children shared by the state and the family. Much of this literature was triggered by *Wisconsin v.*

Yoder and more recently by *Mozert v. Hawkins County*. Prominent among scholars who have addressed this controversy are Amy Gutmann, Stephen Macedo, William Galston, Shelley Burtt, Nomi Maya Stolzenberg, Stephen Bates, Richard Arneson, and Ian Shapiro.

8. Cass Sunstein, "Sexual Equality vs. Religion: What Should the Law Do?" in *Is Multiculturalism Bad for Women?* ed. Joshua Cohen, Matthew Howard, and Martha C. Nussbaum, 85–94.

9. *Bollenbach v. Board of Education of Monroe Woodbury Center School District*, 659 F. Supp. 1450 (1987).

10. Recent noteworthy scholarship includes Nancy Rosenblum, *Membership and Morals: The Personal Uses of Pluralism in America* (Princeton, N.J.: Princeton Univ. Press, 2000); and Amy Gutmann, ed., *Freedom of Association* (Princeton, N.J.: Princeton Univ. Press, 1998).

11. Will Kymlicka is a strong advocate for the political recognition of minority cultures. He does, however, favor those groups that are internally liberal and democratic.

12. Jonathan Boyarin, "Circumscribing Constitutional Identities in Kiryas Joel," *Yale Law Journal* 106, no. 5 (1997): 1537–70.

13. Martha Minow, "The Constitution and the Subgroup Question," *Indiana Law Journal* 71 (Winter 1995): 1.

14. Robert M. Cover, "The Supreme Court, 1982 Term-Forward: Nomos and Narrative," *Harvard Law Review* 97 (1983): 4.

15. *Board of Education of Kiryas Joel Village School District v. Grumet*, 114 S. Ct. 2481 (1994).

16. *Lemon v. Kurtzman*, 403 U.S. 602 (1971).

17. Christopher L. Eisgruber, "The Constitutional Value of Assimilation," *Columbia Law Review* 96 (1996): 87.

18. Ira C. Lupu, "Uncovering the Village of Kiryas Joel," *Columbia Law Review* 96, no. 104 (1996): 104–20.

19. Jeff Spinner, *The Boundaries of Citizenship: Race, Ethnicity, and Nationality in the Liberal State* (Baltimore: Johns Hopkins Univ. Press, 1994), uses the concept of "partial citizenship" (95) and "exit" (112), whereas Abner S. Greene uses the concept of "partial exit" approvingly in making a case for permeable sovereignty. "Kiryas Joel and Two Mistakes about Equality," *Columbia Law Review* 96, no. 1 (Jan. 1996): 4–51.

20. For further discussion of this idea, see Ayelet Shachar, *Multicultural Jurisdictions: Cultural Differences and Women's Rights* (Cambridge, U.K.: Cambridge Univ. Press, 2001).

Diverse Religious Practices and the Limits of Liberal Tolerance

POLYCARP IKUENOBE

INTRODUCTION

As a normative theory, liberalism seeks to account for and justify (1) individual freedom to choose a conception of the good, (2) limits on political institutions and the
political actions of individuals and governments, and (3) state's neutrality and tolerance of individuals' choices of beliefs, values, and practices. Liberalism is historically and conceptually connected to neutrality and religious tolerance, because liberal ideas emerged in the West in part from the incessant and violent religious
conflicts between Catholics and Protestants. Freedom of conscience, neutrality, and
tolerance are essential elements of a liberal account of individual rights to choose
and practice a religion within the context of political institutions and actions. Tolerance and neutrality imply that individuals should be free to choose a rational life
plan and conception of the good, including religious beliefs and practices. In this
regard, John Rawls says, "the state is not to do anything that makes it more likely
that individuals accept any particular conception rather than another."[1] That is,
the state should equally respect and protect the rights and freedoms of all individuals; this will engender religious and cultural diversity and pluralism. It is in this
sense that liberalism appears to be consistent with religious diversity.

Debates in liberal theories about the status of culture, its relation to individual
rights, and the justification for cultural pluralism raise the following vexing question: Is it theoretically and practically possible for liberal democracies to be *truly*
tolerant and neutral, so as to preserve freedom of diverse cultural and religious
expressions, especially minority cultures? I examine this question and argue that a
plausible idea of freedom of religion that can engender diversity of religious practices must be construed broadly in terms of cultural recognition and freedom of

cultural expressions. If freedom of religion is so construed, then the traditional liberal approach of separating state and church, which requires neutrality and tolerance, becomes inadequate in addressing the rights of minority cultures. This is because the notion of tolerance involves a vertical and asymmetrical relationship between the powerful majority (tolerator) and the powerless minorities (tolerated). This relationship, which assumes the normative structures or values of the tolerator as the basis for placing limits on tolerance, indicates a limitation in the ability of tolerance to engender religious diversity. I examine some liberal accounts of the nature of freedom of cultural and religious practices. I argue that these liberal accounts, as exemplified in Western democracies, can neither tolerate diverse religious practices nor preserve the rights of minorities to practice diverse religions. I suggest in passing that what is required for diversity of religious practices ranges from acceptance, understanding, and recognition to rational engagement.

LIBERALISM AND FREEDOM OF RELIGIOUS PRACTICE

Liberalism as a broad normative political theory may be seen as (1) a theory about acceptable political procedures or structures, (2) a theory about acceptable outcomes, and (3) a theory about both acceptable procedures and outcomes. Liberalism is a theory about procedures, in the sense that it provides a framework regarding how the rights and freedom of individuals can be fairly protected from the power of the state. As a theory about acceptable procedures for protecting individual rights, it emphasizes the right over the good. Liberalism may also be seen as a theory about achieving the outcome of equality, justice, and safeguarding of individual rights and freedom as goods. As an outcome theory, it emphasizes the good but does not emphasize how the good or outcome may be achieved. However, a more plausible view of liberalism is that it is both an outcome and a procedural theory: there is no priority of good over right, nor is there a priority of right over good. Thus W. Connolly remarks, "Current liberalism cannot be defined merely through its commitment to freedom, rights, dissent, and justice. It must be understood, as well, through the institutional arrangements it endorses."[2] Liberalism in this sense seeks to achieve the good or outcome of freedom, rights, and justice, as well as to provide adequate structures and procedures for achieving the requisite outcome. This set of procedures may not guarantee the achievement of the requisite outcome, but it makes their achievement more likely or probable.

This plausible view of liberalism implies that if the adequate procedures are not able to achieve the requisite outcome due to human fallibility, then there are built-in procedures to rectify or improve it in order to achieve the outcomes: it is an internally self-rectifying process for achieving requisite outcomes. Within this broad characterization of liberalism is the dominant liberal individualistic view of the nature of rights, the relationship between individuals and culture, and the status of group and cultural rights. This view, which argues that only individuals are "concrete entities" that can be substantively identified as having valid right claims, can be found in the works of John Locke, J. S. Mill, John Rawls, and Ronald Dworkin.[3] This view does not recognize individuals' cultural membership because of its ontological assumptions about (1) the nature of rights, (2) the kind of entities that have rights, and (3) the nature of values. With respect to the nature of values, liberalism assumes value skepticism, fallibilism, and subjectivism. This view suggests that we do not know the true value; as such, each individual must be free to choose her values and revise them when necessary. Liberalism insists that cultural membership is a private issue to which the state is neutral and that groups have attenuated rights only in virtue of the rights of its individual members, who are free to "revise" their choice to be members of a group. Groups do not have valid right claims because they cannot be identified as determinate by any set of features. People are identified as members of a group via different sets of features. This idea is articulated by court decisions in the United States, that freedom of conscience is protected by the First Amendment and that the right to choose any religion or none at all is supported not only in respect for an individual's freedom of conscience but also by the view that religious beliefs are products of free or voluntary choices.

The liberal individualist account of rights, which has no room for group rights, indicates that once individuals have their rights and are treated equally, the state has no further obligation to the cultural groups to which they belong. This idea, in James Ceaser's view, which represents "the national ideal, or 'best statement' of American liberal democracy—not always recognized in fact, to be sure—has been one that involved formally recognized individuals, not cultural groups, as the core of the compact of society. The highest principle was that of all persons being created equal, with the rights and privileges attaching in the first instance to individuals."[4] The liberal idea of ascribing rights only to individuals is articulated as a basis for secularism and freedom of conscience. Freedom of conscience is an element of secularism and religious tolerance that is enshrined in the American Constitution by the free exercise clause. According to Walter Berns, "The Constitution [of the United States] speaks not of Christian, Jew, or Muslim, but consistently only of undifferentiated 'persons.' . . . By so speaking, it seeks to discourage religious (and antireligious) parties in favor of secular political parties. It expects us—whatever our religion, and whatever our cultural 'identity'—to be able to come together in those parties."[5] Liberal individualism construes freedom of religion narrowly as an individual right that is obtained in the private realm. Thus it addresses the issue of freedom of religion by (1) separating church and state, (2) separating private and public realms, and (3) prescribing neutrality and tolerance.

An essential element of this view is the distinction between the private and public realms, the idea that the issue of the membership of a culture or religious group should be a private issue over which the state has no legitimate jurisdiction. This view defends tolerance and neutrality regarding religion and cultures in terms of the procedures and outcomes of protecting *individual* rights and freedoms. Liberalism is thus characterized by a kind of abstract individualism or atomism, where individuals as atomic facts are abstracted from society and cultures and considered to be the ultimate units to which rights and moral values can be ascribed. This is because only human beings are capable of actions and choices regarding the achievement of ends and interests, whose ability to make choices and to act ought to be protected. Rawls makes this point by arguing that only individual persons can be considered as "self-originating sources of valid claims."[6] The ontological assumption by this view of liberalism that only individuals have rights is bolstered by its egalitarian import, which implies that every person has equal moral value, deriving from the moral worth of their freedom and autonomy to make choices and decisions.

Liberalism indicates, from a neutral stance, that the state has a duty to treat equally without preference everyone and his or her conceptions of the good.[7] This liberal idea is ambiguously indicated in the American Constitution and laws. On the one hand, the free exercise clause gives credence to some sense of religious diversity, because it indicates neutrality and tolerance of diverse religions and cultures. If a state and its constitution or set of laws recognize cultural and religious groups, then, in some sense, it lacks neutrality. It assumes, by such recognition, the specific conceptions of the good that the cultural and religious groups represent. On the other hand, the constitution and laws are inconsistent with diversity of religions and cultures in that they primarily do not recognize cultural and religious groups as entities with valid right claims. Liberal individualism seeks a constitutional or normative framework for social unity, which provides the basis for assimilating and integrating individuals as citizens of a state. This principle ensures equal liberty and justice for all, avoids discrimination, and limits a state's power against individuals. This view assumes that there are no significant cultural differences that could trump the normative basis for assimilation, thus indicating an indifference to the legitimate existence of cultural groups. The focus by liberal individualism on individual rights, according to Will Kymlicka, has resulted in, or has been, a cover for injustices to minority cultures.[8] This is because it does not adequately appreciate that the deeper issues raised by freedom of religious practices are about freedom of cultural expression and identity.

Religious practices involve broad cultural expressions. Therefore freedom of religion and diversity of religious practices require the legal recognition of broad cultural expressions in the public realm by political institutions. It is thus pertinent to distinguish between "institutional tolerance" of cultural and religious practices, based on the structures, laws, and principles of an institution, and "individual tolerance" of other people's beliefs and actions in or outside of an institution. Institutional tolerance may influence individual tolerance, but one does not necessarily lead to the other. Robust religious practice may go beyond the latter to the former, and liberal individualism has not appreciated the former as a legitimate issue. Thus it is questionable whether the model of granting individual rights by separating church and state, in the context of the distinction between private and public realms, is adequate for dealing with the broader issues of religious practices, cultural identity, or expressions and the rights of minority cultures. If this model of neutrality and tolerance cannot address issues of cultural differences, and religion is an essential aspect of a culture, then such a model cannot accommodate diversity of religious practices. Liberal individualism seems not to see religion as an integral part of a culture in that it does not see religious practices as a form of cultural expression. I understand culture here in the anthropological sense, which involves a set of values, practices, beliefs, modes of expression, and ways of life, typical among which are language and religion. As such, it does not appreciate that tolerance could operate differently in two contexts: tolerating individual's actions and tolerating cultural practices.[9]

Liberalism does not appreciate the broad issues of cultural differences with respect to freedom of religion because many liberal theorists assume for the sake of citizenship that liberal states are nation-states with a homogeneous culture. J. S. Mill, among others, argues that liberal democracy cannot succeed in a multinational state. States with many different cultures should assimilate or integrate the minority cultures into the majority culture, and if assimilation fails, then the minorities should secede to form another state.[10] This is illuminating because it is *easier* for people to be tolerant of each other's religious differences, such as Catholics and Protestants, in a nation-state with a homogenous culture, because the religions emerged from one culture. Tolerance is more difficult if religious differences derive from substantially different cultures, ethnicity, or nationalities. For instance, it is more difficult for Catholics or some other Christian denominations to tolerate Muslim's practices such as polygamy because the two religions involve substantial cultural and value differences. Assimilation is difficult, as Rawls recognizes, because people have strong attachments to their cultures and are rarely willing to give them up: "The attachments formed to persons and places, to associations and communities, as well as cultural ties, are normally too strong to be given up."[11] This may explain the insistence by liberal theorists that in order for a liberal democracy to succeed in cultivating citizenship, it must be founded on a common culture to provide the normative basis for social unity and political solidarity.

Rawls underscores the difficulty of assimilation by insisting that the value structures of a society, which may include culture and religion, must be "a scheme into which people are born and are expected to lead a complete life."[12] He assumes that this scheme is permanent and should not change; he does not expect people to be easily assimilated into a different culture. He appreciates the important role that culture plays in people's lives; according to him, we use the language of cultures "in speech and thought to express and understand ourselves, our aims, goals, and values. . . . [W]e depend on [it] to find our place in the social world."[13] He excludes culture in his theory of justice because calculations regarding interests, values, and aims deriving from cultures strongly influence people's choices and conception of the good. Such calculations will offset his impartial view of justice, which is based on the liberal abstract conception of individual rights: thus, he says, "calculations that typically influence agreements within society have no place in the original position."[14] Rawls fails to appreciate the essential role of culture in his theory because he thinks that these calculations are not essential in determining what is just and fair. This is because he assumes a semblance of a nation-state where everyone is socially equal in that there are no differences arising from vertical and asymmetrical relations between cultural majority and minorities.

Many liberal theories do not only assume a nation-state with a dominant normative basis and culture, but many Western liberal democracies also operate as a nation-state with a *dominant* Judeo-Christian cultural tradition. This tradition represents the norm of the majority, which assimilates or in some cases represses minority cultures and religions. The process of assimilation does not accept diversity of religions and cultures; it requires minorities to change their fundamental practices to cohere with the Judeo-Christian tradition. The idea of assimilation is usually couched in terms of a melting pot. Western democracies are the pots with the heat and substance that melt other cultures to blend into the main substance of the Judeo-Christian cultural tradition. The metaphorical heat includes legal and constitutional provisions that do not allow for certain religious practices. These laws and the normative basis for assimilation, which reflect the dominant culture, indicate that they are not neutral. James Ceaser argues that there cannot be neutrality among cultures; they are usually in conflict because the way of life preferred by one culture is rejected by the other. If the ways of life were not in some respect inconsistent, they would not be different cultures. According to Ceaser, "The constitution does not say, for example, that English is the national language in the United States, . . . but the nation is not really 'neutral' about this fact."[15] This nonneutrality is indicated in the U.S. immigration law, which says that people below the age of fifty-five who are not proficient in the English language cannot be naturalized U.S. citizens.

One may justify the English language requirement on practical grounds, in that one needs the language to live a meaningful life in the United States. However, there is another argument, which is problematic on liberal grounds: it says that, as a condition for citizenship and social unity, one has to be assimilated into the American culture and ways of life, which is a conception of the good life. Assimilating minorities into the dominant culture has resulted in a situation where minority cultures are not tolerated at their "core" but only at their "peripheries." The free exercise clause grants Muslims freedom to practice their faith and provides the legal framework for tolerance. However, the law against bigamy does not give Muslims the freedom to practice polygamy, which is a core aspect of their culture. This is because liberalism construes freedom of religion very narrowly as an individual right issue in the private realm and not broadly as an issue of freedom of cultural expression and identity in the public realm in relation to one's conception of the good. So, although Islam is not tolerated at its core because of the law against bigamy, it is tolerated at its periphery in that Muslims are allowed to practice some elements of their faith. (My reference to polygamy is just one example to indicate a general problem: that is, limitations in the theories and practices of liberal tolerance in its ability to adequately address religious freedom and diversity.)

John Locke defends religious tolerance by indicating that repression is not an effective public policy for controlling religious beliefs; because such beliefs cannot be altered from the outside, they must be altered from one's internal motivations. He argues that it is also not within the province and jurisdiction of the state to control religious practices.[16] The state ought not to be involved in private matters of religious beliefs and practices, except where it harms others. This is the basis for the liberal argument against legislating morality, that is, laws that regulate private or self-regarding actions or the kind of criminal acts that are characterized as victimless crimes. I accept the harm argument as a plausible basis for placing limits on tolerance, if "harm" is reasonably defined. But the cultural and religious issues here do not cause harm in some relevant sense. If this argument is plausible, then one could make a case for polygamy for Muslims and a case against the legal prohibition of bigamy by the laws of the United States. One may make the case by arguing that marriage is a private and voluntary arrangement between two or more adults. The relevant beliefs and values cannot be altered from the outside. The people who hold these values and beliefs ought to be free to articulate and choose a conception of the good that is consistent with their values, which in this case includes polygamous marriage. No one is particularly harmed by this private and free decision by adults. Given the cases of English language requirement and polygamy, it is reasonable to question whether the United States exemplifies *true* liberal tolerance and neutrality.

In America, Islam is not tolerated at its core and Muslims do not enjoy equal rights and freedoms that Christians enjoy. Islam's polygamy and Christianity's monogamy are a reflection of diversity of religious practices and cultural expressions. It is problematic to reduce such cultural differences to mere moral disagreements.

The disapproval of polygamy by the Christian majority, which is supported by laws, cannot be couched in purely moral terms. The law against bigamy vitiates true tolerance of Muslims, their freedom, and their diversity of religious practices, which the free exercise clause is supposed to guarantee. One paradoxical way to indicate political neutrality and institutional tolerance of polygamy is for the state to disapprove of the practice, as indicated in the law against bigamy, but to decide not to prosecute Muslims who freely choose polygamous marriage. This will imply that the United States should refrain from using state power to repress what it dislikes. This is implausible because laws do not simply indicate what is morally disliked; they constitute, in their enforcement, "positive acts" of prohibitions. Such laws and their enforcement indicate false tolerance and neutrality, and the laws prevent or repress some people's freedom and ability to *truly* practice their religion in a way that matches their own conceptions of the good.

To borrow an expression from George Orwell's *Animal Farm*, it appears that some choices, values, and conceptions of the good in Western liberal democracies and liberalism are "more equal than others" or more tolerable than others, because they match liberal values or conceptions of human society. This implies that in order for a liberal society to continue to exist as a liberal society, it can only be tolerant of the forms of life that are conducive to the preservation of the liberal ways of life. So a liberal society must be *intolerant* of and *nonneutral* toward the forms of life that are inconsistent with or threatening to its liberal values of human society and the values necessary for its preservation. Thus Robert Paul Wolff doubts whether there is true tolerance and pluralism in American politics:

> There is a sharp distinction in the public domain between legitimate interests and those which are absolutely beyond the pale. If a group or interest is within the framework of acceptability, then it can be sure of winning some measure of what it seeks, for the process of national politics is distributive and compromising. On the other hand, if an interest falls outside the circle of the acceptable, it receives no attention whatsoever and its proponents are treated as crackpots, extremists, or foreign agents.[17]

American liberalism assumes normative and cultural values on the basis of which acceptable limits of tolerance are determined, thus raising questions about whether such tolerance is *true* tolerance. For Wolff, tolerance has become a way of "discriminating not only against certain social groups or interests but also against certain sorts of proposals for the solution of social problems."[18] He suggests that people must transcend mere tolerance, which places social limitations on groups or individuals, to a communal politics of mutual acceptance and respect.

True tolerance and neutrality imply that there is no presupposition about a conception of the good or an institutional framework about what is acceptable, which is not revisable. This involves a dilemma: a liberal must either stretch his tolerance to tolerate what he finds intolerable, which may threaten his way of life, or repress what he finds intolerable because it threatens his way of life. The fact that liberalism must theoretically assume a liberal conception of the good that is consistent with liberal values implies that it cannot be truly tolerant or neutral, because to be truly tolerant is to be tolerant of values and practices that may threaten one's assumed way of life. This raises the issue of whether one can articulate a coherent theory of liberalism that places institutional and normative limits on tolerance, without assuming a conception of the good that determines what is reasonable to tolerate. Such difficulty indicates problems in theories of liberalism, that is, if liberalism is defined essentially in terms of tolerance, neutrality, and individuals' freedom to choose and revise their conceptions of the good, then it is problematic.[19] This problem implies that a liberal account of a state that is truly neutral or both neutral and tolerant is incoherent.[20] However, liberal perfectionists have tried to rescue liberalism from this problem of the conflict between neutrality and tolerance by indicating that liberalism may be tolerant but need not be neutral, because it must assume a liberal conception of the good and cannot be neutral toward every, especially illiberal, conceptions of the good.[21]

Liberal perfectionists argue that liberalism does not require neutrality, because the normative basis for a liberal state, procedures, and laws are a set of liberal principles that must be preserved. Liberal tolerance demands that political actions and states' laws and procedures must exhibit reasonableness and evenhandedness in dealing with different ideas and practices that do not fall within the ambit of the generally accepted liberal principles. In this sense, perfectionist liberalism does not have the same kind of problem that the liberal neutralist will face. However, it does raise questions regarding the extent to which liberal perfectionism is truly liberal, granting that it presupposes a liberal conception of the good as the true social and political values, such that it is only tolerant of ideas that do not threaten the preservation of these values. Any conception of the good that is inconsistent with liberal values is considered false, but it must be dealt with in an evenhanded manner. As such, it does not substantially allow individuals to freely and independently articulate, choose, and revise their own conception of the good. If it is reasonable to have a nonneutral and limited view of tolerance as a plausible view of liberalism, then these issues must be addressed: What is tolerance? Why is tolerance limited in its ability to address the issues of religious diversity and freedom of religion, construed as freedom of cultural expression? In what way are current liberal views of tolerance repressive or cosmetic?

The notion of tolerance implies that X (the tolerator) finds Y (the tolerated) or Y's actions or ideas with respect to a significant issue to be deeply objectionable; X has the power or legitimate authority to repress Y's actions or ideas but refrains from doing so; instead, X "puts up with" Y or Y's action or ideas.[22] To understand the idea of liberal tolerance, it is pertinent to distinguish between its moral and political senses. Steven Lukes understands "tolerance" in the moral sense as a virtue, which requires restraint in spite of one's power to repress what one morally dislikes. "Toleration" in the political sense involves the political practice of not using the power of the state, its institutions, or political authority to repress what one finds morally objectionable.[23] Usually, the political sense of toleration is ascribed to liberalism, in the sense that liberalism involves neutrality, which implies that the state should not favor any conception of the good and that it must refrain from using its power to support or repress any value. I consider these two senses or levels to be coextensive and mutually supportive in that the political action of toleration may engender the moral attitude of tolerance, and if people have the virtue of tolerance, then they are more likely to make it part of their political practice. Political toleration is, in a justificatory sense, dependent on moral tolerance in that toleration is justifiable because it involves the virtue of tolerance.

In Peter Nicholson's view, "toleration is the virtue of refraining from exercising one's power to interfere with others' opinion or action although that deviates from one's own over something important and although one morally disapproves of it."[24] Tolerance involves the negative attitude of dislike and the restraint from acting on such an attitude, and a vertical and asymmetrical relationship between the powerful (tolerator) and the powerless (tolerated). As such, the perspective of the tolerator is given logical and moral priority. Tolerance is seen as a moral virtue because it logically assumes the perspective of the tolerator who has forbearance or restrains from repressing an action or view that is disliked. Ernesto Garzon Valdes argues, "Toleration conceptually presupposes the existence of an underlying, basic normative system in which the act to be tolerated is prohibited; if there is no such system, it does not make sense to speak of toleration."[25] The idea of X tolerating Y is usually deemed morally praiseworthy, without due examination of the rationality and moral validity of X's position, in virtue of which he finds Y's view repugnant. The emphasis is on the restraint from acting in accordance with a negative attitude of disapproval and not the validity of the attitude itself. This view of tolerance allows X to get away with tolerance when the reasonable option is for X either to change his position or to respect and accept the position of Y, because Y's position is morally valid. This view implies that tolerance is not necessarily good; hence toleration may not be the appropriate way to address the problem of religious freedom and diversity of religious practices. The legitimate moral demands of minority cultures are not to be tolerated but recognized and accepted on equal terms with those of the majority.

The moral demand for recognition or acceptance by the tolerated, less powerful minorities can be justified from the perspectives of equality of human dignity and value and an appreciation of the role of culture in shaping human choices, values, and dignity. One should not put up with another value—as demanded by tolerance—without subjecting one's own views to rational examination; and one cannot disapprove of a practice simply because it is considered morally different from the dominant values. The notions of recognition and acceptance imply that cultures be taken seriously and rationally engaged and that rational efforts be made to understand them. The implication of the analysis of tolerance as a negative attitude and a vertical asymmetrical relationship is that it involves a moral choice. It is significantly different from the attitude of indifference and from the attitude of acceptance, respect, valuing, or recognition. Tolerance is a rational attitude of choice, requiring a deliberate consideration of reasons for putting up with and refraining from repressing ideas or actions that one finds objectionable. The notion of tolerance implies, according to Valdes, two normative systems: one is the Basic Normative system, which specifies what is morally acceptable and what can be morally disapproved of, and the other, the Justifying Normative system, specifies the justification for restraining from repressing what one disapproves of.[26]

Valdes's view implies that there is a conflict between these two normative systems and that this conflict is resolved in favor of tolerance, which is justified by the higher moral principle that engenders restraint on the part of the tolerator. These principles represent some conceptions of the good, which reflect the ethos of the tolerator or majority, on the basis of which the limits and scope of what is to be tolerated is determined. So toleration does not take seriously or give credence to the moral perspective of the tolerated or consider its adequacy and merit. Because tolerance does not place any moral strictures on the adequacy of the view of the tolerator, it does not require the tolerator to understand or take the view of the tolerated seriously or rationally engage it. In this regard, tolerance only implies, according to Newey, that "the tolerator has to feel the competing pull of reasons for intervention and reasons for restraint."[27] However, feeling the competing pull of reasons as a condition for tolerance does not require that the reasons be adequate. Tolerance is different from indifference because to be indifferent is to fail to engage in a rational deliberation and consideration of reasons regarding whether to find an action or idea objectionable and whether to repress or refrain from repressing such an idea or action. Indifference implies that one has not rationally considered whether and why one dislikes or disapproves of another's action, because such a rational consideration will lead one to some moral conviction. This means that one has not rationally considered one's own moral conviction in order to see whether such a conviction is inconsistent with another point of view that one ought to morally disapprove of. It also means that one does not feel the competing pull of reasons for intervening and restraining that is required by tolerance.

To accept an idea or action rationally is to engage in some deliberation, consideration of reasons, and a decision on justifiable grounds that there should be no disapproval and therefore no reason to refrain from repressing it. In this sense, the idea of acceptance is inconsistent with a dislike that one needs to put up with or tolerate. As such, one cannot, as many have done, analyze the notion of tolerance to include the notion of acceptance.[28] In my view, they are logically distinct. Acceptance requires a rational and critical engagement in an attempt to understand and arrive at a deliberate and conscious judgment. Tolerance does not require understanding or rational engagement because it does not require critical examination of one's own moral stance for disliking what is to be tolerated.[29] Thus the usual argument for the moral view of tolerance is that X, who tolerates Y, has the power to repress Y but refrains from doing so. Such restraint is deemed morally praiseworthy because its opposite, intolerance or repression, is not. For Peter Nicholson, "The opposite of toleration is intolerance."[30] The emphasis is on the opposite.

My view is that tolerance is seen by liberalism as a virtue, a moral ideal, and morally praiseworthy only because it falsely assumes that intolerance is the opposite of or contradictory to tolerance and that intolerance involves not having the restraint to use one's power to repress what one dislikes. Intolerance, which is coextensive with repression, and its cognates, authoritarianism and totalitarianism, are seen as necessarily bad. If intolerance or repression is morally bad and repression is contradictory to tolerance, then the moral unacceptability of repression implies the moral acceptability of tolerance. Liberal theorists defend tolerance by assuming the moral unacceptability of its opposite or contradictory as a basis for its moral acceptability; thus they focus mainly on criticizing repression. My view is that tolerance is, logically, not a moral contradiction of intolerance or repression, but rather they are, logically, moral contraries. If they are seen as moral contradictions, the implication is that the moral unacceptability of persecution or intolerance implies the moral acceptability of tolerance, and vice versa. However, when they are seen as moral contraries, the logical implication is that both cannot be morally acceptable, but both can be morally unacceptable. As moral contraries, the moral unacceptability of persecution does not necessarily imply the moral acceptability of tolerance because tolerance and persecution can be both morally unacceptable. This argument involves a false dichotomy because there are other alternatives of tolerance, such as valuing, accepting, respecting, and recognizing.

George Fletcher makes a similar point by arguing that the two alternatives of tolerance are indifference and respect or acceptance.[31] He accepts that there are cases when tolerance is morally unacceptable; rather, respect or acceptance will be the morally acceptable view. He argues that if disapproval of one's culture—which may be a basis for a better form of life—is based on illegitimate cultural hegemony, then tolerance is unacceptable. Indeed, more than tolerance is needed. Perhaps, acceptance is more appropriate than tolerance in such a situation because, according to Marcuse, "When tolerance . . . serves to neutralize opposition and to render men immune against other and better forms of life, then tolerance has been perverted."[32] Fletcher goes on to argue, "One might say that a minority culture is entitled to more than tolerance. The minority's language, religion, and lifestyle should be accepted, and respected."[33] If one tolerates or represses a view when one ought to accept and respect it, then both toleration or neutrality and repression would be morally unacceptable. However, he concludes that the idea of respect or acceptance cannot be a plausible alternative approach for addressing the issue of diversity of religious and cultural practices if they engender moral disapproval. He says, "When tolerance is born of moral disapproval, one cannot expect the perceived moral order to yield pluralistic respect."[34]

This suggests that the normative limits on tolerance allow liberalism to repress cultural or religious practices because the moral basis for one's disapproval of some cultural and religious expressions cannot yield diversity of views. But Fletcher's argument fails to provide adequate reasons for moral disapproval, but simply assumes, perhaps, on relativist and subjectivist grounds, that such moral disapproval is valid. Fletcher argues that tolerance is the best of the three alternatives of tolerance, indifference, and acceptance, partly because "the notions of acceptance and respect are simply too vague in most cases to undercut the virtue of disapproving or distancing oneself from the behavior of others without trying to suppress what they are doing."[35] He fails to fully appreciate that the notion of tolerance is also vague: in fact, some racists may claim to be tolerant, because there is no constraint on the adequacy of the reason for disapproval. So tolerance is morally unacceptable if there is no legitimate basis for moral disapproval. One may morally dislike something because one is ignorant, prejudiced, or arrogant; these do not constitute a legitimate basis for disapproval. Suppose one dislikes an action because of cultural hegemony or simply because it is different from the "normal" or dominant view of the cultural majority. Suppose one dislikes polygamy as a cultural or religious practice of Muslims because one *simply assumes* monogamy as the "normal" practice because the Judeo-Christian cultural values of the majority say so. Is toleration proper in such a context where adequate moral justification is not available for disliking the practice?[36]

It is clear that if a person tolerates under these conditions, then such tolerance cannot be morally praiseworthy. But how should one determine what to tolerate and what not to? According to Anna Elisabetta Galeotti, the problem with the vertical and asymmetrical view of toleration is that "none of the reasons backing toleration gives due weight to the importance of that difference for the person who is tolerated."[37] There is the need to examine the moral basis for the action of the person being tolerated and whether such a person has any legitimate moral basis for her action that is disapproved of by the tolerator. The fact that someone has not acted on the reason for disapproval, in that such a person is tolerant, does not by itself vitiate or annul the force of the other reasons that the tolerant person has for disliking the action to be tolerated.[38] It is true that the reason for restraining one's action has a greater force, but the reason for disliking the action is also important to an understanding of the notion of tolerance. In order for an act of tolerance to be morally justifiable, there must be legitimate moral reasons for disapproval. Such a legitimate basis must be couched in some universal principles that do not assume the validity or truth of any cultural value or the culture of the majority—the tolerator.

For instance, Rawls offers the idea of "justice as fairness" as a universal normative basis for tolerance in that it "presents itself as a conception of justice that may be shared by citizens as a basis for a reasoned, informed, and willing political agreement."[39] People are able to arrive at this agreement because they have similar normative views of reasonableness or principles for a well-ordered society, which culminate in an overlapping consensus and the basis for social unity. By relying on a normative basis for a state, Locke defends the idea of placing limits on tolerance by insisting that the state should limit the propagation of "opinions contrary to human society, or to those moral rules which are necessary to the preservation of civil society."[40] Such opinions include religious opinions or cultural views or practices that are deemed harmful to others, in that avoiding harm is necessary for the preservation of civil society. By assuming principles of justice as the normative basis of tolerance, Rawls echoes Locke's view by arguing that although a tolerant religious sect does not have the right to suppress an intolerant sect, it can do so in a situation where greater injustices are avoided and greater freedom for all is enhanced.[41] Kymlicka rejects this view by arguing that a liberal state should not prevent or be intolerant of illiberal ideas or cultures, but should seek to influence the people to liberalize.[42] But the idea of "influencing" people to liberalize may involve subtle forms of repression in that it presumptuously assumes that there are *true* conceptions of the good, true liberal, and illiberal values, and that liberal values are the only true values.

The conception of a good society and the moral rules that are necessary for its preservation *must* be, and are indeed, presupposed by every liberal society. The normative basis for tolerance and its honorific view have the following two implausible implications: one should tolerate something that one obviously ought not to or should not, and one can appeal to the apparent honorific idea of tolerance to justify it; and one may merely tolerate things that one ought to, but respect, value, accept, and endorse, by appealing to the assumed honorific notion of toleration. In this sense, tolerance becomes an excuse for not making true, valid, and rational commitments. This is bolstered by the liberal notion of neutrality, which implies that there is a normative vacuum. Such a normative vacuum provides a justification for an individual's freedom to articulate, in any form, her own conception of the good, consistent with her own individual values, which is not encumbered by any predetermined social value. However, the ethos of the dominant majority culture in a state—be it liberal or otherwise, on the basis of which other views or actions are tolerated or not—represents a nonneutral point of view. Thus, Glen Newey argues, "Since toleration requires that the tolerator have reasons for disapproving of the practice, and must nonetheless have reasons for regarding non-intervention as good, the normative vacuum is filled, and neutrality disappears."[43] If this is the case, then no society can be tolerant of every conception of the good. Therefore liberalism must either do away with the idea of neutrality and tolerance, which means it cannot tolerate every conception of the good, or accept that its view of neutrality and tolerance, which assumes the value and ethos of the dominant majority, involves false or cosmetic tolerance and neutrality. Liberal individualism involves cosmetic tolerance, because it usually relies on the falsely *assumed* honorific notion of tolerance as a basis for excusing its attitude of false tolerance instead of acceptance or recognition.

Thus, liberal individualism and its view of religious freedom and tolerance are limited in the effort by liberalism to engender religious and cultural diversity. Cultural differences in Western democracies have, within the ambit of vertical and asymmetrical models of tolerance, culminated in inequality and lack of freedom for minorities. Rawls's liberal theory of justice is inadequate in dealing with the broad view of freedom of religion as a form of cultural identity and expression, because it presupposes that citizens in a social cooperation must see each other as free and equal partners. The notion of tolerance and the moral disapproval of another's action that one is willing to put up with—irrespective of the moral (in)adequacy of the tolerator's position—does not imply moral equality; instead it implies moral asymmetry between the tolerator and tolerated. Galeotti argues that when vertical and asymmetrical tolerance is applied as a political principle, it could undermine reciprocity and mutuality because the equality of the one who is tolerated is not recognized.[44] The problem with the current attitude of liberalism and Western democracies with respect to freedom of religion and religious diversity is not whether they apply principles of justice to individuals who are not equals, but whether they need to recognize and elevate those who belong to the groups that are not recognized to equal status with the majority. The liberal, individualistic, narrow view of freedom of religion, as the right of the individual who is atomistic and abstracted from culture and society, does not address the substantive background conditions of some individuals and their status as cultural minorities, which do not allow them to relate to the dominant majority on the basis of equality and mutuality. This renders suspect the idea that tolerance is justified because it involves respect for individual autonomy and the ability to make free moral choices.

Respect for autonomy is usually provided as the moral foundation for liberal defense of individual rights, such as conscience and religion, in that freedom is a political and legal "recognition" of one's moral autonomy. A problem that confronts liberal tolerance is that of making individuals equal partners, that is, providing background equality in order for the principles of justice and tolerance to be applicable. The assumption is that the principles of justice and tolerance are applicable in a situation where all citizens are equal and autonomous partners in a social cooperation. Rawls's principles of justice cannot be applied to constitutional Western democracies because they do not and cannot provide background equality. As indicated by Galeotti, the normative structure Western democracies assume a distinction between "normal" and "different" individuals or groups. Certain individuals who belong to the dominant majority are "normal," and to them the rules of society fairly apply. The others, the minorities, are "different"; the rules of society do not fairly apply to them. Moreover, "the liberal tradition has developed a well-defined interpretive framework and a highly refined normative doctrine, which have been constitutionally granted and firmly entrenched in the culture and practice of liberal democracy."[45] This suggests that there cannot be genuine freedom that will allow for diversity of religious practices because such diversity can only exist in the context of the normative structures of some specified contents regarding what is tolerable, which are specified in the constitution. If the primary problem of equality is addressed and there is no moral priority of the "normal" majority (tolerator) over "different" minorities (tolerated), that is, if everyone is morally and socially equal, then the principles of justice can be equally applied to everyone. To address these concerns, the normative system that determines what is institutionally tolerable, its justification and limits, must include respect and recognition of values, practices, and conceptions of the good, which derive from minority cultures and religions.

The current liberal individualistic notion and practice of tolerance does not involve a relationship among equals, and as such it is not an adequate attitude or process for dealing with religious freedom and differences. In order for true liberal tolerance to operate adequately in a democracy, in conjunction with liberal principles of justice, it must involve a relationship among free and equal individuals. Tolerance must involve mutual acceptance among equal citizens in order to engender diversity. Valdes argues that such acceptance involves a horizontal sense of tolerance, where the relationship between the tolerator and tolerated is that of reciprocity and mutuality. Such toleration involves a situation "where two persons of equal rank reciprocally tolerated one another's acts, . . . a person A tolerating an act

X of person B, under certain circumstances c, and person B tolerating an act Z of person A, under circumstances c, 'where the tolerated acts X and Z may differ in substance just as the circumstances c and c.'"[46] He argues that the idea of horizontal toleration is consistent with the idea of a social contract, where people who are equal in rank and status freely agree to certain normative terms of social cooperation for the sake of peace. The terms of cooperation and the goal of peace provide the justifying normative basis for tolerance. This kind of horizontal tolerance, which involves consent and social contract among equals, he argues, is a necessary condition for liberal democracy.

Valdes's fundamental point is that the notion of vertical toleration is inconsistent with democracy and that a violation of the spirit and principles of mutual toleration will inflict significant damage on the principles of democracy. He argues that the principles of mutual toleration provide reasonable limits on the scope of toleration, in that the class of actions that cannot be tolerated are those that violate the principles of mutual toleration. This idea implies that a democratic society cannot tolerate people who are intolerant: such intolerance violates mutuality. Using this principle of horizontal and mutual tolerance and the limits it specifies, Valdes argues that it will be inconsistent with democratic principles to deny minority cultures the rights to practice their religion, except that the minorities are intolerant of the majority. Although this analysis of mutual and horizontal tolerance has an advantage over the vertical variant, it is problematic in that it does not address how people who are not equals, such as cultural minorities and a dominant majority, can be mutually tolerant, strictly speaking, of one another. As Marcuse indicates, "The function and value of tolerance depend on the equality prevalent in the society in which tolerance is practiced."[47] It is clear that minorities and the dominant majority in many Western democracies are not equals and cannot be mutually tolerant. So tolerance is limited in its ability to address freedom of religion or to allow for diversity of religious practices, if such practices are construed broadly in terms of cultural expression or identity.

Liberal Multiculturalism and Diversity of Religious Practices

The broader problem of cultural expression and identity in Western democracies is how to maintain equal democratic participation by all citizens, in the face of not only cultural and religious differences, but also the vertical relation between the dominant cultural majority and minorities. The liberal individualistic view of rights, freedom, and tolerance, namely, the constitutional guarantee and noninterference with individual rights, cannot address the concern of minority cultures in multicultural states. Some multiculturalists have charged that "the injustices that have been visited upon various minorities during the course of American history are evidence not of America's failure to live up to its democratic principles in practice, but of the spurious or defective character of those principles themselves."[48] Galeotti has called for an expansion and a reconceptualization of the notion of liberal tolerance to include the positive recognition of minority cultures and their religious differences, so that minorities can enjoy full and equal democratic participation in the public realm.[49] Tolerance in this expanded sense "means literally nothing more than granting the liberty to be and to express one's culture and identity in a given public space."[50] If individual members of minority cultures are to be able to equally participate publicly and fully in the democratic process and not to be penalized for their differences, liberalism must recognize and give them substantive rights so that they will have the same rights as those who belong to the dominant majority culture.

The question is whether the liberal individualistic notion of tolerance can be reconceptualized to include the acceptance of minority cultures and their diverse religious and cultural expressions. I raise this issue because, as indicated earlier, the notions of recognition and acceptance are different from or opposed to the notion of tolerance. A reconceptualization of tolerance, in my view, cannot rescue liberalism from its inadequacies with respect to how it deals with the rights of people who belong to minority cultures. However, Will Kymlicka, among others, has articulated a different view of liberalism that avoids the problems with the liberal individualistic account of rights and religious freedom.[51] This view, which is liberal multiculturalism, argues that one's conception of the good is a function of one's cultural values and that liberalism can defend the rights of cultural and religious groups. Liberal multiculturalism defends the rights of cultures, especially minority cultures, by arguing that one's ability to utilize one's freedoms to articulate and choose one's conception of the good and rationally pursue such a conception, which is a liberal ideal, is dependent on one's culture. One's rights and freedom are meaningless independent of one's cultural identity or membership of a culture. Cultures circumscribe the scope of rational choices and life-plan options; they provide the framework for making free and meaningful rational choices. In this sense, liberalism gives credence to cultural groups, insofar as such groups make individuals' rational free choices meaningful and possible.

For Kymlicka, "Cultures are valuable, not in and of themselves, but because it is only through having access to a societal culture that people have access to a range of meaningful options."[52] Cultural structures provide options as well as the capacity to reflect on and make sense of these options; they give people their sense of value, in virtue of which their options and choices make sense. Kymlicka considers language and religion essential in defining features of a cultural group, and religious practices and values are essential to one's cultural identity, in virtue of which one is able to live a meaningful life. One's freedom to *fully* practice one's religion as an exemplification of one's membership of a culture is important for liberalism and its account of the relationship between individuals and cultures. Kymlicka argues that there are two distinct kinds of cultural minority groups in a state in virtue of which the state is characterized as multicultural: these are *national* and *ethnic* groups. A multicultural state may consist of *polyethnic* or *multinational* groups, or both, and it is important to understand the characteristics and sources of the differences between these cultural groups—ethnicity and nationality—in order to delimit and defend the kinds of rights that they can claim under liberalism. A national group is a distinct ethnic group of people occupying a territory that constitutes their homeland. They are a minority group as a component part of a country, either voluntarily, by association such as federalism, or involuntarily, by colonialism or imperial conquest.

An ethnic group, on the other hand, is a loose group of people that coalesces around some ethnic characteristics in a foreign country because they voluntarily migrated to another country that is not their homeland. Ethnic groups typically want to be accepted in the country to which they have migrated, and at the same time, they want to maintain some unique ethnic identity. Kymlicka argues that various minority cultures are entitled to some special rights. For national groups, some of the defensible group rights include self-government or special democratic representation. As for ethnic groups, they include financial support, legal recognition, and protection with respect to certain religious or cultural practices. These group-differentiated rights seek to protect individuals and their freedom to make meaningful choices. These rights protect people from being discriminated against and prevent *undesired* assimilation, which may deny them their distinct cultural identities that are necessary for meaningful freedom. For instance, immigrants should have the freedom to choose whether they want to maintain or change their cultural values and identities and the conceptions of the good that are consistent with their values. As such, the recognition of some special cultural rights, including religious practices, is a way to provide equal protection for the rights of individuals, which they will otherwise not have because of their minority status.

Institutional recognition of cultures gives individuals substantive rights to cultural and religious expression; it allows people to preserve their cultural and religious values, which in Kymlicka's view, are elements of primary goods. He extends Rawls's argument to show that culture may be considered a primary good and a precondition for and an essential element of self-respect, which is a necessary basis for one's ability to see one's rational life plan and interest as valuable and worth pursuing and one's ability to have confidence in oneself to be able to pursue such a plan. Culture is important for liberalism because it is essential to one's ability and freedom to pursue one's interest, the good life, and a rational life plan in that one's values and beliefs make one's rational life plan meaningful.[53] Kymlicka disagrees with the liberal individualistic view that the values and principles that form the unifying basis for citizenship in a liberal state must be neutral regarding individual's culture and religions. He rejects the view that people are citizens of a liberal state, not in virtue of their culture or religion, but in virtue of their commitment to some principles or moral ideals such as freedom, equality, or justice. Kymlicka's approach to the broader issue of diversity of religious practices and cultural expressions indicates that minority cultures should be granted special rights and recognition with respect to some cultural practices and that some of the practices of minority cultures have to be tolerated.

The problem with Kymlicka's brand of liberalism is that to grant special rights to some cultures is inconsistent with the liberal principles of neutrality and egalitarianism, which require that all rights be treated equally and that no preference should be given to anyone's rights. If these principles are violated by granting special rights to individuals who belong to some cultures, in the name of justice, then it creates a problem for liberalism and its conception of justice, impartiality, and equality. A liberal account of minority rights, some argue, should not violate principles of distributive justice and equality. Minorities cannot have rights that others do not have: all they can legitimately demand is to have equal rights as everyone else.[54] Granting special rights to minorities is problematic, on the one hand, because it gives them preference. On the other, such an approach may not be enough in that it is merely cosmetic and symbolic. This is because the problem is that the theoretical assumptions of liberalism and the liberal institutional structures are faulty in the way that they deal with minorities and will need to be modified to accommodate minorities. To operate within these structures to meet the needs of minorities may violate the fundamental normative principles of liberalism or provide a cosmetic fix that does not address the fundamental problems with liberalism. Critics argue that liberalism cannot, from the perspective of equality, recognize minority cultures or grant them special rights, because it is impossible to argue for the equality of cultural values or cultures: this is what liberal multiculturalist proponents of diversity of cultural and religious practices demand.

According to Wilson McWilliams, the idea of liberalism implies that some cultures, those which accept liberal values, are better than others.[55] The idea of equality of cultures—that liberal values are not better than repressive values—is a rival theory to liberalism. The idea of cultural equality implies cultural relativism, thus denying that there is a legitimate normative basis for one culture or religion to criticize another. This is a problem for Kymlicka's liberalism, which argues that minority cultures should be given special rights that will enable them to be equal to other cultures. Kymlicka's view of liberalism is, in my view, theoretically implausible because it represents a way of life and conception of the good, which must place limits on tolerance in order to be sustained. These limits are derived from assumed normative conceptions of the good or society, which have priority over individual cultures. As a normative theory, liberal multiculturalism must have elements of intolerance toward some kinds of cultures. It must theoretically assume limits on its view of tolerance—what it can or cannot tolerate based on its normative assumption—in order to exist and flourish as a culture of liberal diversity. So if tolerance and diversity are essential elements of liberal multiculturalism and, as a normative view, it requires limits on tolerance based on its values, then it is incoherent in that it clearly cannot allow for free exercise of diverse religious practices that are inconsistent with the assumed values and principles.

Kymlicka argues that minority cultures cannot have all they want in terms of special rights and that there are limits on the kinds of practices that can be tolerated and recognized. According to him, the limits of liberal tolerance imply that "the demands of some groups exceed what liberalism can accept. Liberal democracies can accommodate and embrace many forms of cultural diversity, but not all."[56] This is because liberalism, as a normative principle, accepts a specific idea of tolerance, which involves the freedom of individuals to autonomously act and make choices and to articulate their own conception of the good. Rawls accepts that although liberalism should be neutral toward different conceptions of the good or ways of life, "no society can include within itself all forms of life."[57] Kymlicka justifies placing limitations on tolerance of certain polyethnic group rights and privileges in favor of integration and assimilation. He insists that anyone who decides to migrate to another country is aware of the situation and has made a conscious choice, in some sense, to accept the way of life in that country and to try not to change it. One cannot expect to be granted all the cultural and religious rights that one would otherwise enjoy in one's native homeland.[58] This kind of argument may be a reasonable basis for outlawing polygamy in the United States and not tolerating it, in spite of the fact that it is an inherent way of life and a plausible conception of the good that Muslims ought to be able to freely choose as a rational life plan.

Such an argument is not convincing if a society claims to be truly liberal, neutral, and tolerant. A truly liberal and tolerant society must respect people's autonomy and grant freedom for individuals to make independent rational choices about their life plan, consistent with their own conception of the good. Such a society should not prevent people from making such choices by legal restrictions that are overreaching. If people want to make specific choices on pragmatic grounds regarding polygamy and language requirements as opposed to the legal restrictions, in that learning English will enable them to live a meaningful life in the United States, it should be their free choice. For a state to impose such restrictions, as indicated in the laws of many Western democracies, is to be institutionally intolerant or to lack neutrality. Borrowing from Stanley Fish's idea of "boutique multiculturalism" and Herbert Marcuse's notion of "repressive tolerance,"[59] it appears that current liberal theories and practices, which require normative and institutionally limited tolerance of cultural and religious practices, involve forms of "boutique liberalism, neutrality, and tolerance," and "repressive tolerance." The idea or practice of boutique liberalism or repressive tolerance suggests an internal incoherence in liberalism.

What currently exists in Western democracies, as indicated by the law against bigamy in the United States, is the kind of toleration that Marcuse calls repressive tolerance, whereby minority groups and individuals who belong to these groups are "repressively tolerated." This kind of tolerance, which Guy Haarscher calls passive tolerance, he argues, is coextensive with racism and similar attitudes that call for segregation, exclusion, or mere coexistence with people instead of actually accepting, recognizing, and giving them equal and full participation in public democratic citizenship. He argues that the similarity between racism and passive tolerance has to do with the idea, "In both cases the 'other' is not really perceived as an *alter ego*; at most, one coexists with him, and at the very worst one crushes or deports him when one finds a way of doing it."[60] He insists that this kind of passive tolerance cannot sustain a democratic society of free and equal citizens. What is needed is active tolerance, that is, the recognition of the other in his or her difference. This implies antiethnocentrism, that is, "the rejection of any domination of one culture by another: This is the meaning, in our contemporary 'multicultural' societies, of the requirement of respect and 'tolerance' for the other culture."[61] He understands this kind of multicultural "tolerance" to be the active form of accepting and respecting culture as a *holistic entity*. This implies that we avoid the superficial, peripheral, or boutique tolerance of cultures that we find in current theories and practices of liberalism, where only some peripheral practices of a culture are tolerated, and not its core values.

This kind of tolerance or liberalism, which I refer to as "boutique tolerance or liberalism," is similar to Fish's idea of "boutique multiculturalism." According to Fish,

> Boutique multiculturalism is characterized by its superficial or cosmetic relationship to the objects of its affection. Boutique multiculturalists admire or appreciate or enjoy or sympathize with or (at the very most) 'recognize the legitimacy of' the traditions of cultures other than their own; but boutique multiculturalists will always stop short of approving other cultures at a point where some value at those cultures' center generates an act that offends against the canons of civilized decency, as they have been either declared or assumed.... A boutique multiculturalist may honor the tenets of religions other than his own, but he will draw the line when the adherents of a religion engage in the practice of polygamy.[62]

A boutique liberal will resist any effort to expand his view in order to recognize and accept a different culture at its core; he is willing to tolerate another culture only at its periphery. The reason is that such a boutique liberal does not take seriously core cultural differences that give rise to the need for tolerance. What he sees as cultural differences, which are at the periphery of a culture, are symbolic manifestations such as clothing, music, and cuisine. He sees differences simply as matters of lifestyle: he will listen to rap music, admire African attires, and patronize soul food or Chinese restaurants. For such a boutique liberal who is engaged in boutique tolerance, these differences should not be allowed to overshadow what really matters: that is, the rational ability for people to see equality, freedom, and justice as universal values and to use them to articulate and choose a conception of the good. Anyone's conception of the good that is inconsistent with these values cannot be tolerated by the boutique liberal. In fact, he will consider such a person to be irrational or less of a human being.

Fish denies the plausibility of multiculturalism that can be defended within the ambit of liberal tolerance and neutrality. He argues that multiculturalism—and in my view any form of liberalism—cannot plausibly articulate tolerance as an overriding principle of political action. To specify tolerance as an overriding principle is problematic, according to Fish, because one cannot afford to be unfaithful to it, even if there are intolerable things that cannot be tolerated. A tolerant person is bound to come face-to-face with some core aspects of another culture or value—in virtue of which it is distinct from his—that he will find intolerable. So there is a sense in which, according to Fish, all religions and cultures—liberal or otherwise— are at their core intolerant of alternative practices because they presuppose that the core of their own cultures represent the only reasonable, if not the true, conception of the good, which determines the limits and scope of tolerance. What is required of liberalism to have diversity of religious practices, as a form of cultural expression, is acceptance. This requires understanding and rational engagement. Such acceptance should not only be on the part of individuals but must also be reflected in the institutional principles of a society. This will require Western liberal democracies to change laws that, for instance, penalize polygamy or some other cultural and religious practices.

Liberal theories and practices in Western liberal democracies, as their laws indicate, have not adequately appreciated the need for true cultural and religious diversity, which requires holistic understanding and acceptance. Herbert Marcuse argues that tolerance in modern liberal states is a repressive tolerance: "What is proclaimed and practiced as tolerance today, is in many of its most effective manifestations serving the cause of oppression."[63] The groups that suffer repressive tolerance are cultural and religious minorities, and such repressive tolerance places limits on the amount and extent of diversity of religious practices. Marcuse argues that the range and limits of tolerance cannot be defined in terms of the respective societal values.[64] He argues that tolerance is an end in itself; it cannot be limited by societal values. To assume a societal conception of the good as a basis for characterizing and limiting tolerance is circular. The idea of liberalism, tolerance, or impartiality in Western democracies, which assumes Judeo-Christian tradition and liberal values, in Marcuse's view, "serves to minimize or even absolve prevailing intolerance and suppression."[65]

CONCLUSION

The idea here is that *true* tolerance, which should be the goal of liberalism, as opposed to boutique tolerance or repressive tolerance, includes having deep respect for different cultural and religious expressions in a holistic form—both at their cores and peripheries. True tolerance suggests that people should holistically value diverse religious expressions. A boutique liberal that is cosmetically tolerant only accords superficial respect for other cultures and religious expressions. He will withdraw such respect when he finds that particular practices of other cultures and religious expressions are inconsistent with his own religious and cultural values. Without critically examining his own values or conception of the good, he illegitimately presupposes his own values as the basis for defining tolerance. As opposed to mere tolerance, the true liberal ought to try to understand, engage, and, in some sense, holistically accept cultural and religious expressions because they are valid. A true liberal ought to also respect individuals' autonomy, rights, and freedom to form their own identities and to articulate or nourish their own cultural identities and structures, which shape their conceptions of the good and rational life plan.

NOTES

1. John Rawls, *Political Liberalism* (New York: Columbia Univ. Press, 1993), 193.

2. William Connolly, "The Dilemma of Legitimacy," in *Legitimacy and State*, ed. William Connolly (Oxford, U.K.: Blackwell, 1984), 233.

3. John Locke, *Second Treatise of Government*, ed. C. B. Macpherson (Indianapolis, Ind.: Hackett, 1980); J. S. Mill, *On Liberty*, ed. G. Himmelfarb (Hammondsworth, U.K.: Penguin, 1982); John Rawls, *A Theory of Justice*, rev. ed. (Cambridge, Mass.: Harvard Univ. Press, 1999), and "Kantian Constructivism in Moral Theory," *Journal of Philosophy* 77 (1980): 515–72; Ronald Dworkin, *Taking Rights Seriously* (Cambridge, Mass.: Harvard Univ. Press, 1977), and "In Defense of Equality," *Social Philosophy and Policy* 1 (1983): 24–40.

4. James Ceaser, "Multiculturalism and American Liberal Democracy," in *Multiculturalism and American Democracy*, ed. Arthur M. Melzer, Jerry Weinberger, and M. Richard Zinman (Lawrence: Kansas Univ. Press, 1998), 152.

5. Walter Berns, "Constitutionalism and Multiculturalism," in *Multiculturalism and American Democracy*, 102.

6. Rawls, "Kantian Constructivism in Moral Theory," 543.

7. Dworkin, "In Defense of Equality," 24, and Rawls, *A Theory of Justice*, 511.

8. Will Kymlicka, *Multicultural Citizenship: A Liberal Theory of Minority Rights* (Oxford, U.K.: Clarendon, 1995), 195.

9. Will Kymlicka, "Two Models of Pluralism and Tolerance" and T. M. Scanlon "The Difficulty of Tolerance" in *Toleration*, ed. David Heyd (Princeton, N.J.: Princeton Univ. Press, 1996), draw attention to the difference in the notion of tolerance when applied to individuals in their dealings with others and to groups with respect to their ability to take part in social and political institutions.

10. J. S. Mill, "Consideration on Representative Government," in *Utilitarianism, Liberty, Representative Government*, ed. H. Acton (London: J. M. Dent, 1972), 230–33. Many theorists argue that in order for people to be citizens of a state, they must share or have in common fundamental values that provide the basis for social unity.

11. Rawls, *Political Liberalism*, 277.

12. Ibid.

13. Ibid., 222.

14. Ibid., 277.

15. Ceaser, "Multiculturalism and American Liberal Democracy," 152.

16. John Locke, *A Letter Concerning Toleration* (Indianapolis, Ind.: Library of Liberal Arts, 1955).

17. Robert Paul Wolff, "Beyond Tolerance," in *A Critique of Pure Tolerance*, ed. Robert Paul Wolff, Barrington Moore Jr., and Herbert Marcuse (Boston: Beacon, 1965), 44.

18. Ibid., 49.

19. Rawls, *Political Liberalism*; C. Larmore, *Patterns of Moral Complexity* (Cambridge, N.Y.: Cambridge Univ. Press, 1987); and Thomas Nagel, *Equality and Partiality* (New York: Oxford Univ. Press, 1991) do not make any distinction between tolerance and neutrality; they sometimes use them interchangeably or assume that one implies the other.

20. Saldin Meckled-Garcia, "Toleration and Neutrality: Incompatible Ideal?" *Res Publica* 7 (2001): 292–313.

21. See, among others, Joseph Raz, *The Morality of Freedom* (Oxford, U.K.: Clarendon, 1986), and Stephen Macedo, *Liberal Virtues: Citizenship, Virtue, and Community in Liberal Constitutionalism* (Oxford, U.K.: Clarendon, 1990).

22. This view is commonplace. See Peter P. Nicholson, "Toleration as a Moral Ideal," in *Aspects of Toleration: Philosophical Studies*, ed. John Horton and Susan Mendus (New York: Methuen, 1985), 158–73; Anna Elisabetta Galeotti, "Do We Need Toleration as a Moral Virtue?" *Res Publica* 7 (2001): 273–92; Glen Newey, "Is Democratic Toleration a Rubber Duck?" *Res Publica* 7 (2001): 315–36; Ernesto Garzon Valdes, "Some Remarks on the Concept of Toleration," *Ratio Juris* 10 (June 1997): 127–38; and Meckled Garcia, "Toleration and Neutrality: Incompatible Ideal?"

23. Steven Lukes, "Toleration and Recognition," *Ratio Juris* 10 (June 1997), 214n 2; Galeotti, "Do We Need Toleration?" 273n 1; David Heyd, introduction to *Toleration*, 17n 1, says *tolerance* and *toleration* may be used interchangeably.

24. Nicholson, "Toleration as a Moral Ideal," 158–73.

25. Valdes, "Some Remarks on the Concept of Toleration," 133.

26. Ibid., 130.

27. Newey, "Is Democratic Toleration a Rubber Duck?" 317.

28. See Anna Elisabetta Galeotti, "Contemporary Pluralism and Toleration," *Ratio Juris* 10 (June 1997): 223–35; Michael Walzer, "The Politics of Difference: Statehood and Toleration in a Multicultural World," *Ratio Juris* 10 (June 1997): 165–76; Lukes, "Toleration and Recognition"; Valdes, "Some Remarks on the Concept of Toleration."

29. For a similar view, see Barbara Herman, "Pluralism and the Community of Moral Judgment," in *Toleration*, 60–80.

30. Nicholson, "Toleration as a Moral Ideal," 158–73.

31. George P. Fletcher, "The Case for Tolerance," in *The Communitarian Challenge to Liberalism*, ed. Ellen Frankel Paul, Fred O. Miller Jr., and Jeffrey Paul (Cambridge, N.Y.: Cambridge Univ. Press, 1996), 229–39.

32. Herbert Marcuse, "Repressive Tolerance," in *A Critique of Pure Tolerance*, 111.

33. Fletcher, "The Case for Tolerance," 238.

34. Ibid.

35. Ibid., 239.

36. I cannot address the issue of whether polygamy is morally wrong. I do this elsewhere. I argue that monogamy is anchored in the idea of a selfish, acquisitive, and possessive view of romantic love and the extreme jealousy of not wanting another person to share in what we love and that we have acquired and want to possess exclusively.

37. Galeotti, "Do We Need Toleration as a Moral Virtue?" 275.

38. Newey, "Is Democratic Toleration a Rubber Duck?" 317.

39. Rawls, *Political Liberalism*, 9.

40. Locke, *A Letter Concerning Toleration*, 45.

41. This principle can be found in John Rawls's argument for limiting freedom of conscience: you can justifiably limit freedom or be intolerant for the sake of ensuring greater freedom for all or preventing greater injustice. See Rawls, *A Theory of Justice*, 186–94.

42. Kymlicka, *Multicultural Citizenship*, 94–95.

43. Newey, "Is Democratic Toleration a Rubber Duck?" 326.

44. Galeotti, "Do We Need Toleration as a Moral Virtue?" 290.

45. Galeotti, "Contemporary Pluralism and Toleration," 224. Also see 230–33 for a discussion of how the liberal neutralist does not appreciate this distinction between cultural "difference" and "normality."

46. Valdes, "Some Remarks on the Concept of Toleration," 129.

47. Marcuse, "Repressive Tolerance," 84.

48. Marc F. Platter, "Liberal Democracy, Universalism, and Multiculturalism," in *Multiculturalism and American Democracy*, ed. Arthur M. Melzer, Jerry Weinberger, and M. Richard Zinman, 160.

49. Galeotti, "Contemporary Pluralism and Toleration," and "Do We Need Toleration as a Moral Virtue?"

50. Galeotti, "Contemporary Pluralism and Toleration," 231.

51. Kymlicka, *Multicultural Citizenship*, and *Liberalism, Community, and Culture* (Oxford, U.K.: Clarendon Press, 1989); Jeff Spinner, *The Boundaries of Citizenship*; Charles Taylor, "The Politics of Recognition," in *Multiculturalism and the Politics of Recognition*, ed. Amy Gutman (Princeton, N. J.: Princeton Univ. Press, 1992), 27–73; Iris Marion Young, *Justice and the Politics of Difference* (Princeton, N. J.: Princeton Univ. Press, 1990); Joseph Raz, "Multiculturalism: A Liberal Perspective," *Dissent* (winter 1994): 67–79.

52. Kymlicka, *Multicultural Citizenship*, 83.

53. Kymlicka, *Liberalism, Community, and Culture*, chap. 8.

54. See Alon Harel, "The Boundaries of Justifiable Tolerance: A Liberal Perspective," in *Tolerance*, ed. David Heyd, 114–26.

55. Wilson McWilliams, "Democratic Multiculturalism," in *Multiculturalism and American Democracy*, ed. Arthur M. Melzer, Jerry Weinberger, and M. Richard Zinman, 124.

56. Kymlicka, *Multicultural Citizenship*, 152.

57. Rawls, *Political Liberalism*, 197.

58. Kymlicka, *Multicultural Citizenship*, 95–97.

59. See Stanley Fish, "Boutique Multiculturalism," in *Multiculturalism and American Democracy*, ed. Arthur M. Melzer, Jerry Weinberger, and M. Richard Zinman, 69–88, and Marcuse, "Repressive Tolerance," 81–123. I accept Marcuse's analysis of the current state of tolerance in Western liberal democracies,

but I do not accept his idea of withdrawing tolerance at the stage of communication before deeds. My view is that more than tolerance is needed.

60. Guy Haarscher, "Tolerance of the Intolerant?" *Ratio Juris* 10 (June 1997): 238.
61. Ibid., 239.
62. Fish, "Boutique Multiculturalism," 69.
63. Marcuse, "Repressive Tolerance," 81.
64. Ibid., 84.
65. Ibid., 98.

Dealing with the Unfinished Business of America

Fighting Bias, Bigotry, and Racism in the Twenty-first Century

SANFORD CLOUD JR.

THE NATIONAL CONFERENCE FOR COMMUNITY AND JUSTICE: ITS HISTORY AND WORK

The National Conference for Community and Justice (NCCJ) is a human relations organization. Its mission is "to fight bias, bigotry and racism and to promote understanding and respect among races, religions and cultures through advocacy, conflict resolution and education."

Although you may not recognize the name, NCCJ has a long history. It was founded in 1927 by people who were concerned about religious intolerance, racial injustice, and social injustice. Among its founders were leaders in their day, including Charles Evans Hughes, later a U.S. Supreme Court chief justice, Jane Addams, Benjamin Cardoza, and Roger W. Straus.

One of their motivations for creating the National Conference of Jews and Christians for the Advancement of Justice, Amity and Peace, as it was first called, was the religious intolerance directed toward Alfred E. Smith, governor of New York, when he ran for the office of president of the United States. Al Smith was Catholic, and a movement against him developed because of his religious affiliation, with fears that the pope might influence the decision making of the state. During this same period in the late 1920s, the Ku Klux Klan was strong, and there was also growing anti-Semitism and racial injustice toward African Americans.

Over the years, the National Conference of Christian and Jews, as the organization was called for much of its history, focused on religious tolerance and interfaith engagement, issues of integration, and police-community relations.

In the early 1990s, it changed its name to the National Conference, to show that its mission was to battle bias wherever it occurred. But that name didn't quite provide enough meaning. So a few years ago, in 1998, we changed it to the National Conference for Community and Justice, to better reflect the breadth and depth of its mission, the growing diversity of the country and our need to be more inclusive.

NCCJ has a vision to make America a better place for all of us, not just some of us. Our mission-focused work lifts up the theme of transforming communities through institutional change by empowering leaders. NCCJ presently focuses on six sectors of leadership: faith, business and philanthropy, government, education, media and advertising, and youth and emerging leaders. We pursue our work through programmatic strategies, research, and advocacy. We do our work in different ways at different times. For example, our Faith Leaders Initiative, which President Clinton asked us to lead—has us working with a diverse group of faith leaders to collectively use their voices and faith institutions to fight racism. Together, we declared racism a sin, a problem of the heart, an evil that must be eradicated; we have encouraged these faith leaders to guide their denominations, congregations, and communities toward institutional change. They are also focused on their individual reflections regarding their own biases and prejudices. We all have stereotypes, biases, and prejudices that mar our vision. True reflection by leaders allows them to be better-empowered leaders, more able to make our communities whole, just, and inclusive.

NCCJ also promotes civil—but honest—dialogue among diverse leadership, regarding the disparities in health, education, and economic opportunity across the divides of race and what can be done about it. Partners include Aetna Incorporated, Tenet Healthcare, Bank of America, the W. K. Kellogg Foundation, and other progressive companies and organizations. Our advocacy includes fighting for a federal hate crimes bill with other major civil and human rights organizations. All of this work is informed by research, because there is so much uninformed rhetoric regarding bias, bigotry, and racism.

My personal passion and focus is building bridges of understanding and respect across the divides on racial healing and reconciliation and engaging in the fight against other "isms."

September 11: The Challenge and Opportunity

As I watched on television with horror the second plane crashing into the South Twin Tower, my instincts told me that this was not an accident but an act of terror. But by whom? Who could be that bold and daring to attack the United States so directly?

Next came a report that the Pentagon had been hit; and then, not much later, a report that the Twin Towers had fallen to the ground; and that a plane had gone down in the countryside of Pennsylvania.

Later that day, knowing that my own family and our colleagues at NCCJ were safe—I reflected on the loss of the other families. For those who did not know whether their loved ones were safe—the anxiety of not knowing and then the pain of knowing they would not return—makes one pause; it makes one pause to appreciate the blessings of life, of family, of friends, of the work we are able to pursue; to be thankful for what we have and enjoy; to pay homage and honor to those who gave their lives trying to save others—those fire, police, and medical services people; the heroes of United Flight 93 who stopped another intended hit; the man who led a Pentagon colleague, whom he did not know, to safety against great odds, challenged by smoke and fire—to shed a tear for the three children and three teachers on the plane that hit the Pentagon who were on their way to the Channel Islands off the coast of Santa Barbara to study the environment (they were being honored for their academic achievement by National Geographic).

On that day, the world in which we live, work, and pursue our dreams dramatically changed. It would change us individually, institutionally, as a country and our collective world perspective, and how we, as a nation, should engage the global community.

The horrific events of September 11 strongly indicate that we still have much work to do. During these trying times, is it possible for us to do a better job in the world helping to build community across the divides of race, ethnicity, faith, and culture? I believe it is—but not without some further, deeper reflection and understanding about how we can play a more effective role in advancing civil societies around the globe, consistent with their cultures and, to the extent possible, our own values. It may well be that the United States has a bigger role to play in nation building than we had previously thought. NCCJ may have, over time, an appropriate role to play in assisting leaders in other countries to build just and inclusive communities across the divides. Until then, we have a considerable amount of unfinished business in the United States on which to focus.

Racial and ethnic profiling continue to challenge us as Muslims, Arabs, and South Asians become its new victims in the aftermath of September 11. Their civil liberties are challenged. Hate crimes continue to torment segments of our communities. Disparities in access to, and quality of, health care continue across racial and ethnic lines. Recent reports suggest that there is resegregation occurring in our public school systems. Discrimination still occurs too often in our workplaces and in the broader arena of economic opportunity.

We are a diverse country, becoming ever more so. We are now a nation of some 270 million people; by 2030, we will be a nation of approximately 330 million, with one third of this new anticipated growth coming from Central and South America and South and East Asia. By 2050, we will be a nation one-half white and one-half people of color. Latinos continue to grow in population, surpassing African Americans as the largest community of color. We are also becoming more diverse in religious and faith communities.

America's population of Hindus has grown from 225,000 in 1990 to more than one million today. Buddhism is rapidly expanding in the United States with some 2,400,000 at present. Islam is now thought to be the fastest growing organized faith in America—soon to be the second largest numerically in our nation. In fact, the number of Muslims today is at least four million and may be as large as seven million. This ever-growing diversity can be utilized as a tool toward strengthening our democracy, or it can create major tensions and weaken it. If we are to celebrate this growing diversity, we must start by taking the time to pause and to learn the histories, culture, and religions of other peoples. In return, they must come to learn and understand ours, including, but not limited to, the matter of slavery, its legacy and impact on all of us. We may do some of this through education and study. But, above all, we need conversation.

NCCJ, in partnership with the Aetna Foundation, just held its seventh and most successful Voice of Conscience: Annual National Conversation on Race, Ethnicity and Culture in January of 2001. This year's conversation, moderated by Juan Williams, focused on the evolving role of religion in our society. It was held at the National Press Club on January 15, 2001, Martin Luther King Jr.'s birthday, and was carried live and rebroadcast throughout the following weeks by C-Span. It was an extraordinary conversation with very diverse views. In connection with this conversation, we released powerful pieces of informed knowledge, *Denouncing Racism: A Resource Guide of Faith-Based Principles and Faith Leaders on Intergroup Relations: Perspectives and Challenges,* the next piece in NCCJ's Occasional Papers monograph series. These are tools that can be utilized to enhance understanding and respect. I urge you to read them and share them widely with your colleagues.

The Voice of Conscience Conversation provides further opportunity for NCCJ to bring together leaders of the faith communities, not only to better understand each other's faith but also to take their rightful place of leadership in the process of engaging the social justice issues of the day.

Faith leaders must not only plan interfaith services but also do the harder work of bringing newer faith communities and cultures increasingly present in our society into the mainstream of civic service and the broader community life. Otherwise they will become isolated from it, and we all lose by their lack of involvement.

Faith leaders must advocate for enactment of hate crimes legislation wherever it is lacking and speak out against racial and ethnic profiling wherever it may surface.

Faith leaders must probe leadership about why there continues to be such disparity in the achievement of young people across racial, ethnic, and religious divides and question the push for "English only" legislation that adversely impacts Latinos, the largest growing population segment in our country.

Faith leaders must be vigilant against gender discrimination, homophobia, and anti-Semitism: they must also question those in leadership positions about why they think that it is all right to continue to humiliate and stereotype the American Indian people by using their images as sports symbols and mascots.

Obviously, there is still far too much bias, bigotry, and racism today as we move into the twenty-first century.

WHY THE CONVERSATION IS NEEDED

It is fair to ask why this conversation is needed. John Hope Franklin, noted historian and chairman of the Advisory Board for President Clinton's Initiative on Race, said it best in his book, *The Color Line: Legacy for the Twenty-first Century*:

> Without any pretense of originality, . . . with less than a decade left in this century, I venture to state categorically that the problem of the twenty-first century will be the problem of the color line. This conclusion arises from the fact that by any standard of measurement or evaluation the problem has not been solved in the twentieth century, and this becomes a part of the legacy and burden of the next century. Consequently, it follows the pattern that the nineteenth century bequeathed to the twentieth century and that the eighteenth century handed to its successor.[1]

A look at a few statistics and the disparities that they indicate underscores the correctness of Dr. Franklin's belief and the need for an enhanced set of conversations and new actions resulting, in part, from the legacy of slavery.

Take health care, of which Martin Luther King Jr. said, "Of all the forms of inequality, injustice in health care is the most shocking and inhumane." The statistics tell the story of disparity based on race:

• Did you know that heart disease strikes nearly twice as many African American women as compared to whites?

- Or that 37 percent of all AIDS cases reported are African American, even though we account for only 12 percent of the population?
- Or that in 2000 the U.S. Census Bureau's Current Population Survey found that African Americans were nearly twice as likely as whites to be without health insurance?

Disparities are evident in the area of education as well. About one in six blacks, or 17 percent, have completed college, compared with 28 percent of all whites. Eighty-eight percent of whites are high school graduates, compared with 79 percent of blacks twenty-five years or older.

In the area of economic opportunity, African Americans are about "twice as likely as whites—23 versus 12 percent—to hold lower paying, less prestigious service jobs." African Americans are also "more than twice as likely to be unemployed; in May [2001], the jobless rate for Blacks stood at 8 percent, compared with 3.8 percent among whites." African Americans are "about half as likely as whites to have money invested in stocks, bonds or mutual funds."[2]

If you add to these disparities the continuing housing segregation and criminal justice issues disproportionately impacting the black community, one could reasonably conclude that racism is still alive and well and that the legacy of slavery has played a role in what we see happening today in black communities and communities of other people of color.

DISCRIMINATION CONTINUES

I grew up during the civil rights movement, and it made a deep impression on me. The movement gave structure to dreams. It made me believe that social transformation was possible and that men and women of faith—and lawyers—could lead the way, if only we had the right laws. If only we had the right leaders to enforce them.

In some ways, we were right. Legal remedies have made a difference. The obvious legacies of slavery, the ones easy to see, were dismantled, as "colored-only" drinking fountains and literacy tests for voting became things of the past. But the civil rights laws did not solve the challenges of discrimination. And today we know that laws alone are an incomplete solution—even when they are upheld.

And so, notwithstanding the progress we have made toward a more equitable and inclusive society, we continue to be divided by different life experiences, depending on our color and ethnicity, our economic class, and our faith.

I know this because of my daily experiences, because of what I read, and because of the results of a recent nationwide survey conducted by NCCJ.

Just over a year ago, NCCJ released a follow-up to our 1993 groundbreaking survey,

Taking America's Pulse II. The survey (TAP II) showed that Americans now recognize that discrimination—not just prejudiced beliefs—affects a wide range of groups, from the elderly, illiterate, disabled, and poor to gays and lesbians, African Americans, Asians, Hispanics, and some whites. And we recognize inequality in ways we didn't before the civil rights movement. For example, many respondents concluded that African Americans, Hispanics, and Asians do *not* have equality of opportunity with whites. Stated another way, the survey establishes that people are still divided by discrimination *and* by a lack of access.

As I travel around the nation, my experiences confirm these findings. We still live in communities of isolation—and we still have vastly different realities.

Today, people of Middle Eastern descent are being profiled because of fears. They are now targeted like African Americans and Hispanics, who have been telling us for years about daily racial profiling on highways, whereas some police across the country often deny its existence and object to checking it out—through data collection.

Our interfaith movement has been strong, but we remain isolated across the lines of faith. Disturbingly, the NCCJ survey showed that—of all categories—people are least familiar with different religious groups, in particular, fundamentalist Christians and *especially* Muslims. When asked about closeness with different groups, 36 percent said that they did not even know enough to form an opinion about Muslims, and only 24 percent had ever had contact with a Muslim. We still do not know one another. And maybe that is in large part the reason why we resorted so easily to profiling of this group when terror struck.

Isolated, our social fabric is being torn by discrimination that continues to be "embedded in the bones and blood of the body politic." I share Franklin's belief and suggest the need for an enhanced set of conversations regarding bias, bigotry, and racism, including that which is connected to the legacy of slavery.

The Required Leadership Role

The question is whether faith leaders are prepared to host the forums and promote the dialogues in our communities regarding the legacy of slavery and its impact on all of us. We will never have fuller healing and reconciliation across the racial divides without a serious set of conversations regarding this issue.

The next step required for our country is bold, if we can actually take it. We must engage in a conversation that leads to remedial actions for the conditions resulting from the continuing legacy of slavery. This should include, but not necessarily be limited to, a serious discussion and enactment of H.R. 40, Commission to Study Reparation Proposals for African Americans Act, introduced by Rep. John

Conyers Jr. of Michigan. The bill, which he has introduced in every Congress since 1989 and now has more than forty cosponsors, would address the following issues:

- acknowledge the fundamental injustice and inhumanity of slavery
- establish a commission to study slavery and its subsequent racial and economic discrimination against freed slaves
- study the impact of those forces on today's African Americans
- make recommendations to Congress on appropriate remedies to redress the harm inflicted on living African Americans

As Congressman Conyers has noted,

> Many of the most pressing issues, which have heretofore not been broached on any broad scale, would be addressed. Issues such as the lingering negative effects of the institution of slavery, whether an apology is owed, whether compensation is warranted and, if so, in what form and who should [be] eligible would also be delved into.[3]

A groundswell is occurring around the country for our stalled conversations to continue. They are reflected by resolutions and bills before various city councils and state legislatures regarding acknowledgment of the wrong that slavery did and suggested appropriate remedies. This is heartening. It needs to continue to grow.

In the course of these conversations, it is time to allow for the discussion of reparations. Indeed, reparations may well become the subject of a class action suit against the federal government and certain private sector organizations. Certain corporations have already been targeted. I believe that this venue is unlikely to provide the healing and reconciliation required. I doubt that reparations, without the broader discussion suggested by H.R. 40, is the answer that will move our nation toward reaching its fuller potential.

What More Is Required of Us Now?

Are faith leaders prepared to create safe harbors where the issues that challenge and separate Jews and Muslims and others can be discussed and to promote understanding and respect? Can faith leaders provide a place for a discussion on U.S. Middle East policy without being called anti-Semitic or Palestine haters? Can faith leaders provide a place where we can ask why Muslims, Arabs, and South Asians should enjoy fewer civil liberties than the rest of us?

As we look to the future and consider the issue of racial reconciliation and the social transformation that must occur, we must remember what we have learned, understand the subtle realities of institutionalized racism, and recognize the implications. And then, we must act.

To move us forward, I look to the leaders of our nation, particularly the leaders of our faith communities, because they provide the moral voice of leadership to help close the disparities across the racial divides.

We must do this work. It will not be easy.

As King observed,

Human progress is neither automatic nor inevitable. Even a superficial look at history reveals that no level of human progress goes in on the wheels of inevitability. Rather, it seems clear that every step towards the goals of justice requires sacrifice, suffering, and struggle. Social progress is never attained by passive waiting. It comes only through the tireless efforts and passionate concern of dedicated individuals. Without this persistent work, time itself becomes an ally of the insurgent and primitive forces of irrational emotionalism and social stagnation. So we are challenged to work . . . for the full realization of the dream of brotherhood and integration. This is no time for apathy nor complacency. This is a time for positive action.[4]

But these are complicated and rapidly changing times. Our very nation is quickly being redefined.

BUILDING INCLUSIVE COMMUNITIES

We must be committed leaders. But there is more that we can do to overcome racism.

If we look to another of the findings from TAP II, we learn that there is a correlation between contact, feelings of closeness, and intergroup understanding. Or, to present it in a simpler way, the more contact a person has with different groups, the more likely he or she is to feel close to people who are different from them, and the more likely that person will have a deep understanding of prejudice and discrimination. People who engage those who are different and believe differently from themselves are more likely to conclude that improving our human relations should be a national priority.

In other words, contact is a necessary step to building understanding, to achieving racial reconciliation, and to creating social transformation. If transformation is to occur, we need leaders to come to know those who are different from them, to better understand the depth of prejudice, how discrimination operates in workplaces and other institutions—and why racial healing and social transformation must be a national priority. A nationwide discussion is one way. Reaching out to include and to cross the barriers of difference is another.

Whether from our institutions of faith, law, government, education, media, or the workplace—leaders have influence. They influence the attitudes and behavior of the people in their institutions. And they influence the practices and policies of institutions that can maintain the status quo—or change them to become more inclusive.

When leaders understand—deeply understand—things can change. But to understand how wrongs are perpetrated—how they play out day to day—requires information and the ability to see discrimination in all its subtleties. It requires insight and action by a community of faith leaders committed to building—and preserving—a more just and inclusive society.

- It is time for leaders who are white and who exercise power and influence to understand that they may benefit from white privilege and entitlement.
- It is time for all leaders to understand their own biases. We all have them. But this takes time and a willingness to delve into politically incorrect places in our hearts and souls.
- And finally, our leaders need to learn how to see and how to change institutional racism and prejudice, the institutional racism that occurs when dominant groups create systems to maintain power and influence, preventing the ever-illusive level playing field from becoming our reality.

After these points have occurred, our leaders will be empowered with new understandings and the ability to make a difference. Moving beyond good intentions to action, these leaders—across the sectors—become the agents of change—changing institutions, transforming communities, moving beyond their diversity—to make them more just, more inclusive. We can envision what such transformed communities will look like. They will be more interconnected, and we will see more people assuming communal responsibility. Playing fields will be level—not just in theory but in practice; the tone of the environment will change. Trust will replace fear. Profiling will not be the automatic knee-jerk reaction to a horrific act of terror. And violence will decrease.

We will move to a new level of understanding, collaboration, respect, and commitment. The choice is ours to make.

Are you prepared to act? As leaders yourselves—who can make a personal and professional difference—are you prepared to be part of a bigger movement that sees the need for and insists upon changes that include all people?

I hope you are. I trust you are. Because the racial reconciliation and the ultimate social transformation needed must start with men and women like you. I believe in our collective future.

I am reminded of a speech given by my friend and mentor John Gardner, who died recently at age ninety. He was making a point regarding the leadership that is appropriate for what our responsibility and duty is for community building:

> I keep running into highly capable potential leaders all over this country who literally never give a thought to the well being of their community. And I keep wondering who gave them permission to stand aside! I'm asking you to issue a wake up call to those people—a bugle call right in their ear.
>
> And I want you to tell them that this nation could die a comfortable indifference to the problems that only citizens can solve. Tell them that.[5]

I believe John Gardner was suggesting that "The American Experiment" is still unfolding and still fragile and that upholding the Democratic compact is now particularly up to us. He summarized that compact by saying "freedom and responsibility, liberty and duty, that's the deal."

Let us lead people and institutions where they may not have dared to go before—continuing always to work to become better leaders and colleagues. In doing so, we will change institutions, transform communities to make them more whole and just.

It will be challenging. To do it, we must be ready to learn new skills, to listen in new ways, to hear the merits of what is said with openness and without stereotypes or fear.

We must remember Gandhi's admonition when he said, "We must become the change we want to see." We need to commit ourselves to this effort and learn to live in a way that reflects the transformation that we seek. Only then will we have accepted the responsibility for the future and become accountable for transforming our communities and nation into a model—for our increasingly interconnected globe.

It is up to you. And I call on you—on each of you—to serve as the empowered leaders of a transformed nation, where intergroup relationships are characterized by respect and understanding for all of us; where justice, peace, and equality prevail; where love, freedom, and dignity are the centering core values for all of us. Embrace these principles and values, seize the opportunity, and make America a better place for all of us, not just some of us.

NOTES

1. John Hope Franklin, *The Color Line: Legacy for the Twenty-first Century* (Columbia: Univ. of Missouri Press, 1993), 5.

2. Richard Morin, "Misperceptions Cloud Whites' View of Blacks," *Washington Post*, July 11, 2001.

3. John Conyers Jr., "Reparations: The Commission to Study Reparations Proposals for African American Act," on "Major Issues" Web site for the 14th Congressional District of Michigan, www.house.gov/conyers/news_reparations.htm, April 2002.

4. Martin Luther King Jr., "Address Delivered at the National Biennial Convention of the American Jewish Congress," in *Symbol of the Movement: January 1957–December 1958*, vol. 4 of *The Papers of Martin Luther King, Jr*, ed. Clayborne Carson, Ralph E. Luker, and Penny A. Russell (Berkeley: Univ. of California Press, 2000), 409–10.

5. John Gardner, unpublished speech presented before the San Jose Rotary Club, September 2001.

Selected Bibliography

The cultural, religious, social, and linguistic differences (to name but a few) exhibited in this text enrich the study of democracy and religion. But such plurality also complicates attempts to provide the reader with standard citation information for easy access to the sources. In some instances authors drew on the raw data of experience, while others drew on shared cultural or social knowledge, including oral narratives that do not avail themselves to standard practices of citation. Some citations of print material were neither available nor included in standard indexes. Several authors drew on Web-based sources that did not duplicate print medium and that do not provide basic bibliographical or contact information beyond a Web address (in some cases given the controversial nature of the material, the lack of information may have served to protect the organization or authors from political and economic repercussions). For these unavoidable inadequacies of the bibliography, the editor assumes responsibility.

Achtemeier, Paul J. *Inspiration and Authority: Nature and Function of Christian Scripture.* Peabody, Mass.: Hendrickson, 1999.

Ackerman, Bruce. *Social Justice in the Liberal State.* New Haven, Conn.: Yale Univ. Press, 1980.

Adams, Arlin M., and Charles J. Emmerich. *A Nation Dedicated to Religious Liberty: The Constitutional Heritage of the Religion Clauses.* Philadelphia: Univ. of Pennsylvania Press, 1990.

Ahlstrom, Sydney E. *A Religious History of the American People.* Vol. 2. Garden City, N.Y.: Image, 1975.

Ahmad, Mumtaz. *An Introduction to the Jamaat-i-Islami Pakistan.* Lahore, Pakistan: Jamaat-i-Islami, 1978.

———. "Islamic Fundamentalism in South Asia: The Jamaat-i-Islami and the Tablighi Jamaat of South Asia." In *Fundamentalisms Observed: A Study Conducted by the American Academy of Arts and Sciences,* ed. Martin E. Marty and R. Scott Appleby. Chicago: Univ. of Chicago Press, 1991.

Ajami, Fouad. "The Way We Live Now: 10–01–01; Out of Egypt." *New York Times Magazine*, October 7, 2001.

al-Hirbri, Azizah Y. Interview with Bill Moyers. *Now* (Public Broadcasting Service), February 15, 2002. www.pbs.org/now/transcript/transcript_alhibri.html (accessed December 5, 2003).

Aldridge, Alan. *Religion in the Contemporary World: A Sociological Introduction*. Malden, Mass.: Blackwell, 2000.

Ali, Abdullah Yusuf, trans. *The Glorious Qur'an*. New Delhi, India: Islamic Book Service, 2002.

Ali, Necip. "Halkevleri Yildönümünde Necip Ali Bey'in Nutku" ("Necip Ali Bey's Speech at the Anniversary of the People's Houses"). *Ülkü* 1, no. 2 (1933).

———. "İnkilap ve Türk Kanunu Medenisi" ("Revolution and Turkish Civil Law"). *Ülkü* 2, no. 9 (1933).

Almond, Gabriel A., R. Scott Appleby, and Emmanuel Sivan. *Strong Religion: The Rise of Fundamentalism around the World*. Chicago: Univ. of Chicago Press, 2003.

Althholz, Josef L. *The Churches in the Nineteenth Century*. New York: Bobbs-Merrill, 1967.

Anner, John, ed. *Beyond Identity Politics: Emerging Social Justice Issues in Communities of Color*. Boston, Mass.: South End, 1996.

Antieu, Chester James, Arthur L. Downey, and Edward C. Roberts. *Freedom from Federal Establishment: Formation and Early History of the First Amendment Religions Clauses*. Milwaukee, Wis.: Bruce, 1964.

Appleby, R. Scott. *The Ambivalence of the Sacred: Religion, Violence, and Reconciliation*. Lanham, Md.: Rowman and Littlefield, 2000.

Arinze, Francis A. *Religions for Peace: A Call for Solidarity to the Religions of the World*. New York: Doubleday, 2002.

Armstrong, Karen. *The Battle for God*. New York: Random House, 2000.

———. "The True, Peaceful Face of Islam." *Time*, October 1, 2001.

Arrington, Leonard J. *Brigham Young: American Moses*. New York: Knopf, 1985.

Asim, Ahmet. "Türk İnkilabinin Mana ve Mahiyeti" ("Meaning and True Nature of the Turkish Revolution"). *Ayin Tarihi* (March 1934): 74–75.

Ayubi, Nazih N. *Political Islam: Religion and Politics in the Arab World*. New York: Routledge, 1991.

Barber, Benjamin R. *An Aristocracy of Everyone: The Politics of Education and the Future of America*. New York: Ballantine, 1992.

———. *Jihad vs. McWorld*. New York: Ballantine, 2001.

Barlas, Asma. "Jihad Versus Terrorism: Interpretive Confusion or Exceptionalism," Paper delivered at International Conference on Islam, Lahore, Pakistan, November 2001.

———. "Will the 'Real' Islam Please Stand Up?" Text of talk delivered at the Master's Tea, Sillman College, Yale University, February 21, 2002.

Barr, James. *Fundamentalism*. Philadelphia, Pa.: Westminster, 1978.

Barth, Karl. *Church Dogmatics*. Vol. 1/2. *The Doctrine of the Word of God*. Trans. G. T. Thomson and Harold Knight. Edinburgh, Scotland: T. and T. Clark, 1956.

Becker, Theodore K., and Richard A. Couto, eds. *Teaching Democracy by Being Democratic*. Westport, Conn.: Praeger, 1996.

Bellah, Robert N. *The Broken Covenant: American Civil Religion in Time of Trial.* 2d ed. Chicago: Univ. of Chicago Press, 1975.

Bellah, Robert, ed. *Habits of the Heart: Individualism and Commitment in American Life.* Berkeley: Univ. of California Press, 1985.

Ben-Rafael, Eliezer, and Yitzhak Sternberg, eds. *Identity, Culture and Globalization.* Boston, Mass.: Brill, 2001.

Berger, Peter L. *The Heretical Imperative: Contemporary Possibilities of Religious Affirmation.* Garden City, N.Y.: Anchor/Doubleday, 1979.

———. *The Sacred Canopy: Elements of a Sociological Theory of Religion.* Garden City, N.Y.: Doubleday, 1967.

Berkes, Niyazi. *The Development of Secularism in Turkey.* Montreal, Canada: McGill Univ. Press, 1966.

Berns, Walter. "Constitutionalism and Multiculturalism." In *Multiculturalism and American Democracy,* ed. Arthur M. Melzer, Jerry Weinberger, and M. Richard Zinman, 91–111. Lawrence: Kansas Univ. Press, 1998.

———. *The First Amendment and the Future of American Democracy.* New York: Basic, 1976.

Berry, Jeffrey M. *The Interest Group Society.* Glenview, Ill.: Scott Foresman, 1989.

———. *The New Liberalism: The Rising Power of Citizens Groups.* Washington, D.C.: Brookings Institution, 1999.

Black, Anthony. *The History of Islamic Political Thought: From the Prophet to the Present.* New York: Routledge, 2001.

Black, Henry Campbell. *Black's Law Dictionary.* 4th rev. ed. St. Paul, Minn.: West, 1968.

Blanshard, Paul. *American Freedom and Catholic Power.* Boston: Beacon, 1949.

Blumer, Herbert. *Symbolic Interactionism: Perspective and Method.* Englewood Cliffs, N.J.: Prentice-Hall, 1969.

Boisard, Marcel. *Humanism in Islam.* Indianapolis, Ind.: American Trust, 1988.

Bolt, Robert. *A Man for All Seasons: A Play in Two Acts.* New York: Vintage, 1962.

Boniface, Fr. Michael. "Real Islam vs. Imaginary Islam." *Angelus* (Oct. 2001): 3–4.

Boone, Kathleen C. *The Bible Tells Them So: The Discourse of Protestant Fundamentalism.* Albany: State Univ. of New York Press, 1989.

Bozdoğan, Sibel, and Reşat Kasaba. Introduction to *Rethinking Modernity and National Identity in Turkey,* ed. S. Bozdoan and R. Kasaba, 3–14. Seattle: Univ. of Washington Press, 1997.

Boyarin, Jonathan. "Circumscribing Constitutional Identities in Kiryas Joel." *Yale Law Journal* 106 (March 1997): 1537–70.

Brink, Judy, and Joan Mencher, eds. *Mixed Blessings: Gender and Religious Fundamentalism Cross Culturally.* New York: Routledge, 1997.

Brodie, Fawn M. *No Man Knows My History.* New York: Knopf, 1945.

Brown, Dee. *Bury My Heart at Wounded Knee.* New York: Holt, Rinehart, and Winston, 1970.

Brown, Robert McAfee. *Religion and Violence: A Primer for White Americans.* Philadelphia, Pa.: Westminster, 1973.

Buchanan, Pat. *The Death of the West: How Dying Populations and Immigrant Invasions Imperil Our Country and Civilization.* New York: Dunne, 2001.

Buckley, Thomas. *Church and State in Revolutionary Virginia, 1776–1787.* Charlottesville: Univ. Press of Virginia, 1977.

Bunting, Charles C. "An Afternoon with Walker Percy." In *Conversations with Walker Percy,* ed. Lewis Lawson and Victor A. Kramer, 40–55. Jackson: Univ. Press of Mississippi, 1985.

Burgess, John P. *Why Scripture Matters: Reading the Bible in a Time of Church Conflict.* Louisville, Ky.: Westminster John Knox, 1998.

Burns, John F. "Bin Laden Stirs Struggle on Meaning of Jihad." *New York Times on the Web,* January 27, 2002. www.nytimes.com/2002.

Burton, John. *Conflict: Resolution and Prevention.* New York: St. Martin's, 1990.

Butler, Jon. "Why Revolutionary America Wasn't a 'Christian Nation.'" In *Religion and the New Republic,* ed. James H. Hutson, 187–212. Lanham, Md.: Rowman and Littlefield, 2000.

Calvin, John. *Institutes of the Christian Religion.* Ed. John T. McNeill. Philadelphia, Pa.: Westminster, 1960.

———. *Sermons on the Ten Commandments.* Ed. and trans. Benjamin W. Farley. Grand Rapids, Mich.: Baker, 1980.

Campbell, Eugene E. "Governmental Beginnings." In *Utah's History,* ed. Richard D. Poll, 153–73. Provo, Utah: Brigham Young Univ. Press, 1989.

Carey, Patrick W. *The Roman Catholics in America.* Westport, Conn.: Praeger, 1996.

Carter, Stephen L. *The Culture of Disbelief: How American Law and Politics Trivialize American Devotion.* New York: Basic, 1994.

CBS News. "Falwell Sorry for Bashing Muhammad." *CBS News Online,* October 14, 2002. www.cbsnews.com/stories/2002/10/11/60minutes/main525316.shtml.

Ceaser, James. "Multiculturalism and American Liberal Democracy." In *Multiculturalism and American Democracy,* ed. Arthur M. Melzer, Jerry Weinberger, and M. Richard Zinman, 139–56.

Charlesworth, Max. "Universal and Local Elements in Religion." In *Religious Inventions: Four Essays,* 81–104. Cambridge, N.Y.: Cambridge Univ. Press, 1997.

Çinar, Alev. "National History as a Contested Site: The Conquest of Istanbul and Islamist Negotiations of the Nation." *Comparative Studies in Society and History* 43, no. 2 (2001): 364–91.

Çinar, Menderes. "Postmodern Zamanların Kemalist Projesi." *Birikim* (1996).

Ciuba, Gary. *Walker Percy: Books of Revelations.* Athens: Univ. of Georgia Press, 1992.

Coleman, James S. *Foundations of Social Theory.* Cambridge, Mass.: Belknap, Harvard Univ. Press, 1990.

Coleman, William S. E. *Voices of Wounded Knee.* Lincoln: Univ. of Nebraska Press, 2000.

Connolly, William, ed. *Legitimacy and State.* Oxford, U.K.: Blackwell, 1984.

Cookson, Catharine. *Encyclopedia of Religious Freedom.* Religion and Society Series. Vol. 5. New York: Routledge, 2003.

———. *Regulating Religion: The Courts and the Free Exercise Clause.* New York: Oxford Univ. Press, 2001.

Cord, Robert L. *Separation of Church and State: Historical Fact and Current Fiction.* New York: Lambeth, 1982.

Cover, Robert M. "The Supreme Court, 1982 Term-Forward: Nomos and Narrative." *Harvard Law Review* 97 (1983): 4–68.

Coy, Patrick G., and Lynne M. Woehrle, eds. *Social Conflicts and Collective Identities*. Lanham, Md.: Rowman and Littlefield, 2000.

Daneshvar, Parviz. *Revolution in Iran*. London: Macmillan, 1996.

Davis, Derek H. "The Ten Commandments as Public Ritual." *Journal of Church and State* 44, no. 2 (Spring 2002): 221–28.

———. "Virtue and the Continental Congress." In *Religion and the Continental Congress, 1774–1789: Contributions to Original Intent*. New York: Oxford Univ. Press, 2000.

Davis, Derek, and Barry Hankins. *Welfare Reform and Faith-based Organizations*. Waco, Tex.: J. M. Dawson Institute of Church-State Studies, 1999.

Davis, O. L., et al. *Looking at History: A Review of Major U.S. History Textbooks*. Washington, D.C.: People for the American Way, 1986.

Davison, Andrew. *Secularism and Revivalism in Turkey: A Hermeneutic Reconsideration*. New Haven, Conn.: Yale Univ. Press, 1998.

Deeb, Mary-Jane. "Militant Islam and the Politics of Redemption." *The Annals of American Academy of Political and Social Sciences* 524 (Nov. 1992): 52–65.

Deloria, Vine, Jr. *Custer Died for Your Sins: An Indian Manifesto*. New York: Macmillan, 1969.

Denny, Frederick Mathewson. "The Fundamentalist Project: An Islamic Scholar's Perspective." *Religious Studies Review* 24 (Jan. 1998): 8–9.

De Yoe, Jeffrey. "Homegrown Extremism." *Christian Century* 118, no. 29 (Oct. 2001): 7.

Di Palma, Giuseppe. *To Craft Democracies: An Essay on Democratic Transitions*. Berkeley: Univ. of California Press, 1990.

Divakaruni, Chitra Banerjee. *Black Candle: Poems about Women from India, Pakistan, and Bangladesh*. Corvallis, Ore.: Calyx, 2000.

Doi, 'Abdur Rahman I. *Shari'ah: The Islamic Law*. London: Ta Ha, 1984.

Durkheim, Emile. *The Elementary Forms of the Religious Life*. Rev. ed. New York: Free Press, 1965.

Dryfoos, Joy. "Partnering: Full-Service Community Schools: Creating New Institutions," *Phi Delta Kappan* 83, no. 5 (2002): 393–99.

Duran, Burhaneddin. "Approaching the Kurdish Question via Adil D‚zen: An Islamist Formula of the Welfare Party for Ethnic Coexistence." *Journal of Muslim Minority Affairs* 18, no. 1 (1998): 111–28.

Durkheim, Emile. *The Elementary Forms of the Religious Life*. Rev. ed. New York: Free Press, 1965.

Dürr, Hans-Peter. "Peace as the Crisis." Speech delivered at the meeting of the Institute of Peace Research and Security Policy at the University of Hamburg and the Association of German Scientists, Berlin, October 12, 2001.

Dworkin, Ronald. "In Defense of Equality." *Social Philosophy and Policy* 1 (1983): 24–40.

———. *Taking Rights Seriously*. Cambridge, Mass.: Harvard Univ. Press, 1977.

Easwaran, Eknath. *Nonviolent Soldier of Islam: Badshah Khan, A Man to Match His Mountains*. Petaluma, Calif.: Nilgiri, 1999.

Ebersole, Luke Eugene. *Church Lobbying in the Nation's Capital*. New York: Macmillan, 1951.

Eck, Diana. *Encountering God: A Spiritual Journey from Bozeman to Banaras*. New York: Beacon, 1993.

———. "Neighboring Faiths." *Harvard* 99, no. 1 (Sept.–Oct. 1996): 38–44.

———. *A New Religious America*. San Francisco: Harper, 2001.

Eisgruber, Christopher L. "The Constitutional Value of Assimilation." *Columbia Law Review* 96, no. 1 (1996): 87–103.

El-Awa, Mohamed S. *On the Political System of the Islamic State.* Indianapolis, Ind.: American Trust, 1980.

Ellison, Grace. *Turkey To-Day.* London: Hutchinson, 1929.

Emily, Jacque. "On the Topic of Islam." *Angelus* (Dec. 2001): 20–29.

Engineer, Asghar Ali. "Islamic Ethic." Institute of Islamic Studies and Center for Study of Society and Secularism, January 2000. www.ecumene.org/IIS/csss24.htm (accessed January 24, 2002).

Esposito, John L. *Islam: The Straight Path.* New York: Oxford Univ. Press, 1996.

———. *The Islamic Threat: Myth or Reality?* New York: Oxford Univ. Press, 1992.

———. "Political Islam: Beyond the Green Menace," *Current History* 93, no. 579 (1994): 19–24.

———, and John O. Voll. *Islam and Democracy.* New York: Oxford Univ. Press, 1996.

Estep, William R. *Revolution within the Revolution: The First Amendment in Historical Context, 1612–1789.* Grand Rapids, Mich.: Eerdmans, 1990.

Etzioni, Amitai. *The New Golden Rule: Community and Morality in a Democratic Society.* New York: Basic, 1996.

Fakhry, Majid. "Philosophy and Theology from the Eighth Century C.E. to the Present." In *The Oxford History of Islam,* ed. John L. Esposito, 289–90. Oxford: Oxford Univ. Press, 1999.

Ferguson, John. "Religion in Public Schools: Who Decides?" *Liberty Magazine* 96, no. 3 (2001).

Ferguson, Naill. "2001." *New York Times Magazine,* October 28, 2001, 19.

Fish, Stanley. "Boutique Multiculturalism." In *Multiculturalism and American Democracy,* ed. Arthur M. Melzer, Jerry Weinberger, and M. Richard Zinman, 69–88.

———. *Is There a Text in This Class? The Authority of Interpretive Communities.* Cambridge, Mass.: Harvard Univ. Press, 1980.

———. "Postmodern Warfare." *Harper's* 305, no. 1826 (July 2002): 33–40.

Fitzmier, John R. "The Fundamentalist Project: An American Perspective." *Religious Studies Review* 24 (Jan. 1998): 3–8.

Fletcher, George P. "The Case for Tolerance." In *The Communitarian Challenge to Liberalism,* ed. Ellen Frankel Paul, Fred O. Miller Jr., and Jeffrey Paul, 229–39. New York: Cambridge Univ. Press, 1996.

Flood, Gavin. *An Introduction to Hinduism.* Cambridge, N.Y.: Cambridge Univ. Press, 1996.

Franklin, John Hope. *The Color Line: Legacy for the Twenty-first Century.* Columbia: Univ. of Missouri Press, 1993.

Freire, Paulo. *Education for Critical Consciousness.* New York: Continuum, 1990.

———. *Teachers as Cultural Workers: Letters to Those Who Dare to Teach.* Boulder, Colo.: Westview, 1998.

Galeotti, Anna Elisabetta. "Contemporary Pluralism and Toleration." *Ratio Juris* 10 (June 1997): 223–35.

———. "Do We Need Toleration as a Moral Virtue?" *Res Publica* 7 (2001): 273–92.

Galtung, Johan. *Peace by Peaceful Means: Peace and Conflict, Development and Civilization.* Thousand Oaks, Calif.: Sage, 1997.

————. "Three Approaches to Peace: Peacekeeping, Peacemaking and Peacebuilding." In *Essays in Peace Research: War, Peace, Defence*, ed. Johan Galtung, 282–304. Copenhagen, Denmark: Christian Ejlers, 1976.

Garnett, Nicole Stelle, and Richard W. Garnett. "School Choice, the First Amendment, and Social Justice." *Texas Review of Law and Politics* 4 (2000): 305–6.

Gaston, Paul L. "The Revelation of Walker Percy." *Colorado Quarterly* 20 (Spring 1972): 459–70.

Gaustad, Edwin S., ed. *A Documentary History of Religion in America to the Civil War*. Grand Rapids, Mich.: Eerdmans, 1982.

Gerle, Elisabeth. "Contemporary Globalization and Its Ethical Challenges." *Ecumenical Review* 52, no. 2 (April 2000): 158–71.

Giddens, Anthony. *The Consequences of Modernity*. Stanford, Calif.: Stanford Univ. Press, 1990.

Gilkey, Langdon. *Creationism on Trial: Evolution and God at Little Rock*. Minneapolis, Minn.: Winston, 1985.

Girard, Rene. *Violence and the Sacred*. Trans. Patrick Gregory. Baltimore, Md.: Johns Hopkins Univ. Press, 1972.

Glendon, Mary Ann. *Rights Talk: The Impoverishment of Political Discourse*. New York: Free Press, 1991.

Global Hindu Electronic Networks. "The Hindu Universe Festivals of Bharat," July 20, 1999. www.hindunet.org/festivals.

Goffman, Erving. *Frame Analysis*. Cambridge, Mass.: Harvard Univ. Press, 1974.

Göle, Nilüfer. "The Freedom of Seduction for Muslim Women." *New Perspectives Quarterly* 15, no. 3 (1998): 43–49.

Greene, Abner S. "Kirvas Joel and Two Mistakes about Equality." *Columbia Law Review* 96, no. 1 (Jan. 1996): 4–51.

Greenawalt, Kent. *Religious Convictions and Political Choice*. New York: Oxford Univ. Press, 1988.

Guillaume, Alfred. *Islam*. 2d rev. ed. Harmondsworth, U.K.: Penguin, 1954.

Gülalp, Haldun. "Globalization and Political Islam: The Social Basis of Turkey's Welfare Party." *International Journal of Middle East Studies* 33 (2001): 433–48.

Gunneman, John. "Naming the Terror." *Christian Century* 118, no. 26 (Sept.–Oct. 2001): 4–6.

Gutmann, Amy, ed. *Freedom of Association*. Princeton, N.J.: Princeton Univ. Press, 1998.

Haarscher, Guy. "Tolerance of the Intolerant?" *Ratio Juris* 10 (June 1997): 236–47.

Haeri, Fadhlalla. *The Elements of Sufism*. Rockport, Mass.: Element, 1990.

Hall, Timothy L. "Omnibus Protections of Religious Liberty and the Establishment Clause." *Cardozo Law Review* 21 (1999): 539–64.

Halliday, Fred. *Islam and the Myth of Confrontation: Religion and Politics in the Middle East*. New York: Tauris, 1995.

Hardacre, Helen. "The Impact of Fundamentalism on Women, the Family, and Interpersonal Relations." In *Fundamentalisms and Society: Reclaiming the Sciences, the Family, and Education*, ed. Martin E. Marty and R. Scott Appleby, 294–312. Chicago: Univ. of Chicago Press, 1993.

Harel, Alon. "The Boundaries of Justifiable Tolerance: A Liberal Perspective." In *Toleration: An Elusive Virtue*, ed. David Heyd, 114–26. Princeton, N.J.: Princeton Univ. Press, 1996.

Hassan, Riffat. "The Burgeoning of Islamic Fundamentalism: Toward an Understanding of the Phenomenon." In *The Fundamentalist Phenomenon*, ed. Norman J. Cohen, 151–71. Grand Rapids, Mich.: Eerdmans, 1990.

Hasselstrom, Linda. *Bison: Monarch of the Plains*. Portland, Ore.: Graphic Arts Center, 1998.

Hatch, Nathan O. *The Democratization of American Christianity*. New Haven, Conn.: Yale Univ. Press, 1989.

Hatfield, Mark. *Between a Rock and a Hard Place*. Waco, Tex.: Word, 1976.

Hauerwas, Stanley, and William H. Willimon. *The Truth about God: The Ten Commandments in Christian Life*. Nashville, Tenn.: Abingdon, 1999.

Haynes, Charles. "Religion in the Public Schools." *School Administrator* (Jan. 1999): 6–11.

Haynes, Charles C. *Teaching about Religious Freedom in American Secondary Schools*. Silver Spring, Md.: Americans United Research Foundation, 1985.

Haynes, Jeff. *Religion in Third World Politics*. Boulder, Colo.: Lynne Reiner, 1994.

Hays, Richard B. *The Moral Vision of the New Testament*. San Francisco: HarperSanFrancisco, 1996.

Hehir, J. Bryan. "Religious Activism for Human Rights: A Christian Case Study." In *Religious Human Rights in Global Perspectives: Religious Perspectives*, ed. John Witte Jr. and Johan D. van der Vyver, 97–119. The Hague, Netherlands: Martinus Nijhoff, 1996.

Hening, William Waller. *The Statutes at Large, Being a Collection of All the Laws of Virginia, from the First Session of the Legislature in the Year 1619*. Vol. 12. Facsimile reprint (Charlottesville: Univ. Press of Virginia, 1969).

Hennesey, James. *American Catholics: A History of the Roman Catholic Community in the United States*. New York: Oxford Univ. Press, 1981.

Herberg, Will. *Protestant, Catholic, Jew: An Essay in American Religious Sociology*. Rev. ed. Garden City, N.Y.: Anchor, 1960.

Herman, Barbara. "Pluralism and the Community of Moral Judgment." In *Toleration*, ed. David Heyd, 60–80. Princeton, N.J.: Princeton Univ. Press, 1996.

Hertzke, Allen D. *Representing God in Washington: The Role of Religious Lobbies in the American Polity*. Knoxville: Univ. of Tennessee Press, 1988.

Heyd, David, ed. *Toleration*. Princeton, N.J.: Princeton Univ. Press, 1996.

Hirschkind, Charles. "What Is Political Islam?" *Middle East Report* 27, no. 4 (Oct.–Dec. 1997): 12–15.

Hirshson, Stanley P. *The Lion of the Lord: A Biography of Brigham Young*. New York: Knopf, 1969.

Hofrenning, Daniel J. B. *In Washington, but Not of It: The Prophetic Politics of Religious Lobbyists*. Philadelphia, Pa.: Temple Univ. Press, 1995.

Hofstadter, Richard, and Michael Wallace, eds. *American Violence: A Documentary History*. New York: Knopf, 1970.

Hollenbach, David. "The Growing End of an Argument." *America* 30 (November 1985).

Holler, Clyde. *Black Elk's Religion: The Sun Dance and Lakota Catholicism*. Syracuse, N.Y.: Syracuse Univ. Press, 1995.

Holmes, Arthur F. *Contours of a World View*. Grand Rapids, Mich.: Eerdmans, 1983.

hooks, bell. *Teaching to Transgress: Education as the Practice of Freedom*. New York: Routledge, 1994.

Hooper, J. Leon. "The Theological Sources of John Courtney Murray's Ethics." In *John Courtney Murray and the Growth of Tradition*, ed. J. Leon Hooper and Todd David Whitmore, 106–25. Kansas City, Mo.: Sheed and Ward, 1997.

Hrebenar, Ronald J., and Ruth K. Scott. *Interest Group Politics in America*. Englewood Cliffs, N.J.: Prentice Hall, 1982.

Humaid, bin Sheikh Abdullah bin Muhammad. "Jihad in the Qu'ran and Sunnah." The Islam Age. www.islamworld.net (accessed December 23, 2003).

Humphreys, R. Stephen. *Between Memory and Desire: The Middle East in a Troubled Age*. Berkeley: Univ. of California Press, 1999.

Hunter, James Davison. *Culture Wars: The Battle to Define America*. New York: Basic, 1991.

Huntington, Samuel P. "The Clash of Civilizations?" *Foreign Affairs* 72, no. 2 (Summer 1993): 22–28.

———. *The Clash of Civilizations and the Remaking of World Order*. New York: Simon and Schuster, 1993.

Hutson, James H., ed. *Religion and the New Republic: Faith in the Founding of America*. Lanham, Md.: Rowman and Littlefield, 2000.

Ignatieff, Michael. "Barbarians at the Gates." Review of *The Lessons of Terror: A History of Warfare against Civilians: Why It Has Always Failed and Why It Will Fail Again*, by Caleb Carr. *New York Times Book Review*, February 17, 2002.

Introvigne, Massimo. "There Is No Place for Us to Go but Up: New Religious Movements and Violence." Paper delivered at the Twenty-sixth Conference of the International Society for the Sociology of Religion, Ixtapan de la Sal, Mexico, August 2001.

"The Islamic Threat." *Economist*, March 13, 1993.

Janson, Torsten. "Muslim Meaning Maintenance: Problematizations of Islamic Value Reconstruction in a Globalized Setting." Paper presented at the First Nordic Conference on Middle Eastern Studies: The Middle East in a Globalized World. Oslo, Norway, August 13–16, 1998.

Jefferies, John C., Jr., and James E. Ryan. "A Political History of the Establishment Clause." *Michigan Law Review* 100 (Nov. 2001): 279–97.

Jefferson, Thomas. *The Writings of Thomas Jefferson*. Memorial Edition. 20 vols. Ed. Andrew A. Lipscomb and Albert E. Bergh. Washington, D.C.: Thomas Jefferson Memorial Association , 1903–4.

Jehl, Douglas. "Prominent Muslim Militant Is Named a Suspect in Pear Case." *New York Times on the Web*, February 7, 2002. www.nytimes.com/2002.

Jenkins, Philip. *Mystics and Messiahs: Cults and New Religions in American History*. New York: Oxford Univ. Press, 2000.

Jones, Robert L. "A Conversation with Russell Means." Interview conducted March 15, 2000, www.home.flash.net/~park29/means_1.htm (accessed June 2000).

Jorgenson, Lloyd P. *The State and the Non-Public School: 1825–1925*. Columbia: Univ. of Missouri Press, 1987.

Juergensmeyer, Mark. *Fighting with Gandhi*. San Francisco: Harper and Row, 1984.

———. *Terror in the Mind of God: The Global Rise of Religious Violence*. Berkeley: Univ. of California Press, 2000.

Kagan, Carole F. "Squeezing the Juice from Lemon: Toward a Consistent Test for the Establishment Clause." *North Kentucky Law Review* 22 (1995): 621, 632–33.

Kahraman, Hasan Bülent. "A Journey of Rupture and Conflict: The Culture in Purgatory." *Privateview* 2, no. 5 (Autumn 1997). www.tusiad.org/yayin/private/autumn97/html.

Kannapell, Andrea. "The Festival Man." *New York Times*, October 19, 1997.

Kaplan, Lawrence, ed. *Fundamentalism in Comparative Perspective.* Amherst: Univ. of Massachusetts Press, 1992.

Kaplan, Robert, D. "Looking the World in the Eye," *Atlantic Monthly* 288, no. 5 (Dec. 2000): 68–82.

Keen, Sam. *Faces of the Enemy: Reflections of the Hostile Imagination.* San Francisco: Harper and Row, 1991.

Kelsay, John. "Saudi Arabia, Pakistan, and the Universal Declaration of Human Rights." In *Human Rights and the Conflicts of Culture: Western and Islamic Perspectives on Religious Liberty,* ed. David Little, John Kelsay, and Abdulaziz Sachedina, 33–52. Columbia: Univ. of South Carolina Press, 1988.

Kelsay, John, and James Turner, eds. *Just War and Jihad: Historical and Theoretical Perspectives on War and Peace in Western and Islamic Traditions.* New York: Greenwood, 1991.

Kemal, Nusret. "Halkçilik" (Populism). *Ülkü* 1, no. 3 (1933).

Kennedy, Paul. Review of *What Went Wrong? Western Impact and Middle East Response,* by Bernard Lewis, *New York Times Book Review,* January 27, 2002.

Khan, M. A. Muqtedar. "Muslim to Muslim," *Christian Century* 118, no. 30 (Nov. 2001), 5–6.

Khan, Maulana Wahiduddin. "Islam and Peace." Al Risala Forum International. www.alrisala.org (updated December 23, 2003).

———. "Non-violence in Islam." Paper presented at the Symposium on Islam and Peace, American University, Washington, D.C., February 6–7, 1998. www.alrisala.org (accessed January 24, 2002).

———. "The Principles of Success in the Light of Seerah." Al Risala Forum International. www.alrisala.org (updated December 23, 2003).

Kimball, Charles A. "Examining Islamic Militancy: Roots of Rancor." *Christian Century* 118, no. 28 (Oct. 2001): 18–23.

King, Martin Luther, Jr. "Address Delivered at the National Biennial Convention of the American Jewish Congress." In *Symbol of the Movement: January 1957–December 1958,* vol. 4 of *The Papers of Martin Luther King, Jr.,* ed. Clayborne Carson, Ralph E. Luker, and Penny A. Russell. Berkeley: Univ. of California Press, 2000.

Khomeini, Sayed Ruhollah. *Islam and Revolution: Writings and Declarations of Imam Khomeini.* Trans. and ed. Hamid Algar. London: KAI, 1985.

Knight, David B. "People Together, Yet Apart: Rethinking Territory, Sovereignty, and Identities." In *Reordering the World: Geopolitical Perspectives on the Twenty-First Century,* ed. George J. Demko and William B. Wood, 2d ed., 209–26. Boulder, Colo.: Westview, 1999.

Kopel, David B., and Paul H. Blackman. *No More Wacos: What's Wrong with Federal Law Enforcement and How to Fix It.* Amherst, N.Y.: Prometheus, 1997.

Köymen, Nusret. "Köy Misyonerliği" ("Village Missionarism"). *Ülkü* 2, no. 7 (1933).

Krauthammer, Charles. "The New Crescent of Crisis: Global Intifada." *Washington Post,* January 1, 1993.

Kramnick, Isaac, and R. Laurence Moore. *The Godless Constitution: The Case against Religious Correctness.* New York: Norton, 1996.

Kriesberg, Louis. *Constructive Conflicts: From Escalation to Resolution.* 2d ed. Lanham, Md.: Rowman and Littlefield, 2002.

Küenzeln, G. "Fundamentalismus und säkulare Kultur." In *Fundamentalismus in der verweltlichten Welt,* ed. H. Hemminger, 196–221. Stuttgart: Quell, 1991.

Kugel, James L. *The Bible as It Was.* Cambridge, Mass.: Belknap, 1997.

Kurdi, Abdulrahman Abdulkadir. *The Islamic State: A Study Based on the Islamic Holy Constitution.* London: Mansell, 1984.

Kymlicka, Will. *Liberalism, Community, and Culture.* Oxford, U.K.: Clarendon, 1989.

———. *Multicultural Citizenship: A Liberal Theory of Minority Rights.* Oxford, U.K.: Clarendon, 1995.

———. "Two Models of Pluralism and Tolerance." In *Toleration,* ed. David Heyd, 81–105.

LaBarre, Weston. *The Ghost Dance: Origins of Religion.* London: Allen and Unwin, 1972.

Lambton, Ann K. S. *State and Government in Medieval Islam: An Introduction to the Study of Islamic Political Theory: The Jurists.* Oxford, N.Y.: Oxford Univ. Press, 1981.

Laqueur, Walter. "A Failure of Intelligence." Review of *Jihad* by Guilles Kepel. *Atlantic Monthly* 289, no. 3 (March 2002): 127–30.

Larmore, C. *Patterns of Moral Complexity.* Cambridge, N.Y.: Cambridge Univ. Press, 1987.

Lawrence, Bruce B. *Defenders of God: The Fundamentalist Revolt against the Modern Age.* San Francisco: Harper and Row, 1989.

Laycock, Douglas. "A Survey of Religious Liberty in the United States." *Ohio State Law Journal* 47 (1986): 409, 449–50.

Lessinger, Johanna. *From the Ganges to the Hudson: Indian Immigrants in New York City.* Boston: Allyn and Bacon, 1995.

Levitt, David M. "East Indians Find Niche." *News Tribune,* January 1, 1996.

Levy, Leonard. *The Establishment Clause: Religion and the First Amendment.* New York: Macmillan, 1986.

Lewis, Bernard. *Cultures in Conflict: Christians, Muslims and Jews in the Age of Discovery.* New York: Oxford Univ. Press, 1995.

———. *The Political Language of Islam.* Chicago: Univ. of Chicago Press, 1988.

———. "The Revolt of Islam: When Did the Conflict with the West Begin, and When Will It End?" *New Yorker* (Nov. 19, 2001): 50–59.

———. "The Roots of Muslim Rage," *Atlantic Monthly* 266, no. 3 (Sept. 1990): 47–60.

———. *What Went Wrong? Western Impact and Middle Eastern Response.* New York: Oxford Univ. Press, 2001.

Liebman, Charles S. "Extremism as a Religious Norm." *Journal for the Scientific Study of Religion* 22 (1983): 75–86.

Lifton, Robert J. *Death in Life: Survivors of Hiroshima.* Chapel Hill: Univ. of North Carolina Press, 1968.

Lindbeck, George A. *The Nature of Doctrine: Religion and Theology in a Postliberal Age.* Philadelphia, Pa.: Westminster, 1984.

Lipkin, Robert Justin. "Liberalism and the Possibility of Multicultural Constitutionalism: The Distinction between Deliberative and Dedicated Cultures." *University of Richmond Law Review* 29, no. 5 (Dec. 1995): 1263–325.

Lippman, Thomas W. *Understanding Islam: An Introduction to the Muslim World.* 2d rev. ed. New York: Meridian, 1995.

Lipset, Martin Seymour. *American Exceptionalism: A Double-Edged Sword.* New York: Norton, 1997.

Locke, John. *A Letter Concerning Toleration.* Ed. James H. Tully. Indianapolis, Ind.: Hackett, 1983.

———. *Second Treatise of Government.* Ed. C. B. Macpherson. Indianapolis, Ind.: Hackett, 1980.

Loetscher, Lefferts A. *The Broadening Church: A Study of Theological Issues in the Presbyterian Church since 1869.* Philadelphia: Univ. of Pennsylvania Press, 1954.

Long, Charles H. *Significations: Signs, Symbols, and Images in the Interpretation of Religion.* Philadelphia, Pa.: Fortress, 1986.

Longfield, Bradley J. *The Presbyterian Controversy: Fundamentalists, Modernists, and Moderates.* New York: Oxford Univ. Press, 1991.

Lukes, Steven. "Toleration and Recognition," *Ratio Juris* 10 (June 1997): 213–23.

Lupu, Ira C. "Uncovering the Village of Kiryas Joel." *Columbia Law Review* 96, no. 1 (1996): 104–20.

Macartney, Clarence Edward. *Christianity and Common Sense: A Dialogue of Faith.* Philadelphia, Pa.: Winston, 1927.

Macedo, Stephen. *Liberal Virtues: Citizenship, Virtue, and Community in Liberal Constitutionalism.* Oxford, U.K.: Clarendon, 1990.

MacFarquhar, Neil. "Forces of Islam: Bin Laden's Wildfire Threatens Saudi Rulers." *New York Times,* November 6, 2001.

Machen, J. Gresham. *Christianity and Liberalism.* Grand Rapids, Mich.: Eerdmans, 1923.

Maddigan, Michael M. "The Establishment Clause, Civil Religion, and the Public Church." *California Law Review* 81 (1993): 293–349.

Madison, James. "A Memorial and Remonstrance." 1785. Reprinted in William Lee Miller, *The First Liberty: Religion and the American Republic.* App. 2. New York: Knopf, 1986.

Malbin, Michael J. *Religion and Politics: The Intentions of the Authors of the First Amendment.* Washington, D.C.: American Enterprise Institute for Public Policy Research, 1978.

Manheim, Jarol B., Richard C. Rich, and Lars Willnat, eds. *Empirical Political Analysis: Research Methods in Political Science.* 5th ed. New York: Longman, 2002.

Mani, Lakshmi. "Newspaper Debut Coincides with Navratri: Offers New Voice for Indian Community." *Community India News* (September 1993): 1.

Margalit, Avishai, and Ian Buruma. "Occidentalism." *New York Review of Book,* January 17, 2002.

Marsden, George M. *Fundamentalism and American Culture: The Shaping of Twentieth-Century Evangelicalism, 1870–1925.* New York: Oxford Univ. Press, 1980.

———. *Reforming Fundamentalism: Fuller Seminary and the New Evangelicalism.* Grand Rapids, Mich.: Eerdmans, 1987.

———. *Understanding Fundamentalism and Evangelicalism.* Grand Rapids, Mich.: Eerdmans, 1991.

Martin, David. *Tongues of Fire: The Explosion of Protestantism in Latin America.* Oxford, U.K.: Basil Blackwell, 1990.

Marty, Martin E., and R. Scott Appleby, eds. *Accounting for Fundamentalisms.* Chicago: Univ. of Chicago Press, 1994.

————. *Fundamentalisms and Society: Reclaiming the Sciences, the Family, and Education.* Chicago: Univ. of Chicago Press, 1993.

————. *Fundamentalisms and the State.* Chicago: Univ. of Chicago Press, 1993.

————. *Fundamentalisms Comprehended.* Chicago: Univ. of Chicago Press, 1995.

————. *Fundamentalisms Observed: A Study Conducted by the American Academy of Arts and Sciences.* Chicago: Univ. of Chicago Press, 1991.

Marquand, Robert. "A Special Report on the Ideology of Jihad and the Rise of Islamic Militancy." *Christian Science Monitor,* October 18, 2001.

Marx, Karl. "Zur Kritik der Hegelschen Rechtsphilosophie." In *Deutsch-Französische Jahrbücher (1844),* ed. Arnold Ruge and Karl Marx, 150–51. Leipzig, Germany: Verlag Philipp Reclam, 1981.

Mason, Whit. "The Future of Political Islam in Turkey." *World Policy Journal* 17, no. 2 (2000): 56–70.

Matthiessen, Peter. *In the Spirit of Crazy Horse.* New York: Penguin, 1992.

McBrien, Richard P. *Lives of the Popes: The Pontiffs from St. Peter to John Paul II.* New York: Harper Collins, 1997.

McClosky, Herbert, and John Zaller. *The American Ethos: Public Attitudes toward Capitalism and Democracy.* Cambridge, Mass.: Harvard Univ. Press, 1984.

McConnell, Michael W. "The Origins and Historical Understanding of Free Exercise," 103 *Harvard Law Review* 103, no. 5 (1990): 1409–1519.

Mead, George Herbert. *Mind, Self, and Society: From the Standpoint of a Social Behaviorist.* Chicago: Univ. of Chicago Press, 1934.

Mead, Sidney. *The Nation with the Soul of a Church.* New York: Harper and Row, 1975.

Meckled-Garcia, Saldin. "Toleration and Neutrality: Incompatible Ideal?" *Res Publica* 7 (2001): 292–313.

Meilaender, Gilbert. "After September 11." *Christian Century* 118, no. 26 (Sept.–Oct. 2001): 7–8.

Melwani, Lavina. "The Indian American Family: Cracks in the Mask." *Little India* 9, no. 7 (July 1999): 11–18.

Melzer, Arthur M., Jerry Weinberger, and M. Richard Zinman, eds. *Multiculturalism and American Democracy.* Lawrence: Univ. Press of Kansas, 1998.

Mill, J. S. "Consideration on Representative Government." In *Utilitarianism, Liberty, Representative Government,* ed. H. Acton, 230–33. London: J. M. Dent, 1972.

————. *On Liberty.* Ed. G. Himmelfarb. Hammondsworth, U.K.: Penguin, 1982.

Miller, Donald E. *Reinventing American Protestantism: Christianity in the New Millennium.* Berkeley: Univ. of California Press, 1997.

Miller, John. "Hunting bin Laden." *Frontline,* April 1999. www.pbs.org/wgbh/frontline/ shows (accessed January 16, 2002).

Miller, William Lee. *The First Liberty: Religion and the American Republic.* New York: Knopf, 1986.

Minow, Martha. "The Constitution and the Subgroup Question." *Indiana Law Journal* 71, no. 1 (Winter 1995): 1–26.

Mirsky, Yehudah. "Civil Religion and the Establishment Clause." *Yale Law Journal* 95 (1986): 1237–57.

Mooney, James. *The Ghost-Dance Religion and Wounded Knee.* New York: Dover, 1973.

Morin, Richard. "Misperceptions Cloud Whites' View of Blacks." *Washington Post,* July 11, 2001.

Morgan, Robin. *The Demon Lover: On the Sexuality of Terrorism.* New York: Norton, 1989.

Moussalli, Ahmad S. *Radical Islamic Fundamentalism: The Ideological and Political Discourse of Sayyid Qutb.* Beirut, Lebanon: American University of Beirut, 1992.

Moten, Abdul Rashid. *Political Science: An Islamic Perspective.* Houndsmils, U.K.: Macmillan, 1996.

Mottahedeh, Roy. "Islam and the Opposition to Terrorism." *New York Times,* September 30, 2001.

Moussalli, Ahmad S. *Radical Islamic Fundamentalism: The Ideological and Political Discourse of Sayyid Qutb.* Beirut, Lebanon: American University of Beirut, 1992.

Murray, John Courtney. "The Problem of Religious Freedom." *Theological Studies* 25 (1964): 503–75.

Mutahhari, Ayatullah Morteza. *Jihad: The Holy War of Islam and Its Legitimacy in the Quran.* Trans. Mohammad Salman Tawhidi. Tehran, Iran: Islamic Propagation Organization, 1985.

Nagel, Thomas. *Equality and Partiality.* New York: Oxford Univ. Press, 1991.

———. "Moral Conflict and Political Legitimacy." *Philosophy and Public Affairs* 16 (Summer 1987): 215–40.

Naipaul, V. S. Interview in *New York Times Magazine,* October 28, 2001.

Nankani, Sandhya. "Bride Shopping on the Net." *Little India* 9, no. 5 (May 1999): 2–8.

Naparstek, Michael E. "Falwell and Robertson Stumble." *Religion in the News* 5 (Fall 2001): 28.

National Center for Educational Statistics. *Findings from the Condition of Education 1997: Public and Private Schools: How Do They Differ?* Report NCES 97–983 (July 1997).

"The National Prospect." *Commentary* 100, no. 5 (1995): 23–116.

Neihardt, John G. *Black Elk Speaks: Being the Life Story of a Holy Man of the Oglala Sioux.* Lincoln: Univ. of Nebraska Press, 1979.

Newey, Glen. "Is Democratic Toleration a Rubber Duck?" *Res Publica* 7 (2001): 315–36.

Nicholson, Peter P. "Toleration as a Moral Ideal." In *Aspects of Toleration: Philosophical Studies,* ed. John Horton and Susan Mendus, 158–73. New York: Methuen, 1985.

Niebuhr, Gustav. "Muslim Group Seeks to Meet Billy Graham's Son." *New York Times,* November 20, 2001.

Niebuhr, Reinhold. *The Children of Light and the Children of Darkness.* New York: Scribner Sons, 1953.

Ninian, Alex. "Hindu and Muslim Strife in India." *Contemporary Review* 280 (June 2002): 340–43.

Noll, Mark. "Evangelicals in the American Founding." In *Religion and the New Republic,* ed. James H. Hutson, 137–58. Lanham, Md.: Rowman and Littlefield, 2000.

———, ed. *The Princeton Theology: 1812–1921.* Grand Rapids, Mich.: Baker Book House, 1983.

Noonan, John T., Jr. *The Luster of Our Country: The American Experience of Religious Freedom*. Berkeley: Univ. of California Press, 1998.

Nord, Warren A. *Religion and American Education: Rethinking a National Dilemma*. Chapel Hill: Univ. of North Carolina Press, 1995.

Nord, Warren, and Charles Haynes. *Taking Religion Seriously across the Curriculum*. Alexandria, Va.: Association for Supervision and Curriculum Development, 1998.

Nova. "The Controversial Dr. Koop." Aired on PBS October 10, 1989. Show 1612.

Novak, Michael. "The Influence of Judaism and Christianity on the American Founding." In *Religion and the New Republic: Faith in the Founding of America*, ed. James H. Hutson, 159–86. Lanham, Md.: Rowman and Littlefield, 2000.

O'Brien, Molly. "Free at Last, Charter Schools and Deregulated Curriculum." *Akron Law Review* 34 (2000): 137, 169–70.

Okin, Susan Moller. "Is Multiculturalism Bad for Women?" In *Is Multiculturalism Bad for Women?: Susan Moller Okin with Respondents*, ed. Joshua Cohen, Matthew Howard, and Martha C. Nussbaum, 7–26. Princeton, N.J.: Princeton University Press, 1999.

Özbudun, Ergun. *Contemporary Turkish Politics*. Boulder, Colo.: Lynne Reinner, 2000.

———. "Turkey: Crises, Interruptions, and Reequilibrations." In *Politics in Developing Countries*, ed. Larry Diamond, Juan Linz, and Seymour Lipset, 259. Boulder, Colo.: Lynne Rienner, 1995.

Parla, Taha. *Türkiye'de Siyasal Kültürün Resmi Kaynaklari, Cilt I Atatürk'ün Nutuk'u (The Sources of Political Culture in Turkey, vol. 1, Atatürk's Speech)*. İstanbul, Turkey: İletişim, 1991.

Peker, Recep. *İnkilap Tarihi Ders Notlari (Lecture Notes of History of Revolution)*. İstanbul, Turkey: İletişim Yayınları, 1984.

Pelikan, Jaroslav. "Fundamentalism and/or Orthodoxy? Toward an Understanding of the Fundamentalist Phenomenon." In *The Fundamentalist Phenomenon: A View from Within; a Response from Without*, ed. Norman J. Cohen, 6–7. Grand Rapids, Mich.: Eerdmans, 1990.

Percy, Walker. *Love in the Ruins*. New York: Farrar, Straus and Giroux, 1971.

———. *Signposts in a Strange Land*, ed. Patrick Samway. New York: Farrar, Straus and Giroux, 1991.

Peterson, Paul E. "School Choice: A Report Card." *Virginia Journal of Social Policy and Law* 6, no. 1 (Fall 1998): 47–80.

Pettys, Gregory L., and Pallassana R. Balgopal. "Multigenerational Conflicts and New Immigrants: An Indo-American Experience." *Families in Society: The Journal of Contemporary Human Services* 79, no. 4 (1998): 410–22.

Pfaff, William. "Seeds of War: What Drives Islamic Fundamentalists." *Commonweal* 128, no. 18 (Oct. 2001): 9–11.

Pfeffer, Leo. *Church, State and Freedom*. 2d ed. Boston: Beacon, 1967.

Phillips, W. Gary, and William E. Brown, *Making Sense of Your World*. Chicago: Moody, 1991.

Piscatori, James P. *Islam in a World of Nation-States*. Cambridge, N.Y.: Cambridge Univ. Press, 1986.

Platter, Marc F. "Liberal Democracy, Universalism, and Multiculturalism." In *Multiculturalism and American Democracy*, ed. Arthur M. Melzer, Jerry Weinberger, and M. Richard Zinman, 157–64.

Postman, Neil. *Technopoly: The Surrender of Culture to Technology.* New York: Knopf, 1992.

Poulton, Hugh. *Top Hat, Grey Wolf and Crescent: Turkish Nationalism and the Turkish Republic.* London: Hurst, 1997.

Qur'an. The Tajwidi Qur'an: Transliterated by A. Nooruddeen Durkee with Meanings Rendered in Contemporary American English. Charlottesville, Va.: an-Noor Educational Foundation, 2003.

Qutb, Sayyid. "Paving the Way." *Nida'ul Islam* (April–May 1998). www.islam.org.au (accessed February 9, 2002).

———. "The Right to Judge." www.islamworld.net/justice.

Rahman, Fazur. *Islam.* New York: Anchor, 1968.

Rahnema, A., ed. *Pioneers of Islamic Revival.* London: Zed, 1994.

Ram-Prasad, C. "Hindutva Ideology: Extracting the Fundamentals." *Contemporary South Asia* 2, no. 3 (1993): 285–309.

Ranstorp, Magnus. "Terrorism in the Name of Religion." *Journal of International Affairs* 50, no. 1 (Summer 1996): 41–62.

Rashid, Ahmed. *Taliban: Militant Islam, Oil and Fundamentalism in Central Asia.* New Haven, Conn.: Yale Univ. Press, 2000.

Rashid, Ahmed Abdur. "Islam's Commitment to Peace and Nonviolence." Lecture delivered at Johns Hopkins University, Baltimore, Maryland, March 9, 2001.

Rawls, John. "Kantian Constructivism in Moral Theory." *Journal of Philosophy* 77 (1980): 515–72.

———. *Political Liberalism.* New York: Columbia Univ. Press, 1993.

———. "The Priority of Right and Ideas of the Good." *Philosophy and Public Affairs* 17, no. 4 (1988): 251–76.

———. *A Theory of Justice.* Cambridge, Mass.: Harvard Univ. Press, 1971.

Raz, Joseph. *The Morality of Freedom.* Oxford, U.K.: Clarendon, 1986.

———. "Multiculturalism: A Liberal Perspective." *Dissent* (Winter 1994): 67–79.

Razi, G. Hossein. "Legitimacy, Religion, and Nationalism in the Middle East," *American Political Science Review* 84, no. 1 (March 1990): 69–91.

Reichley, James. *Religion in American Public Life.* Washington, D.C.: Brookings Institution, 1985.

Richey, Russell E., and Donald G. Jones, eds. *American Civil Religion.* New York: Harper and Row, 1974.

Riesebrodt, Martin. *Pious Passion: The Emergence of Modern Fundamentalism in the United States and Iran.* Trans. Don Reneau. Berkeley: Univ. of California Press, 1993.

Robbins, Tom, and Susan J. Palmer, eds. *Millennium, Messiahs, and Mayhem: Contemporary Apocalyptic Movements.* New York: Routledge, 1997.

Roof, Wade Clark. *Spiritual Marketplace: Baby Boomers and the Remaking of American Religion.* Princeton, N.J.: Princeton Univ. Press, 1999.

Rosenblum, Nancy. *Membership and Morals: The Personal Uses of Pluralism in America.* Princeton, N.J.: Princeton Univ. Press, 2000.

Rouleau, Eric. "Turkey's Dream of Democracy." *Foreign Affairs* 76, no. 6 (Nov.–Dec. 2000): 100–115.

Roy, O. R. *The Failure of Political Islam.* Cambridge, Mass.: Harvard Univ. Press, 1994.

Ruthven, Malise. "Islamic Politics in the Middle East and North Africa." In *The Middle East and North Africa,* Europa Year Book, vol. 30, 93–98. London: Europa Publications, 1998.

Ryan, John A., and Francis J. Boland. *Catholic Principles of Politics.* New York: Macmillan, 1948.

Ryan, Patrick J. "Islamic Fundamentalism: A Questionable Category." *America* 29 (Dec. 1984): 437–40.

Sadik, Necmeddin. "Laik Ne Demektir?" ("What Is Laicism?"). *Ülkü* 2, no. 12 (1933).

Saffet, Mehmet. "İnklap Terbiyesi" ("Revolutionary Education"). *Ülkü* 2, no. 8 (1933).

———. "Kültür İnklabimiz" ("Our Cultural Revolution"). *Ülkü* 1, no. 5 (1933).

Şahin, Muzaffer, ed. *MGK 28 Şubat Öncesi ve Sonrasi (MGK Before and After February 28).* Ankara, Turkey: Ufuk Kitabevi, 1997.

Said, Edward. "Backlash and Backtrack." *Al Ahram Weekly Online* (Sept. 7–Oct. 3, 2001). http://weekly.Ahram.org.eg.

———. "The Clash of Ignorance." *Nation* (Oct. 22, 2001): 11–14.

———. *Orientalism.* New York: Vintage, 1979.

Salt, Jeremy. "Turkey's Military 'Democracy.'" *Current History* (Feb. 1999): 72–78.

Sandeen, Ernest R. *The Roots of Fundamentalism: British and American Millenarianism, 1800–1930.* Chicago: Univ. of Chicago Press, 1970.

Scanlon, T. M. "The Difficulty of Tolerance." In *Toleration,* ed. David Heyd, 226–40.

Shafer, Byron, ed. *Is America Different? A New Look at American Exceptionalism.* London: Oxford Univ. Press, 1991.

Schall, James V. *Jacques Maritain: The Philosopher in Society.* Lanham, Md.: Rowman and Littlefield, 1998.

Shachar, Ayelet. *Multicultural Jurisdictions: Cultural Differences and Women's Rights.* Cambridge, N.Y.: Cambridge Univ. Press, 2001.

Shukrallah, Hani. "What Is Terrorism?" *Al Ahram Weekly Online* (Nov. 8–14, 2001). http://weekly.Ahram.org.eg.

Sigmund, Paul E., ed., *St. Thomas Aquinas on Politics and Ethics.* New York: Norton, 1988.

Silk, Mark. "Islam Is Everywhere." *Religion in the News* 28 (Fall 2001): 6–8.

Sire, James W. *The Universe Next Door: A Basic World View Catalog.* 2d ed. Downers Grove, Ill.: InterVarsity, 1988.

Sivanandan, A. "The Three Faces of British Racism: A Special Report." *Race and Class* 43, no. 2 (Oct.–Dec. 2001): 1–5.

Smith, Wilfred Cantwell. *What Is Scripture? A Comparative Approach.* Minneapolis, Minn.: Augsburg Fortress, 1993.

Soloveitchik, Haym. "Migration, Acculturation, and the New Role of Texts in the Haredi World." In *Accounting for Fundamentalisms,* ed. Martin E. Marty and Scott Appleby, 197–235.

Spinner-Halev, Jeff. *The Boundaries of Citizenship: Race, Ethnicity, and Nationality in the Liberal State.* Baltimore, Md.: Johns Hopkins Univ. Press, 1994.

Stalker, Peter. *The No-Nonsense Guide to International Migration.* Oxford, U.K.: New Internationalist, 2001.

Stark, Rodney. *One True God: Historical Consequences of Monotheism.* Princeton, N.J.: Princeton Univ. Press, 2002.

Stark, Rodney, and Roger Finke. *Acts of Faith: Explaining the Human Side of Religion*. Berkeley: Univ. of California Press, 2000.

Stokes, Anson Phelps. *Church and State in the United States: Historical Development and Contemporary Problems of Religious Freedom under the Constitution*. 3 vols. New York: Harper and Brothers, 1950.

Stolzenberg, Nomi Maya. "'He Drew a Circle That Shut Me Out': Assimilation, Indoctrination, and the Paradox of a Liberal Education." *Harvard Law Review* 106 (1993): 581–667.

Story, Joseph. *A Familiar Exposition of the Constitution of the United States*. 1859. Reprint, Lake Bluff, Ill.: Regnery Gateway, 1986.

Stump, Roger W. *Boundaries of Faith: Geographical Perspectives on Religious Fundamentalism*. Lanham, Md.: Rowman and Littlefield, 2000.

Sullivan, Andrew. "This *Is* a Religious War," *New York Times Magazine*, October 7, 2001.

Sullivan, Kathleen. "Religion and Liberal Democracy." *University of Chicago Law Review* 59 (1992): 159–223.

Sunstein, Cass. "Should Sex Equality Law Apply to Religious Institutions?" In *Is Multiculturalism Bad for Women?: Susan Moller Okin with Respondents*, ed. Joshua Cohen, Matthew Howard, and Martha C. Nussbaum, 85–94.

Tabor, James D., and Eugene V. Gallagher. *Why Waco? Cults and the Battle for Religious Freedom in America*. Berkeley: Univ. of California Press, 1995.

Takaki, Ronald. *A Different Mirror: A History of Multicultural America*. Boston, Mass.: Little Brown, 1993.

———. *Strangers from a Different Shore*. New York: Penguin, 1989.

Talmon, Jacob L. *The Origins of Totalitarian Democracy*. Suffolk, U.K.: Penguin, 1952.

Tamadonfar, Mehran. *The Islamic Polity and Political Leadership: Fundamentalism, Sectarianism, and Pragmatism*. Boulder, Colo.: Westview, 1989.

Taylor, Charles. "The Politics of Recognition." In *Multiculturalism and the Politics of Recognition*, ed. Amy Gutman, 27–73. Princeton, N.J.: Princeton University Press, 1992.

Thompson, Bard. *Liturgies of the Western Church*. Philadelphia, Pa.: Fortress, 1961.

Tibi, B. *Islam and the Cultural Accommodation of Social Change*. Boulder, Colo.: Westview, 1990.

Tolson, Jay. "Defender of the Faith: Portrait: Khaled Abou El Fadl." *U.S. News and World Report*, April 15, 2002.

———. "Unholy War: How Islamic Radicals Are Hijacking One of the World's Great Religions." *U.S. News and World Report*, October 15, 2001.

Tolson, Jay, ed. *The Correspondence of Shelby Foote and Walker Percy*. New York: DoubleTake, 1997.

U.S. Congress, House, Committee on International Relations, and Senate, Committee on Foreign Relations. *Annual Report, International Religious Freedom, 1999*. 106th Cong., 2d sess., 2000. 350–56.

U.S. House. *Acknowledgment of God and the Christian Religion in the Constitution*. 43d Cong., 1st sess., 1874. H. Rept. 143.

Valdes, Ernesto Garzon. "Some Remarks on the Concept of Toleration." *Ratio Juris* 10 (June 1997): 127–38.

Van Bruinessen, Martin. "Muslim Fundamentalism: Something to Be Understood or to Be Explained Away?" *Islam and Christian-Muslim Relations* 6 (1995): 157–71.

Vegh, Steven. "Interfaith Services Worry Some: Concerned Christians Fear Prayers of Unity Sanctify All Gods." *Virginian Pilot,* December 2, 2001.

Vitz, Paul C. *Censorship: Evidence of Bias in Our Children's Textbooks.* Ann Arbor, Mich.: Servant, 1986.

Wagaman, Brian. Review of John William Sayer, *Ghost Dancing and the Law: The Wounded Knee Trials,* H-PCAACA, H-Net Reviews, December 1998. www.h-net.msu.edu/reviews/ showrev.cgi?path=21313913131882.

Walker, Edward W. "Islam in Chechnya." Lecture delivered at the Berkeley-Stanford Conference, Religion and Spirituality in Eastern Europe and the Former Soviet Union, Stanford, California, March 13, 1998. *Contemporary Caucasus Newsletter,* no. 6 (Fall 1998): 10–15.

Walsh, Brian J., and Richard J. Middleton. *The Transforming Vision: Shaping a Christian World View.* Downers Grove, Ill.: InterVarsity, 1984.

Walzer, Michael. "The Politics of Difference: Statehood and Toleration in a Multicultural World." *Ratio Juris* 10 (June 1997): 165–76.

Weigel, George. *The Final Revolution: The Resistance Church and the Collapse of Communism.* New York: Oxford Univ. Press, 1992.

Weinrich, Michael. *Kirche Glauben: Annäherungen an eine ökumenische Ekklesiologie.* Wuppertal, Germany: Foedus-Verlag, 1998.

Wessinger, Catherine. *Millennialism, Persecution, and Violence: A Documentary History.* Syracuse, N.Y.: Syracuse Univ. Press, 2001.

Westerlund, David, and Eva Evers Rosander, eds. *African Islam and Islam in Africa: Encounters between Sufis and Islamists.* Athens: Ohio Univ. Press, 1997.

White, Jenny B. "Pragmatists or Ideologues? Turkey's Welfare Party in Power." *Current History* (Jan. 1997): 27.

Whitmore, Todd David. "Immunity or Empowerment?: John Courtney Murray and the Question of Religious Liberty." In *John Courtney Murray and the Growth of Tradition,* ed. J. Leon Hooper and Todd David Whitmore, 149–74. Kansas City, Mo.: Sheed and Ward, 1997.

Williams, Rhys H. "Movement Dynamics and Social Change: Transforming Fundamentalist Ideology and Organizations." In *Accounting for Fundamentalisms,* ed. Martin E. Marty and R. Scott Appleby, 785–833.

Wilson, B. R. *Religion in Secular Society: A Sociological Comment.* London: Watts, 1966.

Wolff, Robert Paul, Barrington Moore Jr., and Herbert Marcuse, eds. *A Critique of Pure Tolerance.* Boston: Beacon, 1965.

Wuthnow, Robert. *The Restructuring of American Religion: Society and Faith since World War II.* Princeton, N.J.: Princeton Univ. Press, 1988.

Wuthnow, Robert, and Matthew P. Lawson. "Imagining the Last Days: The Politics of Apocalyptic Language." In *Accounting for Fundamentalisms,* ed. Martin E. Marty and Scott Appleby, 18–56.

Yael, Navaro-Yashin. "Travesty and Truth: Politics of Culture and Fantasies of the State in Turkey." Unpublished Ph.D. diss., Princeton University, January 1998.

Yavuz, M. Hakan. "Political Islam and the Welfare (*Refah*) Party in Turkey." *Comparative Politics* (Oct. 1997): 73–76.

Young, Iris Marion. *Justice and the Politics of Difference.* Princeton, N.J.: Princeton Univ. Press, 1990.

Zakaria, Fareed. "The Allies Who Made Our Foes." *Newsweek,* October 1, 2001, 34.

———— "Why Do They Hate Us?" *Newsweek,* October 15, 2001, 40.

Zakaria, Rafiq. *The Struggle within Islam: The Conflict between Islam and Politics.* New York: Penguin, 1988.

Zasr, S. V. R. *The Vanguard of the Islamic Revolution: Jama'at-I Islami of Pakistan.* Berkeley: Univ. of California Press, 1994.

Zübeyr, Hamit. "Halk Terbiyesi Vasitalari" ("The Means of People Education"). *Ülkü* 1, no. 2 (1933).

Contributors

Vivodh Z. J. Anand is the communications director for the Indo-American Cultural Society, serves on the philosophy and religion studies faculty at Hofstra University, and is a diversity consultant. Anand served as a New Jersey civil rights commissioner from 1994 to 2003. Anand received his Ph.D. from New York University and presently resides in New York City, where he is working on an oral history project of New Jersey's Indian immigrants. Anand is an affiliate of the Pluralism Project at Harvard University.

R. Scott Appleby is the John M. Regan Jr. Director of the Joan B. Kroc Institute for International Peace Studies and professor of history at the University of Notre Dame. Appleby received the Ph.D. from the University of Chicago in 1985, is the author of *The Ambivalence of the Sacred: Religion, Violence and Reconciliation,* and is the editor of *Spokesman for the Despised: Fundamentalist Leaders of the Middle East.* From 1988 to 1993 Appleby was codirector with Martin E. Marty of the Fundamentalism Project, an international public policy study conducted by the American Academy of Arts and Sciences, and coedited the five-volume Fundamentalism Project.

Ertan Aydin is a member of the faculty of the Department of Political Science and International Relations of Çankaya University in Ankara, Turkey. Aydin received his Ph.D. from Bilkent University in 2003. He primarily works in the areas of political theory, political culture, and revolutionary politics, concentrating on the People's Houses as the major ideological institutions of the Turkish Revolution in the 1930s.

John P. Burgess is associate professor of theology at Pittsburgh Theological Seminary. Burgess received his Ph.D. from the University of Chicago in 1986. He is the author of *Why Scripture Matters* and *The East German Church and the End of Communism.*

SANFORD CLOUD JR. has served as the president and CEO of the National Conference for Community and Justice (formerly known as the National Conference of Christians and Jews) since 1994. As president, Cloud convened leading thinkers in six nationally telecast discussions known as the *National Conversation on Race, Ethnicity, and Gender.* He helped to create a collaboration of national organizations to combat prejudice and build healthy intergroup relations and is an internationally recognized speaker who addressed the United Nations Millennium World Peace Summit. Cloud is a 1969 graduate of Howard University Law School and in 1992 received an M.A. in religious studies from Hartford Seminary. In 1998 Cloud received the Spirit of Anne Frank Outstanding Citizen Award from the Anne Frank Center U.S.A. as one who has stepped forward and actively confronted anti-Semitism, racism, prejudice, and bias-related violence. He has taught corporate social responsibility as a lecturer of law at the University of Connecticut Law School, is a former two-term Connecticut state senator, and through much of the 1980s worked for Aetna Incorporated as vice president, corporate public involvement, and executive director of the Aetna Foundation.

YILMAZ ÇOLAK is assistant professor in the Department of Political Science and Public Administration in the Eastern Mediterranean University. The focus of his research and teaching is Turkish politics. Çolak received his Ph.D. from Bilkent University, Northern Cyprus, in 2000. He authored a piece that appeared in *Studies in Ethnicity and Nationalism.*

CATHARINE COOKSON is assistant professor in the Department of Religious Studies and is the Joan P. and Macon F. Brock Jr. Director, Center for the Study of Religious Freedom, Virginia Wesleyan College. Cookson received a law degree from Rutgers School of Law in 1980 and a Ph.D. from Indiana University in 1997. She authored *Regulating Religion: The Courts and the Free Exercise Clause* and edited the *Encyclopedia of Religious Freedom.*

PATRICK G. COY is associate professor in the Political Science Department and the Center for Applied Conflict Management at Kent State University. Coy received his Ph.D. from the Maxwell School of Citizenship and Public Affairs at Syracuse University in 1997. Coy is the editor of the annual volume *Research in Social Movements, Conflicts, and Change* and *A Revolution of the Heart: Essays on the Catholic Worker* and coedited *Social Conflicts and Collective Identities.* His research and teaching foci include conflict resolution, human rights, social movements, religion and politics, public policy and dispute resolution.

DEREK H. DAVIS is director of the J. M. Dawson Institute of Church-State Studies, Baylor University and authored *Original Intent: Chief Justice Rehnquist and the Course of American Church-State Relations* and *Religion and the Continental Congress, 1774–1789: Contributions to Original Intent.* He is the editor of the *Journal of Church and State* and has edited, coedited, or coauthored eight other books, including *The Role of Religion in the Making of Public Policy* and *Welfare Reform and Faith-Based Organizations.* Davis received his law degree at Baylor Law School and a Ph.D. from the University of Texas at Dallas. Prior to joining the institute in 1990, Davis was a practicing law partner in a Texas law firm.

WILLIAM D. DINGES is associate professor in the School of Theology and Religious Studies at the Catholic University of America. Dinges received a Ph.D. in 1983 from the University of Kansas. His research interests include American religion and culture. He was a participant and contributor to the Fundamentalist Project of the American Academy of Arts and Sciences and coauthored *Young Adult Catholics: Religion in the Culture of Choice*.

JAN FELDMAN is associate professor in the Political Science Department at the University of Vermont. Feldman received her Ph.D. in 1982 from Cornell University. She specializes in political theory and political culture and has published in the field of Soviet political theory, post-Soviet transition to democracy, trade policy, and population theory. She authored *Lubavitchers As Citizens: A Paradox of Liberal Democracy* in 2003.

JOHN E. FERGUSON JR. is a religious-liberty lawyer and the education coordinator for the Freedom Forum's First Amendment Center at Vanderbilt University. Ferguson is a graduate of Vanderbilt University's Law and Divinity schools, where he earned his J.D. and M.T.S. degrees. He is a member of the Tennessee, Washington, D.C., and Supreme Court bars and is coauthor of *The First Amendment in Schools*.

PAUL L. GASTON is professor of English and Provost of Kent State University. Gaston earned his Ph.D. from the University of Virginia, where he was a Woodrow Wilson Fellow, a DuPont Fellow, and a Woodrow Wilson Dissertation Fellow. He is the author of two books and of articles on subjects ranging from interart analogies, the poetry of George Herbert, and the fiction of Walker Percy.

GARY S. GILDIN is professor of law, holds the Hon. G. Thomas and Anne G. Miller Chair in Advocacy, and is the director of the Miller Center for Public Interest Advocacy at the Dickinson School of Law of the Pennsylvania State University. Gildin received a J.D. from Stanford University Law School. A noted scholar in the field of religious liberty, his recent articles in the *University of Pennsylvania Journal of Constitutional Law* and the *Harvard Journal of Law and Public Policy* have explored ways in which religious freedom might be more extensively protected by state constitutions than by the First Amendment to the United States Constitution.

POLYCARP IKUENOBE is associate professor of philosophy at Kent State University. He received his Ph.D. in 1993 from Wayne State University. Ikuenobe's research and teaching interests focus on philosophy of law, social and political philosophy, and African philosophy. Ikuenobe has edited several volumes in the series Symposia: Reading in Philosophy and authored articles that have appeared in *Philosophy East and West* and *Journal of Social Philosophy*.

SAKAH SAIDU MAHMUD is associate professor of political science at Transylvania University. He received his Ph.D. in 1992 from Denver University. His research and teaching interest include comparative political economy with special attention to sub-Saharan Africa, Asia, and the Middle East. He is the author of *State, Class, and Underdevelopment in Nigeria and Early Meiji Japan* and numerous articles.

DAVID W. ODELL-SCOTT is associate professor and chair of the Department of Philosophy at Kent State University and coordinator of the Religion Studies Program. Odell-Scott received a Ph.D. in philosophy from Vanderbilt University in 1989. He authored two books, *Paul's Critique of Theocracy* and *A Post-Patriarchal Christology* and is codirector of the Ohio Pluralism Project, an affiliate of the Pluralism Project at Harvard University.

J. E. RASH (Ahmed Abdur Rashid) is founder of Legacy International, a nonprofit organization that develops domestic and international programs in crosscultural relations and intercommunity dialogue. In 2000 he served as a delegate to the Millennium World Peace Summit of Religious and Spiritual Leaders at the United Nations. A member of the Muslim Peace Fellowship, his articles have appeared in *World Affairs, Education and Urban Society*, and *Sufism Journal*.

AMIRA SONBOL is associate professor of Islamic history, law, and society in the Center for Muslim-Christian Understanding at Georgetown University. Sonbol received her Ph.D. from Georgetown University. Her research and teaching foci include women, gender, and Islam. She has authored several books, including *The New Mamluks, Women, Family Law, and Divorce in Islamic History; The Creation of a Medical Profession in Egypt: 1800–1922*; and *The Memoirs of Abbas Hilmi II: Sovereign of Egypt*, and is coeditor of *Islam and Christian-Muslim Relations*.

MARY ZEISS STANGE is associate professor of women's studies and religion at Skidmore College. She received her Ph.D. from Syracuse University. Her areas of research and teaching include feminism, theology, religion and culture studies, and environmental studies. She has authored *Woman the Hunter* and *Heart Shots: Women Write about Hunting* and coauthored *Gun Women: Firearms and Feminism in Contemporary America*.

ROGER W. STUMP is professor of geography and religious studies at the University of New York at Albany. Stump received a Ph.D. from the University of Kansas in 1981. He authored *Boundaries of Faith: Geographical Perspectives on Religious Fundamentalism*. The foci of his research and teaching are religious conflict and the contextuality and spatiality of religions.

Index

Abbasid dynasty, 142–43
Abington v. Schempp, 35, 53, 81n64
abortion, 37
Abou El Fadl, Khaled, 147–48, 152
academia: disdain for religion, 248
activism. *See* social activism
Addams, Jane, 336
Afghanistan, 123
Africa, 4–5, 271
African Americans, 339, 341–43
Agostini v. Felton, 61, 68, 70–71, 74–76
Aguilar v. Felton, 61
Ahmad, Jalal Al-e, 12
Ahmadiya sect, 131
Ajami, Fouad, 134
Alalwani, Taha, 152
Aldridge, Alan, 252
Alexander, Archibald, 231
Al-Hibri, Azizah, 152
Al Qaeda, 254, 258; demonization of, 168–69;
    fundamentalist characteristics of, 244,
    250; relation to religion, 245–46
American Indian Movement (AIM), 166
American Indians: massacre at Wounded
    Knee, 164–66; religion of, 163–64; U.S.
    government *vs.*, 163, 173n21
American rights dialect, 4–5
Americans, 81n58 53; used to mean Protes-
    tant, 51–52, 80n35. *See also* United States;
    definition of
Anand, Vivodh Z. J., 270, 279–80

Anarchy, 20–21, 28n1
Anderson, Lisa, 123–24
antidiscrimination laws, 28n4, 300
Appleby, R. Scott, 248, 250, 260
Aquinas, Thomas, 28n1
Arabs: communities of, 271, 274, 277; U.S. ste-
    reotypes about, 169
Armstrong, Karen, 121
Arnold, Philip, 161
Arrington, Leonard J., 172n2
Ashcroft, John, 111, 114n12, 168
Asia, 4–5
assimilation, 327; difficulty of, 313–14; as di-
    lemma, 272–75; expectation of, 298, 312;
    influences on, 271, 276–77; pressure for,
    269, 273–74, 293, 307; resistance to, 270,
    272, 275–76, 284, 294–95
Atta, Mohamed, 134, 263n12
authority: in fundamentalism *vs.* democracy,
    196–97; of sacred texts, 225–27, 229–32,
    237–38, 239n2, 304; of state, 204–5, 303–6
autonomy, respect for, 324, 332
Azzam, Abdullah, 133

Bahais, persecution of, 193
Bakr, Abu, 142, 149
Banks, Dennis, 166
Barber, Benjamin, 140, 168–69
Barth, Karl, 226–27
Beecher, Lyman, 52
Bellah, Robert, 39–40

"benevolent neutrality" policy, 47n49. *See also* neutrality

Bennett, John Cook, 158

Berg, Thomas C., 305

Berns, Walter, 311

Bible, 252; beliefs about, 225–36; read in schools, 51–53, 80n40. *See also* sacred texts

Bin Laden, Osama, 115–16, 122–23, 133–34, 139, 253; demonization of, 168–69; influence of, 136n1, 150; as religious fundamentalist, 244, 250, 252; strain of Islam of, 256, 258; use of religious rhetoric, 245–46, 253

Bin Sultan, Prince Bandar, 253

Black, Justice Hugo L., 56–59, 82n91

Black Fox, 165

blacklisting, 112

Blackman, Paul H., 172n14

Bolt, Robert, 113

Bourne, Jenny, 291

Bowen v. Roy, 99n13

Boyarin, Jonathan, 302–3

Branch Davidians, 157, 159, 167, 173n16; massacre of, 110–11, 166, 171, 172n14; U.S. government *vs.*, 160–61

Brandeis, Louis, 96, 171

Breault, Marc, 159–61

Breyer, Stephen G., 72, 78, 87n267

Brodie, Fawn, 159

Bryan, William Jennings, 247

Buchanan, Pat, 278

Burgess, John, 190

Buruma, Ian, 170

Bush, George W., 26, 111, 168–70, 253, 279

Calvinism, 231

Cardoza, Benjamin, 336

Carter, Stephen, 38

Catholic Church, 2, 5–9

Catholics, 259; against communism, 9, 15n20; discrimination against, 51–52, 76, 80n35, 80n40, 80n49, 336; parochial schools, 52, 54, 76, 80n49

Ceaser, James, 311, 314

charitable choice legislation, 35

Chassidic Jews, 270, 272, 297, 299, 304; history of, 293–94; migrations, 274–76; preference for public religion, 294–95; rela-

tions with state, 300, 306–7; relation to group, 302–3, 305; resistance to assimilation, 294–95

Chechnya, 143, 155n24

Christian democracy, 7–8

Christian Right. *See* Religious Right

Christianity, 51, 136n4, 235, 247; fundamentalism in, 81n74, 186, 190, 197–98, 224–25, 247, 251–52; and U.S. foreign policy, 167–69. *See also* Catholics; Protestants; religious fundamentalism

Christians, 146, 163, 277

Church of Jesus Christ of Latter-Day Saints (Mormons), 159, 17n22, 200n9; leaders of, 157–59; propaganda against, 157–58

church-state relations, 8, 28n7, 29n8, 33, 82n100; accommodation in, 39–44, 64–65; interactions of religion and politics, 36–39; and Islam, 10–11; in Turkey, 203–5. *See also* church-state separation; school voucher programs

church-state separation, 33, 45n4; arguments for, 7, 21–22, 64; in *Everson v. Board of Education*, 56–58; incomplete, 37–38; institutional, 34–36; in *Love in Ruins*, 178–79; as protection for religious freedom, 310, 311

City of Boerne v. Flores, 93–94, 96–97

Ciuba, Gary, 175

civic responsibility, 5

civil liberties, 37, 112, 338; and civil rights movement, 341; and cost of national citizenship rights, 270, 294–95, 307; effects of war on terrorism on, 109, 111; Jews fighting for, 275, 294; protecting individuals,' 310–12; religious parties in Turkey demanding, 216–17

civil order: requirements for, 21, 23–24, 27; state's duty to, 19, 281. *See also* human rights

civil religion, 25–26, 296; accommodation of, 33, 39–44; courts on, 40–43; in schools, Supreme Court eliminating in schools, 53

civil rights. *See* civil liberties

civil society, group affiliations in, 301–2

Clark, Tom, 35

clash of civilizations, 109, 139–40, 170, 265n62

Clash of Civilizations, The (Huntington), 278

class, social, 270, 276–78

Cleveland, school voucher program, 23, 25, 49–50. *See also Zelman v. Simmons-Harris*

clothing, 270–71, 278, 293

coercion test: of establishment clause, 82n82

Cohen, Felix, 166

cold war, 168

Collins, Mary, 164

colonialism, 150, 250

Color Line: Legacy for the Twenty-first Century, The (Franklin), 340

Committee for Public Education and Religious Liberty v. Nyquist. See Nyquist

common good, 38, 44, 195; religious sects suppressed for, 156–57, 159; and school voucher programs, 23–24, 78

Communism, 9, 15n20

communitarian groups, 157, 159; Chassidim as, 302–3; on value of groups, 301–2

communities, 274, 284–85, 291; celebrated in Navratri festival, 283–84; of Chassidic Jews, 294–95, 305; finding meaning within Islam, 118–19; steps to improve, 337, 345–46

compelling interest test, 94–96, 99n22, 100n34, 100n40; *vs.* rational basis test, 91–93

Congress, U.S., 99n28, 343; and Religious Freedom Restoration Act of 1993, 92–93, 99n19; and states' rights, 93–94; Supreme Court's relations with, 93–94

Connolly, W., 310

conscience: freedom of, 7, 64; *vs.* law, 196–97

Constitution, U.S., 52; focused on individuals, 301, 311–12; protection for minorities in, 90, 273; religion in, 22, 31n13, 38; religious neutrality in, 39, 296, 298; *vs.* state constitutions, 94–95, 100n38

Conyers, John, Jr., 343

Coughlin, Charles, 106, 113n1

courts, 50, 291; on civil religion, 40–43; Edison Town Council *vs.* Indo-American Society in, 289–90. *See also* state courts; Supreme Court

Cover, Robert, 303–4

Crazy Horse, 164

creation science, 228, 232, 247

crime: religious obligation as intent, 19–20

critical consciousness, 108

Crow, Karim, 145–46

Crow Dog, Leonard, 166

cultural diversity, 139–41, 293, 295, 307, 323, 339; calling for introspection, 319–20; equality *vs.* toleration of, 324; institutional *vs.* individual tolerance of, 312–13; opposition to, 278, 298; valuing *vs.* tolerating, 332

cultural institutions, 291; leadership of, 345–46; in Turkey, 205–8

cultural minorities, 323–24; and boutique multiculturalism, 330–31; national *vs.* ethnic, 327; needs of, 325–26; special privileges for, 327–28

cultural relativism, 227; fundamentalists' opposition to, 186, 195–98, 224

culture, 210, 222, 314, 327; decay of, 178, 189; deliberative *vs.* dedicated, 296–98; diversity *vs.* homogenization of, 139–41, 198; dominant *vs.* minority, 269–70, 272–73, 277–78, 281, 305–6; exceptionalism in U.S., 270–71, 278, 280; freedom of, 273, 326; heterogeneity of, 194; homogeneity of, 192–93, 313; national, 40, 44; Occidentalist assumptions about, 255–56; religion's role in, 209, 244, 312–14; sexual freedom in U.S., 278–80; shared democratic, 306; struggle for Turkey's, 208–9, 214, 217. *See also* assimilation

Culture of Disbelief, The (Carter), 38

Darrow, Clarence, 247

Davis, Derek, 24–25

Dearborn, Mich., 274

Death of the West, The (Buchanan), 278

democracy: conflict of religious fundamentalism with, 189, 195–200; education's relation with, 106–9; February 28 process as crisis in Turkey's, 214–17; infringement on minority rights as price of, 92–93, 98, 99n18; Islamic extremists' negation of, 145; Islam's compatibility with, 1, 9, 141–42, 152; Kemalist views of, 205–9; liberalism's tension with, 269–70, 298, 306; in *Love in Ruins*, 175, 177–78; meanings of, 192–95, 269; minorities in, 194, 291, 313, 325–26; religion and, 2–3, 9, 14, 224, 300, 314; religious freedom under, 19, 89, 185, 324–25; religious fundamentalism as problem for, 185–86,

193, 238; religious fundamentalism's relation to, 190–91, 195, 199–200, 221–22, 238–
39; repressive tolerance in, 331; secularity
of, 202–3; shared culture in, 306; thick *vs.*
thin models of, 204; types of, 192–93; undemocratic means to achieve, 194, 214; in
U.S., 109, 142–43, 153–54, 181

Democrat Party government (Turkey), 208

Democratic Left Party (Turkey), 216

democratic spiritualities, 107

Democratic Turkey Party, 216

democratization, 14; means of, 206–8; religions' role in, 4, 15n20; in Turkey, 203–4,
208–9, 217

demographics, 150

Denouncing Racism: A Resource Guide (NCCJ),
339

Dietz, Park, 161, 172n15

Dignitatis Humanae (ecumenical council), 8–9

Dinges, William, 189

direct-aid cases, 70, 74–75

discrimination, 277, 300, 342; against Catholics, 51–52, 80n49, 336; civil rights laws inadequate against, 341–42; against immigrants, 271–72, 281; intentional *vs.*
unintentional, 89–90; law enforcement
profiling as, 279, 338, 342; against
Navratri festival, 287–88, 290; in levels of
religion, 270–71; prejudice based on, 282;
against religious minorities, 97–98, 274;
working against, 336–38, 340–41, 344–45.
See also racism

diversity. *See* cultural diversity; cultural minorities; religious diversity; religious minorities

Dobson, James, 255

Doomsday cults, 161–62

Douglas, William O., 39

Draper, Andrew S., 51

dualisms, manipulation of, 111

Durkheim, Emile, 40

Dürr, Hans-Peter, 113n5, 140–41

Dworkin, Ronald, 311

Eastern Europe, 4, 9, 15n20, 274–75

economy, 214, 284

Edison, N.J., 285–90

education, 54, 81n74; adult, 206–8; bias

against religion in, 53–54, 76, 81n58; discrimination against Catholics in, 51–52,
80n40, 80n49; in formation of Jewish
fundamentalist identity, 222–23; goals of
public, 51, 81n58; interactions of religion
and politics over, 36, 51–53; for Jewish immigrants, 275, 304; as mode of state intervention, 299, 307n7; by private religious
schools, 52, 54–55; racial inequalities in,
341; relation to assimilation, 276–77; relation with democracy, 106–9; religious activity in, 228; religious activity in schools,
34–35, 40–42, 53, 81n64; role of teachers
in religious development, 105–8, 124, 133;
secularization of, 53, 232; state control of,
214. *See also* religious schools; school
voucher programs

Eisenhower, Dwight D., 26

Emily, Jacque, 259

Employment Division v. Smith, 19, 87n270, 91–
93, 99n15, 99n18; and states' rights, 94,
96, 98

endorsement, 70; perception of, 67–69, 74,
76, 88n279, 88n297

endorsement test, 72, 82n82; of establishment clause, 63–66; Justice O'Connor
and, 72, 74–76

Engle v. Vitale, 25, 53, 81n64

Enlightenment, 294, 296

equality, 24, 322–25, 328

Erbakan, Necmettin, 212, 216

Esposito, John, 118

establishment clause, 39, 82n82, 294, 304;
and accommodation of civil religion, 41–
43; and arguments opposing school
vouchers, 66–69, 74, 83n113; and arguments supporting school vouchers, 23–25;
in criteria for education issues, 55–66; free
exercise clause *vs.*, 20, 24, 74, 299–300;
goals of, 36, 57, 296; interpretations of,
21–22, 27; Supreme Court cases on, 77,
85n184; violations of, 50, 74, 76

Europe, 283; Chassidic Jews in, 293–94; immigrants from, 271, 274–75

Evangelical Protestantism, 22

*Everson v. Board of Education of Township of
Ewing*, 55–59, 69–70, 78, 83n106

expression, religious. *See* free exercise clause

Fadlallah, Sheikh, 148
Fagan, Livingstone, 173n16
Falwell, Jerry, 114n12, 170–71, 255, 265n50
FBI, 160–62, 166, 279
February 28 process: in Turkey, 203, 210, 214–17
federal courts, 50. *See also* Supreme Court
federalism, 95–96
Feldman, Jan, 272, 275–76, 280
feminists, 298; on gender relations, 279–81; inconsistency on women's choice, 278, 299; on women's power, 279–80, 299
Finke, Roger, 248
firearms: of Mormons and Branch Davidians, 157–58, 160, 17n24
First Amendment, 33, 89; and debate over civil religion, 41–42; state aid to religious schools in violation of, 55–56. *See also* establishment clause; free exercise clause
Fish, Stanley, 2, 329–31
Fletcher, George, 320–21
Foote, Shelby, 175
foreign policy, U.S., 167–69
Forsyth, James, 164–65
Forte, David F., 258
Fourteenth Amendment, 78, 82n81, 97, 299
frames, religious ideologies as, 244, 261–62
Franklin, Benjamin, 141, 145
Franklin, John Hope, 340
free exercise clause: establishment clause *vs.*, 20, 24, 299–300; goals of, 36, 91; and government officials, 26–27, 39; influences on, 87n270, 93; interpretations of, 21, 29n8, 91, 197; limits on, 27, 284, 314–16; and no aid to religion, 72; protection for individuals, 311–12; protection of religious groups' internal norms, 299–300; religious minorities not protected by, 89, 93; state *vs.* federal protection for, 95, 97–98. *See also* religious freedom
freedom of conscience, 7, 64. *See also* free exercise clause
Freire, Paulo, 107, 108
Friedman, Thomas L., 257–58
fundamentalism. *See* religious fundamentalism
Fundamentalism Project (American Academy of Arts and Science), 186, 187–88, 222, 248–51, 259, 261

Galeotti, Anna Elisabetta, 321–24, 326
Gallagher, Eugene, 160–61, 167
Galtung, Johan, 113n5
Gardner, John, 346
Gaston, Paul, 107–9
gender, 256, 278; as dilemma for liberalism, 279–81; women celebrated in Navratri festival, 283–84
gender relations, in Judaism, 280, 298–99
Ghost Dance, 162–66, 173n20
Gildin, Gary, 20
Gilkey, Langdon, 232
Ginsburg, Justice Ruth Bader, 72, 78, 83113
globalization, 107, 140–41, 209–11, 216
Goffman, Erving, 244
good, conceptions of, 309, 312, 317, 319, 323, 329, 331–32
government, state: accommodation of religious practices by, 197–98, 299–300, 304–5, 307; accommodation of cultural minorities, 327–28; decay of, 178–79, 189; definitions of, 176, 178–80; and endorsement test, 63–64, 67–69; expansion of, 58, 64; incompetence of Muslim countries', 250–51; intervention in religions, 20, 298–99, 303, 316; involvement with religion, 28n7, 29n8, 61, 64–65, 67–69, 85n180, 316; lack of power over religion, 21–22, 25, 47n49; under people's authority, 39; power used by dominant culture, 273–74; Qur'an on, 141–42; relation of Chassidic Jews to, 293–94; relation with people, 142–43; religious minorities' relations with, 90–92, 156–58, 167, 306–7; role of, 19, 27, 281, 36, 193; self-, 294. *See also* church-state relations; church-state separation; religion, government aid to; religious schools, government aid to
government, Turkey's, 205, 209, 214–17
government, U.S.: Indian Wars by, 163, 164–66; *vs.* American Indian Movement (AIM), 166; *vs.* Branch Davidians, 159, 160–61, 172n14; *vs.* Mormons, 159
government officials, 26–27, 39
Graham, Franklin, Jr., 136n4
Greene, Abner, 305
Gregory XVI, Pope, 5–6
Gujarati Indians, 270, 274; communities of,

272, 282–83; Navratri festival of, 282, 284–88

Gül Abdullah, 212

Haarscher, Guy, 330
Haeri, Fadhlalla, 144
Hall, Timothy, 90
Hardacre, Helen, 2
Hasselstrom, Linda, 173n21
hate-crimes legislation, 337–38, 340
Hatfield, Mark, 43
hatred: religious, 23, 25
Haynes, Charles, 54
healthcare inequalities, 338, 340–41
Henry, Patrick, 21–22, 287
Hindus, 339; fundamentalist, 190, 194, 198
Hodge, Charles, 231
holiday celebrations, religion in, 40–41, 63
Hughes, Charles Evans, 336
human rights, 14, 15n18, 284; Catholic Church's support for, 5, 8–9; and Muslims, 9, 149, 152–53; religious activism for, 4; religious freedom as, 185; and tolerance vs. acceptance, 326; used for undemocratic ends, 195. See also civil liberties
Hunter, James Davison, 225, 233
Huntington, Samuel, 109, 170, 265n62, 278

Ibn Hazm, 145
Ibn Taymiyah, 145
identity, 211; cultural, 205–6, 326–27; and identity groups, 194, 218; national, 192, 198, 209–10, 213; of religious fundamentalists, 222–24, 249
Ignatieff, Michael, 124
Ikinci Mesrutiyet, 210
Ikuenobe, Polycarp, 270, 273
immigrants, 271–72, 279, 294; class of, 276–78; discrimination against, 51–52, 282–83; dominant culture vs., 277–78, 284; gender relations of, 280–81; violence against, 284–85
Immigration Act of America (1965), 282, 284
Immortale Dei (Pope Leo XIII), 6
incorporation doctrine, 78, 82n81
India, 194, 282; Hindu fundamentalists in, 198–99; immigrants from, 277, 285; Navratri festival in, 283. See also Gujarati Indians

Indian Wars, 163–64
individual benefits cases, 69–70, 74
individualism, 211; and discomfort with groups, 300–303; lack of importance to Chassidim, 302–3; and relations with society, 178–80; and religious freedom, 323–24; and tolerance of difference, 312–13; in U.S. culture, 5, 270–71
individuals, protecting rights of, 310–12
Indo-American Cultural Society, 285–89, 291
Indo-American Cultural Society v. Township of Edison, 282
injustice. See justice
Inkilap Dersleri (Revolutionary Courses) (Peker), 206
Inside the Cult (documentary), 159–60
Institutes of the Christian Religion (Calvin), 231
intellectuals, 277–78
interfaith prayer services, 25–26
Iran, 193
Iranian Revolution, 115
Islam, 2, 210; absolutism and exclusivism in, 256–58; compatibility with democracy, 1, 5, 9, 107, 135, 141–42, 152; criticisms of, 213, 258–59; demonization of, 114n12, 136n4, 139; differing interpretations of, 106, 126–28, 132, 135, 149–51; extremism vs. moderation in, 139, 146–48, 151, 153; extremists in, 111, 120–22, 145–46, 149–50; finding meaning within, 118–20, 134–35; fundamentalism in, 120–22, 194, 244–45, 250–52, 263n15; fundamentalism vs. extremism in, 136n2, 260; and human rights, 5, 9; importance of teachers in, 106, 132; and jihad, 128–29, 131; justifying political positions through, 121–24, 126, 134–35, 136n1, 155n24; Kemalists suppressing, 202–3, 214–18; lack of leaders, 154, 155n30; leaders, 125–26, 128, 132–33, 142, 149–50, 152, 251; Mormonism compared to, 158–59; and other religions, 136n9, 145–46; Qur'an in, 128, 187; reforms of, 205, 250–51; relation to Sept. 11 attacks, 253–59; role in state, 10–11; sects of, 143, 145–46, 150–51, 254, 258; Sufis in, 113n6, 144; tasks of, 130–31; tenets of, 136n6, 154n9; and terrorism, 115–16, 171, 245–46, 257; tolerance of peripheries vs.

Islam (*cont.*)
  core, 315–16; totality of, 125–26, 135, 257–
  58; in Turkey, 191, 194, 197, 203–5, 209, 211;
  and U.S., 111, 151–53, 169, 342; use of term
  "fundamentalism" in, 187, 251, 264n33; and
  violence, 105, 111, 116–18, 124–26, 133–34,
  136n4, 148–49, 256; worldviews of, 117–18,
  120, 122–24, 135, 138n62
Islamists, 214; as obstacle to modernization,
  210–11; *vs.* Kemalists in Turkey, 198–99,
  210, 217
Israel, 276, 277; religion *vs.* secular democracy
  in, 194, 197–99, 201n13

Jackson, Robert H., 85n184
Jamaat-i-Islami (JI), 10–11
Jefferson, Thomas, 30n9, 56–58, 141–43, 153
Jenkins, Philip, 160–62
jihad, 127, 131, 245, 253; in Islamic
  worldviews, 133–34; in Qur'an and
  Sunnah, 128–30
Jihad vs. McWorld (Barber), 168–69
John Paul II, Pope, 9
John XXIII, Pope, 8
Judaism, 146, 294, 304; discrimination
  against, 274–75; fundamentalism in, 197–
  98, 201n13, 222–24, 228; gender relations
  in, 280, 298–99; religious *vs.* secular democracy in Israel, 197–99, 201n13; resistance to assimilation, 270, 272. *See also*
  Chassidic Jews
Juergensmeyer, Mark, 167, 260–61
justice, 211; as basis of tolerance, 322–23;
  lacking in health care, 340–41; Muslims
  seeking, 125–26

Kaftaro, Shaykh Ahmad, 139, 148
Kavakci, Merve, 216
Kazan, Şevket, 212, 216
Kemalism: in Turkey, 218n4; democracy of,
  192–93, 205–6, 206–8; Islamists *vs.*, 194,
  198–99, 202–4, 214–16; modernization by,
  204–5; opposition to, 210, 212; reforms of,
  208–9; secularism of, 203–4, 217; undemocratic means to achieve democracy
  by, 194, 214
Kennedy, Anthony, 82n82; on civil religion,
  42–43; on school voucher programs, 67,
  72, 78

Khan, Maulana Wahiduddin, 130
Kharajites, 145
Khomeini, Ayatollah, 120–21, 193
Kiryas Joel Sc. Dist. v. Grumet, 304
Kişlali, Ahmet Taner, 214
King, Martin, 159–60
King, Martin Luther, Jr., 340–41, 344
Koop, C. Everett, 27
Kopel, David B., 172n14
Koresh, David, 107; compared to Joseph
  Smith, 156–57; demonization of, 159, 161,
  172n15; killing of, 156–57; propaganda
  against, 159–60; on violence and self-de-
  fense, 160–61
Kothari, Pradip (Peter), 285
Kugel, James, 229–30
Kurdish movement: in Turkey, 209–10, 212
Kymlicka, Will, 273, 312, 322, 326–29, 333n9

Laicism. *See* Kemalism: in Turkey
Lamennais, Félicité de, 5–6
language, 262n7, 282, 314, 326–27
Laquer, Walter, 122
Latimer, Steve, 289
Latin America, 4
Latinos/Hispanics, 276, 339–40, 342
law: civil rights movement working for, 341–42;
  effects on religious minorities, 90–92, 92–
  93, 97; and fundamentalism, 190, 221–24;
  fundamentalism *vs.* democracy on, 196–97,
  224, 237–38; limits on free exercise in, 314–
  16; restricting religious practices, 287–88,
  314, 329–31; sacred texts as, 232, 237; secularity of, 38–39; state authority over, 303–4;
  states', and religious minorities, 93–94,
  101n48; *vs.* religious obligation, 19–20
Lee v. Weisman, 42, 82n82
Lemon v. Kurtzman: and *Lemon* test, 38–39,
  60–63, 75, 300, 304
Leo XIII, Pope, 6
Lewis, Bernard, 121, 169, 250, 257, 264n33
liberalism, 250, 296, 314, 332; assimilation as
  dilemma for, 272–73; comprehensive *vs.*
  political, 297; discomfort with groups,
  301–3, 311; gender as dilemma for, 279–81;
  and limits of tolerance, 316–25, 329–30;
  and minority rights, 310–12, 326, 328; and
  multiculturalism, 293, 295–96, 330–31; tenets of, 309–10; tension with democracy,

269–70, 306; and virtue of tolerance, 320, 322; *vs.* fundamentalism, 247, 252

"Life and Times of Institutional Racism, The" (Bourne), 291

Lifland, John C., 289–90

Lipkin, Robert, 296, 305

Lippman, Thomas, 118, 125–26

Lipset, Seymour Martin, 270

lobbying: by religious groups, 37, 45n18

Locke, John, 284, 311, 315, 322

Long, Charles, 244–45

Loughlin, Michaelene, 289

Love in Ruins (Percy), 107–9, 112–13, 175–80

Lukes, Steven, 318

Lynch v. Donnelly, 63–65, 75

Machen, J. Gresham, 252

MacIntyre, Alisdair, 3

Madison, James, 21–22, 24, 298, 56–58, 141

Mahmud, Sakah Saidu, 105–6, 111

Man for All Seasons, A (Bolt), 113

Marcuse, Herbert, 321, 325, 329–32

Margalit, Avishai, 170

Maritain, Jacques, 7–8

Marsden, George, 231

Marsh v. Chambers, 42

Marshall, Thurgood, 60

Marty, Martin, 248

Marx, Karl, 239

Marxism: as non-Western democracy, 192

matriarchy, 279–81

Matthiessen, Peter, 166

Matto, Kenneth, 290

Mawdudi, Mawlana Sayyid Abul A'la, 10–11, 193

McDaniel v. Paty, 37

McGillycuddy, Valentine, 163–64

McVeigh, Timothy, 171, 279

McWilliams, Wilson, 328

Means, Russell, 162, 166

media, 277; on Koresh and Branch Davidians, 159, 160; military intervention in Turkey through, 214–15; on Muslims and Arabs, 169–70; on religious extremists, 106, 150; on religious fundamentalism, 247–48; on religious minorities, 156, 158–59

Memorial and Remonstrance (Madison), 56

Middle East, 152, 342; human rights discussions in, 4–5; social conditions in, 116, 133–34

Middlesex County, N.J., 283

Middleton, Richard, 120

military: in Turkey, 209, 212–17

Mill, J. S., 311, 313

Miller, John, 133

Mincberg, Elliot, 67

minority groups, 273, 312; assimilation of, 272–75. *See also* cultural diversity; cultural minorities; religious minorities

Minow, Martha, 305

Mirari vos (Pope Gregory XVI), 5

Miron, Murray, 161

missionaries: to Indians, 163–64

Mitchell v. Helms, 57–58, 82n83, 83n113

modernism, 217; accommodation of religion to, 248–49; fundamentalists' opposition to, 188, 195, 251–52; pluralism of, 257–58; and religious fundamentalism, 190–92, 221, 224, 227–28, 236–37; use by religious fundamentalism to antimodernist ends, 237–38

modernization: religion seen as obstacle to, 210–11, 213, 218–9; in Turkey, 204–5, 208

Mody, Navroze, 285

More, Thomas (Dr.), 175–81

More, Thomas (St.), 113, 176

Mormons. *See* Church of Jesus Christ of Latter-Day Saints (Mormons)

Motherland Party (Turkey), 209, 216

Mount Carmel community. *See* Branch Davidians; Koresh, David

Mozert v. Hawkins County, 307–8n7

Mueller v. Allen, 59, 69

Muhammad (prophet), 126–27, 145, 154n13; on fighting, 130, 149; and Islam's compatibility with democracy, 141–42; on religious moderation, 146–48

multiculturalism. *See* cultural diversity

Murray, John Courtney, 6–9

Muslims, 171, 279, 281; relations with Christians, 146; U.S., 151–53, 253–54, 256, 276, 279. *See also* Islam

National Conference for Christians and Jews. *See* National Conference for Community and Justice (NCCJ)

National Conference for Community and Justice (NCCJ), 336, 338; conversations sponsored by, 339–40, 342–44; goals of, 336–37; name changes of, 336–37; *Taking America's Pulse* survey, 342, 344

National Salvation Party (Turkey), 210–11
nationalism, 204, 250
Nativists, 51–52, 80n49
natural law, 8–9
Navratri festival, 279–80, 282–84; attempts to address concerns about, 286–87; legal steps against, 285–88
Neisser, Eric, 291
neutrality, 47n49, 307, 323; and establishment clause, 62–63, 65, 76, 296; and liberalism, 309, 317, 328; limits on, 314, 329; as protection for religious freedom, 311–12; question of state intervening despite, 298–99, 303; in school voucher cases, 70, 78
Nicholson, Peter, 318
Niebuhr, Reinhold, 171
No Man Knows My History (Brodie), 159
"Nomos and Narrative" (Cover), 303
nonmainstream sects. *See* religious minorities
Nord, Warren A., 51, 54
norms, 110; protection of religious groups', 299–300; of radical communitarian groups, 156–57
Norquist, Grover, 256
novels, 107–9
Nyquist, 59, 66, 71; needing to be clarified or overturned, 71, 75; school vouchers said to violate, 66–69; used in *Zelman*, 71–72, 74–75

Occidentalism. *See* Orientalism/Occidentalism
O'Connor, Sandra Day, 58, 97, 99n18; and endorsement test, 63, 75–76; fear of government involvement in religion, 65; and *Lemon* test, 61; and neutrality test, 63; on school voucher programs, 68, 72, 78
Okin, Susan, 280, 298
Oklahoma City bombing, 171
Orientalism/Occidentalism, 169–70, 255–56
"Otherness," 270; of African Americans, 271; of Chassidim, 305; of Gujarati Indians, 272, 284–85, 291
Ottoman legacy, 204
Özal, Turgut, 209
Özbudun, Ergun, 204, 208

Pacem in Terris (Pope John XXIII), 8–9, 15n18
Pakistan, 10–11, 277
Palmer, A. Mitchell, 112
parents: role in education, 24–25

Patel, Chandrakant, 285
patriarchy, 2, 279–81
Patriot Act, 111–12
peace, 107, 113n5, 130, 140; danger of religious extremists to, 144–45; and Islam, 116, 145
Peace Policy: toward Indians, 163
Peker, Recep, 206
Pelikan, Jaroslav, 230–31
people, the: beliefs about, 141–44; effects of Taliban's rigidity on, 146, 148; government's relation with, 142–43
Percy, Walker, 107–9, 112–13, 175–76, 181
Philippines, 9
Pius IX, Pope, 6
pluralism, 218, 233, 235, 316; in biblical interpretation, 225–30; in democracies, 192–93; within religions, 14; religious extremists *vs.*, 11–12; religious fundamentalism and, 224, 227, 239n1; *vs.* dangers of totality, 257–58. *See also* religious freedom
political messiansim, 207–8
political parties, 279; in Turkey, 208–13, 216
politics, 256–57, 301; Catholic Church on, 6–7; Chassidim in, 295, 297; interactions with religion, 3, 33, 36–39, 170, 253, 294; and Islam, 9–10, 120–23, 126, 134, 149–50; Islam used as justification for positions in, 121–24; over Navratri festival, 288–89; and religious fundamentalists, 13, 249; and Supreme Court decisions, 77, 94; in Turkey, 209, 213–17; use of term "fundamentalist" in, 187, 247–48
polygamy: of Mormons, 156–59; of Muslims, 315–16, 321, 329
postmodernism, 214; accommodation of religion to, 248–49; opposition of fundamentalists to, 186, 188, 195; and religious fundamentalism, 190–92, 227
poverty, 133–34
Powell, Lewis F., Jr., 66
power: and tolerance, 306, 310, 318, 323–25
Prashad, M. G., 289
Presbyterians, 229
Princeton School, 231
private *vs.* public spheres, 53, 296; fundamentalism *vs.* democracy on, 197–98, 232–33; as protection for religious freedom, 311–12. *See also* religion, public
profiling, racial and ethnic, 279, 338, 342

Protestants, 231; discrimination against
Catholics by, 6, 51–52; fundamentalism
in, 224–25, 229; fundamentalists' assumptions about Bible, 225–36; use of term
"fundamentalism" by, 246, 251. *See also*
religious schools
psychology: on causes of Sept. 11, 256
public interest. *See* common good

Quanta cura (Pope Pius IX), 6
quantam physics, 140
Qur'an: compatibility with democracy, 141–42;
covering totality of life, 125; in development of Muslim worldview, 117, 119; differing interpretations of, 149–50; on fighting,
148–49; importance of, 128, 252; jihad in,
128–31; on power relations, 126–27; primacy in Islam, 187; Sept 11 violating ethics
of, 253; on tolerance of differing beliefs,
145–46; on violence, 125; violence in, 132
Qutb, Sayyid, 121–22, 131

racism, 271, 282, 330; continuation of, 340–
41; efforts to overcome, 336–37, 344–45; in
levels of discrimination, 270–71. *See also*
discrimination
Rahman, Fazlur, 119
Ranstorp, Magnus, 148
Rash, J. E., 106, 107, 111; on Islam, 111, 113–
14n6; on peace, 107, 113n5
rational-basis test, 91–92
Rawls, John, 323, 327, 329; on assimilation, 313–
14; on freedom, 309, 334n41; on individuals'
rights, 311–12; on liberalism, 38, 297
Red scare, 112
reforms: of Islam, 205, 250–51; in Turkey,
211–12
Rehnquist, William H., 59, 67, 72, 78
religion, 299; adaptiveness of/changes in, 2–4,
127, 199, 235, 248–49, 254; bias against, 53–
54, 76, 248; as common good, 21–22, 36, 38;
conflicts in doctrine *vs.* practice, 251–52;
criticisms of, 1–2, 218n9; in deliberative *vs.*
dedicated cultures, 297; effects of government aid to, 57, 64–65; engagement
among, 336–37; extremists in, 11–12, 106–7,
111, 144, 148, 260, 262; free choice of, 302,
311; government aid to, 51, 57, 64–65; government entanglement with, 25, 61, 64–65,

85n180; government's lack of power over,
21–22, 57; and holy wars, 128–29; and identity, 193–94, 326–27; interactions with politics, 33, 36–39, 45n18, 170; and irreverence,
178–79; Kemalism's attempt to reduce public, 203, 212, 214, 217–18; leaders of, 339–
40, 342–45; of American Indians, 162–64;
in Navratri festival, 283–84, 287–88, 290;
no aid to, 56, 64, 72, 78, 83n113; public, 275,
294–95; public role of, 53, 65, 197–98; relation to national citizenship rights, 272,
294–95; role in cultures, 209, 244, 312–14;
role in state, 5, 281; role in war against terrorism, 171; role of teachers in development of, 105–8; sincerity of fundamentalists', 161, 249. *See also* church-state
relations; church-state separation; civil religion; religious minorities
religious diversity, 136n9, 233; accommodation of, 95, 291; equality *vs.* toleration of,
324–25; liberalism's relation to, 309, 323;
within religions, 3–4, 14; tolerance of, 90,
145–46, 171
religious freedom, 309, 99n15, 185, 273, 275
Catholic Church on, 5–6, 8–9; democracy's
as hospitable to, 19, 89; equality *vs.* tolerance in, 322–24; and Muslim Americans,
151–53; possibility of, 309–10; selectivity
about, 166–67; state legislation on, 94–95,
97–98, 100n29; in U.S. history, 82n91, 90;
in *Zelman v. Simmons-Harris*, 50. *See also* establishment clause; free exercise clause;
pluralism;
Religious Freedom Restoration Act of 1993,
92–93, 96, 99nn19, 22; ruled unconstitutional, 93–94, 99n28
religious fundamentalism, 13; appeal of, 224–
25, 233, 236; definition of, 11–12, 239n1;
extremists *vs.*, 260, 262; goals of, 189;
leaders of, 249; meanings of, 186–92, 245–
49; in national identity, 198; negative connotations of, 187, 246–48; as problem for
democracy, 185–86, 190–91, 193, 238; relation to extremism, 136n2, 260; relation to
Sept. 11 attacks, 189, 252–53, 260, 262; relation to violence, 260–61; relations with
democracy, 195–200, 221–22, 238–39; sacred texts and laws in, 236–38, 239n2;
traits and values of, 2, 12–13, 188, 191–92,

religious fundamentalism (*cont.*)
231, 249; use of term, 251, 259, 261,
264n33. *See also* Fundamentalism Project;
specific religions
Religious Land Use and Institutionalized Persons Act of 2000, 99n28
religious literacy, 112, 120
religious minorities, 300; accommodation of,
97, 340; discrimination against, 97–98, 167;
government hindrance of, 89, 90–92,
99n15; leaders of, 156–57, 159, 163;
marginalization of, 249, 342; persecution
of, 156–57, 170–71, 193; protection for, 92–
98, 193; special privileges for, 327–28; state
courts on, 20, 100n34; state legislation for,
93–98, 101n48; tolerance for, 166–67, 306–7,
312–13, 318–19, 332; in U.S., 156–57, 168, 339
religious obligation, 19–20
religious practices: government accommodation of, 299–300, 304–5, 307; laws restricting, 329–31; liberalism's limited tolerance for, 316–25
Religious Right, 247–48, 255, 258–59
religious schools, 71; discrimination against,
51–52, 76, 80n49; and free choice with
school voucher money, 68–70, 73–74, 78;
indoctrination by, 67, 70–71, 75; numbers/percentage receiving voucher
money, 67–69, 86n202, 87n274; parents'
belief in superiority of, 54–55
religious schools, government aid to, 73, 78,
83n106, 83n109; direct *vs.* indirect aid, 58–
60, 70, 74–75; establishment clause criteria for, 55–66; limiting factors on, 66–67;
no-aid to religion paradigm, 64, 72, 78,
83n113; resistance to, 52, 54; through
voucher programs, 23–25, 48, 55. *See also*
school voucher programs; *Zelman v.
Simmons-Harris*
reparations: for African Americans, 343
Republican Party (U.S.), 279
Republican regime, in Turkey, 204–8
republicanism, 205–8, 210, 213
resources, 109, 163
Revelation, 1–2
Riesebrodt, Martin, 2
Robertson, Pat, 255, 265n49
Roof, Wade Clark, 233
Russia, 294

Ruthven, Malise, 126
Rutledge, Wiley, 36

sacred texts, 252, 297, 304; in formation of
Jewish fundamentalist identity, 222–24,
228; interaction with custom, 222; in religious fundamentalism, 186–88, 221, 225,
236–37, 239–40n2. *See also* Bible; Qur'an
Sadik, Necmeddin, 218n9
Said, Edward, 116, 169
*San Antonio Independent School District v.
Rodriguez*, 96
satire, purpose of, 108
Savaş, Vural, 216–17
Scalia, Antonin, 61; on endorsement, 76,
88n297; on school vouchers, 72, 78
school voucher programs, 48, 80n50; arguments supporting, 23–25; in Cleveland,
49–50; free choice in, 67–70, 73–74, 78; opposing, 22–23, 26; Supreme Court on, 77,
87n267. *See also Zelman v. Simmons-Harris*
science, 1, 53, 232, 246–47; influence of
worldviews, 140
Scopes "Monkey trial," 247
Scottish Common Sense Realism, 231
Second Great Awakening, 22
Second Vatican Council (1962–65), 5
secularism, 250, 255, 296, 298, 311; effects of,
217, 235; interaction with religious fundamentalism, 227, 231; Islam's resistance to,
250–51; Jewish immigrants working for,
275, 294; religious fundamentalism *vs.*,
195–98, 233, 239n1; in Turkey, 193, 202–3,
209, 212, 214, 217
secularization, 232; opposition to, 12, 186, 188
separation: of church and state. *See* church-
state separation
separatism, 304
Sept. 11 attacks: causes of, 170, 255–56, 259;
effects of, 115, 153, 337–38; relation to Islam, 115, 253–61; relation to religion, 243–
44, 245; relation to religious fundamentalism, 168–69, 189, 248, 250, 252–53, 260,
262. *See also* terrorism
Seventh-Day Adventist Church, 157, 159, 161
sexuality, 156–59, 278–80
Shachar, Ayelet, 307
Shari'a, 10–11, 126
Sheikh Omar, Ahmed, 123

Sherbert v. Verner, 92
Sheridan, Philip, 163, 173n21
Sitting Bull, 164
skeptical secularist argument, 1–2
slavery, 36, 342–43
Smith. See Employment Division v. Smith
Smith, Al, 336
Smith, Joseph, 107, 172n2; arsenal of, 157–58;
    David Koresh compared to, 156–57; lead-
    ership by, 157–59; lynching of, 156–57
Smith, Wilfred Cantwell, 226
social activism: interactions of religion and
    politics over, 36–37; within religions, 4; re-
    ligions calling for, 143–44; of religious
    fundamentalists, 188–89, 233, 295
social conditions: effects of, 150, 163, 235, 255;
    in Middle East, 116, 133–34, 250–51
social protest, lack of opportunity for, 250
social science: disdain for religion, 248
social service programs, 35, 57
society, 178–80, 270. *See also* culture; state, the
Soloveitchik, Haym, 222–24, 227–28
Souter, Justice David H., 72, 78, 83113
South Asia, 187
South Korea, 9
Stange, Mary Zeiss, 107, 109–11
Stark, Rodney, 248
state, the, 318; group affiliations in, 301–2; as
    liberal *vs.* religious, 38–39, 58; multina-
    tional, 313; religion's role in, 5–9; as sole
    authority, 204–5; *vs.* society, 7; *vs.*
    subnational loyalties, 301, 303–6. *See also*
    church-state relations; church-state sepa-
    ration; government
state courts, 20, 50, 96, 100n34, 100n40
states, U.S., 96; ability to expand rights, 94–96;
    constitutions of, 80n50, 100n38; incorpo-
    ration doctrine in, 78, 82n81; protection of
    religious minorities by, 89, 93–98, 10148;
    religious freedom acts by, 97–98, 100n29
state-sponsored prayer, 26
Stein v. Plainwell Community Schools, 41–43
Stevens, John Paul, 72, 78, 83n113
Stolzenberg, Maya Nomi, 305
Straus, Roger W., 336
Stump, Roger, 233, 260
Sufism, 113n6, 143–44, 154n9
Sullivan, Andrew, 115–16, 170, 256–57
Sun Dance, 163

Sunnah. *See* Qur'an
Supreme Court, U.S., 37, 77; on civil religion,
    40–43, 53; establishment clause criteria
    for education issues, 55–66; federalism's
    effects on, 95–96; interpretations of First
    Amendment, 33, 47n49, 91; need to clarify
    Nyquist or overturn, 71, 75; relations with
    Congress, 93–94; on religious minorities,
    91–92, 96, 304; on school voucher pro-
    grams, 25, 66, 69, 72, 77, 87n267; and
    Zelman v. Simmons-Harris, 48, 50, 77–78.
    See also specific cases
symbols: Bible as, 228–30; national, 210, 213;
    religious, 206, 212, 215–17, 217–18

Tabor, James, 160–61, 167
Taking America's Pulse (NCCJ survey), 342, 344
Taliban, rigidity of, 146, 148
tax exemptions, for religious groups, 37
temperance, 36
Ten Commandments, 232, 234–35
terrorism, 139, 195, 244; Islam's relation to,
    115, 245–46, 257; relation to religious fun-
    damentalism, 187, 189, 250; religion used
    to justify, 130, 136n1, 253. *See also* Sept. 11
    attacks; terrorism, war on; violence
terrorism, war on, 167; Christian rhetoric in,
    168–69; effects of, 109–11
theo-democracy, 10–11, 193, 200n9
Theory of Justice, A (Rawls), 38
"This *Is* a Religious War" (Sullivan), 115, 256–57
Thomas, Cal, 114n12
Thomas, Clarence, 72, 78
tolerance, 313; acceptance *vs.*, 319–20, 323–24,
    326, 330–31; active *vs.* passive, 330–31; al-
    ternatives to, 13, 320–21; of individuals *vs.*
    groups, 33n39; institutional *vs.* individual,
    312–13; liberalism and, 316–25; limits of,
    316–25, 328–31; and needs of cultural mi-
    norities, 325–26; peripheral *vs.* core, 315–
    16; power inequality and, 318, 321–22; re-
    pressive, 330–31; respect *vs.*, 318–19;
    vertical and horizontal, 325
Toobin, Jeffrey, 168
True Path Party (Turkey), 211, 216
truth, 1, 7; and absolutism of religious funda-
    mentalism, 228–29, 257; in deliberative *vs.*
    dedicated cultures, 296–98; of fundamental-
    ism *vs.* secular democratic orders, 221, 231

Turkey: democracy in, 203, 208–9; Islamists
in, 191, 197; Islamists *vs.* Kemalists in, 194,
198–99, 203–4; Kurdish movement in,
209–10; military intervention in, 214–17;
political parties in, 209–13; republicanism
in, 204–8; secularism in, 203–4, 217; secularization of, 202–3
Turkish Republic, 215
Turkish Revolution, 204
Turkish Revolutionary elite, 202–3, 206–8.
See also Kemalism, in Turkey

United Nations, 151n8
United States, 276, 339; and al Qaeda, 123,
254, 255; American rights dialect in, 4–5;
democracy in, 109, 142–43, 153–54; disintegration in *Love in Ruins*, 175–77;
exceptionalism in culture of, 270–71, 278,
280; increasing polarization of, 178, 181;
international role of, 338; Islamic war
against, 115–16, 122–23, 245–46; limited
tolerance and pluralism in, 315–16; prejudice in, 282–83; religion in, 198, 235; stereotypes of Islam and Muslims in, 106,
136n4, 150, 169; treatment of religious minorities in, 167–68, 170–71. *See also* government, U.S
USSR, 168

Valdes, Ernesto Garzon, 318–19, 325
values, 236, 307n7; changes of, 178, 209–10;
diversity *vs.* homogenization of, 139–41;
of Islam, 256–57; liberal, 311, 322; pluralistic, 233, 305; traditional, 210, 212–13
violence, 148, 206; causes of, 116, 133–34; fear
of weapons of Mormons and Branch
Davidians, 157–58, 160, 172n4; gratuitous
vs. goal-oriented, 189; Islam on, 111, 125–
26, 128–32, 148–49; Islam's relation to,
105, 116–18, 124–25, 134, 136n2, 138n62,
256; by Kemalists, 203, 218; by and
against Mormons and Branch Davidians,
159, 162, 172n2; relation to fundamentalism, 136n2, 260–61; religion's relation to,
243, 259, 261–62; religious justification of,
13, 134, 190. *See also* terrorism

"Virginia Bill for Religious Liberty"
(Jefferson), 56
Virtue Party (Turkey), 216–17
Voices of Conscience Conversation, 339–40

Waco, massacre. *See* Branch Davidians;
Koresh, David
Walker Percy: Books of Revelation (Ciuba), 175
Walsh, Brian, 120
Walz v. Tax Commission, 37, 47n49
war, 37
war against terrorism. *See* terrorism, war on
war policy: against American Indians, 163–64
Warfield, Benjamin, 231
Washington, George, 142
Washington v. Glucksberg, 94
Weinrich, Michael, 224–25
Welfare Party (Turkey), 210–13, 216
West, 255–56, 259, 278
Westernization, 204–5
Williams, Juan, 339
Williams, Patricia, 169
Wisconsin v. Yoder, 92, 307n7
Witters v. Washington, 59–60, 66–69, 88n289
Wolff, Robert Paul, 316
worldviews, 140; apocalyptic, 159, 161–63; bi-
nary, 168–70; fundamentalist, 189–90,
199; Islam and development of, 117–18,
120, 123–24, 133–34; Islamic, 122, 132, 133,
150; in *Zelman v. Simmons-Harris*, 50
Wounded Knee, massacre at, 110–11, 164–66
Wovoka: and Ghost Dance, 162–64

Yang v. Sturner, 92, 97
Yellow Bird, 165
Yilmaz, Mesut, 216
Young, Brigham, 157–59

Zelman v. Simmons-Harris, 23, 48; background
of, 49–50; endorsement test in, 64; petitioners' arguments in, 69–72, 74–75; respondents' arguments in, 66–69, 72–75;
Supreme Court decision on, 77–78;
worldviews in, 50